Michael Smith is a former Cold War codebreaker who is now Defence Correspondent of the *Daily Telegraph*. He is the author of the number-one bestseller *Station X* and *The Emperor's Codes*.

Ralph Erskine, a retired lawyer, is widely acknowledged among academics and codebreakers as a leading historian of wartime codebreaking. He is a frequent contributor to journals such as *Intelligence and National Security* and *Cryptologia*.

www.**booksattransworld**.co.uk

ACTION THIS DAY

Bletchley Park from the breaking of the Enigma Code
to the birth of the modern computer

EDITED BY
Ralph Erskine and Michael Smith

BANTAM PRESS
LONDON · NEW YORK · TORONTO · SYDNEY · AUCKLAND

TRANSWORLD PUBLISHERS
61–63 Uxbridge Road, London W5 5SA
a division of The Random House Group Ltd

RANDOM HOUSE AUSTRALIA (PTY) LTD
20 Alfred Street, Milsons Point, Sydney,
New South Wales 2061, Australia

RANDOM HOUSE NEW ZEALAND LTD
18 Poland Road, Glenfield, Auckland 10, New Zealand

RANDOM HOUSE SOUTH AFRICA (PTY) LTD
Endulini, 5a Jubilee Road, Parktown 2193, South Africa

First published 2001 by Bantam Press
This paperback edition published 2002
Bantam Press is a division of Transworld Publishers

A catalogue record for this book is available from the British Library.
ISBN 0593 049829

Set in 11/15pt Sabon by Falcon Oast Graphic Art Ltd.

Printed in Great Britain
by Mackays of Chatham PLC, Chatham, Kent

1 3 5 7 9 10 8 6 4 2

Contents

Acknowledgements

The editors are grateful to the contributors for so readily agreeing to donate their work to the Bletchley Park Trust (which is a registered charity), and for meeting a very demanding timetable without complaint.

Michael Smith would like to thank his wife, Hayley, and his family for their patience, while Ralph Erskine is indebted to his wife, Joan, for her forbearance when he is engrossed in Sigint history, especially during the editing of this book. The editors found the project a rewarding one, and hope that readers will enjoy the result.

On 21 October 1941, four of the leading codebreakers at Bletchley Park wrote to the Prime Minister, Winston Churchill:

Secret and Confidential
Prime Minister only

Hut 6 and Hut 8,
(Bletchley Park)
21st October 1941

Dear Prime Minister,

Some weeks ago you paid us the honour of a visit, and we believe that you regard our work as important. You will have seen that, thanks largely to the energy and foresight of Commander Travis, we have been well supplied with the 'bombes' for the breaking of the German Enigma codes. We think, however, that you ought to know that this work is being held up, and in some cases is not being done at all, principally because we cannot get sufficient staff to deal with it. Our reason for writing to you direct is that for months we have done everything that we possibly can through the normal channels, and that we despair of any early improvement without your intervention. No doubt in the long run these particular requirements will be met, but meanwhile still more precious months will have been wasted, and as our needs are continually expanding we see little hope of ever being adequately staffed.

We realize that there is a tremendous demand for labour of all kinds and that its allocation is a matter of priorities. The trouble to our mind is that as we are a very small section with numerically trivial requirements it is very difficult to bring home to the authorities finally responsible either the importance of what is done here or the urgent necessity of dealing promptly with our requests. At the same time we find it hard to believe that it is really impossible to produce quickly the additional staff that we need, even if this meant interfering with the normal machinery of allocations.

We do not wish to burden you with a detailed list of our difficulties, but the following are the bottlenecks which are causing us the most acute anxiety.

1. <u>Breaking of Naval Enigma (Hut 8)</u>

Owing to shortage of staff and the overworking of his present team the Hollerith section here under Mr Freeborn has had to stop working night shifts. The effect of this is that the finding of the naval keys is being delayed at least twelve hours every day. In order to enable him to start night shifts again Freeborn needs immediately about twenty more untrained Grade III women clerks. To put himself in a really adequate position to deal with any likely demands he will want a good many more.

A further serious danger now threatening us is that some of the skilled male staff, both with the British Tabulating Company at Letchworth and in Freeborn's section here, who have so far been exempt from military service, are now liable to be called up.

2. <u>Military and Air Force Enigma (Hut 6)</u>

We are intercepting quite a substantial proportion of wireless traffic in the Middle East which cannot be picked up by our intercepting stations here. This contains among other things a good deal of new 'Light Blue' intelligence. Owing to shortage of trained typists, however, and the fatigue of our present decoding staff, we cannot get all this traffic decoded. This has been the state of affairs since May. Yet all that we need to put matters right is about twenty trained typists.

3. <u>Bombe testing, Hut 6 and Hut 8</u>
In July we were promised that the testing of the 'stories' produced by the bombes would be taken over by the WRNS in the bombe hut and that sufficient WRNS would be provided for this purpose. It is now late in October and nothing has been done. We do not wish to stress this so strongly as the two preceding points, because it has not actually delayed us in delivering the goods. It has, however, meant that staff in Huts 6 and 8 who are needed for other jobs have had to do the testing themselves. We cannot help feeling that with a Service matter of this kind it should have been possible to detail a body of WRNS for this purpose, if sufficiently urgent instructions had been sent to the right quarters.

4. Apart altogether from staff matters, there are a number of other directions in which it seems to us that we have met with unnecessary impediments. It would take too long to set these out in full, and we realize that some of the matters involved are controversial. The cumulative effect, however, has been to drive us to the conviction that the importance of the work is not being impressed with sufficient force upon those outside authorities with whom we have to deal.

We have written this letter entirely on our own initiative. We do not know who or what is responsible for our difficulties, and most emphatically we do not want to be taken as criticizing Commander Travis who has all along done his utmost to help us in every possible way. But if we are to do our job as well as it could and should be done it is absolutely vital that our wants, small as they are, should be promptly attended to. We have felt that we should be failing in our duty if we did not draw your attention to the facts and to the effects which they are having and must continue to have on our work, unless immediate action is taken.

A. M. Turing

W. G. Welchman

C H O' D Alexander

P. S. Milner-Barry

We are, Sir, Your obedient servants,

On receipt of this letter, the Prime Minister minuted as follows to General Ismay on 22 October 1941 (reproduced in facsimile on the opposite page; PRO HW 1/155):

Secret

In a locked box

Gen. Ismay

Make sure they have all they want on extreme priority and report to me that this has been done.

WSC

22.x

ACTION THIS DAY

Secret

In a locked box

Gen. Ismay.

Make sure they have all they want on extreme priority & report to me that this has been done.

WSC
22.X

Dramatis Personae

Hugh Alexander joined Hut 6 in February 1940. He became deputy head of Hut 8 in March 1941, and its head during the autumn of 1942. He later worked on Japanese naval codes and cipher machines.

Gustave Bertrand was a member of French military intelligence, in its cryptology section. He supplied vital documents on Enigma to Polish intelligence and the Government Code and Cypher School (GC&CS).

Frank Birch joined the German naval section at Bletchley Park in September 1939, and later became the head of the naval section.

Joshua (Josh) Cooper joined GC&CS in October 1925 to specialize in Russian codes and ciphers, later becoming head of the air section.

Alastair Denniston was the Deputy Director of GC&CS from its establishment until February 1942. He was then appointed the Deputy Director (Civil) (DD(C)) in charge of the section responsible for diplomatic and commercial codebreaking. He retired in 1945.

Thomas (Tommy) Flowers was the engineer at the Post Office Research Station who designed Colossus.

Hugh Foss joined GC&CS in December 1924. He devised a method to solve non-plugboard Enigma in the late 1920s, and was head of the Japanese naval section in 1942 and 1943.

William Friedman was the founder of the US Army Signal Intelligence Service (SIS), and its head until 1941. He was appointed the Director of Communications Research in November 1942.

Harold (Doc) Keen was an engineer at the British Tabulating Machine Company, which made the British bombe. He was responsible for the detailed design of the bombes.

Dillwyn (Dilly) Knox was the chief cryptographer (cryptanalyst) at GC&CS. He was severely ill from 1941 onwards, and died in February 1943. He specialized in breaking non-plugboard versions of Enigma.

Stewart Menzies ('C') became the head of MI6 in 1939 and, as such, was also the Director of GC&CS (Director General from March 1944).

Stuart Milner-Barry joined Hut 6 in early 1940, becoming its head in September 1943.

Maxwell (Max) Newman was the head of a GC&CS section known as 'the Newmanry', which attacked the Tunny cipher machine.

Marian Rejewski was the Polish cryptanalyst who first solved plugboard Enigma, in 1932.

Telford Taylor was a lawyer who joined US Army Intelligence in 1942. He made an extended visit to GC&CS in April 1943, and later worked in Hut 3.

John Tiltman was the head of the military wing at Bletchley Park, and GC&CS's top cryptanalyst on non-machine ciphers. He was appointed chief cryptographer in 1944.

Alan Turing joined GC&CS in September 1939, and was head of Hut 8 until autumn 1942. He also worked on Tunny.

Edward Travis was a deputy to Alastair Denniston until February 1942, when he was appointed Deputy Director (Services) (DD(S)) in charge of the services' side of GC&CS. He became the Director of GC&CS in March 1944 (when Menzies' title was changed).

Gordon Welchman was the head of Hut 6 from its establishment until about the autumn of 1943, when he became the Assistant Director, Mechanicisation.

1

Bletchley Park in Pre-War Perspective

CHRISTOPHER ANDREW

Bletchley Park may well have been the best-kept secret in modern British history. The 10,000 men and women who worked there were, in Churchill's famous phrase, 'the geese who laid the golden eggs and never cackled'. Ultra, the intelligence produced at Bletchley Park from the breaking of high-grade enemy ciphers and the analysis of intercepted signals, was the best intelligence in the history of warfare. But if the secret had leaked out, Ultra would have been worthless. At the end of the Second World War most of those who had been 'indoctrinated' into Ultra believed that it would never be revealed. Not until the secret was declassified in the mid-1970s did the geese begin to cackle. A student at my Cambridge college told me how, together with his parents and his sister, he had watched the first BBC documentary on Bletchley Park which showed wartime Wrens (members of the Women's Royal Naval Service) operating the 'bombes' used to break the German 'Enigma' machine ciphers. At the end of the programme, his mother turned to the rest of the family and told them, 'That's where I worked. That's what I did.' Until that moment neither her husband nor her children had had any idea that she had been a wartime codebreaker. The most extraordinary thing about this extraordinary episode is that, so far as the codebreakers were concerned, it was not unusual. Shortly before the publication in 1979 of the first volume of Sir Harry Hinsley's official history, *British Intelligence in the Second World War*, he addressed a large reunion of Bletchley Park veterans and their spouses. After the address, the husbands of a number of former Wrens told Hinsley, 'She never breathed a word to me.'

For the mostly youthful wartime recruits to Bletchley Park indoctrination into Ultra was an unforgettable emotional experience which had few, if any, previous parallels in the entire course of British history. Until their recruitment, hardly any of these people were even aware that Britain had a signals intelligence (Sigint) agency. Yet they suddenly found themselves, during Britain's 'finest hour', in possession of a secret whose revelation might do irreparable damage to the war effort. No wonder that some, perhaps many, suffered from nightmares in which they unwittingly gave the secret away. The extraordinary success with which the Ultra secret was kept for so long reflected in part a national culture which embodied far greater respect for official secrecy and deference to authority than is imaginable today. Despite joining the anti-war movement only six years before he arrived at Bletchley Park, Alan Turing, one of the greatest of the wartime codebreakers, seems to have been untroubled even by peacetime doubts about the essential importance of official secrecy. During the Abdication Crisis of 1936, though at first 'wholly in favour of the King [Edward VIII] marrying Mrs Simpson', Turing had second thoughts after 'It appear[ed] that the King was extremely lax about state documents, leaving them about and letting Mrs Simpson and friends see them.'

In itself, however, a traditional national culture of official secrecy is an inadequate explanation for the extraordinary success with which the Ultra secret was maintained for so long. Some of the secrets of British codebreaking during the First World War had begun to leak out almost as soon as the war was over. In his great history of the war, *The World Crisis*, Winston Churchill, later among the staunchest defenders of the Ultra secret, vividly recalled his excitement while First Lord of the Admiralty for the first nine months of the war at receiving decrypted German naval radio messages which, on occasion, were delivered to him even in his bath, where he eagerly 'grasped [them] with dripping hand'. During the 1920s, some of the early successes of Britain's newly established peacetime Sigint agency, the Government Code and Cypher School (GC&CS), against the Soviet Union were revealed in both the press and government statements. Churchill's own attitude to Sigint security at the time now seems remarkably naive. He wrote in the summer of 1920 that the 'perfidy and treachery' contained in Soviet diplomatic decrypts was such that their contents should be made public:

> I have carefully weighed the pros and cons of this question, and I am convinced that the danger to the State which has been wrought by the intrigues of these revolutionaries and the disastrous effect which will be produced on their plans by the exposure of their methods outweighs all other considerations.

In September 1920, the *Daily Mail* and the *Morning Post* published details from the decrypts of secret Soviet subsidies to the socialist *Daily Herald*. In May 1923, the Cabinet authorized the Foreign Secretary, Lord Curzon, to quote Soviet diplomatic decrypts in a protest note to Moscow, chiefly concerned with Soviet subversion in India and India's neighbours. The protest note, swiftly christened the 'Curzon ultimatum', was unprecedented in the history of British diplomacy. Not content with quoting from Soviet decrypts, Curzon repeatedly taunted Moscow with the fact that its secret telegrams had been successfully intercepted and decrypted by the British:

> The Russian Commissariat for Foreign Affairs will no doubt recognize the following communication dated 21st February 1923, which they received from M. Raskolnikov . . . The Commissariat for Foreign Affairs will also doubtless recognize a communication received by them from Kabul, dated the 8th November, 1922 . . . Nor will they have forgotten a communication, dated the 16th March 1923, from M. Karakhan, the Assistant Commissary for Foreign Affairs, to M. Raskolnikov . . .

The new ciphers, introduced by Moscow in an attempt to make its diplomatic traffic more secure after the Curzon ultimatum and other British breaches of Sigint security in the early 1920s, were successfully broken by British cryptanalysts after varying intervals. In 1927, however, Britain's ability to decrypt Soviet diplomatic traffic was fatally undermined by another extraordinary governmental indiscretion. The Baldwin Cabinet, of which Churchill was a member, decided to publish a selection of Soviet intercepts in order to justify its decision to break off diplomatic relations with Moscow. Austen Chamberlain, the Foreign Secretary, gave his message to the Soviet chargé d'affaires breaking off relations a remarkably personal point by quoting a decrypted telegram from the chargé to Moscow 'in which you request material to enable you to support a political campaign against His Majesty's Government'. A. G. Denniston, the operational head of GC&CS, wrote bitterly that Baldwin's government had deemed it 'necessary to compromise our work beyond question'. Henceforth Moscow adopted the theoretically unbreakable 'one-time pad' for its diplomatic traffic. For the next twenty years British cryptanalysts were able to decrypt almost no high-grade Soviet diplomatic traffic (though they continued to have some success with communications of the Communist International).

The lessons learned from the Sigint catastrophe of 1927, as a result of which Britain lost its most valuable interwar intelligence source, were crucial to the later protection of the Ultra secret. No politician took those lessons more to heart than Winston Churchill. After he became prime minister, at his personal insistence the circle of those who shared the secret of the cryptanalysts' 'golden eggs' was limited to only half a dozen of his thirty-six ministers. The Special Liaison Units set up to pass Ultra to commanders in the field were the most sophisticated system yet devised to protect the wartime secrecy of military intelligence. The profound change in Churchill's attitude to Sigint security is epitomized by the contrast between his published accounts of the two world wars. In his memoirs of the First World War, Churchill had written lyrically of the importance of Sigint; in his memoirs of the Second World War there is no mention of Ultra.

As well as being crucially dependent on the lessons learned in 1927, Ultra also owed much to precedents set in the First World War. The creation of GC&CS in 1919 was itself a consequence of the fact that Sigint had proved its value during the war. Without the expertise painstakingly built up by Denniston on minimal resources between the wars, Bletchley Park's wartime triumphs would have been impossible – despite the invaluable assistance provided by the Poles and French on the eve of war. The breaking of Enigma in its wartime variations required a major new intelligence recruitment. In 1937, the Chief of the Secret Service, Admiral Sir Hugh 'Quex' Sinclair, told Denniston that he was now 'convinced of the inevitability of war' and gave 'instructions for the earmarking of the right type of recruit immediately on the outbreak of war' – chief among them what were quaintly called 'men of the professor type'. The most active recruiters of 'professor types' were two Fellows of King's College, Cambridge, who had served in Room 40, the main First World War Sigint agency: Frank Adcock (later knighted), Professor of Ancient History, and the historian Frank Birch, who left Cambridge for the stage in the 1930s. Both inevitably looked for recruits in the places they knew best: Cambridge colleges in general and King's in particular. A total of twelve King's dons served at Bletchley during the Second World War. By great good fortune the King's Fellowship included Alan Turing, still only twenty-seven at the outbreak of war, one of the very few academics anywhere in the world to have carried out research into both computing and cryptography. Turing's pioneering paper, 'Computable Numbers', now recognized as one of the key texts in the early history of modern computer science, was published early in 1937, though it attracted little interest at the time. Three months before its publication Turing, then at Princeton, wrote to tell his mother that he had also made a major breakthrough in the construction of codes. In view of his later exploits at Bletchley Park, Turing's letter now seems wonderfully ironic:

> I expect I could sell [the codes] to HM Government for quite a substantial sum, but am rather doubtful about the morality of such things. What do you think?

Turing went on to become the chief inventor of the 'bombes' used to break Enigma.

The search for 'professor types', of whom Turing was probably the most remarkable, even in a highly distinguished field, followed two important precedents established during the selection of British codebreakers in the First World War: the recruitment of unusually youthful talent and of original minds who would have been regarded as too eccentric for employment by most official bureaucracies. (The two categories, of course, overlapped.) Two of Britain's leading codebreakers in the two world wars, Dillwyn 'Dilly' Knox and Alan Turing, both Fellows of King's, were also among the most eccentric. Knox, a classicist, did some of his best work for Room 40 lying in a bath in Room 53 at the Admiralty Old Building on Whitehall, claiming that codes were most easily cracked in an atmosphere of soap and steam. Frank Birch wrote affectionately of Knox in his classified satirical history of Room 40, *Alice in ID25*:

> The sailor in Room 53
> Has never, it's true, been to sea
> But though not in a boat
> He has served afloat –
> In a bath in the Admiralty.

Knox's bathtime cryptanalysis continued during his time at Bletchley Park, once causing fellow lodgers at his billet, when he failed to respond to shouted appeals through the bathroom door, to break down the door for fear that he might have passed out and drowned in the bath.

Turing's eccentricities make such engaging anecdotes that they are sometimes exaggerated, but there can be no doubt about their reality. His ability from a very early age to disappear into a world of his own is wonderfully captured by a drawing of him at prep school by Turing's mother, which she presented to the school matron. The drawing, entitled 'Hockey or Watching the Daisies Grow', shows the ten-year-old Turing, oblivious of the vigorous game of hockey taking place around him, bending over in the middle of the pitch to inspect a clump of daisies. At Bletchley Park he chained his coffee mug to a radiator to prevent theft, sometimes cycled to work wearing a gas mask to guard against pollen, and converted his life savings into silver ingots which he buried in two locations in nearby woods. Sadly, he failed to find the ingots when the war was over. The informality and absence of rigid hierarchy at Bletchley Park enabled it to exploit the talents of unconventional and eccentric personalities who would have found it difficult to conform to military discipline or civil service routine.

Most of the dons and other professionals recruited by Room 40 had been young. The 'professor types' selected by Bletchley Park were, on average, younger still. In the summer of 1939, Alastair

Denniston wrote to the heads of about ten Cambridge and Oxford colleges, asking for the names of able undergraduates who could be interviewed for unspecified secret war work. Among the twenty or so recruited during the first round of interviews (repeated on a number of later occasions during the war) was the twenty-year-old Harry Hinsley, who was about to begin his third year as an undergraduate historian at St John's College, Cambridge. After Pearl Harbor, when Bletchley Park needed more cryptanalysts and linguists to take newly devised crash courses in the Japanese language, the recruitment included sixth-formers as well as undergraduates – among them Alan Stripp, recruited after winning a classics scholarship to Trinity College, Cambridge, who later co-edited with Hinsley a volume of memoirs on Bletchley Park. During a visit to Bletchley, Churchill is said to have remarked ironically to Denniston, as he surveyed the unusually youthful staff, 'I told you to leave no stone unturned to get staff, but I had no idea you had taken me literally.'

Recruitment to Bletchley Park broke with one important but misguided precedent established during the First World War. Room 40 had made no attempt to recruit professional mathematicians, whose supposedly introverted personalities were thought to be too far removed even from the realities of daily life for them to engage with the horrendous problems posed by the First World War. Though a prejudice normally associated with arts graduates, this jaundiced view of mathematicians appears to have been shared by the Director of Naval Education, Sir Alfred Ewing, a former Fellow of King's and Professor of Engineering at Cambridge, who seems to have been chiefly responsible for the recruitment from King's (where his son-in-law remained a Fellow) of Adcock, Birch and Knox. Despite his own mathematical training, Ewing evidently considered the experience of classicists, historians and linguists in making sense of difficult and complex texts a more relevant skill for cryptanalysis than mathematical expertise. Similar prejudices continued to influence the recruitment of British cryptanalysts between the wars.

Polish military intelligence realized at the end of the 1920s that the attempt to break Enigma would require the recruitment of professional mathematicians (one of whom, Marian Rejewski, was to make the first major breakthrough in the attack on it). In the summer of 1938, Denniston finally reached a similar conclusion and began including a limited number of mathematicians among the 'professor types' who were being earmarked for Bletchley Park. Initially, however, the mathematicians were treated with considerable caution and some suspicion. The first mathematics graduate recruited by GC&CS, Peter Twinn of Brasenose College, Oxford, was told after he began work early in 1939, that 'there had been some doubts about the wisdom of recruiting a mathematician as they were regarded as strange fellows, notoriously unpractical'. Twinn owed his recruitment, at least in part, to his postgraduate work in physics. Physicists, he was told, 'might be expected to have at least some appreciation of the real world' – unlike, it was believed, most mathematicians.

Though the first wave of 'professor types' to arrive at Bletchley Park at the outbreak of war consisted chiefly of linguists, classicists and historians, it also included two brilliant Cambridge mathematicians: Turing from King's and Gordon Welchman from Sidney Sussex College, who may originally have been earmarked because his mathematical brilliance was combined with skill at chess. According to the Cambridge Professor of Italian, E. R. 'Vinca' Vincent – probably the first 'professor type' to be selected – 'Someone had had the excellent idea that of all people who might be good at an art that needs the patient consideration of endless permutations, chess players fitted the bill.' Among other chess experts to arrive at Bletchley Park in the early months of the war were Hugh Alexander and Stuart Milner-Barry. Turing, Welchman, Alexander and Milner-Barry were jointly to sign the celebrated Trafalgar Day memorandum in 1941, which Churchill minuted, 'Action This Day'. Whatever the original reasons for their recruitment, the first professional mathematicians at Bletchley Park made themselves indispensable so quickly that the recruiting drive was rapidly extended to mathematicians without a reputation as chess players.

Though GC&CS operated on a very much larger scale after its wartime move to Bletchley Park than it had done between the wars, at least one aspect of its original organization remained both of crucial importance and considerably ahead of its time. Denniston considered the 'official jealousy' which had prevented any collaboration between naval and military cryptanalysts from October 1914 to the spring of 1917 'the most regrettable fact' in the history of British wartime Sigint. The establishment of GC&CS in 1919 was intended to avoid any repetition of such interdepartmental feuding. Within a few years of its foundation the new agency achieved the successful co-ordination of diplomatic and service cryptanalysis under overall Foreign Office control, though for most of the interwar years diplomatic decrypts yielded much more valuable intelligence than service traffic. That co-ordination, equalled by no other major Sigint agency abroad, was one of the secrets of Bletchley Park's success.

For much of the 1930s the bitter rivalry between US naval and military Sigint agencies closely resembled that between their British counterparts during the First World War. Each sought to crack independently the same diplomatic codes and ciphers in order, according to a declassified official history, to 'gain credit for itself as the agency by which the information obtained was made available to the Government'. Though there was limited interservice collaboration at the end of the decade, the rivalry resumed after the breaking of the Japanese Purple diplomatic cipher by military cryptanalysts in September 1940, as naval codebreakers sought to prevent the Army from monopolizing Magic (Japanese diplomatic decrypts). After lengthy negotiations, an absurd bureaucratic compromise was agreed, allowing the military Signal Intelligence Service (SIS) to produce Magic on even dates, and its naval counterpart, OP-20-G, to do so on odd dates. This bizarre arrangement continued to cause confusion until the very eve of Pearl Harbor. On the morning of Saturday 6 December, a naval listening post near Seattle successfully intercepted thirteen parts of a fourteen-part message from Tokyo to the Japanese embassy in Washington, rejecting US terms for a resolution of the crisis and making clear that there was no longer any prospect of a peaceful settlement. (The fourteenth part was intercepted on the following day.) This critically important intercept was forwarded by teleprinter to the Navy Department in Washington. But since 6 December was an even date, the Navy Department was obliged to forward the message to the military SIS for decryption shortly after midday. SIS, however, found itself in a deeply embarrassing position since its civilian translators and other staff, as usual on a Saturday, had left at midday and there was no provision for overtime. Doubtless to its immense chagrin, SIS was thus forced to return the intercept to the Navy. While OP-20-G began the decryption, SIS spent the afternoon gaining permission for its first Saturday evening civilian shift. By the time the shift started, however, it was too late for SIS to reclaim the partly decrypted intercept from OP-20-G. And so, for the first time, on the eve of Pearl Harbor, the rival agencies produced Magic together. SIS was able to decrypt two of the thirteen parts of the intercepted Japanese message, though the typing was done by the Navy. The Sigint confusion in Washington, at one of the most critical moments in American history, highlights the immense importance of the successful resolution of interservice rivalry by GC&CS two decades earlier.

Equally essential to Bletchley Park's success was Churchill's passion for Sigint. By a remarkable – and fortunate – coincidence, Churchill became war leader shortly after the first Enigma decrypts, one of the most valuable intelligence sources in British history, began to come onstream. Churchill's passion for Ultra was equalled only by his determination to put it to good use. On the tenth anniversary in 1924 of the founding of Room 40, he had described Sigint as more important to the making of foreign and defence policy than 'any other source of knowledge at the disposal of the state'. He was also well aware that, despite some successes during the First World War, the advantage gained by breaking German codes had sometimes been wasted. The indecisive battle of Jutland in 1916, the greatest naval battle of the war, might well have ended in a decisive British victory if the Sigint provided by Room 40 had been properly used by the Admiralty. Churchill's own use of Ultra during the Second World War was, of course, far from infallible. The exaggerated sense of Rommel's weakness in North Africa which he derived from his over-optimistic interpretation of Enigma decrypts, for example, made him too quick to urge both Wavell and Auchinleck to go on the offensive.

Even when due account is taken of Churchill's limitations, however, he still remains head and shoulders above any other contemporary war leader or any previous British statesman in his grasp of Sigint's value. That grasp depended on an experience of Sigint which went back to the founding of Room 40 early in the First World War and on his ability to learn from his mistakes in the handling of it. Had Churchill come to power in May 1940 without previous experience of Sigint, Bletchley Park might well have found his untutored enthusiasm for Ultra a dubious asset.

Great war leader though he was in most other respects, President Franklin D. Roosevelt was simply not in Churchill's class when it came to Sigint. Despite a general awareness of the importance of wartime intelligence and a particular fascination with espionage, dating back to his experience of naval intelligence in the First World War, Roosevelt failed to grasp the importance of Sigint. Though Magic provided by far the best guide to Japanese policy during the year before Pearl Harbor, he showed only a limited interest in it. As well as sanctioning the absurd odd–even date division of labour between naval and military cryptanalysts, he also agreed to a further bizarre arrangement by which his naval and military aides took turns in supplying him with Magic in alternate months. This arrangement led to predictable confusion, including the suspension of the Magic supply in July 1941, after FDR's military aide breached Sigint security by absentmindedly leaving Japanese decrypts in his wastepaper basket. Not until November did the President finally lose patience and insist that Magic henceforth be communicated to him exclusively through his naval aide, Captain John R. Beardall. When shown Japanese decrypts, Roosevelt very rarely commented on them. Not until three days before Pearl Harbor did he discuss with Beardall the significance of any of the Magic revelations.

Churchill would never have tolerated the confusion allowed by Roosevelt in both the production and the distribution of Magic. He also showed far greater appreciation both of his cryptanalysts and the intelligence which they produced. Captain Malcolm Kennedy, one of the leading Japanese experts at Bletchley Park, wrote in his diary on 6 December 1941:

> . . . The All Highest (. . . Churchill) is all over himself at the moment for latest information and indications re Japan's intentions and rings up at all hours of the day and night, except for the 4 hours in each 24 (2 to 6 a.m.) when he sleeps. For a man of his age, he has the most amazing vitality.

It would never have occurred to Roosevelt to ring up his cryptanalysts for the latest news. (Had he done so on 6 December, he would have discovered the confusion in the decryption of the fourteen-part Japanese telegram caused by the odd–even day arrangement.) Churchill also showed far greater determination than Roosevelt to ensure that his cryptanalysts had adequate resources. The American intelligence failure to provide advance warning of the Japanese attack on Pearl Harbor was due primarily to the difficulties in reading the latest variant of the main Japanese naval code, JN-25B. Though Magic contained no clear indication of plans for the surprise attack, undecrypted naval messages did. 'If the Japanese navy messages had enjoyed a higher priority and [had been] assigned more analytic resources,' writes the official historian of the NSA (the current US Sigint agency), Frederick Parker, 'could the U. S. Navy have predicted the Japanese attack on Pearl Harbor? Most emphatically yes!' JN-25B was not read to any great extent before Pearl Harbor because only a total of between two and five cryptanalysts had ever been assigned to work on it. The success in breaking Japanese naval codes, when the number of cryptanalysts was increased after Pearl Harbor, was a crucial element in the US victory at Midway only six months later.

In the months before Pearl Harbor, when OP-20-G lacked the resources required to read JN-25B more fully, it did not occur to American naval cryptanalysts to appeal directly to Roosevelt. At exactly the same time, faced with a less critical though still serious shortage of resources, Bletchley Park's leading cryptanalysts appealed directly to Churchill. The most junior of them, Stuart Milner-Barry, delivered the message personally to Number 10. Churchill's response was immediate: 'ACTION THIS DAY. Make sure they have all they want on extreme priority and report to me that this has been done.'

2

The Government Code and Cypher School and the First Cold War

MICHAEL SMITH

Introduction

Our view of espionage is now so dominated by the period known as the Cold War, that it is easy to forget that between the First and Second World Wars, Britain and the Soviet Union fought a first Cold War every bit as bitter as the second. The predecessors of the KGB regarded Britain as 'the main adversary' and there were widespread attempts to collect intelligence, to subvert British society, and to recruit agents within the British establishment, of whom the members of the Cambridge spy ring were only the most prominent. The following chapter traces the early beginnings of GC&CS and examines the part played by the British codebreakers in this first Cold War. It also dismantles the myth that once the Germans turned on the Russians – in June 1941 – the British stopped collecting intelligence on their newfound Soviet allies. Although their armies were united in the 'hot war' against Germany, the intelligence services on both sides would very soon be positioning themselves to fight the new Cold War that would follow the victory over the Nazis.

MS

Britain's codebreakers enjoyed a very successful First World War. Perhaps the best known of their achievements was the breaking, by the Royal Navy's Room 40, of the Zimmermann Telegram, which brought the United States into the war. But even before Room 40 was created, on the orders of the then First Lord of the Admiralty, Winston Churchill, the Army's MI1b had achieved considerable success against German military codes and ciphers.

The Army and Navy codebreaking units rarely spoke to each other, engaging in a turf war apparently fuelled by the Army's resentment of the greater influence of the upstart in the Admiralty. Alastair Denniston, who for much of the war led Room 40, or NID25, as it was more correctly known, later bemoaned 'the loss of efficiency to both departments caused originally by mere official jealousy'. The two departments finally began to exchange results in 1917, but there remained little love lost and the situation came to a head a year after the Armistice, when the question of whether or not there should be a peacetime codebreaking organization was under consideration.

Although there were inevitably some within government who were keen to axe the codebreakers as part of a peace dividend, there were many more who were just as eager to continue to receive the intelligence they were providing. It was decided to amalgamate the two organizations and a conference was held at the Admiralty in August 1919 to consider who should be in charge of the new body. The War Office wanted their man, Major Malcolm Hay, the head of MI1b, while the Navy was equally determined that Denniston was the worthier candidate.

But Hay appears to have overplayed his hand, insisting he was not prepared to work under Denniston, while the latter expressed a willingness to do whatever was asked of him. The generals were embarrassed by Hay's attitude. It was not for junior officers to decide who they were or were not prepared to serve under. Denniston was subsequently given charge of what was to be known as the Government Code and Cypher School (GC&CS),

with a staff of just over fifty employees, of whom only a half were codebreakers. 'The public function was "to advise as to the security of codes and cyphers used by all Government departments and to assist in their provision",' Denniston later recalled. 'The secret directive was "to study the methods of cypher communications used by foreign powers".'

GC&CS came under the control of the Director of Naval Intelligence, Admiral Hugh 'Quex' Sinclair, a noted bon viveur who installed the School in London's fashionable Strand, close to the Savoy Grill, his favourite restaurant. The material it dealt with was almost entirely diplomatic traffic. Its main target countries were America, France, Japan and Russia, with the latter providing what Denniston said was 'the only real operational intelligence'.

'The Revolutionary Government in 1919 had no codes and did not risk using the Tsarist codes, which they must have inherited,' Denniston said. 'They began with simple transposition of plain Russian and gradually developed systems of increasing difficulty.' One of the reasons that the Bolsheviks were unwilling to use the old Tsarist codes was the presence among the British codebreakers of the man responsible for devising a number of them. Ernst Fetterlein had once been the Tsar's leading codebreaker, solving not just German and Austrian codes but also those of the British.

'Fetterlein was a devotee of his art,' one of his former colleagues in the Russian *Cabinet Noir* recalled. 'I was told that once, when he was sent to London with dispatches, he sat morosely through breakfast until suddenly a complete change took place. He beamed, began to laugh and jest, and when one of the embassy officials asked him what the matter was, confessed that he had been worried by an indecipherable word which occurred in one of the English telegrams he had deciphered. Someone had in conversation mentioned the name of a small English castle to which the King had gone to shoot and this was the word in the telegrams which had bothered him.' He sported a large ruby ring given to him by Tsar Nicholas in gratitude for his achievements, which included deciphering a message that led to the sinking of a number of German ships in the Baltic in 1914. This had a valuable spin-off for Fetterlein's future employers. The Russians recovered a naval codebook from the light cruiser the *Magdeburg*, which they passed on to the British.

Fetterlein fled from Russia during the October Revolution on board a Swedish ship. He and his wife narrowly evaded a search of the ship by the Russians, one of his new colleagues recalled him saying. 'As the top cryptographer in Russia he held the rank of admiral and his stories of the day the revolution occurred, when workmen stripped him of many decorations and bullets narrowly missed him, were exciting. It is said that the French and the British organization were anxious to get him and Fetterlein simply sat there and said: "Well gentlemen, who will pay me the most?" '

The British evidently offered the most money. Fetterlein was recruited by Room 40 in June 1918, working on Bolshevik, Georgian and Austrian codes. 'Fetty, as we addressed him, would arrive precisely at 9.30 and read his *Times* until 10 when he would adjust a pair of thick-lensed glasses and look to us expecting work to be given to him. He was a brilliant cryptographer. On book cipher and anything where insight was vital he was quite the best. He was a fine linguist and he would usually get an answer no matter the language.'

Fetterlein and his team, which included two female refugees from Russia and the occasional British Consul thrown out by the Bolsheviks, were easily able to keep on top of the relatively simple Bolshevik ciphers. This allowed them to ensure that the government of David Lloyd George was fully informed of the machinations of various elements of the Russian Trade Delegation, led by the Bolshevik Commissar for Foreign Trade, Leonid Krasin, which arrived in London in May 1920.

The messages decrypted by GC&CS were known as BJs because

they were circulated in blue-jacketed files, as opposed to the red files used for reports from the Secret Intelligence Service (SIS), now better known as MI6. The Russian BJs showed Lenin telling Krasin that he must be tough with the British. 'That swine Lloyd George has no scruples or shame in the way he deceives,' said the Soviet leader. 'Don't believe a word he says and gull him three times as much.' Lev Kamenev, the head of the Moscow Communist Party, was sent to London to take charge of the delegation. Very soon the decrypts showed that he was actively involved in the setting up of 'Councils of Action' across Britain, with the intention of using them, like the Russian Soviets, to prepare for a communist revolution in Britain. They also disclosed that the Russians were pouring money into the London-based *Daily Herald* newspaper.

To many of those in authority, it appeared that Britain was perilously close to its own communist insurrection. Field Marshal Sir Henry Wilson, the Chief of the Imperial General Staff, wrote a furious memorandum to Lloyd George. The telegrams showed 'beyond all possibility of doubt . . . that Kamenev and Krasin, while enjoying the hospitality of England, are engaged, with the Soviet Government, in a plot to create red revolution and ruin this country'. He received support from Admiral Sinclair, who surprisingly urged the Government to publish the decrypted telegrams. 'Even if the publication of the telegrams was to result in not another message being decoded, then the present situation would fully justify it,' claimed Sinclair.

Lloyd George then sanctioned the publication of eight of the telegrams as long as the newspapers claimed to have obtained them from 'a neutral country'. But *The Times* ignored the official requests to keep the true source secret, starting its report with the words: 'The following telegrams have been intercepted by the British Government.' The Prime Minister called in Kamenev, who was due to return to Russia for consultations and told him there was 'irrefutable evidence' that he had committed 'a gross breach of faith'. He would not be allowed back into the country.

Despite the *Times* report, and further press leaks after Kamenev's departure, the Russians did not change their ciphers. There was no doubt that they were aware of what had happened. Krasin told Maxim Litvinov, the Bolshevik Deputy Commissioner for Foreign Affairs, that the British 'had complete knowledge of all your ciphered telegrams . . . which had strengthened the suspicion that Kamenev is the teacher of revolutionary Marxism and was sent here with the express purpose of inspiring, organizing and subsidizing English Soviets'.

But the Russian ciphers were still not changed until three months later, when Mikhail Frunze, Commander-in-Chief of the Bolshevik forces fighting the White Russians in the Crimea, reported that 'absolutely all our ciphers are being deciphered by the enemy in consequence of their simplicity'. He singled out the British as one of the main perpetrators. 'All our enemies, particularly England, have all this time been entirely in the know about our internal military operational and diplomatic work,' he added. A week later, the trade delegation in London was told to send correspondence by courier until they received new ciphers. They arrived in January 1921 and by April, Fetterlein had broken them.

The main source of the coded messages coming into GC&CS was the international cable companies. Under a section added to the 1920 Official Secrets Act, they were obliged to hand over any cables passing through the United Kingdom – a requirement that was quite openly put down to the 'general state of world unrest' created by communist attempts to replicate the October Revolution across Europe. But many of the messages emanating from Moscow were intercepted by Royal Naval intercept sites – based at Pembroke and Scarborough – and Army sites at Chatham, Baghdad and Constantinople. Although GC&CS remained under Admiralty control, the vast bulk of the messages it decrypted were now diplomatic rather than military or naval and in 1922, Lord Curzon, the Foreign Secretary, decided that the

Foreign Office should take charge of the codebreakers. One senior member of staff attributed this to a conversation with the French ambassador during which the Foreign Secretary 'expressed certain views which did not coincide with the views of his colleagues in the cabinet'. These were duly passed back to Paris, decrypted by GC&CS and circulated among Curzon's cabinet colleagues. The codebreakers were moved from their Strand headquarters to 178 Queen's Gate and a year later again put under the control of Admiral Sinclair, who was now the Chief of MI6.

Despite his interest in the codebreakers' intelligence product, Curzon showed little regard for its security. When further evidence of the Russian attempts to subvert Britain and its empire emerged in 1923, he used the deciphered telegrams to draft a protest note to the Soviet Government – the so-called Curzon ultimatum – which not only quoted the telegrams verbatim but made absolutely clear that they were intercepts, most of them passing between Moscow and its envoy in Kabul. These were almost certainly intercepted, and probably deciphered, in India where there was a well-established signals intelligence operation.

The leading cryptographer in India at the time was Captain John Tiltman, who was undoubtedly one of the best codebreakers in Britain, if not the world. He had been offered a place at Oxford at the age of thirteen but had been unable to accept. He subsequently served with the King's Own Scottish Borderers in France during the First World War, where he won the Military Cross, and spent a year with GC&CS before being posted to the Indian Army headquarters at Simla in 1921. There was already a military intercept site at Pishin on the Baluchistan–Afghan border and Tiltman's arrival coincided with the opening of another intercept station at Cherat, on the North West Frontier.

Tiltman later recalled that he was part of a small section of no more than five people based at Simla. It not only deciphered the messages, but also garnered intelligence from the locations of the transmitters – which were determined by direction finding – from the way they operated, and from the routine communications, a process still known today as traffic analysis. 'We were employed almost entirely on one task, to read as currently as possible the Russian diplomatic cipher traffic between Moscow, Kabul in Afghanistan and Tashkent in Turkestan,' he said. 'From about 1925 onwards, I found myself very frequently involved in all aspects of the work – directing the interception and encouraging the operators at our intercept stations on the North West Frontier of India, doing all the rudimentary traffic analysis that was necessary, diagnosing the cipher systems when the frequent changes occurred, stripping the long additive keys, recovering the codebooks, translating the messages and arguing their significance with the Intelligence Branch of the General Staff. I realize that I was exceptionally lucky to have this opportunity and that very few others have had the chance of acquiring this kind of general working experience. Between 1921 and 1924, I paid three visits to the corresponding unit in Baghdad and on several occasions, sitting amongst operators in the set-room of the Baghdad intercept station, worked directly on the red forms fresh off the sets, to the benefit not only of my own experience but also to the morale of the operators.'

The Indian signals intelligence operation, which was regarded as part of Sinclair's overall organization, took any Russian traffic it could, including the communications of the OGPU, forerunner of the KGB. It achieved 'very considerable cryptographic success', according to one military official. A Wireless Experimental Station was opened at Abbottabad on the North West Frontier with a further intercept site at Quetta. Meanwhile, the site in Constantinople was withdrawn to Sarafand, near Jaffa, in Palestine, as No. 1 section of 2 Wireless Company with Baghdad forming No. 2 section. Like the Indian operation, Sarafand had its own cryptographers, producing intelligence for the British

Middle East Command. It also sent raw Russian traffic back to London where it was passed on to GC&CS, considerably increasing the amount of Russian traffic available to Fetterlein and his assistants.

The increased amount of traffic coincided with yet another change in the Soviet ciphers, leading to calls for more Russian experts. One of those recruited as a result was J. E. S. 'Josh' Cooper, who was to become another leading light at Bletchley Park. He heard of the openings at GC&CS through a friend, the novelist Charles Morgan. 'I joined as a Junior Assistant in October 1925. Like many other recruits, I had heard of the job through a personal introduction – advertisement of posts was, at that time, unthinkable. I was one year down from University of London, King's College, with a first in Russian and had nothing better to do than teach at a preparatory school at Margate. My father was bewailing this at tea with the Morgans one day, and one of Charles's sisters said she had a friend who worked at a place in Queen's Gate where Russian linguists were wanted.'

Cooper already knew Fetterlein, having been introduced to him by one of the teaching staff at King's College. 'His experience and reputation were both great, and I was fortunate to find myself assigned to work with him on Soviet diplomatic, which at that time consisted of book ciphers, mostly one part, reciphered with a 1,000 group additive key. He took very little notice of me and left it to an army officer who had been attached to GC&CS, Capt. [A. C.] Stuart Smith, to explain the problem and set me to recover some Russian additive key. Traffic was scanty and it was hard to get adequate depth. Also the book I was working with had been solved in India by Tiltman and Col. Jeffrey and nobody had worked on it at home. It took me some time to realize that almost every group had two meanings. After about six weeks' work, during which I rubbed holes in the paper with endless corrections, at last I read my first message which was from Moscow to the

Soviet representative in Washington and was concerned with repudiation of debts by American states.'

Despite Cooper's problems with the cipher he was put to work on, the amount of Soviet messages continued to increase with the opening of a new Royal Navy intercept site at Flowerdown, near Winchester, an army site at Chatham, and an RAF site at Waddington, in Lincolnshire. Sinclair moved both the codebreakers and his MI6 staff to a new joint headquarters at 54 Broadway, close to Whitehall, in 1925. He also added to the intercept facilities by co-opting the resources of a small Metropolitan Police intercept operation, which was run by Harold Kenworthy, an employee of Marconi who was on indefinite loan to the police. It operated out of the attic at Scotland Yard, employing a number of ex-naval telegraphists to intercept illicit radio stations.

The Metropolitan Police unit had first shown its capabilities during the 1926 General Strike. Although the strike broke out largely for socio-economic reasons, the BJs had shown the Soviet Government keen to provoke industrial action to the extent of subsidizing the striking miners to the tune of £2 million. It was scarcely surprising therefore that when, on the first day of the General Strike, the Metropolitan Police operators intercepted an unusual wireless transmission using apparently false callsigns and emanating from somewhere in London, there were suspicions of Russian foul play. Kenworthy informed the assistant commissioner in charge of the Special Branch who in turn contacted Admiral Sinclair. The MI6 Chief sent over the GC&CS radio expert Leslie Lambert, better known as the BBC 'wireless personality' A. J. Alan, and together they constructed a miniature direction-finding device small enough to fit into a Gladstone bag, Kenworthy recalled.

> The portable set was put to good use. Influence by Assistant Commissioner and SIS [MI6] made it possible to get access to roofs of buildings in the vicinity of the suspected source of signal which had been roughly located by taking a completely empty van and

> sitting on the floor with the Gladstone bag. It was gratifying that the work put in was finally rewarded by actually 'walking in' from the roof tops into the top of a building housing the transmitter whilst the operator was using it. The result was an anti-climax as the transmitter had been set up by the *Daily Mail*, who thinking that *Post* and *Telegraph* personnel would be joining the strike at any moment, decided to try and be ready for a 'coup'. The call sign AHA was derived from [the newspaper's proprietor] Alfred Harmsworth. As a matter of high policy nothing was ever published about this exploit.

The illicit radio transmitter may not have been run by the Russians, but the General Strike and Moscow's attempts to inspire revolution in China and to take control of Afghanistan – and thereby threaten India – increased the general feeling within the Conservative-led establishment that the Bolsheviks were determined to subvert Britain and its Empire.

Government ministers were also influenced by MI5 and Special Branch reports of Soviet espionage centred on 'the firm', a cover name for the All-Russian Co-operative Society (ARCOS) based in Moorgate, ostensibly set up to facilitate trade between Britain and Russia. None were anywhere near as successful as the later Cambridge spy ring, but their attempts to obtain military and naval intelligence outraged those like the intensely anti-Bolshevik Home Secretary Sir William Joynson-Hicks, who put pressure on the then Foreign Secretary Sir Austen Chamberlain to back action against Russia. Throughout 1926, Chamberlain continued to defend his policy of pragmatic dealing with Moscow rather than lose the new trade links. But by 19 January 1927, he accepted that there was a need 'to review in Cabinet our relations with Russia', asking the President of the Board of Trade what Britain's 'actual trade interests' amounted to, and for some sense of 'the sentiment of traders' about them. Five days later, he drafted a protest note to the Russians. He suspected that it would not satisfy Joynson-

Hicks, or the other hardliners like Winston Churchill, now Chancellor of the Exchequer, and he was right. But it was the start of a process that would soon lead to a complete diplomatic break with Moscow.

What exactly made Chamberlain accept the need for action is still unclear. But some time during 1926, the codebreakers had received a new source of telegrams. MI6 had already managed to acquire the Bolshevik cables passing through the Tehran post office, of crucial interest with regard to Russian threats to Afghanistan. Now it supplied the Soviet telegrams sent via Peking, allowing the codebreakers to break complete substitution tables for the first time and producing a rich harvest of intelligence for the cabinet hardliners. The addition of Alfred Dillwyn 'Dilly' Knox to Fetterlein's team may well have contributed to this success. Dilly's early promise at Eton – he beat John Maynard Keynes to take first place in the scholarship for King's College, Cambridge – had been confirmed by his work in Room 40, where he and Nigel de Grey broke the Zimmermann Telegram in January 1917. Six days before Chamberlain's letter to the President of the Board of Trade, Knox's work had given him an unexplained reason to celebrate. He bought himself a new Burberry overcoat and ordered dinner at an expensive restaurant. 'These expenses might pass as unremarkable,' his niece Penelope Fitzgerald recorded in *The Knox Brothers*. 'But with Dilly they could only mean celebration and it is at least possible that the Government had agreed, in his own phrase, to "get something from the post office".'

Whatever the celebration was about, the messages obtained from the Peking post office were to have a devastating effect on Anglo-Soviet relations. Over the ensuing weeks, further examples of Soviet espionage were detected and on 12 May, the police raided the ARCOS headquarters. The Russians had been warned of the impending raid and, despite three days of searching by the police, nothing of significance was discovered.

In order to justify the decision to break with Moscow, the Prime Minister Stanley Baldwin resorted to reading out the text of some of the deciphered Peking telegrams in parliament. He was followed two days later by Chamberlain who, reminding MPs that there had been a recent anti-British demonstration outside the British embassy in Washington, read an extract from a message sent a month earlier by Moscow to its representatives abroad. Clearly taken from a deciphered intercept, it said: 'It is absolutely essential to organize in the shortest possible space of time meetings against England and to demonstrate where possible in front of British embassies and legations.' Chamberlain followed this extract from one of the decrypts with a succession of other examples. Although these were at least paraphrased rather than quoted verbatim, the Russians had got the message. Where they had previously been slow to change their cipher systems, they now adopted the one-time pad system (OTP), which if used properly was impossible to break.

The codebreakers were horrified. There was a brief period during which the old ciphers continued to be used in more remote places like Central Asia. But very soon the decipherable diplomatic messages dried up. 'HMG found it necessary to compromise our work beyond any question,' recalled Denniston. 'From that time, the Soviet Government introduced OTP for their diplomatic and commercial traffic to all capitals where they had diplomatic representatives.'

Josh Cooper, speaking with the benefit of hindsight, after misuse of the system had led to at least two other one-time pad systems being broken, said that it might have been possible to break the Soviet diplomatic system if only there had been enough codebreakers to allow 'long shots'. 'Tiltman went so far as to read a few groups of "wrapover" texts when a pad was used to a depth of two at the end of some messages. This we felt to be interesting but of little practical value. It might, however, if persisted in, have led to the discovery of re-use of pads. We knew from previous experience of their old diplomatic systems that the Russians were capable of re-using additive tables.'

Although the Russian diplomatic material had dried up, the Soviet Union provided GC&CS with a second interwar success via the communications of the Comintern, the organization set up in 1919 to promote communism and revolution around the world. It controlled all of the various communist parties, each of which formed a so-called 'Section' of the Comintern and was bound to follow its direction. They were also required to set up parallel 'illegal', or more accurately underground, organizations that would be controlled by the Comintern in order to prepare for a general strike and armed insurrection that it was hoped would precede fresh revolutions. An additional role of these 'illegal' organizations was to carry out espionage.

The first sign of illicit transmissions linking the Communist Party of Great Britain to Moscow came in early 1930, when the various intercept units began picking up a large number of unauthorized radio transmissions between London and Moscow. 'Peacetime GC&CS did have one experience of successful work on clandestine traffic,' Denniston recalled. 'This, unlike the diplomatic, necessitated close co-operation between interception, T/A [Traffic Analysis] and cryptography before the final results were made available only to a small select intelligence section of SIS.' The operation, codenamed Mask, was run by Tiltman, who had returned from India in 1929 with a great deal of experience in Soviet wireless and cipher practice. 'The analysis of this traffic was studied closely and from it emerged a world-wide network of clandestine stations controlled by a station near Moscow,' Denniston recalled. 'It turned out to be the Comintern network.' The attack on the Comintern ciphers 'met with complete success', he said.

The 'small, select' MI6 section to which the decrypted material was sent was the two-man counter-espionage department known as Section V (five). It was led by Major Valentine Vivian, a former

Indian police officer. The material was also discussed with B Branch of MI5, which at the time was responsible for Soviet subversion and espionage. J. C. 'Jack' Curry, who was in charge of MI5 operations against subversion for part of the 1930s, recalled that the messages dealt with a variety of subjects. 'The London/Moscow transmissions were part of a large network with a number of stations in different parts of the world and the material dealt with a variety of the affairs of the Comintern and its sections in different countries. Those from Moscow included directions and instructions regarding the line to be taken in propaganda and in party policy generally. They gave, among other things, details regarding subsidies to be paid by Moscow, a large part being allocated to the *Daily Worker*.'

Many of the messages were obscure and difficult to understand without an appreciation of the context and the cover names of those to whom they referred, Curry said. 'Major Vivian was, however, able to extract useful intelligence from a number of messages and, in particular, obtained a certain picture of some of the details of Comintern finance and its measures for subsidising its Sections in other countries. Information about the names of couriers and active Communists, including certain British crypto-communists, was obtained from this source.'

The information culled from the Comintern decrypts appears to have allowed MI6 to recruit a number of agents inside the Comintern in France, Holland and Scandinavia. But the best source it had within the Comintern was a 'walk-in', a spy who offered his services to MI6. Johann Heinrich de Graf (Jonny X), was a German communist who was recruited by Soviet Army intelligence, the GRU. He walked into the MI6 station in Berlin to volunteer his services and was run by its head, Frank Foley, who was to become far better known for his work in helping Jews to escape from Nazi Germany. Jonny X had been involved in the organization of the Comintern 'illegal' network in Britain and was able to provide vital information not only on the workings of the Comintern but also on its attempts to subvert the governments of Britain, China and Brazil.

There was often no love lost between MI6 and MI5 during this period, but Curry was full of praise for the 'close and fruitful collaboration' on the Comintern. The intelligence from the MI6 agents, and particularly from Jonny X, whom he singled out as 'very valuable', were augmented and amplified by the intercepted Comintern messages.

As Denniston suggested, the Mask operation was also notable as a rare early example of close collaboration between the codebreakers and the Metropolitan Police intercept operators, who during the early 1930s moved to a new location in the grounds of the Metropolitan Police Nursing Home at Denmark Hill, south London. Harold Kenworthy and Leslie Lambert set out to track down the source of the London messages, as they had with the *Daily Mail*'s transmitter. Since the radio messages were always sent at night, their early attempts to home in on the signal met with suspicion from ordinary police officers and they were handicapped in any explanation by the need to keep what they were doing secret.

MI6 supplied a van in which they could place the direction-finding equipment while driving around London looking for the transmitter. But Kenworthy recalled that they had to be provided with a special pass after the very act of loading the equipment sparked off a police investigation into an assumed robbery. 'Some exciting moments were experienced – particularly on one occasion, after going round a neighbourhood for some time a police car stopped us. On being asked: "What have you got in that parcel?" – the parcel being a portable short-wave set, Mr Lambert said: "I don't want to tell you." After that remark, there was nothing to it but for the pass to be shown. On another occasion, we spotted a PC waiting for us in the middle of a narrow crossing. We literally backed out of this by reversing round a corner and making off in another direction.'

They used a large direction-finding (DF) set in the van to find the general direction and then deployed the portable set to 'walk in' on the transmitter. 'It took a long time to get final results,' Kenworthy recalled. 'The search for the unauthorised wireless station went on for some months. We were only one and often after all the preparations the London station would be on the air perhaps two minutes only and then off until the following evening. These chancy sort of conditions made the effort a very long drawn out affair, but it was finally rewarded by locating the station in Wimbledon.'

An MI5 surveillance operation was then set up. The house was found to belong to Stephen James Wheeton, a Communist Party member. MI5 officers followed him to regular meetings with Alice Holland, a prominent party member, at which the messages were handed over and collected. The transmitter was later moved to north London but it was not long before Kenworthy and Lambert again located it in the home of another party member called William Morrison.

The Mask operation was inadvertently sabotaged in 1933 when the Moscow station began interfering with a frequency used by the GPO to send telegrams. Since the call sign used by Moscow was similar to those used by the Admiralty for sending diplomatic signals, the GPO rang Henry Maine (the official in charge of liaison with the Post Office to obtain drop copies of enciphered telegrams). The GPO official asked Maine if he knew what station used that particular call sign. 'He did, and not thinking it necessary to warn them not to take action, told them it was Moscow. The GPO immediately sent a service message to Traffic Controller Moscow Commercial Services to the effect that the transmitter was causing interference to one of their frequencies and would they please shift its frequency.' Moscow denied any knowledge of the station, Kenworthy said, but it immediately went off the air and did not return for many months. 'When it did, a completely new system had been devised using more frequencies, numerous call signs and of course an entirely new cipher.'

This period saw the first co-operation between the British and French codebreakers that was to be so helpful to the later attempts to break the German Enigma machine cipher. Tiltman recalled going to Paris with the then Assistant Chief of MI6, Colonel Stewart Menzies, to meet Colonel Gustave Bertrand, the head of the French codebreaking unit. 'An arrangement had been made for the exchange of information regarding Russian cipher systems between the Government Code and Cypher School and French cryptanalysts. I had worked for 10 years on Russian ciphers, nearly nine years in India, and three years on Comintern ciphers and Commander Denniston, the Director of GC&CS, chose me to go to Paris as having more general knowledge of Russian systems than anyone else in the office (except perhaps Ernst Fetterlein). I flew to Paris on May 24 1933 with General, then Colonel, Stewart Menzies. I spent the whole of May 25 with Bertrand and two other Frenchmen.

'I had been instructed before leaving England that I was not to disclose any knowledge of Russian use of long additives or of one-time pads unless I was satisfied that the French were aware of this usage. I was also told not to discuss Comintern cipher systems at all. It was characteristic of Bertrand as I got to know him later that, immediately after I was introduced to him, he handed me a typewritten statement to the effect that the French were fully aware of the nature of Russian high grade systems. I was therefore free to describe for them the various Russian systems (nearly all diplomatic) I had worked on since joining GC&CS in London in 1920, particularly in India 1921–1929. Much of this was new to them – I don't remember that they told me anything significant that I didn't know already.'

The Mask operation led by Tiltman continued until the middle of 1937. Its significance is confirmed not just by Curry but by Josh Cooper who remarked that while the work carried out by Kenworthy's police unit was of no particular interest to the police it was 'of great importance to the future GCHQ'.

Exploitation of Soviet armed forces traffic during the interwar period appears to have been less systematic and therefore less successful than that of the diplomatic and Comintern networks. It is not clear how much military material was deciphered in India. But both Simla and Sarafand had limited success with Russian military ciphers. There was also some early work on the ciphers of the KGB. But during the 1920s and early 1930s, the main focus inside GC&CS with regard to Soviet armed forces was on the Russian Navy.

William 'Nobby' Clarke, a former member of Room 40, was one of a number of GC&CS members unhappy at the way in which the codebreakers and the intercept operators were increasingly being asked to work on diplomatic material at the expense of service traffic. He managed to persuade the Admiralty that there should be a naval section within GC&CS and then made the rounds of Royal Navy establishments and ships, coaxing a number of officers into agreeing to intercept Russian, French and Japanese wireless communications in their spare time while at sea. The Royal Navy intercept station at Flowerdown also began taking Russian naval material and the Army station in Sarafand covered the Black Sea Fleet. But the use of one-time pads and a lack of depth ensured that few messages were deciphered.

Clarke's report on Naval Section work for 1927 admitted that there had been very little naval traffic intercepted, all of it between shore-based establishments. There had, however, been some success in solving a super-enciphered system in which encoded messages were reciphered before transmission, a practice designed to make them more difficult for an eavesdropper to read. The messages were first encoded using a codebook, which provided groups of randomly selected figures for common words or phrases. This produced a series of groups of figures, normally uniformly four-figure or five-figure groups. The operator then took a stream of predetermined but randomly selected figures, placed them underneath his encoded message, and added the two together figure by figure, using non-carrying arithmetic, to produce the reciphered message.

In an attempt to find out whether it was worthwhile continuing to work on the Russian Navy ciphers, Clarke decided to see the problems faced by his volunteer intercept operators for himself: 'In the hope of clearing up the problem of Russian naval ciphers, I joined HMS *Curacao* for the Baltic cruise of the 2nd Light Cruiser Squadron . . . Unfortunately the amount of intercepts available does not permit of much work being undertaken on this kind of traffic nor is it considered that it would be profitable.' The situation improved slightly in 1929. Although no messages had been broken, enough intercepts were coming in to allow some limited traffic analysis.

During late 1929 and 1930, the Naval Section launched a concerted effort to try to solve the Russian naval codes and ciphers. Josh Cooper was sent to Sarafand to carry out a fifteen-month investigation of Black Sea Fleet communications while Lieutenant-Commander G. A. 'Titts' Titterton, a former member of the Naval Section, returned from a Russian interpreter's course to work on Russian Navy material in London.

Cooper's report shows that there were a number of different codes and ciphers in use, ranging from relatively simple systems to high-grade ciphers. But while the lower grade systems proved vulnerable he was not able to break any of the high-grade systems and Titterton seems to have had even less success. He left GC&CS briefly in December 1932 and, as one senior codebreaker noted, was replaced by another officer whose 'skirmish with Russian was also short and unsuccessful'. The lack of success and the need to divert resources to Italian systems as a result of the 1935 Abyssinia Crisis eventually led to Russian Navy coverage being dropped.

But as the attack on Russian Navy systems waned, the Army

Section of GC&CS, set up in 1930 under John Tiltman, was beginning to get to grips with an upsurge of Russian Army traffic. This had become available in 1933 as a result of an arrangement with Estonia's codebreakers, who offered all the material they were intercepting in return for radio equipment. With Tiltman busy, first on the Comintern traffic and later on super-enciphered Japanese army systems, P. K. Fetterlein, the brother of Ernst, was recruited to work on the Estonian material. The creation in 1936 of an Air Section of GC&CS, led by Cooper, gave fresh impetus to this work. Cooper's experience of Russian material and Tiltman's preoccupation with Japanese systems appear to have been the main reasons for the Air Section being asked to deal with the Estonian material, since little if any of it was from Russian Air Force units. 'The Russian traffic was a mess,' Cooper said. 'What we received was a mixed bag from a wide range of stations (some of them in the Leningrad Military District, just over the border, some from at least as far away as the Ukraine), with little or no continuity. Some of the material was in very low-grade systems, which had usually been broken by the Estonians before we got it; the content was of no face value. There was also a variety of higher-grade systems but never enough of any one line to make a crypt attack possible. Controlled interception of selected lines of traffic with good T/A backup might at this time have produced very interesting results, but we could not control the Estonians.'

By 1938, with war against Germany beginning to look inevitable, the main priority had become the breaking of the German Enigma machine cipher, although Russia still remained high on the GC&CS list of target countries. Lieutenant-Commander Titterton had now returned to Broadway and the Home Fleet had resumed interception of Russian Navy traffic. As late as mid-1938, two new junior assistants were recruited solely for their knowledge of Russian, one of them being Alexis Vlasto, whose *A Linguistic History of Russia to the End of the Eighteenth Century* remains a standard textbook. Russia also remained a high priority in India, where the codebreakers had broken the Soviet secret service super-enciphered code.

The responsibility for the Russian material was subsequently handed back to the military section, together with the services of P. K. Fetterlein. The 1939 co-operation with the Polish and French codebreakers, that was to be of immense importance in the breaking of the German Enigma machine cipher, had the added bonus of providing a batch of material from Lithuanian and Latvian codebreakers, Cooper recalled. 'The raw material was similar in quality to the Estonian and work on this untidy mass of miscellaneous Soviet services was co-ordinated in the Military Section with Vlasto as Air Section's contribution. There was only one consignment of Lithuanian and Latvian. Estonian went on, I think, for a while with deliveries by diplomatic bag.'

By now, the codebreakers had been moved out of London to the MI6 'War Station' at Bletchley Park, designated Station X. This was not, as is sometimes supposed, a mark of mystery, but simply because it was the tenth in a number of properties acquired by MI6, all of which were designated using Roman numerals. The number of staff remained limited – only 137 of those who went to Bletchley in August 1939 were members of the GC&CS codebreaking sections. But the alliance between Stalin and Hitler continued to ensure that Russian material retained a high priority. Co-operation with the French was expanded. A dedicated Russian section was set up under Tiltman's tutelage at Wavendon, a country house close to Bletchley Park, and another Russian section was set up at Sarafand, in Palestine.

The crucial breakthrough on Russian armed forces material came during the Russo-Finnish War in late 1939 and early 1940. The large amount of traffic created by the Russian Army's invasion of Finland, and the Finns' determined defence of their territory, gave the codebreakers enough depth to solve two high-grade Russian systems: the Soviet Army's GKK super-enciphered code and the OKF super-enciphered naval code.

It is not clear who made the break into the two Russian high-grade systems, but it seems likely that Tiltman was yet again involved. He was in charge of the section, had worked on a number of similar Japanese Army systems and, the previous year, had broken the Japanese Navy's main super-enciphered code, known to the Allies as JN-25, within weeks of its introduction. It was also Tiltman who set up an arrangement with the Finnish Army's codebreaking unit in order to obtain as much of the Russian traffic as possible to allow further recovery of the system. 'He had the foresight to note the extreme importance of Finnish collaboration in our Russian work,' Denniston said. 'He spent a fortnight in Finland and established a close and friendly liaison with their cryptographic unit and his persistent drive . . . may well seal an alliance which should prove of the greatest value to the intelligence departments of all three services.'

Tiltman agreed a similar deal to that with Estonia, promising to provide radio equipment in return for the traffic. Unfortunately, there were immediate complications. No sooner had he returned to England than the Russo-Finnish War came to an end. Nevertheless, the Finns insisted that they were still determined to expand their Sigint operations against the Russians. There was then difficulty persuading Stewart Menzies, who had succeeded Sinclair as Chief of MI6, to pay for the Finnish equipment. Even once he had agreed, some of the wireless receivers went missing. But eventually the arrangement began to work and the Finns provided an increased flow of Russian military and KGB traffic as well as five captured codebooks: three Russian Army codebooks – two of which had already been partially worked out by the Russian section – and two Soviet Navy codebooks. These were the KKF2 code used by the Black Sea Fleet and the KKF3 code used in the Baltic, which the British had broken a few months earlier but had not totally reconstructed.

This provided fresh impetus to the work against the Russian Navy. Russian armed forces traffic now became the subject of a major effort by GC&CS and its outstations. Radio receivers were installed in the British Legation in Stockholm. Scarborough joined Flowerdown in monitoring Russian Navy frequencies. Vlasto was sent out to bolster the Russian section at Sarafand which, along with India, weighed in with a full range of interception, traffic analysis and codebreaking, sending high-grade cipher back to England via the diplomatic bag. The RAF set up an experimental intercept site in Baghdad to target Russian army and air circuits in the Caucasus. It also monitored Russian Navy intercepts from Cairo. The Royal Navy intercept sites at Dingli in Malta, Alexandria in northern Egypt, and Ismailia on the Suez Canal took Russian Navy material and fixed locations of the transmitters using direction finding. The Far East Combined Bureau (FECB), the main British Sigint outpost in the Far East, began taking Russian traffic from the Vladivostok area and kept watch on Baltic Fleet frequencies. It even asked the Australian and New Zealand Navy intercept organizations to provide any Russian naval material they could. At GC&CS itself, French naval codebreakers, who had been transferred to Britain, began working on high-grade Baltic and Black Sea Fleet ciphers.

The flow of material from Estonia dried up in June 1940 when Russia occupied the Baltic States. But the fall of France brought willing replacements in the form of Polish wireless operators and codebreakers who, having escaped Poland to work with Gustave Bertrand, had now been forced to flee the German *Blitzkrieg* for a second time. Based at Stanmore in west London, they found they were able to monitor Russian material from the Ukraine and were co-opted by Denniston to provide more material for the Russian section.

The increased effort brought yet another break, this time at Sarafand where the KKF4 Black Sea Fleet super-enciphered code was broken in November 1940. A few weeks later, the British and Americans exchanged Sigint material primarily relating to the Axis countries. The exchange took place at Bletchley Park in

February 1941 and as part of their contribution, the British handed over four Russian codebooks: the OKF high-grade Baltic Fleet super-enciphered code broken at Wavendon and Bletchley; the EPRON codebook used by the Russian Navy Salvage Corps, which had also been worked out by GC&CS; the KKF4 Black Sea Fleet codebook broken at Sarafand; and the KKF3 Black Sea Fleet codebook provided by the Finns.

The British operation against the Russian armed forces traffic was subsequently disrupted by a major change in codes and ciphers. But Denniston told Menzies that there was no doubt that it had 'benefited largely by the increased interception from the Poles and that our Finnish liaison is becoming really attractive. This liaison, owing to recent changes in all Russian codes, is of first importance.' By the beginning of June, there was serious concern that the increasing collaboration between the Finnish and German General Staffs might compromise the arrangement with Finland, leading the Germans to question how vulnerable their own ciphers were. The Poles were asked to reinforce their Stanmore operation and Tiltman even sought the advice of the MI6 Head of Station in Helsinki as to whether the Finns could be trusted to keep the secret. However this debate was overtaken by events, in the shape of Operation Barbarossa – the German invasion of Russia – which began on 22 June.

According to the official history of intelligence, all intelligence operations against the Soviet Union now came to an abrupt halt on Winston Churchill's orders. The reality was nowhere near as clear-cut. Indeed, initially, coverage was increased. There was a long drawn-out debate over whether or not to drop Soviet traffic. The codebreakers in India were only too happy to dispose of their Russian Air Force and KGB tasks which had produced 'nothing of intelligence value'. But there were concerns that the lack of continuity would hamper attempts to break the Russian codes and ciphers in the future. As a result, it was not until December 1941 that the Russian section was closed down. Even then the

Poles were told to continue intercepting traffic and trying to break it, while the British kept two sets monitoring known Russian frequencies at the Scarborough Royal Navy site and the RAF station in Cheadle.

Within weeks, the Metropolitan Police intercept site at Denmark Hill and the Radio Security Service, an organization set up to monitor clandestine radio stations which now came under the aegis of MI6, had begun to pick up messages between Moscow and its agents in Europe. Despite the Churchill edict, MI5 had continued to keep a watch on the Russians and their links to the CPGB. But it was unaware of the 'bundles of Russian traffic' that had been intercepted until February 1943 when it discovered through its own sources within the party that Jean Jefferson, a party member, had been asked to resign in order to take an 'illegal' post operating the radio link to Moscow. Sir David Petrie, the Director-General of MI5, had a fraught discussion with Menzies at which it was agreed that Soviet espionage links should be monitored. This was subsequently refined to interception and decryption of the links between Moscow and communist parties across Europe. A small Russian team was secretly set up at a GC&CS outpost overlooking London's Park Lane to break the cipher. The keys were taken from an English edition of Shakespeare's plays, in order to avoid the risk of the operator being caught with a codebook. By the late summer of 1943, less than two years after they had closed their Russian section, ostensibly for the duration of the war, the British codebreakers were again reading Soviet traffic. The end of the Second World War was almost two years away, but the preparations for the second Cold War had already begun.

3

Reminiscences on the Enigma

HUGH FOSS

Introduction

Although Bolshevik codes and ciphers had been the main target of the interwar years, by the time the codebreakers moved to Bletchley Park in late August 1939, these had been replaced by the attempts to break Enigma. It has been suggested that it was not until shortly before the war that the GC&CS codebreakers began to make any effort to break an Enigma machine. Although it is certainly true that Enigma had not enjoyed the highest priority during the interwar years, it was far from ignored. As the late Hugh Foss, who joined GC&CS in 1924, explains in the following chapter, he first looked into the possibility of breaking the machine in 1927, paradoxically with a view to seeing whether the British might want to use it themselves.

The workings of the machine will be explained in later chapters. But for those as yet unfamiliar with the subject, it looked essentially like a small typewriter in a wooden box. On most models, there was a standard continental QWERTZU keyboard, as opposed to the British QWERTY, and above that a lampboard with a series of lights, one for each letter of the alphabet. Inside the machine were a series of three, or sometimes four, rotors, which were the main elements of the encipherment system. The operator typed in the letters of the plain-text message. The action of depressing the key sent an electrical impulse through the machine and the enciphered letters lit up on the lampboard. On the later Wehrmacht *models, there was a plugboard, or* Stecker *system, which increased the variations of encipherment to around 159 million million million possible settings. Put like that, it seemed impossible to break. But the reality was that there were still only twenty-six letters in the German alphabet and that gave the codebreakers a chance. Examining the commercial C Model he was given, where the number of different possible settings was merely several million, Foss decided that it had a high degree of security but, given certain conditions, it could be broken. If you knew a piece of original plain-text, a 'crib', that was at least 180 letters long, the wiring of the first two wheels could be worked out; and if the wiring was known, a crib of just fifteen letters would be sufficient to break the machine settings.*

GC&CS did a very small amount of work on the machine during the early 1930s. But it was not until the Spanish Civil War in 1936 that there was any real attempt to break live Enigma traffic. After some initial work by Josh Cooper, an Enigma machine, given by the Germans to the Italians and Spanish (the K Model), was broken by Dilly Knox on 24 April 1937, using an improved version of the system recommended by Foss ten years earlier.

Here, in a paper written in September 1949, Foss describes the early British work on the commercial 'C Model' Enigma, and the beginning of the contacts with the French and Poles that were to become so important to the subsequent British breaks. The mention of the QWERTZU, or diagonal, in this paper is a reference to the order of the wiring between the keyboard and the first set of contacts inside the machine. The British had been unable to work out the order in which the keys were connected to the 'entry plate' in the Wehrmacht's *plugboard machine. Given the enormous number of different permutations available to the Germans, Foss and Knox had not imagined that it might simply be in alphabetical order. This was probably the most important single piece of information that the Poles provided.*

MS

My earliest recollections of the Enigma date back to 1926. We then knew of two models: large typing [B model] and small index [C model]. I never saw the large machine and don't know if it was ever widely used. It was the small index model that was later developed and used by German services and others.

It will be best to dispose of the large Enigma in a few paragraphs to avoid confusion. Its UK patent specification was 231,502, application date 25 March 1925, convention date (Germany) 25 March 1924. A letter from the Aeronautical Committee of Guarantee, Berlin, to the Air Ministry, dated 19 June 1924, said: 'The invention, in an incomplete state, was examined in about 1921 by Lieutenant Hume, Office of the Military Attaché, British Embassy, Berlin, and it is believed, an expert was sent out from the War Office.'

[A letter from] Hume to [Edward] Travis, 29 July 1926, says that the company have informed him that they have sold out all the big machines and no more of this pattern will be manufactured. An improved model may be ready in 10 months' time. Perhaps the Admiralty would meanwhile like to buy a model of the small machine. The improved model of the large machine was on view in 1928.

There is a brochure in French '*La Machine à Chiffrer, Enigma*' issued by *Chiffriermaschinen Aktiengesellschaft*, Berlin W, 35 (undated, but presumed about 1924). This deals with the machine from the user's point of view and gives no details (apart from the usual astronomical number of key variations) of the ciphering. There is also a brochure in German.

An undated report describes a demonstration of the large machine at the Foreign Office on 27 March (possibly 1926). It was a typewriting model (called the 'Typing Machine' as opposed to the small 'Index' machine) and worked from the main current (DC). It had previously been demonstrated in Stockholm. It was a one-way machine (i.e. it had no reflector wheel), with four drums which were moved by four 'gap-tooth' cog wheels with different numbers of teeth on each, some of the teeth being operative and others not.

Sometime in 1927 or so Travis gave me a small machine to examine. I was not told where it came from, but presumed it had been bought as a sample. This was the Enigma referred to [in the GC&CS history] *German Abwehr Cryptographic Systems and their Solution* vol. 1 (*The Unsteckered Enigma*).

> A worker [Keith Batey] on the SD (*Sicherheitsdienst*) Enigma having recovered the upright, the next most natural step to take was to see whether any known machine had a wheel defined by this upright. This led to a most surprising discovery: that the wheel recovered was identical with wheel I of a certain commercial machine said to have been purchased by Mr [Dilly] Knox in Vienna in 1925. It had in fact been lying in a cupboard behind the person who made the original break.

The only difference between the two machines was that the turnover notch had been transferred to the tyre [ring] [in the SD machine]. I don't know when this model [the small (Index) machine] was first made. It had movable tyres but the turnover notch was on the wheel and not on the tyre. Incidentally, the Air Ministry used this model as an inspiration for Typex* which also had turnover notches on the wheel and not on the tyres.

I wrote a paper entitled 'The Reciprocal Enigma' (the large

Enigma was not reciprocal) in which I showed how, if the wiring was known, a crib of fifteen letters would give away the identity and setting of the right-hand wheel and how, if the wiring was unknown, a crib of 180 letters would give away the wiring of the right-hand and middle wheels. The methods I used were rather clumsy as they were geometrical rather than algebraical and, when Dilly Knox came to study the subject ten years later, he invented the 'rods' and the process known as 'buttoning up', which used the same properties as I had done, but did so in a more effective way.

In January 1939, the French cryptanalysts showed Denniston, Knox and myself their methods, which were even clumsier than mine, and ended with a flourish and a dramatic '*Voici la méthode Française*'. They asked Knox if he had understood and he replied in a very bored way '*Pas du tout*', meaning (I think) '*Pas du tout à fait*' [sic]. Denniston and I rushed in with conciliatory remarks. The French were, however, delighted with the rods when Knox explained them and by the next interview had made a set of '*réglettes*' of their own.

At these two interviews, the Poles were mainly silent but one of them gave a lengthy description in German of the recovery of throw-on indicators when the operators used pronounceable settings. During this exposition Knox kept muttering to Denniston, 'But this is what Tiltman did', while Denniston hushed him and told him to listen politely. Knox went and looked out of the window.

Some time in 1938 or 1939, I can't remember when – Josh Cooper places the time as the autumn of 1938 and that suits me – we were given by the Poles or French cribs of four long steckered Enigma messages and, I believe, the *Stecker*-pairings. I think that at the time we did know how the *Stecker* worked, but I can't remember who told us. There is an undated translation of

* The high-grade cipher machine used by the British armed forces during the Second World War.

a secret German document published in 1930 which describes the method of plugging of the *Stecker*, but does not give the cryptographic effect. This may have been the document given us by the French in 1931. Knox, [Oliver] Strachey, R. R. Jackson and I all worked on it in an effort to reconstruct the wiring, including the basic 'diagonal', which on the steckered Enigma was ABCD . . . Z and not QWERTZU . . . I don't know why the others failed, but the reason I failed was because I assumed the turnover notch was on the wheel and not on the tyre. I believe Knox and Strachey were allowing for the turnover notch to be on the tyre. Later on, at Warsaw, the Poles, who must have considered us all very stupid, gave us the complete answer.

30.IX.49
[PRO HW 25/10]

4

Breaking Air Force and Army Enigma

RALPH ERSKINE

Introduction

GC&CS's wartime solutions of plugboard Enigma owe much to Polish cryptanalysts, who were the first to solve it – in 1932. As is now well known, the Poles gave GC&CS a clone of plugboard Enigma in August 1939, following a meeting in Warsaw at the end of July. But it was not until January 1940 that GC&CS was able to solve any Enigma using new rotors that had come into service in December 1938. Hut 6, as it became known, did so using Polish methods until May 1940, when the Heer *(German Army) and* Luftwaffe *(German Air Force) changed the indicating system used with Enigma. But even before then, Dilly Knox had improved significantly on the Polish methods. Alan Turing had also invented the British 'bombe', which bore little resemblance to the Polish* bomba *and was the basis of virtually all GC&CS's successes against Enigma during the war after 1940.*

Chapter 4 illustrates the fundamental importance of good intercept facilities, which were in short supply for much of the war. Indeed, Hut 6's successes ultimately depended on the skills of the humble intercept operator and good, easily operated intercept sets. Although the contribution of the US Navy bombes to Hut 6's work is now better known, it is not generally appreciated that the British intercept stations had enough high-quality sets only because of superior American production facilities and know-how. A British history of the important Army intercept station at Beaumanor concluded that the intercept war 'was won, in a very large measure, as a result of the availability of American communication receivers'.

Breaking Enigma is sometimes thought to have been a task carried out by a few cryptanalysts, working on their own in back rooms. In fact, most of the work was done by relatively unskilled staff, and the cryptanalysts were very much in a minority – and seldom eccentric. There was so much traffic that Hut 6 had to adopt production-line methods to deal with it. Running Hut 6 as a well-organized and flexible unit, while maintaining staff morale at a high level, required considerable leadership and management skills, especially since many staff were doing boring and monotonous work under difficult conditions. Fortunately, Gordon Welchman, the first head of Hut 6, and his successor, Stuart Milner-Barry, rose to the challenge well. Not every unit at Bletchley was so well managed.

It is sometimes claimed that Hut 6 was completely on top of Enigma by the end of 1944, and that it was often quickly and easily broken then. Chapter 4 shows that nothing could be further from the truth. In November 1944, when Hut 6 was attacking about sixty-five Heer *and* Luftwaffe *Enigma ciphers, Hut 6's demands for bombe time became prodigious, and it required considerable help from US Navy bombes in Washington. The US Navy had generously agreed in November 1943 to handle Hut 6 ciphers on its bombes on exactly the same basis as* Kriegsmarine *(German Navy) ciphers, except for the main naval cipher, Shark: it kept to that decision for the rest of the war, despite being worried about impinging on the functions of the US*

Army codebreakers, which was always a highly sensitive issue.

Chapter 4 describes the methods used by Hut 6 to penetrate Heer *and* Luftwaffe *Enigma, and shows the many difficulties that they faced, especially with* Heer *ciphers. It was a close-run thing, especially in late 1944 and 1945, when Milner-Barry thought that Hut 6 was on the verge of losing its hold on Enigma.*

RE

The Polish Cipher Bureau, Bureau Szyfrow (BS), had attacked German codes successfully in the 1920s until 1926, when the German Navy adopted two simple versions of Enigma. In 1928, the Bureau became blind against much of the German Army traffic, which had also started to use Enigma. The Cipher Bureau realized that a machine cipher required special talents to solve it, and in 1929 gave selected mathematics students a course in cryptology. The only three to complete the course, Jerzy Rozycki, Henryk Zygalski and Marian Rejewski, were recruited by the Bureau, although initially they worked only on a part-time basis.

The German Army added a plugboard to Enigma in 1930, but it was not until September 1932 that Rejewski, who was the star among the young cryptanalysts, was given the plugboard Enigma to attack on his own – the older cryptanalysts in the Bureau had been trying to solve it since its introduction, but had completely failed. By the end of that year, Rejewski had reconstructed the wiring of Enigma's rotors mathematically, using permutation theory, in an outstanding feat of cryptanalysis. The fatal flaw in Enigma had been its indicating system, which used doubly enciphered message keys (see Appendix II). Rejewski described the system as 'the third secret' of military Enigma, although he also received invaluable help from Enigma key-lists which had been received from Gustave Bertrand, in French military intelligence: Bertrand had bought them from Hans-Thilo Schmidt, who was working in the German Defence Ministry's *Chiffrierstelle* (Cipher Centre). The indicating system was also exploited by the Poles to solve Enigma traffic in 1938 and 1939 using electro-mechanical machinery known as *bombas* (bombes), and a system of perforated sheets invented by Zygalski. Rejewski also reconstructed the wiring of rotors IV and V when they were introduced in December 1938.

Plugboard Enigma, which was the only type used by the *Wehrmacht* during the war, measured about 28 × 35 × 15 cm (11 × 14 × 6 in) and weighed about 12 kg (26 lb). Its main components were a keyboard, lampboard, rotors, reflector (*Umkehrwalze*) and plugboard. A battery provided the electric current for the internal circuitry (see Figure 4.1). The standard machine used three rotors, which during the war were chosen from a set of five for the army, or eight for the navy. Rotor turnover notches were in a different place on rotors I to V – a weakness that was later to be exploited by Huts 6 and 8. Double notches in the special naval rotors, VI to VIII, were in the same positions in all three rotors, which made it impossible for Hut 8 to differentiate between them in a procedure known as Banburismus. Unlike the rotors, the reflector in three-rotor *Wehrmacht* Enigma could not move. A later version of naval Enigma, M4, used a rotor as part of a settable reflector, but it did not rotate during use.

The plugboard contained twenty-six dual sockets, into which cables with jacks were inserted to connect pairs of letters – A to P, B to K, and so on. It was reciprocal: in the previous examples, P swapped for A, and K for B. Ten pairs of letters were generally connected during the war, although eleven pairs would have produced the maximum number of combinations. Without a plugboard, Enigma was relatively easy to solve, but the plugboard version was a very impressive machine.

Dilly Knox, GC&CS's chief cryptanalyst, and other members of GC&CS tried to reconstruct *Wehrmacht* Enigma's wiring in

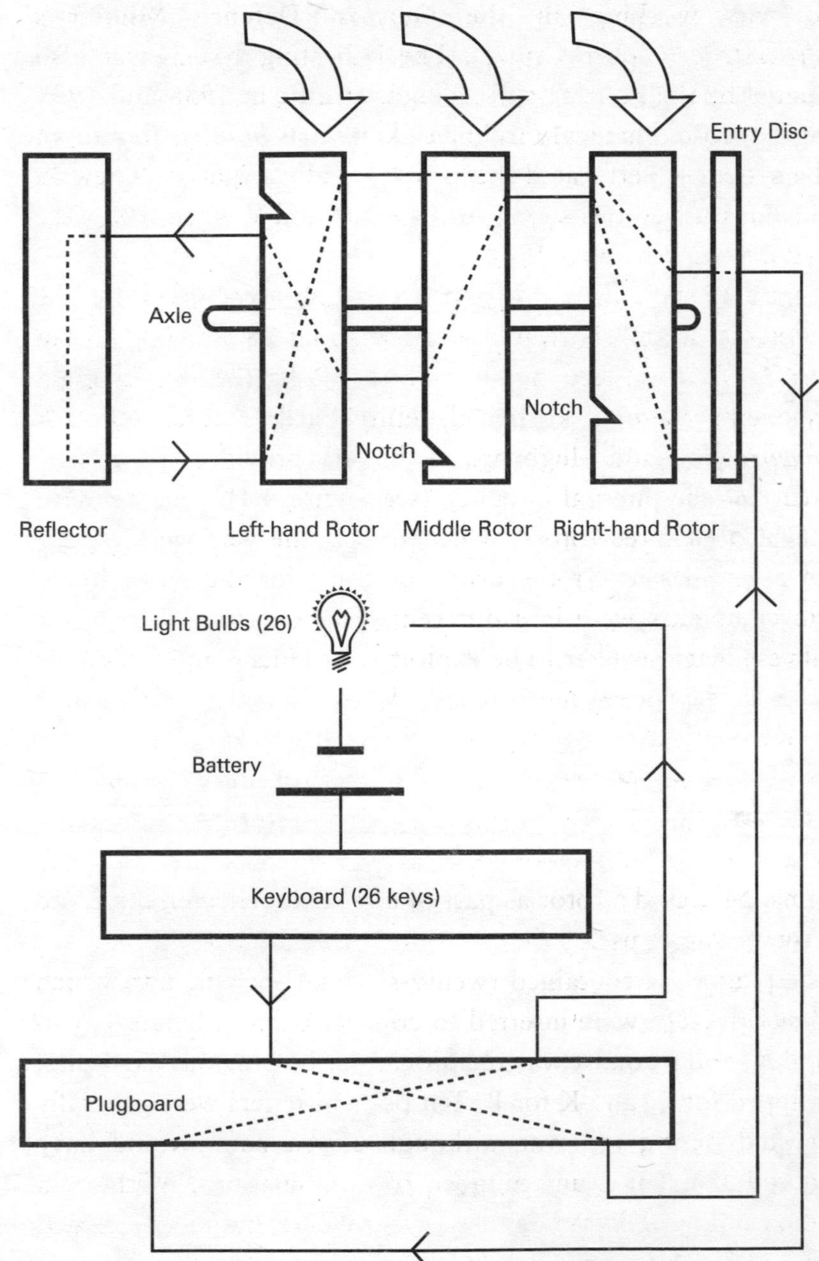

Figure 4.1 **Path of current through Enigma**

the 1930s, but were thwarted by one factor – the wiring to Enigma's entry disc or rotor (the *Eintrittwalze*). Knox called the wiring the 'QWERTZU', on account of its link to Enigma's keyboard. It had also stalled Rejewski, although only for a relatively short time. In January 1939, three representatives from GC&CS, including Knox, met two senior members of the Polish Cipher Bureau and Bertrand in Paris, but the Poles were under orders to disclose nothing substantive about their successes. They did well: one of the GC&CS party wrote about the Poles: 'Practical knowledge of [*Wehrmacht*] enigma nil.' However, Knox and Alastair Denniston, the operational head of GC&CS, together with Bertrand and a French cryptanalyst, were invited by the Poles to Warsaw at the end of July. To their great surprise, a Polish clone of Enigma was revealed to them on 26 July at the Cipher Bureau's centre at Pyry, outside Warsaw, and they were told that the wiring to the entry rotor was the identity permutation (A wired to A, B to B, and so on). Knox was far from pleased that the Poles had beaten him to it, maintaining 'a stony silence' during the conference. The Polish methods to solve Enigma signals were explained at some length; the visitors were shown the *bombas* during the second part of the conference. Fortunately, when they met the Poles the next day, 'Knox was his own bright self & won the hearts & admiration of the young men with whom he was in touch.'

Surprisingly, one cryptanalyst at GC&CS, a 'Mrs B. B.' (it has not been possible to identify her) 'had seriously contemplated' that the wiring was indeed an identity. But she had not been given a crib (known plain-text) supplied to GC&CS by Bertrand, either because organization was not Knox's forte, or because he thought that she would be wasting her time in following it up: she had therefore been unable to make any progress. Even more surprisingly, although Knox understood her hypothesis about its wiring, he had not pursued it himself, probably because he could not believe that the Germans had been so stupid. Knox wrote that 'had she worked on the crib we should be teaching them [the Poles]'. However, in this he was somewhat over-optimistic, since it is most unlikely that GC&CS could have recovered the wiring of rotors IV and V. Rejewski had been able to do so only because the *Sicherheitsdienst* (SD) continued to use a pre-15 September 1938 indicating system when the new rotors were introduced. It is almost certain that the British were unable to intercept the SD traffic at that stage, since it seems to have been sent at low-power, and British intercept facilities were very thin on the ground.

The Poles disclosed the design of the Zygalski sheets (called '*Netz verfahren*' – net method) at the Warsaw meeting, and sent Enigma clones to London and Paris in August. GC&CS soon began to prepare two sets of sheets, based on Zygalski's design, although the actual punching of the sheets could not start until mid-November, since a special machine to print the positions of certain repeated indicator letters, known as 'females', had first to be made. The first set of Zygalski sheets was completed around late December 1939, in one third of the time predicted by Knox. Making the sheets so quickly was a major achievement, since sixty sets (one for each rotor order), each with twenty-six sheets, had to be prepared, with many of the sheets containing about 1,000 holes cut precisely to give the relevant co-ordinates. Knox apparently had to resort to subterfuge and contravene Denniston's orders for preparing them, in order for them to be ready so soon.

The British cryptanalysts must have been dismayed when they started to use the sheets, since they could not solve any Enigma traffic with them. Unknown to GC&CS, crucial data received from the Poles about rotors IV and V had been incorrect. GC&CS's failure with the sheets may have been the reason why Denniston asked Brigadier Stewart Menzies ('C', who was also the director of GC&CS) to see whether Rejewski and his colleagues could visit GC&CS to help with Enigma. Menzies duly wrote to Colonel Louis Rivet, the head of the *Cinquième Bureau de l'État Major de l'Armée* (Fifth Section of the Army General Staff – the *Services de Renseignements et de Contre-Espionnage militaire*), whose functions included radio intelligence. But Rivet was unwilling to send the Polish cryptanalysts, who were working with the French Army at the Château de Vignolles, in Gretz-Armainvillers, near Paris, after escaping from Poland. He felt that since his Service was paying the Poles, it was entitled to keep them.

Part of a second set of Zygalski sheets was sent to the Poles in France on 28 December 1939, together with a set of Jeffreys sheets (which were a punched sheet catalogue of the effect of two rotors and the reflector). Alan Turing took the balance of the Zygalski sheets soon after they were completed around 7 January 1940. According to Knox's accounts, Denniston did not want the balance to be sent, perhaps for reasons of security. Knox had to threaten to resign unless they were sent immediately. It was fortunate that he took such a strong line, since GC&CS would not otherwise have learned the correct data for rotors IV and V so quickly, which might well have had disastrous consequences for its attack on Enigma. The Poles used the sheets to make the first break into wartime Enigma on 17 January, when they solved Green (the cipher used by the *Heer* in Germany's military districts, the *Wehrkreis*) for 28 October. At around this time, the GC&CS Enigma section moved into Hut 6, pursuant to a decision taken in early December 1939.

Hut 6 solved Green for 25 October, the first wartime key to be broken in Britain, almost immediately after Turing's return from France with the correct information about rotors IV and V. There was great relief when soon afterwards it broke Red (the main *Luftwaffe* cipher, which was widely employed for operational and administrative purposes) for 6 January, since there had been fears that the indicating system might have changed on 1 January. Hut 6 solved about fifty daily keys in Red, Green and Blue (a *Luftwaffe* practice cipher) between mid-January and late March

1940 using the Zygalski sheets. A new cipher, Yellow, was first heard on 10 April, during the Norwegian campaign, and was then broken each day until it went out of service on 14 May. Yellow carried both *Luftwaffe* and *Heer* traffic, and also gave some information about ship movements and German intentions. However, little use could be made of the decrypts operationally. Hut 3, which was responsible for analysing and collating the intelligence contained in the decrypts, as well as translating them, was formed into three eight-hour watches. At this stage its staff were mostly 'amateur soldiers and airmen, unversed in the ways of military intelligence', and lacking the necessary experience to deal with the plethora of codenames, abbreviations, arcane technical terms and other mysteries in the decrypts. There were not even enough staff or teleprinters to handle the flood of intelligence from Yellow and Red. To compound matters, the service departments had been expecting a silent war where radio silence ruled, and were insufficiently organized to handle the copious intelligence produced by Huts 3 and 6.

On 1 May, the inevitable happened: all the ciphers except Yellow dropped doubly enciphered message keys. The Germans had at last realized that doubly enciphered message keys made Enigma vulnerable. All Enigma except Yellow became unreadable until 22 May, when Red for 20 May was solved using a highly ingenious method called 'cillies' (see Appendix IV), which had been discovered by Knox around late January 1940. Hut 6 abandoned work on other Enigma to solve about 1,000 messages on Red each day for the rest of May. The resulting flood of operational intelligence was teleprinted to Whitehall much more quickly than during the Norwegian campaign, and this time Whitehall was ready to forward it to the operational commands. Hut 6 depended completely upon cillies and related methods until the first bombe with a diagonal board entered service in August 1940, and continued to rely on them substantially for the remainder of 1940, and yet later whenever it had no other cribs.

Red remained breakable with practically no gaps throughout the war, and was always the largest source by far of Hut 6 Ultra.

At the July meeting with the Poles, Knox had realized immediately that the Polish methods were completely vulnerable to a change in the indicating system, since they depended upon doubly enciphered message keys. Knox and Turing therefore decided to develop a British bombe which would be immune to any such change. The first British bombe was ordered before 1 November 1939. It was completely different from the Polish model, since it used cribs to test certain assumptions about a key's components, and did not merely check for 'females', which was the technique used by the Polish *bombas*. 'Doc' Harold Keen of the British Tabulating Machine Company at Letchworth was responsible for its detailed design, although the basic design concept, which defeated the all-important *Stecker* with their 150 million million key space, was the product of Turing's genius. The bombes were not, despite some claims to the contrary, even remote forerunners of the computer, since their internal architecture bore not the slightest resemblance to that of a computer. Nor was Colossus (the Bletchley Park electronic computer) ever used against Enigma, as is sometimes suggested.

The first bombe, named Victory, entered service on 14 March 1940, but it lacked the diagonal board designed by Gordon Welchman, and therefore produced far too many 'stops', which had to be tested by hand – a very time-consuming process. It was therefore only used against naval Enigma in a somewhat basic way, and not in attacking *Luftwaffe* or *Heer* Enigma. The first improved bombe (named Agnus, later corrupted to Agnes), with a diagonal board, came into service in mid-August 1940. Bombes comprised thirty-six banks of high-speed electrically driven Enigmas (except for a few early models, which had thirty banks), with three or more diagonal boards. The diagonal board made it much easier to devise bombe menus, and reduced the number of false stops by 99 per cent – from 676 to four with an eleven-letter menu giving two 'closures'. Depending on the composition of a menu, up to three rotor orders could be run on a single bombe. Setting up a bombe menu took thirty-five to fifty minutes, and changing a wheel order, ten minutes. A complete bombe run lasted about fifteen minutes, after the bombe was set up. Each bombe had two Wrens assigned to it: an operator and a tester, who made a preliminary check on the stop data to see whether they should be sent to a 'testing party' in Hut 6 for further examination. The two bombes in service in 1940 broke about 180 daily keys, all but a few (probably under ten) being *Luftwaffe* Enigma – mostly Red, which comprised about 120 keys. The daily keys (including naval Enigma keys) solved by the British bombes rose to a peak of 9,064 in 1943, and declined slightly to 8,444 in 1944, when US Navy bombes also solved a substantial number of keys.

From about the end of 1940 onwards, the bombes were the essential basis of Hut 6's solutions of *Heer* and *Luftwaffe* Enigma. Bombes at Bletchley Park were an inter-service resource, and were not 'owned' by any one Hut. Demands for bombe time by Hut 8 therefore had to be fitted in with the much more complex situation on Hut 6 ciphers. When Hut 8 suddenly needed a large number of machines, it could badly disturb the Hut 6 programme. Fortunately, very few issues of bombe priority had to be referred to Whitehall for guidance, since it would have been far too time-consuming a process: one example was at the end of March 1942 when the Y Board (which was responsible for overall Sigint policy) considered a proposal to allot six bombes out of about twenty then available, to work on Shark (the four-rotor cipher used by the Atlantic U-boats) for about twenty-five days. In the event, only 7 per cent of the total bombe time was allocated to Shark in April – about forty-two bombe days out of 600. It was just as well, since the original proposal would have severely disrupted Hut 6's work. Another major decision on priorities was taken in July 1942, when the PQ 17 convoy was under way and the fighting in North Africa had also become critical. It was decided that the threat to PQ 17 justified priority being given to the naval work on Dolphin. There were remarkably few disputes about bombes, partly due to the close friendship between Stuart Milner-Barry in Hut 6 and Hugh Alexander in Hut 8, and the fact that Milner-Barry fully appreciated the critical importance of the Battle of the Atlantic. A panel of five 'bombe controllers' – Milner-Barry, John Manisty and John Monroe from Hut 6, and Shaun Wylie and Hugh Alexander from Hut 8 – was established in mid-1942. The controller on duty settled all questions of bombe priority without leading to any friction between the two Huts.

By May 1943, fifty-eight 'standard' three-rotor bombes, which did not print stop data, and fourteen 'Jumbos', which gave a print-out, were being run by 900 Wrens and maintained by seventy-five RAF mechanics. By May 1945, 1,675 Wrens and about 265 men, virtually all from the RAF, were running and maintaining 211 bombes, including sixty-six four-rotor bombes for naval work. The bombe efficiency rate (the number of possible solutions, less those missed due to a bombe fault) hovered around 96 per cent throughout the war. Since each bombe contained about eleven miles of wire and 1,000,000 soldered contacts and received no preventative maintenance it was a minor miracle that they worked so well, twenty-four hours a day, seven days a week. A US Army contingent, the 6812th Signal Security Detachment, arrived in February 1944 to operate a bank of about eight bombes in the Eastcote bombe outstation from October onwards. The 6812th achieved a high degree of efficiency, with a daily average of 71.5 runs in April 1945 (twenty minutes per run, including the set-up time, etc.). It was a considerable accomplishment, since the theoretical maximum was seventy-two – the highest recorded figure by the Wrens was fifty-seven (twenty-six minutes per run).

A good crib for the bombes consisted of between twenty and thirty letters, but about fifteen would do at a pinch (for example,

'*Geraetklarmeldung*' – equipment ready). Cribs comprising as many as seventy-five letters were not uncommon, while occasionally they were 200 or more letters long. Considering that for all practical purposes cribs had to be letter perfect, it is amazing that so many long cribs were found. The following crib was part of a series called 'Sultan's Meldung', which broke Red on no fewer than six separate days in April 1943:

> EINS X MELDUNG KLAM X LUDWIG KLAM YY . . . YY SULTAN X ROEM X EINS CAESAR X GEHEIM [One Report. (Ludwig) . . . Sultan Roman one Caesar [=Ic (the intelligence officer)]. Secret]

It was easily recognizable, since it was transmitted daily on specific frequencies at three set times by the *Luftwaffe*'s *Fliegerkorps* X (codenamed 'Sultan').

A frequent crib on Phoenix, which was used by *Panzerarmee* Afrika for its high-level operational communications between divisions and Corps, read:

> NAQT RUHIG YY KEINE BESONDEREN VORKOMMNISSE YY [Quiet night. Nothing special to report.]

To Welchman's regret, the general responsible for the unit sending it was captured, with the result that the crib died out.

Hut 6 benefited greatly from the German reluctance to make the *Stecker* in *Heer* and *Luftwaffe* key-lists completely random. *Stecker* were not repeated on two successive days: if B and X were connected on Friday, that combination was not used on Saturday. The compilers of *Luftwaffe* key-lists also had a rule by which a letter was not connected to the next letter in the alphabet (B was not connected to C, C to D, and so on). Bletchley added a 'Consecutive *Stecker* Knockout' (CSKO) modification to the bombes to take account of this restriction, by eliminating stops which included consecutively steckered letters. A different rule prevented any rotor being used on consecutive days in the same position in the machine. Thus in the day before and after rotor order II, V, I was used, rotor II could not be used in the left-hand (slow) position, rotor V in the middle position or I in the fast (right-hand) position, reducing the rotor orders to be tested to thirty-two, instead of sixty. In addition, a rule under which no rotor order was used more than once a month was very helpful, especially towards the end of a month. And some ciphers started to use only half the available rotor orders, which became known as 'Nigelian' wheel orders (possibly being named after Nigel Forward, a member of Hut 6).

Hut 6 also derived considerable help from the following basic mistakes by the German cipher operators:

a) 'Psillies' – psychological cillies. In an indicator such as ROMXLV, XLV would probably be the enciphered message key 'MEL' (making ROMMEL when combined with the *Grundstellung* 'ROM'), while TOBKST might be derived from TOBRUK.
b) 'Nearnesses', which occurred when a cipher clerk, after selecting the *Grundstellung* (say HTB), calculated what the rotor positions would be three letters later (HTE here, if no rotor turnover was involved), typed them, producing, for example, DXX as the enciphered message key. Since his rotors were then at HTE, he did not have to reset them, and could therefore start typing the message text straightaway. The message key was then very 'near' to the *Grundstellung* – three letters away, so that this particular type of nearness was sometimes known as a '003'.

The ROMMEL type of psilli and nearnesses each gave a three-letter crib, linking the unenciphered and enciphered message key.

In September 1940, Hut 6 had broken Brown, which was used

by the *Luftwaffe*'s KGr 100, a pathfinder type unit, and by the Sixth Company of the *Luftwaffe*'s Signals Experimental Regiment. Until Brown ceased in late 1941, it gave indirect warnings of many KGr 100 raids, as well as information which later enabled an advanced 'beam' radio bombing system known as the *X-Gerät* to be jammed. The Brown radio operators were so 'peculiarly incautious in their radio chat' that quite a lot of the intelligence attributed to Brown in fact came merely from 'scarcely disguised plain language' and not from decrypts. Daily keys could sometimes be solved by hand, especially on Brown, since it employed only six or seven pairs of *Stecker* instead of the usual ten. Moreover, Brown days were paired, with the letters linked by *Stecker* not being repeated on the second day of a pair.

Heer Enigma was always much more difficult to break than *Luftwaffe* traffic, because *Heer* cipher discipline was always much higher than in the *Luftwaffe*, although the *Luftwaffe* improved in 1943. *Heer* Enigma included few cillies, or stereotyped beginnings or endings. Even in mid-1943, Dennis Babbage, the chief cryptanalyst in Hut 6, was worried that increased security precautions, such as the inclusion of 'padding' words at the start of messages and 'burying' addresses instead of leaving them at the start of signals, would soon prevent most *Heer* and *Luftwaffe* Enigma from being broken. Hut 6 wanted to find purely cryptanalytic or statistical methods to solve Enigma, but was never able to do so. Its worries and problems were to increase greatly as the war went on.

In January 1942, Hut 6 was receiving about 1,400 intercepts per day (43,600 per month), including Railway Enigma traffic, and producing 580 decrypts each day (18,000 per month). By May 1943, the number of daily intercepts varied between 3,300 and 6,000 – between 102,000 and 186,000 per month. No figure for decrypts is available for May 1943, but it would probably have been about half of the intercepts. To handle so much traffic clearly required a very efficient and flexible organization. By May 1943 (the period to which the description in the next four paragraphs relates), Hut 6 had evolved into five main sections, with a total of about 400 staff: a central party known as No. VI Intelligence School (later renamed Sixta), control party, operations group, operational watch and research party (see Figure 4.2).

The traffic intercepted by the Y service intercept stations was sent to Hut 6 by teleprinter so far as possible: the signals were preceded by a register with their preambles, which were transmitted immediately a full page was ready. Incoming traffic was first sorted by an identification party in the Hut 6 watch registration section into operational traffic, which was processed urgently, and non-operational, which had to wait. Operational messages then went to Registration Room No. 1, where a 'discriminatrix' sorted them by cipher system, using their discriminants and other data. Their preambles were then registered in a 'blist' (Banister list).

Operational messages were examined immediately by the cryptanalytic operational watch, which selected some from which to construct bombe menus. When a key was found by the bombes, the traffic using it was sent to the decoding room, where the signals were run through British Typex cipher machines, which had been converted to emulate Enigma. This part of deciphering the traffic was far from being a straightforward process: up to two-thirds of the messages could present deciphering difficulties – so-called 'duds' – messages which would not decipher, generally because they had the wrong indicators or contained garbled cipher text. The resulting decrypts were first routed through a room called the 'cubicle' for indexing, before being sent to Hut 3 for translation and analysis. A small section in the bombe control room (which was part of Hut 11A, where the Bletchley Park bombes were housed) processed duds. If the section could not decipher a message, it was sent to the log readers in the central party. By late 1944, the number of 'tries and duds' being attempted by Hut 6 had increased enormously, to an

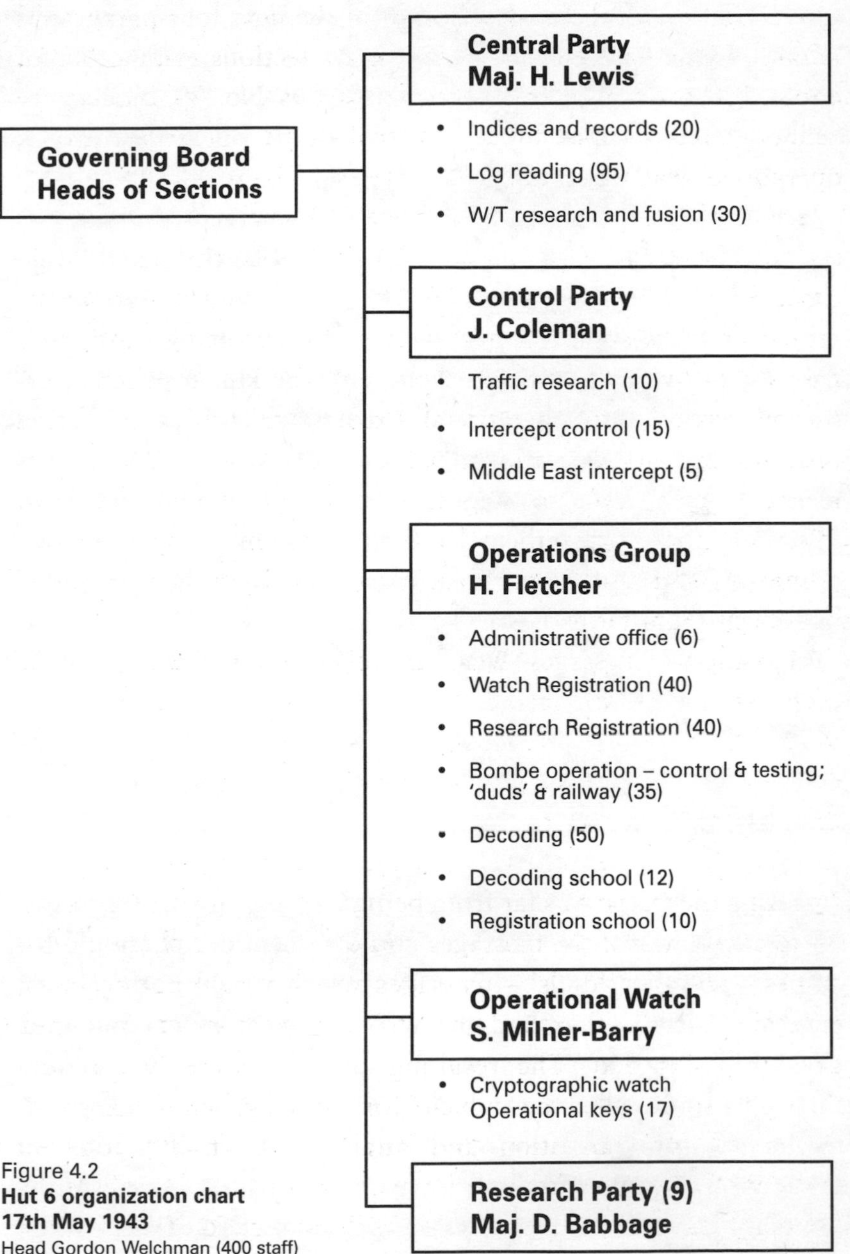

Figure 4.2
Hut 6 organization chart
17th May 1943
Head Gordon Welchman (400 staff)

average of 1,125 per day (compared with 2,050 decrypts) in the week ending 7 October. Stuart Milner-Barry, the head of Hut 6 from September 1943 onwards, considered that a 2:1 ratio was about 'the best that we can do under favourable circumstances'.

The central party analysed the logs kept by the intercept operators in order to build up a geographical picture of the complex German radio nets, which constantly changed call signs and frequencies in order to outwit the British. Since Enigma cryptanalysis was inseparable from traffic analysis, the central party's work made an indispensable contribution to Hut 6's successes. By early 1943, it was a far cry from the days when GC&CS 'did not think that the results of traffic analysis were ever likely to help cryptanalysts', and when Gordon Welchman was 'deeply suspicious of Colonel Butler's efforts to expand the W/TI [traffic analysis] organization'. John Coleman's traffic research section in the control party was responsible for identifying the call signs used by the German transmitting stations under an intricate allocation system.

The log-reading section in the central party was the biggest single unit in Hut 6, with ninety-five staff in May 1943. The log readers also looked for re-encipherments, routine cribs, cillies and 'giveaways' (cryptographic information in operators' plain-language chat). Sometimes even the rotor orders or the *Stecker* were revealed by giveaways – operators on Brown were notorious for doing so. Re-encipherments occurred when a signal had to be sent from one cipher net, such as a *Fliegerkorps*, to another; they were more frequent at the beginning of a month, when new key-lists took effect. Re-encipherments could be identified from their times of origin, which were the same as the original signal, and their lengths, which were similar. The heads of the log-reading groups, with a few assistants, staffed the Fusion Room, which combined information from traffic analysis and cryptanalysis to build a complete picture of the Enigma radio nets, and fed it back in a unified form to the groups sending data to it.

*

Hut 6's successes ultimately depended upon the comprehensive and accurate coverage of the *Heer* and *Luftwaffe* radio nets by the Y service, but regrettably the story of interception in 1939 and for much of 1940 'is not a pretty one'. In September 1939, there were twenty-five sets, manned by civilians, at the War Office intercept station at Chatham, which initially was the main intercept station for Enigma. In November 1939 and February 1940 the War Office warned Group Captain L. F. Blandy, the head of AI1e (which was responsible for interception in the Royal Air Force (RAF)), that if a major offensive began on the Western Front, Chatham would drop *Luftwaffe* Enigma traffic, which the RAF would then have to intercept. In April 1940, Denniston informed Blandy and Colonel D. A. Butler, of MI8, that 'it is now of the highest importance that Y stations should concentrate as far as possible on German Enigma traffic (Air and Army) . . . I should be very grateful if you would issue orders to that effect'.

The Air Ministry agreed to intercept the Enigma traffic on 2 March 1940, but Hut 6 received nothing from it for many months. The root of the problem was that AI1e belonged neither to the RAF's Director of Signals, who had some receivers and men but needed them for communications purposes, nor to the Director of Intelligence, who had no responsibility for intercept facilities and seems not to have realized that there was an intercept problem, since he was already receiving a great deal of intelligence – intercepted by the army. In April 1940, Denniston urged Menzies 'most urgently to call a meeting of your Main Committee [on intercept co-ordination]', adding that 'no action has been taken to improve the position (in regard to interception of Enigma traffic)'. But despite Denniston's plea, little or nothing seems to have happened: the Y Committee did not consider the subject until July. In July, 85 per cent of the Chatham intercept facilities were allocated to Enigma, mostly *Luftwaffe*, yet no *Luftwaffe* Enigma was yet being intercepted by the RAF, which was just about to send forty operators to Chicksands (a naval Y station) for training.

In 1940, the services, mainly the War Office, and not the user (Hut 6), controlled the tasks undertaken by the stations. Around August 1940 Chatham even removed six sets from Enigma cover without notifying GC&CS. Hut 6 protested, but received scant sympathy from the military and Air Force authorities, who considered it 'an act of grace on their part to allow GC and CS any voice in the allocation' of sets. Hut 6 even had to give battle in order to prevent Enigma coverage being transferred from highly skilled Army operators to unskilled RAF personnel, with potentially disastrous results for breaking Enigma. Although RAF Y had not yet started to intercept any *Luftwaffe* ground to ground traffic, Blandy wrote patronizingly about Hut 6's protest: 'My only comment is that the authors of this document have just begun to understand the niceties of wireless interception. If they had all done a course at Chatham or Cheadle they would not have wasted so much paper.'

As more ciphers were broken and as the cover on them improved, more cribs and re-encipherments were discovered, which in turn required more intercept sets to exploit them. Hut 6 ideally needed coverage on every Enigma cipher, however unimportant it appeared to be, but in 1941 it had to complain about 'the [lamentable and inexcusable] failure of the Army authorities to provide an adequate number of trained operators'. It is therefore not surprising that two postwar histories described the expansion of intercept facilities during 1940 as 'astonishingly and lamentably slow' and 'the machinery of the Y services [as] not then functioning well'. By March 1941, Chatham's complement of sets had only increased by two, to twenty-seven, although there was also a second Army station at Harpenden. A newly formed 'E' Sub-Committee of the Y Committee decided in March 1941 that 190 sets were needed for Enigma. One hundred and eighty Army, RAF and Foreign Office sets in Britain and abroad were taking Enigma traffic by November 1941. However, there was a shortage of skilled operators for many months, partly because ex-Post Office operators proved unsuitable. Militarizing personnel at the stations, and forming an ATS intercept unit, was largely to prove the answer for the Army's purposes. It turned out to be a slow process, and it was only in November 1942 that a set room, with thirty-six sets, was completely staffed by ATS at a new Army station, Beaumanor.

In January 1942, the Chiefs of Staff authorized a major expansion of all the Y services, including the recruitment of 7,150 additional personnel, together with the establishment of a much-needed radio network to handle traffic from overseas Y stations and outposts of GC&CS. The sets on Enigma at home and abroad increased from 210 in April 1942 to 322 in January 1943. The Army and Foreign Office provided 64 per cent of the intercept sets, but 60 per cent of the daily keys solved were *Luftwaffe*, and only 26 per cent *Heer*; 10 per cent were Railway daily keys, and 5 per cent were SS. On 3 March 1943, the Chiefs of Staff authorized a second Y expansion programme. By May 1943, the WOYG (War Office Y Group) at Beaumanor had 105 sets on *Heer* and *Luftwaffe* Enigma traffic, and the main RAF station at Chicksands, ninety-nine receivers. There were also sixty sets on Enigma at Foreign Office stations at Whitchurch, Denmark Hill, London (formerly a Metropolitan Police station) and Cupar, an Army station at Harpenden and RAF stations at Shaftesbury and Wick, plus seventy-five sets in the Middle East and the Mediterranean. By June 1944, 515 sets were tasked on *Luftwaffe* and *Heer* Enigma, but even as late as January 1945, Hut 6 was 'as short of sets as ever': minor *Heer* and *Luftwaffe* ciphers were not being intercepted, and no attempt could therefore be made to break them.

The service authorities came to accept Hut 6's view that Enigma interception was an indivisible problem, and allocated Army sets to *Luftwaffe* traffic, and RAF sets to *Heer* signals.

Later, they also relinquished control of tasking the Army and RAF sets. In May 1943 Hut 6's intercept control section under John Coleman specified the Enigma tasks to be taken by the intercept stations, and the number of sets to be allocated, but the stations remained under the administrative control of their parent services. Coleman's section also co-ordinated interception in the Middle East with interception in Britain.

Accurate interception was essential when attacking Enigma, since hours could be lost because of a single wrong letter or call sign, or even a mistake in measuring the frequency. Hut 6 was unable to break Yellow for 5 May 1940, because of a single incorrect letter in the intercept, although the Poles broke it on 7 May. When resources allowed, radio nets were therefore often covered by two (or sometimes even six) sets to ensure that signals were precisely recorded. Only first-rate operators could deal with very faint signals coupled with interference, and drifting or split frequencies, but they were still in short supply even in December 1942. Hut 6 estimated that only about one third of the operators then at Beaumanor and Chicksands were first rate, and another third, second rate. Taking a burst of Morse from 'a distant signal underneath the cacophony of different Morse transmissions, a diva singing grand opera in German, [and] a high-speed Morse transmission' required a very high degree of skill.

Breaking Red was Hut 6's most important task throughout the war, as can be seen from the number of radio receivers allocated to intercepting it: in July 1941, sixty-eight sets were taking Red – over half the 119 sets in Britain tasked on Enigma, although the proportion had declined slightly, to about 35 per cent (fifty sets) in October. The average daily traffic on Red of 380 *Teile* (message parts) from June to November 1942 was 65 per cent of the total combined traffic (590 *Teile*) intercepted on all the Army and SS cipher nets, while the average daily total of the *Luftwaffe* traffic

(1,400 *Teile*) was over double that of the *Heer* and SS. Red was easy to break once continuity had been established: the net was so widespread that if one crib went down there was a good chance of finding another to replace it. Red's links to many other *Luftwaffe* keys made it possible to penetrate them by cribs from re-encipherments, which were known as 'kisses' in Bletchley Park parlance, because the relevant signals were marked with 'xx'. Red was also an invaluable source of intelligence on *Heer* topics in North Africa and elsewhere.

Hut 6 solved the *Luftwaffe* Light Blue cipher, which provided intelligence about the *Heer* and *Luftwaffe* in Libya, within about eight weeks of its introduction in January 1941, and read it daily until it went out of service at the end of 1941. The only other *Luftwaffe* cipher intercepted in 1941, Mustard, the field cipher on the eastern front of the *Luftwaffe* Sigint service, the *Funkaufklärungsdienst* (Radio Reconnaissance Service), was solved for twelve days in the late summer, and from April 1942. It proved useful in giving the order of battle of the Soviet Army and Air Force, and by revealing the very considerable insecurity of Soviet ciphers.

In 1942 all *Luftwaffe* Enigma key-lists except Brown were apparently prepared by one man, who often merged different components of previous keys (for example, *Stecker*) when preparing new key-lists. The April Foxglove keys combined parts of the January Red and March Mustard keys, with the remainders being used to make up the April Red key-list. In June, Locust, Mosquito, Snowdrop, Hornet and Garlic also consisted of partial key repeats. Key repeats died out at the end of 1942, but were briefly revived between March and June 1943, when ciphers used by certain *Luftgau* (*Luftwaffe* administrative units) were allotted different discriminants, but some key components were identical, for example, Daffodil, Gorse, Lily and Speedwell formed one group.

Primrose, the cipher for *Luftgau* XXVIII, the *Luftwaffe* supply unit in Africa, yielded between 140 and 290 decrypts daily, mainly on logistics, on most days between June and November 1942 – almost as many decrypts as the prolific Red, whose total varied from 350 to 445 daily. Primrose was doubly useful since it also provided complete key repeats, although in random order, for Scorpion (employed by *Luftwaffe* close support units and *Luftwaffe* liaison officers with the Afrika Korps) for each month from June to November. Scorpion was very difficult to intercept in Britain, since it was transmitted with low power on medium frequencies by units near the fighting. Special arrangements were made to decipher it at Heliopolis, near Cairo, as well as at GC&CS, since it produced a great deal of intelligence about *Luftwaffe* plans and the ground fighting. The daily keys were available in advance so that messages in it could therefore be deciphered immediately they reached the Heliopolis centre.

In complete contrast to the *Luftwaffe*, *Heer* traffic in 1941 was divided into small, unrelated groups, with few re-encipherments, and light traffic. Hut 6 broke very little *Heer* Enigma before September 1941. Thus, although Vulture (used on the Russian front) was first read on 27 June 1941, shortly after the invasion of Russia, Hut 6 broke no Vulture keys for August, and only one for September. It solved only twelve *Heer* daily keys in August, all in Kestrel. By November Hut 6 was breaking both Vulture, which was the first *Heer* cipher to be broken regularly, and Chaffinch, but then lost them for four months after the Vulture traffic was reduced when the *Heer* began to rely more on land lines.

Heer ciphers in North Africa were initially very difficult to solve. Hut 6 broke Chaffinch II (used between *Panzerarmee* Afrika and Rome and Berlin) for nine days in September 1941, and for part of October and from 2 November to 6 December, although often a week or more later. Traffic on Phoenix, which rose from twenty-five to over 200 messages daily during fighting in Libya, could only be taken by forward intercept sets with the 8th Army, since it was also transmitted at low power on medium frequencies. When it was broken, delays in sending the traffic back from 8th Army to Heliopolis for transmission to GC&CS led to considerable hold-ups, until arrangements were made for Hut 6 to send key-lists to Heliopolis. Hut 6's solution of the *Heer* Mediterranean ciphers, such as Chaffinch, Phoenix and Thrush (which carried information about the air transport of supplies and reinforcements), increased considerably after April 1942. Even so, only 2,800 *Heer* signals were decrypted in May 1942 out of 10,300 *Heer* intercepts, compared with 19,400 *Luftwaffe* decrypts from 31,000 intercepts, illustrating just how difficult it was to solve *Heer* Enigma.

Hut 6 found that many of the twenty-two *Luftwaffe* ciphers it was regularly breaking by the summer of 1942 were interrelated: the fifty *Heer* and *Luftwaffe* Enigma ciphers then being used presented it with a single, indivisible problem. It therefore had to try to break every single cipher, however unimportant for intelligence purposes, since there was no way of telling in advance which would prove the entry point to a different cipher. Even *Heer* Mediterranean ciphers, such as Mallard (a Rome administrative cipher), were sometimes broken by re-encipherments from Red and Scorpion. All the Mediterranean *Heer* keys solved in 1942 were linked by re-encipherments, but the only *Heer* cipher to produce cillies consistently in 1942 was Osprey which, although classified as a *Heer* cipher by Hut 6, was really the cipher of the Todt construction organization, which may explain its poor operating practices.

No repeats of key-lists were discovered in *Heer* traffic in 1941 or 1942. The success rate (decrypts as a percentage of the signals intercepted) against *Luftwaffe* traffic fell from 92 per cent in November 1941 to 50 per cent in November 1942, largely because Light Blue went out of service in January 1942, and the main *Luftwaffe* traffic started to use eight or more ciphers. During 1942, the success rate against *Heer* traffic was only 0.6 per cent (a mere thirty decrypts) in January but rose to 27 per cent in May. Intercepts of all Hut 6 traffic increased from 32,000 per month in September 1941 to 82,000 in November 1942. The overall percentage of the traffic (*Luftwaffe*, *Heer* and Railway) broken by Hut 6 remained around 50 per cent of the total intercepts in 1942. Unidentified traffic, where Hut 6 did not know which cipher was being used, was reduced from 17 per cent of the total traffic in September 1941 to only 2.4 per cent in November 1942, illustrating Hut 6's and the Y service's increasing mastery of the *Luftwaffe* and *Heer* radio nets, and their skill in reconstructing the extensive lists of cipher discriminants used by them.

SS decrypts increased considerably in 1942 following the discovery in April that daily reports (codenamed HOR-HUG by Bletchley Park) of concentration camp numbers provided half the Orange *Stecker*. The HOR-HUG reports gave the numbers of people in certain concentration camps, which were encoded by a letter for digit substitution (so providing ten letters – the first five *Stecker* pairs), but ceased in early 1943, after which the reports were sent by land line. Orange keys could often be broken with an unused part of a bombe, while the other parts were being used for a different cipher.

Hut 6 also solved the Railway traffic in eastern Europe (later codenamed Rocket) in 1941 and 1942. The traffic used a rewired version of commercial Enigma, without *Stecker*, and was therefore relatively easy to solve using hand methods. Lt.-Col. John Tiltman first broke the traffic around the end of July 1940, after which the wiring of the machine was solved by Hut 8, which became responsible for reading the traffic until the work was later transferred to Hut 6. All 2,300 messages received in July and August 1940 were solved. The traffic ceased at the end of August, but began to be intercepted again in February 1941. The 90 per cent success rate against it in 1942 was the highest for all Hut 6 Enigma.

Hut 6 largely consolidated its position during 1943. However, it faced a significant challenge when the *Heer* stopped using discriminants in Enigma traffic on 1 September, and the *Luftwaffe* followed suit on 1 November. The small change represented a major improvement in security, since Hut 6 was now faced with 3,000 or so signals daily, all of which apparently used the same cipher but which in fact employed up to ninety different ciphers. The new procedure slowed Hut 6 quite considerably, and required it to increase its registration and decoding room staff substantially, from about 220 to 300. Hut 6 and the Y service were able to meet the challenge only because they had become highly experienced and very flexible organizations, capable of responding to any change quickly and efficiently.

In addition Hut 6 had to prepare for the second front in late 1943 and early 1944. It identified many of the *Heer*'s Enigma ciphers and their related frequencies and call signs with the help of the Y service, although it had little success in solving them before the Normandy landings in June, and thought that most of its intelligence on the *Heer* might have to be derived from Red and Flivo (*Heer-Luftwaffe* liaison) ciphers. Fortunately, some of the *Heer* ciphers being used in France were solved after the landings, although initially there were not many decrypts. However, following the Allied break-out in Normandy at the start of August, there was a massive increase in *Heer* traffic, which led to about five *Heer* ciphers being read daily and a huge rise in *Heer* decrypts, although the decrypts declined in September 1944 when the land war became static. So did *Luftwaffe* decrypts, when *Luftwaffe* operations were restricted, largely due to a shortage of fuel and trained pilots.

Throughout 1944 Hut 6 was very apprehensive that a new rewirable reflector, *Umkehrwalze* D (Dora – UKD), which had first appeared in some *Luftwaffe* ciphers in January, would be brought into general use, and blind it almost completely. Providentially, despite warnings that UKD would be widely used on 1 August, that did not happen. UKD was employed with about twenty-five *Luftwaffe* ciphers by March 1945, but seldom to the total exclusion of the standard reflector in the same cipher, which was a classic *Luftwaffe* blunder of the first order. But for the *Luftwaffe*'s bungles UKD would have had a devastating effect on Hut 6 and the production of Ultra.

The *Heer* brought an unbreakable system of enciphered call signs into service on 1 November 1944. This was a much-feared step, but it led to an only temporary drop in solutions of *Heer* Enigma, such were the combined capabilities of the Y service and Hut 6, who were greatly helped by the fact that major nets retained their fixed frequencies, confining the problem to about half of the *Heer* traffic. Almost four times as much bombe time was required to break *Heer* Enigma in November 1944, compared with November 1942, and more than twice as much for *Luftwaffe* Enigma (see Figure 4.3). Hut 6's production of decrypts in 1944 would almost certainly have declined significantly if US Navy bombes had not been available, since they more than doubled the three-rotor bombe capacity available to Hut 6.

By early 1945 the *Heer* was employing only a few Enigma ciphers, which greatly expanded the traffic they carried. In turn, this resulted in many more re-encipherments and mistakes by operators – and in a considerable increase in the *Heer* decrypts. However, Hut 6 suffered what was perhaps its worst blow of the war on 1 February 1945, when the *Luftwaffe* implemented a system under which call signs were enciphered daily, and frequencies changed every third day. Although these precautions had been anticipated, they threatened the interception and solution of all *Luftwaffe* traffic, both Enigma and low-grade: *Luftwaffe* Enigma decrypts fell from 1,800 to 1,000 daily. A post-war history concluded that 'if this internal German reform . . . had been a little more thorough, far reaching, and rigidly enforced . . . German messages henceforward would have become largely unbreakable'. Since it had been known in advance that the frequencies would usually be more easily identified by reference to the attributes of the low-grade codes being used than those of

	Sets	Traffic taken	Traffic broken	% broken	Daily keys broken: Current month	Previous months	Total	Bombe hours	Bombe hours per daily key
Luftwaffe (January 1942)		30324	16840	56					
Army-Air (January 1942)		2255	73	3					
Luftwaffe (November 1942)		52860			157	43	200	9375	47
Luftwaffe (November 1944)	281	87390	66966	77	430	36	466	52323	112
Heer (January 1942)		5000	30	0.6					
Heer: Mediterranean ciphers (November 1942)		10650			47		47	5289	113
Heer: other ciphers (November 1942)		6720			89	4	93	8479	91
Heer (November 1944)	229	51951	12600	24	149	21	170	69968	412
SS (January 1942)		1544	20	1					
SS (November 1942)		3810			22	2	24	1276	53
SS (November 1944)	24	10700	3623	34	36	3	39	14610	375
Railway (January 1942)		1216	986	81			30	none	none
Railway (November 1942)		1470			26	3	29	none	none
Railway (November 1944)		2191	1460	67	36	2	38	9082	239
Search	101								

Figure 4.3 **Enigma breaks (Hut 6): 1942 and 1944**

Enigma, a special 'traffic watch' was established by the Air Section in Hut 10 to sort and identify the traffic and pass its details to Hut 6. A combined Sixta and Air Section research party built up a number of frequency continuities by mid-February, but Hut 6 did not recover fully until around mid-March, when documents with details of the new systems were captured. *Heer* and *Luftwaffe* Ultra began to dry up in April, as Germany disintegrated.

From very small beginnings, Hut 6 evolved into a large, well-managed and highly adaptable unit. Only by doing so was it able to counter German measures that would have defeated a less flexible organization. The Y service operators also reached a very high degree of efficiency as the war progressed. Without their help, Hut 6 would have been greatly handicapped, especially when the *Heer* and *Luftwaffe* made significant changes to their radio procedures, as with enciphered call signs. Few *Heer* Enigma ciphers were easy to break at any time. Hut 6 gave considerable attention to Green, but solved it on only thirteen occasions throughout the war – and even then some of the breaks required the help of prisoners of war. If the *Luftwaffe*'s Enigma operators had been as well trained as their *Heer* counterparts, or if some German security procedures had been introduced early in the war, there would have been much less Ultra from Enigma. And while it is unwise to claim too much for Ultra, it was undoubtedly the prime source of intelligence for the Allies, and helped significantly to alter the course of the war in their favour.

5

Hut 6 From the Inside

DEREK TAUNT

Introduction

In Chapter 5, Derek Taunt gives an insightful view of working in Hut 6. Hut 6's main purpose was to provide Hut 3 with intelligence in the form of decrypts. A small section in Hut 3, known as 3L, advised the various sections in Hut 6 on priorities, such as the most urgent ciphers to be attacked, the radio frequencies to be covered, and so on. This had been something of a problem initially, when 'an exaggerated view of security made liaison between Hut 3 and Hut 6 difficult' so that, for example, there was little intelligence input into intercept cover, which 'was not at first satisfactory'. When there was a balance between efficiency and security, the latter tended to predominate. That was certainly the position in relation to the Ultra indoctrination of senior staff at the intercept stations where, for example, at the Beaumanor Army intercept station, only the commanding officer was initially told about Ultra. Right up to the end of the war, only officers at intercept stations were officially informed, to the detriment of efficiency. The irony is that official security was illusory. On one occasion, when the teleprinter staff at Beaumanor enquired on the phone about a background of cheers in Hut 6, they were told that it was because the main Luftwaffe *cipher had just been broken. After that, the teleprinter room always realized why they were being told to stop sending a particular register. There is not the slightest indication that security suffered, and there may well have been a gain in efficiency.*

Derek Taunt refers to the arrival of the US Army's 6813th Signal Security Detachment under Captain Bill Bundy. Although Stuart Milner-Barry initially 'viewed the prospect with some consternation', because Hut 6 'was faced with technical problems which would make it difficult to find the time for training', the gifted American contingent made a real contribution to Hut 6's work. Milner-Barry later described their arrival as 'one of the luckiest things that happened to Hut 6'.

Gordon Welchman's The Hut Six Story *emphasized the importance not only of a good management team but of ensuring that each individual member of staff was kept informed about how his or her work had 'contributed to some specific improvement'. Reports gave 'all Hut 6 staff members a feeling of what was going on', while the supervisory staff ensured that 'everyone knew how he or she fitted into the overall picture'. The views expressed on this subject in Welchman's book are not the product of mere hindsight. Milner-Barry, who worked closely with him throughout the war, has written about 'his practical gifts for planning and organization', and that 'without the vision which again and again proved his intuition correct . . . the task of converting the original break-through into an effective organization for the production of up-to-date intelligence could [not] have been achieved'. It was 'a classic example of the hour producing the man'.*

Derek Taunt's chapter is further confirmation that Hut 6 was indeed well managed. Much is owed to Welchman, who has not received the full recognition he deserves. Without him, Hut 6 would almost certainly not have evolved so quickly, or performed as well as it did, while the bombes would have been much, much weaker unless and until someone else had his flash of inspiration about the 'diagonal board' that transformed them into such potent weapons against Enigma.

RE

I was an undergraduate at Jesus College from 1936 to 1939, reading for the mathematical tripos and specializing in 'pure' mathematics. In the summer of 1939 I made overtures to the great Trinity mathematician Professor G. H. Hardy, whose lectures on Analysis I had attended and greatly enjoyed; he agreed to take me on as a research student. But the project was postponed by the outbreak of war, and I registered with the Joint Recruiting Board. By Christmas I had been allocated to work in the Ordnance Board at Kemnal Manor, Chislehurst, analysing trial firings of new guns and ammunition and drawing up range tables for them.

In Hardy's minor classic, *A Mathematician's Apology*, which came out in 1940, too late to deflect me from Chislehurst, he wrote:

> There is one comforting conclusion which is easy for a real mathematician. Real mathematics has no effects on war. No one has yet discovered any warlike purposes to be served by the theory of numbers or relativity, and it seems unlikely that anyone will do so for many years. It is true that there are branches of applied mathematics, such as ballistics and aerodynamics, which have been developed deliberately for war and demand a quite elaborate technique: it is perhaps hard to call them 'trivial', but none of them has any claim to rank as 'real'. They are indeed repulsively ugly and intolerably dull; even Littlewood could not make ballistics

> respectable, and if he could not who can? So a real mathematician has his conscience clear . . . mathematics is a 'harmless and innocent' occupation.

Perhaps real mathematics (i.e. abstract mathematics) *is* a harmless occupation; but in wartime real mathematicians, such as I hoped to become, with Hardy as my guru, have to buckle down to harmful activities, be they ever so ugly and dull. External ballistics, as practised at Kemnal Manor, was indeed both – even though the influence of Littlewood was still apparent there, in a method we used which bore his name. (Littlewood and Hardy were great collaborators: Littlewood had outstanding flair and inspiration, while Hardy had patience and impeccable technique. Littlewood claimed to have had sixty seconds of inspiration during his career, each one lasting one-tenth of a second. Hardy spotted the genius of the untaught Indian mathematician, Ramanujan, and over many years provided proofs for most of his fabulous flashes of inspiration.)

But it was not its dullness or ugliness that made me want to seek another and more challenging outlet for my particular talents, it was the essential triviality of the methods we applied, more like advanced arithmetic than real mathematics. So I sought escape, and found myself at Bletchley Park in August 1941, where I had the very good fortune to land in Hut 6.

At that time it was still a single-storey wooden hut, linked to its neighbour Hut 3 by a makeshift hatchway along which trays of documents could be pulled as occasion required. In Hut 6 messages enciphered on the German Enigma machine were cracked, while in Hut 3 the plain-text we produced was edited and translated, and military intelligence extracted from it. Hut 3 was full of German linguists. As for Hut 6, we were a mixed bag of mathematicians, classics scholars, chess players, bank staff, actresses, with an average age of perhaps twenty-three due to the high proportion of recent graduates and undergraduates (both male and female) and even school-leavers. It was difficult to guess how many staff there were – Hut 6 was manned for twenty-four hours in three shifts – perhaps something approaching one hundred in all. Prior to my recruitment most of the staff had been found through the 'old boy network' (including many old and young girls), a procedure which would now be regarded as politically incorrect but at the time was a highly effective way of identifying intelligent and trustworthy people to take on an unknown, top secret task, after being assured by someone they knew well that it was both important and challenging, and about which no detail could be divulged. By mid-1941 the law of diminishing returns had affected the network, and the success of Bletchley Park and the hotting up of the war made ever greater demands for staff. My application for release from the non-real activity of ballistics went through the newly set up 'usual channels', headed by C. P. Snow, who had been charged with finding and allocating various talents into appropriate niches in the war effort.

When I arrived in Hut 6 its head was Gordon Welchman, a geometer from Trinity College, Cambridge, who had become a mathematics don at Sidney Sussex College. His second-in-command and successor was Stuart Milner-Barry, a close friend and exact contemporary of Welchman's at Trinity, a classicist rather than a mathematician, who was well known as a leading chess player and who had been out of his element as a peace-time stockbroker. The technical wizard was Dennis Babbage, the Magdalene member of the well-known Cambridge firm of geometers Hodge, Todd & Babbage, and a close friend and colleague of Welchman (who tried unsuccessfully to match him at tennis, squash and billiards. Dennis was a 'natural' when it came to ball games, as I discovered to my cost back in Cambridge after the war.) Other mature figures (i.e. aged at least thirty) included the Scottish Chess Champion Dr Aitken, and John Manisty, from Welchman's old school Marlborough College (later at

Winchester), a mathematician who first appeared in the uniform of an officer in his school Officer Training Corps, until transferred into the Intelligence Corps.

The rest of the *dramatis personae* were young – some very young – friendly, energetic, devoted to the task of outwitting the enemy and happy to be part of a complicated organization designed to do just that. Everyone – with the sole exception, I seem to remember, of Dr Aitken – was known by Christian name or nickname, as were departments (such as the Duddery, the Quatsch, and some colleagues from outside who dealt in call signs and were known as 'the Bathroom boys') and even forms (such as the 'blists' and the 'hankies'). The Hut operated like a factory which never switched off its assembly line. Raw material, in the form of intercepts of messages sent over the air by German air force and army units, enciphered on their Enigma machines, came in a ceaseless flow to one end of the conveyor belt. There they were sorted and listed, with their essential features highlighted, by the girls in the Registration Room, on forms always known as 'blists' (a name not derived, as one might have supposed, from 'those b— lists', but as an abbreviation of 'Banister lists', after Michael Banister, the Cambridge cricket blue from King's College who had designed them). The blists of breakable keys would be scrutinized by the next link in the chain of deciphering – the cryptanalysts who comprised the Watch, who attempted to spot the cribs or re-encodements on which breaks depended. The term 'key' was applied both to a network using a common cipher and to the actual daily set-up of the machines in that grouping; thus 'Red' was the key in general use by the German air force, and 'Light Blue' an air force key in North Africa. The shout 'Red out!' would convey the news that the day's key for the Red network had been found. One standard colour – Dark Blue – had been rendered useless when it was discovered that its traffic was purely used as practice and of no operational significance. Before long the supply of differently coloured pencils ran out and we had to have recourse to names of birds, animals, flowers and even vegetables to specify different keys. Eventually we would be breaking between fifteen and twenty of them daily.

When a suitable message for breaking had been identified, the Watch would produce a 'menu' for the bombes to test. The menus were not just straight conjectured plain-text for given stretches of cipher text, but configurations of letters and connections derived from such conjectures. The bombes were electro-mechanical machines, manned invariably by Wrens, which simulated the Enigma machines and rapidly tested which of the million-odd possible wheel-orders-cum-ringsettings were consistent with the menu. When consistent settings showed up, the bombe would stop and the wheels involved and their relative positions were read off for further testing in the Hut 6 Machine Room. Many stops were fortuitous – but when a genuine, causal stop was found the rest of the key was readily deduced. Then 'Red out' (or Light Blue or Chaffinch or – with less enthusiasm – Beetroot) was proclaimed and the Hut 6 Decoding Room sprang into action to turn the raw material into 'plain-text', which, with its numerous abbreviations and technical terms, needed all the expertise of our colleagues in Hut 3 to interpret. But we depended on the actual letters used in a crib or re-encipherment, not the meaning, and we kept records of the (hopefully not too variable) usage in recognizable messages such as weather forecasts, situation reports and tuning messages (such as ABSTIMMSPRUQYYRESTXOHNEXSINN – 'Tuning signal. Remainder nonsense'). As the machine (unlike a typewriter) had no numbers or punctuation marks these had to be spelt out or otherwise denoted; a gap between words was usually denoted by an X and a full stop by YY, but these offered many opportunities for variants (such as Q for CH). Also, irrelevant nonsense words were inserted at the beginning of messages to create uncertainty as to where the real content actually began.

At the shout 'Red out' people might ask which favoured crib or re-encipherment had done the trick, but not who had produced the menu from it. This was irrelevant: everyone recognized that all successes were due to the team, not to individuals. This was true in particular because it was largely a matter of chance which menu turned up trumps – so many things could go wrong, and no single menu had a certainty of success. A 30 per cent chance for a single menu, or 60 per cent for a pair of menus linked to avoid the hazard of a middle-wheel turnover, was as good as you could normally hope for. Since the supply of bombes was never – until very late in the war – adequate to demand, the Watch staff had to exert their judgement on priorities and probabilities. Indeed, a natural feel for probabilities, akin to an appreciation of orders of magnitude, was one of the few specific mathematical talents used in our everyday activities in Hut 6. Knowledge of the twenty-six times table, though useful, could not be regarded as real mathematics!

The Enigma machine was believed by the German experts to be unbreakable if used correctly, even if the enemy had specimen machines and knew the methods adopted for using them. Indeed, it would have been secure if used properly but a) official usages could be insecure, and b) even if they were secure, misuse by operators could be fatal. I can speak only of air force and army and liaison between them, which were dealt with in Hut 6. A regimen of 'need to know' was rigidly observed at Bletchley Park, and while heads of departments would discuss their problems when they affected each other (e.g. the navy cryptanalysts in Hut 8, led by Hugh Alexander, the only English chess player at Bletchley Park ranking above Stuart Milner-Barry, shared the use of the bombes with Hut 6), the rank-and-file did not discuss their work outside the confines of their own huts. The form of Enigma attacked in Hut 6 – most particularly Red – had been used before 1 May 1940 in an inherently insecure way, so long as enough messages (say one hundred or so) were sent on any one day's key. After that date a change of usage completely shut out the theoretical vulnerability and we became dependent on operators' misuse and the introduction of machinery to help us exploit known habits. The essential principle was to maintain the continuity of breaking: 'nothing succeeds like success' in this game. The clean break of continuity in method of attack left Hut 6 in a Catch-22 situation: we needed continuity to achieve breaks, but we needed plenty of breaks to establish continuity (and of course we needed bombes – and by the end of 1940 there were at most only two). How could Hut 6 bridge this gap and restore continuity?

Two essential features of Enigma, its reciprocity (if A encoded to V, V encoded to A) and the fact that a letter could not encipher to itself, were exploited by cryptanalysts both in fitting cribs against cipher text and in drawing up menus – but also crucially in the design of the bombes which tested the menus to find positions of the wheels consistent with them, from the million possibilities.

Alhough Alan Turing did not impinge directly on my Hut 6 experience, it was his genius that made our success possible. And he gave a clear rebuttal of Hardy's 'harmlessness of real mathematics'! Turing, a research fellow of King's College, Cambridge, was the most brilliant and most 'real' of Bletchley Park's mathematicians attacking Enigma. His subject was the logical foundation of mathematics, which had been thrown into turmoil a decade earlier by the Czech mathematician Gödel, who had proved that any consistent system of mathematics, defined by axioms, must be incomplete – which means that there must exist meaningful statements in it that cannot be either proved or disproved. This raised the so-called 'decision problem': given a meaningful statement in such a system, was there any standard procedure for establishing whether it was provable or unprovable? Turing had shown that the answer to this problem was 'No'. He did this by describing a routine process (or 'thought machine') by which the truth of any provable statement could be established in a finite sequence of steps selected from a small number of possibilities. He then showed the existence of meaningful statements which the machine could not decide as true or false. This 'thought machine' became known as a 'Turing machine'. The same mind conceived the basic design of the far from abstract bombes which were the indispensable weapons against Enigma and in fighting the war.

It is time to revert to May 1940. There were two forms of operator breach of regulations which gave us a chance. The first (the 'Herivel tip') depended on a considerable number of operators taking the same short cut. The other (the 'cilli') depended on one operator making two independent breaches of discipline in a single sequence of half-a-dozen or more consecutive messages (see Appendix IV). John Herivel, a young mathematical recruit from Sidney Sussex College, put himself into the position of a sleepy Enigma operator setting up his machine at the beginning of the day, and asked himself what he might do to save some bother. If enough operators followed the same procedure, their actions could be detected from scrutiny of the first message sent by all operators that day. This would reduce the range of likely *Ringstellungen* from over 17,000 to perhaps six. With cillies (not 'sillies', as Welchman misremembered them in his *The Hut Six Story* forty years later), each breach of the rules was by itself both harmless and undetectable, but the two together could not only give evidence about the day's wheel-order but also (especially if supported by a Herivel tip) lead to a breaking of the key without recourse to the bombes (i.e. by hand methods). So, by one means and another, Hut 6 survived until the arrival of the bombes made it much easier to achieve the essential continuity.

Why were German operators, especially those in the *Luftwaffe*, so careless as to allow us to escape from our Catch-22 situation? I believe it was partly due to their belief that with over 150 million million million different possible ways of setting up the Enigma machine, the enemy's task in choosing the right one was impossible. But here the idea of safety in large numbers falls down. There are over two million times as many different simple substitution ciphers as Enigma machine keys, yet any intelligent youngster, faced with a message of 250 letters (the standard length of an Enigma message) encoded by such a cipher could unravel it in half an hour. If the possible different Enigma keys were tested at the rate of one per second, it would take five million million years to try them all. So how could Alan Turing's ingeniously designed bombe make any impact, however fast it ran? The answer was that it filtered out the *Stecker*, leaving only a million possibilities – say twelve hours running-time at twenty-five tests per second.

On arrival in Hut 6 in August 1941 I was assigned to Control, the first point on the conveyor-belt. Like all of us concerned with the breaking or interpretation of ciphers (as opposed to administration), those of us in Control covered all twenty-four hours every day in three shifts (as I remember 12–9, 9–4, 4–12). Those outside easy cycling range of Bletchley Park were conveyed to and from their billets by a fleet of estate cars (later augmented by superannuated coaches). My first billet was at the home of a railwayman's family in Stony Stratford, some eight miles away up Watling Street, one of several dozen villages eventually colonized by Bletchley Park workers. Stony Stratford was celebrated for one thing only – as the reputed origin of the phrase 'a cock and bull story', supposedly originating from the pair of almost adjacent coaching inns, the Cock and the Bull, and immortalized in the final sentence of *Tristram Shandy*.

In Control, we kept in regular touch with the intercept stations and with both the codebreakers in the Hut 6 Watch and interpreters in Hut 3, making sure that frequencies important either cryptographically or intelligence-wise were double-banked, checking details and generally ensuring that the necessary raw material for the production of Ultra – the top-secret inside information about enemy formations and intentions – was forthcoming. It was not the most glamorous or most mathematically 'real' activity, but gave a very good introduction to the various sub-departments in Hut 6 and their leading personalities. Our work suited the three-shift pattern – one just handed over the interception charts and the current situation to the next shift without any loss of continuity. But life was different in the Watch, to which I was transferred after a year or so in Control. By the end of the shift one might be in the middle of turning a recalcitrant crib or re-encipherment into the form of a pair of runnable menus, and be rather unwilling to hand over in midstream to a fresh mind (which might well follow up the dead-ends which you had tried and rejected). Thus living in or near Bletchley was a real advantage, and members of the Watch were given priority when local billets were available. For the rest of my time at Bletchley Park I was not restricted by the need to catch an end-of-shift bus home.

This was even more useful in my final role as a member of the Q-watch (pronounced 'Quatsch', the German word for 'nonsense'). The Qwatch was a back-room which tackled intractable and longer-term problems. My two colleagues there (for whom I acted as best man when they married in 1947) were Bob Roseveare – who had joined Bletchley Park straight from Marlborough College and had endless enthusiasm and energy – and Ione Jay, whose calm efficiency in keeping us both in order was essential to our effectiveness. We kept tabs on some rather sinister scientists at Peenemünde on the Baltic coast, whose interest in heavy water and rocketry emphasized the need for the allies to get their retaliation in first for the V3 weapon (which fortunately never appeared). We made contingency plans for expected horrors (such as the pluggable *Umkehrwalze*) which threatened but never interrupted the flow of Ultra. One of our more satisfying encounters was with the *Notschlüssel*, or emergency keys. A routine laid down by the Germans for creating a complete Enigma key from a long key-word had been uncovered, and we were able to reconstruct the key-words from broken keys (which showed clear indications of their origin if they had been generated in this way). We could use the key-words if they subsequently reappeared, sometimes written backwards.

There was a strong sense of comradeship in Hut 6, and a feeling that we were all contributing to a great enterprise. This was strikingly expressed much later by Bill Bundy, the officer-in-charge of the USA contingent attached to Bletchley Park from August 1943. He was the older brother of the better-known McGeorge Bundy; both brothers became high-level advisers to successive presidents. Bill had led a US Army unit known as the 6813th Signals Security Detachment to work at Bletchley Park alongside the indigenous staff, and with a handful of others he had joined Hut 6. In a BBC interview in 1999 Bill said: 'Although I have done many interesting things and known many interesting people, my work at Bletchley was the most satisfying of my career.' He had sensed the special ambience of the outfit, quite unlike that of the American stereotype of conventional British reserve and its difference from any other hierarchical organization in Britain or the USA (especially the American Army!). In a talk Bill gave in 1982 to the American Cryptogram Association he said:

> I think the level of performance in Hut 6 was as near perfect as anything I have ever been or ever expect to be associated with . . . There just weren't mistakes. You didn't send down programs that didn't fit. They might not have been the wisest ones; that was a question of judgment, of course. Things were not mis-sorted. Making mistakes in testing could have meant that you'd missed the fact that the key had been solved.

This comment reflects an important point: when undertaking something as intricate and significant as Hut 6 did, you needed staff of high intelligence and integrity to tackle even simple, routine jobs accurately. This had been achieved in Hut 6 in two ways: by recruitment of suitable staff, either by the old boy/girl network or (from 1941) by C. P. Snow's allocation organization; and by making sure that everyone in a particular department (such as Hut 6) knew what was going on throughout that unit and realized how important to its success was the part played by every individual member. Contrariwise, it was essential to maintain confidentiality outside the immediate circle, even within Bletchley Park. This explains why such a small part of what I now know about Bletchley Park comes from my memory at the time – one only discovered what colleagues in other departments were doing on a 'need-to-know' basis.

It is an extraordinary fact that, for at least thirty years after 1945, little hint of what was achieved, and none at all of how it had been done, became public knowledge. It is perhaps less surprising that the secrets were kept in wartime, as the dangers of 'loose talk' were appreciated by everyone. In fact, enemy awareness of our success with Enigma was zero, as the many unsuccessful German attempts to discover why we were so well-informed attest. Among the 8,000–10,000 workers at Bletchley Park, only one, John Cairncross, was an authenticated spy, and he gave information only to our allies, the Russians. Perhaps he felt that they were being unjustly excluded from our secrets; in fact it was because of their known poor cipher security.

A short while ago I received a letter from an old Jesus College man, who had been a pupil of mine fifty years ago and had spent most of the interim years in the USA. He had read *Codebreakers*, to which I contributed a chapter, and commented:

> It is remarkable that so little is said about turf wars and personality clashes. The impression left, by your chapter particularly, is of a remarkably civilized community at BP. This must have taken a strong, continuing and deliberate effort to achieve – and most necessary, or the free flow of imaginative ideas, and the attention to fault-free work, would have been wrecked.

If by 'turf wars' he meant struggles for individual or sectional territory, they were not mentioned because there weren't any! I am not claiming a regime of universal love, but the fact was that no 'strong, continuing, deliberate effort' was needed to achieve harmony. We had a strong awareness of common purpose, and a recruitment process which produced a range not only of the diverse talents needed, but also of tolerant, understanding personalities (most notably that of Stuart Milner-Barry, our boss). Too much has been made of eccentrics at Bletchley Park. In fact there was no greater proportion of eccentrics than in the average Cambridge faculty (staff and students), though at Bletchley Park they dressed less conventionally and sported more beards and long hair than was usual at that time.

However, memory is notoriously selective and unreliable. I shared with Dennis Babbage (who was far more machine-literate than I) the same false memory of the detailed turnover sequence of the machine's wheels. Welchman himself gave a garbled account of the phenomenon of cillies in his trail-breaking book, and many other inaccurate accounts have been given since. (In 1993 I was prevented from including the true story of cillies in my chapter in *Codebreakers* by the censor!) I have seen a reference to rifle practice in the woods between Bletchley Park and the railway line – a crazy place for amateur shooting – when in fact the Home Guard practised in a deep brick-clay pit near at hand, which gave a passable imitation of the Somme in 1916.

We civilians took pride in being more competent in military matters than our Intelligence Corps colleagues, and we must have formed the youngest Home Guard company in the country. Before we disbanded at Christmas 1944 I had become second-in-command to the dashing Michael Banister, so I can claim to be one of the few surviving former captains in 'Dad's Army', most of whose members at large were old sweats from the First World War. There was indeed a small contingent of military police at Bletchley Park for security duty, but although we had a large variety of service people sprinkled among us – Army (mostly Intelligence Corps), Navy, RAF, WRNS (mostly working the bombes), ATS and WAAF, and not forgetting the US Army – we were the least military outfit you could imagine, forming an unforgettable (and hopefully unrepeatable) mixture.

With VE Day the function of Hut 6 ceased. A few were left behind to write the official (but top secret) history of its work, some stayed on to re-emerge in GCHQ at Cheltenham, others to find new ways of contributing to the war effort. For three months I became a genuine mathematician again, working on the other subject condemned by Hardy as 'ugly and dull' – aerodynamics – at the Admiralty Research Laboratory at Teddington. With the unexpectedly rapid conclusion of the Japanese war I was free to return to Cambridge in time for the Michaelmas term. I hoped that Hardy would forgive me for my treason to real mathematics, so I approached him to resume as my research supervisor. But in the meantime he had retired, and he sent me a letter that I can quote verbatim to this day:

> Dear Taunt
> There is much to be said for being a professor at Cambridge, and much to be said for being retired – but absolutely nothing to be said for being retired and undertaking the duties of a professor. I'm sorry, but I cannot now take you on.
> Yours sincerely
> GHH

So I abandoned Mathematical Analysis for Abstract Algebra, an equally esteemed branch of real mathematics, and was most fortunate in being accepted as a research student by Philip Hall. He was as eminent a mathematician as Hardy, but much younger, and for the rest of his life he remained a valued colleague and a close personal and family friend. My own active membership of Jesus College resumed after the six-year break and, having in my career there played many different roles, in 1982 I attained a status that Hardy would have approved of, that of Emeritus Fellow, with most of the privileges and none of the duties of a Fellow. And for the past decade my fading memories of Bletchley Park have constantly been refreshed by new public revelations of what actually went on there in that distant era.

6

Breaking Italian Naval Enigma

MAVIS BATEY

Introduction

The Battle of Matapan was a much needed victory at a time when Britain badly required some good news. It was also the Royal Navy's first victory in a fleet action since Trafalgar, and the first operation in the Mediterranean to be started on the basis of Sigint.

During the Spanish Civil War the Italian Navy adopted a version of the commercial Enigma cipher machine, the K model (which lacked a plugboard), with differently wired rotors: Dilly Knox solved it in 1937. However, very few units, most of them shore commands, were issued with the K machines in the Second World War. They also used the machine very little, which greatly increased the problem for Knox and his co-workers at Bletchley in attempting to read such traffic as there was. Fortunately, Mavis Lever (as she then was) was up to the challenge, even though she was only nineteen when she joined GC&CS and received no formal training in cryptanalysis. She was virtually self-taught, since Knox was not noted for being a good tutor, or imparting information.

Mavis Lever made the first break into the traffic sent on the wartime machine. In addition, she reconstructed the wiring of a new wartime rotor, with the help of her prospective husband, Keith Batey. But perhaps her biggest achievement, in terms of the results achieved, was to solve the first signals revealing the Italian Navy's operational plans before Matapan. In consequence, Admiral A. B. Cunningham was sufficiently forewarned to set to sea on the evening of 27 March to confront the battle fleet of Admiral Angelo Iachino, consisting of about twenty ships, including his flagship, the formidable Vittorio Veneto *(41,000 tons).*

The Vittorio Veneto *and a cruiser, the* Pola, *were damaged in daytime attacks on the 28th, which led Iachino to send two cruisers and four destroyers to assist* Pola. *During the night, good work by a keen-eyed radar operator on the British cruiser* Orion *led to his squadron sailing towards* Pola *and her rescuers. Lacking radar, the Italian ships were caught completely by surprise, with their guns trained fore and aft: all three cruisers and two of the destroyers were sunk. The Italian Navy never again risked putting a fleet to sea during the war, and ceased to be the very real threat that it had once been. The immediate result was to protect British naval forces against surface attacks during the evacuations from Crete in May 1941, which undoubtedly saved them from further heavy casualties, in addition to the fearful losses they suffered by attacks from the air.*

In the following chapter, Mavis Batey tells how Dilly's 'girls' broke the signals that paved the way for Cunningham's victory, which was to be the last fleet action ever fought by the Royal Navy. She also describes the background to those breaks, and working with the endearing Dilly Knox, who was rightly proud of his girls and what they achieved.

RE

Bletchley Park codebreakers, for security reasons, were seldom able to follow through their successful breaks to see what operational effects they might have had; for the most part, we had to wait thirty years for releases to the Public Record Office and the official history to discover that. The Matapan signals break in the Cottage was different. Almost as soon as the last shot was fired, Admiral John Godfrey, the Director of Naval Intelligence, rang through to Bletchley Park with the message: 'Tell Dilly that we have won a great victory in the Mediterranean and it is entirely due to him and his girls.' A few days later we saw it all on the news reel in the local cinema, guns blazing and Admiral A. B. Cunningham, the Nelson of the day, looking dashing on the quarter deck of his flagship *Warspite*. Our sense of elation knew no bounds when Cunningham came down in person to congratulate us a few weeks later. Somebody rushed down to the Eight Bells public house to get a couple of bottles of wine, and if it was not up to the standard the C-in-C Mediterranean was used to, he didn't show it when he toasted 'Dilly and his girls'. 'Dilly' was Dillwyn Knox, a classical scholar, papyrologist and brilliant cryptographer from the First World War and I was one of his 'girls'.

Dilly Knox's tutor at King's College, Cambridge, Walter Headlam, had inspired him with a great love of Greek literature and when Dilly became a Fellow in 1909 he inherited the then deceased Headlam's work on Herodas. He applied himself to the fragmentary texts of the Herodas papyri in the British Museum with the same determination, scholarship and inspired guesswork that was to be his forte in his future cryptographic career. Soon after war broke out in 1914 he was asked to join the department of naval intelligence known as Room 40. By the time this had been expanded into ID25 in 1917, Dilly had succeeded in breaking much of the German admiral's flag code; his 'way in' being through linguistic patterns. His ear for metre had detected lines of poetry in the repeated bigrams of a message:

....en ... .en ... ...en
....en .. ..en

He suspected dactyls and a rhyme and as this was undoubtedly a sentimental German operator given to romantic poetry there was bound to be some roses around. A German professor down the corridor agreed and identified the lines as Schiller's

Ehret die Frauen; sie flechten und weben
Himmliche Rosen in erdliche Leben.

Dilly's lifelong friend and companion, whose career was parallel with his own – Fellow of King's College, ID25 in the First World War and Bletchley Park in the Second World War – was Frank Birch. To add to his other skills, Frank was a born comedian, both writer and pantomime actor; he produced a skit entitled *Alice in ID25*, to which Dilly, who featured as the Dodo, contributed the verses. Alice, who had fallen down a Whitehall grating, suddenly found herself amongst a lot of odd cantankerous creatures who were 'researching' by staring blankly at the tables in front of them and then scribbling away furiously on pieces of paper; of these odd creatures Alice thought that Dilly the Dodo was 'the queerest bird she had ever seen. He was so long and lean, and he had outgrown his clothes, and his face was like a pang of hunger.' Whilst Alice was there the news came through that the war was over and the creatures were asked the questions: 1. Do you want to go? or 2. Do you want to stay? or 3. Both. If so, state which. Dilly, Alastair Denniston and Frank Birch opted to stay; indeed it seems they couldn't bear to go; in Dilly the Dodo's words:

Oh, if a time should ever come when we're demobilized
How we shall miss the interests which once life comprised!

Dilly saw great possibilities in peacetime cryptography in the reorganized Government Code and Cypher School, under the auspices of the Foreign Office, with Denniston in charge; flexible periods of research into cryptographic methods of foreign embassies would allow him to continue his work on the Herodas papyri. The Headlam–Knox Herodas was finally published in 1922. As John Chadwick, who did such brilliant work on the decipherment of Linear B, would later discover, similar attitudes and methods could be applied to breaking unreadable scripts and encoded messages.

In 1936 Dilly's family detected a noticeable change in his habits; not only was he obsessively preoccupied but that year for the first time he declined to go to the King's Founders' Feast for fear of disclosing his new secret over the port. Breaking the Enigma machine and its variations was the new secret challenge which would absorb him until his death in 1943. The operational urgency was necessitated by Mussolini's invasion of Abyssinia in 1935 and the intervention of Italy and Nazi Germany in the Spanish Civil War in 1936; with Mussolini calling the Mediterranean *mare nostrum*, Gibraltar was at risk. There was much wireless activity and the Italian Navy increased security by introducing the commercial version of the cipher machine, but with rewired wheels. GC&CS already had a model of the basic commercial machine. Although this machine, known as 'Enigma', had been on the market it was thought to be absolutely safe as it was impossible to decipher a message until the whole key was known and there were about three million possible ways of setting it up. Dilly Knox was able to work out a theoretical method of reproducing the internal wiring of the Italian Enigma wheels on 'rods', which were small strips of cardboard with letters on them (for a technical explanation see page 313); although more complicated than Room 40 hand ciphers they ensured that messages could be broken textually, given a 'way in'.

However, it soon became clear that Germany had introduced a

more complicated Enigma machine which defeated Dilly's rodding method. The story of the Polish contribution to its solution has been told, but it is worth recalling that at the Warsaw meeting in July 1939, which Dilly attended as the GC&CS chief cryptographer, an instant bond sprang up between him and Marian Rejewski, the mathematician who was largely responsible for the Polish success. Mathematics had hitherto played no part in Room 40's scheme of things and when the first American code-breaking unit sought advice on the right kind of recruit it was told that what was needed was 'an active, well-trained and scholarly mind, not mathematical but classical'. When Peter Twinn, an Oxford mathematician, was recruited in early 1939 to assist Dilly with his attempts to break Enigma he found that GC&CS still consisted mainly of classics professors who regarded mathematicians as 'very strange beasts indeed, unlikely to be of much help'. That was to change after the visit to Poland.

In spite of their differences of approach to Enigma theory – Rejewski through permutation theory and Dilly through linguistics – the rapport was instant. In an interview in 1978, Marian Rejewski said: 'Knox grasped everything very quickly, almost quick as lightning. It was evident that the British had really been working on Enigma . . . So they didn't require explanations. They were specialists of a different kind – of a different class.' Although having originally worked on the commercial machine, Rejewski did not seem to have experimented with the textual rod approach; in the early 1930s, the Poles realized that the German Enigma had been complicated by the introduction of the plugboard. When Dilly returned home he wrote in Polish to the mathematicians he had met to send 'my sincere thanks for your cooperation and patience'. He enclosed a set of rods and by way of congratulations a silk scarf with a view of a Derby horse winning the race. 'I don't know how Knox's method was supposed to work,' Rejewski later commented, 'most likely he had hoped to vanquish Enigma with the bâtons [rods]. Unfortunately we beat him to it.'

A few weeks later Dilly and Peter Twinn were in the advance party when GC&CS transferred cipher operations from Broadway, near St James's Park, to Bletchley Park. The administration had settled in the mansion and they established their quarters in the cottage in the stableyard. Three Cambridge mathematicians, Alan Turing, Gordon Welchman and John Jeffreys, were recruited and contact was resumed with the Polish mathematicians who had escaped to Paris from now occupied Poland. In January 1940, the first Enigma key was broken. Immediately the Cottage was placed out of bounds for the rest of Bletchley Park to keep the breaking of Enigma absolutely secret. Welchman, who had given much thought to the necessary organizational methods once Enigma had been broken, now put this into operation with Edward Travis, Denniston's deputy. More staff were recruited and by March the new hut system was in place. Welchman and Jeffreys would run Hut 6, breaking army and air force codes, with neighbouring Hut 3 processing intelligence. Turing and Twinn were put in charge of naval Enigma, which was still unbroken in its wartime form, in Hut 8. Dilly, who must have known that organization was not his forte, still felt the need to protest about the arrangement. Denniston recalled later that at this time he had told Dilly that 'you could not exploit your own success and run Huts 6 and 3. I was right – you broke new ground while the building on your foundation was carried out by Travis etc, who, I say, were better adapted to this process than you . . . The exploitation of your results can be left to others so long as there are new fields for you to explore.'

Clearly there would have to be some reorganization to appease Dilly, who could not be left as a mere cog in the hut system. He was given charge of a new Cottage research unit to break untried Enigma variations, the most successful of which would be the *Abwehr* machine. Dilly had insisted on choosing his own team and decided that it would be ideal this time to have it entirely composed of young women. He didn't want any débutantes whose daddies had got them into Bletchley through knowing someone in the Foreign Office, nor 'a yard of Wrens'. Dilly did now appreciate the value of the mathematical input, however, and solved the problem by recruiting one of the few Bletchley female mathematicians to join him as one of 'the Cottage girls'. Margaret Rock was a splendid choice and a great asset to Dilly and the Cottage. We always made sure that whatever the time of day, even with his erratic working hours, one of his girls was there to support Dilly if only to track down his spectacles and tobacco tin, which used to get lost beneath piles of messages. We got on with code breaking as best we could ourselves and sometimes made our own contributions. Dilly's explanations of his methods belonged to Alice's Room 40 world, but the intuitive leaps required to comprehend them were a good training for cryptography.

When I appeared on the scene in early May 1940 the unit was still small and consisted of Jean Perrin, Clare Harding, Rachel Ronald and Elisabeth Granger, but our numbers would soon increase. I had been reading German at University College, London, but didn't feel I should be evacuated to Aberystwyth to continue my studies in German romantic poets, and said I would train as a nurse. However, somebody stepped in and I was sent first to Broadway and then, when the phoney war ended, to the expanding Bletchley. When Penelope Fitzgerald, Edmund 'Evoe' Knox's daughter, was writing her book, *The Knox Brothers*, she asked me if I could remember her uncle's first words to me and my introduction to breaking Enigma. I recalled they were: 'Hello, we're breaking machines. Have you got a pencil? Here, have a go.' I was then handed a pile of utter gibberish, made worse by Dilly's scrawls all over them. 'But I am afraid it's all Greek to me,' I said, at which he burst into delighted laughter and replied, 'I wish it were'. I couldn't understand what Penelope meant when she said, 'Half a moment; you know what you are saying, don't you? That's exactly what Alice said when she met Dilly for the first time in Room 40 in World War I.' She then produced a copy of *Alice in ID25*, which I have treasured ever since. At the time we were sitting in my husband's rooms at Christ Church overlooking Alice in Wonderland's Deanery garden.

I have always felt a bond with Dilly, who was for me Alice's White Knight, endearingly eccentric and concerned about my welfare. Staying with the Knoxes at their Chiltern home of Courns Wood is a particularly happy memory, except for the horrendous drive from Bletchley with Dilly gesticulating and quoting Herodas and '*himmliche Rosen*' ad lib, with total disregard of the oncoming traffic. Dilly was not a good driver. He had asked me over at that time as the avenue he had planted, aligned on the guest room, with alternating Scots pine and wild cherry, was then in full flower – a wonderful sight. Olive Knox was most apologetic that the laundry hadn't turned up and she hadn't been able to change the sheets. 'I'm awfully sorry,' she said, 'but it was Ronnie who was in them last and he's very clean.' Dilly ventured the information that his brother was a 'Roman' and that he was helping him with translating his new version of the Bible. A remarkable family – Dilly, Evoe, Wilfred and Ronnie – by any standards, as Penelope Fitzgerald has shown in her book.

May 1940 was perhaps the tensest month in Britain's history. It was brought home starkly to us when after Dunkirk the trains taking exhausted soldiers up north all stopped at Bletchley on the way. Bletchley Park was right near the station and a cry went out from the forces canteen for help. I remember the smell of my hair after I had cooked my 'finest hour' chips in between shifts all day. The fierce woman in charge had ordained that the young girls should be confined to the kitchen stove out of sight and that only the godly matrons would take out the tea and the chips to the troops in the trains. We thought that they would have preferred it the other way round; certainly we would have done. Before the canteen was built we all ate in the hall of the mansion and I remember that I was sitting next to a Frenchman when the fall of

Paris was announced over the radio. I wasn't sure what to do when he burst into tears so I went on eating my sausages; he must have thought me heartless, but with a long shift ahead and now the possibility of invasion, starving wouldn't have helped.

In June Mussolini joined the war and it was imperative to find out which of the Enigma machines he would be using; fortunately for their Naval High Command, or Supermarina as we would soon find it was called, it proved to be the machine without a plugboard, used by the Italian Navy in the Spanish Civil War – for which Dilly had already worked out his theoretical rodding solution. Having the rods for each wheel may seem to make the problem trivial but it was a very tedious process to set up twenty-six positions for each of the three wheels in turn without a reliable crib to limit the possibilities. When traffic is broken cribs greatly assist any kind of subsequent decipherment, especially rodding. Our messages were infrequent so that there was not the advantage of having several on the same setting on a day as there had been with Dilly's Spanish traffic.

Having no such easy 'ways in', Dilly suggested that we should try something as simple as PERX (for) at the beginning of each message, disregarding those that 'crashed' (that is to say, had those letters in the enciphered text where the crib was needed, it not being possible for a letter to encipher as itself). The encoded text was written out on squared paper across the page and the appropriate rods set up under it, the letters on the rod fitting the same size squares. This went on tediously and unsuccessfully for months until finally, alone on the evening shift, I disobeyed instructions and when S, rejecting X, appeared of its own accord from the first coupling I did not discard the position but decided that PERSONALE might pay off as a guess. It did. Fortunately there was a run before the wheel turnover and a 'beetle' (two letters side by side), which meant that one of the remaining bigrams in the column would have to be used, suggesting other words to try. I was able to take this word over the turnover and so put up a new set of couplings on the other side. I then began to get an idea of how the machine really worked and, just as Dilly had said, got down to breaking it with a pencil. I have recently read Turing's 'Treatise on the Enigma' in relation to breaking by rodding and feel sure that if I had seen it then I would have decided it was all too difficult. However, it seemed obvious enough that evening and I just took the couplings from one side of the turnover and found a position on one of the other wheels where the other couplings would lie side by side and then everything fell into place. Being trained on Dilly's *Alice in Wonderland* thought processes was, it seems after all, better than wrestling with a Turing treatise. Dilly was amazed in the morning to find that I had produced not just the right-hand position of the wheel as instructed but the whole setting and had read the message. I was promoted which was a relief as I was only getting thirty shillings (£1.50) a week and had to pay a guinea (£1.05) for my billet.

The good thing was the psychological effect of knowing that we were no longer working in the dark and that we had the right machine. A few months later, however, to increase security, Supermarina changed the wiring of one of the wheels but a slack operator soon gave us a perfect crib, which enabled us to ascertain the new wiring. As soon as I picked up one long message, I could see that it had no L in it; as traffic was so infrequent operators were told to send out the occasional dummy message and this one had just put his finger on the last letter of the keyboard, probably relaxing with a fag in his mouth. The usual Saga method of recovering the wiring by 'buttoning up' on the QWERTZU diagonal was proving very difficult owing to the repetitive nature of the crib. Once again I was alone on the evening shift in the Cottage and this time I sought the help of what Dilly called 'one of the clever Cambridge mathematicians in Hut 6'; as luck would have it, it was Keith Batey. We put our heads together and in the calmer light of logic, and much ersatz coffee, solved the problem. Perhaps Welchman had a point when he said that 'the work did not really need mathematics but mathematicians tended to be good at it'. Dilly made no objections to my having sought such help and even took it in his stride when, after a decent interval, I told him I was going to marry the 'clever mathematician from Hut 6'. He gave us a lovely wedding present.

As our familiarity with the texts increased we could make charts of 'clicks' of key crib words, such as Supermarina; this covered not only 'beetles' but also 'starfish' where the text and hoped-for crib letter criss-crossed. The encoded message was written out vertically on squared paper and slid down the chart to locate clicks. To our delight we read a message dated 25 March 1941, which simply said 'Today is X–3' with a little top and tailing. Amazingly enough, in such a short telegraphic message they had used XALTX, which indicated a full stop, three times. We had a chart showing every possible position for this and an added bonus was that clicks might be found at appropriately staggered distances throughout the message. We were 'exalted' (Dilly's quip) by the break and worked full out night and day to find what they were up to.

Each of the three days had a different setting, of course, and each message had to be broken separately. This was the Cottage triumph of the Battle of Matapan. When Cunningham came down to see us he was particularly anxious to see the actual encoded messages to his opposite number Admiral Iachino, on the strength of which he had made his battle plan. As a decoy he had been able to send his Force B to the actual rendezvous position, given in our message as 20 miles south of the island of Gaudo at 7 a.m., to intercept the Trieste division bent on attacking one of our convoys to Crete. Having effectively dealt with them, the Light Forces were to join Cunningham's battle squadron from Alexandria to tackle the main Italian fleet where Admiral Iachino was on the newly built *Vittorio Veneto* flagship. Cunningham was quite proud of his own secret service tactics and told us the now famous story of how he had gone ashore on the evening of X–1 [X minus 1] with a suitcase, as if intending an overnight stay, and spent some time on the golf course in Alexandria making sure that he was within sight of the Japanese consul, who was certain to report on his movements. Under cover of darkness he had slipped back to his flagship *Warspite* and the fleet sailed silently out of harbour. The consul must have been dumbfounded when he saw the harbour empty the next morning.

Dilly was ready with a poem to celebrate the occasion. Each verse began 'When Cunningham won at Matapan by the grace of God and . . .', mentioning all his girls with a rhyming tribute; the rhyme for Mavis conveniently being the flattering 'rara avis'. All very heady stuff for a nineteen-year-old. Dilly was considered by some to see cryptography only as a theoretical problem unrelated to real events; but that was a mistake. Undoubtedly aerial reconnaissance played an important part in allowing Cunningham to draw up his battle plan, but it was Dilly who rang the Admiralty immediately to make sure that when the battle was reported in the press its success should be accredited entirely to reconnaissance to cover the real source. He chuckled in his poem when he referred to the reconnaissance 'cottage aeroplane'. Clare as usual had organized shifts and kept our spirits up and so was given a special tribute.

> When Cunningham won at Matapan by the grace of God and Clare
> For she pilots well the aeroplane that spotted their fleet from the air.

Tribute was also paid to Margaret whose aim 'straddled the target' and, amongst others, to Hilda who 'sank the *Vittorio Veneto* – or at least they can't rebuild her'.

In 1974, *The Ultra Secret* by Frederick Winterbotham appeared with a picture of Bletchley Park on the front. All those who had kept the secret for thirty years were amazed. Could we now tell the family why we were so good at anagrams, Scrabble and crossword puzzles? But what was this 'Ultra' the jacket cover told us went on at Bletchley? We could never remember using the word. Dilly's 'girls', some of them now grandmothers, eagerly looked in the index for some mention, but not a squeak about the Cottage, and Matapan was credited to a *Luftwaffe* break in Hut 6, as Winterbotham had only known about air force intelligence. What about the rods and the drink with Cunningham? Maybe Dilly's mentor, Lewis Carroll, had been right after all and life was but a dream.

Fortunately, it was the Italians who came to our rescue and proved it was real after all. The Germans had always accused the Italians of having traitors in their midst, which was made worse when, in 1966, H. Montgomery Hyde published the story of the beautiful spy, Cynthia, who had seduced Admiral Lais, the naval attaché in the Italian Embassy in Washington, and obtained the codebook from him which resulted in the Italian defeat at Matapan. As one reviewer observed, 'treason in bed and death at sea made a libretto which sold well', and the Admiral's family felt obliged to take out a libel action, such a course being permitted in Italy on behalf of the dead. Montgomery Hyde was found guilty but the real evidence was not then available.

When *The Ultra Secret* was published, however, the Italians were delighted as it paid off an old score by proving that it was the Germans and not the Italians who were the culprits. They wanted to have Winterbotham's book translated into Italian at once. However, Dr Giulio Divita, who was asked to edit the book, was determined to investigate the matter more fully and, when records were released in 1978, he found ample evidence that it was in fact decoded Italian and not German messages that had given the game away. The BBC ran its *Spy!* series in 1980 with an accompanying book, rehashing the Cynthia story of seduction and treason, now that it was official that breaking Italian ciphers had been responsible for Matapan; it was she after all who sent the codebooks to the Admiralty, which allowed the signals to be read. Dr Divita wrote to *The Times* about this misrepresentation of the facts, having by then decided to end the matter by tracking down the Bletchley Cynthia, or at least one of them. This wasn't difficult as Ronald Lewin had already mentioned names in his book *Ultra Goes to War*, the first book about Bletchley since the release of official records.

I was able to scupper the idea that we had been given codebooks captured by Cynthia or anybody else; if we had had such books we shouldn't have needed codebreakers as it would have been child's play, given that we had a simulated machine. The Italian messages began with a five-figure number to which the operator referred in his list of keys and then inserted the wheels in the given order, adjusted the clips on the side of them and put up the setting in the four windows as directed. Not having such a list, we had to break every message separately by Dilly's rodding method as has been described. At last the Italians had got what they needed to exonerate poor Admiral Lais. They asked me if they brought the actual Matapan battle messages from Rome whether I would show them how they had been broken individually without a codebook. I warned them that as this all happened forty years ago there wasn't much chance of my remembering the actual break.

Nevertheless, losing no time, Dr Divita brought the Admiral in charge of naval history to see me and when I held the message headed SUPERMARINA in my hand it seemed as if time had stood still and I was nineteen again and wearing a green jumper. I spotted the word *incrociatore*, the Italian for 'cruiser', for which we had a chart and remembered that it was a new recruit, Phillida Cross, who had found the clinching click with a lovely starfish and earned herself an honourable mention in Dilly's poem. The Admiral would have been amazed that a starfish could have sunk a cruiser if I had been able to tell him so. Margaret Rock and I had been able to rod out enough of the rest of the message to ensure that we had the right wheel position. It had been raining all day and was still pelting when I rushed it over to the machine room. Dilly was rung up at home and came in to take charge of any further messages and the 'girls' on duty went thankfully home to bed. Cynthia was finally put to bed too; no seduction and no codebooks but just hard cryptographic slogging and a lucky break, or as Dilly put it in his epitaph on Matapan to Mussolini:

> These have knelled your fall and ruin, but your ears were far away
> English lassies rustling papers through the sodden Bletchley day.

My new Admiral friend drank the health of 'Dilly and his girls', just as Admiral Cunningham had done in the Cottage forty years before. On his return to Supermarina, the Admiral wrote a charming letter of thanks, but, with the lesson of Cynthia still in mind, he ended on a cautious note: 'Hoping to be given the opportunity of meeting you again, on work matters.'

There has been a tendency of late to relegate Dillwyn Knox to the status of an old-time professor who did brilliant work on ciphers in Room 40 but was defeated by Enigma, the credit for the breaking of which must go entirely to Turing and Welchman. It is to be hoped that this book will go some way to redressing the balance and that when Bletchley Park's restoration plan goes ahead, the Cottage will be dedicated to his memory. 'Nobby Clarke', an old friend of Dilly's since Room 40 days, who was in overall command of the naval section at Bletchley Park at the time of Matapan, summed up the situation when he added a verse to Dilly's Matapan poem.

> When Cunningham won at Matapan
> By the grace of God and Dilly,
> He was the brains behind them all
> And should ne'er be forgotten. Will he?

7

A Biographical Fragment: 1942–5

JOHN CHADWICK

Introduction

In Chapter 7, the late John Chadwick relates his experiences in breaking several Italian naval codes, while serving in the Royal Navy in the Mediterranean. His account is all the more remarkable, since he had no formal training whatsoever in cryptanalysis, and knew no Italian – only Latin. However, his later work at Bletchley as a Japanese translator, which he also describes, was probably even more difficult than codebreaking.

Chadwick attended one of the six-month courses introduced in 1942 by Brigadier John Tiltman in a desperate attempt to increase the number of Japanese interpreters, who were in very short supply throughout the war. The London School of Oriental and African Studies had advised that no course could produce useful results in less than two years, but Tiltman's unorthodox views were completely vindicated by the success of the courses, which were mainly taken by bright young Classics students. Tiltman even achieved considerable popularity at Oxford and Cambridge because he was then the only person in England who wanted their young scholars purely on account of their skills in Greek and Latin.

Many of the signals translated by John Chadwick's section at Bletchley Park had been sent by Japanese naval missions abroad using the Coral cipher machine, since no codebook could cope with the technical subjects covered by their reports. The signals sent from Berlin, in particular, were highly technical, since they dealt with all aspects of German wartime scientific research, covering radar sets, infra-red search devices (in which Germany was more advanced than the Allies), jet aircraft (including 'sweep-back' on wings), advanced adhesives, and much more. The translations of the technical decrypts from the Japanese Navy's technical mission in Berlin provide a fascinating overview of German technology and production. They are by no means easy to understand without a good knowledge of the subject being dealt with, yet the translators appear to have lacked any technical training, and the many ambiguities of Japanese words were greatly increased by the phonetic form required for signals being transmitted by radio. The decrypts therefore presented the translators with a most formidable challenge, but they met it fully: the translated decrypts are superb examples of the translators' art. John Chadwick, who later acquired an international reputation as a philologist, has rightly paid tribute to their vital work, which until now has gone virtually unrecognized.

John Chadwick later achieved world renown for his most famous feat of codebreaking, which had nothing to do with Sigint. He collaborated with Michael Ventris in the 1950s to decipher the ancient Minoan script called Linear B. They proved it to be a form of early Greek, contrary to the views of established scholars who had been attempting to solve its mysteries for decades.

RE

In May 1942, I was an Able Seaman serving on board HMS *Coventry*, an anti-aircraft cruiser attached to the Eastern Mediterranean Fleet based in Alexandria. I had been trying in various ways to improve my position, and one of the things I had done was to acquire a reasonable degree of competence in speaking modern Greek. This was a much rarer accomplishment than it is today. I was therefore not unduly surprised when on putting into Alexandria after a long absence I received orders to go ashore and report to an office in the naval base called COIS. No one told me what those letters stood for, but since it bore some resemblance to the Arabic word for 'good', I took it for a favourable omen. When I found the place, I discovered that it stood for 'Chief of the Intelligence Staff'. To my astonishment I was interviewed by the COIS himself (Captain Bousfield, RN), who had with him a middle-aged English civilian. I assumed he was there to test my knowledge of Greek.

But I was puzzled by the questions I was asked. They seemed quite uninterested in my linguistic ability and Greek was never mentioned; they concentrated on my schooling and my first year as an undergraduate at Cambridge. I had abandoned my course in Classics to join up after the fall of France in 1940. I was even more perplexed when I was asked to demonstrate my ability to write small numerals clearly. However, after a short delay I was given to understand I had passed the test, whatever it was, and I was sent back to my ship with orders for my immediate transfer to HMS *Nile*, the naval base.

Two days later I reported for work (at the absurdly late hour of 0900) and was directed to another office, where I met the head of the section I was to join. He had apparently been absent when I was interviewed. His name was Commander 'Jock' Murray, RN. As I learned later, he had had as his confidential clerk an English lady who was the wife of the Fleet Engineer Officer. Murray was well known for his violent temper, and he had been sufficiently provoked to call this lady a liar, whereupon she had walked out.

It occurred to the COIS that if he had a rating as his clerk, he could call him any name he chose without creating another incident.

He gave me a long lecture on security, and explained that I must keep what I was doing secret from my messmates, not an easy thing on the lower deck. When he was satisfied I had grasped its importance, he calmly told me that his section was trying to decipher Italian naval signals. 'You say you know Latin,' he remarked, 'so you shouldn't have much difficulty with Italian.' He then produced a large pile of old intercepts, an Italian codebook (the *Cifrario Mengarini*) and some recipherment tables. He demonstrated how to use them and left me to decode the remainder. After making a few mistakes I soon learned how to do this, although of course I could not understand all the telegraphic Italian that emerged. There was no sort of Italian dictionary in the office, not even the unilingual one we later acquired.

After a few days I was initiated into the art of indexing (hence the need for small numerals), building a 'depth' and eventually reconstructing the recipherment key. This was of course much more interesting and I soon picked up enough Italian to follow what was coming out. But before I had gone very far, the news from the Western Desert became alarming; the British forces had been driven out of Cyrenaica and Rommel was invading Egypt. The Army announced its intention of holding him at a place no one had ever heard of, called El Alamein. The Navy promptly ordered the evacuation of Alexandria, and overnight not only did the fleet sail, but all the auxiliary and depot ships too; we awoke next morning to find the harbour empty except for a single minesweeper.

There were two civilians working for the Commander, the one I had met at my interview, W. Stanley Backhouse, and a lady, Pauline Smith, who was the wife of an army officer. At this stage I had no idea what their duties were. When the panic started we were ordered to pack up our work in sacks labelled with innocuous tags like 'Baccy' meaning Backhouse, and to stand by to move at a moment's notice. Next day the order came to destroy all confidential documents, so the sacks were unpacked again and I helped incinerate thousands of intercepts and indexes made from them. I quite expected to be abandoned to take part in the defence of the naval base while my superiors got away, but in fact I was ordered to accompany them on a journey by train to Cairo. We were taken to Heliopolis Museum, the main outpost of Bletchley Park in the Middle East. My arrival created administrative chaos, since I was a lone naval rating attached to an Army Intelligence Corps unit, itself attached to an RAF station. There was no work to do, but we had not long to wait before we were moved again. We had the impression that the German Air Force were aware of our location; one night they dropped a stick of bombs which straddled the building, fortunately with little damage.

The 'I' Corps unit to which I had been attached received orders to leave and took me with them; we travelled by train to Ismailia on the Suez Canal, were ferried across, and then began a most uncomfortable journey in a train of covered goods wagons across the Eastern Desert. When we reached Gaza, in what was then called Palestine, we were taken to a tented camp. Conditions there were quite tolerable since it was summer, though we had nothing to do; and in little more than a fortnight we repeated the journey in reverse, but this time in slightly more comfort. From Cairo I was sent back to Alexandria by train.

The unit now reassembled and had to start afresh with only the latest intercepts to work on, together with the information stored in the memories of the workers. We were also disrupted by the move of the naval base to new quarters in a suburb of Alexandria, about five miles to the east. A luxurious villa (the Villa Laurens) was taken over for the main HQ, and various adjacent buildings were included in a secure perimeter for offices. We were allocated a small bungalow. We had not been there long before

Commander Murray announced that he was leaving, for what reason I never learned. Mr Backhouse was left in charge and proved a much easier person to work for. He had, before the war, been a shipping agent in Naples, so he spoke the language fluently and I learned a lot from him. Our duties were now reorganized, and I became his assistant, working mainly on a low-grade code we all called 'Ouzo', although the name was a risky allusion to its Italian name, *Cifrario per Uso di Mare*. I was to spend a long time on this, so it may be worth describing in some detail.

The signals sent in this code were easily recognizable, since each group consisted of a letter and three figures. The letter normally stood at the beginning of the group, but occasionally occupied other positions. Mr Backhouse had worked on it for some time before the evacuation and established that it was unreciphered, but cleverly designed to make penetration difficult without a very large amount of traffic. It was divided into twelve sections or 'pages', each of which was indicated by the letter in the group; there were two letters for each page, to be varied arbitrarily, and from time to time these were shuffled. This change caused us little trouble, once we had grasped the procedure.

On each 'page', each word in the book was supplied with ten three-figure code groups, one beginning with each digit from 9, 8, 7, and so on to 0. Thus in theory the encoder had a choice of twenty code groups for each word, but since it was easy to pair the letters, in practice we had ten codes to break simultaneously. We were able to reconstruct the arrangement of the columns of figures on the page, since, human nature being what it is, the 900 column was the one most frequently used, and the frequency of each column fell off regularly as the columns stood further and further away from the list of words. Only the 000 column showed a slight rise in frequency.

This now became my chief task, and Mr Backhouse left me more and more to myself, though he constantly checked and verified my work. What I found difficult to believe was that a book so regularly constructed would have ten decode sections on each page, since the various groups for each word appeared to be randomly selected within the hundred possibilities. I suggested therefore that the book was in fact so constructed that it would be easy to find where on the page each numerical group might be located, so that there would be no separate section for decoding. But Mr Backhouse would not hear of this.

My first success was to work out that each 'page' had the numbers divided into two classes. Those of the first class always preceded those of the second, so that each 'page' represented a double-page spread. All the groups on the left-hand side and all on the right shared a common feature. On the left-hand pages the first and last digits of every group were both odd or both even; on the right-hand pages, if the first digit was odd, the last was even, and if the first was even, the last was odd. The rule could be expressed by saying that if the sum of the first and last digit of a group was even, it belonged on the left-hand page; if odd, on the right-hand page.

This suggested that the arrangement of the numbers in each column, now of fifty, not a hundred groups, was also methodical. We had established the value of enough groups in the 900, 800 and 700 columns to be able to see the numerical connections between the groups with the same meanings in different columns. By this means I discovered that there were only three arbitrary factors to be worked out for each column: the starting point, whether the next group was that following in ascending or descending order, and a break point somewhere in the columns. Thus if the 900 column began with 939, the group for the next line would be either 941 or 937. The sequence then continued until it reached 999 or 901 or the break-point occurred. If the break came at 963, the next group would be either 999 and continue descending to 997, 995, etc.; or it would be 901 followed by 903, 905, etc.:

939	995
941	993
943	991 and so on to
945	983
947 and so on to	981
961	965
963	967
999	969 and so on to
997	979

Having established this principle, I was able to reconstruct a whole column by identifying only three or four groups in it. It was hard work convincing Mr Backhouse of this, but eventually he accepted some decodes on the basis of this method. Unfortunately the traffic dried up before we had been able to glean intelligence of any value. Since it was used in the Italian-held Dodecanese islands, it would have been invaluable if Allied operations had been launched in that area. As it happened, the decision was made to invade Sicily and then Italy, leaving the Italian overseas garrisons to their fate.

However, long before that date, in September 1942, a signal from Admiralty in London announced that Able Seaman J. Chadwick was promoted Temporary Sub-Lieutenant (Special Branch) RNVSR. Before Commander Murray left, he had told me that he had recommended me for promotion, but I hardly expected this. From what I could piece together afterwards I suspect the story went something like this. Having initiated me into the work and discovered my aptitude for it, my superiors suddenly realized that the material I was handling was officially classed 'Officers Only'. On enquiring whether I could be made an officer, the Commander was told yes; I should be sent back to England for training and would be returned to service in Alexandria in about six months. This provoked the famous Murray temper, and as a result of the explosion the C-in-C was compelled to ask Admiralty for an immediate commission so that I could remain on the spot. The change of status brought about a very welcome improvement in my living conditions, but made not the slightest difference to the work I was doing.

About the same time we were joined by another new recruit, F. W. Ponting, a Sub-Lieutenant of the Fleet Air Arm, who had been trained as aircrew but to his immense disgust was then grounded for medical reasons. He had been an undergraduate at Christ Church, Oxford, reading mathematics, so he proved adept at the procedures needed to break recipherment keys. After the war he became a lecturer in mathematics at the University of Aberdeen.

Our best success was not the result of our own work, but of the capture of an Italian submarine named *Perla* with all its code-books. For about six weeks we were able to decipher and read every signal sent to its submarines by the Italian Admiralty in Rome. Unlike their German allies, but like our own, the submarines were instructed to keep radio silence while on patrol, so there were no signals from them. The recipherment key changed too frequently to be broken even with the benefit of the code-book, but at least we were able to prove that traffic analysis as applied to this code was useless, since on any one day the proportion of dummy messages varied from zero to 100 per cent. The information on patrol areas gleaned from these signals was of course very useful in keeping our shipping out of trouble.

The result of the decision to by-pass the area of our interest was that traffic declined, and I found myself under-employed. Mr Backhouse had no work to give me, and since I declined to remain idle for about half my time, I cast envious eyes on a pile of intercepts which was growing untouched in my office. They were received regularly from Malta, where there was a unit intercepting Italian naval radio telephone (R/T) signals. With some difficulty I prevailed on Mr Backhouse to allow me to take a look at this traffic. His reluctance was due to the fact that his orders from Bletchley were to leave this to them, but I was able to point out that there was a good naval tradition of ignoring orders when they seemed inappropriate to the man on the spot. I had no illusions that this traffic would contain any intelligence of value, but I thought that any fresh examples of naval signals might offer parallels which would make it easier to understand our assignment. So in my spare time I started to analyse these R/T signals.

Each began with a prefixed word: DRAPI, GIOVE or DELFO. It was soon clear that GIOVE and DELFO were alternative indicators for one code, but that DRAPI indicated a different one. Since there was less traffic in this, I put it aside and concentrated on the more frequently used code. I had hardly begun the indexing when news reached us that a sweep by units of the Western Mediterranean Fleet from Gibraltar had captured a small Italian auxiliary vessel, together with its documents. These revealed the existence of a chain of observation posts on fishing boats in positions at sea to cover the approaches to the Italian mainland and give warning of air raids. Among the documents was the code for the western chain with the prefix DRAPI. But instead of immediately circulating these documents to other intelligence units, the officer in charge at Gibraltar decided to have them translated, and he then sent us a copy of his translation. It is obviously ludicrous to try to translate a codebook, since without context the meaning of many words would be ambiguous. So the first thing I had to do on receiving this was to translate it back into Italian, guessing as best I could what the original was which had given rise to the translated word. I could then decode the traffic we had.

As I expected, there was nothing in it of interest. But the routine signals provided an easy key for the solution of the other code (GIOVE/DELFO) for the eastern chain, covering the straits of Otranto and the extreme south of the Italian peninsula. Therefore I was quickly able to read the routine traffic, but my attention was caught by a very long and obviously exceptional message of quite recent date. It used a number of groups which did not appear elsewhere in the traffic, so only a partial decode was possible. However, after working on it with Mr Backhouse we were able to translate enough to establish two facts. It dealt with a sunken 'enemy' (i.e. Allied) submarine. Now a British submarine was overdue from a patrol in this area, and had been presumed lost. Here was the first confirmation that it had been sunk, not far from the big Italian base at Taranto. Secondly, it seemed that the reason for the signal was to inform all units at sea that efforts were being made to salvage the vessel. This was of major importance, since if successful the enemy might well recover a copy of the British submarine code. Mr Backhouse reported this immediately, and a signal was sent to Admiralty in London relaying these facts.

When it was received, an enquiry was made of Bletchley Park why the news had come from Alexandria and not the home station. As I learned much later, there were some red faces in the naval section. After the war, when I had resumed my studies at Cambridge, I was sent for a supervision to Patrick Wilkinson at King's; to my astonishment he greeted me with the words GIOVE, DELFO. It took me some time to grasp what he was talking about.

The Italian surrender in September 1943 brought our work to an abrupt end. There were a few days immediately afterwards when a transmitter in Rhodes started sending *en clair*, and we were able to submit translations. What happened was that Rhodes then had a garrison of about 25,000 Italians and 5,000 Germans. The Germans had an air base on the east coast, from where their bombers could reach Egypt. But they succeeded in disarming and rounding up the much larger Italian garrison, no doubt by this time thoroughly demoralized. The naval personnel where the transmitter was located were isolated and sent out appeals for help; the Germans apparently adopted salami tactics and came at intervals and took away a few men at a time. The last message declared that there were only five of them left, and when the transmitter went off the air that would be an indication that they too had been taken. We were unable to do anything to help them.

However, elsewhere in the Dodecanese there were no Germans, and the Italian authorities at the other naval base in Leros, much further north, offered to co-operate with the Allies. Contact was established and a tiny British force was sent to stiffen the Italian garrison. But the only means by which the Navy could transport them there was by destroyers, each carrying only a small quantity of men and equipment. The destroyers sailed from Alexandria about 1600 hours and proceeding at top speed reached the straits leading to the Aegean after dark, arriving in Leros around 0200. They had two hours to unload, then had to sail again and take refuge for the following day in a bay on the Turkish coast. Here they were protected by the conventions governing territorial waters; but the German Air Force of course located them, and then amused themselves by making dummy attacks, hoping the ships would open fire, and thus expose themselves to real attack. Then the following night they had to make good their escape back to Alexandria. Several runs were successfully completed, but on one occasion the Italians were only informed of the arrival of the British destroyers after they had sent out their squadron of motor torpedo boats to patrol the approaches. They therefore sent them a signal giving the time of arrival and route to be followed by the British ships. They had taken the precaution of making a small change in the code (the special MAS code), but it took me less than half an hour to penetrate this, and I have no doubt that the German naval codebreakers were equally efficient.

As a result of this incident, I volunteered to go on the next mission to act as liaison with the Italian Navy in Leros, in the hope of preventing any further breaches of security. My suggestion was rejected, and I was told brutally that my superiors did not mind if I were killed, but they were unwilling to take the risk of my being taken prisoner. Although I was never on the Ultra list (people receiving high-grade signals intelligence), I had inevitably gathered a certain amount of information about it, and with hindsight this was a wise decision. But at the time I was annoyed at not being allowed to resume a more active form of service.

In any case, the next mission was the last. A force of four destroyers ran into a newly laid minefield off Kalymnos; one sank and another had to be beached on the Turkish coast. At the same time, against all expectations, the Germans in Greece managed to scrape together an invasion force and transport them on caiques and other small craft to Leros, so the operation was short-lived. It was as well I was not allowed to go.

After the Italian surrender I was for a time employed on general intelligence duties in the naval headquarters, but at the beginning of 1944 I was sent home by air from Cairo to London and, after my first leave for three years, started on a Japanese language course at Bletchley Park. This was run by a diplomat named John Lloyd, who had studied the language in Japan before the war; it was specifically designed to teach us to read written Japanese naval documents. Our main textbook was a photostat copy of the captured logbook of a destroyer squadron. Being handwritten it was a severe test of our ability to recognize characters. I was billeted in Bedford and had to travel to Bletchley by train each day; the work was arduous and the hours long. At the end of six months we were given an examination, and I was one of the two best students on the course; the other was another classics scholar. As a result I was assigned, not as I hoped and expected to cryptography, but to the very specialized unit which had the task of translating the decodes of the Japanese naval attaché machine cipher, JNA 20. We had no contact with the experts who had broken the system, a variant of the Japanese Purple machine. We merely received the signals as processed by a party of Wrens, who had machines for the purpose.

The personnel of this unit were most unusual. Nominally in charge, though he was frequently absent for unexplained reasons, was Lieutenant-Commander Nichol, RN, presumably retired, but rumoured to be employed by some branch of the Secret Service. How he had acquired his knowledge of Japanese I never discovered. The other two, named Watts and Pickles, were both diplomats who had served in Japan, and so had a good command of the language. So I found myself, the veriest beginner, in the company of three of the very scarce experts in the language. Naturally I was given all the uninteresting messages to translate, thus allowing the experts to work on the important ones.

At this time there were only two sources in Europe from which messages were sent to Tokyo: Berlin and Stockholm. It was my task to translate the dull bits of information gleaned by the man in Stockholm, very often by reading English newspapers and magazines. He was a regular subscriber to the periodical called *Aeroplane* and sent his masters any details about naval aviation which had been passed for publication by the British censor. When I asked why we should translate such material, I was told that it might be of interest to see what he had been told to look out for.

The real gems, of course, came from Berlin. The naval attaché was given many of the secret reports prepared by the German Navy on all kinds of technical matters. These were carefully translated into Japanese and a digest was sent to Tokyo in a long series of signals. We were well aware that some of the technical information was of the highest value, both in disclosing the research activity of the enemy, and telling our boffins how far the Germans had been able to discover the secrets of our latest weapons. I remember one particularly difficult set of messages, which I was allowed to handle, dealt with the details of the latest Allied airborne radar, which had been installed in an American bomber brought down sufficiently intact for the German experts to be able to study its construction. The technicalities were almost wholly incomprehensible to anyone without a good background in advanced radio engineering, and we eventually succeeded in obtaining a copy of the manual for this set, but even with this crib it was still very hard to make a good translation. Fortunately we were relieved from this need by the end of the war in August 1945.

I can recall two technical subjects – though I did not do the translation myself. They gave an account of the German experiments in connection with the design of acoustic mines; they had laid out a pattern of microphones on the sea-bed in relatively shallow water, and then run a variety of ships over them at different speeds, recording the volume of propeller-noise at different ranges. All this information was contained in our signals. We were told that if the Allies had performed such an experiment, it would have cost (in those days) well over £100,000 (in present values several millions). All this information was presented to our experts for next to nothing.

Even more vital was the account of the new generation of U-boats the German Navy was building in 1945. These were of revolutionary design, since they were the first submarines with a high underwater speed. The messages gave full details of their performance. Fortunately very few of them had become fully operational by the time of the German surrender; but if we had had to deal with them at sea, it would have been very valuable to know their capability so exactly.

We occasionally had items of more general interest, when the officer in Berlin was able to pick up information which related to Germany's ability to carry on the war. During the winter of 1944–5, the Japanese Ambassador called in his military and naval attachés for a serious appraisal of this subject, and after an exchange of information and views each sent his own report to his masters in Tokyo. The naval attaché's version passed through our hands, and must have been of vital interest to the strategists directing the Allied war effort.

In order to encipher Japanese by machine it was necessary first to write the text phonetically in the roman alphabet, something no Japanese would normally do. There was an official system of romanization, called *romaji*, which differed from the more common one, as for instance in the Kenkyusha Japanese–English Dictionary which we regularly used. However, once you got used to it, this was no obstacle, any more than the special conventions adopted to help disguise the patterning of texts. The real problem lay in the technical terms, most of which were of too recent invention to appear in the dictionary. The Japanese were able to devise their own terminology by creating new compounds out of Chinese characters. Thus to describe a radar set, they came up with a new word *dempatanshingi*. This was written with five characters: *DEN* – 'electric', *HA* – 'wave', *TAN* – 'search', *SHIN* – 'find', *GI* – 'apparatus'. It was easy enough to work out the meaning of such a compound, provided you knew which the characters were. The trouble was that when written phonetically many characters had the same phonetic form, so each syllable might represent any of several characters, and in the worst cases there might be as many as twenty or thirty alternatives. For instance, DEN literally means 'lightning' but can be used to mean 'electricity', and could equally well be translated as 'rice-field'.

Watts and Pickles both had their own indexes of compounds they had encountered and successfully solved, and I began to build one of my own – which I still possess, having illegally retained it at the end of the war. A short selection of the English equivalents will give some idea of the kind of material we had to translate. None of these terms was in any dictionary available to us: prevention of espionage; yield (of a mechanical process); tail-plane; cordon sanitaire; superimpose; (electric) earth; warming up (of an aircraft engine); (electrical) wave-guide; (in optics) pupil-diameter; silver paper; angle of incidence; synthetic oil; magnetron; gun-turret; quadrilateral; reducing solution; stall (of aircraft); cavity resonator; Order of the Rising Sun; lens tube;

suicide squad; combustibility; screw cap; coal slag; directional; catapult; sensitive nose fuse; temporary disbursing officer; laminar flow; cloud height; oils and fats; Trans-Siberian railway.

The *suikan* story is worth telling, though it was not mine. Pickles spent a long time wrestling with a report describing night-vision for fighter-pilots, but he could make nothing of a word which occurred repeatedly, spelled *suikan*. We were familiar enough with *sensuikan* ('submarine'), but clearly this was made up of very different characters. *SUI* offered few possibilities, and almost always it meant 'water' or 'liquid' as in the word for submarine. But *KAN* was one of our worst horrors, with something like thirty characters to choose from. Only after scouring local libraries was he able to find a book on anatomy, which gave an account of the microscopic structure of the retina of the eye, where he met for the first time the phrase 'rods and cones', regularly used to describe it. Now one possible value for *SUI* was 'cone', and among the many possible characters for *KAN* was one which meant 'rod'. Once identified it was easy to write the correct characters and thus to understand the passage.

It was a great honour to have been chosen to work, even as a humble assistant, with these men, who performed an invaluable service by providing translations of such recondite material. I never heard of them again after our organization was dissolved at the end of the war, so perhaps this tribute, posthumous as it is likely to be, is an appropriate note on which to end this memoir.

8

An Undervalued Effort: How the British Broke Japan's Codes

MICHAEL SMITH

Introduction

The obsessive secrecy of GCHQ about the historical achievements of Britain's codebreakers, and the contrasting willingness of the US authorities to release their own material, has distorted the history of codebreaking in the first half of the twentieth century. Nowhere has this been more evident than in the British contribution to the war in the Far East. While a few books like Alan Stripp's Codebreaker in the Far East *and the collaborative* Codebreakers *have shed light on the work carried out by the British on Japanese codes and ciphers, they have merely scraped the surface. It was not until the late 1990s that GCHQ finally began to release files on codebreaking operations in the Far East, revealing that the British had been just as successful in this field as the Americans. The work of remarkable men like John Tiltman and Hugh Foss has had to be reassessed in the light of recent releases. Tiltman in particular emerges as a man who truly earned his wartime title as Chief Cryptographer, making the first inroads into the super-enciphered codes adopted by the Japanese in the late 1930s, and breaking the most famous, the main naval code JN-25, within weeks of its appearance. This chapter highlights the British contribution to the codebreaking war in the Far East. It also examines the sometimes fractious relationship between the British codebreakers and the US Navy, an area in which there may be yet more revelations to come.*

MS

Japan was one of the most important targets for GC&CS during the interwar years; indeed for much of that period it was second only to Bolshevik Russia. The Japanese had emerged from the First World War as the third largest naval power behind Britain and America and were determined to expand their influence in the Far East, particularly in China. But despite their arrival as a super-power the Japanese codes and ciphers were relatively unsophisticated, said Alastair Denniston, the head of GC&CS. The codebreakers' Japanese expert, Ernest Hobart-Hampden, a former senior official at the British embassy in Tokyo and co-editor of the leading English–Japanese dictionary, 'soon acquired an uncanny skill in never missing the important', Denniston recalled. 'Throughout the period down to 1931, no big conference was held in Washington, London or Geneva in which he did not contribute all the views of the Japanese government and of their too verbose representatives.'

The first attacks on the codes and ciphers used by the Japanese armed forces were directed against the Imperial Japanese Navy. William 'Nobby' Clarke, one of the former members of the Admiralty's Room 40 codebreaking section, persuaded a number of Royal Navy officers to spend their spare time listening in to messages between Japanese ships and their naval bases. There were a number of inherent problems, one of which was that the Japanese Morse code consisted of many more signs than its English equivalent.

The advent of the telegraph had brought problems for the Japanese, whose written language was based on pictorial characters or ideographs, called *kanji*, and around seventy phonetic symbols called *kana*. The sound of words containing *kanji* can be represented using *kana*. But Japanese has a large number of different words which, while having distinctive written forms, sound the same. So a system of transliteration known as *romaji* developed which allowed the *kana* syllables to be spelled out in Roman letters. The Japanese created their own Morse code, which contained all the *kana* syllables plus the *romaji* letters and was totally different from the standard international system.

Paymaster Lieutenant Commander Harry Shaw, a Royal Navy officer who had just completed a Japanese interpretership at the British embassy in Tokyo was sent to GC&CS to assist Hobart-Hampden. But more Japanese experts were needed and the Royal Navy decided to try to poach a Royal Australian Navy officer who had achieved amazing results on his own interpretership course. Paymaster Lieutenant Eric Nave was now serving on board HMAS *Sydney*, the RAN's flagship, where he had set up his own operation to intercept Japanese messages.

The RAN agreed to lend Nave to the British and he was posted to HMS *Hawkins*, the flagship of the Commander-in-Chief, China Squadron, to act as a Japanese interpreter. He arrived at the British naval base in Shanghai in July 1925 and eventually received his instructions that he was to intercept and decipher Japanese radio messages. 'The extent to which this method of obtaining intelligence can be utilized in war largely depends on a plentiful supply of naval cipher messages in peace time,' the messages from the sea lords said. 'Up to the present, only a small number of naval cipher messages have been received and a great many more are required. The use of a ship as a combined intercepting and deciphering centre appears to offer the best solution.'

Nave was given a trained wireless operator, Petty Officer Gordon Flintham, to intercept the messages. With the assistance of Japanese officers, who believed their language alone made the messages impenetrable, and a Japanese operator who helpfully ran through the complete Japanese Morse code in a practice message, Nave began to intercept Japanese naval messages. They soon made good headway, breaking into the *tasogare*, the basic naval reporting code used by the Japanese to announce the sailings of individual ships. All the information Nave managed to produce, together with any messages he was unable to break, was to be sent back by bag to the Admiralty in London, which passed it straight on to the codebreakers. Any further results were passed back to Nave and by the end of 1928 the Japanese Navy's Main Operational Code could be read without problems.

The early 1930s saw major improvements in the systems of codes and ciphers used by the Japanese. But the increase in traffic resulting from the Japanese occupation of China, and an influx of more Japanese experts, allowed the British codebreakers to keep on top of the problem. There was also a marked increase in Japanese espionage against the British, particularly targeted at the naval base in Singapore and led by the Japanese naval and military attachés in the embassies around the world. The Japanese military attaché code was broken in 1933 by John Tiltman. 'There was a small basic code chart of, I think, 240 units which meant that a large part of the plain-text had to be spelled out in syllables,' he said. 'I don't remember the details of the system except that the code-chart had to be reconstructed and forty different sets of lines and column coordinates recovered.'

In order to disguise the espionage, the Japanese naval attachés began using a cipher machine, but this was broken in September 1934 by Oliver Strachey, a veteran of the Army's First World War codebreaking operations, and Hugh Foss, who had learned Japanese while his father was working as a missionary in Japan. The improvised nature of the British operations at the time is perhaps best demonstrated by the Heath Robinson nature of the first attempts to replicate the Japanese machine. 'The first trial was made in the office using a brown foolscap file cover with a collar stud retrieved from a returning laundry parcel, a piece of string and slots cut in the cover for the letters,' Nave recalled. 'This worked, so we asked the Signal School at Portsmouth to help and received some expertly finished models in Bakelite.' The Japanese diplomatic codes and ciphers were translated by Hobart-Hampden, Harold Parlett and N. K. Roscoe – all of whom were former British consular officers in Japan, as well as J. K. Marsden, a former military attaché in Japan, and Captain Malcolm Kennedy, who had been seconded to the Japanese Army and had also been Reuters correspondent in Tokyo.

By now it was clear that the telegrams carrying the most sensitive information were being enciphered using a machine. The Japanese referred to this as the *angoo-ki taipu a*, the Type A cipher machine. It was very similar to the Japanese naval attaché machine broken by Foss and Strachey, although it used *romaji* letters rather than *kana* syllables. It consisted of two typewriters, one to input the plain-text, the other to type out the enciphered message, a standard telephone exchange plugboard, and the encipherment mechanism. Pressing one of the keys on the input typewriter sent an electrical impulse through the machine producing the enciphered letter on the output typewriter. Basic cryptographic analysis of the messages enciphered on the machine, almost certainly carried out by Foss and Strachey, showed that the keys changed every ten days and that it was extremely vulnerable to attack. By November 1934, they had found a way in. Recovering the messages was likely to prove time-consuming, so the Metropolitan Police signals expert Harold Kenworthy was asked to produce a machine that would allow the codebreakers easy access to the Japanese diplomatic cipher. The 'J Machine', as it was known, was working by August 1935.

Shortly after the breaking of the Type A machine, in November 1934, Britain decided to set up its own espionage operation based in Hong Kong. The Far East Combined Bureau (FECB) was to collect intelligence from every possible source, including Sigint, and an intercept site was set up on Stonecutters Island, four miles across the harbour from the FECB offices, where there was a small team of codebreakers led by Harry Shaw. They focused on the three main Japanese Navy codes and ciphers: the Japanese Naval General Cipher, the Flag Officer Code used by naval staff officers based in China, and the *tasogare*.

There were also military officers and operators attached to the FECB and plenty of military messages arising from the continued occupation of China and frontier clashes with the Russians. Many of these had to be sent back to London where they were deciphered by Tiltman. At the end of 1937, the Japanese again improved their codes and ciphers, going over to a super-enciphered code system. The message was encoded using a four-figure group codebook and then enciphered using an additive book containing 10,000 randomly selected four-figure groups from which a series of groups was selected and then added digit by digit to the encoded message. This was carried out using the Fibonacci system in which no figures are carried over – five plus seven therefore becomes two rather than twelve. The messages were also bisected, cut into two with the second half sent first to disguise the stereotyped preambles and make it more difficult for the codebreakers to read the message. This bisected super-enciphered code was the main type of system used by the Japanese Army and Navy throughout the war. But by the late summer of 1938, Tiltman had managed to break the Japanese military system.

Concern that Japan might further improve its code and cipher systems led in 1938 to the creation of a separate section to attack Japanese commercial systems in order to help keep track of supply convoys. The concerns soon proved justified. Within the space of six months, the main Japanese naval system changed twice. The second system, introduced on 1 June 1939, was similar to the military super-enciphered system broken by Tiltman except that it was based on five-figure groups and used a much larger codebook. It was known to the British as the Japanese Navy General Operational Code but was to become much better known by its American designation – JN-25. Remarkably, Tiltman made the first break into the system within the space of weeks.

Shortly before the outbreak of war with Germany, the FECB moved to Singapore for fear of Japanese attack, leaving a small team of codebreakers and intercept operators in Hong Kong. On the same day, GC&CS moved *en masse* to Bletchley Park. As Bletchley Park concentrated on the battle to break the German Enigma ciphers, the Japanese military and naval sections were stripped of their staff to reinforce the FECB, taking with them the JN-25 groups recovered by Tiltman. The FECB codebreaking section had around forty people working solely on JN-25 and by May 1940 they had enough of the code groups recovered to read simple messages. The largest Japanese section at GC&CS was now the diplomatic section housed in the neighbouring Elmer's School. But the amount of useful intelligence they could produce had been limited by the introduction on all the main links between Tokyo and its embassies abroad of a new Japanese cipher machine, the *angoo-ki taipu b*, the Type B machine. Like the Type A machine, it was electro-mechanical and had two typewriter keyboards. However, the encipherment systems on the Type B ran through a series of telephone stepping switches designed to simulate the action of the rotors used on previous cipher machines such as the Type A or the German Enigma machine. With the British machine specialists putting the main thrust of their efforts into the Enigma ciphers, Bletchley Park made no apparent effort to break the Type B machine. Fortunately, it was being attacked on the other side of the Atlantic by both the US Army and US Navy. It was broken by a team of US Army codebreakers led, not as is commonly supposed by the veteran US cryptanalyst William Friedman, but by Frank Rowlett, a bespectacled former mathematics teacher.

The breakthrough was to provide one of the first bartering

chips in the signals intelligence alliance between Britain and America that exists to this day. A team of four US codebreakers, two from the army and two from the navy, travelled to Britain in January 1941, almost a year before America joined the war. One of the top-secret packages they brought with them to exchange for the British expertise in breaking the German Enigma messages was a Purple machine, designed to decipher the telegrams enciphered using the Type B machine. Two days after the American delegation arrived at Bletchley Park, Admiral John Godfrey, the British Director of Naval Intelligence, authorized a full exchange of Japanese signals intelligence between the Far East Combined Bureau and a US Navy codebreaking and intercept site, on the island of Corregidor in the Philippines. The Americans provided a 'pinch' – a stolen version of the Japanese merchant shipping code, a naval personnel code, a new diplomatic cipher called 'Hagi', and a 'nearly empty' JN-25 codebook. The main British contribution was recoveries of the latest JN-25 super-enciphered code, which were greater in number than those available to the US station.

The Japanese had changed the JN-25 system on 1 December 1940, just two months earlier, introducing a new codebook which the Allies would designate JN-25B. But they had made a serious mistake in not changing the additives at the same time. As a result, the codebreakers had been able to break into the JN-25B immediately, recalled Neil Barham, one of the FECB JN-25 experts: 'The Japanese introduced a new codebook but unfortunately for them, retained in use the current reciphering table and indicator system. These had already been solved in some positions and new codegroups were discovered immediately. But for this mistake on the part of the Japanese the form of the book might have taken a matter of months to discover.'

Harry Shaw gave the Americans a JN-25B codebook with 500 of the groups already recovered, plus 4,000 cipher additive groups and 290 indicator additive groups, all of which were from the old system in use before the codebook changed. Although the additive system had now changed as well, these groups covered the two-month window into the new system created by the Japanese mistake, allowing the codebreakers to use them to recover more groups. These in turn allowed sustained recovery of the new additive and further reconstruction of the JN-25B codebook. But the JN-25 exchange was very much a two-way street. Although the British were in the lead at this stage, Corregidor was better placed to intercept Japanese Navy messages than Singapore, which could only pick up the Combined Fleet, based in Japanese home waters, at night. The two sites exchanged signals every three days, giving lists of the first three groups of every JN-25 message they had intercepted, and then sent on hard copies of the messages the other site had missed on the regular Pan-American Airlines flight between Manila and Singapore.

The increased co-operation allowed both stations to surge ahead with their recoveries. The Americans had developed a highly mechanized system, using punch-card tabulating machines to sort the code groups, and they soon began to catch up with their British counterparts. By April 1941, the combined effort had recovered 30 per cent of the new additive system. There was also collaboration on Japanese military systems between the British codebreakers and the US Army's 'Station 6' intercept site at Fort McKinley, near Manila. Two US Army codebreakers were sent to Singapore, where Peter Marr-Johnson, the chief British Army cryptanalyst, handed them partial solutions of two Japanese Army codes, and Lt. Geoffrey Stevens, the FECB's other military codebreaker, was posted to Washington to liaise with the US Army codebreakers.

However, the British were not just co-operating with the Americans. They set up an exchange arrangement with a Dutch codebreaking unit, known as Kamer 14 (Room 14), which was based at the Bandung Technical College in Java. The technical exchange was limited to information on diplomatic ciphers, but there was also a limited exchange of decrypts and intelligence on military and naval material.

Eric Nave had returned to Australia where he helped to set up a new 'Special Intelligence Bureau'. The RAN had intercept sites at Canberra and Townsville and there was also a small Royal Australian Air Force site at Darwin. The Australians and the Royal New Zealand Navy, which had its own intercept unit, agreed to provide coverage of Japanese and Russian traffic to supplement the FECB's intercepts. Nave and Shaw also agreed an exchange of information on a number of codes and ciphers.

The decrypts from the Purple machine were not just providing details of Japanese intentions but also extremely good intelligence from inside Berlin, where the Japanese Ambassador Oshima Hiroshi was a close confidant of Hitler. As a result, the Purple messages provided some of the first evidence that the Germans were about to turn on their Russian allies and invade the Soviet Union. Confirmation came in Oshima's account of a meeting in April 1941 with Hermann Göring, Hitler's deputy, who briefed the Japanese ambassador in detail on the number of aircraft and divisions that would be used in Operation Barbarossa. The code-breakers at Bletchley Park had been warning for some time that the Germans appeared to be withdrawing units from various parts of Europe and pushing them east towards the Soviet Union. But they were not believed in Whitehall until 10 June, twelve days before the invasion began, when the Japanese diplomatic section in Elmer's School translated two messages from Oshima. The first said that Hitler had told him personally that war with the Soviet Union was now inevitable. The other suggested to his bosses in Tokyo that 'for the time being I think it would be a good idea for you, in some inconspicuous manner, to postpone the departure of Japanese citizens for Europe via Siberia. You will understand why.'

Hitler was anxious to draw the Japanese into a war with the Soviet Union in order to create a second front in the Far East that would drain resources from the war with Germany. But Japan was not prepared to be deflected from its main aim, which was to strike south, taking the European colonies in the Far East, including Hong Kong and Malaya. Confirmation of this came with the results of a full cabinet meeting attended by Emperor Hirohito on 2 July 1941. Two days later, the results of the meeting, which had been sent by telegram to Oshima, were deciphered by Bletchley Park's Japanese diplomatic section. The telegram made clear that Japan was intent on expanding its empire into south-east Asia. The first step was the occupation of the whole of French Indochina, by force if necessary, to provide bases that would allow it to launch attacks against Malaya and the Dutch East Indies. Should Britain or America attempt to interfere, the Japanese would 'brush such interference aside', Oshima was told. A few weeks later, Bletchley Park read a Purple message confirming that Vichy France had agreed to allow the Japanese to occupy southern Indochina, ostensibly to protect it from a possible British attack.

The British codebreakers in Singapore began picking up almost daily intelligence reports from the Japanese Consul in Singapore on the situation in Malaya. By the end of October 1941, the FECB's naval intercepts had left no doubt that the Combined Fleet had been mobilized. Throughout November, a combination of traffic analysis, direction-finding and an improved capability against the JN-25B code enabled the FECB to keep track of a mass of Japanese ships heading south. Although the difficulty in breaking detailed operational messages remained, the codebreakers had now recovered more than 3,000 code groups, and were able to produce 'intelligence covering a wide field'.

The Japanese preparations for war were confirmed in the Purple messages. On 19 November, the Japanese embassy in London was told to await a coded weather message on Japanese overseas radio that would indicate the opening of conflict with either Britain, America or Russia. The message, deciphered at

Bletchley, read: 'With America, the words: *higashi no kaze, ame* (easterly wind, rain). With Soviet, the words: *kita no kaze, kumori* (northerly wind, cloudy). With Britain, including invasion of Thailand, the words: *nishi no kaze, hare* (westerly wind, fine). On receipt of these code words all confidential books are to be burnt.'

On 1 December, the Japanese diplomats in London were ordered to destroy their codes and ciphers and began making preparations to leave. The Japanese Navy now changed both its call signs and the JN-25B additive. But the codebook remained in use, again limiting the damage. The codebreakers had recovered nearly 4,000 code groups, allowing them to get out additive on many of the most common messages and make further inroads into the codebook itself.

It was late on Sunday, 7 December, local time, when Hong Kong reported having heard the coded Winds message that was to precede the declaration of war. It had said: '*higashi no kaze, ame; nishi no kaze, hare* (easterly wind, rain; westerly wind, fine)', indicating that war would be declared on both Britain and America. A few hours later, in the early hours of Monday, 8 December, Singapore time, the first Japanese troops began landing on Kota Bharu beach in northern Malaya. It was the first in a carefully co-ordinated series of attacks against Malaya, the Philippines, Hong Kong and, the only real surprise, Pearl Harbor. (Although the attack on Pearl Harbor, which brought America into the war, took place on Sunday, 7 December, the relative location of Hawaii and Malaya on either side of the international dateline meant that in 'real time' the attack on Malaya occurred first.)

Persistent allegations that the British codebreakers knew of the Pearl Harbor attack and failed to warn America in order to drag her into the war are totally without substance. There were messages that might have indicated the existence of a 'northern force', which had practised the use of torpedoes in shallow water such as would be found at Pearl Harbor. But given the limitations on the Allies' ability to break JN-25B, these could not have been read. Nave, who was quoted as having backed the allegations in his memoirs, actually said the exact opposite, pointing out that the Japanese had used a sophisticated radio deception operation to prevent the Allies from realizing that Pearl Harbor would be attacked. Malcolm Kennedy, who was working in the Japanese diplomatic section at Bletchley, wrote in his diary that the attack came as 'a complete surprise'.

As the Japanese advanced down the Malay peninsula, the Royal Navy codebreakers were evacuated from Singapore to Colombo in Ceylon, while their Army and RAF counterparts went to the newly formed Wireless Experimental Centre at Delhi in India. The small detachment left in Hong Kong was not so lucky. The British colony was captured on Christmas Day 1941 and the staff spent the next four years in Japanese prisoner-of-war camps.

The Royal Navy codebreakers moved into Pembroke College, an Indian boys' school about two miles from Colombo. But the deterioration in reception and the break in continuity had badly damaged their ability to break JN-25, which continued to evolve with new codebooks being introduced on a regular basis. It was to be another two years before they would come anywhere near catching up with the Americans, said John MacInnes, one of the GC&CS codebreakers attached to the Royal Navy unit:

> The original work on this had all been British but from the start of co-operation with Corregidor in 1941, the burden was carried more and more on the broad shoulders of the US stations. Work on the British side was badly dislocated by the move to Colombo. The loss of depth on the cypher table caused by the break in interception during the move, and the subsequent reduction in volume, greatly hampered stripping in bulk. It was at this time that the US Navy first took the lead in cryptanalysis.

The Corregidor unit was itself evacuated to Melbourne, where it effectively took over Nave's RAN unit. The latter's willingness to work with the Australian army units, which had been pulled back from the Middle East to work on Japanese material, led to major disagreements with the administrative head of the new US unit. Like many of his US Navy colleagues, Lieutenant Rudi Fabian regarded co-operation with anyone who was not in the US Navy or under its command as poor security. Not only did this cause problems for Nave, who in the end had to be moved to the Australian army unit, but it would also cause much greater problems for the Royal Navy codebreakers in Colombo, who were now supposed to obtain any US results through Fabian's unit.

Despite the problems thrown up by the move to Colombo, the codebreakers were still able to break some messages as a result of the continued Japanese use of the ageing JN-25B codebook and the same additive tables introduced shortly before the outbreak of war. 'As the life of the cipher table was extended, so more and more readable messages became available,' MacInnes said. 'The table remained in force for nearly six months. The book-building was delayed at first by much new jargon unknown in peacetime but, as regards units, was much helped by the possession of a library of messages going back to early 1941, so covering a period when the callsigns were well identified.'

However, in April 1942, the Royal Navy codebreakers were forced to withdraw to Kilindini, near Mombasa, in Kenya, after an attack by a Japanese task force which they had themselves predicted. George Curnock, one of the senior codebreakers, would later recall how amid confusion over the location of the target, a Japanese operator spelt it out in *kana* syllables 'KO-RO-N-BO', sending an electric shock through what been until that moment a very relaxed office.

The move to Kilindini was a disaster for the Royal Navy codebreakers, according to MacInnes. It put their intercept operators out of reach of all but the strongest Japanese signals, cutting down on the depth of messages available to the codebreakers. 'The moves from Singapore to Colombo, and Colombo to Kilindini, followed by the miserable volume of traffic which was intercepted there, caused an almost complete collapse in this field of work,' MacInnes said. 'When efforts were resumed the leeway was too great. Signals frequently took up to a fortnight to be enciphered, transmitted and deciphered.'

Meanwhile, the Americans were able to push ahead. The US Navy codebreaking unit at Pearl Harbor, under the brilliant Commander Joe Rochefort, enjoyed good reception of the Japanese Navy messages and was breaking JN-25 with ease. As a result, the Americans were able to achieve the extraordinary feat of deciphering the complete Japanese operational orders for Admiral Yamamoto's attempt to draw the US Pacific Fleet into an ambush off the island of Midway, 1,000 miles west of Hawaii. Having obtained the full details of its opponent's plans in advance, the US Navy inflicted a crushing defeat on the Japanese, destroying four irreplaceable aircraft carriers and putting them on the defensive for the rest of the war.

On the other hand, the British codebreakers working on Japanese Navy material were now at their lowest point of the war. The belligerent Fabian blamed security concerns over Nave for his reluctance to exchange material with the British codebreakers at Kilindini. But they were too far away from the action to intercept anything apart from the loudest signals that FRUMEL, the US Navy's Melbourne site, and FRUPAC, the US site in Hawaii, were already able to receive without assistance. Fabian was also completely open over his belief that his unit had no reason to exchange material with anyone who could not give him anything in return. One senior British officer who visited FRUMEL said that 'the most notable feature was the inability of the Americans to appreciate the full meaning of the word "co-operation". The atmosphere was "What is yours is mine, and what is mine is my own".' Having given the Americans the help they needed before the start of the war, the British were now denied the technical assistance they desperately needed to get back on top of JN-25. With Admiral Sir James Somerville, Commander-in-Chief of the Royal Navy's Eastern Fleet, complaining that Kilindini's problems, and the US Navy's concentration on the Pacific at the expense of the Indian Ocean, meant he was not receiving sufficient intelligence, the Admiralty considered the most drastic of measures.

'The lack of US intelligence supply to C-in-C Eastern Fleet led the British to consider ditching the Americans on the Japanese side,' said Frank Birch, the head of the Bletchley Park Naval Section. 'Admiralty was not willing to be dependent on such small scraps as US were willing to provide and the only alternative to sharing all available intelligence between the two countries was for this country to build up independently an organization big enough to provide, without American help, as much intelligence as could be got with American help.'

As a result, the British compromised on their previous 'Europe first' approach and began to expand the Japanese naval section, Hut 7, as well as sending more codebreakers out to Kilindini. Despite their difficulties, the Kilindini codebreakers did have some significant successes, most notably with the Japanese Merchant Shipping Code, dubbed JN-40. This was believed to be a super-enciphered code similar to JN-25. But in September 1942 a textbook error by the Japanese gave John MacInnes and Brian Townend, another of the civilian codebreakers sent to Kilindini by GC&CS, the way in. The Japanese operator omitted a ship's position from a detailed message and instead of sending it separately in a different message, re-enciphered the original with the same keys, this time including the longitude and latitude that had previously been missing. A comparison of the two messages made it immediately clear that JN-40 was not a code at all. It was in fact a transposition cipher. It was based on a daily changing substitution table, containing 100 two-figure groups or dinomes, each representing a *kana* syllable, a *romaji* letter, a figure, or a punctuation mark. The operator wrote out the message in *kana* syllables and then substituted the relevant dinomes. This produced a long sequence of figures, which was written into a 10 by 10 square horizontally and then taken out vertically, thereby splitting up the dinomes and making it more difficult to break. Within weeks, MacInnes and Townend had not only broken it but were able to read all previous traffic and were confident of breaking each message in real time, allowing enemy supplies to be tracked and attacked at will by Allied submarines. What was more, since it was a cipher, there were no code groups to recover and therefore no gaps in any of the messages. Over the next fortnight, they broke two more systems. The first was the previously impenetrable JN-167, another merchant shipping cipher. The second was JN-152, a simple transposition and substitution cipher used for broadcasting navigation warnings.

There had also been a notable British success on a Japanese military code in 1942. The mainline Japanese Army codes had so far evaded the efforts of the Allied codebreakers. But John Tiltman had spent some of the early part of 1942 trying to break the Japanese military attaché (JMA) code. He discovered that it was a digraph code in which the basic *kana* syllables stood for themselves and other two-letter groups stood for certain words or phrases commonly used in military communications, e.g. AB stood for 'west' and AV for 'message continued'. The two-letter groups were then set out in a square grid in adjacent squares, sometimes horizontally and sometimes diagonally, and the letters were read off vertically to form the basis for the encrypted text. They were then enciphered using a prearranged 'literal additive', a series of letters that would be notionally 'added' to the letters taken out of the grid on the basis of a pattern laid down in advance on a separate table. Reading off the enciphered letter along the relevant horizontal line and the 'additive' letter down the appropriate vertical column would produce a super-enciphered letter, which would be transmitted by the operator. 'By March 1942, I and my section had partially recovered the indicating system and had diagnosed the cipher as a literal additive system with indicators which gave the starting and ending points for messages,' Tiltman recalled. 'The normal practice was to tail successive messages rigorously through the additive tables, i.e. to start reciphering each message with the additive group following the last group of the preceding message.'

Tiltman set to work on a large number of JMA messages from one particular embassy, where the cipher clerk had used the additive table again and again, giving a large 'depth' to attack. 'It was clear from the indicators that the sender had tailed right round his additive table five times and it was this depth that I set myself to resolve.' The solution took a lot of work, but with a depth of five on the cipher additive, he eventually managed to break the system. One of the first JMA messages deciphered revealed the Japanese intentions to construct a Burma Railroad. It was not until several months later that it became clear from another Japanese military attaché decrypt that British prisoners-of-war would be used as slave labour to build the railway.

Tiltman set up a small Japanese military section at Bletchley Park in June 1942. It comprised a codebreaking sub-section and a traffic analysis team, but its main purpose was to handle the JMA material. The staff came mainly from a Japanese course set up by Tiltman in Bedford, which confounded the experts by turning out fluent Japanese linguists within the space of six months.

By the beginning of 1943, there were a number of British sites around the world intercepting or decoding Japanese messages. At Bletchley Park, there was the Japanese naval section Hut 7, under the control of Hugh Foss, and Tiltman's military section. Apart from Kilindini, there were a number of Bletchley Park outposts covering Japanese armed forces traffic. The main outpost was a joint RAF and Army intercept and codebreaking operation at the Wireless Experimental Centre (WEC) just outside Delhi. There was also a Wireless Experimental Depot at Abbottabad on the North West Frontier, but this mainly covered diplomatic links. The WEC had two main outposts: the Western Wireless Signal Centre at Bangalore in south-western India, which was merely an intercept site; and the Eastern Wireless Signal Centre at Barrackpore, near Calcutta. The latter site had its own codebreakers and traffic analysts as well as its own forward intercept and codebreaking outpost at Comilla, covering tactical air force communications nets. There was also a British officer, Major Norman Webb, based at the Central Bureau, a joint US and Australian Army codebreaking operation in Brisbane, where Nave was also now working, following his disagreement with Fabian.

The Central Bureau was also facing difficulties in its relationship with FRUMEL. It originally attempted to set up an exchange relationship with the US Navy site, but Fabian was not interested and was backed in his reluctance to exchange material by Admiral Joe Redman, the Director of Naval Communications. This was perhaps unsurprising. For much of the war, the US Navy codebreakers and their US Army counterparts were barely on speaking terms. But Fabian insisted that the Central Bureau could give FRUMEL nothing it needed and it had nothing that could help them. The US Navy unit was 'concerned solely with information on Japanese naval circuits', Fabian said, where 'the Central Bureau was not'. It was not that simple. Few wars had seen more need for complete co-operation between the army and navy. The Japanese Army was forced by the very nature of the campaigns it was fighting, cut off from its home bases by thousands of miles of ocean, to pass messages on naval communications circuits, often in naval codes and ciphers. Messages would be translated from one system to the other, providing a wealth of potential 'cribs' if only they could have been followed through the system.

It is impossible to say how much help this might have given the army codebreakers. In the event, the US Army codebreakers at the Central Bureau and the two main British outposts converged on the solution to the first mainline army code at the same time in March 1943. Some credit Wilfred Noyce, a classicist from King's College, Cambridge, and a prominent mountaineer, who was working at the WEC in Delhi, with having broken the Japanese Army Water Transport Code, *senpaku angosho 2*, assisted by Maurice Allen, an Oxford don. The difficulties of communication between the various codebreaking bases make it difficult to tell for sure whether they were first. They may well have been beaten by Warrant Officer Joe Richard, a US Army codebreaker at the Central Bureau, Brisbane, who also broke it at around the same time. There is even a possibility that Brian Townend, who remarkably was working on it in his spare time at Kilindini, may have broken it first.

Bletchley Park was not in any way involved in what was perhaps the most controversial use of the ability to break the high-level Japanese codes – the shooting down, in April 1943, of an aircraft carrying the Japanese Navy's Commander-in-Chief Admiral Yamamoto Isoruku. A JN-25 message giving the itinerary of a tour by Yamamoto of the Solomon Islands was deciphered by the US Navy codebreakers in Hawaii, allowing US fighters to intercept his aircraft and shoot it down, killing all those on board. The Japanese ordered an investigation but fortunately details of the visit had also been sent on low-level nets and it was assumed that the Allies had intercepted these rather than having been able to decipher the original JN-25 message.

Meanwhile, the Japanese military section, where John Tiltman was leading the research, broke the Army Air Force General Purpose Code, *koku angoo-sho 3*, designated 3366, and began to expand to cope with the increased intelligence expected as a result of the recent successes. It acquired its own Army Air subsection in May 1943, presumably as a direct result of the breaking of the 3366 code, and some weeks later, a military intelligence section was added, reporting direct to MI2, the War Office intelligence section covering the Far East.

The breaking of the first two mainline army codes led Tiltman to call a conference at Bletchley Park in July 1943 to allocate coverage among the various Allied outposts. It was agreed that Bletchley Park and Delhi should concentrate their cryptographic resources on the codes and ciphers of the Japanese Army Air Force. Arlington Hall (headquarters of the SIS) would deal with the high-level systems used by the Japanese ground forces, leaving the Central Bureau to concentrate on the low-level material produced by their forward field units and the Army Water Transport code.

A separate Japanese air intelligence section was set up at Bletchley Park in October 1943, with Leonard 'Joe' Hooper, a future head of the postwar GCHQ, in charge. So many Japanese military messages were now being sent over Japanese naval circuits, and in a number of cases actually using JN-25 and other naval codes and ciphers, that it was decided to co-locate all the Japanese sections. They were moved into Block F, the largest of a series of brick-built blocks designed to cope with the expansion of Bletchley Park. This consisted of a number of wings jutting off a long, central corridor which, as a result of its length and the proliferation of various Japanese subsections in the block, became known as 'the Burma Road'.

The summer of 1943 saw a marked improvement in the relations between the British and the US Navy codebreakers. Redman attended a number of conferences at Bletchley and the Admiralty during which he promised to ensure that the Royal Navy codebreakers would receive all urgent Japanese Navy material and all the American JN-25 recoveries. The Royal Navy codebreakers were to return to Colombo in September to improve their coverage and Redman agreed that the new station would have a direct cipher link to Melbourne.

The new Colombo site was on the Anderson Golf Club. The

Royal Navy codebreakers were soon swamped with Japanese naval messages to work on. But despite Redman's promises the exchanges with Melbourne did not improve. Commander Malcolm Saunders, a former head of Bletchley Park's Hut 3 intelligence-reporting section, toured Allied naval codebreaking sites in the autumn of 1943. He was very impressed with the FRUPAC centre in Hawaii but less so with FRUMEL, where Fabian continued to block co-operation. 'The liaison with Colombo is not nearly as good as it should be,' Saunders said. 'This is partly due to bad communications and insufficient staff at each end, but also due to the present lack of productivity of the Colombo unit, and to lack of a clear-cut statement of policy from Washington in this regard. The security aspect is constantly in mind and there is a constant suspicion of "leakage" to the American military authorities at Brisbane.'

Harry Hinsley, the leading naval intelligence analyst at Bletchley Park, was sent to Washington in late 1943 in an attempt to improve co-operation with the US Navy. The result was an agreement, in January 1944, to set up a comprehensive exchange circuit between the main stations tackling Japanese Navy material, including Bletchley Park and the Royal Navy site at Anderson, 'as early as practicable'.

Perhaps the best example of the new spirit of co-operation came in the breaking of Coral, the successor to the Japanese naval attaché machine cipher broken by Foss and Strachey. With the US Navy now bearing the brunt of the attacks on the German U-boat Enigma, Hugh Alexander, the head of the German naval Enigma section Hut 8, began to examine the Coral cipher. Since it used banks of stepping switches to simulate the rotors of an Enigma-type machine, many of the processes used were similar. At the end of September 1943, the British began to make real headway and Alexander produced a report, which according to the official US history, 'marks the birth of the successful attack on the Coral'.

Alexander flew across to America in early 1944 to help in the final attack on Coral. Since Foss, who had broken Coral's predecessor, had also just arrived in Washington as liaison officer, he may have been involved too in the discussions with Lieutenant-Commander Frank Raven, who was leading the US Navy team. By 11 March, the codebreakers had solved the wiring of the Coral machine and read a few messages. The British codebreakers 'contributed heavily' to what was a joint US–British success, the US history records. Coral, together with the Japanese military attaché code and the Purple diplomatic cipher, would also contribute to the Allies' knowledge of the German defences in Normandy and thus to the success of the D-Day landings.

As the Allies pushed forward on a number of fronts in the Far East, the codebreakers benefited from an increasing number of 'pinches' of Japanese codebooks. One of the most important, and certainly the largest, occurred in early 1944 when the 9th Australian Division overran the positions of the 20th Japanese Division at Sio in northern New Guinea. The division's chief signals officer should have burned its codebooks. Instead he dumped them into a water-filled pit inside a metal container. When it was retrieved it was found to contain the current codebooks for six different mainline systems, allowing the Allies to read the Japanese military codes for the next two months and to keep on top of most of the main military systems after new codebooks were introduced. The Central Bureau was able to provide General Douglas MacArthur, the Allied commander, with full details of the Japanese order of battle in New Guinea, greatly aiding his advance.

Bletchley Park now began to reinforce the Central Bureau with a number of graduates of the Bedford course. Hugh Melinsky, who had been recruited from Christ's College, Cambridge, arrived in April 1944 as one of a dozen or more British reinforcements. He was put to work on the naval air desk, part of Eric Nave's air-ground section. 'What Captain Nave did not know about code-breaking was not worth knowing,' Melinsky said. 'He had a sixth sense which enabled him to sniff out a meaning in what looked to me like a jumble of letters or numbers.' Melinsky and other British codebreakers were sent forward with Australian mobile wireless units to provide MacArthur with up-to-date tactical intelligence as the Allies pushed northwards.

The British and Indian advances in Burma during the second half of 1944 and into 1945 were also aided by mobile signals intelligence units that pushed forward with the Allied troops. But one of the most significant pieces of assistance they received from Sigint was a result of Bletchley Park's breaking of the three-figure super-enciphered code used by the Japanese Army Air Force for its communications with the ground, known as *kuuchi renraku kanji-hyoo 2-goo* to the Japanese and BULBUL to the Allies. The code was broken in the new Japanese air section, which was rapidly expanding, with around 250 people working on army air alone in September 1944, but was exploited in India to great effect.

Michael Kerry was one of the codebreakers assigned to work on the BULBUL code in Comilla. 'The Japanese bombers used to be kept safely down in Bangkok and then when there was a full moon, they were moved forward to the Mingaladon air base in Rangoon. On one occasion we got wind in advance that a raid was going to take place and passed the information on. Most of the time, we had no way of knowing if what we did was a pennyworth of use but in this particular instance the nightfighters got the lot and all night we could hear Mingaladon air base calling for its lost children.'

The US codebreakers' achievement in breaking the Purple cipher, and the fact that they were reading the main Japanese Navy code JN-25, was revealed almost immediately the war ended through a series of leaks and the congressional inquiry into the attack on Pearl Harbor. But the part played by the British codebreakers in the war in the Far East remained secret until the late 1990s when GCHQ began to release the files that recorded the achievements of men like Tiltman, Foss and Nave. As a result, most of the existing literature credits the Americans with having led the way in the breaking of the Japanese codes and ciphers. Only now are the British codebreakers beginning to receive the recognition they deserve.

9

Most Helpful and Co-operative: GC&CS and the Development of American Diplomatic Cryptanalysis, 1941–2

DAVID ALVAREZ

Introduction

In Chapter 9, David Alvarez describes how GC&CS helped the US Army's Signal Intelligence Service (SIS), as it then was, to develop its diplomatic codebreaking capability significantly during the war. Under an inter-service agreement, the US Army had sole responsibility for diplomatic codebreaking, although this was later modified to enable the US Navy to share the load of breaking traffic using the high-level diplomatic cipher machine, codenamed Purple by the Americans. The SIS was in favour of Sigint co-operation with Britain as early as August 1940, whereas the US Navy codebreakers, headed by Commander Laurence Safford, had then set their face against any collaboration on codebreaking.

In February 1942, following a review of GC&CS's functions, Alastair Denniston was moved sideways to become the Deputy Director (Civil), in charge of GC&CS's diplomatic and commercial sections, which moved to Berkeley Street and the nearby Aldford House, respectively, in London. Edward Travis replaced him as the operational head of Bletchley Park, with the title of Deputy Director (Services).

Despite having relatively few staff, GC&CS's diplomatic section produced huge numbers of decrypts. In 1940, a staff of about sixty-five read 70,000 signals out of the 100,000 received, although only 8,500 were actually circulated. The Foreign Office received all of them, with other important clients being the service Ministries and MI5, where the recipient was Major Anthony Blunt, one of the notorious 'Cambridge Five' group of Soviet agents. In 1940, MI5 was sent only 1,200 of the 'BJs', as the diplomatic decrypts were known, on account of their distinctive blue jackets, but by 1943 it was the diplomatic section's second biggest client, receiving 9,300 BJs compared with the 13,000 sent to the Foreign Office. It would be of considerable interest to know how many Blunt passed on to the Russians, and how they used them. The Russians have recently claimed that they too reconstructed the Purple machine in late 1941, although they adduced no evidence. If, as is quite probable, Blunt received the Purple decrypts solved by the British, they would have been valuable to the Russians as cribs in solving Purple. But even if they were not used for cribs, the value of one Purple decrypt to the Russians would have been priceless. On 27 July 1942, when battles were raging on Russia's western front, the Japanese Foreign Minister, Togo Shigenori, informed Japan's ambassador in Berlin, Oshima Hiroshi, that Japan would not attack the Soviet Union. Did Blunt receive the decrypt of that message? We shall have to await the release of the BJs for 1942 to learn the answer.

In contrast to the major difficulties that emerged in 1943 over the US Army's desire to attack Heer *and* Luftwaffe *Enigma, co-operation between Britain and the United States on diplomatic codebreaking was remarkably trouble-free from its start in early 1941. Partly for that reason, and partly no doubt because of the range of countries potentially involved, no formal agreement about diplomatic Sigint was ever concluded between the US War*

Department and GC&CS. Inevitably there were misunderstandings from time to time, but they were resolved, in no small measure due to the wise approach adopted by Alastair Denniston, who was wholeheartedly in favour of Sigint co-operation with the United States. Denniston was a man of vision on this issue, just as he had been in 1938 when he recruited Alan Turing and Gordon Welchman to join GC&CS when war with Germany was declared. Sadly, there has been insufficient recognition of his vital role in laying the foundations of GC&CS's wartime successes and in paving the way for Britain's important Sigint alliances with the United States.

RE

Signals intelligence has fully emerged from the historical shadows of the Second World War. With the release in the past decade of almost 1.5 million pages of cryptologic materials into American and British archives, historians have acquired a documentary base upon which to construct an important story, most of whose chapters had remained among the still-guarded secrets of the war. The new materials have enhanced our understanding of well-known episodes in the signals intelligence history of the war, such as the Battle of Midway and the Battle of the Atlantic. More importantly, they have also revealed previously unknown or only dimly perceived episodes of that history, such as the highly successful Anglo-American cryptanalytic effort against the wartime diplomatic codes and ciphers of a range of friendly, neutral and hostile powers. The revelations have especially surprised American historians who, though well aware of their country's wartime success against Japanese cryptosystems, have been astounded to learn that by the end of the war the US Army's Signal Security Agency, the organization responsible for diplomatic cryptanalysis, was reading the secret communications of more than sixty governments and organizations. They have been even more surprised to discover that this impressive record, which catapulted the United States into the front rank of intelligence powers, was achieved largely because of significant advice and assistance from Britain's signal intelligence service, the Government Code and Cypher School (GC&CS).

In the decade following its creation in 1930, the US Army's codebreaking organization, then known as the Signal Intelligence Service (SIS), had a very limited horizon. Until 1938, the SIS studied the codes and ciphers of only one country: Japan. That country was selected, not because it monopolized American diplomatic attention in the 1930s (it didn't), but because Tokyo's communications represented the path of least resistance for a small and inexperienced cryptanalytic organization. With few personnel (the original staff consisted of five men and one woman, none of whom had any training in cryptology), William Friedman, the pragmatic civilian director of the service, decided to concentrate on the cryptosystems of one country. Without any guidance from the State or War departments, he selected Japan because the SIS had inherited an archive of Japanese cryptologic material from a predecessor agency, the so-called Cipher Bureau that had solved several Japanese ciphers during its brief existence in the 1920s.

Friedman trained his novice cryptanalysts with practical problems from the files of intercepts and solved and unsolved ciphers in the Japanese collection of the defunct Cipher Bureau. Once satisfied that his pupils possessed some basic skills, he tested them against the small stream of current Japanese messages that trickled into the War Department from the army's primitive network of radio intercept stations. Apt pupils, a good teacher, and relatively simple ciphers combined to produce a formula for success. By 1935 the SIS had solved five Japanese diplomatic ciphers; by 1938 it had solved another four, including the so-called Red cipher machine used by the Japanese foreign ministry for its most secret messages.

The Signal Intelligence Service did not abandon its exclusive focus on Japan until the spring of 1938 when, shortly after the *Anschluss* and just as Berlin was opening a political offensive against Czechoslovakia that would culminate in September in the Munich agreement, William Friedman directed Solomon Kullback, one of his original recruits, to open a study of German ciphers. Later that year, Italy and Mexico were added to the target list under the direction, respectively, of Abraham Sinkov, another of Friedman's original recruits, and Herrick 'Frank' Bearce, who had joined the service in 1936.

Unfortunately the triumph against Japan did not translate into widespread success against the new targets. By early 1939 Frank Bearce had solved at least one Mexican cipher and was making rapid progress against three others. German and Italian systems, however, proved harder nuts to crack. The German foreign ministry used several cryptosystems and Solomon Kullback's small team had decided to focus on an unenciphered code, the *Deutsches Satzbuch* (DESAB). When Germany sparked the Second World War by attacking Poland on 1 September 1939, this book had been sufficiently reconstructed that messages in the code could be read. Unfortunately, DESAB carried only 5 per cent of Berlin's diplomatic traffic and then only low-grade consular and administrative messages. The high-grade ciphers that protected Berlin's more important diplomatic communications remained a mystery to the SIS. In the Italian section things were even worse. At the outbreak of war, Abraham Sinkov's team was studying two systems: an unenciphered code known to the Americans as 'X' and an enciphered code known as 'Trujillo' (or TR) because most of the intercepted messages in this system were collected on the Rome–Ciudad Trujillo (Dominican Republic) circuit. Neither of these systems was readable.

In autumn 1939 the sound of distant cannons echoed, if only faintly, down the normally somnolent corridors of American military intelligence. Within weeks of the outbreak of war in

Europe, Army Chief of Staff General George Marshall approved a proposal to expand the Signal Intelligence Service by hiring twenty-six additional personnel, which would more than double the staff of a service that after nine years still numbered fewer than twenty analysts, translators, clerks and machine operators. While welcome, the additional resources had little impact on operations. There was no attempt to expand the target list beyond the four countries studied before the war. Most of the new staff were assigned to the lagging German and Italian problems, but since they required months of training to reach even a modest level of cryptanalytic skill, their presence did little in the short term to accelerate the effort. Fully a year into the European war, the American signals intelligence programme had advanced only marginally beyond its position in the summer of 1939, and in one area it had actually regressed.

Kullback's German desk still struggled with its target. The desk continued to read the low-grade messages in DESAB and had discovered that occasionally this basic code was enciphered with reciprocal bigram tables. Unfortunately, this enciphered version (known as *Spalierverfahren*) was observed only on relatively quiet Caribbean circuits (e.g. Berlin–Havana) and thc low traffic volume undermined solution efforts. Kullback's team had also isolated what it believed to be two different high-grade systems, but had made no progress beyond suspecting that one was enciphered by a string of random additives. The situation in the Italian section was hardly better. By the summer of 1940, Sinkov's team had reconstructed enough of the 'X' code to read most messages in the system, but Rome used the system only for routine administrative traffic, and the intelligence content of the messages was negligible. The team had also identified the encipherment and reconstructed a portion of the codebook for TR, the medium-grade system used by Rome to communicate with its minor Caribbean missions. Traffic in TR was light and only a few messages were read. At least two high-grade Italian systems had been identified, but Sinkov's team was still working on the encipherment and no messages in these systems were readable.

While progress in the German and Italian sections was disappointing, the situation in the Japanese section was disastrous. Long accustomed to reading all of Japan's diplomatic traffic, the section had been alarmed at the end of 1938 by decrypts that suggested that Tokyo was preparing to introduce a new cipher machine. Alarm turned to panic when, on 21 February 1939, SIS intercepted three messages from the Japanese legation in Warsaw that should have been readable but were not. Within a week a trickle of unreadable messages became a flood. The Japanese foreign ministry had introduced a new cipher machine to replace Red. It would take some time for the ministry to distribute the new machine (christened Purple by the Americans) and a few minor posts continued to use the old machine well after the outbreak of war, but by 1940 only a handful of Red messages were intercepted each month as Tokyo entrusted its most secret communications to the unreadable Purple machine. The cryptologic window into Japanese diplomacy had closed.

The inability to solve the Purple machine or advance against high-grade German and Italian ciphers meant that in the desperate first year of the war, as Germany defeated and occupied Poland, Denmark, Norway, France, Belgium, the Netherlands and Luxembourg, and threatened to invade Britain, the Signal Intelligence Service could read the high-grade diplomatic traffic of only one country: Mexico. As President Franklin Roosevelt and his State Department frantically (and futilely) sought to formulate a policy that would contain Nazi aggression, stiffen the resolve of threatened nations, and deter Benito Mussolini from leading Italy into the war alongside Hitler, American signals intelligence provided little support. The foreign ciphers accessible to the SIS revealed little beyond the routine and often trivial work of German, Italian and Mexican embassies and consulates: the

Italian embassy in Washington informed Rome that the United States intended to open a consulate in Greenland; the Mexican foreign ministry authorized its embassy in Brussels to withdraw to Paris as German armies approached the Belgian capital; the German embassy in Guatemala informed Berlin that its staff had donated a large sum of money to the Reich Red Cross. With Tokyo's most important messages wrapped securely in Purple, Japanese decrypts, once the pride of the SIS, were now more likely to reveal negotiations for a textile agreement with Peru than the latest perspective on Germany's intentions toward Britain. The few political messages transmitted to Tokyo in secondary ciphers revealed little that was not also reported by American diplomats and journalists in Europe.

In their warren of cramped offices in the Munitions Building on the Washington Mall, the army codebreakers cast about for a way to regain the cryptanalytic initiative. Increased effort against Purple might result in a breakthrough, but the personnel in the Japanese section were already logging twelve- and fourteen-hour days. Additional personnel might advance operations, but there was no evidence that the notoriously parsimonious War Department was prepared to be generous. In a gesture that revealed the extent of its desperation, the SIS set aside inter-service rivalry and exchanged observations about Purple with its sister service in the United States Navy, OP-20-G. The Navy's help was welcome, but breakthroughs still eluded the Americans. Then, on 5 September 1940, a message arrived from London that promised an escape from the cryptanalytic wilderness.

After the fall of France, the Roosevelt administration had cast about for a way to support Britain within the limits set by an American public opposed to armed intervention and an American military establishment ill-equipped to support the security of its own country let alone the security of another. In July 1940 President Roosevelt, in consultation with Secretary of War Henry Stimson and Secretary of the Navy Frank Knox, accepted a

British proposal that military representatives of the two governments convene a joint staff conference in London. Within a month, an 'American Military Observer Mission' arrived in the British capital ostensibly to study 'standardization of arms', but really to discuss co-operation between the armed services of the two countries.

On 31 August 1940, the army representative on the American observer mission, General George Strong, startled his hosts (as well as his American colleagues) by announcing that the US Army was working on Axis codes and ciphers and proposing that London and Washington exchange information on their cryptanalytic operations. The British were particularly surprised by Strong's proposal, since the Royal Navy had been rather curtly rebuffed by the US Navy in October 1939 when it suggested sharing information on Japanese naval communications. Having had one door slammed in their face, the British were now pleasantly surprised to have another door opened even before they had knocked. Within days they accepted General Strong's invitation. On 5 September Strong sent the War Department the telegram that would electrify the Signal Intelligence Service: 'Are you prepared to exchange full information on all German, Italian, and Japanese code[s] and cryptographic information therewith? Are you prepared to agree to a continuous exchange of important intercept in connection with the above? Please expedite reply.'

The Signal Intelligence Service was more than prepared to pursue any opportunity to advance its lagging cryptanalytic programme. Indeed, even before Strong's message reached Washington, William Friedman and Colonel Spencer Akin, the military commander of the service, may have already concluded that co-operation with the British promised a short cut to success. About the time that Strong was proposing cryptanalytic co-operation to his astonished British and American colleagues in London, Friedman and Akin were preparing a memorandum, 'Proposed Exchange Basis with the British', that recommended the exchange of 'any and all material that we have on a basis of complete reciprocity', and explicitly stated that the SIS was interested in information concerning specific foreign codes and ciphers.

It is easy to understand the SIS's enthusiasm for establishing links to GC&CS. When Akin and Friedman composed their memorandum, Japanese traffic was still America's only productive source of diplomatic signals intelligence. Unfortunately, even this source had declined significantly in value after Tokyo's introduction of the yet unsolved Purple cipher machine. The low-grade German and Italian traffic accessible to American codebreakers produced negligible intelligence and would continue to do so as long as Berlin's and Rome's high-grade ciphers remained impenetrable. The potentially useful communications of powers such as China, Russia and Vichy France had not even been studied let alone exploited. A connection to the British might provide short cuts to success against all these targets. Given the secrecy that surrounded GC&CS, American codebreakers knew nothing about operations at Bletchley Park, the wartime home of the British codebreakers, but through Friedman they were vaguely aware of Britain's cryptanalytic achievements during the First World War and assumed that GC&CS was working hard to repeat those successes in the present war. Perhaps the British were already reading high-grade German and Italian ciphers. An exchange of 'any and all material' might well produce just the information necessary for an American entry into Nazi and Fascist communications. With luck an exchange might even help the effort against Purple.

The Americans were correct in assuming that in the early autumn of 1940 the Government Code and Cypher School (which admittedly had been playing the game longer and harder than its American counterpart) was significantly ahead of the Signal Intelligence Service in most areas of diplomatic signals intelligence; indeed the SIS was not even playing in the same league.

In 1940, when the SIS was covering only four targets, GC&CS was working the diplomatic communications of twenty-six countries.

Figure 9.1 **Diplomatic Cryptosystems Read at GC&CS and SIS, 1940**

Systems	GC&CS	SIS
Japanese	19*	15*
German	1**	1**
Italian	7	2
French (Vichy)	10	0
Chinese	6	0
Russian	0	0
Latin American	47[a]	4[o]
Balkan	12§	0
Near Eastern	65¶	0

* Includes Red but not Purple
** DESAB
[a] Includes Argentina, Bolivia, Brazil, Chile, Colombia, Ecuador, Mexico
[o] Mexico only
§ Bulgaria, Romania, and Yugoslavia
¶ Iran, Iraq, Saudi Arabia, and Turkey

Sources: Untitled table of foreign codes and ciphers, PRO HW 14/11; 'The Status of the Cryptanalysis of Japanese, German, Italian, and Mexican Systems, August 1940', NACP HCC box 587.

Figure 9.1 compares the records of GC&CS and SIS against some of those countries. British codebreakers, for example, had solved high-grade Italian ciphers while the Americans were struggling to master low-grade versions. GC&CS was reading several Vichy French diplomatic ciphers at a time when the SIS was hoping that the next staff increase might free up one or two officers to open a French section. GC&CS routinely solved Balkan and Near

Eastern systems that did not even appear on the cryptologic horizon of the SIS. Even in the matter of Japanese codes and ciphers (an American speciality) the British were reading more systems (including Red) than the Americans, although GC&CS had had no more luck with Purple than their cousins across the Atlantic. Only in the area of German and Russian communications were the prospective partners equal. In their efforts against Berlin's diplomatic systems neither had been able to advance beyond the reconstruction of the DESAB code. As for Russian systems, neither was studying Moscow's diplomatic ciphers, although GC&CS was reading a few Red Army and Comintern systems.

There can be little doubt that the United States stood to benefit significantly from any collaboration with Britain. Of course, General Strong's proposal called for an exchange; the British would certainly expect some return for any secrets they shared with the Americans. It wasn't clear, however, that the SIS had anything GC&CS might need. The principal product that the SIS could bring to the exchange was information on American progress against Japanese diplomatic ciphers. What if GC&CS had already solved these ciphers? In the midst of a life-and-death struggle against the Axis would the British share the secrets of German and Italian cryptography in return for a copy of the cipher used by the Mexican finance ministry? SIS stood to benefit disproportionately from collaboration, but it needed something big to bring to the table. By the end of September it had something big.

For eighteen months the battle to solve the Purple machine had consumed the SIS. Under the direction of Frank Rowlett, the Japanese section routinely logged fourteen-hour workdays as they struggled under great pressure to find a weak spot in the cryptographic armour that protected Tokyo's most sensitive diplomatic communications. On 20 September 1940 the perseverance and hard work paid off. On that day, Genevieve

Grotjan, a studious young statistician who had come to the SIS from the Railroad Retirement Board in 1939, noticed certain patterns in the cipher alphabets so far reconstructed by the American team. It was the breakthrough. One week later Frank Rowlett handed William Friedman the first two decrypted Purple messages.

The solution of Purple reopened access to Tokyo's high-grade diplomatic traffic and significantly improved America's bargaining position in any exchanges with Britain. The Americans had no way of knowing if GC&CS had broken Purple for itself, but even if it had it would immediately understand that the solution of the Japanese machine was an impressive accomplishment that established the United States as a potentially valuable partner in the signals war. The SIS believed that Purple would purchase any number of British secrets.

On 11 September, almost two weeks before the solution of Purple, the Army Chief of Staff, General George Marshall, had approved the exchange of cryptanalytic information with Britain. The US Navy cryptanalysts, however, suspected British intentions and managed to block the plan to pass American Sigint secrets to London until December when the combined political power of the President of the United States, the Secretary of War and the Secretary of the Navy finally quashed their opposition. To open the collaboration the Army and Navy signals intelligence services each selected two of their officers to form a joint mission to Britain. Still a reluctant participant, the Navy gave its representatives, Lieutenant Prescott Currier and Ensign Robert Weeks, no guidance beyond a general injunction 'to get whatever you think we should get and have a look around'. As their contribution to the exchange the naval officers carried the latest version of the Imperial Japanese Navy's fleet code to the extent that it had been reconstructed by OP-20-G. The latest version of this system, JN-25B, had been in service less than two months and naval cryptanalysts had as yet recovered so few code values that the codebook carried by Currier and Weeks was 'almost empty'. For its part, the Army, always more enthusiastic about connections with the British, stripped bare its cryptanalytic cupboard. The most precious gift in the baggage of the military representatives, Abraham Sinkov and Leo Rosen, was an analogue of the Purple cipher machine designed and built by Frank Rowlett's Japanese section. Lacking any information concerning GC&CS operations and successes, Sinkov and Rosen packed anything else that might help or impress the British: a copy of Japan's Red cipher machine, several additional Japanese diplomatic systems solved by the SIS in the 1930s, a complete copy of DESAB as confiscated by the Army from a clandestine German courier transiting the Panama Canal, the Italian systems X and TR as reconstructed by the SIS, and four Mexican diplomatic systems.

The American mission reached Bletchley Park on 7 February 1941 and over the next several weeks they toured GC&CS facilities, visited intercept stations, examined equipment, and generally talked shop with their British hosts. Much of the controversy surrounding the 'Sinkov Mission' has revolved around the question of whether the British reciprocated the gift of a Purple machine by revealing to their guests their success against the German Enigma cipher machine (they did). In the debate over what the British told the Americans about Enigma, it is easy to lose sight of what the hosts told their guests about a range of other cryptologic subjects.

A broader perspective seems especially appropriate in view of the fact that in early 1941 Enigma was not a priority for the Signal Intelligence Service. Germany used the famous cipher machine for army, navy, and air force traffic. At the time of the American mission, however, the SIS was not even intercepting, let alone studying, the service traffic of Germany or any other country. It focused exclusively on diplomatic ciphers, and no foreign ministry except the Swiss used Enigma. Of course, any insight into the German machine would have been welcomed by

Sinkov and Rosen (who were collecting insights into *everything*), but the success of their mission did not turn on how much Enigma material they could cram into their return baggage. In any event, that luggage was already full. It is often difficult to weigh the relative value of contributions in a collaborative relationship. This is especially the case in intelligence history. Still, one might plausibly argue that, given the current priorities of the SIS, the Sinkov mission departed Bletchley Park with more than they brought.

The American analogue of the Purple machine allowed Britain access to Tokyo's high-grade diplomatic traffic for the first time since the spring of 1939, and this valuable gift was most certainly welcome at GC&CS. The (very) partially reconstructed JN-25B codebook from OP-20-G may also have been useful, though GC&CS's outstation at Singapore, the Far East Combined Bureau, had been working this system and may well have progressed as far, if not further, than the US Navy cryptanalysts. The Sinkov mission's other offerings were less impressive. Bletchley's German section was already familiar with the DESAB code. Similarly, the low-grade Italian diplomatic systems were already read at Bletchley as were probably the Mexican systems, which in any event were hardly a priority for British signals intelligence. In contrast, the items that the American mission carried back to Washington contained much that was new to American codebreakers: insights into German, Italian and Russian systems, a new Mexican cipher, a complete Brazilian codebook and partially reconstructed Argentine and Chilean books. Evaluating the importance of these items, Sinkov concluded, 'The material . . . will result in a saving of several years of labor on the part of a fairly large staff.'

The impact was most dramatic in the Italian section. Before the Sinkov mission, the section was reading two Italian diplomatic systems, neither of which produced significant intelligence. At Bletchley, Sinkov acquired information (including reconstructed codebooks) concerning two high-grade diplomatic systems hitherto unknown to the Americans, as well as details concerning a new version of TR, one of the systems already under study at the SIS. This information so accelerated the work against Rome's communications that in the Munitions Building six analysts were added to the four already committed to the Italian problem. By the summer of 1941 they were decrypting messages in IMPERO, the first high-grade Italian cipher read by the SIS, and the number of decrypted Italian messages deemed worthy of circulation began to increase.

Some of the material contributed by GC&CS (e.g. Red Army codes) could not be immediately exploited by the Americans because the SIS lacked the necessary staff or could not intercept traffic. Other material further illuminated difficult problems even if it did not provide a key to solutions. Although GC&CS had not cracked high-grade German diplomatic ciphers, the British had determined the nature of these systems. They confirmed for the Americans that the Reich foreign ministry used four different systems and that all used the same codebook (DESAB), each differing only in the encipherment applied to that code. At the SIS, Solomon Kullback's German section had reconstructed the codebook, but for lack of traffic was struggling with the enciphered version known as *Spalierverfahren*. The British also lacked sufficient traffic to make much progress against *Spalierverfahren*, but they provided information about the encipherment and actually donated a set of cipher tables recovered from the German consulate in Reykjavik during the British occupation of Iceland. From his new friends at Bletchley Park, Kullback also learned that Berlin's high-grade diplomatic system enciphered DESAB with a one-time pad, while the next system in importance (dubbed Floradora by the British) enciphered with a long additive. GC&CS told the Americans that, for the moment, it had abandoned work on these formidable ciphers, but at least the Americans now knew what they were facing.

As both London and Washington intended, the Sinkov mission launched a programme of cryptanalytic exchanges. For its part, the SIS wasted little time in exploiting the new relationship. Sinkov and Rosen had hardly unpacked their bags before the SIS was asking GC&CS for information regarding Vichy French diplomatic ciphers, especially those used on the circuits connecting Vichy and French territories in the western hemisphere. In return, the SIS began sending to Bletchley Park cryptanalytic observations regarding German, Italian and Japanese systems. These contributions, while earnest, were not always relevant to the problem at hand. An early consignment of German material included American observations relating to ciphers used by Germany in the First World War.

In August 1941, Commander Alastair Denniston, the director of GC&CS, crossed the Atlantic to observe American cryptanalytic operations and discuss further collaboration. At the SIS (he also visited OP-20-G) Denniston was pleased to note that collaboration on German diplomatic ciphers was making progress towards solving a problem that had seemed intractable. He was less sanguine about the new Vichy French and Latin American sections that the SIS had opened with the assistance of material from GC&CS. Here, too, collaboration was promising, but Denniston hoped that the Americans would concentrate their resources on Japan and not be distracted by forays against secondary targets that the British could cover well on their own.

By the end of 1941, collaboration against diplomatic targets was sufficiently established that the Japanese attack on Pearl Harbor on 7 December had little impact on SIS–GC&CS relations beyond accelerating the pace of co-operation. For example, by March 1942, when Lieutenant-Colonel John Tiltman, chief of the military section at Bletchley Park, arrived in Washington for a four-week visit to American signals intelligence facilities, GC&CS had added to its list of items passed to the SIS all the Vichy French codes and ciphers it was reading, as well as the basic codebook used by the Spanish foreign ministry and a description of its encipherment for high-grade traffic. Tiltman brought additional gifts. Instructed by Alastair Denniston to effect a 'complete interchange of all technical knowledge available and in particular to hand over to [the Americans] all our technical documents', Tiltman arrived with a 'considerable quantity' of material from the various sections at GC&CS, including three more Vichy codebooks, microfilms of Floradora material generated by GC&CS and 'descriptions of the methods used for the solution of 3 or 4 different complex ciphers by our Research Section'. Tiltman also offered to produce upon request Brazilian and Portuguese codebooks.

In May 1942 the Americans further exploited British cryptanalytic experience when the Signal Intelligence Service despatched another mission to the Government Code and Cypher School. The American team, Major Solomon Kullback (senior SIS civilians had been given military ranks for the duration of the war) and Captain Harold Brown, spent most of their time at Bletchley Park, but they also visited the centre for diplomatic cryptanalysis recently established by GC&CS in Berkeley Street, London. At Berkeley Street, Kullback and Brown visited the sections working German, Japanese, Italian, French, Spanish, Chinese, Swedish, Near Eastern and Latin American diplomatic systems. Upon the mission's return to the United States in July, Kullback could assure his colleagues, 'I found the British most helpful and co-operative . . . They were completely frank, open and aboveboard with me and kept no detail of their operation, procedures, techniques, or results from me.'

By the end of 1942 the Signal Intelligence Service (now ensconced in new headquarters at Arlington Hall, a former girls' school outside Washington) had significantly expanded the range of its diplomatic operations. Much of this expansion can, of course, be attributed to a dramatic increase in staff and resources after Pearl Harbor. The British connection, however, was a crucial factor behind the increasingly impressive performance of the SIS. Indeed, it would not be an exaggeration to say that in the period 1941–2, GC&CS fuelled American diplomatic cryptanalysis by generously sharing its experience and material. In many ways, the collaboration that emerged in that period was one-sided. With the exception of the Japanese problem (and that is an important exception), the American contribution to the common effort remained relatively modest throughout 1942, mainly because the American cryptanalytic record against targets other than Japan was relatively modest. In the early stages of the joint effort against important targets – Germany, Italy, France, the neutrals – GC&CS simply had more to contribute.

It is perhaps indicative of the early history of co-operation that when Tiltman visited Washington in the spring of 1942 he brought a bag full of cryptanalytic gifts, but when he returned to Bletchley Park he arrived empty-handed. On the other hand, through the missions of Sinkov and Kullback, Denniston and Tiltman, GC&CS certainly obtained from its ally useful insights into particularly recalcitrant problems, such as the high-grade German diplomatic ciphers. On at least one occasion the British codebreakers frankly acknowledged that liaison with the Americans on the German systems, particularly Floradora, had been especially fruitful. Still, the British may be forgiven if they sometimes felt in this early period that they were contributing to the relationship more than they were receiving. Often the Americans were so unrevealing about their own work that GC&CS was not sure which foreign ciphers the SIS was reading. In the spring of 1942, for example, GC&CS complained that it required such information in order to determine what French, Italian, Spanish and Latin American material should be passed to the SIS. As late as December 1942 Alastair Denniston felt compelled to ask his liaison officer in Washington: 'Strictly between ourselves, are the Americans making a massive library of foreign government systems for filing purposes, or do they actually work on the stuff which we send them? We hear so little about Spanish and even French results that sometimes we wonder if they are actually deeply interested.'

Despite such occasional frustrations, Anglo-American co-operation in diplomatic cryptanalysis was generally smooth. Indeed, fruitful wartime collaboration continued long after the Signal Intelligence Service (renamed first the Signal Security Service and then the Signal Security Agency) evolved into a large organization employing thousands of staff and directing a world-wide intercept network. As American diplomatic cryptanalysis matured, GC&CS continued to provide important support usually in response to direct requests for assistance. In early 1943, for example, Berkeley Street passed to Arlington Hall what British codebreakers knew about the wheel wirings of the Enigma machine used by the Swiss foreign ministry. In August of that year, Berkeley Street provided additional information concerning the Swiss machine as well as full information on the Dutch Hagelin diplomatic cipher machine. In 1944, British contributions included full information (often together with reconstructed codebooks and cipher tables) concerning Bulgarian, Burmese, Greek, Hungarian, Iranian and Iraqi diplomatic systems. Such assistance was particularly welcome as Arlington Hall expanded its operations by opening Balkan and Middle Eastern sections.

Both parties were so satisfied with the state of co-operation that disagreements in other areas of signals intelligence collaboration, such as the famous 'Enigma Crisis' of 1943, hardly rippled the waters of diplomatic operations. By that time co-operation against diplomatic targets was taken so much for granted that the SIS felt comfortable asking its operational sections to submit lists of what they needed from GC&CS in the full expectation that those needs would be satisfied. Further, the curious omission of any reference to diplomatic targets in the so-called BRUSA Agreement of 1943 – apportioning responsibilities for Axis military traffic – suggests that the informal exchange arrangements in the diplomatic area were so mutually satisfactory and non-controversial as to require no formal delimitation.

As might be expected, though, the collaboration was never perfect. Occasionally (especially towards the end of the war) one party would decline to share information. In the summer of 1944, for example, the Foreign Office hesitated to disclose to the Americans the contents of the so-called Reserved Series of intercepts, revealing foreign diplomats reporting the comments of British officials on various topics, including American policies. Later that year, the Foreign Office became increasingly skittish about Berkeley Street giving the Americans cryptanalytic information regarding certain countries, such as Egypt, that London considered clients. On one occasion GC&CS felt honour-bound to refuse an American request for a Polish codebook because the Poles had given the British a copy under a promise of security. For their part, the Americans were less inclined as the war wound down to share information about South American systems. Less frequently, one party would launch an operation without informing the other, as in February 1943, when the SIS created a highly secret section to study Russian ciphers. Ironically, the Americans remained unaware that in late 1944 GC&CS established its own secret unit to study Russian internal traffic (civil and military) in Sloane Square, London. Of course, signals intelligence methods and successes have always been among the most precious secrets of any government. What is remarkable is not that London or Washington would hesitate or equivocate before exchanging such secrets, but that such hesitancy and equivocation were so rare.

By the end of the war, the United States had developed a large and productive signals intelligence organization that was reading the diplomatic traffic of almost every government in the world from Afghanistan to Yugoslavia. Much of this success was due to the diligence and skill of American cryptanalysts. No small part, however, was played by the British codebreakers at the Government Code and Cypher School. Throughout the war GC&CS provided timely advice and assistance that significantly advanced the American programme in diplomatic signals intelligence. The value of the British contribution was accurately summarized by the US Signal Security Agency in a postwar review of operations: 'It is doubtful whether success in solution of certain diplomatic systems could have been achieved in time to be useful had not the British supplied the necessary information . . . The debt of the SSA to GC&CS in shortening the period between the beginning of study and the production of translations was in the case of the diplomatic traffic of certain governments very great indeed.' Without doubt, the British had been most helpful and co-operative.

10

Breaking German Naval Enigma on Both Sides of the Atlantic

RALPH ERSKINE

Introduction

Chapter 10 describes how Hut 8 and its US Navy counterpart broke naval Enigma. Decrypts from Hut 8 were sent to Hut 4 (Naval Section) for translation and analysis, from where they were sent to the Admiralty's Naval Intelligence Division in Whitehall. However, Hut 8's relationship with Hut 4 was initially a somewhat uneasy one. Frank Birch, in Hut 4's German subsection, desperately wanted to help Alan Turing, who he did not regard as 'a practical man', to find a way into naval Enigma in 1940. But Birch did not fully understand the complexities involved in breaking Enigma, and Dilly Knox had not had time to explain the process to him in 1939. At one stage, Birch's anxieties led to a proposal to put Turing under Birch's wing, which would have been disastrous. Even Knox found that Turing was 'very difficult to anchor down. He is very clever but quite irresponsible & throws out a mass of suggestions of all degrees of merit. I have just, but only just, enough authority & ability to keep him & his ideas in some sort of order & discipline.' Birch would have found it impossible to do so.

Although Birch did not at first fully understand how Enigma could be broken, he did appreciate Hut 8's desperate need for more bombes, and he fought hard to get them. He was understandably frustrated: bombes were said to be expensive and to require 'a lot of skilled labour to make and a lot of labour to run'. Even their need for more electric power at Bletchley was raised as a problem. Bletchley had not pressed hard enough for more bombes, and Stewart Menzies, GC&CS's somewhat nominal director, had not taken the trouble to find out about its needs. Birch saw the issue clearly:

> *It has been argued that a large number of bombes would cost a lot of money. Well, the issue is a simple one. Tot up the difficulties and balance them against the value to the Nation of being able to read current Enigma.*

It took many long and bitter battles, fought mainly by Edward Travis and Birch, before GC&CS acquired more bombes. Later, British manufacturing capacity was so over-extended that, when the Kriegsmarine *applied the four-rotor version of Enigma to most of its ciphers during the course of 1944 (having already done so for its Atlantic U-boat cipher in 1942), Hut 8 had to rely largely on US Navy bombes for its attacks on these ciphers. Fortunately, good cable communications with OP-20-G enabled Hut 8 to use the OP-20-G bombes 'almost as conveniently as if they had been at one of our outstations 20 or 30 miles away'. And Hut 8's dependency on OP-20-G's hardware had indirect benefits in the long run: Hut 8's virtual partnership with OP-20-G on naval Enigma helped to pave the way for the important postwar UK–USA pact on Anglo-American Sigint co-operation.*

RE

Like all navies in the Second World War, the *Kriegsmarine* had to rely extensively on radio communications. In particular, U-boat pack tactics in the Atlantic were completely dependent on the use of radio. The Admiral Commanding U-boats – *Befehlshaber der U-Boote* (BdU) – directed the packs on the basis of sightings and other reports from the U-boats, which he collated with all the other intelligence available to him. To protect its signals, the *Kriegsmarine* employed the three-rotor Enigma machine, M3, with the three additional naval rotors, VI, VII and VIII, although it also used some manual ciphers, when security was not all important. At least twenty naval Enigma ciphers came into service during the war. The principal cipher in 1940 and 1941, *Heimisch* (later renamed Hydra, and called Dolphin by Bletchley Park), was used by U-boats and surface ships in home waters, including the Atlantic. Some naval ciphers, such as *Ausserheimisch* (Foreign Waters, later known as *Aegir* – codenamed Pike by Bletchley) were never broken during the war, although OP-20-G (the US Navy's codebreaking unit) later devoted much effort to attacking Pike in 1944. In addition to *Allgemein* (general) keys, most naval Enigma ciphers had doubly enciphered *Offizier* (Officer) keys, which were especially difficult to break. A few had *Stab* (Staff) keys, which Hut 8 (Bletchley Park's naval Enigma section) broke on only one occasion.

Despite the fact that the Poles had given GC&CS a reconstructed Enigma and rotors I to V in August 1939, probably only two people at Bletchley Park believed in the autumn of 1939 that naval Enigma could be broken: Frank Birch, the head of the German naval subsection, and Alan Turing. Birch thought it could be broken because it had to be, even though Alastair Denniston, the operational head of Bletchley, had told him at the outbreak of the war that 'all German codes were unbreakable'. Turing had become interested in naval Enigma when he arrived at Bletchley in September 1939, 'because . . . I could have it to myself'. Despite Denniston's forebodings, Turing solved the complex naval indicating system (which is described in Appendix III) in December 1939, using some Polish decrypts for 1 to 8 May 1937. However, since he did not have the bigram tables used with the system, he could make no progress against wartime traffic. He therefore decided to tackle signals that had been intercepted in November 1938. After two weeks' work, five days' traffic was broken. It was found that six *Stecker* (plugboard connections) were still being used, and that no letter was steckered for two days in succession, which eliminated twelve letters on each second day. Turing hoped that this would allow him to make progress quickly, but he had made little headway by May 1940.

New wartime rotors, VI and VII, were recovered from the crew of U-33 in February 1940, but Dolphin proved much more resistant to attack than the *Luftwaffe* Enigma ciphers. In May and June 1940, using papers captured from the patrol boat *Schiff 26*, Hut 8 solved six days of April Dolphin traffic, with help from the first British bombe, 'Victory'. Rotor VIII was captured in August 1940, after which Bletchley held all eight rotors. In November, after months of work, Hugh Foss broke the key for 8 May, which became known as 'Foss's day', using the bombe. The key for 7 May was quickly broken, but only about three other daily keys were solved before February 1941.

None of the ten or so Dolphin daily keys solved in 1940 was broken in time to provide operationally useful intelligence. Hut 8 faced two main problems in trying to break Dolphin after the first bombe with Gordon Welchman's diagonal board entered service in August 1940: first, it lacked cribs, which were needed on a daily basis to provide menus for the bombes. But none would be available until it had read a substantial amount of traffic, which it could not hope to break. Secondly, GC&CS had only two bombes at the end of 1940, which were seldom available for naval use. Birch complained bitterly that Hut 8 was not getting 'fair does', but to little avail. Without a short cut, M3's eight rotors imposed an impossibly heavy load on the bombes, since up to 336 rotor combinations had to be tested, taking around eighty hours (excluding the time to change rotors) – almost six times longer than a comparable attack on the sixty rotor combinations involved in *Heer* or *Luftwaffe* Enigma. The resulting delay of four days or more would have rendered the decrypts useless for operational purposes. Moreover, at least two bombes would have been constantly required, and Bletchley could not spare them from other work for so long. Hut 8 therefore required some method of reducing the number of rotor orders to be checked.

Turing had in fact already invented a Bayesian probability process called Banburismus to solve the difficulty. Banburismus reduced the number of M3 rotor orders to be tested from 336 to a manageable number, usually between forty and sixty, by ascertaining which rotors were in M3's right-hand and middle slots. However, to use Banburismus Hut 8 needed a complete set of the bigram tables for encoding Dolphin message indicators. Without the tables, Hut 8 had no prospect of aligning Dolphin signals 'in depth' by correctly superimposing cipher texts enciphered with the same key, which was the basis of Banburismus. However, Hut 8 lacked both the bigram tables and enough solved traffic to reconstruct them. To solve Dolphin it required an extensive corpus of Dolphin plain traffic. This was a singularly vicious circle from which Hut 8 could escape only if the Royal Navy captured the tables or Enigma key-lists to allow Hut 8 to read the traffic in order to recreate the tables.

On 12 March 1941, Hut 8 received an Enigma key-list for February 1941, which had been snatched from the German armed trawler *Krebs* during a commando raid in the Lofoten Islands. Hut 8 had read most naval Enigma for February and had broken about eight days' April traffic by 10 May. Although the decrypts were not available in time to be operationally useful to the Admiralty's Operational Intelligence Centre (OIC), they enabled

Hut 8 to reconstruct the 'Bach' bigram tables then in force.

Weather signals were transmitted daily by designated Atlantic U-boats, as an essential part of the German war effort, since so much of European weather moves from west to east. The signals were encoded on the *Wetterkurzschlüssel*, a short signal book, in order to shorten them as a precaution against shore high-frequency direction-finding (HF-DF), before they were enciphered on Enigma. The weather data was then rebroadcast by the powerful *Kriegsmarine* transmitter at Norddeich (call-sign DAN), after being enciphered in the *Kriegsmarine* manual cipher called 'Germet 3' by Bletchley (and also known by it as 'the DAN meteorological cipher'). Bletchley Park's meteorological subsection in Hut 10 broke the DAN meteorological cipher from February 1941 onwards. On 10 May 1941, Hut 8 received the 1940 edition of the *Wetterkurzschlüssel*, which had been seized from the weather ship *München* in a specially planned operation. Hut 8 could now reconstruct the exact plain-text of the encoded weather short signals from the U-boats, giving it a further invaluable source for bombe menus.

Enigma key-lists for June and July seized from *München* and another weather ship, *Lauenburg*, proved a godsend. The resulting decrypts familiarized Hut 8 with naval Enigma sufficiently for it to solve the August Dolphin keys with an average delay of fifty hours. The lists also greatly eased the task of reconstructing a set of new bigram tables, codenamed '*Fluss*', which came into force on 15 June. Hundreds of bombe runs would otherwise have been required to help build up the new tables. Since there were then only about six bombes, Hut 8 would probably have been unable to break naval Enigma currently for a further two months – until October – but for the key-lists. The traffic also enabled Hut 8 to assess the extent to which the *Kriegsmarine* was sending dummy signals consisting of nonsense, in order to defeat traffic analysis: the signals would otherwise have falsified many of its language statistics, which were a vital part of Banburismus.

Despite its new-found knowledge, Hut 8 was unable to solve the Dolphin keys for 1 to 6 August and 18 and 19 September. However, those were the only days on which it failed to break Dolphin during the rest of the war. In finding naval keys, Hut 8 was helped because the inner settings (the rotor mix and ring settings) were changed only every two days, presumably because only officers were permitted to alter the inner settings, saving Bletchley a considerable amount of bombe time. In addition, since Hut 8 knew the rotor order for the second day, it did not have to carry out Banburismus, which was a time-consuming process, on the second day. This almost halved its work but, more importantly, it greatly speeded up the solution of Dolphin for second days. If a crib was available on the second day, a few bombe runs could therefore find the settings very quickly, since only a single rotor order had to be tested. After August 1941, Hut 8 broke most Dolphin traffic within thirty-six hours during the remainder of the war. Hut 8 took about three days to solve the settings for the first of a pair of days' traffic in August, and under twenty-four hours for the second day. In October 1941, Dolphin took seventy-five hours to solve on the first day of a pair, but only a few hours on the second.

The June and July decrypts also enabled GC&CS's Naval Section in Hut 4 to spot a breach of cipher security in the inter-connected German signal nets. Because some small *Kriegsmarine* units were not issued with Enigma, signals were sometimes enciphered on a manual system known as the *Werftschlüssel* (dockyard cipher), as well as Enigma. Hut 4 first penetrated the *Werftschlüssel* in mid-1940 and was breaking it more or less currently by March 1941. The deciphered *Werft* versions of the signals provided Hut 8 with a second source of cribs. On occasion, minelaying operations (known as 'Gardening') were carried out by the Royal Air Force to provide Hut 8 with *Werftschlüssel* cribs. The *Kriegsmarine* then sent signals in Dolphin and the *Werftschlüssel* about the re-opening of the relevant sea lanes after sweeping them for mines.

Shark (codenamed Triton by the Germans), a special cipher for the Atlantic and Mediterranean U-boats, was introduced on M3 as an interim security measure on 5 October 1941, but only thwarted Hut 8 for a few days. When Hut 8 initially could not solve Shark for a few days in early October, it found, by using a re-encodement, that Shark now had a completely different *Grundstellung* from Dolphin. Previously the U-boats had merely used the reverse of the Dolphin *Grund* (e.g. DFT instead of TFD). The change made little difference to solving Shark, but it was a harbinger of the threat to come.

On 29 November the bigram tables and *Kenngruppenbuch* (known to Hut 8 as 'the K book') used with them changed. However, the fifteen bombes available in December helped Hut 8 to build up the tables quite quickly. Turing was about to start the laborious task of reconstructing the new K book, when both the book and the tables were captured from *Geier*, a German trawler, on 26 December 1941.

Hut 8 had been aware since early 1941 that there was a four-rotor naval Enigma – M4. In September 1941, it learned that some U-boats had been issued with the new machine, when an M4 lid was recovered from U-570, which had surrendered to an aircraft on 27 August. It was therefore far from a complete surprise when M4 came into operation on Shark on 1 February 1942. Hut 8 had in fact already solved the wiring of the new rotor, beta, and its associated thin reflector, Bruno, in December 1941, after M4 was used accidentally on several occasions. But the combination of M4, a separate cipher (Shark) and the introduction of a second edition of the *Wetterkurzschlüssel* on 20 January 1942 were calamitous for Hut 8. Deprived of cribs and without four-rotor bombes, it became blind against Shark, solving only three Shark keys during the next ten months.

However, M4 was not a true four-rotor machine, since beta was the right-hand half of a split reflector. Being thinner than rotors I to VIII, beta was not interchangeable with them. Beta could be set (although it did not rotate during encipherment), giving M4 the equivalent of twenty-six different reflectors (in conjunction with thin reflector B), but M4's rotors could still only be permuted in 336 (8×7×6×1) different ways – not 3,024 (9×8×7×6). Given cribs, three-rotor bombes could therefore attack Shark in M4 form. However, Hut 8 needed twenty-six times as many bombes to do so effectively, but held only about twenty three-rotor bombes in February 1942, and thirty in August. Few could be spared from their work on other keys to mount parallel attacks on standard M4 Shark signals. In March 1942, a proposal to release bombes from other work to attack Shark had to be referred to the Y Board for decision, which required the Chief of the Imperial General Staff, among others, to be briefed on the issue.

Soaring shipping losses on the Atlantic convoy routes from the autumn of 1942 onwards led the Admiralty to become somewhat disheartened. On 22 November 1942, the OIC urged Hut 8 to focus 'a little more attention' on Shark, thereby demonstrating that it had completely failed to understand the difficulties confronting Hut 8, which was helpless without cribs. Fortunately, Hut 8 was almost ready to defeat Shark.

On 30 October 1942, the second edition of the *Wetterkurzschlüssel* was seized by Lieutenant Anthony Fasson, Able Seaman Colin Grazier and a sixteen-year-old canteen assistant, Tommy Brown (all from HMS *Petard*), from U-559 before it sank north-east of Port Said. Tragically, Fasson and Grazier were drowned when the U-boat went down suddenly. They were awarded posthumous George Crosses, while Tommy Brown, who survived, became the youngest holder of the George Medal. The *Wetterkurzschlüssel* reached Hut 8 on 24 November. By 2 December, Hut 8 believed that it could soon re-enter Shark through the weather short signals. In order to ensure compatibility with existing machines, M4 emulated M3 at one setting of beta, which was Shark's undoing. Moreover, Germet 3 additive tables, consisting of several sets of ten tables, were repeated, although in a different order, during the second of a pair of months. When this happened, Germet 3 could be broken with few delays. But in December Hut 8 had to wait for the 100 reciphering tables used in November with Germet 3 to begin to be repeated on 8 December before it could confirm its hunch, and for the tables to be 'hotted up' by being broken more fully. Hut 8 then found, after numerous bombe runs, that M4 was in M3 emulation mode when enciphering the weather short signals. A full three-rotor bombe run against M4 in M3 mode, using a menu derived from the weather signals, took about four bombe days, instead of the 100 or so required when M4 used its full potential. It was easy to test the setting for the fourth rotor, and the key for a second day in a pair could generally be solved by three-rotor bombes in under twenty-four hours.

On 13 December 1942, Hut 4 sent a teleprint to the OIC, listing the positions of over twelve Atlantic U-boats, as established from Shark weather signals for 5 to 7 December. It was the end of the Shark black-out: eighty-eight out of the following ninety-nine days' traffic on Shark were solved with the aid of the weather short signals and the DAN weather broadcasts broken by Hut 10, although sometimes there were significant delays.

Hut 8's use of the *Wetterkurzschlüssel* against Shark only lasted for about three months. On 8 March 1943 Commodore E. G. N. Rushbrooke, the Director of Naval Intelligence, pessimistically advised the Admiralty that GC&CS would be blinded against Shark for 'some considerable period, perhaps extending to months', presumably after learning that from Bletchley Park. On 10 March, a third edition of the weather short signal book came into operation, again depriving Hut 8 of Shark cribs. Hut 8 reconstructed the substantially revised edition of the *Wetterkurzschlüssel* quickly, but could not build the monthly indicator tables used with it quickly enough to make much use of the signals. However, by using cribs based on U-boat short signal reports about convoys (which were encoded with a codebook known as the *Kurzsignalheft*), Hut 8 broke into Shark again on 19 March. Hut 8 solved Shark for 90 out of the 112 days from 10 March to 30 June, mostly with cribs from the sighting short signals. The sighting reports also used M4 in M3 mode – and a copy of the *Kurzsignalheft* had been captured from U-559.

The short sighting signals seldom provided cribs longer than seven letters, but they could be combined with other data to form bombe menus. Using the signals as cribs stretched Allied HF-DF and other intelligence-gathering resources to the limit. In Hut 4, a section under Edgar Jackson helped to assemble all the available evidence. Jackson's mastery of the mass of raw material proved invaluable, especially since garbles, mistakes by intercept operators and unusual short signals laid many false trails.

A severe drop in the Shark traffic in the summer months, following the withdrawal of the U-boats from the North Atlantic convoy routes, coupled with the adoption by M4 of a new 'Greek' rotor, gamma (with thin reflector *Cäsar*), on 1 July 1943, led to serious delays in breaking Shark until September. British and US Navy production four-rotor bombes entered service in June and August 1943 respectively, but some July and August keys still took up to twenty-six days to solve. However, from September on, Shark was often broken within twenty-four hours (especially on the second day of a pair), although there were some difficulties and delays, especially when cribs were in short supply, as in October 1944, when the average delay in solving it was forty-five hours.

Hut 8's successes owed much to the drive and energy of Hugh Alexander, who became its head around November 1942, when Alan Turing was in America. He had been the acting head for some time, since Turing was, to put it mildly, uninterested in administration. Alexander had moved to Hut 8 in March 1941, as deputy head under Turing, when naval Enigma started to take off after the Lofoten captures. Alexander was both a superbly skilled cryptanalyst and an excellent manager, who transformed Hut 8 into an outstanding machine for delivering decrypts speedily to Hut 4.

Alexander was keenly interested in staff morale. He applied 'need to know' in a positive way by telling the Hut 8 clerical staff, most of whom were doing monotonous (but vital) jobs, as much as possible about the operational results of their work, in order to help them appreciate that they were a crucial part of the machine. This worked well, and his trust was fully rewarded. Interestingly, Richard Feynman adopted exactly the same approach with some junior staff while working on the atom bomb at Los Alamos. The Hut 8 cryptanalysts were constantly in contact with the clerical staff, so that it was always clear to them that their work was being used, and not just being filed away. Unlike Alexander's counterparts in Hut 6, he did not employ university graduates on clerical work, since he found that it led to dissatisfaction.

Alexander seems to have acquired organizational skills during the short period when he was in business before the war. Under his leadership, Hut 8 constantly refined its techniques for dealing with various tasks. In particular, Banburismus was broken down into as many separate modules as possible. Charts prepared for the necessary calculations transformed a highly sophisticated Bayesian system into one in which the ground work could largely be carried out by unskilled clerks. When Banburismus began in mid-1941, 'scoring' tetras (repeated groups of four letters or more) in decibans (a unit of calculation invented by Turing) was too time-consuming even for skilled cryptanalysts. Later, a series of tables enabled two clerks to score over 100 tetras in a shift quite easily merely by looking up the tables, with the only mathematics required being simple addition and subtraction. Decibans played a vital part in Banburismus. Jack Good, another member of Hut 8, found that by changing the unit to half-decibans whole numbers could be used, instead of decimals. The change saved an immense amount of time and, more importantly, enabled Hut 8 'to succeed where it would otherwise have failed'.

Initially, Hut 8 consisted of two subsections: an inner room with the cryptanalysts, and a 'Big Room' with the supporting clerical staff who prepared work for the Banburists, kept traffic records, and tested the results from the bombes. As the work grew, the subsections were subdivided. There was first a 'Banburists' room' and a crib room, then a research section was added and later a research crib room was created. A separate registration room was set up when traffic began to be teleprinted from the Scarborough intercept centre in April 1941. When bombes became plentiful, a separate bombe testing room was formed. The machine room decoding was at first done by Hut 6; it was later dealt with part-time by Big Room typists, and eventually a separate decoding room was established.

The solution of a cipher known as Porpoise in late summer 1942 meant that the registration room had to deal with a further 250 messages each day, and that the clerical staff were hard pressed. However, the main problems with Dolphin and Porpoise had been solved – breaking them was largely a matter of refining the 'production line' dealing with them – and the purely cryptanalytic work eased off. Three cryptanalysts (Harry Golombek, Leslie Yoxall and Perkins) were therefore transferred to other sections in October and November 1942. Alexander believed in keeping staff busy, not only to keep them interested, but also because he thought that work tended to be done poorly if they were underemployed.

Hut 8 broke many other ciphers besides Dolphin and Shark. However, one of its eventual successes was later a source of considerable embarrassment to it, being an episode over which Hut 8 'would gladly draw a veil of considerable opacity'. About 100 messages a day of Mediterranean traffic had been sent to Naval Section by bag during 1941 and early 1942 but, since the traffic did not use the Dolphin bigram tables, Hut 8 did not examine it closely. By 1942, 200 to 300 signals were being intercepted each day, which led Hut 8 to study the traffic for a few days in the early summer. It found that if the second letters of the indicators in two or more messages agreed, so did the sixth; the same applied to the third and seventh and the fourth and eighth letters (e.g. with XFZT IPAM and OFGS EPQS, F 'throws-on' to P in the same place in each indicator). Even so, Hut 8 thought that bigram tables were involved until a visitor from Hut 6 pointed out that it was a 'throw-on' system, such as was used by army and air force traffic before 15 September 1938, and in naval Enigma before 1 May 1937, with the *Grund* being set out in the key-lists, and not chosen by the operator (see Appendix II).

Throw-on systems were relatively easy to break given 100 or more messages a day. It was even possible to do so given between ten and fifteen messages. Moreover, the system was the only form of service Enigma that could be solved entirely without cribs, since it could be broken using only the enciphered indicators. Hut 8 quickly developed systems for breaking the cipher, whose German codename was *Süd* (codenamed Porpoise by Bletchley). Since no K book was involved, the operator was permitted to choose his own message key, subject to a few very basic rules.

While the German blunder is astonishing, it is also surprising that Hut 8 did not spot the nature of the indicating system, since when describing the weaknesses of the throw-on system in 'Prof's Book' Alan Turing had written:

> This phenomenon [of patterns in the indicators] enables us to tell very quickly with any cipher whether the Boxing form of indication is being used.

Hut 8's failure to spot the nature of the system earlier also shows that Turing himself had been taking comparatively little interest in the day-to-day work of Hut 8 from at least early 1942 onwards. He would almost certainly have recognized the nature of the indicating system immediately if he had studied the indicators for even a few minutes.

Süd eventually split into three separate ciphers: Grampus (German codename, Poseidon), Trumpeter (Uranus) and Porpoise (Hermes, formerly *Süd*). All used doubly enciphered message keys, as did three further ciphers. Porpoise and Grampus did not abandon the throw-on system until 1 June 1944. Sunfish (whose German codename was Tibet), a cipher used by the blockade runners returning from Japan, was broken by Hut 8 in August 1943, largely at the instigation of OP-20-GM (the US Navy's naval Enigma section), which had made detailed studies of the traffic. Hut 8 had thought that Sunfish used a form of unsteckered Enigma, but it turned out to be another throw-on cipher. However, the US Navy bombes could not run menus derived from throw-on indicators, since they had only sixteen banks of Enigmas, and throw-on menus required about thirty-two. OP-20-GM therefore asked Hut 8 to run a menu on the Bletchley bombes, which contained thirty-six banks. All throw-on menus were expensive in bombe time, since the bombes stopped much more often than with ordinary menus. Hut 8 therefore attacked the traffic only when a blockade runner was returning home, and largely left Sunfish to OP-20-GM, especially after January 1944, when they were able to use their '800' double bombes to attack the throw-on systems.

Hut 8 then broke Seahorse (whose German codename was Bertok, derived from 'Ber[lin]-Tok[io]') in September 1943, again at the request of OP-20-GM, following an extensive examination of the traffic. Seahorse was employed for communications with the German naval attaché in Tokyo, Vice-Admiral Paul Wenneker, and was called '*Kriegsmarine*' by OP-20-GM. It, too, used a throw-on indicator system, and turned out to be an M4 cipher.

The final throw-on system attacked by Hut 8 was Bonito (German codename, *Eichendorff*), which was first broken, '[a]fter a certain amount of trouble', in May 1944. Bonito provided intelligence on midget submarines and saboteurs. The traffic increased from five to ten messages daily in April 1944 to 100 a day in spring 1945.

The use of doubly enciphered message keys was a catastrophic blunder by the *Kriegsmarine*. Such a basic security error is almost incomprehensible, especially since the *Heer* and the *Luftwaffe* had abandoned double-encipherment on 1 May 1940 because they had become aware that it made Enigma very vulnerable. The *Kriegsmarine* was definitely fully informed about that decision, but still adopted a completely flawed system. In consequence, Hut 8 and OP-20-GM penetrated no fewer than six ciphers, some of which they probably could not otherwise have broken, since no cribs were available for them. *Süd* and its subsets alone ultimately yielded over 115,000 decrypts, containing a considerable amount of intelligence about the areas they covered.

The traffic handled by Hut 8 increased considerably as the war went on. On average about 460 intercepts were dealt with each day in 1941 and 1942, 980 in 1943, 1,560 in 1944 and 1,790 in 1945. The principal naval intercept station, Scarborough, had about sixty-five receivers on German naval traffic in April 1942, most of them taking naval Enigma. There were also a number of sets abroad on naval work, including some in the Commonwealth, and a small station in Murmansk, in northern Russia. Traffic often had to be double banked, since bombe menus depended upon accurate message texts, preferably with no omissions; sometimes Hut 8 even requested treble or quadruple banking, particularly for keys in the Mediterranean, where intercept conditions were very poor. Hut 8 did not control the intercept sets, unlike Hut 6. Instead, it requested special coverage through Hut 4, but the different system worked well in practice.

In addition to being a significant source of intelligence, shore high-frequency direction-finding (HF-DF) was Hut 8's vital ally, especially when using the weather and sighting short signals as cribs. Moreover, without shore HF-DF it is highly probable that

Banburismus would have been impossible. The only weak point in the K book indicating system was its use of a single *Grundstellung* each day in any one cipher. The *Kriegsmarine* could easily have provided for different *Grund*, but doing so early in the war would probably have increased the length of signals, making them more vulnerable to shore HF-DF. There can be little doubt that the *Kriegsmarine*'s fear of shore HF-DF strongly influenced its decision to adopt a common *Grundstellung* procedure. Shore HF-DF therefore indirectly advanced the production of operational intelligence from Dolphin by about one year, since only Banburismus enabled Hut 8 to overcome the shortage of bombes for naval work before mid-1943. By September 1942, seventeen naval HF-DF stations had been established in the United Kingdom. By May 1943, there were about twenty-three British and Commonwealth stations on the Atlantic seaboard. The US Navy also had a substantial number of Atlantic stations.

Other forms of Sigint, such as Tina (the identification of radio operators from the characteristics of their morse-sending) and radio finger-printing (RFP), which used cathode ray screens to identify individual radio transmitters, were of less assistance to Hut 8. So far as U-boats were concerned, RFP could seldom do more than distinguish between the transmitters used by the large Type XB and Type XIV boats, and those in the general mass of U-boats. Due to the high standard of German transmitters, RFP could not identify the transmitters of specific boats, which in 1944 led Naval Section to conclude that all attempts to do so should be abandoned as an aid to the production of Ultra from Enigma, although not for the purposes of general intelligence. Curiously, OP-20-G took the opposite view so far as using RFP and Tina combined to produce cribs for Shark was concerned, even though US Navy RFP gave worse results than in Britain. Intelligence derived by Hut 4 from traffic analysis – the study of the external characteristics of signals, such as their indicators (for example, 'w w' for weather short signals), the volume of traffic, the radio frequencies used and so on – also helped Hut 8 on occasion.

Hut 8 in the long run gained much from its eventual close co-operation with OP-20-G but the relationship took some time to come to fruition. Mrs Agnes Driscoll, a celebrated US Navy codebreaker, and a small section in OP-20-G had begun an attack on Dolphin in November 1940, but did not have the slightest success. Following various disputes with GC&CS during the course of 1942 over the role to be taken by OP-20-G in attacking Shark, Commander Joseph Wenger, the head of OP-20-G, became exasperated by GC&CS's failure to build four-rotor bombes. On Wenger's recommendation, Vice-Admiral Frederic J. Horne, the US Navy Vice Chief of Naval Operations, therefore decided on 4 September 1942 that OP-20-G should embark on an extensive bombe programme, tentatively costed at $2,000,000 (the eventual cost was $6,000,000, about $48,000 (£12,000) per bombe). By 17 September, Joseph Desch, of the National Cash Register Company in Dayton, Ohio, had completed a twelve-page report setting out an outline design of a four-rotor bombe for the US Navy.

In October 1942 Travis and Captain Carl F. Holden, the US Navy's Director of Communications, concluded the wide-ranging 'Holden Agreement' (sometimes referred to as the Travis–Wenger Agreement) on naval Sigint. Under the Agreement, work against Shark became the subject of 'full collaboration' between GC&CS and OP-20-G. GC&CS was to help the US Navy to develop 'analytical machinery' (the bombes) and there was to be a complete exchange of technical information on *Kriegsmarine* ciphers. The Agreement was the first to establish the vital Sigint relationship between the two countries during the war.

The British official history errs in claiming that 'in September [1942] the Navy Department announced that it had developed a more advanced machine [i.e. a bombe] of its own, [and] would have built 360 copies of it by the end of the year', and that the Agreement included a 'compromise' under which the 'Navy Department . . . undertook to construct only 100 Bombes'. No US Navy bombe of any kind had been developed by September 1942. Neither the original US Navy directive for the bombe project nor the Holden Agreement specified the number of bombes to be built. OP-20-G's decision to build only about ninety-five bombes was not taken until March 1943.

One of the first two US Navy bombe prototypes, named Adam (the other was 'Eve'), was delivered to the Navy Computing Laboratory in Dayton on 26 May 1943 to begin tests. There were countless problems, with both machines, especially with 'shorts', 'opens' and oil leaks. Neither machine was running well as late as July 1943. However, the problems were eventually sorted out, and production models began to be shipped to Washington, DC, in late August. Some production bombes were in 'semi-continuous operation' by 11 August, with six operating by 7 September.

The standard US Navy bombe, known as a '530', was about 2 ft wide, 8 ft long and 7 ft high and weighed 5,000 pounds. The British three-rotor bombe was a few inches smaller, but weighed only about 2,200 pounds. The Navy bombe had at least three hundred valves – quite a large number for that time. The Navy's 530 type bombes only had sixteen banks of Enigmas – eight on each side (see page 7 of the plate section). They could therefore only run short menus, with a maximum of sixteen letters. OP-20-GM eventually built three double unit bombes, known as the 800 bombe (nicknamed 'grand-dad'), which contained thirty-two banks of Enigmas, to tackle ciphers such as Seahorse. The first 800 unit became operational at the end of January 1944.

About ninety-five of the Navy 530 type bombes were made, including eight inverted machines. A 530 bombe ran a three-rotor menu in a mere fifty seconds, and a four-rotor menu in twenty minutes. However, due to the time required to set up a bombe menu and change rotors between runs, the average production per watch of eight hours was between forty-eight and sixty three-rotor runs (known as short runs) or twelve four-rotor runs. Twenty-three units of an improved model, the 1530, with circuitry which reduced the number of false 'stops', were also built. The US Navy also used a number of 'black boxes', called 'grenades' (being small bombes), which were attached to bombes to deal with various Enigma problems where the *Stecker* were known. The standard grenade, for example, was used to locate the rotor starting positions when the rotor order, ring settings and *Stecker* had been found.

Once the Navy bombes were moved to Washington, they worked well, and were extremely reliable. Thus in April 1944, when eighty-seven Navy bombes were in service, their down-time was about 2.7 per cent, while routine maintenance required about 2.5 per cent. This was just as well, since the British four-rotor bombes were far from reliable. In early 1944, only twenty-five or so four-rotor bombes had been installed at GC&CS. In March, their performance was described by Hugh Alexander as 'still poor, and likely to remain so'. Very few, perhaps only three, were actually operational then. In consequence, GC&CS decided that future British bombe production would be concentrated on making three-rotor bombes, although a further eighteen or so four-rotor bombes were in fact made.

The US Navy bombe figures for maintenance and reliability were maintained consistently throughout 1944 and 1945, each being under 3 per cent. Like some British bombes, some US Navy bombes continued to operate after the end of the war in Europe: one Navy bombe was still attacking old wartime ciphers in March 1946. It has even been claimed that some were brought out of storage to tackle an East German version of Enigma in the early 1950s.

After Hut 8 re-entered Shark in mid-December 1942, OP-20-G broke a few keys manually. By the end of 1943, with about seventy-five bombes in service and considerable experience under its belt, OP-20-GM was allocated responsibility for breaking Shark. At first, OP-20-G used cribs sent by Hut 8. However, they soon started to devise their own cribs. By August 1944, Hut 8 had only four cryptanalysts (Rolf Noskwith, Joan Clarke (one of Bletchley's very few female cryptanalysts), Patrick Mahon and Richard Pendered) – very few, bearing in mind that a three-shift system operated, and that there had been sixteen in February 1942. The number of Shark keys solved by Hut 8 gradually diminished. It solved only five Shark keys in January 1945, none in February and one in March.

The US Navy bombes very soon had spare capacity. Although the Navy was very apprehensive about trespassing on the US Army's preserves, it agreed to run Hut 6 (Army and Air Force) problems (codenamed Bovril). However, tackling this work for Hut 6 ran counter to an allocation agreement with the Army on the division of work that had been agreed by President Roosevelt in 1942. Eventually, a somewhat reluctant Travis was pressed by Rear Admiral Joseph Redman to obtain the approval of Colonel Carter Clarke, the chief of the Army's Special Branch, for the work being done by the Navy. Clarke agreed, but gently chided Travis and Redman for having put the work 'into operation without our prior knowledge'. In January 1944, about 45 per cent of the Navy's seventy-five bombes were on Hut 6 work, while about 60 per cent of its 115 bombes were so engaged in January 1945. The number of Navy bombes on Hut 6 jobs therefore rose from roughly about thirty to seventy during 1944.

GC&CS had about seventy three-rotor bombes in service in January 1944, and 140 in January 1945. Allowing for set-up times, and changing rotors, one US Navy four-rotor bombe could do about three times the work of a GC&CS three-rotor bombe. The seventy Navy bombes on Hut 6 work in January 1945 were therefore equivalent to about 210 GC&CS three-rotor bombes, increasing GC&CS's three-rotor bombe capacity by 150 per cent. This was extremely fortunate, since GC&CS needed all the bombes it could get. Indeed, in February 1944, GC&CS had asked OP-20-G to order fifty additional bombes. They were duly requisitioned, and started to enter service in mid-August. However, the existing US Navy bombes were found to be so efficient that the additional order was reduced to twenty-five in September.

From June 1943 to June 1944, OP-20-GM recovered:

236 Shark keys (65 per cent of the total)
266 special Shark keys (65 per cent of the total) – these were probably keys modified by the use of a special cue-word (*Stichwort*) procedure
448 other *Kriegsmarine* keys
581 German Army and Air Force keys.

The *Kriegsmarine* began to issue special Enigma ciphers (*Sonderschlüssel*) to individual U-boats in mid-1944, but did not use them until mid-November. *Sonderschlüssel* were virtually unbreakable, since very few cribs were available: it took 5,300 bombe hours and about six weeks' work before *Sonderschlüssel* 161 succumbed in early April 1945, and only three *Sonderschlüssel* were broken, all by OP-20-G. The widespread use of *Sonderschlüssel* from February 1945 onwards deprived the Allies of virtually all operational intelligence on the U-boats. However, even worse was to come. On 1 April 1945 Plaice, a cipher used in the Baltic, implemented 'one of the most formidable changes' made by the *Kriegsmarine*, by employing a set of 288 *Grundstellungen* for April, instead of a single daily *Grund*. Hut 8 had to break a considerable number of individual messages in order to reconstruct the list of *Grundstellungen*, and could do so only because a new machine, Filibuster, was available. Hut 8's problems were compounded when Dolphin adopted the new system on 1 May – and a fresh set of 288 *Grundstellungen* took effect for Plaice. Hugh Alexander was by no means certain that Hut 8 could have survived these changes. At least twenty-four more examples of Filibuster and another machine (Hypo) would have been required, as well as a greatly increased staff. Even then, the outlook would have been uncertain.

Anglo-American co-operation on naval Enigma proved extremely successful, due to the excellent relations between Hut 8 and OP-20-GM. Without the help of OP-20-G's superb four-rotor bombes, Shark and the other M4 ciphers could not have been consistently broken after mid-1943. Hut 8 broke about 1,120,000 out of the 1,550,000 *Kriegsmarine* Enigma signals intercepted during the war, although only 530,000 decrypts were sent to the Admiralty, since many dealt with weather forecasts and other matters which did not affect operations, even indirectly. It was a magnificent performance, given that Hut 8's complement never exceeded about 150 staff. Naval Ultra was the most important of the many intelligence sources, including photo-reconnaissance and the invaluable HF-DF fixes, available to naval intelligence during the war. Without Ultra from Shark, in particular, the course of the war would have been very different, since it must be very doubtful whether the Allies could have established naval supremacy in the Atlantic until the second half of 1943. Ultra was only one of many factors, including shipbuilding capacity, modern sensors and weapons, trained seamen and airmen, which contributed to the Allied victory, but Hut 8's crowning achievement was to save countless lives, on both sides of the conflict, by helping to shorten the war.

11

Hut 8 from the Inside

ROLF NOSKWITH

Introduction

Chapter 11 gives an insider's views on breaking naval Enigma. Rolf Noskwith was a young Cambridge mathematics graduate when he was recruited for Bletchley under a new system headed by C. P. Snow.

He joined Hut 8 in June 1941, when it was starting to get into its stride, and was assigned to its crib room because of his fluent German. Hut 4 (Naval Section) had attempted to provide cribs until Hut 8 set up its own crib room in 1941, even though there was very little plain-text in 1940 from past decrypts, and virtually no continuity in breaking the few Enigma daily keys that had been solved. Frank Birch had erroneously believed that if Alan Turing, in Hut 8, tried out cribs with the bombes 'systematically they would work'. But Birch had misunderstood the problems involved in using cribs, largely because Turing was 'a lamentable explainer'. Some of Birch's suggestions would have involved testing tens of thousands of results for a single crib, which would have been completely beyond Hut 8's scant resources in 1940 –

and the capacity of the sole bombe that was available until towards the end of the year.

However, as Hut 4 gained experience and more decrypts became available, Hut 8 came to appreciate the very close co-operation that developed between its crib room and Naval Section, including the latter's intelligence sub-sections, a unit breaking hand ciphers and the U-boat plotting room there. When a second black-out threatened to develop in March 1943 on Shark, the cipher used by the North Atlantic U-boats, sterling work in Naval Section helped to save the day, and to prevent the black-out from lasting for the several months originally forecast.

Hut 8 would probably not have solved the Porpoise naval cipher when it did if Hut 4 had not kept pressing it to investigate the traffic, which Hut 8 thought used a much more complex system than emerged. Fortunately, the liaison between Huts 4 and 8 on all topics became much closer and more successful as the war progressed, although surprisingly it was not until May 1943 that regular meetings began between Hut 8 and the relevant parts of Naval Section. Happily, at the end of the war in Europe, Birch was able to write to the head of Hut 8, Patrick Mahon, of 'two independent entities so closely, continuously, and cordially united as our two Sections'. Co-operation, whether with other Huts at Bletchley, with OP-20-G, or with GC&CS's outposts, was the key to the many superb Allied successes in the codebreaking war.

RE

At the outbreak of the Second World War I was an undergraduate at Cambridge, reading mathematics. As I also spoke German I thought that I had some qualifications for 'decoding' work. This view was accepted by the University Recruiting Board and included in a wider recommendation for my war service. There was then a setback when I failed two medicals. I therefore continued with my studies and in 1940 I was interviewed for work at what I later recognized to be Bletchley Park – but my appointment was vetoed because of my foreign birth. In 1941 I had a similar interview with C. P. Snow (the future novelist who was then a Civil Service Commissioner) and Hugh Alexander. The rules had since changed. I was appointed at a salary of £250 per annum as a Junior Assistant (later Junior Administrative Officer) at the Foreign Office which had jurisdiction over GC&CS.

I arrived at Bletchley on 20 June 1941, the day after my twenty-second birthday. Alexander met me at the station and took me through the Park entrance to one of the Nissen-type huts which had been erected in the grounds of the Victorian mansion. This was Hut 8, the unit of which Alexander was acting head and for which he had recruited me. It was only then that I was told that our task was to break the ciphers used by the German Navy. Despite my talk about decoding I had no conception of the work I would be doing and I entered a completely new world when I learned that the German Navy enciphered its signals using a machine called Enigma, which was also used by the German Army and Air Force.

I joined the crib section of Hut 8, headed by Shaun Wylie. We were known as cribsters and our function was to produce cribs, a crib being a guess of what a portion of a particular signal might be saying. A correct crib, tested on the bombes (the electro-mechanical machines developed by Alan Turing), would lead to the solution of a day's keys.

Next door to us was a section, staffed mostly by mathematicians, which used a sophisticated application of probability theory, designed by Turing to reduce the number of variables which the bombes had to test. The process required the manipulation of big sheets of paper, each with punched holes representing an individual signal. These sheets were manufactured in Banbury: the process was therefore called Banburismus and the people doing the work were known as Banburists. There were ways in which cribsters and Banburists could help each other.

When I arrived in Hut 8, the keys for June and July 1941 had been captured by 'pinches', i.e. successful raids on German naval units, mostly small ships stationed in the remote North Atlantic to supply weather reports. Until 1 August we were therefore reading Enigma messages almost as quickly as the Germans for whom they were intended. While valuable intelligence was obtained from this material we studied it carefully in order to identify potential cribs.

A significant proportion of the messages turned out to be 'dummies', consisting of nonsense words like DONAU DAMPFSCHIFF FAHRTS GESELLSCHAFTS KAPITAEN (Danube steamship navigation company captain), further text such as 'intended to deceive the enemy' and finally a jumble of letters. Their purpose was to maintain a fairly even flow of traffic so that no inferences would be drawn from an upsurge in the number of signals when some special activity was planned.

The most common cribs were derived from weather reports. The Germans sent out regular messages, usually twice a day, from weather stations at various ports, e.g. Boulogne, Hook of Holland, Royan etc. A typical message would read 'from weather station Boulogne x weather forecast for', followed by the area and period of time covered by the forecast. The operator sending out such a signal had strict orders to vary the text from message to message, but not uncommonly these orders were disregarded so that the same text appeared day after day. At other times it was possible to discern a shift system, three operators on a rota, each with his pet text which then occurred at predictable intervals.

Even then there could be numerous variations in the wording of a weather report. It was possible to narrow the choice by making use of an important characteristic of Enigma: a letter in the plain-text could be encrypted as any other letter but never as itself. For example, if a signal had 'V' as its first letter, the underlying message could not start with 'von', the German for 'from'. If we had a crib for the message starting with VON, we would say that it 'crashed'. Conversely, if we had a long crib, say twenty-five or more letters, which did not crash, there would be an increased chance that it might be correct.

The captured material ran out at the end of July so that 1 August 1941 brought a great challenge for Hut 8. By an apparent stroke of amazing good fortune the day produced two probable weather messages (identified by frequency, code sign and time) which had both been encrypted with the same starting position of the wheels in the machine. Their beginnings were:

1. M O N . O 2. M V V . E

It seemed highly probable that the decrypts would begin as follows:

1.	M	O	N	.	O	.
	V	V	V	(W)	E	.
2.	M	V	V	.	E	.
	V	O	N	V	O	N

This was a perfect example of a 'depth crib', combining the probable plain-text of two or more signals, where the starting positions were identical or in close proximity. The letters MV in the first column illustrated a 'click', where a common letter in both signals had to have a common decrypt. The subsequent parts OV/VO, NV/VN, OE/EO were known as 'reciprocoggers', i.e. paired letters which might be encrypts/decrypts of each other: such pairs increased the probability that the solution was correct. VVV and VONVON were alternative forms used in signals to mean 'from', and the messages were likely to continue with the

German for weather station, i.e. WETTERWARTE or, more frequently, WEWA. This led to a small number of permutations which were almost certain to include a crib of sufficient length for the bombes. Despite this hopeful start we failed to achieve a break, and 1 and 2 August remained among the very few days which were never read.

This was an exceptional disappointment: for the next six months we demonstrated the efficiency of Banburismus, cribs and bombes by breaking almost every day, sometimes very quickly, occasionally with a few days' delay. We had the satisfaction of learning that the resulting intelligence, used with great discretion in order not to compromise the source, led to a dramatic reduction of sinkings of merchant ships by U-boats in the Atlantic.

It was during this period that I was lucky to find a successful crib for an *Offizier* message. Such messages, thought to require a higher degree of secrecy, were encrypted by an officer using different pluggings (*Stecker*) and one of twenty-six starting positions of the wheels. At that time, the pluggings changed every day and the twenty-six positions every month. The encrypted result was then encrypted a second time by the regular operator with the normal key for the day, with a preamble featuring the word *Offizier* and a name (Anton for A, Berta for B, etc.) indicating the starting position.

I was not expecting to be successful and went home on leave before the testing on a bombe was complete. Wylie promised to confirm a positive result by sending me a telegram containing the name of a fish. When a telegram arrived with the word 'pompano' I had to look it up in a dictionary to make sure that 'pompano' *was* a fish. The breakthrough resulted in more knowledge about the content of *Offizier* messages which subsequently helped us to read most of these signals without great difficulty.

We dealt successfully with a change in October 1941 when the Germans split the traffic into two keys, one for U-boats in the Atlantic and one for the rest. We called the U-boat key Shark and the other Dolphin. For some reason the U-boats in the Arctic, north of Norway, remained on Dolphin.

We were forewarned by some messages that a more serious change would occur on 1 February 1942. On that day, the Enigma machines used for Shark started to use a fourth wheel. The change multiplied by twenty-six the number of combinations of variables to be tested by the bombes – it also made Banburismus impossible. Except on rare occasions we did not, at that time, have enough bombe capacity to try possible cribs. We therefore broke only three Shark keys between February and mid-December 1942. The consequence was an upsurge in the number of sinkings, which reached dangerous levels for the rest of that year.

I have been asked whether our prolonged inability to break Shark gave us a sense of guilt. While we knew the seriousness of the situation I cannot say that we felt guilty. First, we genuinely felt that, without more captured material, there was no short-term solution. Secondly we knew that there was a long-term solution because of plans, in collaboration with the Americans, to build more powerful bombes capable of coping with the four-wheel machines. Thirdly we were still regularly breaking Dolphin (the other main key) as well as, from the summer of 1942, a separate key called Porpoise used for traffic in the Mediterranean. We did have a sad time in July when we were late in breaking a crucial day while the Arctic convoy PQ17 was being slaughtered by U-boats and aircraft.

In his chapter on 'Breaking Naval Enigma', Ralph Erskine has given an account of the steps which enabled Hut 8 to resume its breaking of Shark from mid-December 1942 to June 1943 with the aid of 'short signals' used by U-boats for weather reports (WWs) and operational reports (B-bars). This success could not have been achieved without the men from HMS *Petard*, who gave their lives in capturing the necessary codebooks from U-559.

The construction of successful cribs for WWs was then

dependent on the breaking of a meteorological cipher in Hut 10 under Philip Archer; the result became known in Hut 8 as Archery. In the later stages essential information relating to B-bars was provided by Edgar Jackson, head of one of the Naval Intelligence sections in Hut 4 (afterwards Block B). Within Hut 8 a major contribution to this work was made by Michael Ashcroft whose promising post-war career at the Treasury was tragically cut short by his death from cancer in 1949.

June 1943 marked the beginning of a new era for Hut 8. The first of the new bombes had arrived, capable of dealing with the variables of a four-wheel Enigma machine. Quite soon we had a growing arsenal of three-wheel and four-wheel bombes. This meant that we could do all the key breaking by cribs, without the help of Banburismus, even on Dolphin, which stuck to three wheels until 1944. In the following months there was a gradual exodus of talent from Hut 8: Wylie, Ashcroft and others left to join the Tunny section (Block F) under Max Newman, where they contributed to another of the great Bletchley successes. Finally, in autumn 1944, Alexander was transferred to work on Japanese naval codes and Patrick Mahon became head of Hut 8.

In the last twelve months of the war all the breaking of naval keys was done by four cribsters: Patrick Mahon, Joan Clarke (later Murray), Richard Pendered and myself; we worked on a shift rota around the clock. All the main keys were broken regularly during this period. While some of the cribbing became routine we enjoyed our tasks after the bombes had identified a key's wheel order and pluggings. We still had to work out the *Ringstellung* and the *Grundstellung*.

With growing participation by OP-20-G, our opposite numbers in the US Navy, we coped successfully with the introduction of many new keys: they included Plaice for ships in the Baltic, Grampus for ships in the Black Sea, Narwhal for U-boats in the Arctic, Sunfish for blockade runners, etc. In one way this prolifer-ation was helpful because the same announcement was often sent out in several keys. Having broken one of these we had a reliable crib for the others.

Apart from these re-encodements, weather messages remained our most frequent source of cribs. On D-Day in 1944 we broke Dolphin at daybreak thanks to an undisciplined German operator who began his report day after day with WETTERVORHERSAGEBISKAYA. At other times the disciplines must have been reimposed so that reliable weather cribs disappeared for a time. We then had to turn to other sources, including the 'gardening' procedure described in Chapter 10. The areas where the RAF dropped mines were carefully chosen so that the German naval grid references contained no numbers for which there were alternative spellings (NUL or NULL for '0', FUNF or FUENF for '5').

One day, while on duty in the morning, I was told by Intelligence that it was very important for us to read the next day's messages as early as possible. Would gardening improve the chances of an early break? I thought about it and gave the answer 'yes'. That night was stormy and I lay in bed worrying whether my judgement had been correct or whether I had needlessly endangered the lives of the air crews. I was extremely relieved when I heard next day that there had been no flying because of the bad weather.

On rare occasions a successful crib was based on a guess that a message might contain an important topical announcement. The outstanding example occurred when the battleship *Tirpitz* was sunk by Bomber Command in north Norway in November 1944. We guessed that a certain signal might say '*Tirpitz* capsized'. It did and we were able to break one of the day's keys.

Although in the last phase the number of cryptanalysts in Hut 8 had dwindled to four, we were always dependent on a big supporting cast. First of all there were the wireless operators at the various interception stations who did a fantastic job. Picking up and accurately recording a short signal, lasting only a few seconds, must have required great skill and concentration. Then there were the ladies in Hut 8 itself, eventually about 130 of them, doing the clerical work and the typing; in the days of Banburismus they also had to punch the holes in the Banbury sheets. Finally, there was the work of running the bombes, which were located in several big houses around Bletchley. This was done by Wrens working under very spartan conditions. Looking back, I think that we did not give enough credit to all these people without whom we could not have functioned.

The Germans responsible for Enigma security had tolerated all kinds of flaws but they became extremely active at the very end of the war. A complicated new system for determining the starting positions of signals was introduced on Dolphin in May 1945. We made plans to meet this challenge but it would undoubtedly have caused delays and it was perhaps fortunate that the war ended before the new procedures became effective.

At the peak there were about 9,000 people working at Bletchley Park. With, I believe, only one exception, the confidentiality of the work was never breached either then or for about thirty years after the war. We had all signed the Official Secrets Act and never doubted that we could not talk about what we did during the war. Is it conceivable that such secrecy could be maintained amid the present culture of constant leaks?

Robert Harris's *Enigma* is a very good novel but it paints far too drab a picture of life at Bletchley. No doubt the meals served in the canteen featured dried egg, Spam, and other wartime delicacies: they may have been stodgy but they were perfectly palatable. Most of us were billeted on householders in a wide area around Bletchley and I do not remember many complaints. I have fond memories of the elderly couple with whom I lodged in Newport Pagnell; the wife was a wonderful lady who had been maid to a duchess. No duchess could have received better care than I did.

Many of us had come straight from university and it was in many ways like having an extra four years of university life. We did work hard, taking unsocial hours for granted, but there was also a good social life. An active Dramatic Society put on plays and satirical revues of a high standard, there was a lot of music, and we played chess and bridge. Most men went about in old sports jackets and shabby corduroy trousers. Once when a visiting Admiral was taken around the site by the Director he is reported to have asked: 'What are all these velvet arsed bastards doing here?'

I had a happy time at Bletchley, not only because of the work but because Hut 8 was always a friendly place. There really was a spirit of camaraderie among the cryptanalysts and a sense of a common purpose. I can recall no personality clashes or big outbursts of temper. I attribute this to the fascination of the work, the satisfaction of getting results, exemplary leadership and, above all, the personalities of the individuals. I would like to conclude this account with recollections of some of them.

From addressing each other by our surnames we soon switched to first names. There were two exceptions: one of these was Alan Turing, without whom Hut 8 might not have existed. It was he who, building on pre-war discoveries by the Poles, originated the methods by which the naval Enigma was broken. We all recognized his genius; perhaps for this reason he was known as 'Prof'. We regarded him as eccentric but I cannot remember any specific eccentricities. By the time of my arrival in Hut 8 the basic principles of the work were well established so that there was less scope for his genius. He therefore spent more and more time on assignments outside Hut 8 and left altogether in late 1942. While he was with us he was always approachable and ready to help with technical problems. It may have been my fault that I did not find it easy to communicate with him.

I could always communicate with Hugh Alexander, the former British Chess Champion, who had come in as acting head of

Hut 8 because Turing's great abilities did not include a talent for administration. He had a wonderfully quick mind combined with tremendous energy and enthusiasm. I still think of him as the model manager, always leading from the front. He treated us as colleagues but he could be very firm when it was necessary.

Turing and Alexander have since died but Shaun Wylie remains active in his eighties. Alexander rightly described him as 'easily the best all-rounder in the section, astonishingly quick and resourceful'. He was an outstanding leader who always set higher standards for himself than for anyone else. I have continued to admire his intellect and his integrity, more recently his superior skill in solving the weekly 'Listener' crossword in *The Times* to which we are both addicted.

I have already mentioned the part played by Michael Ashcroft when breaking Shark was resumed in 1942–3 with the aid of short signals. He would now be described as a caring man; he had helped to rescue and educate at least one Jewish boy from Germany. At Oxford he was active in centre-left politics. We shared various interests and met frequently after the war. I felt a great loss when he died.

Patrick Mahon was the obvious choice as head of Hut 8 when Alexander left in September 1944. He was exceptional among the cryptanalysts in being a linguist, not a mathematician. If this was a handicap, he amply compensated for it by great energy and a very methodical mind. It was he who discovered the shift system worked by some operators sending weather messages. He was given to strong views, with some youthful intolerance, but he was always popular because he had great personal charm. After the war he had a successful career in the John Lewis Partnership. We kept in touch but sadly his health failed and he died prematurely in 1972.

Richard Pendered was the brightest of the younger cryptanalysts in Hut 8. He had a memorable success when he broke

Shark for 27 May 1943, using a long crib, by a purely manual method, which he himself had refined. It was a superb technical achievement: the method was used again to find the wiring of a new fourth wheel and reflector which the Germans introduced on 1 July 1943.

Joan Clarke, later Murray, was an excellent Banburist who later became an excellent cribster. It was a tribute to her ability that her equality with the men was never in question, even in those unenlightened days. She was kind and always good-tempered, but rather reserved. It was known that she had been close to Alan Turing but that nothing had come of the relationship. She never spoke about it, but when I met her again in 1993, at the launch of *Codebreakers* (the book of reminiscences of Bletchley, edited by Harry Hinsley and Alan Stripp), she said that she had not seen Hugh Whitemore's play *Breaking the Code* because it would have been too painful.

The other exception to the use of first names was Kendrick. I never knew what the initials F. A. stood for and it was something of a shock to find him listed in the index of *Codebreakers* as 'Kendrick, Tony'. He was a member of Hut 8 from early 1940 until July 1942; it was said that any new suggestion had already been proposed by Kendrick at some earlier date. Severely crippled by polio, he was a very private man but he was courteous and kind, and he had a fine sense of humour. He was an even shabbier dresser than the rest of us; strips of tattered lining were seen to protrude from his threadbare suit. It was believed that this was his protest, as a career civil servant, against the abandonment of pinstriped trousers after GC&CS moved to Bletchley. Some time after the war I met him at a concert; he was working at the Ministry of Defence. 'England is safe then,' I said. 'Yes,' he replied. 'I don't interfere much.'

When the war ended I could not tear myself away from decoding and spent a further year working on other ciphers. When I finally left to join the family business created by my father, I made sure that I could come back if a six months' trial did not work out. The option was unnecessary: I am still involved in the business.

Being at Bletchley during the war was a prime example of my good fortune in life. While most of my contemporaries were risking death or injury and enduring hardship I was living comfortably and doing exciting work. At the same time I could maintain my self-respect because the work was important. I know that I was very lucky.

12

Bletchley Park and the Birth of the Very Special Relationship

STEPHEN BUDIANSKY

Introduction

Chapter 12 describes the wartime events that gave birth to the unprecedented – and, more than a half century later, still enduring – 'special relationship' between the British and American signals intelligence services. Through a combination of wartime necessity, some shrewd political calculation, and not a few deft acts of individual diplomacy, Britain and the United States agreed to throw open the doors to one another on many of their most closely guarded secrets. It was far from a foregone conclusion that they would. Even after the two allies subscribed to formal arrangements on Sigint co-operation during the course of the war – the Holden Agreement (on naval Sigint) and BRUSA (on attacking the army, air force and secret service codes and ciphers of the Axis powers) – there were many forces at work to prevent co-operation from becoming anything more than symbolic. The British on several occasions sought to keep control of the dissemination of Sigint from Enigma firmly in their hands; the Americans, for their part, completely refused to share with their ally the US Navy's extremely secure Electric Cipher Machine Mk. II (the Army's Sigaba), even when that refusal severely hampered the Allied war effort. Yet through all of the mutual suspicions, tensions and jockeying for position that inevitably occurred, a genuinely co-operative relationship was forged, that paid off dramatically during the war (and afterwards). This was particularly true of the mobilization of American industrial might to produce the much-needed four-rotor bombes that took over the solution of the Atlantic U-boat Enigma problem during the last two years of the war.

Surprisingly, the US Army and Navy were at times prepared to trust their ally more than they trusted each other. Dr George McVittie, the head of GC&CS's meteorological subsection, was astonished to find, during a visit to the United States in September 1942, that Commander Joseph Wenger in OP-20-G was willing to reveal secrets to him which he would not pass on to two Army codebreakers. GC&CS had to be very careful not to disclose the contents of the Navy's Sigint pact to the Army and vice versa: the Navy did not send a copy of the Holden Agreement to the Army until mid-1944, two years after it was signed.

Chapter 12 tells a truly remarkable story, which reflects greatly to the credit of three men in particular, William Friedman, Telford Taylor and John Tiltman: they are shown to have been men of real vision, blessed with good judgement – and to have been much needed at the time.

RE

In July 1942, a Bletchley Park liaison officer arrived in Washington and immediately began venting his considerable annoyance with Britain's ally in a series of increasingly exasperated despatches. There was the unbearable 'regimental gossip' of American wives at dinner parties. There was an absurd and tedious picnic he was dragged to in Washington's Rock Creek Park. There was 'our fat friend Kully' – Solomon Kullback, one of the US Army's leading cryptanalysts – who over-organized his section, placed obstacles in the way of British requests for information, and had the habit, 'which I am sure you must have observed in some degree, of shouting people down to contradict something they have no intention of saying'. By September the British official was writing home:

> Sometimes I think they are just a lot of kids playing at 'Office'. You must have noticed yourself how very many childish qualities the American male has: his taste in women, motor-cars, and drink, his demonstrative patriotism, his bullying assertion of his Rights, his complete pig-selfishness in public manners and his incredible friendliness and generosity when he likes you – Hell! anyone would think I didn't like them. But perhaps it is as well I'm fond of children.

Even with America's entry into the war in December 1941, it was far from inevitable that the two allies would forge any real or meaningful co-operation in cryptanalysis and signals intelligence. There was certainly a lot working against it. For a start, the British were convinced that the Americans were simply incapable of safeguarding important secrets. Many Bletchley Park officials were loath to share their monopoly over the control and distribution of intelligence derived from the breaking of the German Enigma ciphers. On the American side, the US Navy might have finally forgotten the war of 1812 and the press-ganging of American sailors, but nonetheless harboured a widespread distrust and resentment of the British, and was particularly touchy about anything that might imply that America was a junior partner taking orders from the British. Moreover, many American officials (with good reason, given past practice of GC&CS) were suspicious that the British would exploit cryptologic co-operation to gain access to American codes in order to read confidential US diplomatic communications.

Finally, there was the simple transatlantic culture gap – far greater then than now – that led to repeated misunderstandings, friction and enmity on a personal level, of the sort so richly exemplified by Bletchley Park's liaison officer, who, when he was not penning poisonous despatches, was irking the US Army code-breakers at Arlington Hall with what many took to be his pompous and overbearing manner. (One Arlington Hall veteran recalled that this officer always appeared with Sam Browne belt, polished riding boots and swagger stick.)

In the end it was a combination of practical necessity and personal diplomacy that overcame these many obstacles and helped to launch the 'special relationship' between the British and American intelligence agencies, which endures to this day. The pooling of talent, effort and technology by British and American cryptanalysts proved to be of the first importance in the breaking of the German U-boat ciphers and diplomatic codes and the Japanese naval and military codes in particular. But it was a long haul, and were it not for a few far-sighted and level-headed men on both sides of the Atlantic who prevailed at critical junctures, the relationship would never have progressed beyond the 'make polite noises' stage at which it was largely stuck for the first couple of years of the war. The real heroes of this tale are John Tiltman on the British side and William Friedman and Telford Taylor on the American side, and perhaps even more importantly, the many lower-ranking technical experts on both sides who began working with one another at a very practical level and forged personal ties that did much to overcome the mutual suspicion and incomprehension that had threatened to poison the relationship before it had even started.

The half century that has passed since the Second World War has brought about such a thorough revolution in travel and communication that it is difficult for us today to realize just how insular Britain and America were in 1940, and the extent to which cultural differences posed a significant obstacle to establishing co-operation. The knowledge that even many well-educated Britons had of Americans was limited to the actors they had seen on movie screens. Within official circles in Britain, Americans were frequently portrayed in the broadest caricatures: naive in the ways of the world and incapable of keeping a secret.

On 15 November 1940, in a memorandum discussing the first feelers for co-operation with the US signals intelligence agencies, Alastair Denniston – then the operational head of GC&CS – warned that 'we are entitled to recall that the Americans sent over at the end of the last war the now notorious Colonel [Herbert O.] Yardley for purposes of co-operation. He went so far as to publish the story of his co-operation in book form.' Even after the US Navy had begun convoying merchant ships to Iceland and had become engaged in what was for all intents and purposes an undeclared war in the Atlantic in 1941, British officialdom was set against sharing the fruits of signals intelligence with the United States. Brigadier Stewart Menzies, who as 'C' oversaw both GC&CS and the Secret Intelligence Service (MI6), wrote to Prime Minister Winston Churchill on 24 June 1941 that he had considered the matter 'from all angles'; true, US Navy units *were* being chased by U-boats – just four days earlier U-203 had pursued the American battleship *Texas* for 140 miles between Greenland and Iceland and had repeatedly tried to manoeuvre into position to fire a torpedo – and, true, GC&CS was reading Enigma traffic that contained orders from the German Admiral Commanding U-boats to his captains at sea, which might give vital warning to the Americans. But, 'C' concluded:

> I find myself unable to devise any safe means of wrapping up the information in a manner which would not imperil this source . . . it [is] well nigh impossible that the information could have been secured by an agent, and however much we insist that it came from

> a highly placed source, I greatly doubt the enemy being for a moment deceived, should there be any indiscretion in the USA. That this might occur, cannot be ruled out, as the Americans are not in any sense as security-minded as one would wish, and I need only draw your attention to the attached cutting from to-day's '*Daily Express*' on a matter which, in my opinion, should not have been made public if the two Secret Services are to work together.

The attached article that had caught 'C''s attention reported that Colonel William 'Wild Bill' Donovan 'has a new hush-hush mission – to supervise the United States Secret Service and ally it with the British Secret Service . . . The American "Mr. X", as he is known privately, will report direct to the President.' It wasn't exactly 'hush-hush' by the time the story had appeared in the *Daily Express*, and 'C' had a point.

Although the US Army's Signal Intelligence Service, under the direction of the renowned cryptanalyst William Friedman, was eager to initiate a sharing of technical data with GC&CS in the autumn of 1940, the US Navy was almost completely opposed to all of Friedman's recommendations. Commander Laurence Safford, Friedman's counterpart as head of the Navy's OP-20-G, rejected any exchange of cryptanalytic data and techniques or training materials. Neither Friedman nor Safford, however, was interested in letting the British in on American *cryptographic* secrets – that is, the business of codemaking as opposed to codebreaking. In particular, Friedman ruled out giving the British 'information of any kind' relating to America's SIGABA cipher machine, even the very fact of its existence. There was considerable suspicion – again not unjustified, as it happened – that the British were attempting to read American codes. Even while proposing an intimate exchange of highly secret material on codebreaking Friedman was not going to give the British anything that might help them break American systems. (After America's entry into the war following the Pearl Harbor attack, Churchill felt he needed to warn his new ally about the insecurity of her diplomatic codes; in a letter to President Roosevelt on 25 February 1942, the Prime Minister wrote:

> Some time ago . . . our experts claimed to have discovered the system and constructed some tables used by your Diplomatic Corps. From the moment when we became allies, I gave instructions that this work should cease. However, danger of our enemies having achieved a measure of success cannot, I am advised, be dismissed.

On the one hand it was a considerate gesture, but it also confirmed the US experts' worst fears about the British. The following year, Colonel Alfred McCormack, a US military intelligence officer, visited the British radio intercept station at Beaumanor, and while the station's commander was showing him around he casually remarked that he used to read the US State Department ciphers and that it had been 'lots of fun'.)

Of course, a far greater obstacle was that the British and American signals intelligence establishments had very different aims; each wanted to extract something quite different from the other, and some of those goals were mutually exclusive. When the first technical exchanges between the two sides began in February 1941 with the arrival of a combined US Army–Navy liaison mission, Britain's chief concern was gaining assistance in dealing with Japanese codes. Though the British had begun in the 1930s to intercept Japanese naval traffic from a station in Hong Kong (the station moved to Singapore in September 1939 and Kilindini, Kenya, in 1942 as the Japanese Army advanced through South Asia) – and though they had made some progress against the main Japanese naval operations code (the system that would later be known as JN-25) – Britain had a critical shortage of Japanese linguists. The codebook change that the Japanese Navy introduced in December 1940, replacing the JN-25A code with the much more complex JN-25B code, was a considerable setback, and the British frankly conceded that they very much needed American assistance. In fact, the British offered to turn over their entire Far East codebreaking operation to the Americans if the United States would supply the needed translators.

In its efforts against the high-level Japanese diplomatic cipher, Purple, which was generated by a machine roughly equivalent in complexity to the German Enigma, GC&CS was also stymied and very eager for US help. GC&CS had broken the relatively simple Japanese Red machine, which had been used for diplomatic traffic for much of the 1930s, but had actually given up trying to solve the more complex Purple machine, which came into use on 20 February 1938. From the start, the British consistently sought to keep Anglo-American cryptanalytical co-operation principally limited to the one area where they knew they needed help – Japan.

At a higher level of diplomatic calculation, Britain also was seeking to budge America away from her neutrality, and Churchill in particular saw technical exchanges among military experts in many areas as one way to do so. In a frank speech to the House of Commons, Churchill said his aim was to see the United States and Britain 'somewhat mixed up together'. In growing numbers, American military experts began arriving in Britain in the summer of 1940 to study how the British military was performing in the fight against Germany, and they were handed reams of data on the effectiveness of fighter and bomber aircraft, on radar, and other extremely secret information. Co-operation on intelligence was just one dimension of a much broader British charm offensive, and it apparently so overwhelmed American Brigadier General George V. Strong (who in August had cabled back that Britain was 'a gold mine' of technical information) that in September Strong, on his own initiative, asked the British if they would be interested in a full exchange of codebreaking results, including US work on Japanese diplomatic ciphers. The British staff officials were astonished, but immediately accepted.

Strong then had to convince Washington. He cabled, asking for an urgent reply. William Friedman at the SIS immediately saw the advantages. Though he did not know of British progress against the Enigma, he was well aware how behind the United States was in dealing with German military traffic in general. German signals were impossible to pick up from the continental United States, and the Army was essentially devoid of knowledge about the German military cryptographic systems. The US Army had not even begun paying much attention to German traffic, military or diplomatic, until October 1939, concentrating instead on Japan, Russia and Mexico. The benefits of an exchange of raw traffic, at a minimum, were manifest. Friedman was more cautious about the idea of exchanging cryptanalytic research or results, but thought it might work on a strict item-by-item quid pro quo.

The US Navy, for its part, had been able to intercept some Enigma signals from the east coast of the United States, but had made no significant progress in decrypting the material – and it had a growing need for operational intelligence about German U-boats. Yet the Navy was so suspicious of British motives that Safford would agree to nothing beyond an exchange of traffic.

By the late autumn of 1940, the US Navy had at last agreed to go along with Friedman's proposal to exchange technical data with GC&CS, and the British had agreed to accept a visit by American technical experts. Roosevelt gave his blessing on 24 October and the next day the US Army's chief signal officer, General Mauborgne, forwarded to the US Army staff a list of what the SIS proposed giving to the British – including its solution of the Purple machine. But this was far from constituting a formal agreement. The planned visit by the American technical experts was viewed by both sides as really just an initial exploratory conversation. And internal British memoranda make abundantly clear that the British plan was to stonewall if questions about the Enigma came up: the British directors of military, air and naval intelligence conferred and concluded that 'a full interchange on

Germany and Italy cannot be entertained at this stage'. Instead, when the American 'expert' arrived, 'steps will be taken to steer him away from our most secret subjects':

> Should this expert make a favourable impression, we could consider opening out on the Italian material, and possibly discuss generally 'Y' work problems as regards Germany, upon which subject their assistance might be valuable . . . I would add that the matter has been discussed with Sir A[lexander] Cadogan [the permanent undersecretary of the Foreign Office], who concurs that we cannot possibly divulge our innermost secrets at this stage, but that if the Americans return to the charge, it might become necessary to refer the question of policy to the Prime Minister.

'Y' referred to the interception and direction-finding of enemy signals and to the decryption of low-level tactical and field codes, and most definitely did not include the 'innermost secret' of the Enigma. It was not until after the four American cryptanalysts – Abraham Sinkov and Leo Rosen from the Army, and Prescott Currier and Robert Weeks of the Navy – had been in the country three weeks that a decision was finally made to reveal to them that the Enigma was in the process of being broken and the methods that were being used. A memorandum from 'C' to Churchill dated 26 February 1941, reported that the British Chiefs of Staff 'on balance' now favoured 'revealing to our American colleagues the progress which we have made in probing the German Armed Force cryptography'. But 'C' assured the Prime Minister that the discussions would be on technical aspects of cryptanalysis only and would not extend to 'the results', i.e., actual intelligence derived from Enigma traffic. A handwritten note from Churchill at the bottom of the memo reads 'As proposed. WSC. 27.2'.

On 3 March 1941, the Americans were informed of the British success against the Enigma. But there were strict limitations. A handwritten agreement dated that same day and signed by Weeks stated that they should inform no one of the information they had acquired, except the head of their section, Commander Safford, and him 'by word of mouth only'. (The Army representatives agreed to a similar restriction.) The Americans would be given the wiring of the naval Enigma rotors, but agreed to 'disclose that only when it is decided to work on the problem'.

There has been considerable controversy in subsequent years over the exact nature of the exchange of information that occurred during this visit. An account by Safford, written many years later, claimed that the Americans had been double-crossed; the United States gave the British its most closely held secrets about Japanese codes, even supplying a copy of the Japanese Purple machine that the US Army cryptanalysts had reconstructed, while the British gave the Americans nothing in return.

But the true situation was more complex. Co-operation on Japanese codes began almost immediately and was definitely a two-way street. Even while the Sinkov mission was at GC&CS, the British cipher unit in Singapore received radioed orders to begin sharing information on JN-25 with the US Navy's intercept and decrypting unit at Cavite in the Philippines, known as Station Cast. In February 1941, the two bureaux in the Far East exchanged liaison officers and thereafter regularly sent each other recovered code groups. (By June 1941 only about 1,100 code groups of the 55,000 used in the new JN-25B codebook had been identified between the two units, and these were mostly groups that stood for numbers and other mundane and common words or symbols that yielded little of intelligence value. By the time of Pearl Harbor the total of recovered groups was still under 4,000, and a change on 1 August in the additive book used to conceal the code groups' identities in actual messages further blocked attempts to read traffic. At the time of Pearl Harbor not a single JN-25 message had ever been read currently, and since the

December 1940 codebook change no JN-25 messages had yielded more than fragments, of no intelligence value.)

Co-operation between the British and American codebreakers, in the true sense of the word, also began on German diplomatic codes. On Enigma, however, the British drew a careful line between 'research' and 'exploitation'. It was one thing to have a technical discussion about cryptanalytic theory; it was quite another to let anyone else in on the actual intelligence operation – the system that transformed intercepted German military communications into military intelligence. The Americans were told about the Enigma and were shown the bombes, the electro-mechanical devices Bletchley Park had developed to recover the daily Enigma settings. But the visitors were not permitted to take notes, nor was GC&CS terribly quick in replying to subsequent requests for further details. On 15 July 1941, Washington requested information about daily Enigma settings; a month later the material 'was still being copied'. Denniston was meanwhile 'aghast' to receive a letter from the United States asking for a copy of the bombe, explaining that 'we avoid as far as possible putting anything on paper on this subject'.

Denniston was scheduled to travel to Washington on 16 August. 'Perhaps the most important purpose of the visit is to clear up the position concerning E traffic', he wrote in a memorandum to 'C'. Denniston proposed that he should explain to the Americans during his visit that GC&CS had received so far only 6 of the 36 bombes it had ordered and could not spare one. Allowing an American firm to build a bombe was out of the question on security grounds, he wrote; for the American cryptanalysts, the Enigma was at best a 'new and very interesting problem', but for Britain it was 'almost life-blood to our effort'. But perhaps, Denniston suggested, it might be possible for the US codebreaking bureaux to send some 'young mathematicians' to Britain to work with GC&CS directly on the Enigma. 'C' shot down every one of these suggestions. He replied that he was 'a little uneasy about the proposal for young mathematicians' and that 'I should feel inclined not to mention' the bombe situation at all lest that might be used as an argument by the Americans to have them built in the United States, which the British were adamantly opposed to.

On 1 October 1941, Denniston did apparently write Safford a letter supplying the information OP-20-G had been after, but the letter went astray. On 27 November, Admiral Leigh Noyes, the US Director of Naval Communication (under whose jurisdiction OP-20-G fell), sent a long complaint to the British alleging that they had failed to carry out their end of the bargain. The British reply, from 'C', did little to mollify his concerns, for it argued rather jesuitically that on naval Enigma, 'everything asked for has been supplied', which did not exactly seem to the Americans to reflect a spirit of true co-operation. Finally Denniston realized that his letter to Safford had not been received and cleared the matter up; by 12 December the letter had arrived and Noyes stated that everyone was now satisfied.

Nevertheless the British position was untenable in the long run, for it still insisted that neither the US Army nor the US Navy need participate directly in 'exploiting' German Enigma traffic – that is, in decrypting it and distributing the results on an operational basis. When it came to control of the product, that was a British prerogative, period. The Admiralty would 'pass German naval intelligence to Navy Department when U.S.A. was affected', Washington was informed. As for the US Army, they clearly were *not* affected by the ground war in Europe:

> 1. No results are being passed out because they only affect operation in various localities in Europe and Africa in which U.S.A. has only academic interest.
> 2. An undertaking was given to the War Department that our methods which may have led to partial success will be shared with them when they are really interested in the operational results.

'Interested' in this case was clearly meant in the strict sense of the word, that is, when the US Army had an interest at stake in the actual fighting. With the entry of the United States into the war, both OP-20-G and Arlington Hall (as the US Army SIS establishment came to be known after its move in 1942 to the former girls' school of that name in Arlington, Virginia) renewed their demands for direct involvement in decrypting German Enigma traffic. And now British opposition began to assume a different complexion. Knowledge is power, and being able to control the distribution of such a valuable form of knowledge as Enigma intelligence gave the British a not inconsiderable point of leverage in the alliance. It was not so much that the British were out to directly manipulate the information or withhold it when military necessity dictated it be provided to field commanders, British or American. But many decisions in negotiations over military strategy between the new allies were tilted by arguments over the relative contribution each side was making to the war effort, and the Enigma was one bargaining chip: the British monopoly over this intelligence was one thing that made the Americans undeniably beholden to them. By the same token, the growth of a significant independent American capability would make the British – and British views – that much more dispensable.

Denniston was alarmed by the new American demands for fuller participation in the Enigma work, and at once sent a message to the British liaison in Washington:

> In telegram from the War Department A.16 of 18th December, they raise the question of investigating the German Air-Army cypher. During my visit it was agreed that we should be responsible for this investigation and that when U.S.A. were in real need of this work we should invite their party to join ours.
>
> Could you find out if their views on this procedure have changed and if they wish to begin their own investigations now? It

> is devoutly hoped by all here that any such investigations will not interfere with their progress on Japanese work for which we count on them.

For the US Navy, what finally broke the British claim to monopoly was GC&CS's sudden failure to continue reading the Atlantic U-boat traffic. On 1 February 1942, the Atlantic U-boat networks changed from the three-wheel Enigma to a four-wheel machine. Running the bombe through all possible positions for one wheel order of a three-wheel machine typically took about fifteen minutes of machine time (the set-up time for each run added another ten or fifteen minutes, and additional time was required for testing the results of the run). The addition of a fourth wheel meant that the time required for each run on the three-wheel bombes was multiplied by a factor of twenty-six – the machine would have to be run through all possible wheel orders *and* at every possible position of the fourth wheel; testing all 336 wheel orders at all twenty-six positions of the fourth wheel could thus in theory take several thousand hours on a three-wheel bombe. Even with all sixteen bombes that were available at this time running simultaneously, and even exploiting methods that could reduce the number of wheel orders that needed to be tried, recovering each daily setting might take two days or more of effort. But there were other problems as well, notably a lack of suitable cribs. What was needed was a new, four-wheel bombe that could run at much higher speeds.

Lieutenant-Colonel John Tiltman, one of GC&CS's top cryptanalysts, visited the US Navy Department in April 1942 and at once assessed the situation with a clear eye. He began a tactful but straightforward lobbying effort with his new director, Edward Travis, who had replaced Denniston in February as the operational head of Bletchley Park. 'In view of the fact that they are now at war and have a vital interest in submarine traffic they are entitled to results or a detailed statement as to why traffic cannot be read at present and what are prospects for future,' Tiltman cabled to London. 'Unless a rapid and satisfactory solution is found . . . the high command will insist on their naval cryptanalysts attempting to duplicate our work on E [Enigma].' He noted that, as a riposte against the British excuse of concerns over poor American security, OP-20-G was already insisting that the US needed to form a 'skeleton party' with 'some machinery' as insurance, in case the Germans invaded England, or if the *Luftwaffe* bombed Bletchley Park.

Travis cabled back, 'hardly think necessary to form skeleton party as if real danger arose of present facilities being lost we would certainly send experts other side'. But he got the message. On 13 May 1942, Travis informed OP-20-G that 'higher authority has agreed future policy regarding E solution . . . we will continue exploiting but will send you a machine for solution in August or September and lend you a mechanic to instruct in working. We will also give full instructions and try to spare some one to explain our method.' Travis also agreed with Tiltman's suggestion that several US Navy experts who had been working on methods for speeding up the bombes be sent over to Bletchley. Lieutenants Robert Ely and Joseph Eachus arrived on 1 July, and after a few more delays and excuses were finally given what the United States had been seeking since February 1941 – complete wiring diagrams and blueprints of the actual bombes.

The British clearly hoped to assuage the US Navy by allowing it to participate more fully on the research end of things, and even to develop a small independent capability of breaking some of the traffic that could be intercepted from North America, while still keeping fundamental control of the intelligence output themselves. But that last ditch stand had to be abandoned finally in August when, having failed to make good on the promise of providing the US Navy with a bombe, GC&CS was suddenly confronted with a *fait accompli* by the Americans. It was clear the British designs for the four-wheel bombes were running into difficulties in particular in getting the high-speed rotors to make good electrical contact; the new head of OP-20-G, Captain Joseph Wenger, was also apparently convinced, though wrongly, that the British had achieved some success reading current U-boat traffic and were concealing that fact. On 3 September 1942, Wenger proposed to his superiors spending two million dollars – 'it must be understood that it is a gamble', he wrote – to build 360 four-wheel bombes. The British liaison to OP-20-G had tried to head off the American move, protesting that Tiltman promised only to provide results or 'a detailed statement as to why traffic cannot be read', and by doing the latter the British had fulfilled their obligations and the US Navy had no reason to complain. But the fact was that GC&CS only had about thirty bombes built by this point, and there was no doubt that they desperately needed the help. In July and August the demands of trying (still without success) to break the four-wheel naval Enigma keys had overloaded the available bombes, restricting work that could be done on some German Air Force keys. (Even six months later the situation remained almost desperate. On 5 January 1943, Gordon Welchman, who had played a key role in the original design of the bombe and in organizing the system at Bletchley Park for handling Enigma traffic, warned Travis: 'An analysis of probable and possible requirements for bombes during 1943 is most alarming'. At the new year there were 49 machines in operation; Welchman calculated that as many as 120 three-wheel bombes would be needed for 'urgent work' on German Air Force and Army traffic, while breaking the U-boat and other naval keys might take as many as 134 high-speed, four-wheel bombes.)

Faced with the inevitable, Travis and Frank Birch, head of GC&CS's Naval Section, travelled to Washington in September 1942 and negotiated an agreement by which GC&CS and OP-20-G would establish 'full collaboration' on attacking the German naval Enigma – exchanging traffic, recovered settings, and the 'cribs' needed to run the bombes. The US bombes would be patterned on the general British design, but would use an electronic sensor instead of relays to detect when the rotors hit the correct position, an innovation that would allow the rotors to turn at a much faster speed. The Navy quickly contracted with National Cash Register (NCR) in Dayton, Ohio, to build the machines, and work began immediately.

This pact, known informally as the 'Holden Agreement', was a breakthrough for American cryptanalysts; for the first time they had broken the British monopoly over Enigma. But one interesting aspect of the agreement was that the US Army was not consulted. Just because GC&CS had surrendered on one front it saw no reason to do so on the second front. As a GC&CS memorandum in late 1942 noted in relation to German Army and Air Force Enigma traffic, 'it is not proposed to invite the Americans to take part in our work on "E" though the fruits are at present being handed to the Americans in the Mediterranean'. The US Army cryptanalysts were, however, permitted to study the British bombe blueprints that the US Navy had obtained, and within two weeks of the Navy's decision to begin building bombes, the Army was proposing to build its own machine, too. The Navy agreed that NCR could build bombes under an Army contract as well, but the Army had what it thought was a better idea; in place of the rotating drums of the bombe it wanted to use telephone switching relays, and on 15 December 1942, a $530,000 contract with an 'AAA' priority rating was signed with AT&T to build a single huge relay bombe.

The Army intended to produce a *fait accompli* of its own to present the British, but it was clear that Friedman and company had little notion of what was actually involved in creating a signals intelligence operation of the scale needed to handle Enigma traffic. The single Army bombe was the equivalent of 144 Enigmas, about four times the size of one standard British bombe. It was a highly innovative design, and incorporated some features that speeded up the operations considerably, including a system for automatically changing the wheel order; in the British bombes this required physically removing wheels and replacing them, a time-consuming procedure. But its huge cost (which eventually reached a million dollars, equal to the cost of fifty fighter aircraft at that time) made it totally impracticable for the sort of mass production of traffic required for a serious attack on Enigma intercepts. Moreover, without its own intercept capability in the proximity of the Continent, the US Army would be wholly dependent on traffic relayed from Britain in any event. It was inconceivable that the Army could truly create an independent capability of reading Enigma traffic, at least not soon.

Undeterred, the US Army codebreakers pressed ahead, motivated if nothing else by a simple rivalry with the Navy. They had the perfect opportunity just a few weeks later to present their *fait accompli* to the British. Alan Turing had been despatched to America to visit the NCR plant in Dayton and make recommendations. (Turing went to Dayton on 21 December 1942, and did offer several suggestions, the most significant of which was that the American plan to build 336 bombes – one for each wheel order – was wasteful and ill-considered, given the methods available to reduce the number of possible wheel orders to be run for each test and the way the bombes were used on actual problems.)

On 4 January 1943, Arlington Hall received permission to reveal to Turing and Tiltman, who was in America as a liaison officer at this point, 'the fundamental principles and details of the equipment now in development'. Dale Marston, who was then directing the development of the rapid analytical machinery for Arlington Hall, later recalled that when Tiltman was briefed on the work, he immediately said that the Army and GC&CS 'had better get together'. Turing was shown the actual prototype at Bell Laboratories in New York City on 5 February.

The Army at once requested that the British send Enigma intercepts and cribs to Washington; Tiltman tactfully responded that GC&CS objections to doing so were 'dictated entirely by considerations of security and their great fear that present exploitation of this traffic may be jeopardized by allowing such data to leave England'. Of course that was a disingenuous position, since GC&CS had already accepted the principle of sending such data to the US Navy in Washington, and was sending settings, cribs and traffic to OP-20-G on a daily basis at this very time. Cribs supplied by short weather signals had allowed GC&CS to break the four-wheel Enigma traffic in December 1942, and even before the first two US Navy bombes were completed on 3 May 1943 (they solved their first daily key on June 22), OP-20-G was involved in solving Enigma keys by hand methods and sending the results back to GC&CS.

GC&CS tried other tacks: one was to emphasize the wasteful duplication of effort that would result if the US Army began 'exploiting' Enigma traffic on its own; much better and more efficient would be for the United States to concentrate on Japanese traffic. There was some sense to that but of course it was also self-serving; the British were proposing in effect full co-operation in Japanese traffic in exchange for a British monopoly on German traffic. The British had also never expressed concerns over the wasteful 'duplication' of effort on German diplomatic traffic, which was being worked on in both Washington and London.

A better argument was the one that also happened to be true: that GC&CS by this point had more than two years' experience in mastering the myriad subtleties not only of the daily Enigma keys and in using the bombes to their highest efficiency, but, even more important, in correctly translating and interpreting German military terminology and placing it in the broader intelligence context. Bletchley had accumulated thousands of points of reference – the meanings of abbreviations and German military terms and cross-indexes of the names of units and commanders – that Washington could not possibly expect to duplicate without years of work. If the labour were divided, that would mean that inexperienced American intelligence officers would be producing intelligence without supervision and they could easily make erroneous deductions.

An internal GC&CS memorandum on 8 January 1943 laid out the situation. It noted that a 'gentlemen's agreement' had been reached that the exploitation of intelligence would be left in British hands until America was actively engaged in military operations. True, two events had changed matters: American entry into North Africa, with the TORCH landings of 8 November 1942, and U-boat activity along the American coast. But the Admiralty was helping the US Navy meet the U-boat situation by telegraphing relevant decrypts as soon as they were available, and a special party of British intelligence officers, trained at Bletchley Park to handle Enigma intelligence, had been attached to Eisenhower's command in North Africa. Since it was now 'desired that the whole matter be placed on an official basis', the thing to do would be to ask the Americans whether they would agree to leave the exploitation of Enigma in British hands, with results exploited by America only where operations were in proximity to her own seaboard.

This was again an odd and rather jesuitical position: Britain was still claiming a right of absolute and exclusive control over the breaking and distribution of Enigma traffic where joint US–British military operations were concerned; only where American interests alone were at stake – the East Coast of the United States – would they cede a right for America to become involved. Taking the same fallback position they had assumed with the Navy, the British would make it clear they welcomed co-operation 'in the field of research' and had no objection to machinery being built in America, using 'results of British design and manufacture', provided absolute secrecy was maintained. But they insisted that Britain could not cede its vital interests by sharing control over decryption and distribution of the resulting intelligence, and sent a draft formal agreement to that effect.

The opposition to US Army 'exploitation' of Enigma grew increasingly bitter as the spring wore on. A British liaison official in Washington followed up with additional pressure, disparaging the American work on Purple in particular and American signals intelligence in general, and suggesting that Britain was prepared to sever all signals intelligence co-operation if the US Army refused to accept the British terms. Within GC&CS, at least some were even more furious in their opposition to what they saw as a pointless American duplication of their effort: 'It is perfectly appreciated that the Americans wish to participate in an already proven success, so that they may not appear to lag behind the British either in acumen or knowledge', read one of the more acerbic internal memoranda, apparently written by Nigel de Grey, a senior administrator. It concluded that 'the Americans have no contribution to make'. But cooler heads intervened at the crucial moment. Telford Taylor, then a lieutenant-colonel working in signals intelligence, noted that the British threats to sever all contacts were not really worth taking seriously, since neither the British nor the American Chiefs of Staff would permit such a breach. Taylor advised rejecting the British proposal, but cautioned against making unreasonable demands:

> We should not phrase [our proposal] so broadly that it seems to envision a *duplicate* operation at Arlington Hall, or to impose *undue* burdens on the British in supplying us with traffic and other aids. What we really want *at this time* is to gain a foothold in 'Enigma' and develop technical competence, and gradually develop a supplementary operation so as to improve joint coverage. What we *ultimately* want is independence, but if we get the foothold and develop our technique, independence will come anyhow. As our position in Europe gets better established, we will be less dependent on the British for intercept assistance; as our skill in dealing with traffic grows, we will need less help in securing 'cribs'.

Colonel McCormack, who was at Bletchley to help assess the situation for Arlington Hall, cabled back on 13 May, also urging compromise. He noted that it was indeed ridiculous to think of routing to Washington all raw traffic and attempting to duplicate all of the ancillary reference and index material, built up at GC&CS over three years, that was needed to tackle the German traffic: 'if [Colonel Preston] Corderman [the head of Arlington Hall] wants his people to learn what makes this operation tick,' McCormack wrote, 'he had better send them here to learn it, because they never on God's green earth will learn it from anything that Arlington will be able to do in any foreseeable future'. On the British side, Gordon Welchman urged moderation, too; while 'the idea of a separate "E" organization being built up from scratch elsewhere seems to us to be absurd . . . on the other hand it does seem logical that the Americans should take some hand in work on "E" and we certainly need help'.

On 17 May the 'BRUSA Agreement' was completed, providing for full American participation – in Britain – in the interception and solution of Army and Air Force Enigma traffic, though there were still thorny details to be worked out, and only towards the end of 1943 were arrangements finally settled for Telford Taylor to select decrypts for transmission to Washington directly from Bletchley Park.

There were still occasional clouds over the relationship. The Americans remained suspicious that the British were going to exploit the new intimacy to break American codes or pry out uncomfortable secrets. Colonel McCormack noted at one point with some alarm that the Navy was apparently supplying the British Admiralty with the Navy Department's summary of State Department cables:

> It may be that our State Department codes are so secure that they cannot be broken even by someone who has knowledge of the contents of particular messages. To my mind, however, it would be

> foolhardy to make that assumption . . . The British . . . are very realistic people, and depending on the course of events will certainly at some time – possibly while the war is still on – resume work on United States communications.

The British were equally suspicious about American interest in code materials from countries such as Iraq that remained within the British sphere of influence. The BRUSA Agreement of May 1943 discreetly sidestepped the issue of diplomatic traffic; it called for full co-operation and complete exchange of cryptanalytic results and intercepts, but mentioned only the military and air forces of the Axis powers and the *Abwehr*, the German intelligence service. Informally, a good working relationship was forged between Arlington Hall and Denniston's diplomatic section at Berkeley Street. But the British drew a line at providing Washington with copies of neutral countries' diplomatic messages sent via cables that the British controlled. An American liaison officer from Arlington Hall reported in November 1944 that Denniston 'frequently gets the impression that we are utilizing the war to exploit British cryptographic knowledge' in fields unrelated to actually winning the war. The United States, for its part, ceased sending Berkeley Street information about Latin American countries' codes in September 1944. And when Arlington Hall began work on Russian diplomatic codes in 1943, it went to great lengths to conceal the fact from the British, ensconcing the Russian section behind a plywood partition and keeping it off limits from the British liaison officer, Geoffrey Stevens. Only at the end of the war did America and Britain let each other know that each had in fact been working on Russian traffic – projects codenamed Venona in the United States and Iscot in Britain.

In the end, however, what made the relationship work and endure was that both sides truly did gain; indeed when it came to breaking naval Enigma traffic during the last two years of the war, neither side could have done it alone. The contribution that the US Army contingent in Britain made under the BRUSA Agreement was not insignificant – at Bletchley Park and its outstations the US Army supplied manpower to operate bombes and to perform all of the other tasks associated with reading Enigma traffic. But a much more vital contribution was made by the ability to harness US industry to the urgent task of building the desperately needed four-wheel bombes. That would never have happened without the British conceding some operational control to the US Navy, the move they had so long resisted. The US Navy's 100 four-wheel bombes operating in Washington largely took over the entire job of decrypting the U-boat traffic, codenamed 'Shark', by autumn of 1943. The British four-wheel bombes, by GC&CS's own admission, had never functioned as intended, and on 24 March 1944 GC&CS cabled to Washington conceding the four-wheel bombe field to the Americans. In fact, the US Navy bombes worked so well that by spring 1944 they had a huge, excess capacity to spare. Not only were they handling virtually all of the U-boat traffic; about 45 per cent of the US Navy bombe time was being devoted to German Army and Air Force problems being cabled from GC&CS. (By contrast, the US Army relay bombe never did much, and Arlington Hall's Enigma section mainly focused on experimental and theoretical studies. The relay bombe was eventually adapted for 'dudbusting' – recovering the initial rotor setting on Enigma messages whose indicators had been garbled – and Bletchley Park did cable Arlington Hall some problems to be solved on the machine, and it did the job. But it was considered slow and inefficient, and other machines and methods did these jobs just as well, and often better.)

Co-operation between the Allies on German diplomatic codes led to important cryptanalytic results, too, particularly as a result of the intensive and successful research effort at Arlington Hall to harness IBM machines to the task. The sharing of recoveries on Japanese naval codes produced more progress than either side could have achieved alone, especially during the early years of the

Second World War when both were strapped for manpower. And just as the Allies' agreement to centralize German Army and Air Force Enigma work at Bletchley Park was able to draw on the considerable accumulated British expertise in translating this traffic and correctly interpreting it for intelligence value, so the concentration of work on Japanese Army codes at Arlington Hall in the last two years of the war was able to utilize the huge American investment in IBM machines and methods; by 1944 Arlington Hall was not infrequently reading a coded Japanese Army message before its intended recipient was, thanks to a nearly automatic system of decryption using IBM equipment and a number of special-purpose machines.

It took a blend of individual personality, high politics, and even a certain amount of skulduggery to break down the natural suspicions that prevented co-operation between agencies that, by their very nature, are prone to be secretive to the point of paranoia. Neither side was quite willing to admit how much they would gain through co-operation. But once the door was broken down there could be no turning back, for both sides could manifestly see how much they would lose through going it alone.

13

Mihailović or Tito? How the Codebreakers Helped Churchill Choose

JOHN CRIPPS

Introduction

It is often assumed that the Bletchley Park codebreakers were only interested in the armed forces of Germany, Italy, Japan and, for a time, Russia. In fact, they attacked the codes and ciphers of the armed forces of a wide number of different countries, including Romania, Spain, Vichy France, and even China. They also broke a number of ciphers used by the various factions of the resistance in Yugoslavia. In this chapter, John Cripps examines the use of signals intelligence in determining which of the two guerrilla leaders fighting the Germans in Yugoslavia the Allies should back. The choice lay between the royalist Chetniks of General Draza Mihailović and the communist Partisans led by Tito. There were already concerns over the way in which a post-war eastern Europe was likely to be dominated by the Soviet Union, so Churchill's choice of the communist Tito seems on the face of it a surprise. It has been suggested that James Klugman, a communist activist and a KGB agent, who joined the Yugoslav section of SOE Cairo in 1942, was a prime mover behind the decision to back Tito rather than Mihailović. Klugman's role as a KGB agent is no longer in any doubt. He was instrumental in the conversion to communism of his Cambridge contemporary Anthony Blunt, the so-called Fourth Man in the Cambridge spy ring. He also played an active role in the recruitment of John Cairncross, the Fifth Man and for a while a member of Bletchley Park's Hut 3. On his own admission, Klugman acted in the classic manner of a KGB agent of influence. When the section was set up in September 1942, the SOE supported Mihailović's Chetniks and provided no assistance to Tito's Partisans. Klugman described, in conversations monitored by MI5, how after two years of political work and a series of fights with the Foreign Office, the War Office and GHQ Middle East, the situation was completely reversed. He must therefore have played an important part in creating the situation that led to Churchill's decision to back Tito. But as Cripps shows here, it would have been the overwhelming evidence of the Bletchley Park decrypts, Churchill's most favoured source of intelligence, which persuaded Britain's wartime leader that Tito and his Partisans were a much more effective, and reliable, ally in the war against Germany.

MS

Yugoslavia was invaded by the Axis on 6 April 1941. Its armed forces surrendered unconditionally eleven days later: it was then divided up between the occupying powers – Germany, Italy, Hungary and Bulgaria – with the largest part, although subject to military occupation by Germany and Italy, being declared the Independent State of Croatia. King Peter and the Yugoslav government fled, arriving in England in June to be feted as gallant heroes. This image was bolstered later in the year by the British government and the media when it became apparent that a major uprising had broken out in Yugoslavia. There were two major resistance movements fighting the Axis. One, the Chetniks, was led by Draza Mihailović, a regular Yugoslav army colonel who had decided to fight on; the other, the communist Partisans, was led by Josip Broz, who operated under the *nomme de guerre* of Tito.

The British Government, at the time short of good news, and the Yugoslav government-in-exile, gave Mihailović their enthusiastic backing and he was appointed Yugoslav Minister of War in January 1942. However, lack of resources and more important commitments elsewhere meant that support from Britain for the Chetniks was limited almost entirely to words rather than deeds. It was not considered appropriate to give succour to the Partisans who were described in a report by the Director of Military Intelligence, Major General Francis Davidson, to Winston Churchill in June 1942 as 'extreme elements and brigands'. But, less than eighteen months later, the Prime Minister decided, despite the outright opposition of Britain's ally, the Yugoslav government, to withdraw all support from Mihailović and to supply the Partisans with materiel to enable them to prosecute their resistance. This assisted the Allies by tying down Axis forces which would otherwise be deployed in other theatres of the war, but had the inevitable consequence that Yugoslavia would become a communist state after the war. How did this volte-face in policy come about and what information provided the basis for this astonishing change of policy?

The British received intelligence about Yugoslavia during the war from a number of sources. Mihailović established radio contact with his government and this link provided a certain amount of information, albeit entirely from Mihailović's point of view. Reports were received from neutrals who had visited Yugoslavia and from Yugoslavs who had escaped the country. Neutral and Axis wireless station broadcasts, together with those from Radio Free Yugoslavia transmitting from the Soviet Union, were monitored and analysed, as were press reports. But as soon as the organization charged with fostering resistance movements, the Special Operations Executive (SOE), became aware of the revolt, it wanted to know more. It sent liaison officers, initially to Mihailović. But when the British became disenchanted with Mihailović, as they began to perceive his movement was less effective than the Partisans, the SOE sent missions to the Partisans. The first, led by Captain Bill Deakin, was sent to Tito's headquarters in May 1943. He was joined by Brigadier Fitzroy Maclean, a Conservative MP and former diplomat, the following September. Maclean subsequently reported to Anthony Eden, the British Foreign Secretary, and produced his 'blockbuster report', which recommended that the British should transfer support to Tito and sever their links with Mihailović. In the absence until recently of Sigint on Yugoslavia, and in particular of decrypts of signals sent by the *Wehrmacht*'s intelligence service, the *Abwehr*, it has generally been assumed that Maclean's report was the crucial element leading to the change of policy. The vast amount of Sigint relating to wartime Yugoslavia that has now been deposited at the Public Record Office shows that this was not the case.

The German occupying forces, and to a lesser extent the Italians, had little option but to use radio for communications between their units in Yugoslavia and to both the German Army Command in Salonika and the *Oberkommando der Wehrmacht* (OKW – the High Command of the German armed forces). The infrastructure of the country was primitive and was frequently disrupted by the resistance. Radio was, so they thought, a safer and more reliable form of communicating than post or courier. Decrypts were to show that the *Abwehr* had to rely to some extent on pigeons to send messages, probably not terribly dependable but more secure. Bletchley Park was able to decrypt many of the German signals, which led the authors of its internal history of Sigint in Yugoslavia and the Balkans to write in 1945 'that never in the field of Signals Intelligence has so much been decrypted about so little'.

Sigint provided intelligence from many different sources for the policy-makers, not least Churchill, who referred to it as Boniface, the mythical secret agent from whom, for cover purposes, it was supposedly obtained. Before the outbreak of hostilities in Yugoslavia, Bletchley Park had broken German railway Enigma, some air force Enigma ciphers and a very little army Enigma. Some intelligence was forthcoming about German plans for the invasion of Yugoslavia, including the build-up of forces and the exact date and time of the invasion, to the extent that the British were aware when the start time was brought forward, at the eleventh hour, by thirty minutes. After the occupation the amount of decrypted material gradually increased. The army established its headquarters for the Balkans (Army Group E), initially in Athens, and then in Salonika. Bletchley regularly read messages and situation reports passing between the Commander of Army Group E and his subordinate commanders, the German Generals in Zagreb and Belgrade, together with those of the German liaison office with 2nd Italian army, all of whom used Enigma. During 1943, it was also able to read some messages passed on the Fish links (which used teleprinter cipher machines) between Berlin and Salonika and Belgrade, and between Vienna and Salonika, as a result of the development of 'Heath Robinson'. Daily situation reports from Army Group E to Berlin were read regularly. German naval Enigma messages were decrypted, particularly after the Italian capitulation in September 1943 when the German Navy was trying to regain control of the Adriatic islands off the coast of Yugoslavia. *Luftwaffe* Enigma was also decrypted and some Italian Air Force messages using hand ciphers were read. The *Abwehr* had established a presence in Belgrade before the invasion and its radio messages were decrypted. After the occupation of Yugoslavia by the Axis, the *Abwehr* established offices throughout Yugoslavia, which used both hand ciphers and a special version of the Enigma machine to send reports of resistance activity to their area headquarters. Many messages from

Abwehr officers or their agents were read. Others used the *Abwehr* links including the German consul in Dubrovnik, Herr Aelbert. In addition, the Nazi Party's intelligence service, the *Sicherheitsdienst*, operated in Yugoslavia: its messages were read, although in lesser volume than those of the *Abwehr*. In order to try to keep control, the Germans used various arms of their police service, often manned by local ethnic Germans, whose reports by radio were frequently decrypted. By the autumn of 1943, after the Allies had established themselves in southern Italy, a monitoring station was established in Bari, and later on the island of Vis, off the Yugoslav coast, which enabled local traffic between Chetniks, Partisans and Croatian units to be read. This supplemented intelligence from Chetnik and Partisan radio messages, which were summarized in German reports of their own decrypts of intercepted resistance radio messages. Despite Bletchley's own use of the Boniface cover, one of its internal reports described the German efforts to disguise the source of their intelligence, somewhat smugly, as being 'camouflaged rather transparently as information obtained from agents'.

Two other sources were identified and decrypted. Tito and the separate Slovene communist party kept in touch by radio with their masters in Moscow, the Comintern and its Bulgarian Secretary-General, Georgi Dimitrov. The volume of messages intercepted was not great but they yielded significant intelligence and continued with Dimitrov after June 1943, when the Comintern itself was dissolved. For a long time before the outbreak of war, the principal activity of GC&CS had been the decrypting of messages sent between diplomatic missions and their governments. This continued during the war. One of the most useful sources to the British, in terms of German policy in Yugoslavia, was the link between General Oshima Hiroshi, the Japanese ambassador in Berlin, and Tokyo. Oshima frequently reported on his conversations with Hitler and the German Foreign Minister, Joachim von Ribbentrop.

It was realized at a very early stage in the war that the decrypts provided the British with a priceless asset. Every effort was made to protect its security. By 1943, those who received Ultra were far greater in number than the thirty men who were its sole recipients (outside GC&CS and MI6) in 1940. By early 1943, Ultra was being sent to twelve destinations in the Middle East alone. Some of those who received intelligence derived from Sigint were not informed of its source, but as Montgomery's intelligence officer, Brig. E.T. Williams, has written, they must have guessed that it came from wireless intercepts. Nevertheless, some of those responsible for policy, and not just that on Yugoslavia, were denied access to the Bletchley Park material. The SOE in London did not receive any Sigint from any source during the war, let alone Enigma, although its office in Cairo did receive some locally decrypted *Abwehr* material on Yugoslavia in early 1943. MI6 received the decrypts on Yugoslavia. The Military Intelligence section concerned with the Balkans (MI3b) received almost all the relevant decrypts, including diplomatic but not Comintern. The Directorate of Military Operations certainly had summaries from military intelligence. The Joint Intelligence Committee, whose task was to advise the military and the government on major matters of intelligence, had reports based on Sigint, as did the Chiefs of Staff. There were other recipients of Bletchley Park's output of Yugoslav Sigint. The Soviet agent John Cairncross passed some decrypts to the KGB when he was working in Hut 3 at Bletchley and later after being transferred to the MI6 headquarters at Broadway Buildings, which included both *Abwehr* and German Army signals from Yugoslavia. The evidence for this can be found in messages from the Comintern to Tito, giving information that was identical to Bletchley Park decrypts – it is unlikely that the source was the Russians' own decrypts. Thus Tito also benefited from Bletchley's work!

The Foreign Office received some heavily disguised intelligence reports based on Sigint, but did not receive any raw material, other than diplomatic decrypts, until the autumn of 1943. Therefore, the two principal organizations charged with the development of policy towards the Yugoslav resistance – the SOE and the Foreign Office – had either no access, or very limited access, to the decrypts. This inevitably led to much confusion in 1943 between those who wished to continue to support Mihailović – the SOE and the Foreign Office – and those who wanted to switch support to Tito – SOE Cairo, MI6, the Directorates of Military Intelligence and Operations, the Chiefs of Staff and, ultimately, Churchill himself. The dilemma, after months of argument, was only to be resolved by the Prime Minister. Churchill received his daily box of raw decrypts, which frequently included detailed information about the actions of the resistance in Yugoslavia and Axis counter measures. Churchill, using his customary red pen, underlined or ringed items that caught his attention. He was, from time to time, briefed in detail in writing and given advice by military intelligence. He received summaries of decrypts from both military intelligence and air intelligence, some of which have survived, despite being marked 'to be destroyed'. Churchill received regular oral briefings from 'C', and from General Davidson, of which there is no record. It must be presumed that he also received written assessments from MI6, but they have not been released.

Sigint provided a wealth of information about the events that occurred in Yugoslavia as they unfolded. German situation reports provided evidence of the activities of the resistance and of the Axis's attempts to counter them. From the decrypts, it was possible to discern the conflict that amounted to a civil war that raged between the Chetniks and the Partisans from the autumn of 1941 until the end of the war. The opinions held by German military commanders of their allies, the Italians and the Croats in the so-called Independent State of Croatia, were revealed, as were the Germans' own assessments of the Chetniks and the Partisans. The concern of the Germans, including Hitler, to preserve their vital mineral supplies from the Balkans and to keep open communications to Greece, together with their fears that the Allies might invade the Balkans in the summer and autumn of 1943, were described. Decrypts, particularly *Abwehr*, shed much light on the vexed question of collaboration between the resistance and the Axis. The subservience of Tito towards Dimitrov was confirmed. Decrypts also provided material on a lighter note. In April 1943, the *Abwehr* in Dubrovnik asked its office in Sarajevo to use their influence with the Italians on behalf of the owner of the *Zwei Fischer* restaurant to obtain permission for him to fetch a wagonload of wine for his customers.

In June and July 1941, foreign press reports and refugees provided some sketchy evidence that there was unrest in Yugoslavia and that the Serbs in the Independent State of Croatia were being displaced from their homes and killed by the Croats. At the end of July, the first substantive reports of this were received from decrypts. *Abwehr* reports referred to attacks on railway lines and confirmed that Serbs were being shot by the Croats. Italian aircraft were being deployed in Montenegro and in Croatia. German police reports revealed that the communists were making it difficult to maintain law and order along the border with the *Reich*. In early August, the first report was received that German soldiers had been killed and their bodies mutilated. One *Abwehr* report referred to a body of rebels who were well organized and 2,500–3,000 strong and added that, at that time, pacification of Bosnia was out of the question. During September, it was clear that the unrest was continuing. German army reports disclosed that towns were being threatened and that mopping-up operations were being carried out 'to crush the rebellion'. This report was sent to Churchill, who underlined these words in red.

Decrypts in October and November gave the names and locations of the ten Italian divisions based in Yugoslavia. They also disclosed that the Germans had four divisions deployed there. A series of decrypted situation reports provided evidence of the measures being taken by the Germans against guerrillas who were disrupting communications, seizing towns and attacking German, Italian and Croat forces. Decrypts also revealed that there were 'clashes' between Chetniks and Partisans and fighting between them. A decrypt of an *Abwehr* message at the end of November reported a meeting between Croat and Partisan representatives when the Partisans declared 'they would not lay down their arms until the end of the war and that they believed Russia would win in the end'.

The British also had intelligence from Captain D. T. 'Bill' Hudson, an SOE officer who before the war had worked as an engineer in Yugoslavia. He was landed by submarine on the Yugoslav coast in September and briefly visited Tito's headquarters before joining Mihailović. He was able initially to send back reports by radio but after November could not continue to do so for technical reasons and because of a breakdown in relations with Mihailović. Intelligence assessments based on Sigint and Hudson's reports were sent to the Chiefs of Staff who expressed the opinion that 'the revolt was premature but the guerrillas have thrown their caps over the fence and must be supported by all possible means'. The reality was quite different: the British in North Africa were hard pressed and had no materiel to send or the means to send it. A letter from MI6 to MI3b reveals that their view, probably formed from the decrypts, was that Mihailović's forces appeared to be fighting the communists rather than the Germans and that if that were true it was unlikely that the revolt could be maintained. The first doubts about Mihailović were already setting in. Churchill, however, told the Chiefs of Staff on 28 November that 'everything in human power should be done to help the guerrilla fighters in Yugoslavia'. It became clear from the decrypts that, by the end of 1941, the Axis had got the upper hand. Mihailović told his government by radio that he was going to ground. It seemed that for at least the foreseeable future there would be little resistance to the Axis from either the Chetniks or Partisans.

However, decrypts in early 1942 revealed that the Partisans were carrying on the fight. Reports were received of continuing sabotage that necessitated combined operations in January and February by German, Italian and Croat forces against the communists in Bosnia and Herzegovina. A series of situation reports from the German General Glaise von Horstenau, who was attached to the Croat government in Zagreb, revealed that there was resistance activity throughout Croatia and further west in Slovenia. An *Abwehr* officer reported from Sarajevo on 28 February that the Chetniks were being forced out of eastern Bosnia by the Partisans and that 'in future the communists are the only ones to be reckoned with'. At the end of March, a *Luftwaffe* report stated that the situation in the Italian area was becoming steadily worse. Information was sufficient for the officer responsible for the analysis of intelligence from Yugoslavia at MI3b, Major David Talbot Rice, to report that if Mihailović was conserving his forces to strike when the time was right and if he did not receive support from the British, the initiative would pass to the Partisans. MI6 commented that the Partisans' policy was one of all-out offensive.

With the onset of spring, the Partisans continued their resistance. Railway Enigma provided evidence that bans had been imposed on the movements of trains on a number of lines due to sabotage. German army decrypts revealed that a special battle group had been formed to mount a joint operation with the Italians in western Herzegovina 'to smash the resistance as soon as possible'. Churchill continued to read his decrypts and, as a result, was sufficiently interested to ask for a report from General Davidson, which was delivered on 2 June. A map was attached illustrating the reports from Sigint for the five-day period from 26 to 30 May. The Prime Minister was advised that the 'wilder elements' among the Partisans 'embarrassed the enemy' by their attacks, but notwithstanding that Davidson was in no doubt that the British were right in backing Mihailović. Churchill commented 'Good' and asked to be kept informed.

During the course of the summer, decrypts revealed that there were serious disputes between the Germans and the Italians. Von Horstenau reported that the Italians wished to withdraw much of their forces from the hinterland of Herzegovina, Bosnia and Croatia, leaving the Croat armed forces to deal with the resistance. The Germans, as a result, were particularly concerned about the security of supplies from one of their principal sources of bauxite, near Mostar, in Italian-occupied Herzegovina. Von Horstenau also reported that by August the Partisans had seized control of a large area of Croatia, centred on the town of Livno (at its largest, the area they controlled was about the size of Switzerland), and that the Croats would be unable to retake it. Although not revealed by decrypts, Tito was present and in charge of the area. The Commander of Army Group E, General Löhr, reported to OKW in Berlin that 'a really ticklish situation has arisen through the sudden departure of the Italians'. Reports were received of continued sabotage and clashes between the Partisans and the Axis. On 23 August, General Davidson wrote that the bulk of resistance activity was being carried out by the Partisans, but that, in his view, Mihailović was preserving his forces 'to do their part when a general uprising could be staged'.

During September 1942, Hudson was joined by a radio operator. He had been back on speaking terms with Mihailović since the spring but had been granted only limited access to Mihailović's radio. He was now able to send reports more freely, but only from Mihailović's headquarters, and about the Chetniks. This was virtually all the information that the SOE and the Foreign Office received; they decided to send a more senior officer, Colonel Bill Bailey, to join Hudson and to advise them on who to support and on the differences between Mihailović and Tito. Bailey did not arrive until Christmas Day 1942.

In the meantime decrypts provided more intelligence. Von Horstenau demanded that the Italian High Command should take vigorous action to protect the bauxite area. The complete text of a message from the German Supreme Command, incorporating Hitler's decisions following a meeting with the Croat head of government on 23 September, was decrypted. Hitler would not countenance German reinforcements being sent but agreed to further armaments being supplied to the Croat army, now to be placed under German command. Von Horstenau predicted that German soldiers would be 'needlessly sacrificing their blood' unless the Croats proved more capable than they had in the past. Further messages from the German Supreme Command were intercepted, stating that they were putting pressure on the Italians to clean up the Livno area while doubting that they had the means or desire to do so. On 17 October, a message from Hitler to Löhr was intercepted, demanding a full report about an attack on an antimony mine. Löhr then proposed that a joint German–Italian command be established, with himself as commander, and told German Supreme Command that the Italians were refusing to take part in any campaigning against the guerrillas during the winter.

Although not disclosed by decrypts, Hitler was sufficiently concerned about the situation in Yugoslavia to meet the Italian Foreign Minister, Count Ciano, in early December, when it was agreed that joint operations would take place in early 1943 to eliminate first the Partisans and then the Chetniks, who the Germans still feared had the potential to cause them problems. Before the campaign against the Partisans began, decrypts revealed its existence as Operation *Weiss*, and that it would be followed by a similar effort against the Chetniks, Operation *Schwarz*.

During the course of 1943, the volume of decrypts increased enormously. With the tide in the war having turned in the Allies' favour, and with the possibility of the invasion of Italy and Italian capitulation, there was renewed interest in stimulating the Yugoslav revolt. Churchill was sent decrypts relating to *Weiss* while on a visit to the Middle East. In late January, he received the complete German battle orders for *Weiss*; details of the German operational area in Croatia which included the Livno and bauxite areas; and the agreed plans for the disposition of Italian troops. The objective was to surround the Partisans, drive them against a blocking line provided by the Italians and then eliminate them. Churchill must have been excited when he learnt about these plans. At the time, he saw Bill Deakin, his pre-war research assistant who was then working for the SOE in Cairo. The operational head of SOE Cairo, Brigadier Keble, had previously worked for military intelligence in Cairo and was still receiving a limited number of *Abwehr* decrypts, which were analysed by Deakin and his superior officer Basil Davidson. Churchill demanded a report from Keble, who advocated that the Partisans should be contacted.

Talbot Rice reported on the Axis offensive to his superiors in military intelligence, who noted that the Partisans must have been causing the Axis considerable annoyance for them to mount an operation in mid-winter. He advised that if the Axis destroyed the ideological nucleus of the Partisans then it might be possible to reconcile the Partisans and the Chetniks; but if they escaped, their organization would have its prestige and influence enhanced. The decrypts revealed in great detail the progress of *Weiss*. The Partisans offered stiff resistance to the German ground forces and the *Luftwaffe* had to provide bombing support. By 16 February, the first stage of the operation was declared over, but reports indicated that elements of the Partisans had escaped the net, some moving towards the bauxite area and others re-establishing themselves in the cleared areas. Following Keble's report to Churchill, the Chiefs of Staff, who had been sent a copy, decided not to change policy and contact the Partisans, but not before Colonel Bateman of the Directorate of Military Operations had recommended that it was right to support the 'active and vigorous Partisans' rather than the 'dormant and sluggish' Chetniks. However, military intelligence was firmly of the opinion that support for Mihailović should be maintained as were the Foreign Office and the SOE in London. The debate had now commenced in earnest, and decrypts were the only reliable source of information about the Partisans and the actions of the Axis.

The second stage of *Weiss* was now implemented. Decrypts provided evidence that the Partisans from the Livno area and local Partisans were advancing on the bauxite area. The Croat commander in Mostar complained that his forces were inadequately armed; that he was not being assisted by the Italians; and that his left flank was exposed. *Abwehr* decrypts confirmed that neighbouring towns had fallen to the Partisans. Decrypts revealed that proposals from Löhr to the Italians for the conduct of the second phase of *Weiss* were not agreed as the Italians wanted the Germans to provide more forces, which Löhr said he did not have. Decrypts did not reveal how this *impasse* was broken, but Löhr did say that he had used German troops in order to relieve the bauxite area. In fact, Hitler had sent him a directive to move on the bauxite area and temporarily to occupy it, which he did successfully. But the decrypts showed that the Partisans had again largely escaped destruction because once more the Italians had failed to move into position to the south-east of the Germans, allowing the Partisans to move eastwards across Herzegovina towards Montenegro.

The decrypts indicated that the situation on the ground was becoming ever more complex. As the Partisans moved to escape the Germans, the decrypts disclosed that they were confronted by Chetniks who were also intent on their annihilation. The *Abwehr* reported that the Chetniks in Herzegovina and Montenegro were preparing for large-scale operations against the Partisans at the end of March, with all men between the ages of thirteen and sixty being mobilized in the area for this purpose. The decrypts also revealed that there was a close relationship between the Italians and some Chetniks. This was already known to the British as a result of reports from Hudson, but the decrypts showed that the

Italians were seeking the consent of the Germans for the use of Italian-officered Chetnik units against the Partisans. Löhr would not agree, but, as he could not stop the Italian plans, he requested that they make every effort to ensure the Chetniks would not come into contact with Germans advancing from the west, in case Italian officers came under German fire. Decrypts showed that the Italians were supplying the Chetniks with weapons and transporting them in lorries to get into position against the Partisans. In fact, during March the Germans did not advance against the Partisans or attempt any action against the Chetniks. Many years later, it became clear that there had been a ceasefire between the Germans and the Partisans, initially for the exchange of prisoners, but also because the Partisans were negotiating with the Germans for recognition as combatants, and for possible joint action against the Chetniks. Hitler put an end to the negotiations. Two *Abwehr* decrypts had, however, revealed that one of their agents, a German who reported as Dr Baux, was in negotiation with the Partisans, although it was not clear what the negotiations were about.

On 10 March, Talbot Rice prepared an appraisal on *Weiss*. General Davidson consequently advised the Chiefs of Staff and revealed the first signs of doubt about British policy with military intelligence stating that 'it was impossible to advise whether we should stick to our current policy of supporting Mihailović but not the Partisans'. The SOE, military intelligence and the Foreign Office had not been greatly assisted by the reports from Bailey, who had only been able to suggest that the Partisans and the Chetniks should be allocated spheres of activity. Bailey himself accepted this was a forlorn hope. The Chiefs of Staff were provided not only with Talbot Rice's report, but the complete file on *Weiss*. As a result, they decided on 20 March that the Partisans should be contacted, despite opposition from the SOE in London, although to the delight of the SOE in Cairo. During this time, Churchill continued to receive decrypts relating to the major events that were taking place in Yugoslavia and also received a summary of the decrypts from 'C' in March, but the Prime Minister was yet to play a decisive part in the development of British policy.

During the German–Partisan ceasefire, Ultra enabled British intelligence to follow the course of a battle that ensued between the Chetniks and Partisans. In mid-March, a running battle took place along the Neretva river, which the Chetniks were unsuccessfully trying to prevent the Partisans from crossing. A decisive encounter took place around the Montenegrin town of Kalinovik between 20 and 25 March. Bailey had told the SOE that Mihailović had left his headquarters on 16 March without telling Bailey where he was going or for what purpose. Decrypts reported that Mihailović was directing the fight against the Partisans led by Tito around Kalinovik and that the Italians were transporting Chetnik reinforcements to the area. Numerous decrypted signals demonstrated that the fighting was severe. The town fell to the Partisans on 25 March, the battle against the Chetniks having been won. Dr Baux, who was on a mission in the area, reported that Mihailović barely escaped being taken prisoner by the Partisans. Many Montenegrin Chetniks were said to have joined the Partisans, whose numbers in the area were estimated at 30,000. By early April, some of the Partisans were reported by the *Abwehr* to have reached the area in Montenegro around Mount Durmitor, having engaged Italian forces and put them to flight. They were said to have captured large quantities of food, arms, including heavy mortars, and ammunition. On 21 April, the first message from 'Walter' (Tito) to the head of the Comintern was intercepted by the British, although it was not decrypted until many months later. Tito claimed that a large number of regions were under Partisan control and that they were now organizing in the towns and villages in Herzegovina and Montenegro. The *Abwehr* reported that Tito, whose existence was mentioned in their messages, had established his headquarters near Foca.

A report, based on decrypts, was prepared for General Davidson and the Chiefs of Staff by MI3b on 23 April. It advised that Mihailović had gravely prejudiced his long-term position by mobilizing his men for the campaign against the Partisans, and had lost command of Herzegovina and probably Montenegro. It concluded that, despite 200 miles of running battle with German forces, the Partisans had retained sufficient vigour and organization to defeat the Chetniks decisively, that the Germans were still trying to complete the destruction of the Partisans, and that Mihailović and his Chetniks were in danger of becoming further identified with the Axis.

Decrypts also revealed the details of Operation *Schwarz* against the Chetniks. On 2 May, a message sent by General Alfred Jodl, Head of Operations at OKW, to Löhr on Hitler's instructions was intercepted. The operation was to be kept secret from the Italians, as they were not trusted to keep its existence from the Chetniks. An incident would be engineered to justify the Germans moving into Italian-occupied Herzegovina and Montenegro; the Chetniks would be rounded up and placed in prison camps rather than annihilated, as had been the plan with the Partisans in *Weiss*. *Abwehr* decrypts disclosed that fighting was still going on between Partisans and Chetniks and that one of Mihailović's principal commanders, Pavle Djurisić, had fallen out with Mihailović as he wished to assist the Germans against the Partisans, a course of action Mihailović refused to contemplate. The Italians were still supplying the Chetniks and providing transport. On 13 May, the fabricated report that Chetniks had attacked German forces was decrypted as were subsequent German negotiations with the Italians who tried to protect as many of the Chetniks as they could when it became clear that the Germans were moving into their territory. The Germans advanced into Montenegro, taking Chetniks prisoner and disarming them. Decrypts showed that the German forces were also trying to surround and destroy the Partisans (including Tito) now concentrated around Mount Durmitor. As the Germans closed in, Deakin and an MI6 officer, a Captain Hunter, parachuted in to join Tito. Decrypts revealed that for the first time the Partisans were effectively surrounded and were at real risk of being wiped out. *Abwehr* and German army decrypts referred to the bitter fighting and repeated bombing of the Partisans. The battle was over by 14 June but it soon became clear, from the decrypts, that once again a substantial body of Partisans had escaped and that Tito had given orders that they should disperse and reform near Jajce in Bosnia. A decrypted report from Löhr on 22 June reported to the German High Command that 583 German soldiers and 7,489 Partisans had been killed, with the probability that the Partisans had lost another 4,000 men. Chetnik losses were put at 17, with nearly 4,000 taken prisoner. The contrast between the two resistance movements was stark.

Churchill had been kept informed from his own reading of the decrypts and no doubt from briefings. By this time the Allies had decided, at the Trident Conference in Washington in May 1943, that the second front would be launched across the Channel in 1944, but that Sicily could be invaded during that summer with further operations in the Mediterranean if subsequently agreed. Churchill argued in a note circulated at the end of the Conference for the occupation of southern Italy, which would enable munitions and commandos to be sent across the Adriatic to Yugoslavia. On 12 June, after reading his decrypts, he asked for a report from the intelligence services on Yugoslavia. At the time a debate was still raging as to whether the British should provide assistance to the Partisans now that they had been contacted. Probably due to incompetence, the report was prepared by the Foreign Office and the SOE in London, neither of whom had access to Sigint. It recommended the continuation of whole-hearted support for Mihailović, with contact with the Partisans being limited to trying to reconcile the two groups. The Chiefs of Staff wrote to the Foreign Office that they felt the report had given 'insufficient weight to the value of the Partisans as a fighting force against the Axis'. They stated that it was clear from 'information available to the War Office from *Most Secret Sources* that the Chetniks were hopelessly compromised with their relations with the Axis in Herzegovina and Montenegro and that . . . as the most formidable anti-Axis element outside Serbia the Partisans deserve the strongest support'. In their reply the Foreign Office grudgingly climbed down, agreeing to supplies being sent to the Partisans if the Chiefs of Staff were 'satisfied from information at their disposal' that the Partisans were sufficiently well organized and they would not hamper British efforts to unify the resistance.

Churchill had had enough: he summoned a meeting on 22 June to discuss Yugoslavia, stating: 'All this is of the highest importance.' He had also received that day the decrypt of the report by Löhr on Partisan and Chetnik losses. The meeting concluded that military assistance could be sent to the Partisans and support maintained for Mihailović subject to conditions that he must actively offer resistance and refrain from collaboration with the Italians. Churchill now had the bit between his teeth. Three days before the invasion of Sicily, on 7 July, he sent a message to the British commander, General Alexander, saying that he presumed he had read the 'Boniface' about the heavy fighting in Yugoslavia. He also urged the seizing of the mouth of the Adriatic so that ships could be run into Dalmatian and Greek ports, although he recognized that 'this was hunting in the next field'. On 11 July, the Prime Minister, no doubt having chewed the cud further, instructed that a 2,000–3,000-word digest be made of the Sigint reports about Yugoslavia, Albania and Greece, 'showing the great disorder going on in these regions'. The digest is unfortunately not available, but after its receipt Churchill felt so impressed by its contents that he cabled Alexander to say that 'it gave a full account of the marvellous resistance by the followers of Tito and the powerful cold-blooded manoeuvres of Mihailović in Serbia'.

Left: Alan Turing, the mathematical genius who designed the British bombe, and was a co-signatory of the Trafalgar day letter to Churchill.

National Portrait Gallery

Below: Hugh Alexander, a leading Bletchley Park codebreaker (later the head of Hut 8) and co-signatory of the letter.

Sir Michael Alexander

Above: Gordon Welchman, the first head of Hut 6, and co-signatory of the letter.

Gordon Welchman

Right: Stuart Milner-Barry, a Bletchley Park codebreaker (who succeeded Gordon Welchman as the head of Hut 6), and co-signatory of the letter.

Lady Milner-Barry

John Tiltman (right) with Alastair Denniston, the original head of the Government Code and Cypher School (left) and Professor E. R. P. Vincent.

Barbara Eachus

Above: The GC&CS diplomatic and commercial codebreaking operations at 7–9 Berkeley Street, London.

National Archives, College Park, Md

Right: Members of 'Captain Ridley's Shooting Party' arriving at Bletchley Park.

Barbara Eachus

Above: Mavis and Keith Batey, who worked on the *Abwehr* 'counter' Enigma machine (below). Mavis and Keith Batey

Below: The *Schlüsselgerät* 41, invented by Fritz Menzer, which replaced some *Abwehr* Enigmas in late 1944.
NSA Center for Cryptologic History

Above: *Abwehr* Enigma machine (with 'counter' and *Umkehrwalze* that moved when enciphering). David Hamer

Below: Dilly Knox, the veteran codebreaker who broke a number of important codes and cipher machines, including the *Abwehr* 'counter' Enigma (left). Mavis Batey

Below left: Hugh Foss, who was the first person at GC&CS to solve Enigma, in the form of the C model, and also broke the pre-war Japanese naval attaché cipher machine.
Charles G. Foss

Above: Enigma C, known to GC&CS as the 'index machine'.
Public Record Office HW 25/6

Above left: John Chadwick, who solved Italian naval codes in Cairo, and later became a Japanese translator at Bletchley Park. Tony Chadwick

Above right: Rolf Noskwith, who worked on naval Enigma in Hut 8. Rolf Noskwith

Left: Shaun Wylie (who worked on 'Tunny') marrying Odette Murray (then a Wren at Bletchley Park also working on 'Tunny'), in April 1944. Shaun Wylie

Above: Lorenz *Schlüsselzusatz* SZ42 'Tunny' teleprinter cipher attachment, with cover removed. Wolfgang Mache

Above: Colossus, the world's first electronic semi-programmable computer, operational at Bletchley Park from December 1943. It was used to break 'Tunny'. Bletchley Park Trust

Left: Derek Taunt, who was later a codebreaker in Hut 6, at Jesus College, Cambridge, in June 1939. Derek Taunt

Below left: James Thirsk, log reader in 'Sixta', the traffic analysis section of Hut 6. James Thirsk

Above right: Part of Duenna, the US Navy machine which was used to break *Umkehrwalze D*. National Archives, College Park, Md

Right: Wiring core of the rewirable *Umkehrwalze D*, with pin removed. If 'D' had been used properly by the *Luftwaffe* in 1944, it would have dried up Hut 6 Ultra. Philip Marks

Above: US Navy four-rotor bombe, with WAVE. Note the eight vertical banks of Enigma rotors. National Archives, College Park, Md

Left: HMS Anderson, the British intercept and codebreaking site outside Colombo, which intercepted Japanese communications during the Second World War and remained in place into the Cold War, working on Soviet traffic. Public Record Office HW4/3

Right: British three-rotor bombe in the GC&CS outstation at Eastcote, North London. National Archives, College Park, Md

TOP ~~MOST~~ SECRET ULTRA

TO BE KEPT UNDER LOCK AND KEY AND NEVER TO BE REMOVED FROM THE OFFICE
THIS FORM IS TO BE USED FOR AIR INTELLIGENCE MESSAGES ONLY.

A.I. FORM No. 1479

NR. No.	GR. No.		OFFICE SERIAL No.
DATE	TIME OF RECEIPT	TIME OF DESPATCH	SYSTEM

TO

FROM

SENDER'S No.

CX/MSS/T207/41

(T.O.O. 0800/6/6/44) KV/6624

TIME OF DESPATCH 8am 6.6.44

W E S T E U R O P E

UNSIGNED STAMPED ~~0800~~ 8am/6/6 :-

1) ENEMY LANDED WITH STRONG FORCES BETWEEN DIEPPE AND CHERBOURG.

2) ALL-OUT OPERATION NECESSARY.

3) 5 F123 TO EXTEND ITS OWN COASTAL RECCE TO LE HAVRE.
4 F 123 COASTAL RECCE IN THE AREA AS ALREADY ORDERED. RECCE AS OWN COMMITMENT OF PARACHUTE LANDING NEAR MEZIDON.

4) NAG 13 SUBORDINATED TO FLIEGERKORPS (ROMAN) II WITH IMMEDIATE EFFECT. PROJECTED THAT 1 F 121 TAKE OVER TASKS OF NAG 13.

NOTE:

ABOVE ALMOST CERTAINLY FROM F 123.

DISTRIBUTION:

DEGREE OF PRIORITY	TIME OF ORIGIN	SIGNATURE OF ORIGINATOR. NOT TO BE TELEPRINTED	OPERATOR'S RECEIPT

A Hut 3 report of an Enigma decrypt as sent to Churchill, of the German message reporting that the allies had landed on D-Day.

Public Record Office HW 1/2895

Having set out for Alexander the numbers of Axis divisions deployed, he wrote that, in his opinion, 'great progress lay in the Balkan direction'. Churchill was sufficiently enthused with the report to direct that a copy should be delivered by hand to Alexander. Churchill agreed to upgraded missions being sent to both Tito's and Mihailović's headquarters. He personally briefed Fitzroy Maclean, who was being sent to the Partisans, dubbing him an 'ambassador leader'. But the Prime Minister clearly cared not one jot who was to be sent to the Chetniks. While he had not finally made up his mind whether to withdraw support from the Chetniks, it was clear that he was set on a course to provide the Partisans with the maximum support possible, whatever the political consequences for postwar Yugoslavia.

In the meantime, a message from Dimitrov to Tito in early July advised the Partisan leader to conserve his forces for future decisive fighting – a clear indication of the level of control exercised over him by Moscow. *Abwehr* decrypts indicated that Partisan groups were indeed making their way westwards from Mount Durmitor. During July, message after message was decrypted which indicated that the Germans feared an Allied invasion of the Balkans. The *Abwehr* advised Löhr that the Balkans would be 'the main object of an Allied attack'. The German Foreign Ministry advised its Consul in Istanbul that 'the Balkans would be the first to be invaded'. The head of the Italian Secret Service, General Cesare Amè, advised his German opposite number (he was not named in the decrypt but this was presumably Admiral Wilhelm Canaris, head of the *Abwehr*) that if Italy capitulated the Allies would turn their attention on the Balkans – his fears may have come about as a result of British disinformation. The possibility that the Germans feared Italian collapse was confirmed in a decrypted message from Ambassador Oshima to his government in Tokyo on 26 July, when he advised that Hitler had told him 'he recognised the possibility of Italian collapse and was preparing for the worst; and that Germany must strengthen her defences in the Balkans'. The Allies invaded southern Italy on 3 September. The final decision not to invade the Balkans had been taken at an Allied Conference in Quebec in August, which also decided that the Allies' involvement in that part of the world would be limited to supplying arms to the guerrillas, bombing strategic objectives, and minor commando raids.

Prior to this, the decrypts revealed that the Italians were effecting a withdrawal and that the Germans were positioning their limited forces to try to prevent a vacuum which could be exploited by the resistance or the Allies. On 7 August, the German Consul in Dubrovnik reported that the Italians were withdrawing from the hinterland and were moving Chetniks into position to cover their retreat. The German liaison officer with the Italian 2nd Army advised that his impression was that they were making 'a planned evacuation little by little'. *Abwehr* reports indicated that the Italians were offering arms to Chetniks to cover their withdrawal. Messages from the German naval commander were decrypted, which revealed his plans to seize Italian naval installations and ports. The German plans for re-organizing their army commands in north Italy and the Balkans were read. Decrypts disclosed movement of German forces into the Italian zone, and the occupation of Italian airfields. Some Chetniks, seeing the way the wind was blowing, sought to collaborate with the Germans. Intercepted reports from Dr Baux detailed the negotiations that he was having with the Chetnik leader in Herzegovina, Jevdjević, who was offering to deploy 5,000–6,000 Chetniks in co-operation with the Germans against the Partisans. A *Sicherheitsdienst* report confirmed what the British also thought from their intelligence, that Mihailović would only act if and when the Allies invaded the Balkans.

On 9 September, Italy capitulated. A decrypt of a message from the German Foreign Ministry announced that Hitler had foreseen

Italy's collapse, that all measures had been taken and that German troops were marching. German Army Commander South East claimed on 12 September that 'the south east is firmly in our hands'. The decrypts revealed that the reality was different. The SS Prinz Eugen Division, recruited from local ethnic Germans, reported encountering stiff resistance from Italian forces who refused to surrender, although in Dubrovnik, the consul Aelbert signalled that after negotiations 28,000 Italians had decided not to fight. An earlier decrypt of a message sent by Aelbert to the commanding officer of the Prinz Eugen Division shed light on some of its activities. Aelbert complained that those reported to him included the shooting of '25 children as young as eight months', which he described as 'counterproductive' and 'having an extremely bad effect on the population'. The Prinz Eugen Division then fought a sixteen-day battle with Italian troops as it tried to move along the coast to take Split. In Montenegro, decrypts revealed that the Germans fought battles with the Italians until November. Decrypts also disclosed the actions of the resistance. The Partisans seized Split from the Italians, capturing large quantities of arms and supplies, and were joined by many Italians. On the German approach to the town, the Partisans moved away, the *Abwehr* reporting that Tito then intended to carry out 'major operations' in north Croatia and Slovenia. An *Abwehr* officer voiced the opinion, in a report on 21 September, that the 'total situation' in Croatia had got worse as a result of the actions of the Partisans. But decrypts also revealed that the Germans had largely dealt with the Italian problem by mid-October, when a report revealed that over 10,000 Italian officers and a quarter of a million men were being removed from Yugoslavia. There were no reports of Chetnik activity. The British knew from their liaison officers that Mihailović had told his men not to carry out sabotage or engage the Germans. Decrypts also disclosed that the Germans were moving their killing squads, the *Einsatzgruppen*, into the former Italian zone to seize Jews and others.

Decrypts between Tito and Dimitrov subsequently revealed the Partisan leader's complaints that the British had not informed him of the date of Italian capitulation and that the British sent spies to the Partisans rather than supplies – a view that at that time was entirely correct, Maclean having arrived to join Deakin on 18 September. They also revealed that Dimitrov had told Tito the Russians would be sending him a mission. Tito's immediate response was to send a shopping list, including a request for 'several tens of suits for our generals and colonels'. Shortly afterwards, Dimitrov rebuked Tito for sending over-long reports.

At the end of September, Talbot Rice prepared a detailed assessment. He confirmed that there had been only isolated anti-German activity by Mihailović, but that 'the heroes of the hour are undoubtedly the Partisans', who had seized large stretches of the coast. He advised that the Partisans were successfully embarrassing the Germans and that their 'military efforts deserve all the support we can give them'. He further recommended Mihailović should be told to destroy German lines of communication in Serbia and be warned that if he failed to do so, Tito would be the sole recipient of British aid which they were at long last in a position to deliver. In the space of six months, the evidence from Sigint had completely changed the view of Talbot Rice, and MI3b.

Churchill was still very much interested in what was happening in Yugoslavia. On 9 September he minuted the Chiefs of Staff that, with the capture of southern Italy, munitions could soon be sent to the resistance. Although not now available, MI3b prepared a report for the Prime Minister on 12 October, no doubt on the same lines as their assessment at the end of September. Churchill was told by 'C' that the SOE had been asked to report on the provision of supplies to the resistance.

Numerous decrypts during October showed the continuing disorder in Yugoslavia and the Germans' attempts to counter it. German army and police reports referred to the Partisan threat to the major towns of Ljubljana and Zagreb and their interruption to railways radiating from the towns. Communists were resisting the German advance in Slovenia. A major operation was launched by the Germans in the area between Zagreb, Ljubljana and the Italian border at Trieste. According to German reports, the operation resulted in the death of 3,200 Partisans by mid-November. The German commanders launched a series of operations to clear the Partisans from the remaining stretches of coast that they held, and from the Adriatic islands from which they threatened German shipping and supply routes. These operations were followed in detail by Bletchley Park. Air intelligence sent Churchill a breakdown of German efforts to capture the islands compiled from the decrypts. The German Admiral in the Adriatic reported their efforts as 'unsatisfactory'. Decrypts disclosed that the Germans were carrying out further operations to try and keep the bauxite flowing and at least gain control of communications in Herzegovina and Montenegro.

At the end of October, Churchill was sent a further assessment by MI3b, advising him in detail on the situation and concluding that 'the Partisans had been able to take over the initiative over practically all of Yugoslavia'. Mihailović was not mentioned except for the fact that in Montenegro some of his supporters had deserted to the Partisans as 'the more active body'. More reports were received of Chetnik collaboration, the most significant of which was the full text of a treaty signed by one of Mihailović's principal commanders, Lukacević, and the German Commander South East. Lukacević agreed a cessation of hostilities in his area of southern Serbia and joint action against the Partisans. A full copy of the treaty was sent to Churchill.

Maclean delivered his report to Anthony Eden on 7 November, recommending all-out support for the Partisans. This had been the view of military intelligence since at least the end of September, when Talbot Rice's report backed the Partisans, and had also very probably been the view of MI6 for some time. The

Chiefs of Staff advised Churchill on 11 November that measures to support the Partisans should be intensified. The question of what to do about Mihailović had still to be decided. Churchill took the decision to abandon him and his movement. He announced his decision to Stalin – much to his surprise – and Roosevelt at the Tehran Conference at the end of November 1943. The existence of the principal source of Churchill's intelligence could not be revealed – hence the publicity given to Maclean's report – although it told Churchill nothing he did not already know. In fact, the Prime Minister was better informed than Maclean, who knew little of the detail of events over a wide area of Yugoslavia or of the Lukacević treaty. In order to justify the decision to Parliament, to Allied governments, particularly those in exile, and to the press, Mihailović was told to blow up two important bridges in Serbia or lose British support. As expected, he failed to act and British liaison officers were withdrawn from the Chetniks. At the same time a delegation from Tito arrived in Cairo to negotiate with the Yugoslav government-in-exile. The delegation was able to seek instructions from Tito by radio. Dimitrov advised Tito on the negotiations and how the delegation should play its hand. A series of decrypts revealed the exact advice given, particularly on the issue of the future of King Peter. Dimitrov advised Tito 'to show a necessary flexibility with reference to the question of the king to overcome certain difficulties on the side of the British and the Americans in the matter of their material assistance'.

It has been alleged by a number of commentators that 'a conspiracy' at SOE Cairo, having revealed the successes of the Partisans to Churchill, seduced him on to a path that was to lead to all-out support for the Partisans. It has been suggested that James Klugman, a communist activist and KGB agent, who joined SOE Cairo in 1942, was the 'agent of influence' and prime mover behind the decision to back the Partisans rather than the Chetniks. However, in response to these 'wild accusations',

Ralph Bennett, a former duty officer in Hut 3 at Bletchley, and Sir William Deakin and others later put forward the view that Sigint had provided the facts which persuaded Churchill, on military grounds and military grounds alone, to choose Tito in place of Mihailović. It is now indeed clear from the decrypts that the Prime Minister was well aware of what was happening before he saw Deakin and Keble in Cairo and, while interested in what they had to say, was not manoeuvred into ultimate support for the Partisans by anything that emanated from SOE Cairo.

Churchill addressed the House of Commons for the first time in six months on 22 February 1944. He dealt with the situation in Yugoslavia at length. He was unable to justify the decision by reference to the decrypts and the advice he had received based on them, and therefore referred to reports received from Deakin and Maclean. In his peroration he advised that:

> Our feelings, here, as elsewhere, I should like the House to see, follow the principle of keeping good faith with those who keep good faith with us, and of striving, without prejudice or regard for political affections, to aid those who strike for freedom against Nazi rule and thus inflict the greatest injury on the enemy.

With these few words, Churchill publicly dismissed Mihailović and the Chetniks, and embraced Tito and the Partisans. The Partisans continued to harry the enemy, although the Germans were able to keep the bauxite flowing and to keep major communications routes open, allowing their forces in Greece to complete an orderly withdrawal in 1945. The Partisans won the civil war and seized power in the immediate aftermath of German surrender. They hunted down Mihailović and captured him. After a show trial he was shot in 1946.

14

Traffic Analysis: A Log-reader's Tale

JAMES W. THIRSK

Introduction

In Chapter 14, James Thirsk introduces us to the art of traffic analysis – the study of signals to gain intelligence from them without actually reading them.

Traffic analysis using Heer *and* Luftwaffe *signals got off to a very slow start at Bletchley, largely because GC&CS had no suitable intelligence team until Enigma decrypts became available in January 1940. The services were ill-equipped to carry out traffic analysis in the first months of the war, and could not even determine whether one major radio net carried* Heer *or* Luftwaffe *traffic. When Ultra established that it was a* Luftwaffe *net, it was a shock to MI8 to find that virtually all of the Army's fixed intercept receivers had been intercepting traffic which was really an RAF responsibility.*

Intercept stations had two functions: providing 'wireless telegraphy intelligence' (WTI, as traffic analysis was then known), and gathering intercepts for GC&CS. But since no one had decided which should take priority – and therefore who controlled intercept tasks – the stations were almost rudderless. When Josh Cooper, the head of Air Section, suggested that an RAF station should take Enigma, the head of the RAF Y service told him 'My Y Service exists to produce intelligence, not to provide stuff for people at Bletchley to fool about with.' A sub-committee of the 'Y' Committee eventually decided in mid-1941 that WTI and cryptanalysis formed an indivisible whole, and that there was no conflict between them. But the debate rumbled on.

As Cooper pointed out, deriving intelligence about the enemy's intentions from traffic analysis must be carried out very carefully indeed, since it is 'a difficult and dangerous art': cryptanalysts who make false deductions can produce little or nothing, but 'anybody with a flair for detective work can produce theories based on undecypherable traffic and nobody can contradict him'. Good traffic analysis in that wider sense could too easily be thwarted by efficient defensive and offensive radio deception. As the Allies were to find out, the fact that radio traffic did not increase significantly before the Ardennes offensive in December 1944 did not mean that the Germans were not massing the troops to launch it.

In May 1943 a senior member of GC&CS told William Friedman, the legendary American codebreaker, that inference 'solely based upon radio studies is of doubtful value', but 'intelligence concerning the enemy's W/T network and procedures is extremely important'. James Thirsk deals with the latter kind of traffic analysis, and describes the roles of units such as Hut 6's Fusion Room in building a full picture of the complex German radio nets. The humble intercept operators also played an important part in traffic analysis. Their analytic input could be of crucial importance, especially when the Germans made major changes in communications security, as with the introduction by the Luftwaffe *of a new call-sign book on 1 April 1944, just weeks before D-Day.*

RE

As the train steamed into Quorn and Woodhouse station in Leicestershire I wondered whether I had been wise to volunteer for the Intelligence Corps. 'Never volunteer', the old soldiers used to say. But I read one day in Army Council instructions that 'Men with suitable qualifications are required for transfer to the Intelligence Corps'. No more details were offered. Several months later, after two interviews in London, here I was, in April 1942, arriving alone at the little railway station with all my worldly goods, including a heavy kitbag, gas mask, steel helmet and a small suitcase full of books. Outside the station, a young woman from the Auxiliary Territorial Service (ATS), the women's section of the army, was waiting for me in a jeep. I had been told to report to Beaumanor, a large country house less than a mile from the station. As the jeep passed through the imposing gateway, winding its way down a long drive, bordered by ancient trees, I wondered whether I was arriving at the secret headquarters of British Intelligence.

In the entrance hall of this large Victorian mansion, built in the Elizabethan style, I was greeted by Lieutenant Rodney Bax. We sat on a long sofa on a landing at the top of the main staircase. 'I expect you're wondering what you've let yourself in for, Bombardier Thirsk?' he said. After a few enquiries about my civilian job and my army service, he explained that the unit I had joined was a branch of MI8, known as the Central Party, and that its job was to analyse German and other wireless signals or 'traffic'. He explained that at many places all over Great Britain, hundreds of men and women, trained in the Morse code, listened and wrote down on pads of paper everything they heard on different wireless frequencies. These records were called logs and our job was to study this traffic, hoping to construct pictures of German Army and Air Force formations. 'We do not deal with naval traffic,' he added. 'The intercept operators, as we call them, also write down messages on a separate pad which are in cipher,' he said. When I enquired whether the ciphers were broken, he told me that there had been occasional successes with simple ciphers but that we were not concerned with cryptography. He was a good liar. It was not until nearly ten months later that we log-readers were told that the 'impregnable' German Enigma machine ciphers were being regularly decrypted. Lieutenant Bax told me that one of the intercept stations was at Beaumanor, buried away in huts and buildings in the grounds. Some logs came from other intercept stations by despatch rider.

At Beaumanor, we received no training in the art of log-reading. 'I'm afraid that we have to throw you in at the deep end,' said Bax. 'But for a few days you will be working alongside Corporal Newte.' During the following month, I gradually picked up the skill of scanning the logs and picking out the important items. Each separate unit in a German Army or Air Force group used an identifying label, known as a call sign, when sending or receiving traffic. This consisted of a mixture of letters and figures, usually three in number: for example TR7, VLU, 4BK. To outwit enemies intercepting traffic, call signs were changed daily, according to a printed programme.

The German Army and Air Force during the Second World War used five printed call-sign books which they named B, C, D, E and F. Each book contained thousands of call signs, arranged in columns and rows so that a station, knowing the row and column which had been allocated to it, could select its correct call sign for the day. Book B, known to the log-readers as the 'Bird book', was used by the German Air Force from the beginning of the war until 1 April 1944, when it was superseded by Book F (Fox). The Central Party, during 1940–1, before it moved to Beaumanor, had already largely reconstructed the Bird book, by studying the call signs over a whole year. We used a well-thumbed copy daily to identify stations on our networks. It was always missing from the control table in the log-room and a familiar cry would be heard again and again: 'Has anyone seen the Bird book?' A German copy was captured in Libya in December 1941. The other call-sign books C, D, E and F were not used so frequently by the Germans. When the German Army began to encipher call signs in November 1944 we were unable to identify networks by predicting changes of call signs until March 1945, when a copy of the German instructions for enciphering call signs was captured. This information was also of great value to the intercept stations, enabling them again to identify networks even if they had changed frequencies.

The organization responsible for investigating all enemy and neutral communication during the Second World War was known as the Y service. It was responsible for monitoring or intercepting signals, for direction finding (DF) and for the decryption of low-grade ciphers and for plain language traffic. The intercept operators often became so familiar with the 'fist' of a German transmitting in the Morse code that they would make a note on the log, telling us that the German operator today was the same man who had used a different call sign yesterday. One added a note: 'Italian operator' on the log, having allegedly recognized a Latin rhythm in the Morse transmission.

Although some stations intercepted foreign radio signals before the war, many more were needed to cope with the flood of traffic as soon as the war started. Men and women in the Post Office, familiar with the Morse code, having worked in the old telegraphic service, were recruited. But, as many more were needed, it was necessary to train hundreds and later thousands of men and women. The women in the WAAF and the ATS far outnumbered the male soldiers and airmen. Some civilian men and women also joined the service.

The intercept operator's job was arduous: working around the clock on a three- or four-shift timetable, they sat for hour after hour with headphones, transcribing the Morse signals as they arrived. Often atmospheric conditions were poor, stations drifted from their frequencies, other transmitters were heard overlapping and signals faded. Great concentration and patience were essential and the operators had no idea whether their efforts were of any value or not. Beaumanor was one of the largest intercept stations. There were a number of camouflaged buildings, one of them disguised as a cricket pavilion, and spread around the grounds were the wireless masts bearing the aerials. By the end of the war, more than a thousand intercept operators worked at Beaumanor; there were many other such stations in different parts of the country.

At the top of each log, written in pencil on sheets from red printed pads, appeared the operator's initials or codename, the date, the frequency covered, the time of interception and the call signs indicating who was calling whom. Below were written any preambles to messages and the 'chat', which was the name given to everything heard on a frequency other than ciphered messages. 'Keying', usually in the form of a series of letter Vs in the Morse code (...-) was used to maintain contact between stations in the intervals between messages. Also appearing on the log were messages in the Q Code, an international three-letter code with the first letter always the Morse for Q (- -.-). The Germans in the main kept to the standard international meanings; for example, QCB meant 'you are causing delay by answering out of turn'. QSA was 'What is my signal strength?' The reply QSA 5 meant that the signal strength was good, and QSA 1 that it was poor.

The logs were passed to the Central Party, where they were sorted by frequency and allocated to the different groups of log-readers, each studying a section of the German Air Force and Army networks. We never used the terms 'traffic analyst' or 'traffic analysis': we were log-readers reading logs. At the beginning of a shift, each log-reader would collect the logs for his or her networks (there could be as many as a hundred) from a pigeon-hole. The logs were first checked to see if there were any messages in clear German. The next job was checking that all the logs bore the same frequency and were therefore recording the traffic of the same German group or network. Sometimes a log-reader might be studying two or three smaller groups using different frequencies. The Bird book was then used to check all the call signs on the logs, equating those in use yesterday with those in use today.

The most common type of operational group in the German Army or Air Force was in the form of a star (*Stern* in German). This was a group of stations with a headquarters (control) and two or more outstations. In some cases, the outlying stations were allowed to contact each other direct. Another type was in the form of a circle (*Kreis* in German). Here, three or more stations, usually of equal status, communicated with each other. The log-readers drew network diagrams on proforma sheets to show the stations using a particular radio net with lines drawn between various stations that communicated with each other and arrows depicting each message and the direction in which it was being sent. In the mornings, headquarters often checked outstations in turn to make sure that they were awake and alert. We were asked by the cryptanalysts to look out for messages at regular times in the mornings or evenings. These were usually situation reports, which often had standard opening phrases like '*Morgenmeldung*' (morning report) in cipher. This could help the cryptanalysts to decrypt the message by providing a crib. Below the network diagram we wrote notes about the activities of the stations on the radio network during the past twenty-four hours. We also noted any unusual flow of traffic, whatever the direction, and any changes from normal procedure.

Each week, we would compile a weekly report about the networks we were studying. Each one, placed in a folder bearing the name of the group, was passed to the Fusion Room, where the staff identified the individual stations of each group from further information contained in decrypted Enigma messages. Details were then sent to Major Morrison's group, who recorded information in indexes and also diagrammatically on a wall map, which was kept up to date by continuous alterations, additions or

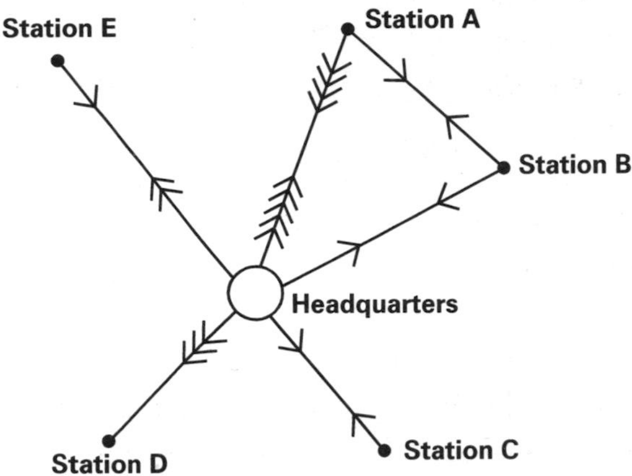

Figure 14.1
Network diagram showing the number and flow of messages passing between a headquarters and its outstations on a *Stern* (star) radio net.

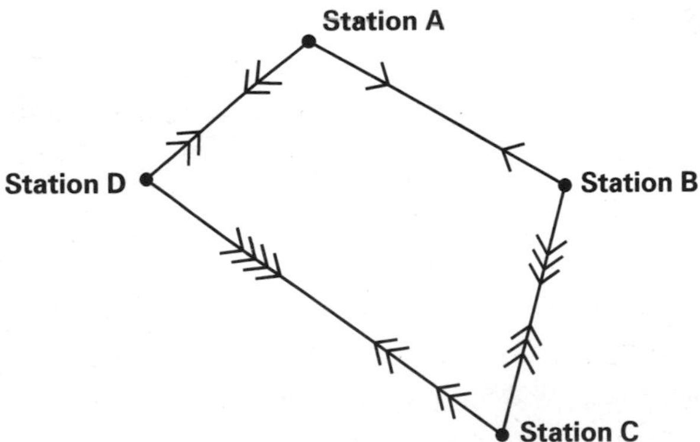

Figure 14.2
Network diagram showing the number and flow of messages passing between stations on a *Kreis* (circle) radio net.

deletions. The dispositions of German Army and Air Force formations were therefore available at any time.

Having written the weekly reports I would get a day off-duty, which I would spend perhaps in London, Oxford, Cambridge or Bedford. Trips to the theatre or the cinema, spending hours in the bookshops, a meal at my favourite restaurant, 'Au petit coin de France', in Camberley Street, Soho, were always welcome breaks from the logs, call signs and frequencies. At times the working days were long and the nights were longer. It was always a relief in the middle of the night to down pencils, stumble across the park in complete darkness and enjoy a cooked dinner in the brightly lit cafeteria, thronged with men and women from other departments.

We log-readers, about fifty in number, mostly non-commissioned officers in the army, were not allowed to go into the Fusion Room. The officers, a few NCOs and some civilians who worked there would sometimes emerge to consult us about the traffic on the networks on which we were working; they sometimes asked questions about the weekly reports we had sent in. Activities were going on which, in the interests of security, could obviously not be revealed. Among ourselves we used to talk about these mysteries, wondering whether the German messages in cipher were being decrypted. But we toiled on in our blinkered fashion, blind to the wider picture known only to those working in the forbidden rooms.

We moved from Beaumanor to Bletchley Park on 3 May 1942. Several large army trucks carried us and all the office furniture and equipment from Leicestershire to Buckinghamshire. Here was another Victorian mansion set in extensive grounds, with formal gardens now ruined by the addition of long huts. Into one of these we unloaded our precious cargo. At the end of the log-readers' hut was another forbidden room out of bounds to us. Among senior staff at Bletchley Park there were some who thought that the log-readers should never be told that German Enigma ciphers were being decrypted. However, wiser counsels prevailed. It was decided that the work of traffic analysis would be more efficient if the log-readers knew more about the German networks they were studying. On 23 January 1943, Gordon Welchman therefore gathered all the log-readers together and told us the full story of the breaking of this machine cipher.

It was a memorable day for all of us, since our log-reading had often been a boring occupation. Now we had a new zest for the work, with access to a wealth of information about the German networks we were studying. Before we were told about Enigma we were trying to construct a picture with a jigsaw lacking many pieces; now we were allowed to see some of the English translations of German messages, which gave us information about who sent the messages, where they were located and what was their function.

The role of the Fusion Room, which was now a section of Hut 6, became clear to us. Its job was to fuse two lots of information. Workers in the room had to study all messages in German together with the reports of the log-readers. With knowledge of the whereabouts of any German transmitter, derived from direction-finding reports, it was possible to construct and keep up to date knowledge of German Army and Air Force networks and movements all over Europe and in other theatres of war as well.

The information revealed was of great help both to the cryptanalysts and to those concerned with guiding the intercept operators. The Fusion Room was able to warn the intercept stations about frequency and call sign changes so that operators could monitor the German stations and watch for changed locations, usually preceded by periods of silence when they moved around. The Fusion Room was staffed by civilians and army officers, male and female, and by some non-commissioned officers of both sexes, most of whom were commissioned later. During the war, fifty-six people worked in the Fusion Room for varying periods; of these thirty-one were men and twenty-five women. Thirty-seven of these arrived after the move from Beaumanor to Bletchley. As the German war expanded into the Balkans and later to North Africa the number of staff working in the Fusion Room increased. More men and women, some civilian, some army, arrived, most of them being fluent in reading German. American male army officers joined the Fusion Room later in the war and several American NCOs came to read logs.

When an Enigma cipher was not being decrypted, the Fusion Room was able to maintain a fairly complete picture by studying the reports of the log-readers, which revealed the quantity of traffic, call sign changes, and the routeing of messages. It also had the results of high-frequency direction-finding. This technique enabled us to locate German transmitters fairly accurately. To find a location all we had to do was to go to a small department at Bletchley Park, armed with the frequencies and the call signs of the stations we wished to locate. Major Firnberg's staff would then pass on the enquiries to Beaumanor, where a direction-finding exchange controlled many DF stations in the United Kingdom, ranging from the Shetlands to Land's End and Northern Ireland. These outstations established the direction from which the radio signals came by rotating an electrical device known as a goniometer until the signal came through at minimum strength. The line bearings were then plotted on a map at Beaumanor. If three DF stations were used, the location of the transmitter was at or near any intersection of the three bearings. Locations were not accurate to a matter of a few miles, but they were near enough to be of great assistance to those who were building a picture of the enemy order of battle.

To avoid duplication of effort a reorganization of the work of traffic analysis took place in November 1943. From that date all parties worked together in Block G, one of the brick buildings provided when the original huts became inadequate. The Central

Party was combined with other parties to form a new organization within Hut 6 called Sixta. The raw material, the logs from the red printed pads on which the operators wrote down in pencil everything they heard, arrived at Bletchley Park every day by despatch rider, unlike the enciphered messages which were teleprinted direct to enable the cryptanalysts to work on them urgently.

At Beaumanor, most of the log-readers – some fifty in number – were men. Soon after our move to Bletchley Park, more log-readers were recruited, many of them young women in the ATS. Several were in the Women's Auxiliary Air Force (WAAF), but we had no Wrens (members of the Women's Royal Naval Service). At its height, there were probably one hundred or more log-readers, from all ranks, from the lowly lance-corporal to the highest non-commissioned rank of regimental-sergeant-major. Among my fellow log-readers were teachers, barristers, librarians, accountants, journalists, bank clerks, parsons' daughters, undergraduates and graduates, male and female, who had recently completed their degrees or had interrupted their university courses.

As the war progressed we were all promoted regularly. I suspect this was partly to bring our army pay to the level of the salaries paid to the civilians, who were on Foreign Office scales. But whenever we were doing the same work, we were totally unconcerned with our different ranks. To those of us who had earlier experience of the crudities of army life it was good to be working with men and women in a friendly atmosphere, with little need for heavy discipline. For the most part we were on friendly terms with everybody. Indeed, some of us became lifelong friends. Several couples married. In my case I met a young subaltern who worked in the Fusion Room. In the days before we were married this led to no problems within Bletchley Park. But when all military personnel were removed from their civilian billets and housed in a newly built army camp adjacent to

Bletchley Park, administered by alien soldiers unused to our free and easy ways, the liaison between a subaltern and a company-sergeant-major was frowned upon.

All of us knew that we were a long way from the real war and we were far from the horrors of the Blitz. The perils of the 8th Army, slogging it out in Italy, the Soviet Army slowly overpowering the mighty German forces, the nightly departure of Allied bombers, some flying to their deaths – at times knowledge of these events made our log-reading seem a bizarre occupation. Yet, although we were only small cogs in an enormous war machine, the combined efforts of all those thousands of men and women who worked at Bletchley Park, together with the work of many others working in the intelligence services all over the world, were helping to win the war.

What was achieved can only be seen in the context of the whole picture. The intercept operators supplied our raw material. Our study of the traffic was combined in the Fusion Room with information from Ultra. The resulting detailed picture of German Army and Air Force formations over the whole of Europe and North Africa helped Hut 3's military and air advisers to prepare intelligence reports based on the decrypts, for transmission to British and American commanders in the field.

Sometimes we doubted the value of our work. It was heartening therefore to read in later years Gordon Welchman's views on traffic analysis at the end of his book *The Hut Six Story*, published in 1982: 'I believe the Central Party that became part of the Hut 6 organization at Bletchley Park had more detailed knowledge of the entire communications system that handled Enigma traffic than anyone in Germany. It followed the movements, changes in control, retransmissions, the handling of different keys, and of course the chit chat that appeared in the logs.'

When the war with Germany ended on 7 May 1945, there were no more logs to read. But before many days had passed more logs appeared, this time from French and Russian traffic. Many of the log-readers, astounded to learn that we were intercepting Allied signals, refused to take part. We formed a group and protested. A captain whose name I do not remember attempted to justify the work, but we could not agree. 'In that case,' he said, 'you are redundant.'

15

Bletchley Park, Double Cross and D-Day

MICHAEL SMITH

Introduction

Although we know a great deal about the activities of British intelligence during the Second World War, even now many details have still to emerge. This is largely a result of the unwillingness of secret services to give away either the identities of their agents, past or present, or methods of operation that might still be useful. But during the 1970s, two major intelligence successes were revealed. Sir John Masterman's 1972 book The Double Cross System in the War of 1939 to 1945 *described how MI5 and, to a lesser extent, MI6, persuaded German spies to work for the Allies as double agents. They sent their* Abwehr *controllers intelligence that deceived them into believing that the main thrust of the D-Day landings would be against the Pas de Calais rather than Normandy and thereby ensured that the* Wehrmacht *was unable to drive the Allied forces back into the sea, as it had planned. It was not until two years later that Frederick Winterbotham's book* The Ultra Secret *revealed the work carried out by Bletchley Park codebreakers. Winterbotham did allude to the part they played in*

Fortitude, the D-Day deception operation. But Masterman was unable for security reasons to mention Bletchley Park's role at all. Yet the parts played by the double agents and the codebreakers were so closely intertwined that the Double Cross story can only properly be told when both are taken into account.

MS

The long-awaited opening of the second front in the war against Hitler came on 6 June 1944, now commonly known as D-Day. Senior administrators at Bletchley Park were well aware that some of the young men working there wondered whether they too should be fighting alongside their friends and relatives, who were now thrust into the thick of battle. Eric Jones, the head of Hut 3, the military and air intelligence reporting section, told his staff that the work they were doing was just as important. One recent report sent out by Hut 3 had shown that enemy dispositions in the Cotentin peninsula in Normandy had changed. US paratroopers had been due to drop right into the middle of a German division, with potentially disastrous consequences. The resultant change to their dropping zone saved the lives of up to 15,000 men, Jones said.

> At this moment, in far the biggest combined operation in history, the first of the airborne troops are down. Sailors and airmen are facing frightful dangers to transport the first ground troops across the Channel and protect them on their way; more sailors and airmen are daring everything to blast holes in the German defences; and the ground troops themselves, in their thousands, will soon be literally throwing away their lives in the main assault by deliberately drawing enemy fire so that others may gain a foothold; and we are in complete, or almost complete, safety; some of us are even enjoying something akin to peace-time comfort.

> It's a thought we cannot avoid and it's a thought that inevitably aggravates an ever-present urge to be doing something more active; to be nearer the battle, sharing at least some of its discomforts and dangers. Such feelings cannot be obliterated but they can be subjugated to a grim resolve to serve those men to the very utmost of our capacity. There is no back-stage organization (and I think of Hut 3, Hut 6, Sixta and the Fish Party as an indissoluble whole) that has done more for past Allied operations and Allied plans for this assault; and none that can contribute more to the development of the invasion once the bloody battles for the beaches have been won.

Jones was right. Although Hut 6 struggled with the *Heer*'s Enigma radio links during the early months of 1944, the British codebreakers still managed to solve most of the new *Luftwaffe* keys, and continued to break the indispensable main *Luftwaffe* key, Red. More importantly, a number of other sources allowed the intelligence analysts in Hut 3 to map out virtually the entire German order of battle in northern France. The most important of these was the enciphered radio teleprinter link between the headquarters of Field Marshal Karl Rudolf von Rundstedt, C-in-C West, and Berlin. Codenamed Jellyfish by the British codebreakers, it had been broken in March, following the introduction of the first Colossus computer. It produced detailed returns for each of Rundstedt's divisions and, crucially, the itinerary of a tour of inspection of all the German armoured units by their commander General Heinz Guderian, updating the Allied assessment of the German military defences. This was already fairly good, based on traffic analysis, photo-reconnaissance and agent reports, as well as a detailed description by General Oshima Hiroshi, the Japanese Ambassador in Berlin, of a tour of the German defences in late 1943. An American working on the Japanese diplomatic machine cipher, known as Purple to the Allies, recalled the excitement of working through the night and into the next day on Oshima's detailed rundown of the Atlantic Wall.

> 'When I picked up the first intercept, I was not sure what I had because it was not part one,' he said. 'But within a few hours . . . the magnitude of what was at hand was apparent. I remained on duty throughout much of the day, continuing to translate along with colleagues who had pitched in to complete the work. I was too electrified to sleep. In the end, we produced what was veritably a pamphlet, an on-the-ground description of the north French defences of "Festung Europa", composed *dictu mirabile* by a general.'

The gaps in Oshima's assessment were filled in by two other messages sent from the Berlin embassy and deciphered at Bletchley Park. Colonel Ito Seiichi, the Japanese military attaché, made his own tour of the entire German coastal defences at the end of 1943, sending a massive thirty-two-part report back to Tokyo. This was deciphered in a marathon six-month operation carried out by the Japanese military section at Bletchley Park and finished just in time for D-Day. The other message was a description by the Japanese naval attaché in Berlin of his own tour of the German defences in May 1944. Sent in the Coral machine cipher, broken only weeks earlier in a remarkable joint US–British operation, his report gave detailed appraisals of the German dispositions and intentions. Field Marshal Erwin von Rommel, who had been appointed to lead the main force resisting an invasion, intended 'to destroy the enemy near the coast, most of all on the beaches, without allowing them to penetrate any considerable distance inland', the naval attaché said. 'As defence against airborne operations he plans to cut communications between seaborne and airborne troops and to destroy them individually.'

These were just some of the very many reports that ensured

that by the beginning of June the British knew almost the entire disposition of the German forces awaiting them in northern France. Ralph Bennett, one of the intelligence reporters working in Hut 3, recalled that there was very little wrong with the British intelligence assessment:

> Remarkably we got the positioning of all the German divisions. We made no mistakes, but you couldn't make a mistake when you get a signal saying this division will be there. There's no mistake we could make about that. We didn't get exactly what one panzer division was going to do, which was to attack the left-hand section of the British landing, and we didn't get the positioning of 352 Division, which was the one that held Omaha beach. We didn't get the detail that it was going to be so close up and if we had we would have warned the American 1st Army that they were going to have a rather sticky time, otherwise we got it just about right.

This in itself was a major contribution towards the success of D-Day. But it was not the only one to be made by Bletchley Park, which played a key role in one of the most remarkable espionage operations of all time, the Double Cross system. The main credit for this system is normally given to MI5 and to a lesser extent MI6. But the role played by the codebreakers, and particularly by Dilly Knox, was absolutely crucial.

The Double Cross system originated from an MI5 plan based on an operation carried out by the French *Deuxième Bureau*. Dick White, a future head of both MI5 and MI6, suggested that captured agents of the German military intelligence service, the *Abwehr*, should be left in place and 'turned' to work as double agents for British intelligence. MI5 would be able to keep complete control over all German espionage activities in Britain and, as a welcome side-effect, the information the agents asked for would tell the British what the *Abwehr* did and did not know. At this early stage, this was the full extent of MI5's ambitions.

One of the earliest opportunities to turn a German agent came with the arrest of Arthur Owens, a Welsh businessman who travelled frequently to Germany and who had volunteered in 1936 to collect intelligence for MI6. But the intelligence he provided was of little use and he was soon dropped. He subsequently got back in touch with MI6 to inform them that he had managed to get himself recruited as an agent by the *Abwehr*, claiming to have done so in order to penetrate the German intelligence service on behalf of the British. But interception of his written correspondence with his German controller threw doubt on this, suggesting that he was playing the two services off against each other. In September 1938, he announced to MI5 that he had now been appointed the *Abwehr*'s chief agent in Britain and that he had been given a special German secret service code with which to encode his messages. On the outbreak of war, he was arrested at Waterloo station and agreed to work as a double agent under the cover name of Snow. His controller was Lt.-Col. Tommy 'Tar' Robertson of MI5, a remarkable man who was to become the key British figure in the Double Cross system, setting up an MI5 section (B1A) to run them.

Snow had been given a radio transmitter by the Germans in January 1939, handing it over to MI5 immediately. He had also been given a very primitive cipher with which to contact the Germans (see Appendix I). This was used to send Snow's 'reports' to his German controller, and was also sent to Bletchley Park for evaluation. An alert MI5 officer, monitoring Snow's frequencies to ensure that he sent exactly what he was told, noticed that the control station appeared to be working to a number of other stations. GC&CS was sent copies of the messages the station was transmitting, which were in a different cipher to that given to Snow. But the codebreaker who looked at them expressed 'considerable disbelief' that they were of any importance, suggesting that they might be Russian telegrams originating from Shanghai.

Despite the scepticism displayed by Bletchley Park, the *Abwehr* radio nets were monitored by the Radio Security Service (RSS), which was run by Major E. W. Gill, a former member of the British Army's signals intelligence organization in the First World War, and was based close to Bletchley at Hanslope Park. It had the services of Post Office intercept operators, plus a small army of volunteers, most of them radio 'hams', who scanned the shortwave frequencies looking for enemy wireless traffic.

Gill and a colleague, Captain Hugh Trevor-Roper (later Lord Dacre), who worked in the Radio Intelligence Service, the analysis section of the RSS based at Barnet, north London, broke one of the ciphers in use. They managed to show that the other messages on Snow's allotted frequency were indeed *Abwehr* traffic. This appears to have been the source of considerable embarrassment at Bletchley and the row over the significance of the traffic went on for some weeks with Trevor-Roper becoming increasingly unpopular with the professional codebreakers. Eventually, a new section was set up at Bletchley, in Elmer's School, to decipher the various messages on the network. It was headed by Oliver Strachey. The *Abwehr*'s cipher instructions given to Snow led to a number of ciphers being broken and the first decrypt was issued on 14 April 1940. Initially codenamed Pear, the decrypts became known as ISOS, standing either for Illicit or Intelligence Services (Oliver Strachey).

The ISOS decrypts enabled MI5 to keep track of the messages of the double agents and spot any other German spies arriving in the country. It also meant that the agents' reports could be designed to allow the codebreakers to follow them through the *Abwehr* radio networks. Hopefully, this would help them break the keys for the Enigma cipher that the German controllers were using to pass the reports on to Hamburg.

By the end of 1940, Robertson had a dozen double agents under his control. At the same time, MI6 was running a number of German spies abroad. 'Basically, MI5 was responsible for security in the UK and MI6 operated overseas,' said Hugh Astor, one of the agent runners. 'Obviously there was a grey area as far as double agents were concerned because they were trained and recruited overseas and at that point were the concern of MI6, while once they arrived here they became the responsibility of MI5.'

A 'Most Secret' committee was set up to decide what information should be fed back to the Germans. Its small select membership included representatives of MI5, MI6, naval, military and air intelligence, HQ Home Forces and the Home Defence Executive, which was in charge of civil defence. The committee was called the XX Committee, although it swiftly became known as the Twenty Committee, or more colloquially, the Twenty Club, from the Roman numeral suggested by the double-cross sign. It met every Wednesday in the MI5 headquarters, initially in Wormwood Scrubs prison, but subsequently at 58 St James's Street, London. 'The XX Committee was chaired by J. C. Masterman,' said Astor. 'Tar Robertson, who ran B1A, really developed the whole thing. He was absolutely splendid, a marvellous man to work for. He and Dick White were the two outstanding people I suppose and Tar collected around him some very bright people who actually ran the agents for him.'

The Twenty Club's job was to decide what information could be fed back to the *Abwehr* without damaging the British cause. Initially, with the threat of a German invasion dominating the atmosphere in London, it was decided that the 'intelligence' provided by the double agents should be used to give an impression of how strong Britain's defences were. But by the beginning of 1941, it was clear that more could be done with the double agents. They could be used to deceive the Germans, to provide them with misleading information that would give Allied forces an advantage in the field.

The MI5 and MI6 officers handling the double agents needed to know what information they could give to their agents to build up their reputations with the Germans. Much of it was 'chicken-feed', unimportant information that would give the *Abwehr* a feel that its agents were doing something and had access to real intelligence, without telling them anything really harmful to the war effort. But mixed among this were key pieces of specious or misleading information, designed to build up a false picture of what the British were doing.

The committee's task was to co-ordinate this work. They supervised the system but they did not run the individual agents. 'They approved the overall plan,' Astor said. 'I was in touch with the Germans probably two or three times a day by radio and so I had to move fairly quickly. So the approving authorities were not the actual Twenty Committee because it only sat once a week. I would get approval from people who were on the committee and every week I and others who were actually active would prepare a short report for the committee saying what we were doing and what we had done.'

But while the system appeared to be working, the Twenty Committee and the agent handlers had a problem. They could not be sure the Germans were fooled. The *Abwehr*'s operations abroad seemed to be unbelievably incompetent. The agents were 'too amateurish' to be genuine. Capturing them and turning them around was so easy that the British suspected that it might be part of an elaborate *Abwehr* deception. Even if this were not the case, the lax system employed by the Germans, who ignored basic security procedures by putting the agents in touch with each other, warned the Twenty Committee when any new agents were sent to Britain. But it also meant that if the *Abwehr* realized that one of its agents was operating under British control, it would have to assume that they were all blown. 'The position at the beginning was largely experimental as no one knew very much about the working of double agents or about the working and general incompetence of the *Abwehr*,' wrote Ewen Montagu, the naval intelligence representative on the committee. 'Later on, after we had had experience of the German Intelligence Service, no incompetence would have surprised us.'

While the response of the *Abwehr* controllers to the double agents' reports helped the Twenty Committee to work out where the gaps in the Germans' knowledge lay, it did not tell them whether or not the misleading intelligence picture they were attempting to build up was believed in Berlin. The only way of finding this out was by deciphering the messages passed between the *Abwehr* outstations in Paris, Madrid, Lisbon and their headquarters. But these links all used the *Abwehr*'s Enigma machine, which was completely different to those used by the other German services.

So the Twenty Club's confidence in their double agents was considerably enhanced in December 1941 when Dilly Knox, who was terminally ill with cancer and working from home, broke the *Abwehr* Enigma. This followed six months of research during which he was assisted by a young Mavis Lever (now Batey) and Margaret Rock. It was to be the last of Knox's remarkable achievements. Just over a year later, in February 1943, and after a long struggle against cancer, he died.

The first of the messages, known as ISK for Illicit (or Intelligence) Services Knox, was issued on Christmas Day 1941. They were invaluable to the Twenty Committee, revealing that the Germans believed the false intelligence the Twenty Committee was feeding them and showing whether or not individual double agents were trusted or under suspicion, in which case steps could be taken to remedy the situation. Two months later, Mavis Lever solved a separate *Abwehr* Enigma machine, known as GGG, which was used near the Spanish border. By the spring of 1942, the information collected from the Bletchley Park decrypts had built up such a good picture of *Abwehr* operations in Britain that Robertson was able to state categorically that MI5 now controlled all the German agents operating in Britain. The Twenty Committee was able to watch the Germans making arrangements to send agents to Britain and discussing the value of their reports, Robertson wrote: 'In two or three cases we have been able to observe the action (which has been rapid and extensive) taken by the Germans upon the basis of these agents' reports.'

Nevertheless, the breaking of the Enigma cipher had brought a new problem for the committee. The release of any material from Bletchley Park was controlled extremely strictly by MI6 in order to safeguard the Ultra secret. The fact that the 'unbreakable' Enigma ciphers had been broken had to be protected at all costs. The MI6 representative on the committee was Felix Cowgill, the head of Section V, the MI6 counter-espionage division. A former Indian Police officer, Cowgill was a shy, slightly built man in his mid-thirties. 'His face gives the impression of intensity coupled with a great weariness,' said Kim Philby, the MI6 officer and KGB spy, in one of his reports to Moscow. 'Although normally quiet in manner, due to shyness, he is combative in his work, always prepared to challenge an office ruling.'

Cowgill defended the Ultra decrypts vigorously, to the extent of refusing to allow the Home Forces and Home Defence Executive representatives on the Twenty Committee to see them at all, while anything that referred to MI6 agents was held back even from MI5. 'Cowgill was so imbued with the idea of security that when he was put in charge for C of this material, he was quite willing to try entirely to prevent its use as intelligence lest it be compromised,' Montagu said. 'These views inevitably caused friction.'

While there was no doubt that some within MI5 were paying scant regard to the necessary restrictions on the Bletchley Park decrypts, Cowgill's attitude made the Twenty Committee's operations almost impossible. Some members were not privy to vital information about the agents on which the others were basing their decisions. The result was potentially far more detrimental to security than the widespread dissemination that Cowgill was trying to prevent. His controls were soon being ignored on a wholesale basis. 'A good deal of bootlegging of information had to take place,' said Montagu. 'Many undesirable "off the record" and "under the table" practices were essential unless work was to stop entirely.'

The situation came to a head over the case of a man who was to become the most valuable of all the Double Cross agents – Juan Pujol Garcia, better known by his codename: Garbo. The Bletchley decrypts had revealed an *Abwehr* agent who claimed to be running a network of agents in Britain. His reports were ridiculously inaccurate. He was clearly a fraud, reporting 'drunken orgies and slack morals in amusement centres' in Liverpool, and Glasgow dockers who were 'prepared to do anything for a litre of wine'. It ought to have been obvious to the Germans that, not only had he never met a Glasgow docker in his life, he had never been to Britain. Yet they believed him wholeheartedly. MI6 became concerned that his false reports might damage the Twenty Club's own plans. Then in early February 1940, the MI6 head of station in Lisbon reported that he had been approached by a Spaniard, claiming to be a top *Abwehr* secret agent. He said he had been disaffected by the Spanish Civil War and was keen to help Britain to fight the Germans. Having been turned down by the MI6 station in Madrid, he had gone to the *Abwehr* equivalent, persuading the officers there that he was a Spanish intelligence officer who had been posted to Britain and offering to act as a German spy.

In fact, Pujol went to Lisbon, where, armed with a Blue Guide to Britain, a Portuguese book on the Royal Navy and an Anglo-French vocabulary of military terms, he produced a series of highly imaginative reports built on his alleged network of agents. Pujol was vehemently anti-Nazi and his reports were apparently designed to disrupt the German intelligence service – he was in effect a freelance double-cross operation in miniature. Cowgill kept him secret from MI5, on the basis that although sending reports ostensibly from British territory and therefore notionally under MI5 jurisdiction, he was actually abroad and the responsibility of MI6.

The fact that an important German agent was sending uncontrolled reports about Britain, however inaccurate, could have caused immense damage if it had not been taken into account in the overall deception plan. So when, at the end of February, senior officers in MI5 discovered that his existence had been hidden from them, they were furious. A few weeks later, they discovered that Cowgill had also been holding back ISOS messages thought to refer to MI6 agents, placing them in a separate series known as ISBA, which was not being circulated to either MI5 or the service intelligence departments.

This was the final straw and Sir David Petrie, the head of MI5, used the row to lobby for MI5 to take over control of Section V. He added all the arguments over the distribution of deciphered intercepts, MI5 criticism of the apparent lack of basic knowledge about Germany among a number of Section V officers, and the fact that it was based in St Albans, too far away from London to make liaison with MI5 as easy as it should have been. Stewart Menzies proposed a compromise. He would set up a new department within Section V called VX to deal exclusively with the Double Cross system. It would be based in London to allow easy liaison with MI5 over the work of the double agents and would be headed by a man with unrivalled knowledge of Germany, Frank Foley, who had been the MI6 head of station in Berlin throughout the 1920s and 1930s.

Foley, now better known for his role in helping tens of thousands of Jews to get to Palestine in contravention of the British rules, replaced Cowgill as the MI6 representative on the Twenty Committee. 'There was an obvious qualitative difference in the way in which the committee worked from then on,' one former MI5 officer said. 'For the first time, the MI6 representative was speaking authoritatively because he was a real operational officer. He knew what he was talking about and it showed.' Masterman, who as secretary of the Twenty Committee was in the perfect position to know, also pointed to the mid-1942 changes as the moment that the Double Cross system really began to take off. 'Broadly speaking, bad men make good institutions bad and good men make bad institutions good,' he said. 'It cannot be denied that there was some friction between MI5 and MI6 in the early days, but this disappeared when the MI6 representative on the committee was changed.'

One of the major problems faced by those running the Double Cross system was that when the British tried to work out what the Germans would do next, they based their judgements on what they would have done in the same situation. But their opponents, and in particular Hitler, had a different view of things. 'It is necessary for the deception staff to think as the enemy thinks and to divorce themselves entirely from being influenced by what we would do if placed in what we imagine to be the enemy's position,' one former deception officer said. 'Again and again, what the deceivers suggested was plausible to the enemy. But both our operations and intelligence staffs maintained that it was not because they were governed strictly by their appreciation of what we would think was plausible in the enemy's place.'

Masterman had been a prisoner of war in Germany during the First World War and he had a better grasp of the German way of thinking than most of the committee, but even he could not match the new MI6 representative. 'Foley knew the Germans backwards,' one former MI6 officer said. 'So if people wanted to know how the Germans would react to any particular deception plan, they would naturally ask him.' Foley swiftly succeeded in turning around the committee's attitude to MI6, which had been so heavily tarnished by Cowgill's restrictions. 'He was not a member of the establishment clique,' said another of Foley's former colleagues. 'But he was a pretty serious chap, feet on the ground, solid, very much the elder statesman, giving useful advice whenever called upon. His exceptional knowledge of the workings of, and personalities in, the *Abwehr*, acquired during years of service in Berlin, made him a tower of strength.'

By the spring of 1943, the Double Cross system had developed deception into a fine art. But one of the Twenty Club's most famous achievements did not involve a double agent at all. The Allied forces were now mopping up in North Africa and preparing to invade southern Europe. The most obvious stepping stone was Sicily, just a short hop across the Mediterranean from Tunisia. The problem was to find a way of giving the Germans the impression that General Eisenhower and his British colleague General Alexander had other plans, forcing the Germans to reinforce other areas and weakening the defences in Sicily.

Charles Cholmondeley, the RAF representative on the Twenty Committee, devised Operation Mincemeat, a plan centred around the known level of collaboration between the Spanish authorities and the Germans. The idea was to drop the body of a dead 'British officer' off the coast of Spain, close enough to ensure it would be washed up on the beach, with the intention of making it look as if it had come from a crashed aircraft. He would be carrying documents indicating that the main thrust of the Allied attack would be somewhere other than Sicily. The Spanish would be bound to pass these on to the Germans who would reinforce their garrisons in the suggested targets at the expense of the real one.

Montagu took charge of the operation, acquiring a suitable body from a London hospital and giving it the identity of Major William Martin, Royal Marines, an official courier. Attached to Martin's wrist by a chain was a briefcase containing a number of documents, including a letter from one senior British general to another, discussing planned assaults on Greece and an unspecified location in the western Mediterranean, for which Sicily was to be a cover. A further letter from Lord Mountbatten, the Chief of Combined Operations, referred jocularly to sardines, which was rightly thought enough of a hint to make the Germans believe the real attack was going to be on Sardinia. The members of the Twenty Committee were highly inventive in their choice of other documents to be planted on the body. Two 'used' West End theatre tickets for a few days before the intended launch of the body were in his pocket to show that he must have been travelling by air. A photograph of Martin's 'fiancée', actually that of a female MI5 clerk, was placed in his wallet. For several weeks, Cholmondeley carried two love letters from the 'fiancée' around in his pocket to give them the proper crumpled look. There was even an irate letter from Martin's bank manager.

The body was floated ashore near the southern Spanish town of Huelva from a submarine. The Allies now had to find out if the Germans had swallowed the bait and the only sure way of knowing was from Sigint. Noel Currer-Briggs was an Intelligence Corps officer in 1 Special Intelligence Section, a mobile Sigint unit operating in Tunisia. 'We were stationed at Bizerta on top of a hill just outside Tunis and I remember we were inspected one day by Alexander and Eisenhower,' he said. 'There we were working away at the German wireless traffic coming from the other side of the Mediterranean and we were saying: "Oh yes. They've moved that division from Sicily to Sardinia and they've moved the other one to the Balkans" and these two generals were jumping up and down like a couple of schoolboys at a football match. We hadn't a clue why. We thought: "Silly old buffers". It wasn't until 1953 when Montagu's book *The Man Who Never Was* came out that we realized we were telling them that the Germans had swallowed the deception hook, line and sinker.'

The Germans had been totally taken in by Mincemeat. Even two months later, when the invasion of Sicily had been launched, German intelligence continued to insist that the original plan had been to attack Sardinia and Greece and that it had only been switched to Sicily at the last moment. The ability the Allies now had, through Ultra, to tell whether or not the enemy had been fooled by deception operations was crucial to the Double Cross system as it prepared its biggest challenge, misleading the Germans over the Allied plans for D-Day. According to Bennett, a military advisor in Hut 3, 'No other source could have proved the efficacy of the deception planners' rumour-mongering so conclusively, relieving the operational commanders' minds as they prepared an amphibious undertaking on an unprecedented scale.'

The running of the Double Cross operations was helped immensely in July 1943 when Section V moved from St Albans to Ryder St, just off St James's St, and a stone's throw from both MI5 headquarters and the offices of the London Controlling Section, which was co-ordinating all deception operations. Now, whenever problems arose, MI5 officers could simply walk across the road to discuss them with their opposite numbers in MI6. 'One always gets the impression of a tremendous rivalry and that sort of thing,' said Hugh Astor. 'And I suppose at the top, there can be rivalry. But at the lower level, one just has to get on with the job and I always found everybody very helpful. Even at the top, one can exaggerate the degree of thigh grabbing. The time scale was so short you couldn't really have a long battle with anybody. I don't think there was really enough time for bad blood to be created.'

Mutual understanding of each other's problems and knowledge of how the German intelligence services operated was fostered by the Radio Security Intelligence Conference which met at the MI5 headquarters every alternate Thursday and was attended by the key players within MI5, MI6, the service intelligence departments, the Radio Intelligence Section and Bletchley Park. Even before Cowgill's replacement, those attending the meetings discussed a wide range of subjects 'off the record'. The relaxation of Cowgill's strict regulations turned the conference into an invaluable forum for discussing every aspect of the German intelligence networks, whether controlled by the British or not, Astor said. 'I knew all that I needed to know about those organizations and the style and characteristics of the agents I was running, the techniques that they used and of course assisted very much by Ultra. One usually got advance information about the arrival of agents through Ultra, so one knew what training they had been through.'

By now the main thrust of the Twenty Club's operations was in preparing for D-Day. Churchill was as fascinated with deception as he was with espionage. At the Tehran Conference in November 1943, when the final decision was made to launch the invasion of Europe in mid-1944, the British Prime Minister told Stalin that 'in wartime, truth is so precious that she should always be attended by a bodyguard of lies'. From that point on, the overall deception plan for D-Day was known as Operation Bodyguard. Planning for the operation came under the control of the Supreme Headquarters Allied Expeditionary Force (SHAEF), based at Norfolk House, St James's Square, close to all the main participants on the Twenty Committee. From then on, the double agent handlers had to think continuously about the various elements of the deception plan and how the agents could be used to convince the Germans they were true. The Double Cross system became like a game of chess, with the agents resembling pieces, each being carefully moved into a position where it could contribute to the opponent's demise.

By the beginning of 1944, the Twenty Committee was controlling fifteen double agents. But only seven of these had wireless sets. Four of them were to be the key players in the deception plan to cover the actual D-Day landings, which was to be called Fortitude South. Although the reports of the letter-writing agents would also be used to point the Germans away from the Allies' real plans, it was only those with wireless sets who could send messages in 'real time'.

Fortitude South evolved rapidly during the early months of 1944, but the bare bones of the plan remained the same. The Germans were to be led to believe that the Normandy landings were a feint attack, aimed at drawing German forces away from the main thrust of the Allied invasion, which would be against the Pas de Calais. This would ensure that the bulk of the German forces would be held back from the Normandy beaches, allowing the Allies time to establish a strong foothold in northern France from which they could break out towards Paris and then on to the German border. A completely mythical formation was invented, the First United States Army Group (FUSAG), supposedly commanded by General George Patton, a hero of the invasion of Sicily and a man whom the Germans would believe must be heavily involved in the invasion of Europe, as indeed he later would be. FUSAG was supposedly grouped in East Anglia and south-eastern England and it was vital that the agents' reports were co-ordinated to show that this was the case, and to down-play the mass of troops waiting in the south and south-west to attack the German defences in Normandy.

The most spectacularly useful of the wireless agents used in the Fortitude South deception plan was Garbo. Although he had now been moved to Britain, his network was so large and so vital to the overall deception picture that virtually everything had to be closely co-ordinated on a day-to-day basis. The most important of the other agents who, in the parlance of the Twenty Committee, 'came up for D-Day', was the triple agent Brutus. Roman Garby-Czerniawski, a Pole, had led the Interallié resistance network in France and, once it was uncovered, volunteered to work for the *Abwehr* in London in order to save the other members of his group from execution. But on arrival in Britain he immediately told the authorities of his mission and was turned against the Germans. Two others should be mentioned as important to Fortitude South: the Yugoslav Dusko Popov, codenamed Tricycle, and Natalie 'Lily' Sergueiev (codenamed Treasure), a French citizen born in Russia, whose family had fled in the wake of the Bolshevik revolution.

All four of these agents helped in building up Fortitude South, the false picture of the intended target of D-Day. Tricycle and

Brutus, who was supposedly a member of a Polish unit attached to FUSAG, provided an order of battle for the fictitious formation so detailed that the Germans were not just supplied with details of individual units, strengths and locations, but even with reproductions of the insignia painted on the side of their vehicles. Treasure's role was to report from the West Country that there were very few troops there, further pushing the Germans towards the view that the main thrust of the attack would be against the Pas de Calais. But she came close to blowing the whole plan. Sent to Lisbon to collect a radio set from the *Abwehr,* she told a former acquaintance she had met in the street that she was now working for the British Secret Service. When she returned, she confessed to considering warning the *Abwehr* as retribution for the British refusal to allow her to bring her dog to the UK without going through quarantine. She was swiftly retired and replaced by an MI5 operator, who had to imitate her distinctive method of sending Morse and loquacious messages. For several months after D-Day, the Treasure character was kept active for no other reason than that her messages were so long-winded that Bletchley Park was able to follow them through the *Abwehr* communications network and use them as cribs. Denys Page, who had taken over from Oliver Strachey as head of the ISOS section in early 1942, told Masterman that the cribs supplied by Treasure and Brutus had 'absolutely saved our bacon' after the Germans introduced more secure systems during 1944.

But by far the most important and complex role was played by Garbo. At one point he had a network of twenty-seven agents, some of whom still survived from his freelance period before the British recruited him. They included a Swiss businessman based in Bootle, who had reported 'drunken orgies and slack morals in amusement centres' in Liverpool, and an enthusiastic Venezuelan living in Glasgow who had noted the willingness of Clydeside dockers to 'do anything for a litre of wine'. The Swiss businessman died of cancer in the autumn of 1942, but his widow continued working for Garbo, becoming virtually his personal assistant. The Venezuelan also grew in stature, becoming Garbo's official deputy and developing his own ring of agents in Scotland, one of whom was an ardent communist who actually believed he was working for the Soviet Union. The *Abwehr* codenamed this group of agents the Benedict Network. Garbo's mistress, a secretary working in the offices of the War Cabinet, provided useful opportunities for valuable pillow talk. She, like the network's wireless operator, believed that her lover was a Spanish Republican. Garbo had also successfully set up a large network of agents in Wales, mostly Welsh Nationalists but led by an ex-seaman, 'a thoroughly undesirable character', who was working for purely mercenary reasons.

It is worth pointing out that – in the words of the official historian – 'the reader should bear in mind that none of these people actually existed'. Nevertheless, they all contributed to the German dependence on Garbo as their most reliable source for intelligence on the Allied plans and set the scene for his key role in Fortitude. The German belief in the existence of FUSAG was steadily built up by a number of means, apart from false reports from the double agents. Dummy invasion craft nicknamed 'Big Bobs' were left out in the open in east-coast ports and mobile wireless vehicles travelling around south-east England broadcast messages from a number of different locations to fool the German radio interception units.

During the second half of May 1944, Garbo told his German controller in Madrid that he had accepted a job in the Ministry of Information, which would give him access to details of all propaganda designed to cover up the invasion plans. By reading these 'in reverse' he would be able to detect the real plans, he said. On 29 May, he sent a message saying that he had now studied all the propaganda directives. 'What I was clearly able to get out of it and what I consider to be of maximum importance is the intention to hide the facts in order to trick us,' he said. He was bringing his Venezuelan deputy down from Scotland to assist him in sending off the messages. This man could not speak German, would they mind if he sent his messages in English. The Germans readily agreed and the stage was set for Garbo's greatest triumph.

In the early hours of 6 June 1944, D-Day, Garbo made repeated attempts to warn his *Abwehr* controller that the Allied forces were on their way. This move was agreed by SHAEF on the basis that it would be too late for the Germans to do anything about it but would ensure that they still believed in Garbo as their best-informed secret agent after the invasion had begun. As predicted, it only served to increase their trust in Garbo and paved the way for the next stage of the deception. Shortly after midnight on 9 June, as the Allied advance faltered, and with the elite 1st SS Panzer division on its way, together with another armoured division, to reinforce the German defences in Normandy, Garbo sent his most important message. Three of his agents were reporting troops massed across East Anglia and Kent and large numbers of troop and tank transporters waiting in the eastern ports, he said.

> After personal consultation on 8th June in London with my agents Donny, Dick and Derrick, whose reports I sent today, I am of the opinion, in view of the strong troop concentrations in south-east and east England, that these operations are a diversionary manoeuvre designed to draw off enemy reserves in order to make an attack at another place. In view of the continued air attacks on the concentration area mentioned, which is a strategically favourable position for this, it may very probably take place in the Pas de Calais area.

Garbo's warning went straight to Hitler, who ordered the two divisions back to the Pas de Calais to defend against what he expected to be the main invasion thrust, and awarded Pujol the Iron Cross. Had the two divisions continued to Normandy, the Allies might well have been thrown back into the sea. On 11 June, Bletchley Park deciphered a message from Berlin to Garbo's controller in Madrid, saying that Garbo's reports 'have been confirmed almost without exception and are to be described as especially valuable. The main line of investigation in future is to be the enemy group of forces in south-eastern and eastern England.'

Even once the war was over, senior German officers still believed that the Allies had intended to make their main assault on the Pas de Calais area and only decided not to because the Germans had massed troops there. During the postwar interrogations of senior *Wehrmacht* officers, one asked: 'All this Patton business wasn't a trick, was it?' 'What do you mean by that?' asked his British interrogator. 'What I mean is this,' the German said. 'Were all those divisions sent to south-east England simply to hold our forces in the Pas de Calais?' 'I certainly imagine,' the British officer replied, 'that if you had denuded the Pas de Calais, they would have been used to attack that place, but since you did not do so, they were equally available to reinforce Montgomery.' 'Ah,' the German said with evident relief. 'That is what we always thought.'

16

How Dilly Knox and his Girls Broke the *Abwehr* Enigma

KEITH BATEY

Introduction

In early 1940, two members of the Radio Security Service (otherwise known as MI8c), Hugh Trevor-Roper (later Lord Dacre) and E. W. B. Gill, who were only amateur cryptanalysts, broke some Abwehr *signals which had been encrypted using simple manual ciphers. GC&CS had initially said it had no interest in the traffic, which it thought was of no relevance to the war. However, the Trevor-Roper and Gill successes kindled the interest of GC&CS, and that of the intelligence services, in the* Abwehr *signals. Bletchley took the work on, and issued its first* Abwehr *decrypt in April 1940.*

The Abwehr *also employed a wide variety of cipher machines: Kryha (a form of geared disc), teleprinter machines such as the Siemens and Halske T52 (Sturgeon), and the Lorenz SZ40/42 (Tunny), and different types of Enigma, including one known as the* Zählwerke *('counter') machine (since it had a letter counter). GC&CS recognized that some of the* Abwehr *traffic was machine-enciphered. When the daily intercepts increased to a modest number, they were given to the legendary Dilly Knox to tackle. In this chapter, Keith Batey explains how Knox solved the counter machine in October 1941 with the help of Mavis Lever and Margaret Rock.*

The first Abwehr *Enigma decrypt was issued on 25 December 1941 in a series that became known as ISK. By the end of the war, over 140,000 ISK decrypts had been circulated. Initially, they did not yield much useful intelligence, but that very soon changed when the volume of traffic increased. In May 1943, for example, they gave information on Chetnik and Partisan operations in Yugoslavia, shipping reports from Spain and Portugal, especially on Gibraltar, agents in various countries, and espionage arrangements generally, including sabotage at Gibraltar. But as Michael Smith has shown in Chapter 15, its most important role lay in revealing what the* Abwehr *really thought about reports from the double agents, such as Garbo, who were being used in the Double Cross operation.*

The ISK operation was an outstanding success. A number of amateurs in Bletchley, backed by a very few professionals, made a major difference to the Allied war effort – and helped to save D-Day.

RE

Intelligence from decrypts of the *Abwehr* (the German Secret Service) was largely responsible for enabling MI5 to control the entire German espionage network in the United Kingdom. It also enabled the organizers of the 'Double Cross' system of playing back German agents to be sure that they were successfully deceiving the Germans and, through strategic deception, played a major part in the success of the D-Day landings.

Radio traffic between various European capitals and Berlin, which had been intercepted – though spasmodically and in small amounts – from late 1939, was thought to be between outstations of the *Abwehr* and its headquarters, and had been diagnosed as having been enciphered on a four-wheel Enigma from its use of eight-letter indicators, such as GIWM XPEB, since that was a common practice when using the four-wheel commercial Enigma (see page 311, paragraph 3). The traffic was referred to Gordon Welchman in Hut 6 early in 1941, but although the number of signals intercepted had increased, following breaks into *Abwehr* hand ciphers in 1940, it remained much too insignificant to offer any prospect of evaluating the indicators, and as no cribs were available Hut 6 made no progress with the problem. Welchman, no doubt not being serious, asked me if sufficient information could quickly be got to break the machine if someone could get into an embassy for the purpose; I was discouraging, and mercifully no such tactic was tried.

As Dilly Knox had handed over his work on the Italian naval Enigma, he was asked to tackle the unsolved traffic around mid-1941 and, remarkably, had made great headway with the solution by October 1941. His note, dated 28 October, reporting his success to Alastair Denniston, the deputy director of GC&CS, is endearingly eccentric and typically obscure; sadly, it ends with a scribbled postscript saying that he would welcome a discussion but would be away on 30 October – in fact his stomach cancer was to keep him away for the rest of his life. Ralph Erskine sent me a copy of the note in 1999 – until then I had no reliable information about how Dilly had solved the problem.

Dilly saw, as had Hut 6, that the number of signals on any one day was too small to make it feasible to evaluate the indicators (i.e. decipher the message settings from them), but he saw that if he could find two days where the same wheel order was used and such that the *Grundstellung* of one day could be got from the other by rotating each wheel and the reflector through the same number of places, he would in effect double the number of indicators available on one setting, because the letter pairings at each position of the *Grundstellungen* would be related by a QWERTZU . . . substitution (see page 316, paragraph 9). He therefore organized a search for two such days with the help of the Bletchley Park card sorting and tabulation section – this must have involved Dilly in some very persuasive negotiations, because the section's resources were usually overloaded. The search was unsuccessful, which Dilly thought suspicious, though why is puzzling: it is doubtful that there were as many as a hundred days of traffic worth working on, implying fewer than sixteen on each of the six possible wheel orders. The probability that two days would have the desired relationship was 1 in 17,576 – but Dilly was disinclined to be troubled by probability calculations (an attitude inculcated in his lieutenants). Freeborn did, however, find a day on which the positions 1–5 and 2–6 fitted the bill – which Dilly reported as 'finding what was wanted standing, like the abomination of desolation, precisely where it should not – on a single setting'. He called the phenomenon a 'crab' on the basis that matters moved sideways. He also said that the discovery came as no surprise to him: presumably by this he meant that he was ready for something odd; if he had had the slightest suspicion that the machine had numerous wheel turnovers he would surely have had each day's indicators carefully looked at, in which case crabs would have been found with little trouble, and Freeborn saved a tiresome task.

The crucial discovery of the crab was pure serendipity, but Dilly took full advantage of it: from the discovery he deduced that:

a) the Enigma had a QWERTZU... diagonal: the sequence from the top right to the bottom left of the rod square when the rod labels are in QWERTZU order (see Figure 16.1 and page 313, paragraph 8);
b) occasionally, between consecutive positions four places apart on the *Grundstellung*, all the wheels and reflector moved together;
c) hence the reflector moved during enciphering – a feature not

previously encountered by GC&CS in an Enigma;
d) the wheels had numerous turnover positions, otherwise crabs would be very rare: this was also a feature not previously met with;
e) 'as everything that has a middle also has a beginning and an end' there would be positions at which all the wheels and reflector turned together without doing the same four places later – this he called a 'lobster', arguing that it was half a crab.

Dilly said that he condemned a crab as useless because, although it was a great help in finding the alphabets at the four positions of the *Grundstellung*, the alphabets could not lead to deductions about rods (see page 314, paragraph 8 (d)) because of the turnovers between each pair. Lobsters were useful because the QWERTZU . . . relation between the two alphabets at the lobster position greatly helped to discover them, so giving the alphabets four places away, which, with luck, would not be separated by a turnover.

At this stage Dilly organized a lobster hunt: he probably restricted the hunt to days with at least ten indicators intercepted; for each day 'chains' were made for places 1–5, 2–6 and so on; if a letter pairing was assumed in, say, place 1, the chains gave deductions about other pairings in 1 and 5, and if a lobster existed 1–2, there would be several pairings implied for 6; it was then easy to see whether these were consistent with the implications of the chain 2–6. Clearly the hunt involved a great deal of careful, tedious work, but Dilly announced with evident pride that 'after two days Miss Lever,* by very good and careful work, succeeded in an evaluation which contained sufficient non-carry units to ascertain the green wheel'.

The evaluation of the first day showed that the operators (no

*The present author married Miss Mavis Lever on 5 November 1942.

doubt contrary to strict instructions) nearly always used Christian names, swear words, or obvious keyboard sequences as message settings, and as this greatly eased the evaluation for other days a fair number of solutions soon accumulated, from which followed recovery of the wiring of two other wheels, one (designated Blue) with 15 turnovers and the other with 17 (Red). With so many turnovers these recoveries were difficult, the Red especially so – it was only recovered by David Rees after a complex operation. Each evaluation produced seven consecutive places at which it was shown whether the wheel had a turnover or not: if a turnover the position was marked by +, if not by – so that the turnovers produced by an evaluation would be shown by a sequence such as – +++ – + –. With evaluations for several days these sequences could be fitted together in a process akin to dendrochronology (though much simpler!) to give the complete sequence of turnovers for the wheel, known as the 'wheel-track'.

Having discovered the wheel wiring and wheel-tracks, it remained to discover how the letters on the wheel tyres related to the turnovers. This necessitated decipherment of a message, a formidable problem which Dilly tackled at home because of his illness. His reports do not say how he accomplished the break, and I was unable to ask him as I only followed David Rees on secondment from Hut 6 (permanent, as it turned out) at the beginning of November 1941. Dilly was helped by Margaret Rock, who stayed with him for some time at his home in Courns Wood, but I never asked her how the solution came about, possibly because she too was off sick for some months from December 1941. Undoubtedly Dilly used rods, since other possible attacks would have involved statistics, which he disliked. Analysis of the first letters in the intercepted messages established that most, if not all, began 'NRX' ('Nr' followed by 'x' as a separator), since N very rarely appeared in the first position, R in the second, or X in the third. Dilly, or Margaret, would have noticed that the Green wheel rod square contained adjacent occurrences of RX on two rods (two letters on the same rod were called beetles by Dilly) and a N*X beetle. On a day with twenty or more messages – according to my recollection quite common in November, probably because more resources had been allocated to interception following Dilly's break – it would be unlucky not to have messages starting at two of the beetle positions, and the message settings would confirm that their relative rod positions were correct; the beetles would be easily found by noting the indicators in which the bigrams associated with the beetles on the rod square appeared as the second two, or the first and third, letters. This process, repeated if necessary on two or three days with the Green wheel in the right-hand (RH) position, would fix the tyre in relation to the rod positions, which would be related to the wheel-track's eleven turnovers by the evaluation of the indicators.

The Blue rod square had NRX on one rod, but no other relevant beetles; finding at the start of a message one of the trigrams in the same column of the rod square as the NRX beetle would make it highly probable that it gave the rod position at the start of the message. There were just three places on the Blue wheel-track which had no turnover in three consecutive positions of the wheel, so that study of the indicator evaluations for several Blue days would, by the process described, fix the tyre in relation to the wheel-track. The same procedure would, though with more trouble, fix the tyre in relation to the Red wheel-track, the Red wheel having a N*X and a RX beetle; Dilly, having sorted out the other two wheels, possibly used rods to read more text in one or two messages.

However Dilly went about the problem, Denniston informed 'C', who was also the director of GC&CS, that 'Knox has again justified his reputation as our most original investigator of Enigma problems . . . He read one message on December 8th. He attributes the success to two young girl members of his staff, Miss Rock and Miss Lever, and he gives them all the credit. He is of course the leader, but no doubt has selected and trained his staff to assist him in his somewhat unusual methods.' Denniston implied that Dilly was being kind, but in fact he greatly valued the work of his two lieutenants, saying 'Give me a Lever and a Rock and I will move the Universe.' This reading of a message completed Dilly's triumph and gave him the satisfaction of being brought into the mainstream again, having been distanced from the work of Hut 6 and Hut 8 (rightly so, because the crib/machine production line methods involved were not his style). Dilly's note of 28 October 1941 said that he expected the recovery of keys to be laborious and he asked for the gradual return of the Cottage staff who had been seconded to Hut 8 during the slack period.

The correspondence that followed with Denniston harked back to the days of the first breaks of wartime Enigma when Dilly wanted to be involved with the intelligence side of codebreaking. 'A scholar is bound to see his research through from the raw material to the final text,' Dilly complained. Denniston's reply on 11 November 1941 reveals their relationship with each other – also Denniston's diplomatic forbearance!

> If you do design a super Rolls-Royce that is no reason why you should yourself drive the thing up to the house of a possible buyer, more especially if you are not a very good driver . . . You are Knox, a scholar with a European reputation, who knows more about the inside of a machine than anyone else. The exigencies of war need that latter gift of yours though few people are aware of it.

Dilly was in fact terminally ill and never did take charge of the section which became known as ISK (Intelligence Services Knox) to his great satisfaction; the name was highly appropriate as the *Abwehr* hand-cipher traffic had been broken in 1940 by Oliver Strachey, Dilly's colleague from the early days of GC&CS, and his section was named ISOS (Intelligence Services Oliver Strachey). It was Peter Twinn, Dilly's first colleague in the Cottage in 1939, who took over the running of the new ISK section early in 1942. Dilly remained at home in Courns Wood, with Margaret Rock liaising between him and Bletchley Park. He worked from his bed until he died on 27 February 1943, only getting up in order to receive the CMG 'for services to his country' from the Palace emissary.

ISK became operational early in 1942 and finally expanded into a staff of over one hundred in one of the new blocks. Four European *Abwehr* networks were attacked by ISK: two in the West and two in the East. As they all used different daily settings a considerable amount of work was involved. In spite of Dilly's initial misgivings, evaluation of settings from doubly enciphered indicators proved fairly easy, and after straightforward rodding it was determined which was the RH wheel, the rod position at the start of the *Grundstellung*, and the wheel-track, which together fixed the RH wheel *Ringstellung*. The rod couplings for the RH wheel at the *Grundstellung* positions in effect gave parts of the alphabets produced by the other two wheels and reflector at those positions, and so enabled the middle wheel and its rod position to be determined, but probably not its wheel-track because only two or three turnover positions would be involved. This meant that determination of the *Ringstellung* depended on rodding out a few letters at the start of a message, which could prove troublesome.

Priority was given to the production of catalogues (on the lines developed by Gordon Welchman for the Railway Enigma), which provided a convenient and quick way of finding which settings of the reflector, LH and middle wheels gave prescribed pairings required by the rod position discovered for the RH wheel. When these catalogues became available, after three or four weeks, the day's key was easily settled once the RH wheel and its rod position at the *Grundstellung* were found. Priority was also given to the conversion of Typex machines to deal with the work of deciphering messages after the day's key was found, because the multiple turnovers of the *Abwehr* machine made deciphering by hand exceedingly slow and barely practicable without a vast staff. This was an inconvenient result from the multiple turnovers which, as just shown, were actually immensely helpful in working out daily keys because the wheel-track fixed the RH wheel *Ringstellung* in relation to the rods.

Very occasionally a day's indicators proved obdurate. To deal with such cases Mavis Lever, in spite of my strong scepticism (long regretted), had charts made for NRXEINS etc., arguing intuitively that the correct rod position of the RH wheel would probably have a chart 'click'. This scheme worked and proved invaluable when the double encipherment of message settings was stopped late in 1942, leaving the NRXEINS cribs as the only entry to the traffic. In 1943 ISK acquired a special four-wheel bombe (known as *Fünf*) to handle days when rodding failed. Charts and bombe together enabled nearly all *Abwehr* Enigma traffic to be deciphered until the end of 1944 when an entirely new machine, the *Schlüsselgerät* 41 (SG 41), was introduced.

Dilly had to start his attack on the unsolved *Abwehr* cipher machine from the initial assumption that a form of commercial Enigma was involved, since at that stage no other kind of four-wheel Enigma was known to GC&CS. The following notes, which relate mainly to the commercial machine, give some of the theory of the machine which he could use in testing that assumption.

Features of Simple Four-Wheel Enigma

1. The Enigma connected a typewriter keyboard to a bank of light-bulbs through a variable electric circuit, so that if a letter – A, say – was pressed a bulb – X, say – would light; the circuit was reciprocal, so that if X was pressed at the same setting A would light.

2. The variable circuit was provided by three wheels coaxially mounted with a reflector on the left and a fixed circular plate (the entry rotor – *Eintrittwalze* – or end-plate) on the right. Each wheel had twenty-six spring-loaded pins equally spaced around one face, each wired through the wheel to one of twenty-six small discs similarly placed around the other; the reflector had twenty-six pins placed like those on the wheels; and the end-plate had twenty-six discs, each wired to one keyboard letter and one bulb. Each wheel and the reflector carried a movable tyre or ring around its rim, lettered A–Z spaced to match the pins and discs; when mounted in the machine each could be set in one of twenty-six positions, each identified by the letter on the tyre which showed through a window in the machine's cover. The tyre could be fixed relative to the body of the wheel or reflector by a clip fixed to the wheel's body at one end and having a small pin at the other, which could be fitted into a hole in the edge of the tyre, identified by the adjacent tyre letter. The wheels could be mounted in the machine in any order, with the pins to the right, and when mounted were pressed together by a lever-operated spring, ensuring effective electrical contact between adjacent sets of pins and discs. When a keyboard letter was pressed, the right-hand (RH – i.e. that next to the end plate) wheel rotated anti-clockwise (viewed from the front right) one place; in each complete rotation of the RH wheel through twenty-six places the middle wheel would move one place, at a position determined by a notch on the RH tyre (called the turnover position); and the left-hand (LH) wheel moved one place for each complete rotation of the middle wheel. The reflector remained stationary during encipherment, but could be set manually.

3. To decipher a message the recipient had to know the order in which the wheels were mounted, the clip positions (*Ringstellungen* (ring settings) to the Germans), and the position of each wheel at the start of encipherment (the message setting). The message setting could not safely be sent in clear: one way of

hiding it, often used by the Germans, was to encipher it twice at a specified basic setting (the *Grundstellung*) and transmit the eight resulting letters as the indicator. Cipher instructions for an *Abwehr* network gave a key for a period, usually a day, specifying the wheel order, *Ringstellung* and *Grundstellung* to be used. Each operator was usually allowed to decide the setting he used for each message; inevitably, instead of using meaningless sets of four letters as intended, many operators chose names, keyboard sequences, or swear words.

4. A system with doubly enciphered indicators was easy to diagnose because study of the indicator starting groups for a day's traffic would quickly reveal eight consecutive places in which each letter in one of the first four places was always followed by the same letter in the place four places later (e.g. A in place 1 always followed by T in place 5 – sometimes the same letter would appear in both places, an occurrence known as a 'female'). If several indicators were available, 'chains' could be constructed joining corresponding letters in places four apart: e.g. if the indicator pairings in places 1, 4 were AM, MN, NT . . . the partial chain AMNT . . . would arise. Given a large enough set of indicators – probably at least thirty, allowing for non-random choice of settings – more or less complete chains could be obtained for each pairing 1–4, 2–5 etc., and from these letter pairings (i.e. alphabets) deduced, especially if some message settings could be guessed. Dilly Knox called this process 'boxing'.

5. To recover the wiring of an unknown Enigma from intercepted traffic some kind of crib – i.e. a cipher text and its *en clair* equivalent – is necessary. No straight crib – e.g. the retransmission of a message deciphered from another system – for the networks using *Abwehr* multi-notched Enigma was discovered, and the best hope of breaking into the traffic was judged to be the attempt to decipher a day's indicators. To do that with truly arbitrary message settings would require a large number of messages, but with slack operators using easily guessed four letters the task was

managed with some 15–20 messages. This happened with the Berlin–Rome *Sicherheitsdienst* link, whose choice of indicators was so helpfully lewd as to produce a reprimand from Berlin to the station head, Kappler, reminding him that young girls had to decipher the messages in Berlin.

6. A property of Enigma machines is that a letter will never be enciphered as itself. This meant that if, for example, it was suspected that messages were all starting in the same way, an analysis of the letters occurring in the first few places of thirty or more cipher texts would show that in each place one letter did not occur, so revealing the plain-text. This process was called a 'boil'.

7. The effect of the RH wheel is to join each disc on the end plate to a pin on the middle wheel, so that if the discs are labelled 1 to 26 clockwise (viewed from the LH side of the entry plate) and the pins on the middle wheel similarly labelled anti-clockwise, the connections made by the RH wheel may be entered in a table containing twenty-six rows and twenty-six columns, in which the entry n_{rs} in row r and column s means that in position s of the RH wheel the disc n_{rs} of the end-plate is joined to pin r of the middle wheel. Each row of the square was known as a 'rod'. If pins x and y of the middle wheel are connected by the wiring through that wheel, the LH wheel and the reflector, then placing the rods x and y together with matching columns will give the numbers of the end-plate discs connected through the machine at each position of the RH wheel for which the other parts of the machine stay the same.

8. Points to note about rods are:

(a) if n_{rs} appears in row r, column s, then $n_{rs}+1$ will appear in row (r+1), column (s+1);

(b) the numbers in each diagonal of the rod square run from top left to bottom right in numerical order;

(c) if the keyboard keys and the light-bulbs are wired to the end-plate in the order QWERTZU . . . reading clockwise viewed from the keyboard – and hence anti-clockwise viewed from the

RH wheel – letters can be substituted for the numbers on the rods using the substitution:

Q	L	M	N	B	. . .
1	2	3	4	5	. . .

The keyboard order is reversed because the end-plate discs are numbered anti-clockwise from the keyboard aspect. This troublesome business of clockwise and anti-clockwise led Dilly on occasion to tease new entrants with the question, 'Which way does a clock go round?'

To complicate matters further, if the rod labels are arranged in the order QWERTZU... the rod square will have diagonals running from top right to bottom left!

(d) If a rod contains two or more letters of a text enciphered with its associated wheel in the RH position and there is no turnover between them, then the associated plain-text letters must also lie on one rod. This fact was especially useful if two adjacent cipher letters were on the same rod, because the deciphered letters must then also lie on one rod; as the bigrams in any two adjacent rod columns were usually unlikely to occur in plain-text (e.g. JT, VQ etc.), this reduced the number of possible decipherments; and with luck and persistence it was sometimes possible to 'rod out' a piece of plain-text and recover the day's key.

(e) Because of the diagonal structure of the rod square (cf. (b) above), if a rod had a bigram AG in places 8, 9, say, then AH was part of column 8, SJ part of column 7, and so on reading down the diagonal. This fact enabled a wheel's wiring to be discovered if five or six sets of letter pairings were available for each of four consecutive positions, because if one assumed, given a pairing FS in position 2 and HL in position 3, say, that FL was a rod bigram then SH would also be a bigram, and so column 1 would contain pairs GW and DK, leading to implications about bigrams at other positions and hence other pairings in column 1; wrong

Figure 16.1 **Rod square for the Green wheel – 3 Beetles (in rows e, t and j) are emboldened and circled**

	1		3		5		7		9		11		13		15		17		19		21		23		25	
q	L	K	C	A	U	E	H	T	O	F	Z	X	B	J	S	M	D	Y	G	S	U	N	W	P	V	I
w	P	V	S	I	R	J	Z	A	G	U	C	N	K	D	L	F	X	H	D	I	M	E	Y	B	O	Q
e	B	D	O	T	K	U	S	H	I	V	M	P	F	Q	G	C	J	F	O	L	**R**	**X**	N	A	W	Y
r	F	A	Z	P	I	D	J	O	B	L	Y	G	W	H	V	K	G	A	Q	T	C	M	S	E	X	N
t	S	U	Y	O	F	K	A	**N**	Q	**X**	H	E	J	B	P	H	S	W	Z	V	L	D	R	C	M	G
z	I	X	A	G	P	S	M	W	C	J	R	K	N	Y	J	D	E	U	B	Q	F	T	V	L	H	D
u	C	S	H	Y	D	L	E	V	K	T	P	M	X	K	F	R	I	N	W	G	Z	B	Q	J	F	O
i	D	J	X	F	Q	R	B	P	Z	Y	L	C	P	G	T	O	M	E	H	U	N	W	K	G	A	V
o	K	C	G	W	T	N	Y	U	X	Q	V	Y	H	Z	A	L	R	J	I	M	E	P	H	S	B	F
a	V	H	E	Z	M	X	I	C	W	B	X	J	U	S	Q	T	K	O	L	R	Y	J	D	N	G	P
s	J	R	U	L	C	O	V	E	N	C	K	I	D	W	Z	P	A	Q	T	X	K	F	M	H	Y	B
d	T	I	Q	V	A	B	R	M	V	P	O	F	E	U	Y	S	W	Z	C	P	G	L	J	X	N	K
f	O	W	B	S	N	T	L	B	Y	A	G	R	I	X	D	E	U	V	Y	H	Q	K	C	M	P	Z
g	E	N	D	M	Z	Q	N	X	S	H	T	O	C	F	R	I	B	X	J	W	P	V	L	Y	U	A
h	M	F	L	U	W	M	C	D	J	Z	A	V	G	T	O	N	C	K	E	Y	B	Q	X	I	S	R
j	G	Q	I	E	L	V	F	K	U	S	B	H	Z	A	M	V	P	**R**	**X**	N	W	C	O	D	T	L
k	W	O	R	Q	B	G	P	I	D	N	J	U	S	L	B	Y	T	C	M	E	V	A	F	Z	Q	H
p	A	T	W	N	H	Y	O	F	M	K	I	D	Q	N	X	Z	V	L	R	B	S	G	U	W	J	E
y	Z	E	M	J	X	A	G	L	P	O	F	W	M	C	U	B	Q	T	N	D	H	I	E	K	R	S
x	R	L	K	C	S	H	Q	Y	A	G	E	L	V	I	N	W	Z	M	F	J	O	R	P	T	D	U
c	Q	P	V	D	J	W	X	S	H	R	Q	B	O	M	E	U	L	G	K	A	T	Y	Z	F	I	T
v	Y	B	F	K	E	C	D	J	T	W	N	A	L	R	I	Q	H	P	S	Z	X	U	G	O	Z	W
b	N	G	P	R	V	F	K	Z	E	M	S	Q	T	O	W	J	Y	D	U	C	I	H	A	U	E	X
n	H	Y	T	B	G	P	U	R	L	D	W	Z	A	E	K	X	F	I	V	O	J	S	I	R	C	M
m	X	Z	N	H	Y	I	T	Q	F	E	U	S	R	P	C	G	O	B	A	K	D	O	T	V	L	J
l	U	M	J	X	O	Z	W	G	R	I	D	T	Y	V	H	A	N	S	P	F	A	Z	B	Q	K	C

assumptions would rapidly lead to contradictory deductions, and a correct assumption would lead to no contradictions.

9. If discs numbered x and y on the end-plate are connected through the machine, then (x+1) and (y+1) will be connected if the three wheels and reflector are each moved one place forward. Using the substitution of numbers by letters as described in paragraph 8(c), it follows that if, for example, letters T and V are connected at the setting ABCD, letters R and C – i.e. the preceding letters in QWERTZU . . . – will be connected at BCDE, and so on; and any setting obtained by rotating all three wheels and reflector by x positions will produce an alphabet got from that at ABCD by replacing each letter by that x positions before it in the QWERTZU . . . sequence. The chains obtained by 'boxing' the alphabets at 1–5, 2–6, 3–7, 4–8 at the second setting will also be obtained from those at ABCD by a QWERTZU . . . substitution.

17

Breaking Tunny and the Birth of Colossus

SHAUN WYLIE

Introduction

The breaking of the Enigma machine ciphers is invariably cited as the great achievement of the Bletchley Park codebreakers. But the breaking of the German enciphered teleprinter traffic, given the generic codename of 'Fish', was a far greater achievement. After an early break by John Tiltman, who yet again succeeded in making something extraordinarily difficult seem very easy, Bill Tutte, another of the unsung British codebreakers, broke the Lorenz SZ 40/42 teleprinter cipher attachment. The solution of this cipher machine and its traffic, codenamed 'Tunny' by GC&CS, must rank as one of the finest cryptanalytical achievements of all time. It also led to the development of Colossus, the world's first semi-programmable electronic computer.

This chapter by Shaun Wylie, who worked on Tunny at Bletchley, gives a real insight into the very considerable effort devoted by GC&CS to its solution. It was more than worthwhile, providing intelligence of the highest grade, including communications from Hitler direct to his frontline commanders during the

Allied invasion of Europe. Tunny decrypts may even have helped the Russians to win the Battle of Kursk, the turning point on the Eastern Front. Stalin was distrustful of the sanitized intelligence being given to him by official British sources, but the raw Tunny decrypts passed to Moscow by John Cairncross, the 'Fifth Man' in the Cambridge spy ring and a member of Hut 3, gave him details of the German battle plans straight from the horse's mouth. Not only did the Tunny decrypts provide high-grade intelligence, they provided it in unprecedented quantity. Walter Jacobs, a US Army codebreaker who worked at Bletchley Park, wrote in an official report on the operation to break Tunny that in March 1945 alone 'upwards of five million letters of current transmission, containing intelligence of the highest order, were deciphered'.

Tunny was not the only German teleprinter cipher broken at Bletchley Park. The British codebreakers also worked on the Siemens and Halske T52 teleprinter cipher machines, codenamed 'Sturgeon'. The T52 had at least four variants. In a little-known operation, GC&CS reconstructed them all, including the T52d, which was a significantly more complex machine than the earlier models. But for a number of reasons, including the fact that the machines were mainly used by the Luftwaffe *– on which Enigma traffic already provided a great deal of information – Bletchley Park decided to concentrate on Tunny.*

MS

In the autumn of 1943, I was moved from Hut 8 of Bletchley Park, where I had been working on naval Enigma, to Hut 11, where I worked on Tunny, the Lorenz SZ 40/42 teleprinter cipher machine. For me, Hut 8 had been fascinating and immediate. I was in a section, part of whose job it was to study the deciphered signals and know as much as possible about them. Suddenly what we did produced the Enigma settings and a day's traffic tumbled out. The satisfaction to be had from the work I was involved in on Tunny was different. We formed part of a process, improving our methods of using machines and devising new approaches; actual plain-text was none of our business, only its statistical features. We were told of the importance of the intelligence derived from Tunny, and we prided ourselves on the efficiency of our part of the operation; but the results weren't immediate. If, however, Tunny was less exciting for me than Enigma, there was one personal bonus that more than compensated: I met and married Odette Murray, who was one of the first batch of Wrens in the section.

Fish

When the Germans invaded Russia, they started to use a new type of enciphered transmission between central headquarters and headquarters in the field. The signal was a string of teleprinter characters: each character consisted of five impulses (or 'bits'), each impulse being either positive (a dot) or negative (a cross). These signals were taken at a station in Knockholt, near Sevenoaks in Kent, where they were painstakingly transcribed. They reached Bletchley Park on teleprinter tape and handwritten on the Red intercept forms.

All such systems were known at Bletchley Park as Fish. There were three kinds: Thrasher, Sturgeon and Tunny. Nothing positive was ever found out about Thrasher. Sturgeon (the Siemens and Halske T52 series of machines) was diagnosed after a remarkable feat of analysis by Michael Crum, an Oxford research mathematician; the system, however, was too complex for this heroic diagnosis to be followed by exploitation. Tunny, on the other hand, was both diagnosed and exploited, with a valuable harvest of intelligence. This chapter is therefore about Tunny.

The Tunny Machine

In Tunny, the cipher stream (Z) is obtained from the stream of plain-text (P) by adding a stream of key (K), character by character. Symbolically Z = P + K. Two characters are added together by adding their corresponding bits level by level; two different bits add to a cross, two equal bits to a dot. So for instance (using the international teleprinter code):

H		N		O		
•		•		•		
•		•		•		
×	+	×	=	•	or	H + N = O
•		×		×		
×		•		×		

Subtraction is the same as addition (making decipherment the same process as encipherment), so that also

H = N + O and N = H + O

The key-stream in its turn was the sum of two streams:

$$K = \chi + \psi'$$

The χ-stream (chi-stream) and the ψ-stream (psi-stream) were generated by twelve wheels in the Tunny machine, each with a different number of pins on its circumference, carrying its pattern of dots and crosses. The operator set the pattern by making each pin active (cross) or inactive (dot). The total number of pins on a wheel determined the length of its pseudo-random pattern.

i) Five of these, called by us the χ-wheels (chi-wheels), moved regularly, producing the chi-stream. The lengths of their patterns were 41, 31, 29, 26 and 23, the wheel of length 41 giving the

χ_1-stream for level 1 in the teleprinter code, the next for level 2, and so on up to level 5.
ii) Another five, the ψ-wheels (psi-wheels), had patterns of lengths 43, 47, 51, 53 and 59. Had they also moved regularly they would have produced a psi-stream. In fact they moved under instruction from a 'total motor' stream of bits; when the bit was a dot, they all stood still; when it was a cross they all moved. That produced the 'extended' stream ψ' (extended psi).
iii) The other two wheels were motor wheels of lengths 61 and 37; the longer μ_{61} moved regularly; when it was at a cross, the shorter μ_{37} moved on one place; when at a dot, μ_{37} stood still. The resulting extended stream μ_{37}' provided the basic motor stream of dots and crosses. In the original Tunny machine it was the basic motor that constituted the total motor. In later versions, a 'limitation' stream was generated from other streams, which combined with the basic motor to give the total motor stream.

The whole contraption, remarkably, was diagnosed from the transmissions themselves.

The Transmissions

Initially there was a single experimental communications link; later links were put into use covering continental Europe and North Africa. The German operator (assumed masculine in what follows), sitting at his teleprinter console, sent information in clear about the initial wheel settings and then switched over to the cipher mode. Whatever he then put on line was automatically enciphered by the Tunny machine and automatically deciphered at the other end. He could input messages that had already been punched onto teleprinter tape (recognized at Knockholt as such and noted as 'Auto' on the red forms), or he could tap out messages himself; in either case he would intersperse the messages with operator chat, doodling and corrections (all noted by Knockholt as 'Hand'). One transmission could include many messages.

To start a new transmission, he could choose new initial wheel positions or (apparently) he could press some gadget that returned the wheels to the starting positions just used. Fortunately for us, he quite often took the easy option, sending two transmissions from the same start. Then (except when the link was using one of two particular limitations) the two transmissions had the same key-stream throughout:

Za = K + Pa and
Zb = K + Pb
So, subtracting, Za – Zb = Pa – Pb.

The observed stream Za – Zb could often be analysed by linguists as Pa – Pb, and the plain-texts of the two transmissions recovered in whole or in part. From that the key-stream can be formed as (for instance) Za – Pa. Such transmissions were said to provide a 'depth'.

The Diagnosis

The diagnosis of Tunny was a triumph of the research section at Bletchley Park. No doubt other members of the section contributed, but the two feats are ascribed to John Tiltman and Bill Tutte. Tiltman was an already revered cryptanalyst, oozing confidence; Tutte was a recently recruited Cambridge research student, on the face of it (but only on the face of it) oozing diffidence.

Exploitation of Tunny traffic depended on three processes:
i) Diagnosis of the machine, once and for all.
ii) Recovery of wheel patterns, once for each link and pattern-period.
iii) Setting of known patterns, once for each transmission.

In early Tunny, the preamble to a transmission would include an indicator, twelve letters sent as Anton, Bertha . . . (A, B, etc., which were spelt out in full phonetically, to reduce garbles and errors). On 30 August 1941, two long transmissions had exactly the same indicator. A previous depth had been partly read on the correct assumption that Z = P + K. Tiltman could therefore attack this new depth on that assumption. After breaking into the beginning by reading likely starts he discovered that both transmissions were hand-sendings of the same message, but with different spacings, misspellings and corrections. This fortunate feature enabled Tiltman to battle his way through the entire depth. So different were the two texts that at the 3,976th character, when the shorter one ended, the longer still had 100 more characters.

The upshot of this was that the research section had (by subtracting the recovered plain-text from its cipher) almost 4,000 characters of key. Their only problem was what to do with it. It was months before they had a smell of a feature, and the final diagnosis did not emerge until January 1942. In what follows, the analysis is ascribed to its chief architect Tutte, although others may have made occasional contributions.

Among the multitude of things tried on this key-stream, Tutte looked at long repeats within levels. He noticed that the distances apart of these long repeats in the first level tended to be multiples of 41. Accordingly, he wrote that level out on a width of 41 so as to place many of the long repeats in the same columns. For each set of five consecutive columns, he made a count of its five-bit characters. The distributions were significantly non-random; moreover, the distribution for one set could be matched well with that of another by adding an appropriate five-bit character throughout. These five-bit addends then turned out to fit together to give a 41-bit pattern.

This cyclic pattern was called χ_1. He subtracted it from the first level of the key-stream to yield a stream (that would later be called ψ'_1). It seemed to be approximately periodic and was correctly diagnosed as an extended pattern of length 43. Calling this pattern ψ_1, the observed stream was the extended ψ'_1.

The same method worked well on the other levels producing

chi-patterns (χ-patterns) of lengths 31, 29, 26 and 23 and associated psi-patterns (ψ-patterns) of lengths 47, 51, 53 and 59. It then emerged that all the psi-patterns could be regarded as having moved or having stood still together, suggesting a motor stream. This was soon diagnosed as a pattern of length 37, called μ_{37}, extended by a regularly moving pattern of length 61, called μ_{61}. The Tiltman–Tutte triumph was complete.

The Usage

This diagnosis determined all that had to be known about the Tunny machine for that pair of transmissions – its structure, the allocation of pattern-lengths to levels and the wheel patterns themselves. The research section then had to find out how long the wheel patterns stayed unchanged, and whether the allocation of lengths to levels could be changed. They had valuable help from a depth sent on 3 July 1941. They had by now (from Tiltman's earlier success with the depth) a long sample of plain-text; with that to help them they read two stretches of lengths 500 and 300 characters of this July depth. Tutte's method was successfully applied to the resulting stretches of key. They found that the allocation of pattern-lengths to levels was unchanged. Another depth of July 1941 was also solved. For all three depths the psi-patterns were the same; for both the July depths the chi-patterns were the same, but different from those in the August depth; and the μ-patterns were all different.

Early Wheel-Setting

There were, of course, many transmissions in July 1941 that were not in depth. The research section had the chi-patterns and psi-patterns and they used a highly laborious method of setting the wheels and so deciphering the transmissions. It involved trying likely cribs as plain-text at the start to give putative key; then subtracting from the putative key the chi-pattern at all possible settings for each level; and hoping to recognize possible fragments of the extended psi-streams. It was a long time before their first success, but by April 1942 they had deciphered several transmissions.

A Change in Tunny

Various features of Tunny that favoured the analyst were, from time to time, abandoned by the Germans. The first of these concerned the psi-patterns, and is best described in terms of an important symbol Δ. Δ before a symbol describing a stream of bits or characters means the stream formed by adding together each pair of consecutive bits or characters. So

If K starts	•	×	×	•
	•	•	×	•
	×	•	×	•
	•	×	•	×
	×	×	×	•

Δ K starts	×	•	×
	•	×	×
	×	×	×
	×	×	×
	•	•	×

In all Tunny ever recovered, both the χ_i and the $\Delta\chi_i$ patterns for the ith level had as nearly as possible equal numbers of dots and crosses. Initially this was also true for the ψ_i and the $\Delta\psi_i$ patterns. It was this feature of the $\Delta\psi_i$ patterns that had let Tutte in. In order for a particular bit in $\Delta\psi_i'$ to be a cross, both the total motor and $\Delta\psi_i$ must be a cross. If *a* is the proportion of crosses in the total motor and b the proportion in $\Delta\psi_i$, then the proportion in $\Delta\psi_i'$ is ab. In early Tunny b was nearly ½, so that ab was much less than ½, and $\Delta\psi_i'$ had considerably more dots than crosses. That meant that $\Delta\chi_i$ was equal to ΔK_i considerably more often than not, so that ΔK_i written on a width appropriate for the ith level would be expected to give a majority of bits in each column that were equal to that bit in $\Delta\chi_i$. That was the feature that allowed Tutte to reconstruct $\Delta\chi_i$ (and so χ_i) for each level separately.

By the end of 1941, the German cryptographers plugged this gap. Thereafter the total motors and psi-patterns were always designed in such a way that $ab \cong ½$.

Second Generation Wheel-Breaking and Setting

After a drought, depths started to reappear in February 1942, and the research section read some of them and tried Tutte's method without success. That was, of course, because by then $ab \cong ½$ and no attack in single streams could work.

They did eventually break the patterns for March and April 1942. In each month, there was a 'near depth', a pair of transmissions whose indicators differed only in the letters that gave the setting for two or three chi-wheels. They contrived a long and highly resourceful method of exploiting the differences of the χ-settings of those wheels, and eventually prised the whole thing open. They found that between March and April both the psi-patterns and the chi-patterns were different. Perhaps the psi-patterns changed quarterly, the chi-patterns monthly, and the μ-patterns daily.

The wheel settings were given by indicator letters, but they were not in letter order. When, however, two indicators had the same letter in a position, the wheel for that position started at the same place for the two transmissions. This meant that wheel-setting during a month gathered pace. The research section had such success setting wheels for March and April 1942 that it became clear that they needed a machine to do the decryption. The first was ordered and was delivered in June 1942.

For any month with no usable near-depth, a new method was needed to break the patterns. Another quite different (and equally laborious and resourceful) method was found. It exploited the twelve-letter indicators, a special feature of what Tunny did at the first few letters of a transmission, and the routine starts to the plain-text. It was used to break the patterns of May, June and July 1942.

The Testery

In July 1942 work on Tunny was handed over to a new section headed by Major Tester and named after him. It was formed from people already at Bletchley Park and they were supplemented by people from the Army and the ATS. The section inherited from the research section various methods but no royal road to success. Moreover, the two methods of wheel-breaking just mentioned were both defeated by German improvements. In August 1942 they began starting their transmission with '*Quatsch*' (meaningless German words), so the method that depended on standard initial cribs was no use. In October 1942, the original experimental Tunny link was closed; in its place they started more and more links (on slightly modified machines) each with its own wheel-patterns. Thereafter, on all links, the clear twelve-letter indicator was replaced by a 'QEP' number; it referred to some list of settings available to the operators but not to Bletchley Park. Depths could be recognized from the repetition of the QEP number; but near-depths could not, even if there were any. So the method of wheel-breaking that used the letter-indicators was also denied to the Testery. Depths were still sent and read but there was at first no way of breaking wheel-patterns from the key-streams they provided.

Turingery

In the summer of 1942, Alan Turing, already a legendary figure of Enigma cryptanalysis, attacked this problem of breaking patterns from key. He worked entirely on $\Delta K = \Delta\chi + \Delta\psi'$, exploiting a weakness of $\Delta\psi'$, namely that the chance that two bits of a character of $\Delta\psi'$ should be the same is *b*. (The two bits can only differ if, for that $\Delta\psi'$ character, there was a total motor cross so that there $\Delta\psi' = \Delta\psi$. The probability, therefore, that they differ is $a \times 2\,b\,(1 - b) = 1 - b$ when $a\,b = \frac{1}{2}$.)

The method started by making the assumption that, at some arbitrarily chosen point, there had been a total motor dot, so that there $\Delta\psi'$ = / (the all dot character – a space in the teleprinter code). If that is right, at that place $\Delta\chi = \Delta K$ and one $\Delta\chi$ bit is known at each level. These bits are cycled through the depth to give (by subtracting from ΔK) isolated bits of $\Delta\psi'$, 'correct' under the initial assumption. Since in a $\Delta\psi'$ character each pair of bits has a probability *b* of being equal, each such 'correct' $\Delta\psi'$ bit spawns putatively equal bits of $\Delta\psi'$ in the other four levels. Each such putative bit gives, by subtraction from ΔK, a putative $\Delta\chi$ bit that has a probability *b* of being right (under the initial assumption). These putative $\Delta\chi$ bits are then assembled onto a blank $\Delta\chi$ pattern for each of the five levels.

For instance, with a depth of 1,000 characters the original assumption places about twenty-four 'correct' $\Delta\chi_1$ bits, about thirty-two $\Delta\chi_2$ bits, about thirty-four $\Delta\chi_3$ bits and about thirty-eight $\Delta\chi_4$ bits. Each spawns a single putative $\Delta\chi_5$ bit, giving nearly 130 putative bits; so there will be five or six putative bits at each place on the twenty-three-long blank $\Delta\chi_5$ pattern.

At this stage for all the levels the number of agreements and disagreements (between putative bits at the same place on a $\Delta\chi$ pattern) is counted. If the agreements do not exceed the disagreements convincingly the initial assumption is rejected, and another place is chosen to start the process and the whole thing is repeated.

Eventually the agreements do exceed the disagreements convincingly; fragmentary $\Delta\chi_i$ patterns can be formed from the places where the putative $\Delta\chi_i$ bits give a clear preference between dot and cross. These fragmentary patterns are then cycled through and subtracted from ΔK to give bits of $\Delta\psi'$. At a place where $\Delta\psi'$ has three probable dots, it is assumed that there has been a motor dot and the remaining bits are taken to be dots, yielding two more $\Delta\chi$ bits. In this way the $\Delta\chi$ patterns are massaged against each other until complete correct $\Delta\chi$ patterns establish themselves. The rest is easy.

With this weapon known as Turingery, the Testery were in a position to break the patterns for each link/month that offered a substantial readable depth. The recovered patterns could be set against any other depth that could be read for twenty or more characters. There remained, however, the important problem of setting the bulk of the transmissions, that were not in depth.

Setting Transmissions

In November 1942 Tutte proposed a way of setting known χ_1 and χ_2 patterns against a long enough stretch of cipher. He suggested comparing $\Delta\chi_1 + \Delta\chi_2$ with $\Delta Z_1 + \Delta Z_2$. The idea is that $(\Delta Z_1 + \Delta Z_2) - (\Delta\chi_1 + \Delta\chi_2) = (\Delta P_1 + \Delta P_2) + (\Delta\psi_1' + \Delta\psi_2')$. For each character the probability that $(\Delta\psi_1' + \Delta\psi_2')$ is a dot is b (when, as now, $ab = ½$). The value of b tended to be about 0.7. Results from statistics of plain-text had shown that $(\Delta P_1 + \Delta P_2)$ is also considerably more likely to be dot than cross. Consequently $(\Delta\chi_1 + \Delta\chi_2)$ is expected to be equal to $(\Delta Z_1 + \Delta Z_2)$ noticeably more often than not.

Tutte devised a way of testing all the possible pairs of settings for χ_1 and χ_2 against a transmission of about 4,000 characters, and found a significantly good answer. The other chi-wheels were then set using similar methods and the psi-wheels and motor wheels followed. This was a striking achievement, but too slow to open an avenue to the goal of setting known patterns in useful quantities. It did, however, in March 1943, play an important part in diagnosing a new motor limitation.

Motor Limitations

In February 1943, the new Tunny machines had new features. These were 'limitations' that influenced the extension of the psi-stream. The basic motor was as before, but the psi-stream was only extended when the basic motor stream was at a dot and also the limitation stream was a cross. On a link known to Bletchley Park as Codfish, when chi- and psi-patterns had been set, the extensions of the psi-stream only partly agreed with any possible μ'_{37}. The Testery analysed the divergences and found that they only came when $\bar{\chi}_2$ (the bit of χ_2 one place back) was a dot; the psi-stream was extended only when μ'_{37} was a dot and $\bar{\chi}_2$ was a cross.

In March 1943, the link known as Herring introduced as the limitation stream $\bar{\chi}_2 + \bar{\bar{P}}_5$, the sum of χ_2 one back and P_5 two back. When in a system the key depends on previous plain-text, it is said to be 'autoclave', self-keying. This has two effects, one serious for us. Two transmissions with the same QEP numbers would have the same starting positions for their wheels, but, having different P_5 bits, they would eventually have different extensions to their psi-wheels and so have different keys. Apparent depths would soon cease to be in depth and could no longer be read. The second feature was unfortunate for the Germans. Poor radio reception would often cause the receiver to get a false Z_5 bit and so a false P_5 bit, which could throw the decipherment out from then on. They had so much trouble with this autoclave feature that it was soon abandoned and only resumed in December 1943.

This limitation might have taken the Testery a long time to diagnose, but fortunately it was introduced in mid-March after the March patterns had been broken from a normal depth.

Among the later unbreakable depths was one 6,000 characters long. They applied Tutte's method by hand and set the known chi-patterns and stripped them. They set the ψ's on both de-chis and compared the total motor patterns for both. Again they noted the discrepancies and found that at all of those $\bar{\bar{P}}_5$ also differed. That enabled them to diagnose the limitation stream as $\bar{\chi}_2 + \bar{\bar{P}}_5$.

The Newmanry

Although Tutte's method of setting known chi-wheels on a long transmission had proved successful, it took too long. In November 1942, Max Newman, an established Cambridge mathematician, was a member of the Tunny team. He pointed out that the 41×31 comparisons of $\Delta\chi_1 + \Delta\chi_2$ with $\Delta Z_1 + \Delta Z_2$ could be made by comparing rotating loops of punched paper tape. One would carry Z and the other, of length 41×31, would carry the 31-fold repetition of χ_1 on one level and the 41-fold repetition of χ_2 on another. These tapes would rotate in step, and (provided the length of the Z tape was prime to 41×31) the start of the Z-stream would eventually come opposite to all possible starts for χ_1 and χ_2. Suitable photo-electrical machinery could count the number of dots in $(\Delta Z_1 + \Delta Z_2) - (\Delta\chi_1 + \Delta\chi_2)$ between the start and the stop signs on the Z tape. Whenever the count exceeded a given threshold (or 'set-total'), it could record the count and the number of rotations the Z tape had made. If the design was flexible enough, it could make fast counts also of other combinations and the other chi-patterns could be set in a similar way.

The scheme was approved and Newman was given the job of implementing it. His first move was to talk to engineers about the machines he needed. The most important was the machine to compare fast-moving loops of tape and to count combinations of bits. It was designed by Dr C. E. Wynn-Williams of the Telecommunications Research Establishment at Malvern and by members of Tommy Flowers' Post Office Research Department at Dollis Hill. The first was specified in January 1943 and delivered to Bletchley Park in June 1943. Apart from Post Office racks it had two systems of adjustable pulleys, called bedsteads, around which loops of paper tape could be threaded. It looked unlikely and was christened Heath Robinson (plain Robinson to its friends).

Other machines were needed and provided. One called Tunny mimicked the German machine and could produce such things as the 41 × 31 long tape of χ_1 and χ_2, and a great deal else. Another had five heads and could combine in various ways up to five inputs to produce four tape outputs. It was known as Mrs Miles in honour of a lady of that name who had leapt to fame by having quadruplets.

By April 1943, Newman had in his section sixteen Wrens and Donald Michie. Michie was an unprecedentedly young recruit: he had won a Classics scholarship at Oxford in the days when most of the brightest boys did Classics. He was outstandingly inventive, open-minded and vigorous, one of the heavyweights in the attack on Tunny. The Wrens were held in a typing school until June 1943 when the machines arrived. They were then divided into four watches and set about learning how to use the machines – and very good at it they became. By that time Jack Good and seven engineers had joined the section. Good came from Hut 8, where, as well as doing the standard things very well, he had helped with an influential statistical review of the material. In the Newmanry, among a mass of other contributions, he took the lead in establishing proper statistical tools for evaluating results. He once told me that he wanted to win the war by himself, and, from the way he set about Tunny, you could tell that he meant it. In the course of time other analysts like me were sent from Huts 6 and 8 and the research section; other engineers came from Dollis Hill, and other Wrens joined the original sixteen.

In the early days, the machines had teething problems and so did the analysts, but eventually the section discovered how to set all the wheels on a long enough transmission. After χ_1 and χ_2 had been set, the other chi-patterns could be attacked, one by one or in pairs. They were subtracted from Z on Tunny to provide the de-chi, D = $\psi' + P$. Strong features of ΔP would appear in ΔD much more strongly against dots than against crosses in μ'_{37} where $\Delta\psi' = /$. The whole length of μ'_{37} was run against ΔD, counting some strong feature of ΔP against dots of μ'_{37}. This set the motor wheels. The D stream was then 'contracted' by omitting the characters that came against motor dots; that gave a stream of 'contracted' P added to the unextended psi-stream. The psi-patterns were set by subtracting them at all settings and counting for dots (say) in levels of the contracted P-stream.

This airy description slides over the surface. Under the surface a lot was going on and a lot was going wrong. We were analysing statistical properties of samples of ΔP, and found great differences between samples. We had to identify robust features and devise efficient strategies for setting the χ's after setting χ_1 and χ_2. Our earliest efforts were often inefficient. At the places where a count exceeded its set-total threshold, the count and the number of revolutions the Z tape had made were shown on a screen and the operator wrote them down. The output of a run was a list of these. The screen, however, was quite hard to read and even the operator's handwriting could be misread. The place on the χ_1 χ_2 tape that corresponded to the number of revolutions could be miscalculated; the stated length of the Z tape could be wrong. The looped tapes could stretch and they could break. It soon became clear that time spent on checking everything was time saved. Checking became an integral part of all the Newmanry routines.

Early on successes came slowly, but eventually it became clear that Robinson could indeed set known patterns in useful quantities. But new Tunny links were coming on the air, each with its own wheel-patterns; there were ten in the autumn of 1943 and eventually twenty-six; and many of them carried important strategic intelligence. Most of the long transmissions could be deciphered if only we could get at them; Robinson was overloaded and more machinery was essential.

More (and improved) Robinsons were ordered and began to arrive in late 1943. More significantly Newman consulted with Flowers about something much more powerful. Flowers had the idea of a machine in which the wheel patterns and how they affected each other could be set up on valves. The cipher text (as with Robinson) was on perforated tape that rotated on a bedstead (but much faster). The scores and wheel-positions were typed out. In their design they went for great flexibility in the combinations that could be counted, which proved to be important. This machine, known as Colossus, was installed in February 1944. After a successful run on Robinson a new tape had to be mounted, and another often had to be made, before the next run. On Colossus you only had to change the plugging; it was liberating.

The Testery and the Newmanry

The Newmanry and the Testery had at first distinct jobs: the Testery read depths and recovered wheel-patterns; the Newmanry set transmissions on these patterns; the Testery handled the deciphering. We realized, however, in November 1943 that the Testery could set the psi- and μ-patterns on any transmission from which the chi-patterns had been correctly subtracted. We gave them the de-chi, $D = P + \psi'$. The Testery analysts could use the skill that enabled them to read depths to split D into its component parts, P and ψ'. It was therefore decided that the Newmanry should content itself with setting the chi-wheels and delivering the de-chis to the Testery. We would also give a character-count of ΔD, and the duty officer responsible for accepting the settings as correct would add his initials. The Testery could (and did) assign priorities, based on the look of the count and the initials that went with it. The decision meant, of course, that more transmissions could be deciphered; Robinson had formed the bottleneck, not the Testery.

About that time, the Newmanry moved from its original intimate hut into lavish accommodation in Block F near to the Testery. It housed the first Colossus, two improved Robinsons, and other improved Colossi as they arrived. The two sections formed a joint Registry, and a non-Morse section of Sixta (which was responsible for traffic analysis) was created. Its job included liaison with our suppliers, Knockholt, and with our customers, the intelligence sections. Knockholt intercepted more transmissions than Bletchley Park could decipher; Sixta, knowing both the intelligence and the cryptanalytic priorities, could get Knockholt to send us the transmission that could be used for wheel-breaking and the decipherable transmission that the customers most wanted to read.

New Wheel-breaking Methods

By the start of 1944 the days of great achievements and inventions had passed. There was a lot we could and did do to improve our methods of exploitation; but for the recovery of wheel-patterns we had so far depended on depths. At about this time, however, some links began re-using autoclave limitations, and for such links depths could not be read. We needed to break the patterns from single transmissions. A method, known as rectangling, derived from one of Tutte's hand experiments, came to our aid.

It used the $\Delta\chi_1 + \Delta\chi_2$ feature that we had been using to set transmissions. If $\Delta Z_1 + \Delta Z_2$ were written out on a width of 41×31, the excess of dots over crosses (positive or negative) in each column gave evidence about whether $\Delta\chi_1$ and $\Delta\chi_2$ at those positions were equal or not. These excesses were written into a rectangle of 31 rows and 41 columns diagonally downwards, reappearing in the obvious way when they came to the bottom or the right-hand end; each row, therefore, referred to a single χ_2 position and each column to a χ_1 position. Any assumed pattern for $\Delta\chi_2$, consisting of 1s for dots, –1s for crosses and 0s for 'don't know' could be applied to each column to assemble a total excess for that bit of $\Delta\chi_1$. From that a fragmentary putative pattern could be deduced for $\Delta\chi_1$. This could, in the same way, give an excess for each bit of $\Delta\chi_2$, and so on. This process, known as crude convergence, continued until believable patterns for $\Delta\chi_1$ and $\Delta\chi_2$ were reached. A bad start was likely to lead to a bad end, and devices were found for getting a good start with a few dots and crosses and a lot of 'don't knows'.

Jack Good provided significance tests. One, on the total excesses arising from the final patterns, determined whether it would be worth proceeding to the next stage. Another (too lengthy until a way was found of calculating it on Colossus) picked out the transmissions whose rectangles were likely to work.

Colossus could be used to provide the original 41 × 31 excesses that were written into the rectangle. Wrens did convergences and became very good at it. Once a convincing pair of patterns was produced, Colossus could be used to get partial patterns for the other chi-wheels, and eventually to give complete patterns. At first this involved Wrens or (much worse) cryptanalysts going behind the machine and fiddling with the gadgets that set up the wheel-patterns. The engineers hated anything like that and soon provided us with panels at the front of some of the Colossi on which we could do the job without risk to the machines.

The method worked well enough and we sent reliable de-chis to the Testery; but we wondered at first whether they could expand their method of ψ-setting to the much harder job of ψ-breaking. We need not have wondered. In February 1944, they had their first such success. The method was to fit a longish crib, say thirty characters long, that gave a plausible stretch of ψ'; to contract this to a stretch of ψ, perhaps twenty long; and to cycle the twenty-long stretches of ψ_1, ψ_2, . . . through one cycle each. The shortest cycle-length is forty-three and the longest fifty-nine, so that there would be four consecutive complete ψ characters.

The analyst could guess whereabouts they would appear, probably extended, and place them by recognizing a fragment of plain-text. From then on it was a question of extending the plain-text and building up the complete psi-patterns.

This first success was rightly hailed as a triumph, but it was repeated confidently on almost all occasions on which we sent a correct de-chi (and even sometimes when it wasn't entirely correct). In one very favourable case, the ψs were recovered in 35 minutes.

So by early 1944, we could break the patterns and decipher transmissions on any link/month that had one long enough transmission or a readable depth. But soon we had an addition to our armoury. Sixta discovered that some messages on perforated tape were sent on more than one link. For this to be fruitful three things had to go right: a pair of such transmissions had to be spotted; one of them had to be deciphered; and the plain-text had to be matched against the correct stretch in the other and the resulting key broken. Sixta had useful clues to spotting a pair. Each message in a transmission carried a serial number, which would, of course, be enciphered; when a transmission had been deciphered by its recipient, he often sent, as a receipt, the last two digits of the serial numbers of each message in the transmission. When Sixta found among the receipts of different links the same pair of digits at similar times there was a chance that they included the same message. Since links generally passed more than a hundred messages each day, there were plenty of coincidences that had not arisen from retransmission. Sixta became familiar with pairs of links liable to be sending the same message, and they could often make use of priority signals and other indications.

They would submit to the Testery crib section daily predictions of retransmissions. This crib section read all deciphered messages and could often pick out a message that was likely to have been retransmitted on another link. They would pass such ideas to

Sixta and could include the enciphered serial number, from which Sixta could often pick out a likely pair. Most of the successful pairings were spotted in this way.

The plain-text to be used was provided by the Testery and sent with the supposed match to the Newmanry crib section. Robinson was the ideal machine to subtract the plain-text at all likely offsets from stretches of the cipher text, and count for some suitable property of key. Many such properties were proposed and used. When a convincing match was found, the resulting stretch of key was broken by standard methods.

All this called for close liaison with Knockholt, painstaking checking both of plain and cipher text, and ingenuity and mathematics to devise the most efficient tests. The Newmanry crib section worked on 250 cases out of nearly 900 suggested by Sixta. Of these 72 were successful.

Exploitation

Throughout the whole Tunny operation, research and experience led to continual improvement. Experience was responsible for one improvement. The Testery deciphered the transmissions that had been set, and they often found it went wrong before the end. They soon discovered that the cipher tape sent by Knockholt sometimes left out or inserted a character or two, generally because of poor radio reception. We called that a 'slide'. A slide, of course, would weaken any statistical effect being used to set patterns. We therefore asked for subsequent Colossi to have the facility to 'span', to restrict its count to any stretch of the cipher tape that we could specify by giving the positions at which to start and to end. A good count could then be repeated on (say) the first two-thirds and again on the last two-thirds of the tape. Often one was strong and the other weak, suggesting a slide; subsequent spans could home in on the approximate position of the slide and later runs could be limited to the largest span available that seemed to be slide-free.

In the Testery, they sharpened their methods and came to know more and more about the cribs useful for the various links. They commissioned and received a machine called Dragon. This was used on a de-chi; a likely crib was 'dragged' against it; it was subtracted at a range of plausible positions to give a stretch of putative ψ'. Dragon removed any repeated characters to give putative unextended ψ, and checked against the known psi-patterns, only recording a possible hit when it could fit all five.

They also refined Turingery by a process (I think Peter Hilton invented it) called Devil Exorcism. In Turingery, characters of $\Delta\psi'$ that look likely to be / are assumed to be so, giving consequent $\Delta\chi$ bits that get cycled throughout. When the assumption is wrong it can proliferate wrong bits of $\Delta\chi$. Devil exorcism was a technique that limited the damage done by such wrong assumptions.

Both sections kept research books for anyone to record bright ideas. The Newmanry produced over forty of these, containing suggestions of new routines, calculations of significance tests, bits of mathematics that seemed relevant, reports of plain-text statistics and much else. In the Newmanry, tea parties were started; anyone could call one, ideas were bandied about, you came if you could and you brought your own tea. Tea parties didn't decide things but they led to action on all fronts. Newman ran a comfortably democratic and friendly section. I was not the only one to persuade one of the Wrens to marry him. Mathematicians had occasional weeks off for research or secondment. I remember with particular pleasure a secondment to the Testery where Hilton guided me through a successful Turingery.

Both sections grew steadily. The Testery recruited from the military, the Newmanry from the Wrens, the universities and from Dollis Hill, which also supplied us with one new Colossus each month, as well as most of the other machines. We depended totally on our engineers, who installed incoming machines and maintained the battery already installed. It was only because of them that we could keep on increasing our output.

The Wrens were housed in the splendour they deserved in Woburn Abbey. We eventually had over 250 of them in the Newmanry, and their contribution (not just socially) was outstanding. They controlled the flow of tapes and ordered the runs to be made, with occasional advice from the analyst who was duty officer. They operated the machines, including the Colossi, with aplomb. Some of them would be in charge of Colossi on their own, moving expertly from run to run. For wheel-breaking, there was always an analyst in charge, but he would be helpless without a Wren to wind the tapes onto the bedstead and plug up the runs.

Several analysts were seconded to us from the US Army and one from the US Navy; we also had highly professional advice at our tea parties from a US liaison officer. Unquestionably the Americans had generously sent us some of their best men. Four of them later held, as civilians, highly important posts in the postwar National Security Agency. They also sent us, near the end of the war, a photographic team. They had developed efficient ways of comparing two streams at all offsets by sliding photographic strips over each other and measuring the amount of light that shone through – instantaneous counting. It had the advantage of speed over Robinson, but came too late to make the impact the equipment deserved.

The Last Months

The Germans saluted the Normandy landings by changing wheel-patterns not monthly but daily. That meant that we had to break the patterns every day for all the links of intelligence interest. Fortunately by then our techniques of converging rectangles and completing the χ-breaking on Colossus were well established; we just had more of it to do. The Newmanry had by then spread into Block H where the wheel-breaking and the crib section were sited. It housed a large roomful of Wrens in Block H, converging rectangles, and the Colossi that had been adapted for wheel-breaking. The Testery had more de-chis from which to break the psi- and μ-patterns; and, as the Germans progressively abandoned the autoclave limitations, more depths to disentangle. The job of setting known psi- and μ-patterns on de-chis was taken back into the Newmanry; Colossus was very well adapted for the job and we then no longer had to make de-chi tapes. That meant that, once a day's patterns had been broken, all the setting was done in the Newmanry (as it had been in September 1943) and the settings were sent to the Testery for them to decipher the transmission.

This period lacked incident except for the fire that we had in one of the Block F rooms. The fire was put out, and on that day, as it so happened, we solved more transmissions than ever before. All-round success persisted; technical advances and refinements continued. We were still getting better at it when the German war came to an end. Soon after that we were happy to be sent a mobile German Tunny machine; it was probably of more detailed interest to the engineers and telecommunication experts than to the rest of us.

After the war some from both scctions joined GCHQ. One Newmanry analyst was rumoured to have set up a bogus university that issued impressive degree documents to anyone willing to buy. Most of the mathematicians ended up teaching at real universities. Two Testery analysts were bold enough to start new organizations: Roy Jenkins later initiated and led the Social Democratic Party; and, most remarkably, Peter Benson started Amnesty, which later became the highly influential Amnesty International. I never lose an opportunity to claim them as war-time colleagues. Whatever we did after the war – ATS, Wrens, engineers, analysts – we all knew that we had been part of a very successful joint venture, and that it had significantly helped the Allied armed forces to win the German war.

18

Colossus and the Dawning of the Computer Age

B. JACK COPELAND

Introduction

Historians describe intelligence as 'the missing dimension'. Without an understanding of the intelligence those in power were receiving and its influence on the decisions they made, any history will be incomplete. It is now easy to see how important the breaking of the Axis codes and ciphers at Bletchley Park was in influencing the Allies' conduct during the Second World War. But while details of many of the Cold War intelligence operations have made their way into the public domain, very little is still known about codebreaking successes during that period. We do not as yet know quite how important Sigint was in the decisions taken by Western politicians during the critical moments of the Cold War such as the Cuban missile crisis, the Soviet invasions of Hungary and Czechoslovakia, and the Solidarity-led industrial unrest in Poland. Sigint remains the 'missing dimension' to any history of the second half of the twentieth century.

But it is not the only 'missing dimension'. The second half of the twentieth century was dominated by the computer age. The tentative first steps taken during the war led initially to widespread use of computers within industry, later to the advent of the personal computer and finally to the construction of the Internet. Computers now dominate virtually every aspect of our lives but until only recently there was a 'missing dimension' to the history of the computer age, and one in which, like the intelligence resulting from the breaking of the Axis codes and ciphers, Bletchley Park played a groundbreaking role.

There were many remarkable people at Bletchley Park. But in early 1943, two extraordinarily gifted men came together to create Colossus, the world's first electronic digital computer. Alan Turing did not, as is sometimes assumed, have any role in the construction of Colossus. A telephone engineer called Tommy Flowers built the computer, working on specifications laid down by Max Newman, a Cambridge mathematician. Told that it might affect the course of the war, Flowers had Colossus up and running by the end of 1943. The full details of that story remained secret until only very recently. Even now, Colossus remains something of a 'missing dimension' in computing history. Books claiming that the American ENIAC computer was the first electronic digital computer continue to be published. This chapter, by the distinguished computer historian Professor Jack Copeland, tells the true story of the birth of the modern computer.

MS

Colossus was the world's first large-scale electronic digital computer. In the hands of the Bletchley Park codebreakers, it gave the Allies access to the most secret German radio communications, including messages from Hitler to his front-line generals. It was built during 1943 by Thomas (Tommy) Flowers and his team of engineers and wiremen, a 'band of brothers' who worked in utmost secrecy and at terrific speed. The construction of the machine took them ten months, working day and night, pushing themselves until (as Flowers said) their 'eyes dropped out'. One day, towards the end of 1943, the racks of electronic components were transferred from Flowers' workshops at the Post Office Research Station at Dollis Hill, north London, to Bletchley Park, where Colossus was assembled by Flowers' engineers. Despite its complexity, and the fact that no such machine had previously been attempted, the computer was in working order almost straight away, with the first trial runs on 8 December 1943 – testimony to the quality of Flowers' design and the accuracy of the engineering work carried out at Dollis Hill. The name 'Colossus', devised a little later by the Wrens who operated the computer, was certainly apt: the machine was the size of a small room and weighed approximately a ton. By February 1944 Colossus was in use by the codebreakers of the Newmanry, a Bletchley section named after its head and founder, Cambridge mathematician Maxwell (Max) Newman.

By the end of the war in Europe, nine additional Colossi were working in the Newmanry, all built by Flowers' team at Dollis Hill, and an eleventh was partly assembled. Most Colossi were broken up once hostilities ceased. Some of the electronic panels – counters, shift-registers, and so forth – were taken to Newman's newly created Computing Machine Laboratory at Manchester University, once all traces of their original use had been removed. An intact Colossus was retained by GCHQ at Cheltenham. The last Colossus is believed to have stopped running in 1960. During its later years it was used for training purposes.

Those who knew of Colossus were forbidden by the Official Secrets Act from sharing this knowledge. A long time passed before the secret came out that Flowers had built the first working electronic computer. During his lifetime (he died in 1998) he never received the full recognition he deserved. Many history books, even recently published ones, claim that the first electronic digital computer was an American machine built by J. Presper Eckert and John Mauchly – the ENIAC. Started in 1943, the ENIAC was designed to calculate the numerical tables used when aiming artillery in the field. However, the ENIAC was not operational until 1945. Before the 1970s, few had any idea that electronic computation had been used successfully during the Second World War. In 1975, the British Government released a set of captioned photographs of Colossus. Also during the 1970s, articles appeared by two former Newmanry codebreakers, Jack Good and Donald Michie, giving the barest outlines of Colossus, and historian Brian Randell published material derived from interviews with Flowers, Newman, Good, Michie, and others. By 1983, Flowers had received clearance from the British Government to publish an account of the hardware of Colossus I. Details of the later Colossi, and of how Flowers' computing machinery was actually used by the cryptanalysts, remained secret. There matters stood, more or less, until 1996, when the US Government released numerous wartime documents concerning Colossus and the cryptanalytical processes in which it figured. Even then, however, one historically vital document, the 'General Report on Tunny', remained classified. This detailed two-volume account of the cryptanalytical work involving Colossus was written in 1945 by Good, Michie, and their colleague Geoffrey Timms. Thanks largely to Michie's tireless campaigning, this report was declassified in 2000, finally ending the secrecy and enabling the full story of Colossus to be told for the first time.

In the original sense of the word, a computer was not a machine at all, but a human being – a mathematical assistant whose task was to calculate by rote, in accordance with a systematic method supplied by an overseer prior to the calculation. The computer, like a filing clerk, might have little detailed knowledge of the end to which his or her work was directed. Many thousands of human computers were employed in business, government, and research establishments, doing some of the sorts of calculating work that nowadays is performed by electronic computers.

The term 'computing machine' was used increasingly from the 1920s to refer to small calculating machines which mechanized elements of the human computer's work. For a complex calculation, several dozen human computers might be required, each equipped with a desk-top computing machine. By the 1940s, however, the scale of some calculations required by physicists and engineers had become so great that the work could not easily be done in a reasonable time by even a roomful of human computers with desk-top computing machines. The need to develop high-speed large-scale computing machinery was pressing.

During the late 1940s and early 1950s, with the advent of electronic computing machines, the phrase 'computing machine' gave way gradually to 'computer'. As Turing stated, the new machines were 'intended to carry out any definite rule of thumb process which could have been done by a human operator working in a disciplined but unintelligent manner'. During the brief period in which the old and new meanings of 'computer' co-existed, the prefix 'electronic' or 'digital' would usually be used to distinguish machine from human.

A computer, in the later sense of the word, is any machine able to do work that could, in principle, be done by a human computer. Mainframes, laptops, pocket calculators, palm-pilots – all are computing machines, carrying out work that a human rote-worker could do, if he or she worked long enough, and had a plentiful enough supply of paper and pencils.

The Victorian Charles Babbage, many decades ahead of his time, was one of the first to grasp the huge potential of the idea of using machinery to compute. Babbage was Lucasian Professor of Mathematics at the University of Cambridge from 1828 to 1839. Babbage's long-time collaborator was Ada, Countess of Lovelace (daughter of the poet Byron). Her vision of the potential of computing machines was perhaps in some respects more far-reaching even than Babbage's own. Lovelace envisaged computing machines going beyond pure number-crunching, suggesting that one of Babbage's planned 'Engines' might be capable of composing elaborate pieces of music.

In about 1820 Babbage proposed an 'Engine' for the automatic production of mathematical tables (such as logarithm tables, tide tables, and astronomical tables). He called it the 'Difference Engine'. This was, of course, the age of the steam engine, and Babbage's Engine was to consist of more accurately machined versions of the types of components then found in railway locomotives and the like – brass gear wheels, rods, ratchets, pinions, and so forth. Decimal numbers were represented by the positions of 10-toothed metal wheels mounted in columns. Babbage exhibited a small working model of the Engine in 1822. He never built the full-scale machine he had designed, but did complete several parts of it. The largest of these – roughly 10 per cent of the planned machine – is on display in the London Science Museum. Babbage used it successfully to calculate various mathematical tables. In 1990, his 'Difference Engine No. 2' was finally built from the original design and is also on display at the London Science Museum – a glorious machine of gleaming brass.

Babbage also proposed the 'Analytical Engine', considerably more ambitious than the Difference Engine. Had it been completed, the Analytical Engine would have been an all-purpose mechanical digital computer (whereas the Difference Engine could perform only a few of the tasks that human computers carried out). A large model of the Analytical Engine was under construction at the time of Babbage's death in 1871, but a full-scale version was never built. The Analytical Engine was to have a memory, or 'store' as Babbage called it, and a central processing unit, or 'mill'. The behaviour of the Analytical Engine would have been controlled by a program of instructions contained on punched cards connected together by ribbons (an idea Babbage adopted from the Jacquard weaving loom). The Analytical Engine would have been able, like Colossus, to select from alternative actions on the basis of the outcomes of its previous actions – a facility nowadays known as 'conditional branching'.

Babbage's idea of a general-purpose calculating engine was well known to some modern pioneers of automatic calculation. In the US during the 1930s, Vannevar Bush and Howard Aiken, both of whom built successful computing machines in the pre-electronic era, spoke of accomplishing what Babbage set out to do. Babbage's ideas were remembered in Britain also, and his proposed computing machinery was on occasion a topic of lively mealtime discussion at Bletchley.

Two key concepts in the development of the modern computer are the 'stored program' and the 'universal computing machine'. As everyone who can operate a personal computer knows, the way to make the machine perform the task you want – word-processing, say – is to open the appropriate program stored in the computer's memory. Life was not always so simple. The Analytical Engine did not store programs in its memory. Nor did Colossus. To set up Colossus for a different job, it was necessary to modify by hand some of the machine's wiring. This modification was done by means of switches and plugs. The larger ENIAC was also programmed in this way. It was something of a nightmare: in order to set up the ENIAC for a fresh job, the operators would have to spend a day or more rerouting cables and setting switches. Colossus, ENIAC, and their like are called 'program-controlled' computers, in order to distinguish them from the modern 'stored-program' computer.

This basic principle of the modern computer, i.e. controlling the machine's operations by means of a program of coded instructions stored in the computer's memory, was thought of by Alan Turing in 1935. At the time, Turing was a shy, eccentric student at Cambridge University. He went up to King's College in October 1931 to read Mathematics and was elected a Fellow of

King's in the spring of 1935, at the age of only twenty-two. In 1936 he left England to study for a Ph.D. in the United States, at Princeton University, returning in 1938. Turing's 'universal computing machine', as he called it – it would soon be known simply as the universal Turing machine – emerged from research that no one would have guessed could have any practical application. In 1935, Turing was working on an obscure problem in mathematical logic, the so-called 'decision problem', which he learned of from lectures on the foundations of mathematics and logic given by Newman. While thinking about this problem, Turing dreamed up an abstract digital computing machine which, as he said, could compute 'all numbers which could naturally be regarded as computable'.

The universal Turing machine consists of a limitless memory in which both data and instructions are stored, in symbolically encoded form, and a scanner that moves back and forth through the memory, symbol by symbol, reading what it finds and writing further symbols. By inserting different programs into the memory, the machine can be made to carry out any calculation that can be done by a human computer. That is why Turing called the machine universal.

It is not known whether Turing had heard of Babbage's work when he invented the universal Turing machine. In their specifics, the Analytical Engine and the universal Turing machine are chalk and cheese. Turing later emphasized that the Analytical Engine was universal (a judgement that was possible only from the vantage point of the mathematical theory of universal machines that Turing himself developed). Nevertheless, there is an important logical difference between the two types of machine. In Turing's machine, but not Babbage's, program and data both consist of symbols in memory, and the machine works on both using exactly the same operations. Reading the program is no different from reading the data. This is the stored-program concept. Implicit in the concept is the possibility of the computer operating on and modifying its own program as it runs, just as it operates on the data in its memory. Turing was later to suggest that this ability of the stored-program computer to modify its own instructions might form the mechanism for computer learning – a topic now at the forefront of research in Artificial Intelligence.

In 1935, the universal Turing machine existed only as an idea. Right from the start, Turing was interested in the possibility of building such a machine, as to some degree was Newman. But it was not until their Bletchley days that the dream of building a miraculously fast general-purpose computing machine took hold of them.

The transition from cogwheel computers to electronic computers took just over a century. Various largeish, purely mechanical computing machines were built, including the Scheutz Difference Engines, modelled on Babbage's, and Bush's (analogue) Differential Analyser, completed at the Massachusetts Institute of Technology in 1931. It took a skilled mechanic equipped with a lead hammer to set up the mechanical Differential Analyser for each new job.

The next generation of computing machines used electro-mechanical technology. Their basic components were small, electrically driven switches called 'relays'. A relay contains a mechanical contact-breaker, consisting of a moving metal rod that opens and closes an electrical circuit. A current in a coil is used to move the rod between the 'on' and 'off' positions. A number of electro-mechanical program-controlled digital computers were built before and during the war. Turing himself built a very small electro-mechanical multiplier (it multiplied binary numbers) while at Princeton.

Electro-mechanical is not electronic. Electronic valves (called 'vacuum tubes' in the US) operate very many times faster than relays, because the valve's only moving part is a beam of electrons. Relays are too slow for effective large-scale general-purpose digital computation. It was the development of high-speed digital techniques using valves that made possible the modern computer. Valves were used originally for purposes such as amplifying radio signals. The output would vary continuously in proportion to a continuously varying input, for example a radio signal representing speech. Digital computation imposes different requirements. What is needed for the purpose of representing the two binary digits, 1 and 0, is not a continuously varying signal but plain 'on' and 'off' (or 'high' and 'low'). It was the novel idea of using the valve as a very fast switch, producing pulses of current – pulse for 1, no pulse for 0 – that was the route to high-speed digital computation. At the outbreak of war in 1939, only a handful of electrical engineers knew anything about this use of valves. One was Flowers, who estimated that there were no more than ten or twenty others in the whole world. When he was summoned to Bletchley – ironically, because of his knowledge of relays, a standard component in telephone equipment – he turned out to be the right man in the right place at the right time.

Flowers had joined the Telephone Branch of the Post Office in 1926, after an apprenticeship at the Royal Arsenal in Woolwich, well known for its precision engineering. He entered the Research Branch at Dollis Hill in 1930 (where he achieved rapid promotion). On his own initiative, he explored the feasibility of using valves to control the making and breaking of telephone connections. His work in this area was, it appears, the earliest extensive use of valves as devices for generating and storing pulses. At this time, the common wisdom was that valves could never be used satisfactorily in large numbers, for they were unreliable and in a large installation too many would fail in too short a time. However, this opinion was based on experience with radio receivers and the like, which were switched on and off frequently. What Flowers discovered was that, so long as valves were switched on and left on, they could operate reliably for very long periods. He recognized that valves were not only potentially very much faster than relays but also, being less prone to wear, actually more reliable.

In 1934, Flowers put the new electronic pulse-techniques he had developed into use, in electronic equipment for the automatic control of connections between telephone exchanges. He used 3,000–4,000 valves in an installation controlling 1,000 telephone lines, each line having three or four valves attached to its end. Flowers' design was accepted by the Post Office and the equipment went into limited operation in 1939. During 1938–9 he worked on an experimental high-speed electronic data store for use in telephone exchanges. His overall aim, achieved only much later, was that electronic equipment should replace all the relay-based systems in telephone exchanges. As Flowers remarked, at the outbreak of war with Germany he was possibly the only person in Britain who realized that valves could be used reliably on a large scale for high-speed computing.

Turing had been working on the problem of Enigma for some months before war broke out. In the period when GC&CS was still located in London, before the move to Bletchley Park, Turing would pay occasional visits to the office in order to compare notes on Enigma with Dilly Knox. At the outbreak of hostilities in September 1939, Turing took up residence at Bletchley. It was here that he would meet Flowers. By the beginning of November, Turing's design for the British bombe – a radically improved form of the Polish *bomba* (both were electro-mechanical) – was in the hands of the engineers at the British Tabulating Machine Company. During the attack on Enigma, Turing approached Dollis Hill to build a relay-based machine to operate in conjunction with the bombe. Dollis Hill sent Flowers to Bletchley. In the end, the machine Flowers built was not used, but Turing was impressed with Flowers, who began thinking about an electronic bombe, although he did not get far.

Newman, meanwhile, spent the early years of the war in Cambridge, at St John's College, where he had been a Fellow since 1923. He and Turing kept in close touch after Turing left Cambridge for Bletchley, writing letters about mathematical logic. (Turing's first letter to Newman, written in March 1940, starts: 'Dear Newman, Very glad to get your letter, as I needed some stimulus to make me start thinking about logic'.) Despite the pressures of codebreaking, Turing found time to collaborate with Newman on an academic paper, published in March 1942. In 1942, Newman was beckoned by Bletchley. He wrote to the Master of St John's to request leave of absence and at the end of August joined Lt.-Col. John Tiltman's Research Section. Tiltman's group was engaged in the attempt to break the German teleprinter cipher machine that the British codenamed 'Tunny'.

The Germans developed several different types of encrypting machine for use in association with teleprinter equipment; the British operators first intercepted enciphered teleprinter messages during the second half of 1940. The British gave these teleprinter cipher machines the general cover name 'Fish'. Three different types of Fish were known to GC&CS: Tunny, Sturgeon and Thrasher. GC&CS focused on Tunny (the Lorenz SZ 40, succeeded by the SZ 42), which was used mainly by the German Army.

An initial experimental Tunny link went into operation in June 1941 between Berlin and Athens/Salonika. By D-Day 1944 there were twenty-six different links. Bletchley gave each link a piscine name: Königsberg–South Russia was Octopus, Berlin–Paris was Jellyfish, Berlin–Zagreb was Gurnard, and so on. The two main central exchanges were Königsberg for the Eastern links and Straussberg, near Berlin, for the Western links. The other ends of the links were usually mobile. Each mobile Tunny unit consisted of two trucks. One carried the radio equipment. The other carried teleprinter equipment and two Tunny machines, one for sending and one for receiving. The links carried messages from Hitler and the High Command to the various Army Group commanders in the field – intelligence of the highest grade.

In January 1942 the research section managed to reverse-engineer the Tunny machine on the basis of a few messages which they had been able to read because of operator error. William Tutte made the crucial break, deducing the structure and function of two of the machine's various internal wheels. At this stage the rest of the research section joined in and soon the whole machine was laid bare, without any of them ever having set eyes on one. It was, to say the least, a remarkable feat. The problem now that they knew the workings of the machine was how to read the message traffic. The difficulty was the wheel settings. Each message had its own wheel settings – its own 'combination', chosen by the German operator before enciphering the message – and could not be read until its combination was known.

In November 1942 Tutte invented a way of discovering wheel settings known as the 'Statistical Method'. The rub was that the method seemed impractical, involving a very large amount of time-consuming work. This was the sort of work that, given enough time, a human computer could carry out – basically, the comparing of two streams of dots and crosses, counting the number of times that each had a dot in the same position. However, given the amount of comparing and counting that the method required, the intelligence in the message would be stale before the work was finished. Tutte explained his method to Newman, who suggested using electronic counters. It was a brilliant idea. In December 1942 Newman was given the job of developing the necessary machinery.

Electronic counters involving small numbers of valves had been in use in Cambridge before the war, in the Cavendish Laboratory, for counting sub-atomic particles. These had been designed by C. E. Wynn-Williams, a Cambridge don, but now involved in research at the Telecommunications Research Establishment (TRE) in Malvern. Newman worked out the cryptanalytical requirements for the planned machine and called in Wynn-Williams to design the electronic counters. Newman also approached Francis Morell, head of the telegraph and teleprinter group at Dollis Hill, to engineer the rest of the machine. (Morell's group was located in the same building as Flowers' switching group.) Turing himself appears to have had no direct involvement in Newman's project, although Newman has remarked in this connection that Turing 'was always full of ideas and he liked to talk about other people's problems'.

Construction started in January 1943, and the machine began operating in June of that year, in Newman's new machine-section, the Newmanry. The Newmanry consisted initially of Newman himself, Michie, two engineers, and 16 Wrens. The section was housed in Hut 11, originally the first bombe room. The machine was soon named 'Heath Robinson' by the Wrens. Smoke rose from it the first time it was switched on (a large resistor overloaded). Part of Heath Robinson consisted of a huge angle-iron metal frame resembling an old-fashioned bedstead standing on end; this became known as the 'bedstead'. Around the bedstead wound two long loops of teleprinter tape. Each loop was made by gluing together the two ends of a single length of tape. The two tapes were supported by a system of pulleys and aluminium wheels of diameter about ten inches. The tapes were driven by sprocket-wheels which engaged a continuous row of sprocket-holes along the centre of each tape. Both tapes were driven by the same drive-shaft so that they moved in synchronization with each other. The speed of the tapes was 1,000-2,000 characters per second.

Each tape had rows of holes punched across its width. Every row was a letter, or other keyboard character, represented in international teleprinter code. In order to describe these patterns on the tape, as well as the pulsed patterns that made up the enciphered transmissions themselves, Bletchley used '×' to mark the position of a hole (or pulse) and '•' to mark the absence of a hole (or no pulse). The hole/no-hole patterns on the tape were read photo-electrically. Once these patterns had been converted by the photo-electric reader into electrical pulses, they were modified and combined in a specified way by a 'combining unit' (a logic unit, in modern terminology). The resulting number of pulses was counted by Wynn-Williams' counting unit. The combining could be varied by means of replugging cables. Dollis Hill made the combining unit and the bedstead, and TRE the counting unit. In all Heath Robinson contained about two dozen valves.

The central idea of Tutte's Statistical Method is as follows. Tunny encrypts each letter of the plain-text by adding another letter to it. The internal mechanism of the Tunny machine produces its own stream of letters, known at Bletchley as the 'key-stream', or simply key. Each letter of the cipher-text is produced by adding a letter from the key-stream to the corresponding letter of the plain-text. Tunny produces its key-stream by adding together two other letter streams which it generates, called the psi-stream and the chi-stream at Bletchley (from the Greek letters Psi and Chi). The psi-stream is produced by a mechanism consisting of five 'psi-wheels' and the chi-stream by a mechanism consisting of five 'chi-wheels'. For example, if the first letter from the chi-wheel mechanism is M (••××× in teleprinter code) and the first letter from the psi-wheel mechanism is N (••××•), then the first letter of the key-stream is M + N, which under the rules of Tunny letter-addition is T (••••×). (Tunny adds letters by adding the individual dots and crosses that compose them.) Finally, supposing that the first letter of the plain-text is e.g. R (•×•×•), the first letter of the cipher-text is R + T, or G (•×•××).

If, say, the plain-text is 4,000 characters long, then 4,000 consecutive characters from the chi-stream are used in the course of forming the cipher-text. These letters from the chi-stream will be referred to simply as 'the chi' of the message. Tutte's method exploits a fatal weakness in the design of Tunny which renders the chi amenable to attack. The method depends on knowing the Tunny machine's wheel-patterns – patterns of cams or 'pins' around the circumference of each wheel. The Research Section established what these patterns were in the course of reverse-engineering the machine, and although the Germans changed the patterns from time to time, Bletchley kept on top of the changes thanks to operator errors. What Tutte discovered was that after some massaging, the chi of the message is recognizable on the basis of the cipher text, provided that the wheel patterns are known. Once the message chi has been found it is an easy step to the settings of the chi-wheels, one part of the message's combination.

What both Robinson and Colossus did, initially, was use Tutte's Statistical Method to find the settings of the chi-wheels (other methods came later). Knowing the settings of the chi-wheels gave the codebreakers enough of a head-start that they were able to discover the settings of the psi-wheels by eye, given 'a knowledge of "Tunny-German" and the power of instantaneous mental addition of letters of the Teleprint alphabet'. Once the settings of all the wheels were known, the codebreakers had the message's 'combination'. From there on it was left to clerks to decipher the complete message.

The crucial massaging required by Tutte's method involves forming what is called the 'delta' of a character stream. The delta is the stream that results from adding together each pair of adjacent letters in the original stream. For example, the delta of the short stream MNT is produced by adding M to N and N to T. The last two columns of the following table contain the delta of the stream MNT. The rules for dot-and-cross addition are: dot plus dot is dot, cross plus cross is dot, dot plus cross is cross, cross plus dot is cross.

M	N	T	M+N	N+T
•	•	•	•	•
•	•	•	•	•
×	×	•	•	×
×	×	•	•	×
×	•	×	×	×

The idea of the delta is that it tracks changes in the original stream. If a dot follows a dot or a cross follows a cross at a particular point in the original stream, then the corresponding point in the delta has a dot. A dot in the delta means 'no change'. If, on the other hand, there is a cross followed by a dot or a dot followed by a cross in the original stream, then the corresponding point in the delta has a cross. A cross in the delta means 'change'. (Tutte cannot now remember who introduced the idea of delta but believes it might have made its first appearance in Turingery.)

Tutte's all-important discovery was that the delta of a message's cipher-text and the delta of the chi usually correspond somewhat: where the one has a dot, so does the other, more often than not.

Here, then, is Tutte's method for finding the chi of a given cipher-text when the wheel-patterns are known. Suppose, for the sake of illustration, that the cipher-text is 4,000 characters long. First, form the delta of the cipher-text. Then, use the patterns of the chi-wheels to start generating chi-stream (as we may imagine, by hand with paper and pencil). It is the patterns of the cams around the circumferences of the chi-wheels that determine which letters the chi-mechanism produces, and if these patterns are known it is possible to calculate the entire chi-stream. Generate 4,000 successive characters of the chi-stream. Form their delta, and compare the result with the delta of the cipher-text, counting how many times the two both have a dot in the same place. Record this score. It probably won't be very good, since the chances are that at the start of the simulated generation of chi-stream, the positions of the chi-wheels were not the same as those used in producing the cipher-text. The five chi-wheels are like the moving parts of a combination lock, and it is only when they are set to the exact combination that the German operator used at the start of enciphering the message that they will produce the chi of the message. The goal of Tutte's method is to find that combination. So now generate the next character in the chi-stream, and compare the delta of the 2nd to the 4001st characters of the stream with the delta of the cipher-text. And so on. Since the motion of the chi-wheels is circular, eventually the complete chi-stream will have been examined. The stretch of chi-stream whose delta matches the delta of the cipher-text more closely than any of the other stretches do (and there may be no more than a 55–60 per cent correspondence) is probably the message chi.

Why do the delta of a message's cipher-text and the delta of the message chi tend to correspond? At bottom, this is because of the all-or-nothing way in which the psi-wheels move – the great weakness of Tunny. The Tunny machine's heart, its twelve wheels, stand side by side in a single row, like plates in a dish rack – the five psis, the five chis, and two motor wheels. The chi-wheels all move forward together one step every time a key is pressed at the keyboard, whereas the psi-wheels may all move forward one step when the key is pressed or may all stand still. Whether the psi-wheels move or not is determined by the motor wheels (or in some versions of the machine, by the motor wheels in conjunction with yet other complicating features). Whenever a stroke at the keyboard is not accompanied by a movement of the psi-wheels, what is added to the letter produced by the chi-wheels is whatever letter the psi-wheels produced on the last occasion when they did move. It follows that the delta of the letters contributed by the psi-wheels will contain a column consisting of five dots every time the psi-wheels stand still and 'miss a turn' (because in this case they contribute the same letter twice, so there is absolutely no change). These columns of dots in the psi's delta produce the correspondence that Tutte discovered. If instead of the psi-wheels either all moving together or all standing still, the designer had arranged for them to move independently, then the delta of the cipher-text and the delta of the chi would not have tended to correspond and the chink that let Tutte in would not have existed.

Colossus generated the chi-stream electronically. The cipher-text was on a loop of tape on a bedstead. In the case of Heath Robinson, the complete chi-stream was punched on one of its tapes before the search commenced, the other tape carrying the cipher-text. The two tapes ran on the Robinson's bedstead in such a way that the tape containing the cipher-text was progressively stepped through the chi-tape, one character at a time. In practice, the search would be simplified by punching onto the chi-tape only the dots and crosses produced by the first and second of the five chi-wheels, resulting in a much shorter tape. Tutte had shown that his method of counting correspondences worked in this case too (and for this reason it was sometimes called the '1+2 break in'). Once the settings of the first two chi-wheels had been found, the settings of the others would be chased by the same procedure.

Heath Robinson was effective, but there were problems. Tapes would stretch, causing them to go out of synchronization, would tear, and would come unglued. It was clear that one machine was not going to be anywhere near enough. Newman proposed to order a dozen more Robinsons from the Post Office. He asked Flowers to suggest improvements to be included in the mass-produced version. Flowers had first been called in, at Turing's suggestion, when Morell's group was having difficulty with the design of the combining unit. Flowers had not been involved in the overall design of the Robinson and did not think much of the machine. The difficulty of keeping two paper tapes in synchronization at high speed was a conspicuous weakness. So was the use of a mixture of valves and relays in the counters, because the relays slowed everything down. Flowers suggested a new machine, all electronic, with only one tape. However, opinion at Bletchley was that a machine containing the number of valves that Flowers was proposing – about 2,000 – would not work reliably. In any case, there was the question of how long the development process would take. Newman decided that his section should press ahead with the Robinsons, and left Flowers to do as he wished. At Dollis Hill Flowers just got on with building the machine that he could see was necessary. Colossus was entirely his idea.

Colossus I had approximately 1,600 valves and operated at 5,000 characters per second. The later models, containing approximately 2,400 valves, processed five streams of dot-and-cross simultaneously in parallel. This boosted the speed to 25,000 characters per second. By means of repluggable cables and a panel of switches, Flowers deliberately built more flexibility than was strictly necessary into the logic stages of Colossus I. These, like the combining unit of Heath Robinson, did the deltaing and the comparing. As a result of this flexibility, new methods could be implemented on Colossus as they were discovered. Michie and Good soon found a way of using Colossus I to discover the wheel patterns themselves. (Prior to the summer of 1944, the Germans changed the cam patterns of the chi-wheels once every month and the cam patterns of the psi-wheels at first quarterly, then monthly from October 1942. After 1 August 1944 wheel patterns changed daily.) Colossus II, installed shortly before D-Day, was supplied with a special panel for use when breaking wheel patterns. Following the delivery of Colossus II, new Colossi arrived in the Newmanry at roughly six-week intervals.

If Flowers could have patented the inventions that he contributed to Ultra, he would probably have become a very rich man. As it was, the personal costs that he incurred in the course of building the Colossi left his bank account overdrawn at the end of the war. Newman was offered an OBE for his contribution to the defeat of Germany, but he turned it down, remarking to ex-colleagues from Bletchley Park that he considered the offer derisory.

Colossus was far from universal. Nevertheless, Flowers had established decisively and for the first time that large-scale electronic computing machinery was practicable. Even in the midst of the attack on Tunny, Newman was thinking about the universal Turing machine. He showed Flowers Turing's 1936 paper about the universal computing machine, 'On Computable Numbers'. (Not being a mathematical logician, Flowers 'didn't really understand much of it'.) There is little doubt that by 1944 Newman had firmly in mind the possibility of building a universal Turing machine using electronic technology. It was just a question of waiting until he 'got out'. In February 1946, a few months after his appointment to the Fielden Chair of Mathematics at the University of Manchester, Newman wrote to the Hungarian–American mathematician John von Neumann (like Newman, considerably influenced by Turing's 1936 paper, and himself playing a leading role in the computing developments taking place in the US):

> I am . . . hoping to embark on a computing machine section here, having got very interested in electronic devices of this kind during the last two or three years. By about eighteen months ago I had decided to try my hand at starting up a machine unit when I got out . . . I am of course in close touch with Turing.

The implication of Flowers' racks of electronic equipment would have been obvious to Turing too. Flowers has said that once Colossus was in operation, it was just a matter of Turing's waiting to see what opportunity might arise to put the idea of his universal computing machine into practice.

Such an opportunity came along in 1945, when John Womersley, head of the Mathematics Division of the National Physical Laboratory (NPL) in London, invited Turing to design and develop an electronic computing machine for general scientific work. Womersley named the proposed computer the

Automatic Computing Engine, or ACE – a homage to Babbage.

During the remainder of 1945 Turing designed his electronic stored-program universal machine, completing his technical report, 'Proposed Electronic Calculator', before the end of 1945. This was the first relatively complete specification of an electronic stored-program general-purpose digital computer. An earlier document (May 1945), 'First Draft of a Report on the EDVAC', written by von Neumann in the US, discussed at length the design of an electronic stored-program universal digital computer, but in fairly abstract terms, saying little about programming, hardware details, or even electronics. Turing's 'Proposed Electronic Calculator', on the other hand, contained specimen programs in machine code, full specifications of hardware units, detailed circuit designs, and even an estimate of the cost of building the machine (£11,200). Turing's ACE and the proposed EDVAC computer differed fundamentally in their design; for example, the EDVAC had what is now called a central processing unit, or cpu, whereas in the ACE, the various logical and arithmetical functions were distributed among different hardware units.

Turing saw that processing speed and memory capacity were the keys to computing, and his design specified a high-speed memory of roughly the same size as the chip memory of an early Macintosh computer (enormous by the standards of his day). Had Turing's ACE been built as he planned, it would have been in a different league from the other early electronic computers. Unfortunately, delays beyond Turing's control resulted in the NPL losing the race to build the world's first electronic stored-program universal digital computer – an honour that went to the University of Manchester, where in Newman's Computing Machine Laboratory the 'Manchester Baby' ran its first program on 21 June 1948.

It was not until May 1950 that a small 'pilot model' of the Automatic Computing Engine executed its first program (some months before the EDVAC was working properly). With an operating speed of 1 MHz, the Pilot Model ACE was for some time the fastest computer in the world. DEUCE, the production version of the Pilot Model ACE, was built by the English Electric Company. Sales of this large and expensive machine exceeded thirty – confounding the suggestion, made in 1946 by Charles Darwin, grandson of the famous naturalist and Director of the NPL, that 'one machine would suffice to solve all the problems that are demanded of it from the whole country'. The fundamentals of Turing's ACE design were later employed by Harry Huskey (at Wayne State University, Detroit) in the Bendix G-15 computer. The G-15 was arguably the first personal computer; over 400 were sold worldwide. DEUCE and the G15 remained in use until about 1970. Another computer deriving from Turing's ACE design, the MOSAIC, played a role in Britain's air defences during the Cold War period; other derivatives include the Packard-Bell PB250 (1961).

The delays that cost the NPL the race with Manchester were not of Turing's making. It had been agreed between the NPL and Dollis Hill in February 1946 that a team under Flowers' direction would carry out the engineering work for the ACE, and in March 1946 Flowers said that a 'minimal ACE' would be ready by August or September of that year. Unfortunately, Dollis Hill was overwhelmed by a backlog of urgent work on the national telephone system. As Flowers has said, his section was 'too busy to do other people's work'. In February 1947, Turing suggested that the NPL set up its own electronics section in order to build the ACE. This was done but, sadly, inter-departmental rivalry hindered the work, and in April 1948 Womersley reported that hardware development was 'probably as far advanced 18 months ago'. Meanwhile, in the autumn of 1947, Turing retreated in disgust to Cambridge for a year's sabbatical leave, during which he did pioneering work on Artificial Intelligence. Before his leave was over, he lost patience with the NPL altogether and Newman's offer of a job lured a 'very fed up' Turing to Manchester University. In May 1948 Turing was appointed Deputy Director of the Computing Machine Laboratory (there being no Director).

Newman had laid plans for his Computing Machine Laboratory following his appointment at Manchester in September 1945, applying to the Royal Society for a sizeable grant in order to develop an electronic stored-program computer. This was approved in July 1946. Newman introduced the electrical engineers Frederick Williams and Thomas Kilburn – newly recruited to Manchester University from TRE – to the idea of the stored-program computer. Williams and Kilburn knew nothing about Colossus. At TRE they had worked during the war on radar and they were expert with electronic pulse-techniques. At the time he left TRE, Williams was developing a technique for storing pulse/no pulse patterns on the face of a cathode ray tube – an idea that, with Kilburn's help, was rapidly to lead to the type of high-speed random access memory (RAM) known as the Williams tube.

Williams' description of Newman's Computing Machine Laboratory is vivid:

> It was one room in a Victorian building whose architectural features are best described as 'late lavatorial'. The walls were of brown glazed brick and the door was labelled 'Magnetism Room'.

Here, Kilburn and Williams built the world's first electronic stored-program digital computer, the 'Manchester Baby'. As its name implies, the Baby was a very small machine. The first program, stored on the face of a Williams tube as a pattern of dots, was just seventeen instructions long. It was inserted manually, digit by digit, using a panel of switches.

Once Turing had arrived in Manchester, he designed the input mechanism and programming system for an expanded machine and wrote a programming manual for it. This expanded machine was known as the Manchester Mark I. At last Turing had his hands on a stored-program computer. He was soon using it to model biological growth, a field nowadays known as 'Artificial Life'. While the rest of the world was just waking up to the idea that electronics was the new way to do binary arithmetic, Turing was talking very seriously about programming digital computers to think.

At the time of the Baby machine and the Mark I, Kilburn and Williams, the men who had translated the logico-mathematical idea of the stored-program computer into hardware, were perhaps given too little credit by the mathematicians at Manchester. They were regarded as excellent engineers, but perhaps not as ideas men. This was unfair, but now the tables have turned. During the official celebrations of the fiftieth anniversary of the Baby, held at Manchester in June 1998, Newman's name was not so much as mentioned. Fortunately the words of the late Williams still exist on tape:

> Now let's be clear before we go any further that neither Tom Kilburn nor I knew the first thing about computers when we arrived in Manchester University . . . Newman explained the whole business of how a computer works to us.

Newman had played a crucial role indeed in the triumph at Manchester. Through him, both Colossus and Turing's abstract universal computing machine of 1935 were vital influences on the Manchester computer.

Meanwhile, momentum was gathering on the other side of the Atlantic. After visiting America in January 1947, Turing reported that the 'number of different computing projects is now so great that it is no longer possible to have a complete list'. The most visible players were Eckert, Mauchly, and von Neumann. Eckert and Mauchly had entered into a contract with the US Army Ordnance Department in June 1943 to build an electronic machine, the ENIAC. Construction got under way at the Moore School of Electrical Engineering at the University of Pennsylvania. Von Neumann was involved in the Manhattan Project at Los Alamos, where human computers armed with desk calculating machines were struggling to carry out the massive calculations required by the physicists. Hearing about ENIAC by chance, he saw to it that he was appointed as a consultant to the Eckert–Mauchly project. By the time he arrived at the Moore School, the design of the program-controlled ENIAC had been frozen in order to complete construction as soon as possible. Programming consisted of re-routing cables and setting switches. Von Neumann brought his knowledge of Turing's 1936 paper to the practical arena of the Moore School. Thanks to Turing's abstract logical work, von Neumann knew that by making use of coded instructions stored in memory, a single machine of fixed structure could in principle carry out any task that can be done by a human computer. It was von Neumann who placed Turing's abstract universal computing machine into the hands of American engineers.

After extensive discussions with Eckert and Mauchly, von Neumann wrote the 'First Draft of a Report on the EDVAC', describing a stored-program computer. The first draft (not quite finished) was circulated, bearing only von Neumann's name. Eckert and Mauchly were outraged, knowing that von Neumann would be given credit for everything in the report – their ideas as well as his own. There was a storm of controversy. As a result, von Neumann abandoned the proposed EDVAC and in 1946 established his own project to build a stored-program computer in the Institute for Advanced Study at Princeton University. Von Neumann gave his engineers Turing's 'On Computable Numbers' to read. The completed machine, with a high-speed memory consisting of forty Williams tubes, was working by the summer of 1951. It had approximately the same number of valves as Colossus II. Known as the IAS computer, this was not the first of the various stored-program computers under construction in the US to work, but it was the most influential, and served as the model for a series of what were called 'Princeton Class' computers.

Von Neumann is sometimes falsely described as the 'inventor of the computer' and the 'inventor of the stored-program concept'. Books and articles that purport to tell the story of the stored-program computer sometimes place von Neumann centre stage and make no mention of Turing. Von Neumann himself, however, repeatedly emphasized the fundamental importance of 'On Computable Numbers'. For example, in a letter to the mathematician Norbert Wiener, von Neumann spoke of 'the great positive contribution of Turing', Turing's mathematical demonstration that 'one, definite mechanism can be "universal"'. In a lecture delivered at the University of Illinois in 1949 (entitled 'Rigorous Theories of Control and Information') von Neumann said:

> The importance of Turing's research is just this: that if you construct an automaton right, then any additional requirements about the automaton can be handled by sufficiently elaborate instructions . . . [A]n automaton of this complexity can, when given suitable instructions, do anything that can be done by automata at all.

The Los Alamos physicist Stanley Frankel, responsible with von Neumann and others for mechanizing the large-scale calculations involved in the design of the atomic and hydrogen bombs, has described von Neumann's attitude to Turing's work:

> I know that in or about 1943 or '44 von Neumann was well aware of the fundamental importance of Turing's paper of 1936 'On computable numbers . . .', which describes in principle the 'Universal Computer' of which every modern computer (perhaps

> not ENIAC as first completed but certainly all later ones) is a realization. Von Neumann introduced me to that paper and at his urging I studied it with care. Many people have acclaimed von Neumann as the 'father of the computer' (in a modern sense of the term) but I am sure that he would never have made that mistake himself. He might well be called the midwife, perhaps, but he firmly emphasized to me, and to others I am sure, that the fundamental conception is owing to Turing – insofar as not anticipated by Babbage, Lovelace, and others. In my view von Neumann's essential role was in making the world aware of these fundamental concepts introduced by Turing and of the development work carried out in the Moore school and elsewhere.

Given our knowledge of the achievements at Dollis Hill and Bletchley Park, the history of computing must be rewritten. Histories written in ignorance of Colossus are not only incomplete, but give a distorted picture of the emergence and development of the idea of the modern computer. Turing's logical work in 1935–6 and Flowers' work at Bletchley led, via Newman's desire to put the concept of the stored-program universal computing machine into practice, to the Manchester Computing Machine Laboratory and the Manchester Mark I computer. From this in turn came another momentous development, the first mass-produced computer to go on sale, a copy of the Mark I. In the US, Turing's work steered von Neumann to the underlying logical principles of the EDVAC and the IAS computer. Technology transferred from Manchester, the Williams tube random-access memory, was crucial to both von Neumann's IAS machine and IBM's first mass-produced stored-program computer, the IBM 701. The 701 was a foretaste of the global transformation soon to flow from this criss-crossing pattern of invention and influence set in motion by Alan Turing in 1935.

19

Enigma's Security: What the Germans Really Knew

RALPH ERSKINE

Introduction

Chapter 19 reveals what the Germans knew about Enigma's security. Plugboard Enigma would have been impregnable if it had been used properly, but with up to about 40,000 Enigmas in service there was little prospect of that happening – the fundamental mistake made by the Wehrmacht *was to think otherwise. However, it should never be forgotten that plugboard Enigma could be broken by purely cryptanalytical means only in one set of circumstances – when it used doubly enciphered message keys. After April 1940, only the* Kriegsmarine *made the catastrophic mistake of employing that very fallible indicating system, with no fewer than six ciphers at that. All other Enigma ciphers could be broken only with a good crib, which had to occur on a daily basis before a cipher would yield to the bombes. Since Hut 6 was attacking over sixty* Heer *and* Luftwaffe *Enigma ciphers at any one time later in the war, the Germans had continually to make a lot of mistakes every day for it to succeed against them. If the* Heer *and* Luftwaffe *had monitored their radio nets more carefully, and given the OKW's radio security organization some real power at an early date, GC&CS would have had many more problems in breaking Enigma – and Hut 6 Ultra would have been thin on the ground. As it was, introducing even the most basic precautions in preparing messages for encipherment made Hut 6's task much more difficult, and sometimes an impossible one: one such change quintupled the amount of bombe time required to break daily keys.*

The Wehrmacht *paid dearly for its decision to make Enigma a standard machine, common to all three of its branches, with only the* Kriegsmarine *employing extra rotors. The British did not make the same mistake with their own cipher machine, Typex, even though it was essentially a copy of commercial Enigma. Perhaps profiting from their experiences in breaking Enigma, there were about twenty different sets of rotors for Typex, which made the Germans give up their attempts to break it (and helped to protect it against US Navy attempts to solve it in 1945). Nor did the Americans overlook the principle that making good codes and ciphers is as important as breaking them. Not only did the United States produce a large number of different rotor sets for the Navy's very advanced Electric Cipher Machine (the Army's Sigaba), but special codebreaking units were tasked with attacking their own cryptographic systems, both in theoretical studies and, more importantly, as they were used in practice. One machine was found to be wanting, but special steps were taken to increase its security.*

Chapter 19 sets out the findings of some of the Kriegsmarine's *many inquiries into Enigma's security. It also describes devices and precautions introduced by the* Wehrmacht *to improve Enigma, including one which would have had devastating effects for Ultra – if only it had been used properly. As Gordon Welchman observed, the Allies were indeed lucky.*

RE

There has long been uncertainty about what the Germans knew about Enigma's security. Fortunately, the release of some important postwar TICOM (Technical Intelligence (sometimes target identification) Committee) interrogation reports of German Sigint personnel has at last thrown considerable light on this issue. Towards the end of the war, TICOM made plans to round up the staff from the numerous German Sigint agencies, in order to find out exactly what they knew about German cipher machines and code-breaking equipment, and the extent to which the Germans had been able to penetrate Allied codes and ciphers. When the war ended, and for some while afterwards, TICOM units combed Germany for Sigint personnel and equipment and made many valuable finds.

The German Foreign Office refused to use Enigma, since it was not convinced that Enigma was secure. Instead, it employed one-time pads to encipher its highest level traffic, in a system known to the Allies as GEE. However, GEE itself was insecure: the pads being used did not contain fully random numbers, since they had been generated by a machine which produced predictable sequences. Cryptanalysts in the US Army's Signal Security Agency exploited this to solve GEE in the winter of 1944–5.

A *Heer* or *Luftwaffe* Enigma key-list comprised the rotor order (*Walzenlage*), ring settings (*Ringstellungen*) and plugboard settings (*Steckerverbindungen*). A naval list also set out the *Grundstellungen*. Cryptanalysts attacking Enigma were therefore confronted by a huge key space: 60 (5×4×3) rotor orders, 676 (26×26) effective ring settings, 150 million million *Stecker* combinations, and 17,576 (26×26×26) message starting positions – a combined total of 1.074×10^{23}. The total was even higher for the standard naval machine M3 (6.0144×10^{23}), and twenty-six times greater again for M4 – 104 times after 1 July 1943, when a second 'Greek' rotor (gamma) and its related thin reflector were introduced.

These are huge numbers, but some experts in the *Kriegsmarine* were not impressed by them. Soon after the beginning of the war, German naval cryptanalysts advised that Enigma was not secure. A report prepared by Wilhelm Tranow, then a senior member of the *Kriegsmarine*'s codebreaking agency, the *B-Dienst*, recommended that the *Kriegsmarine* should replace Enigma by a codebook. At first sight that appears to be an odd recommendation since the *B-Dienst* was already breaking several British enciphered naval codes, and Tranow was fully aware of the weaknesses of such codes generally. However, Germany's circumstances were very different from those of Britain, since its Navy did not have to operate on a global basis. Tranow's recommendation might just have worked, particularly if the enciphering additive tables had not been overused. Once a daily Enigma key was found, all the messages in it fell, but each message in an enciphered code has to be solved separately, and it is a very slow process until the additive book being used can be substantially reconstructed.

The *Kriegsmarine*, in particular, carried out many inquiries into Enigma's security. Captain Ludwig Stummel, of the Marine Communications Service, the *Marinenachrichtendienst* (MND), reported on it following the capture of *Schiff 26* in April 1940, and the loss of U-13 off the coast of Norfolk on 30 May 1940. On both occasions he gave assurances that Enigma was safe to use: all the important documents relating to it were printed on specially absorbent water paper, using water-soluble ink so that they should have been destroyed if a U-boat was sunk. And even if key-lists had been captured, a special *Stichwort* (cue word) procedure, which modified the settings, had been brought into force after the captures. But Admiral Karl Dönitz, the Admiral Commanding U-boats (*Befehlshaber der U-Boote – BdU*) remained deeply uneasy. Following the ambush of U-67 and U-111 by the British submarine HMS *Clyde* in Tarafal Bay in one of the Cape Verde Islands, off the coast of Senegal, on 28 September 1941, he concluded that:

> Either our ciphers have been compromised or it is a case of leakage. A British submarine does not appear by chance in such a remote part of the ocean. The Naval Staff is requested to take the necessary measures to safeguard the cipher system.

In the ensuing inquiry, Rear-Admiral Erhard Maertens, the head of the MND, advised that 'The more important ciphers do not seem to have been compromised.'

As the war progressed, the evasive routeing of Allied convoys, attacks on U-boat rendezvous and evidence from *B-Dienst* decrypts, led the *Kriegsmarine*, especially its U-boat arm, to become increasingly alarmed about cipher security. The *B-Dienst* was solving many of the 'U-boat estimates' promulgated by the British and Americans. Although these were based on Ultra in 1943, they invariably referred to the intelligence being derived from direction-finding (DF), to disguise its true origin. In late March 1943, for example, BdU recorded that:

> according to an American estimate of the U-boat situation on 24 March it is presumed on the basis of inaccurate D/F that 10 to 15 U-boats are sought to be controlling in the area 56 to 61 degs. N and 28 to 36 degs. W. . . . The *Seeteufel* Group with 14 boats was in a patrol line from AD 7986 to AK 3955 up to 2100 on 23 March.

However, as BdU observed, DF could not account for the estimate, since the *Seeteufel* group had not yet sent any signals. Even so, BdU managed to convince himself that the American estimate could have been deduced from a detailed analysis of all the available intelligence, and that it was not the result of the Allies reading the U-boat signals.

BdU's suspicions were again aroused by a series of attacks on U-boats at or near no fewer than ten refuelling rendezvous in mid-Atlantic between 3 and 11 August 1943. These were followed by a highly disturbing report from the *Abwehr* in Switzerland:

> A special office [in England] has dealt exclusively with solving German codes. It has succeeded for some months in reading all orders sent by the *Kriegsmarine* to U-boat commanders, which has very considerably helped the hunt against the U-boats.

The *Abwehr* had received the information from a member of the Swiss intelligence service. The original source was said to be a Swiss-American in an important position in the US Navy Department. BdU's alarm can be imagined, but the experts re-affirmed their earlier advice that the 'continuous current reading of our W/T traffic by the enemy is out of the question', since 'At present no possible way of solving [the plugboard combinations] within a reasonable time is known, even with the maximum amount of labour.'

At the end of February 1944, the MND carried out a further inquiry into how the Allies had found out about three rendezvous, between U-129, U-516 and U-544 on 16 January, the tanker *Charlotte Schliemann* and U-532 on 11 February, and U-518 and the Japanese submarine I-29 on 13 February. However, the committee conducting the inquiry does not seem to have approached its task with an open mind, since it explained its purpose as being 'to explain for what reasons reading of our signals . . . could *not* have taken place' (my emphasis). It completely discounted the possibility that messages had been read with the help of punched card systems, since, for some unexplained reason, it thought the systems 'would have to be applied anew to each signal'. A later investigator, Lt. Hans-Joachim Frowein, did not make the same mistake. The committee concluded that if 'the enemy really was for a limited time in a position to read our traffic currently it is incomprehensible that during this period he should not have interfered with all U-boat operations'. The fact that doing so would have endangered the Allied source seems not to have occurred to them. Since reading the traffic was 'shown to be out of the question', only the usual culprits – 'treachery or discovery by enemy aerial reconnaissance' – could explain the incidents. As it was, the report had scarcely been completed before U-It 22, an ex-Italian freight-carrying U-boat, was sunk on 11 March at a rendezvous some hundreds of miles south of Capetown, and a refuelling tender, *Brake*, was attacked and destroyed by a British destroyer on 12 March, the day after a rendezvous in the Indian Ocean. This immediately led to yet another inquiry, and later to a major report on *Kriegsmarine* cipher security generally.

The *Kriegsmarine*'s investigators continually emphasized the security afforded by the *Stichwort* procedure in protecting key-lists which might have been compromised by capture, since it was obvious that the Allies would use a captured key-list and then try to find message settings by trial and error. The *Kriegsmarine* even believed that the *Stichwort* procedure protected captured key-lists from attacks using 'extensive mechanization'. But the investigators were completely mistaken about the *Stichwort*'s effectiveness, and can scarcely have given it even a cursory analysis. Under the procedure, five numbers were derived from the letters in a secret key-word (*Kennwort*), for example '*baden*' furnished 2, 1, 4, 5, 14. The first number was added to each of the rotors which would otherwise have been used (with 2, rotors III, I, VII became V, III, I), the next three to the *Ringstellung*, and the last number to each *Stecker* letter. An attacking cryptanalyst therefore only had to try a maximum of eight new rotor orders (instead of 336) and a mere twenty-six sets of *Stecker* (instead of 150 million million), which could be done even by hand methods, and would have taken only a few minutes with punched cards. It is amazing that the *Kriegsmarine* placed so much emphasis on such a weak procedure, demonstrating as it does that the people carrying out the inquiries had no cryptographic expertise. Even more surprisingly, it would seem that they did not ask any real experts to examine the procedure carefully.

In finding that Enigma was secure, Stummel and others relied heavily on *B-Dienst* decrypts, which they described as a 'first-class and important source of information'. So they were, until they virtually dried up when Naval Cypher No. 5 replaced Naval Cypher No. 3, which the *B-Dienst* had substantially penetrated, as the combined British–American naval code on 10 June 1943. The decrypts also required rigorous analysis, which Stummel was seemingly ill-equipped to carry out. Largely because the decrypts did not even indirectly refer to Allied solutions of Enigma, he reported that they gave 'infallible confirmation' that the Allies had not solved Enigma, and that:

> no trace or even any hint has been afforded by our cryptographic work [i.e. by the *B-Dienst*] of any results of the decyphering of our own main procedures . . . the success of these [*Kriegsmarine* Enigma] cyphers has been further assured and confirmed by all existing proofs.

Some German signals to the U-boats gave clear indications that they were based on decrypts, by referring to the contents of Allied signals without paraphrasing them. Stummel seems to have expected the Allies to have adopted that highly insecure German procedure, even though *B-Dienst* reports emphasized that they were to be 'disseminated only in cases of emergency and then in paraphrase and without reference to source'. However, a careful reading of some of the Allied signals referring to DF might well have revealed to the *Kriegsmarine* that some were mere cover for Sigint. Some signals which purport to be based on DF were sent twenty-four hours or more after the alleged DF 'fix', and do not cite the frequency of the signals said to have been fixed. Information based on true HF-DF fixes was sent out much more quickly and specified the frequencies involved, to enable the shipborne HF-DF operators to tune to them, if necessary.

As Tranow observed, however, all but one of the MND's investigations were fundamentally flawed: 'the only effective action was to do what the enemy might be expected to do – [carry out] a first class cryptanalytic attack'. No cryptanalyst was assigned to investigate M4's security until July 1944, when Lt. Frowein was lent by department 4 SKL III (cryptanalysis) of the German Admiralty to 4 SKL II (radio, including cipher security) for six months for the purpose. Although neither Frowein nor any of his ten staff had any experience whatsoever of breaking commercial Enigma, or any other machine ciphers, by December he had developed a method to recover M4's inner settings and *Stecker* with a twenty-five-letter crib. His method was slightly artificial, in that it depended on only the right-hand rotor moving during the full length of the crib, which would only happen about once in every forty-two messages with M3 or M4 – only when one of rotors I to V was in the right-hand position and had just passed its turnover position. But it was a start, and proved that *Heer* and *Luftwaffe* Enigma ciphers were more vulnerable in practice, especially from an attack using punched cards. Frowein knew that punched card machinery would have speeded up his methods considerably. He reckoned that a catalogue for M4 would have required four million cards, but that the three-rotor Enigma needed only 70,000 cards. Since M3's rotors were the same throughout the war, punching the cards once would have sufficed. Frowein's findings are said to have led the *Kriegsmarine* to decide that only rotors with two notches (VI to VIII) should be used in the right-hand position from December 1944 onwards. But even that basic step appears not to have been taken. A Shark key-list for June 1945 does not show any of those rotors in that slot.

The failure of the Germans to take additional steps to protect Enigma is all the more astonishing, since they knew that young

Polish mathematicians had solved Enigma before the war, and probably up to May 1940. They had discovered the Polish Cipher Centre at Pyry (codenamed *Wicher*) when they occupied Poland, and had been amazed by its successes. They may even have found decrypts of some pre-war naval Enigma messages in *Wicher*'s files. They carried out various investigations into the work done at *Wicher*, but made little real progress for many months. However, in March 1944, as a follow-up to the earlier inquiries, a German technical commission questioned the former head of the Polish Cipher Bureau, Colonel Gwido Langer, and Major Maksymilian Ciezki, a senior member of the Bureau, who were being held at an SS internment camp, Schloss Eisenberg, near Brüx (now called Most) in Czechoslovakia. Langer and Ciezki learned that the commission clearly knew, from decrypts found after the occupation of Poland, that the Poles had broken Enigma. Langer and Ciezki therefore felt compelled to concede, at least indirectly, that *Wicher* had done so before the war, but fortunately they also convinced the commission that a change in Enigma procedures had made it impossible for the Poles to continue their breaks into Enigma. Although the MND should clearly have been informed about Langer's and Ciezki's testimony, that appears not to have happened, since the MND's major report in mid-1944 on *Kriegsmarine* cipher security does not even mention the commission's findings. That is all the more surprising since the findings undoubtedly received some circulation: one German prisoner of war later told a TICOM team that the Poles had continued to read Enigma in France after the fall of Poland. However, he thought that a change in the indicator system (possibly the dropping of double encipherment in May 1940) had brought the Polish work to an end: 'Solution had stopped, however . . . It was an abrupt ending, as if caused by a change in the system.'

Although an organization known as OKW/Chi (*Amtsgruppe Wehrmachtnachrichtenverbindungswesen Chiffrierabteilung*) became responsible for communications security in the German armed forces in 1943, the relevant order remained a dead letter until mid-1944. But even then, OKW/Chi lacked clout: it had no authority to monitor actual traffic, and the Navy successfully opposed its attempts to take over naval communications security. OKW/Chi experts merely maintained that *Wehrmacht* Enigma was 'secure when used according to regulations'. They were well aware of Enigma's weaknesses and that, in particular, the right-hand rotor moved too uniformly, other rotors moved too seldom, and that Enigma should have held more than three rotors, and been issued with more than five rotors. The *Heer* and *Kriegsmarine* knew that Enigma was theoretically breakable, 'given extraordinary mechanical outlay on the part of the enemy for cryptographic activities', but OKW/Chi investigations on how *Wehrmacht* Enigma could be solved using long catalogues of the enciphered letter 'e' had not been finished by the end of the war. OKW/Chi did not carry out an in-depth study to ascertain whether a practical solution was feasible, partly because no authentic clear and cipher texts were ever made available to it for the purpose.

OKW/Chi knew, of course, that commercial Enigma was insecure and, indeed, the Germans broke a rewired Enigma used by the Swiss during the war. Messages on the rewired versions used by the German post office and railways were therefore supposed to be re-enciphered at a different setting. In practice, that was probably not always done, if at all. GC&CS would probably have been unable to solve Railway Enigma traffic so successfully if the messages had been doubly enciphered. OKW/Chi also knew that the 'counter' Enigma (which used 'multiple notch' rotors) employed by the *Abwehr* could be solved with cribs of only ten letters. Instructions were therefore issued by OKW/Chi to encipher messages on the counter Enigma twice, or to encipher the plain-text manually before doing so on the *Abwehr* Enigma.

The *Heer* and *Luftwaffe* made no physical changes to Enigma for most of the war – they did not even introduce new rotors, even though they knew that rotors had been captured on all fronts. However, Hut 6 was confronted by a potentially devastating problem on 1 January 1944, when the *Luftwaffe* started to use a new reflector with its principal cipher, Red. After quickly solving the reflector's wiring on the first occasion when it was used, the Hut 6 cryptanalysts thought they had seen the end of it. They were therefore dismayed when a differently wired reflector turned up ten days later. Initially, they thought that it might merely be a split reflector, like the beta rotor/thin reflector Bruno combination in M4 Enigma. Such a reflector would not have been too difficult to deal with after the wiring was solved initially. However, it slowly emerged that the reflector, named *Umkehrwalze D* (Dora) by the Germans (UKD), was completely rewirable in the field, which was potentially a Herculean problem, with approximately 3.2 x 10^{11} different possible wirings every ten days (the period after which the wiring generally changed) on each cipher which used it. Interestingly, a rewirable reflector had been added to Typex, the British development of Enigma, as early as November 1941. But no thought seems to have been given at Bletchley to the steps needed to counter a similar development in Enigma, probably because the Bletchley cryptanalysts were kept in the dark about it, as a result of the 'need to know' principle.

Luckily, as usual, the *Luftwaffe* blundered when making a major change in its cipher procedures. Not only was UKD introduced slowly, but it did not entirely displace the standard reflector, B (*Umkehrwalze B* – UKB) on the nets which did use it. Instead, both reflectors (UKB and UKD) were generally used alongside each other in the same cipher net: UKD for highly secret messages, and UKB for other signals. But apart from the reflector, all the other components (rotors, *Ringstellung*, *Stecker*, etc.) of a given daily key were the same for both the UKB and the UKD keys, which greatly reduced the task facing Hut 6. So long as it could solve the UKB key in the usual way, it only had to solve the UKD reflector wiring, which it could easily do given a crib of about eighty letters.

Hut 6's worst nightmare was that the *Luftwaffe* would entirely replace UKB by UKD on all or many of its cipher nets simultaneously. It received warnings that such a step was planned for 1 August and had to make major contingency plans to try to combat the change. Despite the efforts of the US Navy to develop a machine known as Duenna to tackle UKD, there was no prospect of Duenna being available on time to do so. Indeed, the first Duenna did not enter service until November 1944. Hut 6 therefore had to train about 400 relatively unskilled personnel to attack UKD using hand methods. About one hundred staff per shift were to use one hundred letter cribs – if available – in much the same way as planned for Duenna. Sixty of the staff were to be Wrens who normally looked after bombes at the Stanmore bombe outstation; in consequence, four bays of bombes (thirty-two bombes) would be put out of action – something that had never happened before. It represented a major loss of bombe power, and reveals just how seriously Hut 6 treated the threat. Stuart Milner-Barry, the head of Hut 6, thought that only three UKD wirings might be recovered during each ten-day period: in effect, only three *Luftwaffe* keys each day (thirty in ten days) – 'a pathetically meagre result compared with the flood with which we have become accustomed'. Fortunately, the emergency did not happen: the *Luftwaffe*'s use of UKD in August and later turned out to be much less than anticipated, although a large number of UKDs had been issued. And for some reason the *Heer* made very little use of UKD: Greenshank (formerly Green) was the only *Heer* cipher broken by Hut 6 to employ it.

A number of machines were designed or developed to meet the UKD menace. Bletchley's main contribution was Giant, which comprised no fewer than four Bletchley bombes linked together (and so needed very long cribs), but it does not seem to have been a success. The Autoscritcher, which was the brainchild of the US Army Signal Security Agency, entered service in late December 1944. Being electro-mechanical, it was very slow, and only achieved four successful solutions (the first being on 6 March 1945) out of twenty-one problems attacked. A much more advanced electronic machine, the Superscritcher, only became operational after the end of the war. Duenna was the most successful of the wartime machines, but even it solved only eleven keys, out of sixty-two problems attempted. It was electro-mechanical, but also incorporated a number of sophisticated memory arrays. It was developed by National Cash Register of Dayton, Ohio, which also made the US Navy bombes. Duenna tested a single rotor order in about ninety minutes.

Had it not been for the mixing of UKD and UKB on the same cipher net, in particular, the results of introducing UKD would have been much more serious. If UKD had also been brought into service on a widespread scale, it would have had a disastrous effect on GC&CS's production of intelligence. In the almost complete absence of suitable fast machinery to solve UKD, Hut 6 could not have dealt with its widespread and secure deployment by the *Heer* and *Luftwaffe*.

Hut 6 encountered a different change to Enigma on 10 July 1944 when, without any warning, some *Luftwaffe* Enigma decrypts yielded only a number, which was later recognized as an indicator, followed by nonsense. It took Hut 6 about four days from the receipt of the first of the messages to work out the wiring: it realized that a substitution device (called the *Uhr* by the Germans) had been employed between the clear-text and the rotors. Forty such *Stecker* substitutions, of which thirty were non-reciprocal, were eventually isolated and their interrelationship discovered, which then allowed them all to be deduced after one was broken. The *Uhr*, which was later applied to about fifteen *Luftwaffe* ciphers, only had a slight effect on breaking Enigma, since the bombes could still be used, although the diagonal board was rendered useless by the non-reciprocal *Stecker*. The *Uhr* was a nuisance – and not a significant problem – for Hut 6, although interestingly the Germans attached much more importance to it than to UKD, probably because they placed undue reliance on Enigma's plugboard.

The Germans had designed a cipher machine, *Schlüsselgerät* 39 (cipher machine 39 – SG 39), in 1939 to replace Enigma, but it never went into mass production. The SG 39 was an outstanding machine, embodying a rewirable reflector, four variable notch rotors, three mechanical drive wheels, and an entry plugboard. The Allies could not have broken it. The Germans developed a variable-notch rotor (*Lückenfüllerwalze*) for Enigma as an interim measure, pending the introduction of the SG 39. Plans were made in December 1943 to bring one such rotor into service with *Heer* Enigmas 'within a reasonable time', since replacing all the existing rotors would have been a huge logistical task. Although it was a very simple device, the new rotor would almost certainly have foiled the bombes, by making it impossible to know when the middle and right-hand rotors advanced.

OKW/Chi's *Oberinspektor* Fritz Menzer, who was a thorn in the flesh of the ISK Section (*Abwehr* machine ciphers) at Bletchley, developed a Hagelin-type machine, the *Schlüsselgerät* 41 (cipher machine 41 – SG 41). About 11,000 machines were ordered by the *Heer* and *Luftwaffe*, but few were produced. When it was brought into service with the *Abwehr* in late 1944, GC&CS solved a few messages using it by aligning them in depth, but could not reconstruct the machine itself.

However, UKD had posed the greatest potential threat to Ultra. A postwar United States Army study concluded that:

> only a trickle of solutions would have resulted if [UKD] had been adopted universally; and this trickle of solutions would not have contained enough intelligence to furnish the data for cribs needed

> in subsequent solutions. Thus even the trickle would have eventually vanished.

The Allies were very fortunate indeed that Ultra from Enigma did not dry up long before the end of the war, especially since, with better management, the *Wehrmacht* could have greatly increased Enigma's security without undue difficulty.

20

From Amateurs to Professionals: GC&CS and Institution-Building in Sigint

PHILIP H. J. DAVIES

Introduction

Throughout the interwar years GC&CS was a remarkably relaxed organization. It recruited only from within a certain circle of people, virtually everyone who joined had been recommended by a friend of one of the codebreakers. This was deemed to be the only way of ensuring that the codebreakers' work remained secret but, as Josh Cooper recalled, it was not conducive to good organization. 'Recruitment by personal introduction had produced a number of very well-connected officers. At best, they were fine scholar linguists, at worst some of them were, frankly, passengers.'

Alastair Denniston had virtually no resources with which to improve the situation and it was not until 1937 when, with the backing of Admiral Hugh Sinclair, he toured the universities looking for mathematicians and linguists to work on the Enigma ciphers, that the situation began to change. This showed far more prescience than either man has been credited with. 'It would be hard to exaggerate the importance of this course for the future development of GC&CS,' Josh Cooper said. 'Not only had Denniston brought in scholars of the humanities, of the type of many of his own permanent staff, but he had also invited mathematicians of a somewhat different type who were specially attracted by the Enigma problem. I have heard some cynics on the permanent staff scoffing at this. They did not realize that Denniston, for all his diminutive stature, was a bigger man than they.' The new recruits included men like Gordon Welchman and Hugh Alexander. They began to take an interest in the organizational structure of Bletchley Park and introduced measures to improve the process of intelligence production, something that had been anathema to many of the interwar codebreakers, who were only concerned with the solution of the ciphers, not with passing on the intelligence they produced.

This chapter describes the subsequent evolution of GC&CS into the postwar Government Communications Headquarters (GCHQ) and the internal and external pressures that led to the transformation from a small group of 'Gentlemen Codebreakers' to the large-scale, highly organized postwar Sigint organization GCHQ.

MS

It is difficult to really understand an organization like GC&CS outside of its contemporary institutional context of Britain's wartime intelligence community, and its longer term historical context as a phase in the evolution of today's Government Communications Headquarters (GCHQ). To appreciate how GC&CS evolved, why it evolved the way it did, and what that evolution means, it is valuable to compare GC&CS and its sister intelligence and security services, the Secret Intelligence Service (now better known as MI6), and the Security Service (MI5).

Although GCHQ, as a Sigint organization, collects information from a fundamentally different class of sources from MI6 (which concentrates on human agents and local technical operations, usually in conjunction with GCHQ), MI5 has to handle both communications as well as human intelligence domestically (again in concert with GCHQ). However, like MI6, GCHQ is essentially a service provider to consumers in the overt government and as a result is subject to very similar structural and political pressures. By contrast, MI5, which is supposed to be as independent from political interference as possible under both the 1952 Maxwell-Fyffe Directive (which charged it with 'the Defence of the Realm') and the 1989 and 1996 Security Service Acts, does not really serve a brace of intelligence 'consumers' in quite the same way. As a result, GCHQ, like MI6, evolved very much on the basis of consumer demand for a particular kind of intelligence. The pressures of that demand shaped its early loose and informal structure as the interwar GC&CS, and also proved central to the pressures and crises during its most productive years, churning out Ultra during the Second World War. It was out of that period of pressure and transformation that much of what constitutes the modern GCHQ took shape.

Compared with both MI6 and GCHQ, MI5 developed throughout its history as a fairly coherent, hierarchical bureaucracy. In part, one might trace the tighter organizational practice at the Security Service back to the earliest days of Mansfield Cumming and Vernon Kell, founding fathers of the foreign and domestic sides of the Secret Service Bureau. Those two sides would eventually split apart to become MI6 and MI5. Even from the earliest days, Kell, the War Office official, displayed a greater flair for organizational design than the ageing and retired naval commander Cumming. However, such an early influence need not prove pervasive and lasting, and it is fairly easy to show that, regardless of flair, MI6 was as subject to the range of pressures within Whitehall that prevented it from adopting a conventional hierarchy.

The strongest single pressure on MI6 was consumer demand.

The most important thing to understand about consumer demand in terms of Britain's intelligence machinery is that intelligence in the broad sense, that is, any and all information relevant to policy formation and execution, is a departmental concern, and not an agency one. Intelligence, at least in the sense of special or secret intelligence, is essentially one more of a variety of information sources which the overt government can employ in its ordinary course of work. According to Reginald Hibbert, a government official, around 50 per cent of the information used by the Foreign Office is 'drawn from overt published sources'. A further 10 to 20 per cent is 'privileged material which is not strictly speaking classified' or information which is 'classifiable as confidential' and is 'a product of normal diplomatic activity', while of the remainder only around 10 per cent comes from secret sources. Traditionally, the various forms of covert intelligence collection were set up as required more or less independently by the various departments. Hence, during the Napoleonic Wars military intelligence networks were set up, but dismantled after the conflict, just as the Indian Government employed the players of the Great Game on an *ad hoc* basis. Even the long-standing Secret Department of the Post Office had been shut down in 1840. It was not until after the Boer war that there was any effort to set up a permanent secret service, and even that was a very limited undertaking. When the first really permanent secret service was set up in 1909, it was primarily because of concerns expressed by the Admiralty and War Office before the Haldane Committee 'into the question of foreign espionage' that they lacked information about German ports and dockyards, and the ability to deal securely with potential agents.

The importance of customer demand is well illustrated by the fact that, in 1917, Cumming was forced to reorganize his headquarters from a geographical structure to one based on the functional relevance to his consumer departments. Under the so-called MacDonough Scheme, the MI6 HQ was then divided into sections that provided military intelligence for the War Office, economic intelligence for the Ministry of Blockade and political intelligence for the Foreign Office and so forth. This reform, imposed on Cumming by his Whitehall masters, meant two main things. In the first place, it demonstrated that he was not really master in his own home. What the customers in Whitehall and Downing Street wanted would prevail over any internal process. It also flattened the MI6 headquarters structure so that it acted mainly as a distributor of information to those consumers where the first responsibility of the collating sections was to their customers rather than Cumming or his successors as Chief or 'C'. This dynamic of consumer demand was intensified after the First World War by the decision in 1921 to give MI6 exclusive responsibility for collecting intelligence for all three services and a number of government departments. As a quid pro quo for MI6's monopoly, the principal 'consumers' attached sections of their own intelligence branches to MI6 HQ to act as collators, as conduits of requirements (or 'tasking') issued to MI6 by their home departments, and as circulators of intelligence reports from MI6 to their departments. These sections were dubbed Circulating Sections.

The doctrine of 'dual control' (as it would later become known in MI6), originally embodied in the Circulating Sections, meant that senior headquarters officers owed only part loyalty to 'C', and the rest to the War Office, Admiralty or wherever they had come from. This created a precedent of loose and horizontal organization which carried over into the addition of other sections for internal ciphers and radio communications, escape and evasion and so forth. This made the service desperately difficult to manage, especially when the Second World War broke out and staff numbers and additional specialist sections began to multiply. As a consequence, one-time Deputy Chief Valentine Vivian eventually described the service as a loosely affiliated group of 'independent sections . . . known as the SIS'. This weak structure made the service almost impossible to oversee and direct by the middle of the war, and successive attempts at reform eventually led to a postwar scheme in which the service was centrally divided between a 'Production side', which collected information on a geographical basis, and a 'Requirements side', which collated and disseminated it and received consumer requirements, on a functional basis.

By comparison, MI5 has always existed with a certain degree of detachment from the rest of the British machinery of government. Production and dissemination of raw intelligence to consumers in Whitehall and Downing Street were never its main function. Moreover, during its interwar and early wartime years, MI5 was very much without a specific governmental master or ministerial sponsor. Indeed, the Security Service's main consumer is, and has always been, the service itself. As a result, it has never been subject to the same kind of tangential forces that pulled MI6 into a wide, flat, 'organic' structure. On the contrary, the problems experienced by MI5 have generally had to do with excessively rigid bureaucracy rather than overly loose organization. However, MI5 would experience problems of rapid growth and unanticipated success during the Second World War, much as GC&CS did, the crucial difference in their experiences being the fact that the latter's position in the machinery of government was (and in its modern form as GCHQ is) more akin to that of MI6 than MI5.

Like MI6, the key force in the evolution of GC&CS was consumer demand, and the desire of consumers to ensure access to the service's product. Its origins lay in an attempt to regularize the cryptanalytic machinery which had developed during the war, chiefly in the form of the Admiralty's highly successful 'Room 40' staff, and the less dramatic efforts of the War Office cryptanalysis section MI1b. Just as early human intelligence had been run on a departmental, *ad hoc* basis, so wartime codebreaking had been chiefly a departmental concern. This was so much the case that considerable rivalry and hostility existed between the Admiralty and War Office codebreaking teams, undermining the potential advantages to be had from pooling their efforts. Regardless of the risks to security from weakening compartmentalization by co-operating, codebreaking is a field with very real economies of scale where different groups working on different problems can generate results useful to each other as well as to themselves. This was certainly the experience of the First World War, and it was because of this that GC&CS was established on an inter-departmental basis in 1919. That being said, in the first instance, GC&CS came under the authority of the Foreign Office, and under 'C' when Admiral Sir Hugh 'Quex' Sinclair took over that post after the death of the MI6 founder Mansfield Cumming. The original GC&CS consisted of its director, six senior assistants, drawn from the best cryptanalysts of Room 40 and MI1b, eighteen junior assistants and a clerical staff of twenty-eight.

GC&CS was housed with MI6 at 54 Broadway, near Whitehall, where they were known collectively and euphemistically as the Government Communications Bureau (GCB). The original organization was very loosely and informally organized, partly a carry-over of the organizational culture of Room 40 and partly a consequence of its relatively small size. Formal management structure took a back-seat to getting the job done, so much so that one historian has summarized the experience of the interwar GC&CS as a combination of 'technical success and organizational confusion'.

The resulting organization, however, like MI6, was to become profoundly shaped by the role and interests of its consumers as it developed. Rather than being confined to its original single, central cryptanalysis staff under its interwar chief, Alastair Denniston, its original postwar staff was added to in the form of service branch cryptanalytical sections and a Foreign Office-oriented civilian side, which were attached on terms of dual control similar to the circulating sections of MI6. Almost as soon as GC&CS was set up, the service branches began to complain that service cryptanalytical interests and needs were not being properly addressed. A Naval Section was formed in 1924, an Army Section in 1930, and an Air Section in 1936. In 1938, a commercial section was set up to provide intelligence to the Industrial Intelligence Centre (IIC) at the Department of Overseas Trade. From 1937, the 'civil side' included a GPO-manned system of stations intercepting Axis diplomatic traffic for Foreign Office consumption, although GC&CS had had access to pretty much any telegram traffic required from Britain's commercial cable companies throughout the interwar period. Once war broke out, there was even a meteorological section attacking enciphered German weather reports.

It might be tempting to suggest that part of the reason for this weak internal structure was a carry-over from MI6. This would be a substantial misreading of the situation as the two organizations had only a minimum of interaction, the main links being via 'C', who oversaw both, and the MI6 circulating sections which tasked the operational sides of both services. The main factor driving the matrix of dual-control sections that took shape as GC&CS was the individual departmental contributions of staff and resources to the service, and the desire of those departments to make use of its product. However, the internal processes were further complicated by the fact that the MI6 circulating sections also acted as conduits for consumer requirements to GC&CS during the interwar years.

If the demand for intelligence is a crucial input to intelligence service structure in the British model, the lack of demand can be equally telling. Although the War Office, Admiralty and Air Force all contributed to the make-up of GC&CS, this did not make it a highly valued or well-endowed organization. Throughout the interwar period, it suffered the same financial stringency as the other intelligence services and the armed forces under 'the Ten Year Rule' – the assumption that there would be no major war for at least a decade. The result was an acute lack of receivers for intercepting foreign traffic, and therefore a dearth of traffic to study in order to achieve any significant breaks. This problem was intensified by the fact that most continental armed forces adopted relatively fixed, stationary deployments during the inter-war period, and so secure communications moved mainly to landlines leaving relatively trivial and generally unencoded traffic to go by radio.

During mid-1940, Air Intelligence did attach a small traffic analysis team to Bletchley Park's Air Section. This was considerably enhanced when the War Office intercept organization MI8 attached all its traffic analysts to Bletchley as well. Denniston originally resisted this, insisting that GC&CS should remain concerned strictly with cryptanalysis (although he would later insist on a consolidation of all Sigint work in the Middle East theatre). Apart from any issue of the advantages or disadvantages of consolidating Sigint at Bletchley, one factor almost certainly in Denniston's mind was the increasingly crowded circumstances at Bletchley Park. There was, however, external pressure for an amalgamation of Sigint. The Director of Military Intelligence wrote to his fellow service directors of intelligence lamenting the lack of co-ordination between traffic analysis and cryptanalysis, and the overall direction of Sigint. He demanded an investigation of the body responsible for the overall handling of intercept work, the Y Committee, and even suggested subordinating it to the Joint Intelligence Committee (JIC).

The Y Committee's parent body, the Y Board, was reconvened from February to March 1941 and was composed of 'C' and the service directors of intelligence. It examined all interception or Y work including both communicative and non-communicative (e.g. radar and navigation beacons) emissions, and even the study and recognition of individual Morse operators. The Y Board concluded, with regard to GC&CS, that the technical characteristics of cryptanalysis precluded any increasingly direct service branch intervention in its internal operation than already was the case (through the GC&CS service sections and MI6 circulating sections). By the same token, however, it did endorse the closer integration of traffic analysis and cryptanalysis, and in due course traffic analysis proved a very valuable auxiliary method to the production of Ultra. The Y Board in turn was to be responsible for co-ordinating the two sides of the process on behalf of the Chiefs of Staff, and was supposed to meet every six to eight weeks. The service intelligence directorates were each to attach an intelligence officer to a Y sub-committee concerned strictly with interception, and likewise to a cryptanalysis sub-committee intended to be 'run in parallel' with the Y sub-committee. The chairs of the two sub-committees were in turn appointed as members to the Y Board. In the event, the obvious duplication between the two sub-committees eventually led to the crypt analysis sub-committee petering out as its duties were subsumed by an additional Enigma sub-committee created in March 1941.

In an attempt to address the concerns of his consumers in Whitehall about their access to, and control of, cryptanalytical product, Denniston set up an additional section within GC&CS called the Interservice Distribution and Reference Section. This section would also include representatives from the service branches to help ensure that their interests were duly considered in the circulation of GC&CS product. Despite these attempts to incorporate consumer demand into the day-to-day operation of the service, the Admiralty in turn remained relatively dissatisfied. In an effort to increase the forcefulness of their representation at Bletchley, they attached an assistant director of naval intelligence to GC&CS. In practice, however, he was actually based at the Admiralty's Operational Intelligence Centre (OIC), albeit making regular visits to Bletchley, and received daily reports from the navy section by telephone.

One can see, therefore, that GC&CS was very much an assortment of semi-independent sections with divided loyalties and subject to lines of dual control between GC&CS and their departments of origin. The organizational politics of intelligence management were very similar in both GC&CS and MI6. Where the two organizations differed most dramatically was in their relative success as the war developed. While MI6 lost most of its continental assets during the fall of Europe in 1939–40 and spent much of the war trying to regain lost ground, GC&CS developed a chain of successes, central of which was the successful penetration of the Axis high-grade codes and ciphers, now famous as Ultra. Hence, the difficulties of MI6 arose from the unenviable combination of escalating demand and dwindling supply. On the other hand, while GC&CS found itself in possession of a rich vein of raw intelligence (plus or minus occasional ebbs and flows as the fortunes of cryptanalytical war came and went), it was confronted by severe overload of already strained facilities combined with growing demand that actually seemed to outpace even the richest outpouring of the intelligence product. As a result, GC&CS quadrupled in size between late 1939 and early 1941 when it reached a staff of 900. With continued success, its size continued to expand to 1,500 in 1942.

At the outbreak of war, GC&CS had been composed of a combination of Foreign Office and Service Branch professionals coupled to an assortment of ageing but productive Room 40 alumni of First World War vintage. In the new population there was an exotic assortment of civilians, amongst which the official history counts 'professors, lecturers and undergraduates, chess-masters, experts from the principal museums, barristers and antiquarian booksellers'. The result was a struggle to keep up with the flood of new faces and personalities, and to keep some semblance of orderly process. As the official history notes, 'At the beginning of 1941 it was by Whitehall standards poorly organized . . . new sections had to be improvised into existence in response to the needs and opportunities thrown up since the outbreak of war.' The result was 'a loose collection of groups rather than . . . a single tidy organization', words which almost exactly parallel Vivian's description of MI6 in the same period. The situation was intensified by the fact that senior officers still retained the pre-war practice of performing both cryptanalytical as well as administrative tasks. An additional source of friction was the fact that the new and relatively 'undisciplined' wartime staff were less familiar with the traditional departmental and ministry control over intelligence analysis, and were prone to stray into areas of interpretation and assessment consumers viewed as their own domain.

By early 1942, GC&CS found itself all but overcome by its own internal management problems, partly driven by a new and unmanageable size, partly by a progressive erosion of traditional institutional and administrative boundaries, and partly by escalating efforts of the Service customers to keep a hand in the day-to-day operation of the organization. GC&CS reached a crisis point in the autumn of 1941, forcing Menzies to appoint a Joint Committee of Control drawn from both MI6 and GC&CS. However, like so many of Menzies' administrative initiatives, the committee proved unequal to the task, and – despite the obvious dangers of going over the heads of their superiors – four leading cryptanalysts were forced to appeal directly to Churchill. Despite this drastic action, matters remained unresolved until January 1942.

It is worth keeping in mind that this kind of difficulty as a result of too rapid success was not wholly unique to GC&CS. During the same period, and also partly as a result of GC&CS successes, in this case against *Abwehr* ciphers, MI5 experienced a similar overload crisis. With the successful penetration of the German espionage effort against the UK that took the shape of the now-famous Double Cross programme, MI5's operational side, B Division, found itself a vast and tottering mass of *ad hoc* groups and sections, trying to cope with the volume of work brought on by Double Cross. It also experienced management bottlenecks where staff and procedures were not equipped to handle the volume of materials generated by both counter-espionage Sigint, double-agent operations, and a flood of reports from around the British Isles of suspected spies and saboteurs. Where MI5 differed from GC&CS, however, was that it was designed primarily as an investigation service and not as an intelligence producer. MI5 did not have a brace of powerful Cabinet-level customers demanding their respective pounds of flesh, and was not composed of a staff subject to the divided loyalties of dual control between the service and its consumers. The demands of Bletchley Park's consumers intensified its difficulties with overload well beyond that experienced by the Security Service. What MI5 needed was a strong central hand of control, which it eventually received in the form of Sir David Petrie as Director-General. No such solution was available to a GC&CS which existed to serve many masters rather than one. Although the service intelligence branches increasingly ceded direct control of GC&CS to the organization itself and to 'C' prior to 1941, debates over the circulation of what amounted to an embarrassment of Ultra wealth set matters back considerably.

One of the peculiarities of intelligence supply and demand in wartime is the absence or even reversal of the law of diminishing marginal utility. Under this old standard of economic theory, a thirsty man derives more utility from his first mouthful of water than from his last, by which time he is sated and drinking ceases to be a source of pleasure. The additional utility of each additional swallow diminishes until there is no more utility to be had. On the whole, this theory holds quite nicely for most products, from food to household computers to television comedy. In the case of intelligence, and especially in wartime, the process is almost reversed, as each intelligence report of the calibre of Ultra creates an increased appetite for more of the same, with no real upper limit in sight. One cannot really imagine the Admiralty's OIC turning around to Bletchley Park and saying 'that's all the Ultra we need thank you, we've had quite enough now'. The result was that as supply increased, demand increased rather than decreased, and the armed forces' desire for a direct hand in the running of things that had been on hold for a time increased likewise.

As far as the internal workings of GC&CS were concerned, this was particularly apparent with the army and air sections, the Admiralty having made something of a 'separate peace' with Bletchley Park through its appointment of an OIC-based Assistant Director of Naval Intelligence. The army and air sections were subject to a particularly keen sense of divided loyalty between GC&CS and their own services. This was demonstrated most clearly in October 1941, when the Director of Military Intelligence and his RAF counterpart demanded what the official history described as 'total operational control of the staff engaged in translating and elucidating the decrypts, and selecting from them those which should be passed to Whitehall and operational theatres'. To complicate matters, this demand was supported by the military and RAF circulating sections (Sections IV and II respectively) at MI6. The irony of this development was that the Sigint service branch officers themselves fell to quarrelling like thieves over the division of the spoils, and this intervention too ended in deadlock.

As internal solutions to GC&CS's internal problems were not forthcoming, Menzies was forced to initiate an independent inquiry by a former deputy director of military intelligence. In February 1942, Menzies implemented the inquiry's recommendations. The Joint Committee of Control was disbanded, and the civil and military sides of GC&CS were drawn apart into two distinct directorates under 'C'. The sub-division of GC&CS largely resolved the span of control problems which had come with frantic expansion, and relieved some of the crowding problems at Bletchley Park as the civil and diplomatic sections of GC&CS were rehoused in quarters in Berkeley Street, London.

The service sections came under a new post of Deputy Director (Services), filled by Commander Edward Travis, who subsequently received replacements for the civilian administrative staff that had been drawn from MI6 and who relocated to Berkeley Street under Denniston – moved sideways but effectively demoted, to become Deputy Director (Civil). This solution was not, however, without its costs. In creating two Directorates under 'C', the post of a single operational head of GC&CS had to be abolished.

Civilians who remained with the service directorate at Bletchley Park were given formal authority over armed service personnel working under them. Finally, differences over the control of Ultra were to be settled by the appointment of a head of section responsible for distribution and answerable directly and only to Travis.

GC&CS continued to grow rapidly, with continued managerial difficulty resulting, albeit not on the scale of the 1941 crisis. By summer 1943, the staff had increased to 5,052 (from 2,095 the previous summer). In June 1944 they numbered 7,723, of whom 3,371 were civilians and 4,352 service persons. Numbers peaked in January 1945 at 8,995. The solution to these management difficulties can only have served to intensify the friction felt over the 1942 reorganization. Menzies redesignated himself Director-General and promoted Travis as overall Director of GC&CS while Denniston continued to languish in the hierarchy as Deputy Director (C). These arrangements prevailed until the end of the Second World War.

After the war, GCHQ managed to escape from the control of 'C' and disengage itself from the even more fraught internal management problems of MI6. It swallowed up what had been the wartime Radio Security Service, although it was divorced from the London Communications Security Agency until their eventual re-amalgamation in 1969. In looking at the internal structure of the postwar GCHQ, it is impossible not to see the legacy of the hard lessons of Bletchley Park, Ultra and the Second World War.

The Cold War GCHQ continued to serve a brace of consumers in Whitehall, as well as foreign but allied collaborators in the UKUSA 'special relationship'. As such, its structure has still had to cope with the importance of customer requirements, but also take into account the dangers of insistent and intemperate customer demand when it interferes with the bread and butter work of Sigint. As a result, what we see in the Cold War GCHQ is a division – like that of the Cold War MI6 – into five main directorates or Divisions: H Division, consolidating cryptanalysis into a single administrative entity; J and K Divisions handling the operational work of Sigint production, J Division handling the Soviet Bloc and K Division the rest of the world; X Division providing specialized computing services (GC&CS was, of course, the birthplace of the first semi-programmable electronic computer, Colossus, for attacking Tunny signals); and finally Z Division responsible for Requirements and Liaison, handling links between GCHQ and its customers in Whitehall and its allies in the UKUSA Sigint alliance. Under these arrangements, it was able to retain its links to customers in Whitehall and Downing Street through Z Division, but without quite the same problem of divided loyalties, as liaison with consumers was divorced from the practical work of doing Sigint.

The structure of demand in government circles also changed, with an increasingly powerful JIC in the Cabinet Office from 1957. From there the JIC has since been in a position to arbitrate between competing demands for intelligence among customers, and empowered to lay down clear and agreed national intelligence priorities through the annual National Intelligence Requirements Paper. Of course, whether these smoothly oiled mechanisms would run quite as slickly in a case of crisis of national survival comparable to the Second World War has never really been put to the test, and hopefully is unlikely to be so tested in the foreseeable future. Nonetheless, the experience of the Second World War, of the problems and crises created by unexpected success, proved as vital to creating the postwar British intelligence system as the only slightly harder lessons learned from unavoidable failure. During those glory years of Ultra at Bletchley Park, GC&CS and its masters and customers in the British Government were forced to identify genuine weaknesses and difficulties in their traditionally collegial way of doing things. Solutions had to be found that allowed the intrinsic problems to be resolved, or at least minimized, without sacrificing the strengths of that way of doing things. The solutions were not unalloyed good or bad ones, but risks and trade-offs that, overall, served admirably well and provided that vitally necessary institutional setting for what was undoubtedly the jewel in Britain's wartime intelligence crown.

21

Cold War Codebreaking and Beyond: The Legacy of Bletchley Park

RICHARD J. ALDRICH

Introduction

The postwar Soviet Union and the threat it posed to the western democracies dominated future planning for the British intelligence and security services throughout 1944 and 1945. MI6 began looking towards Moscow as the main postwar enemy, setting up a small anti-Soviet section under the service's rising star Kim Philby, later revealed as 'the Third Man' in the Cambridge spy ring. The codebreakers also began looking to their future. Travis set up a small committee comprising Harry Hinsley, now one of his key aides; Gordon Welchman, the head of Hut 6; and Edward Crankshaw, who had spent time in Moscow dealing with the Russians on Sigint. They pressed for a combined foreign intelligence organization, taking in both Sigint and human intelligence, a logical development of the situation that already existed in the control by 'C' of both GC&CS itself and of the distribution of its material. In the event, the opposite occurred. The postwar successor to Bletchley Park discarded both the links to MI6 and its old name, adopting the wartime cover name of

GCHQ as its new title. It moved first to Eastcote in north London, and later to Cheltenham, as an independent Sigint organization, separate from MI6 although still under Foreign Office control. It remained highly secretive. Its existence only became widely known in the 1970s and 80s through a series of trials over leakage of Sigint secrets and a badly handled bout of industrial action, which led to a number of workers being sacked. This chapter by Professor Richard J. Aldrich shows that, despite the obsessive secrecy surrounding GCHQ, there is a good deal that can be learned about it through careful research in the British and US archives.

MS

It is all but impossible to draw a distinction between Bletchley Park's work on wartime Germany and its growing work on the Soviet Union in the 1940s. Knowledge of wartime Germany required the tracking of events on the eastern front and involved learning as much as possible about the Soviet effort. British intelligence began to value the Germans for their knowledge of the Soviet Union as soon as Ultra came onstream. German messages used to send their own Sigint summaries about the Soviet Union back to Berlin were, in turn, intercepted by the British. This 'second-hand' Sigint proved to be London's best source on the performance of the Soviet forces. As early as 1943 the Joint Intelligence Committee (JIC) – Britain's highest intelligence authority – was able to produce detailed and accurate reports on the capabilities of the Soviet Air Force, based on *Luftwaffe* Sigint material.

In July 1944 Whitehall began consulting at Bletchley Park about what material they wished to scoop up from what would soon be occupied Germany. Suitably briefed, by early 1945, Intelligence Assault Units were moving into Germany with the forward elements of Allied formations, looking for all kinds of German documents, experimental weapons and atomic plant. Combined Anglo-American Target Intelligence Committee (TICOM) teams were despatched from Bletchley Park to Germany to seek out cryptographic equipment and Sigint personnel. They were not disappointed. Stopping at various German headquarters along the way they ended up at Hitler's Berchtesgaden, where they found a *Luftwaffe* communications centre and a large amount of communications equipment. Eventually German POWs were persuaded to lead them to a vast haul of materials buried nearby and four large German lorries were loaded to capacity with the contents that were then unearthed. The team returned to Bletchley Park – which was increasingly referred to as 'GCHQ' – with its booty on 6 June 1945.

GCHQ relocated and reorganized at the end of 1945. Some of its wartime equipment was constructed at the laboratories of the Post Office Research Department at Dollis Hill in north London, and it was no coincidence that the Director of GCHQ, Sir Edward Travis, chose to move the organization to a temporary site at Eastcote near Uxbridge in north-west London, only a few miles from Dollis Hill. Here it remained until 1952, when his successor, Eric Jones, oversaw the move to two permanent sites in Cheltenham.

One of the most important battles won by GCHQ during 1945 was its struggle with the Treasury. In the autumn, while Travis was in the United States seeking to sustain the Anglo-American Sigint alliance, one of his deputies, Captain Wilson, was busy arguing for exceptional financial measures to help retain the best senior staff beyond the end of the war. Wilson warned that 'there is a grave danger of us losing key personnel which are irreplaceable'. Accordingly, an early tranche of money was released while officials argued over the request for 260 officers as part of a core GCHQ staff of 1,010 (this compared with a wartime allocation of 8,902 staff). Travis returned in late November 1945 to join the fray. He explained that the large quota of senior staff was essential for a new 'Sigint Centre' at Eastcote, from which he would be able to provide a better service to Whitehall. His blueprint for the new GCHQ at Eastcote envisaged six main groups: Technical (Interception and Communications), Traffic Analysis, Cryptographic Exploitation, Cryptographic Research, Intelligence, and Cipher Security.

By mid-December 1945, Travis had won the argument and had reached a deal with the Treasury that was 'on the whole most satisfactory'. But in conveying these feelings to the Treasury he did not miss an opportunity to lecture them on the importance of affording good staff and facilities for GCHQ:

> The war proved beyond doubt that the more difficult aspects of our work call for staff of the highest calibre, the successes by the Professors and Dons among our temporary staff, especially perhaps the high-grade mathematicians, put that beyond doubt. We cannot expect to attract many men of that calibre but we should have suitable conditions with which to attract them.
>
> From his remarks I do not think Winnifrith [a Treasury official] realizes how in some spheres our work is akin to that of the scientific services. For instance, one of our mathematicians has evolved, and made mostly with his own hands, a prototype model of a telephone scrambler of a unique system, and one which gives very great security, and yet of a size that could be used in an aircraft or a car. Although very much wanted, this is a project on which Government scientific establishments have so far failed. Again, the theory on which some of our very secret instruments have been constructed must surely be regarded as a very considerable scientific achievement.

Travis had rightly anticipated the shape of the main challenge that awaited GCHQ in the 1950s and 1960s, namely to stay ahead in a field that increasingly required cutting-edge developments in physics and electronic engineering, something that was likely to place intense strain on GCHQ's budget.

In the late 1940s, the key target for GCHQ was the Soviet A-bomb. The British Chiefs of Staff were fascinated by the problem of Britain's relative vulnerability to attack by weapons of mass destruction and wanted forecasts on this crucial issue. The JIC ordered Britain's codebreakers to focus their efforts upon this, together with other strategic weapons systems such as chemical and biological programmes, ballistic rockets and air defence. Although the JIC placed these subjects in a special high category of priority, it was to no avail. The Soviet bomb took the Western allies by surprise in late August 1949. Other Soviet activities, including espionage and diplomatic initiatives, constituted second and third priorities for GCHQ, but here too there were thin pickings. Many Soviet messages employed one-time pads which, if correctly used, could not be broken. The extent to which Britain was surprised by the Tito–Stalin split in 1948 underlines the limited success enjoyed against its diplomatic targets. Secure Soviet ciphers were only part of the problem. Moscow and its satellites used landlines, which could not be easily intercepted, instead of wireless transmissions.

The limited headway that Britain and the United States had made with Soviet Bloc communications by the late 1940s, including the Venona programme, which attacked KGB intelligence traffic, was soon nullified by the espionage of William Weisband. Weisband was serving with the US Army Security Agency and was privy to most of what the West was obtaining from Soviet channels. As a result, on Friday, 29 October 1948, the Soviet Union underwent a massive change of code and cipher security, eliminating most of the channels that the West could read, including some machine-based, mid-level military systems. In part it was this catastrophe that prompted the British to follow the Soviets down the path of more extensive physical bugging in the mid-1950s. It also prompted the British and the Americans to accelerate their efforts to intercept Soviet telephone landlines by tunnelling under the Soviet sectors of Berlin and Vienna. Several tunnels are known to have been dug in these locations, but it is not unlikely that there were others.

Difficult Soviet targets aside, GCHQ was nevertheless providing Whitehall with large quantities of material in the late 1940s, albeit of a secondary and tertiary order. They continued to attack the communications of many states with vulnerable cipher systems. Some neutral states were persuaded to adopt Enigma or Enigma-type machines previously used by the Axis, in the belief that these machines provided a secure means of communication. This was a belief that GCHQ did nothing to undermine. The JIC had requested material on subjects such as Arab nationalism and the relations of Arab states with the UK and USA, the attitude of the Soviet Union, France, Italy and the Arab states towards the future of the ex-Italian colonies, especially Libya. GCHQ was also urged to focus on the Zionist movement, including its intelligence services. These subjects proved more accessible. In 1946, Alan Stripp, a codebreaker who had spent the war in India working on Japanese codes, suddenly found himself redeployed to the Iranian border. During the Azerbaijan crisis of 1946, he worked on Iranian and Afghan communications (but not Soviet communications) with considerable success.

Although GCHQ was always the largest postwar British secret service, much of its activity was hidden by the use of the signals units of the armed services for interception. Each of the three services operated half a dozen sites in Britain. GCHQ also had a number of civilian outstations including a Sigint processing centre at 10 Chesterfield Street in London, a listening post covering London at Ivy Farm, Knockholt, in Kent and a listening post at Gilnahirk in Northern Ireland. GCHQ had overseas stations hidden within Embassies and High Commissions overseas. There were also service outposts. In the Middle East, the base of Ayios Nikolaos, just outside Famagusta on Cyprus, became a critical intelligence centre, receiving further Army and RAF Sigint units as they gradually departed from Palestine, Iraq and Egypt. Further east, the Navy maintained its intercept site at HMS Anderson near Colombo in Ceylon, and the Army began reconstruction of its pre-war Sigint site at Singapore. But the main British Sigint centre in Asia after 1945 was Hong Kong, initially staffed by RAF personnel. Here, together with help from their Australian counterparts, they captured Chinese and Soviet radio traffic.

Despite London's decision to give GCHQ the lion's share of British intelligence resources and the tendency to bury some of the programme in other budgets, it was difficult to meet the expanding costs of Sigint. On 22 January 1952, the Chiefs of Staff had met together with the Permanent Under Secretary of the British Foreign Office to review plans for improving British intelligence. GCHQ came out on top in this exercise. Its cutting edge programmes, mostly in the area of computers and 'high speed analytical equipment' for communications intelligence, were given 'highest priority'. The Chiefs of Staff continually reiterated the 'very great importance' of speeding up development and construction in these 'very sensitive' areas. By November 1952 a major review of British intelligence was underway. The process was prolonged by the primitive nature of available managerial instruments. Nevertheless, all were clear that in the short term the emphasis should be 'for Sigint'. Eric Jones, the Director of GCHQ in the 1950s, reported that he was busy filling the 300 extra staff posts recently authorized. GCHQ had proposed a further increment for an extra 366 staff to follow. GCHQ was moving from strength to strength.

As early as 1945, most English-speaking countries had committed themselves to postwar Sigint co-operation. Policy-makers at the highest level had come to expect a world in which a global Sigint alliance rendered enemy intentions almost transparent. They were not about to relinquish that privilege willingly. In the autumn of 1945, when Truman was winding up the Office of

Strategic Services (OSS), America's wartime secret service organization, he was also giving permission for American Sigint activity to continue and approved negotiations on continued Allied co-operation. All desired the maximum option. Yet the way ahead was strewn with obstacles and the package of agreements, letters and memoranda of understanding, often referred to as the UKUSA treaty, that sealed this alliance, was not completed until 1948. As this agreement emerged, Britain derived considerable benefit from her dominance over Commonwealth partners.

The semi-feudal relationship which London enjoyed is no better illustrated than in Australia where Sigint operations were controlled by London. Only in 1940 did Australia establish her own separate organization. When this became the Australian Defence Signals Bureau, formed at Albert Park Barracks in Melbourne on 12 November 1947, it remained in the shadow of GCHQ. Four Australian applicants for the directorship were rejected in favour of Britain's Commander Teddy Poulden, who filled the senior posts with twenty GCHQ staff and communicated with GCHQ in his own special cipher. During the winter of 1946–7, a Commonwealth Sigint conference was held in London, chaired by Edward Travis, during which each country received designated spheres of activity. Canada's Sigint organization, under the long-serving Lieutenant-Colonel Ed Drake, suffered similar treatment. On 13 April 1946 the Canadian Prime Minister, Mackenzie King, authorized the consolidation of a number of wartime organizations into a small postwar unit of about 100 staff, known as the Communications Branch of the National Research Council (CBNRC). Again, the senior post was filled by staff seconded by GCHQ, prompting Canadians to say that CBNRC stood for 'Communications Branch – No Room for Canadians'.

Although GCHQ representatives were often over-awed by the scale of American Sigint resources, matters looked quite different from Washington. With the war over and an economizing

Republican Congress controlling the federal purse-strings, resources for American communications intelligence (Comint) interception activities were remarkably tight before 1950. This led to a state of parlous under-preparedness prior to the Korean War. It also prevented the European expansion that American Sigint had hoped for. In 1949, US Army Security Agency interception units in Europe were still passing their product to GCHQ, rather than back to Washington, for analysis. In the late 1940s and early 1950s, GCHQ retained primary responsibility for areas such as Eastern Europe, the Near East and Africa. This period also saw the development of spheres of influence. For example, relations with Norway were an American responsibility, while relations with the Swedes belonged to GCHQ, although this demarcation was not strictly adhered to. GCHQ enjoyed the benefits of a panoply of bases provided by Britain's imperial and post-imperial presence. Although the empire was shrinking, the very process of retreat often rendered the new successor states more willing to grant limited base facilities to the departing British. These facilities seemed innocuous, being termed 'communications relay facilities', but the reality was often different. Many countries, such as Ceylon, were unwitting hosts to GCHQ collection sites. Island locations, including Britain, were intrinsically attractive because they would be slower to be overrun by the enemy in wartime military operations.

In the 1950s, Anglo-American relations were made easier in the Comint field by the arrival of the National Security Agency (NSA), which imposed some order upon the squabbling of the US armed services. In 1952 the Brownell report had recommended to President Truman the creation of a strong centralizing force. The three separate American armed services fought a desperate rearguard action against the creation of the NSA. General Samford of US Air Force intelligence denounced 'strong central control of the national COMINT effort' as a 'major error'. He also warned darkly about Comint slipping away towards civilian control under the office of the Secretary of Defense. But Truman's mind was made up and the NSA began to reshape American Comint. The efforts of the NSA to extend its control over electronic intelligence (Elint), the interception of electronic signals like radar, and to 'fuse' it with Comint processes would be more troubled and stretched on into the 1960s. American officials often envied the more centralized British model.

The closest Anglo-American intelligence relationship during the immediate postwar period was probably that developed between RAF intelligence and the US Air Force. General Charles Cabell (later Deputy Director of the CIA) was head of US Air Force Intelligence as the USAF became fully independent of the US Army in 1947–8. While establishing an expanded intelligence organization and getting to grips with being a fully independent service, the Americans found RAF intelligence to be an ideal partner. RAF intelligence was headed by the convivial Lawrie Pendred, who was anxious to cement the Anglo-American relationship. This growing friendship also reflected the fact that GCHQ had identified air power as a critical area for Sigint, especially those arcane forms of Sigint associated with strategic bombing. Sigint in the air was one of the major growth areas of the early intelligence Cold War.

Air intelligence was keen to develop Elint. It was invaluable for the operational planning for air attack against the Soviet Union. It was equally invaluable to anyone planning peacetime 'spy-flights' over Soviet airspace and looking for gaps in Soviet radar cover. Thus, in this area, air intelligence collectors were also consumers, not least to protect the security of their own missions. Elint was first developed by the Allies in the face of radio-guided German air raids during the Second World War and was later sited at the Central Signals Establishment at RAF Watton. Towards the end of the war, it continued to be refined against Japan.

Initially, the RAF was ahead in this new field. By 1947 a fleet of specially equipped Lancaster and Lincoln aircraft patrolled the East German border, monitoring Soviet air activity. This was complemented by a programme of monitoring of basic low-level Soviet voice traffic by ground stations at locations such as RAF Gatow in Berlin. British 'Ferrets' began their first forays into the Baltic in June 1948 and the Black Sea in September 1948. In that year they began to be supplemented by American prototype B-29 Ferrets flying missions from Scotland to the Spitzbergen area. B-29 Ferrets were also supplied to the RAF under the Mutual Assistance Act from 1950. By 1948 much of the perimeter of the Soviet Union was covered. A British undercover team was operating in northern Iran, monitoring Soviet radar in the Caucasus as well as Soviet missile tests at Kasputin Yar on the edge of the Caspian Sea. The team conducting this was posing as archaeologists, a favourite British cover for intelligence work.

The Comint and Elint effort against the Soviet Air Force and associated strategic systems was one of GCHQ's key areas of achievement in the first postwar decade. The arrival of the first Soviet atomic bomb in 1949 may have eluded them, but its subsequent operational deployment certainly did not. During the early 1950s the Joint Intelligence Bureau in London and the USAF target intelligence staffs had been busy exchanging sensitive data on 'the mission of blunting the Soviet atomic offensive'. This involved the early counter-force targeting of Soviet nuclear forces in the hope of destroying them on the ground before they could be used. Senior officers in London had given particular attention to this matter because of the vulnerability of the UK. The Americans were impressed by the 'considerable progress that London had made on the counter-atomic problem'. GCHQ and the RAF had amassed 'a significant amount of evaluated intelligence, particularly in the special intelligence field, which would be of the greatest value'. Most of the airfields and the operational procedures for Soviet strategic air forces in the European theatre had been mapped by 1952. The full Anglo-American intelligence exchange in this field was somewhat ironic given the different views held in London and Washington on nuclear strategic issues at this time. However, full intelligence exchange on targets continued regardless.

Between 1956 and 1960 several 'incidents' reverberated upon intelligence-gathering from seaborne and airborne platforms. In each case ministers in London reacted more strongly than their counterparts in Washington, constraining the nature and frequency of subsequent operations. For the practitioners, this underlined the value of working with allies. In the late 1940s and early 1950s the British had been more relaxed about forward operations, such as over-flights, and had passed their dividends to Washington. After 1956 the situation was reversed. London's hesitancy in the face of various flaps and shoot-downs accelerated the shift of momentum in the world of Sigint towards the United States.

The scale of political embarrassment that could be generated by bungled surveillance operations was first underlined by the infamous Commander 'Buster' Crabb incident. In April 1956 operations were mounted against the Soviet cruiser *Ordjoninkidze* during the visit of Marshal Bulgarin and Nikita Khrushchev to Britain. Despite some robust exchanges, the visit went well and the Soviet delegation departed on 27 April 1956. But even as they left the press had begun to speculate about the mysterious disappearance of a British naval diver, Commander Lionel 'Buster' Crabb RNVR, in the vicinity of the visiting Soviet warships. His headless body was later recovered from the sea. Anthony Eden intended to take 'disciplinary action' because the mission had been unauthorized and told the ministers concerned to order their staff to co-operate fully with the inquiry. As a result, John Sinclair, the Chief of MI6, was replaced by Sir Dick White, previously Director-General of MI5.

Sir Edward Bridges, a somewhat nineteenth-century figure, conducted a thorough inquiry, employing the Joint Intelligence

Committee mechanism to help him ferret out all aspects of the Crabb affair. Bridges rightly identified 'certain questions' of a broader nature arising out of this event. On the one hand, intrusive intelligence operations clearly had a capacity to cause international repercussions, but, on the other hand, the systems for their authorization were unclear. Bridges recommended a new and broader inquiry, to review all of Britain's strategic intelligence and surveillance activities. It would assess 'the balance between military intelligence on the one hand, and civil intelligence and political risks on the other'. Eden gave this job to Sir Norman Brook, the Cabinet Secretary, working with Patrick Dean, Chairman of the Joint Intelligence Committee. This review had important consequences for intelligence. In April 1956, simultaneous with Khrushchev's visit to Britain, the first CIA U-2s had arrived at RAF Lakenheath and some U-2 work was Sigint-orientated. Eden now decided that this, and a host of other operations, had to go.

Eden's review also impacted on naval Sigint. Even more secret than the U-2s were joint intelligence operations by British and American navies using submarines. But in the backwash from the Crabb affair, British submarine operations were cancelled and so the British half of the deal on Anglo-American submarine-derived Sigint could not be delivered. British officers in Washington spoke of their 'embarrassment', which would persist 'until we can make good our part of the bargain'. Their underlying concern was that Britain would be eclipsed by similar operations by the American submarine commander in the Atlantic, which they were expanding 'so as not to be outdone by the Pacific submariners'. British Naval Intelligence wanted to keep their stake in the game and so urged not only that current operation be restored, but that it be followed by 'a bigger and better operation'. Admiral Inglis, the British director of Naval Intelligence in London, was agitated. The main scoop provided by this series of American operations had been a choice selection of short-range Comint and Elint:

'considerable' VHF voice, Identification Friend or Foe (IFF), and radar transmission was recorded, mostly from airborne and coastal defences. The take was voluminous. Moreover, while the Soviets seemed prepared to repel 'unfriendly air intrusion', by contrast 'no difficulties were placed in way of submarine visitors' and Soviet anti-submarine capability seemed low. The Commander-in-Chief Pacific Fleet was already pressing Washington to abandon the twelve-mile restriction on operations near the Soviet coast. But the question now was, were there to be any further British operations?

By the end of 1956 the Royal Navy felt things slipping away from them. Admiral Elkins, the senior naval officer at the British Joint Staff Mission in Washington, wrote to Mountbatten to voice his concern. As predicted, the US Navy was beginning its own independent operations off Murmansk. Initially, the American Office of Naval Intelligence had decided that the British Naval Intelligence Division was not to be informed. But Admiral Warder from the secretive American OP 31 section entrusted with this mission decided that it would be foolhardy not to draw on extensive British experience of similar operations in these waters. So the British Commander John Coote, who had been on the Murmansk run several times, was called in to brief the first American crew. But this was only on the understanding that he told no other British naval officers in Washington. These new American submarine intelligence operations off Murmansk had been triggered by two factors. First, the cancellation of British operations: Elkins lamented the fact that 'we are no longer providing sufficient cover in an area where we have hitherto been a reliable and productive source'. Second, the US Navy had used the reports of previous British intelligence operations off Murmansk to persuade the State Department that these activities were valuable while 'the risks of detection are negligible'. Elkins accepted that the British cancellations had been a high-level political decision. But he also warned that British prestige in the operational and intelligence fields, which was currently high, would soon suffer 'unless we resume these activities ourselves'.

In the late 1950s, Harold Macmillan allowed the gradual restoration of intrusive operations using British aircraft, ships and submarines for photography and Sigint. Moreover, between 1956 and 1960 twenty U-2 aircraft were involved in overflights. Some U-2 flights used British bases or pilots. Most of the deep-penetration flights were launched from Adana in Turkey and six RAF pilots were based there. Because Turkey would not allow penetration directly into the Soviet Union, U-2s staged on to Peshawar in Pakistan before crossing the Soviet border. Along the southern border of the Soviet Union, Soviet radar stations were more dispersed and a variety of attractive targets presented themselves, including a range of missile testing centres at Kazakstan and the Caspian Sea and at Kapustin Yar on the Volga. Some of these flights substituted Sigint packages for cameras; however, the Sigint package that the U-2 could carry was fairly light. Serious airborne Sigint activity of an intrusive variety was sometimes carried out by the American-modified version of the British Canberra, the RB-57D which, with improved engines and an improbable wing-span, could reach nearly 60,000 feet, compared with the 70,000 feet available to the U-2.

The loss of the Gary Powers U-2 aircraft occurred in May 1960. A month later, an American RB-47 ferret aircraft engaged in maritime surveillance was lost over the Barents Sea, very close to Soviet airspace. The latter aircraft had been launched from RAF Brize Norton in Britain. American and Norwegian Sigint stations had tracked the aircraft, but disputed its course, plotting it thirty miles and twenty-three miles respectively from the Soviet coast. The aircraft crew had received orders not to go closer than fifty miles. The Soviet coastal limit was twelve miles and the margin for error was small. The twin shoot-downs reverberated in Britain in the early summer of 1960. There was a public furore and questions in the House of Commons. Prime Minister Harold

Macmillan was bitter when the Gary Powers shoot-down contributed to the collapse of the East–West summit in Paris, by which he had set much store. The Soviet Union exploited this to the full, threatening countries such as Britain and Japan, which hosted U-2 and RB-57D flights, with rocket attacks against the bases from which future flights were made over 'Socialist' countries. These threats were first made by the Soviet Minister of Defence, Malinovsky, on 30 May 1960 and were reiterated on 3 June to a packed press conference by Nikita Khrushchev himself. The Joint Intelligence Committee in London concluded that these threats were a bluff, nevertheless they induced a new climate of extreme caution on the part of Harold Macmillan.

The impact of these events in the summer of 1960 was similar to the Crabb affair in 1956. They served to crush a British plan for increased airborne surveillance and Sigint gathering against the Soviet fleet that had been emerging in the weeks and months immediately prior to the loss of the Gary Powers U-2 aircraft. In early 1960, the First Sea Lord had held a meeting with the US Navy's Chief of Naval Operations (CNO) and agreed to an 'increased accent on surveillance'. By March 1961, British plans for increased airborne surveillance of the Soviet fleet were put 'into cold storage indefinitely'. Other long-established British programmes were brought to a close. Macmillan now required the Joint Intelligence Committee to prepare a review of all aerial surveillance and submarine surveillance tasks so that he could assess provisionally the value of the intelligence gained from these sorts of activities. These developments contained an element of irony. In the 1950s, Britain and the United States had increasingly turned to technical means of examining the Soviet armed forces and Soviet scientific-technical developments, because human espionage inside the Soviet Union had proved increasingly hazardous and, with a few exceptions, notably unproductive. Forward technical surveillance was now proving to be less than risk-free.

Somewhat safer alternatives certainly existed. In the early 1950s, the British had begun cultivating an alternative form of seaborne surveillance: the possibility of gathering intelligence on the Soviet fleet from the relative safety of British trawlers operating in northern waters. This was similar to the Soviet Sigint trawler that became ubiquitous by the 1960s. This sort of activity was less provocative, though not without risk. However, the real solution to intelligence collection without provocation lay with American satellites that came on stream in 1964, providing both imagery and Sigint collection. It is often thought that the first intelligence dividends from satellites took the form of imagery provided by the Corona operations in 1964. In fact, Sigint satellites began their activities in 1962 with a series of successful and highly secret US launches codenamed 'Heavy Ferret'. By 1970 they had been replaced by the much more sophisticated Rhyolite satellite. The Rhyolite satellite was able to intercept the 'spillage' from microwave telephone links, even though these were in theory 'line of sight' communications. The resulting information was so plentiful that it required immediate downloading, largely to the NSA sites in Britain at Menwith Hill and in Australia at Pine Gap. Both the NSA and GCHQ struggled to cope with the vast output of the Rhyolite satellite programme which provided astonishing numbers of intercepts.

Despite the advent of satellites, Britain retained a strong need for an airborne Sigint capability. In the 1960s much of this was provided by three specially converted Comet Mk 2 aircraft and four Sigint Canberras operated by 51 Squadron of RAF Signals Command. Their main purpose was to gather intelligence on Soviet air defences in support of the V-Bomber force, Britain's main nuclear deterrent in the mid-1960s. They also carried out interception of telemetry from Soviet missile tests in the southern region of the USSR, a process that could not be conducted from the ground without missing crucial data from the first ninety seconds of the missile's flight. However, by 1966 Whitehall had begun to realize that the Sigint Comets would be coming to the end of their operational life in 1972. A long lead time was required to allow 'time for the fit of special role equipment' to any replacement aircraft. As early as October 1966 a special committee, led by the Chair of the London Signals Intelligence Board and composed of key figures from GCHQ and MoD, had concluded that the way forward was a special Sigint variant of the new Nimrod maritime patrol aircraft. The Chiefs of Staff endorsed this decision on 8 November 1966 and the Nimrod Sigint aircraft programme began to roll forward.

The special Sigint variant of the Nimrod was required partly because of alliance pressures. There was a limited choice of partners to share burdens with, for although the French had an airborne Elint capability, and were members of NATO, there was 'no exchange' with them. Other NATO partners, such as Norway and Turkey, offered 'full co-operation', but only used ground-based stations. At the core was the relationship with the United States. Air Vice Marshal Harold Maguire, the Deputy Chief of Defence Staff for Intelligence, explained that, because of the significant British programme, they were the only NATO country receiving raw American Sigint. Accordingly, they were the only country with the capability 'to make our own assessments in our area of interest and, where necessary, challenge US assessments'. Maguire stressed that this had been 'critical' when discussions on future NATO weapons system requirements had occurred. Moreover, the British airborne Sigint programme simply helped to pay Britain's way in the broader politics of Anglo-American intelligence co-operation: 'We know that our relatively small airborne Elint programme is appreciated by the Americans as a sharing of the collection task, particularly as their resources are stretched because of world-wide commitments. As with other British intelligence activities, such as JARIC [Joint Air Reconnaissance Intelligence Centre], it helps to repay in some degree the enormous quantity of material we receive from them.'

Indeed, some officials worried that the US had come to expect British assistance in the airborne Sigint field in Europe 'and a failure would threaten the massive help they give us in the whole Sigint area'.

The cost of the Nimrod Sigint aircraft programme in the 1970s was considerable, initially estimated at some £14 million. This could not be accommodated within the already tight Sigint budget. On 26 July 1967 this issue was addressed by the committee that supervised the budget of the British intelligence community, the Permanent Secretaries' Committee on the Intelligence Services (PSIS), led by the Cabinet Secretary, Burke Trend. He quickly concluded that the Nimrods were 'unacceptable as part of the Sigint budget'. However, everyone was agreed that they were an essential purchase and increasingly an integral part of Britain's nuclear strategic weapons provision. Accordingly, airborne Sigint would henceforth become a formal part of the RAF vote rather than the Secret Service vote. In reality this decision only confirmed what had been a growing practice. Because of the rising cost of Sigint, much of the required finance had been buried in other budgets, and airborne Sigint provision had already been handled in this way as part of what the RAF called 'our overall contribution to the hidden Sigint costings'.

The rapid growth of GCHQ's interest in electronic intelligence and airborne Sigint in the 1950s and 1960s underlined the fact that Western Sigint was entering a new era in several respects. Comint, Elint and communications security (Comsec) were being joined by the equally technical fields of electronic warfare, radio counter-measures and radio deception. Alongside this there were also very elaborate and powerful efforts in the area of radio propaganda broadcasting and also jamming. The airwaves were becoming increasingly crowded and so in 1953–4, Lord Strang, previously the Permanent Under Secretary at the Foreign Office, led a high-level investigation into the future higher direction of radio in war. GCHQ 'were concerned that they should know the details of any radio deception plans' developed by the services. The London Signals Intelligence Board (LSIB) offered Strang a detailed report on the dangers of different branches of the radio war coming into conflict with one another. They explained that 'jamming of an enemy air force signals on one part of the front might prevent the interception of, say, enemy police force cipher messages from quite a different part of the front; study of these might have made it possible to solve, some months later, the cypher messages of submarines operating throughout the world'. John Sinclair, Chair of the LSIB, urged the necessity of 'rapid, forceful and expert co-ordination of the different aspects of the radio war'. Current proposals would not suffice to provide the control during 'the critical opening phases of a war . . . a grave weakness, which ought to be remedied', but the exact solution was not yet clear. Instead, the 1950s and 1960s saw an increasing proliferation of Cabinet committees and sub-committees. Throughout this period GCHQ itself continued to be managed by the LSIB rather than the Joint Intelligence Committee. Each spring, GCHQ brought forward an annual report 'on measures to improve Sigint' for LSIB approval. The LSIB also prepared for the British Chiefs of Staff a more general annual report on the state of British Sigint. Meanwhile the role of the Joint Intelligence Committee was to provide GCHQ with a broad overall list of targets on an annual basis. There were inevitable tussles between these various committees, with the Joint Intelligence Committee conscious that some of its broader reviews of British intelligence effectiveness 'encroached on the preserves of LSIB'.

During the 1950s, most high-grade ciphers, for example one-time pads, used by the major powers, remained effectively impossible to break by the sweat of direct cryptanalysis, when employed correctly. As a result, increasing efforts were made to tap communications before they were enciphered. The era of large-scale bugging had arrived, accelerated by the development of transistors. Soviet efforts were revealed by the accidental location of a microphone in the office of the British naval attaché in Britain's Moscow Embassy in July 1950. The British air attaché, who was testing a radio receiver, heard the voice of his colleague being broadcast loud and clear from another part of the building. An active search ensued but, alarmingly, the Soviets succeeded in removing the device before it could be found. In 1952 more bugs were found in the office of the American Ambassador, George Kennan, using 'a special British detector'. In 1956, conference rooms in the US European Command Building were found to be seriously compromised by listening devices. Britain had not been slow to retaliate and in October 1952 Churchill ordered British defence scientists to begin a vigorous programme of developing British bugs for offensive use against the Soviets. By the late 1950s this was a busy field of activity.

Bugging, direct tapping of landlines and the breaking of the communications traffic of minor states ensured a stream of Sigint was routinely available to Whitehall. Little of this can be seen in the archives today due to the nature of security procedures attending it. Sigint material and ordinary working files never mixed. Before gaining access to Sigint, Foreign Office officials were required to attend a day course on Sigint security. Foreign Office staff could then go on the circulation list for BJs – Sigint material still being circulated in the same blue jacketed files as they were before the war. This material was never to be referred to in ordinary Foreign Office paperwork and always remained in the distinctive blue jackets. BJs were circulated by special messenger, originating in the Permanent Under Secretary's Department and always returned there after use. There, in a small office in this Department, sat the Communications Security Officer, the work-a-day liaison with GCHQ. More humble files dealing with policy and correspondence lived in the Foreign Office registry. This hermetic separation has ensured the near invisibility of Sigint to postwar diplomatic historians.

Throughout the Cold War the physical entity that constituted

GCHQ continued to expand. In 1952 it had moved to a single site in Cheltenham at what had been a former US Army base at Harthurstfield Farm. This became known as the Benhall site. But soon it was clear that more space was required and a further site on the other side of Cheltenham was acquired at Oakley. Benhall contained much of the technological and development effort, while Oakley contained the language training centre and administrative buildings. Around the main buildings at Oakley were the physical manifestations of continued Cold War growth – an expanding network of low-level temporary buildings and Portakabin-type structures. Much of this work was devoted to defensive communication security as well as the more frequently remarked upon business of Sigint. Moscow maintained an aggressive Sigint programme and in the late 1980s it was estimated that the Soviet Union maintained a capability at least as extensive as that of the United States, deploying some 350,000 people. These were mostly located at some 500 ground stations inside Eastern Bloc countries or at locations such as Cuba.

GCHQ linkage to American facilities has always been important. The largest American Sigint base in Britain is at Menwith Hill, which has recently expanded further to accommodate American programmes withdrawn from Europe. In 1997, a new US Naval Security Group detachment arrived to join a major British Sigint site at RAF Digby, seventeen miles south of Lincoln. This American unit is fully integrated with the RAF 399th Signals Unit. Indeed, Digby constitutes a major all-arms Sigint and Comsec centre, in which members of the three armed services of both countries co-operate in a fully integrated operation. In the United States, the main interface is the National Security Agency Columbia Annex (CANX) at 7200 Riverwood Drive, Maryland. This is a long, low, single-storey building, almost invisible behind its screening, which provides accommodation to the British Liaison Officer to the NSA and his staff, allowing a permanent GCHQ presence at Fort Meade. The long-term future of the

Anglo-American Sigint relationship beyond the end of the Cold War was effectively shaped in the late 1980s. The main factor was the cancellation of the vastly expensive British Zircon Sigint satellite programme in 1987, which had been costed at £500 million for a geo-stationary satellite with a five-year lifespan. The project had been strongly advocated by the GCHQ Director Brian Tovey. Thereafter, Britain reportedly negotiated an agreement whereby she made a substantial contribution to the National Reconnaissance Office programme and was able to make some tasking requests. These developments marked an implicit admission that London was at last giving up any pretensions to being a premier league Sigint player.

The Iraqi attack against Kuwait on 1 August 1990 was arguably an event which GCHQ had been waiting for for three decades. The historic tensions in the area, together with Britain's defence relationship with Kuwait, ensured that Britain had long devoted herself to deterring an Iraqi attack and also to providing some warning of such an attack if deterrence failed. In January 1965, Leonard Hooper took over from Clive Loehnis as Director of GCHQ. One of his first priorities was to discuss the future of a small team of GCHQ staff in Kuwait, whose task was to constantly sweep the airwaves for signs of an Iraqi attack. 'While the team was a reasonable insurance factor in providing timely warning of an external attack,' he explained to the Joint Intelligence Committee, 'it could do little or nothing to give Sigint warning of internal unrest or a coup.' Hooper was pressed for resources elsewhere and wondered whether this task could be transferred to the British facilities in Cyprus. But by monitoring from Cyprus a good deal of local Sigint would be lost and the Joint Intelligence Committee decided the GCHQ team should stay in place, not least because they did not want to suffer the 'loss of tactical Sigint information on the Basra brigade' of the Iraqi army.

During the Gulf War of 1990, one of the first warnings of the Iraqi attack was provided by satellite detection of Iraqi radar activity. Soviet-constructed, long-range radar units, codenamed 'Tall King', became very active on 29 June 1990, having been silent for some months. By mid-July 1990 a considerable programme of satellite monitoring of Iraq – mostly through imagery – had been developed, which was expected to provide somewhere between twelve and twenty-four hours' notice of an attack. But despite warnings of troops massing on the Kuwait border, the prevailing thinking in the White House was that this was a bluff. Once the war began in earnest it became clear that US training offered to Iraq in the 1980s had facilitated very secure communications, including the extensive use of landlines with fibre-optic cables and a great deal of inbuilt communications channel redundancy. It also appears that the Soviets may have given the Iraqis information about the timetable of US satellites passing overhead. British and American Sigint experts then became involved in complex discussion about how much of the Iraqi signals infrastructure should be left intact to permit continued monitoring, perhaps with the intention of locating Saddam Hussein, and also taking into account the additional factor of integrating deception operations which were distributing false orders to Iraqi battalions. The Iraqis were also adept in the field of sophisticated electronic deception, including maintaining silence on key military channels prior to an attack. British forces conducted a successful operational deception of their own, superintended by a unit codenamed 'Rhino Force'. British transmissions from the First Armoured Division were recorded during the weeks of desert exercise before the final invasion. When the final attack was launched and the First Armoured Division moved west to join the US Seventh Army Corps, the messages were replayed in a manner that suggested the Division was moving east. Sigint showed that the Iraqis had bought this deception in its entirety.

The war in Yugoslavia, which followed hard on the heels of the Gulf War, raised very different kinds of questions for GCHQ. In a war which has seen the first head of state arraigned before an international war crimes tribunal, the intelligence services have taken a lead in preparing evidence for these unprecedented proceedings. In the mid-1990s, considerable debate ensued in Whitehall and Westminster as to the extent to which the capabilities of GCHQ should be revealed in the course of bringing war criminals to justice. To present the most compelling types of evidence would also be to reveal the minutiae of what British monitoring could achieve. In the event, a high-level decision was taken to allow some material to be presented before The Hague.

During the 1980s and 1990s, the Sigint agencies of most developed states had a tough time. They were confronted by the increasing use of fibre-optic cables, which provided greater security for communications by states. They also had to address the important issue of public key cryptography by non-state actors and individuals. This is the system that allows most computers to send secure messages to each other without first exchanging ciphers, the basis of today's commercially available cryptography packages and also an essential part of the security in systems for controlling nuclear weapons. The widespread use of increasingly powerful desk-top computers, combined with the availability of 128-bit encryption packages, has increasingly rendered the exponentially growing e-mail traffic impenetrable to the major Sigint agencies. During 1997, GCHQ put forward a complex solution to the problem of public key encryption involving escrow, but this collapsed after protests by private individuals and major corporations alike. In September 1999, the British Government announced that GCHQ would be a partner in a new project designed to address the increasing sophistication of e-mail encryption by criminal users including drug-runners.

There is no doubt that Downing Street is taking the threat of international organized crime very seriously. In early December 1999, Francis Richards, the current director of GCHQ, joined the heads of MI6 and MI5 in an extended meeting at Number 10 on the 'crime emergency' facing Britain and how to tackle what Whitehall increasingly refers to as the 'Red Mafia'. GCHQ will work closely with MI5 and the National Criminal Intelligence Service in a new unit, initially designated the Government Telecommunications Advisory Centre, intended to deal with the growing use of e-mail by organized crime. In July 2000 this was reinforced by the passing of the Regulation of Investigatory Powers Act. This involves GCHQ more closely in the complex and controversial territory of domestic monitoring, which is increasingly inseparable from international communications. It also blurs domains hitherto occupied primarily by the police, the post office and customs and excise.

It now appears that the concept of Public Key Cryptography, perhaps the most important development in secure communications for several centuries, was invented by James Ellis at GCHQ in the 1970s. Some would rank Ellis's discovery alongside the contribution that Alan Turing made to the development of computing. But Ellis's achievement was ahead of its time and so neither GCHQ nor the NSA could initially find any workable method of implementing the idea until a young GCHQ mathematician, Clifford Cocks, made the necessary breakthrough, which was confirmed by Malcolm Williamson, a friend who joined GCHQ later. Shaun Wylie, one of GCHQ's top cryptologists, raised the issue during a visit to Washington, but it did not seem practicable to anyone at the time. Later, Dr Whitfield Diffie discovered public key cryptography independently at a time when the development of desk-top computers rendered it a breakthrough development. Inevitably, some have wondered aloud whether the NSA and GCHQ simply wished to delay the advent of Public Key Cryptography for as long as possible. The advent of Public Key Cryptography and powerful personal computers is now reflected in the fact that one of the most significant developments at Cheltenham in recent years has not been material but organizational. The advent of 'e-commerce' and talk of a knowledge-based economy has heightened the importance of communications security, not only for Government departments but also for major industries and financial institutions in Britain. This has led to the expansion of GCHQ's sister organization, the high-profile Communications Electronics Security Group.

The future shape of GCHQ is round – or to be more precise – bagel-shaped. By 2003 all of GCHQ's activities will be located on the original Benhall site, mostly within a vast new circular building with an open centre. This will provide a state-of-the-art environment for the 4,500 staff of GCHQ, brought together on one site for the first time for many decades. This is the largest government private finance initiative and as a result GCHQ will not own, but instead will lease, its new quarters, the construction of which is costed at £330 million. Capital and running costs over thirty years are estimated at £800 million. This structure will be immense when completed and constitutes not only the largest building project ever initiated by the British Government but also the largest construction currently in progress in Europe. An underground road will be used to service the main building and computer halls and also to allow for the secure movement of documents. Above ground, an inner corridor will lead off the main entrance which will be surfaced with sixteen miles of carpet. When completed it will provide more than a million square feet of office space. Francis Richards described this arrangement as offering 'maximum efficiency, better working conditions and excellent value for money'. However, given that the new MI6 and MI5 headquarters each cost more than three times their original estimated price, the projected figures might be looked on with some scepticism.

The vast space-age GCHQ building at Cheltenham and the expansion of the NSA presence at sites such as Menwith Hill and Digby is not best calculated to reassure all of Britain's European allies. Menwith Hill has been at the centre of charges by the

European Parliament about Anglo-American economic espionage in Europe. The French-led complaints about the UKUSA alliance's so-called Echelon electronic surveillance operations culminated in a front-page article in *Le Monde*. This featured a cartoon of Britain as a mad cow, electronically eavesdropping from inside the European Union on behalf of her Anglo-Saxon intelligence allies. It is hard to resist the observation that French accusations mingle some naivety with a certain hypocrisy. Most states have openly asserted the importance of intelligence-gathering for the purpose of securing their economic well-being over a period of several decades and so these 'revelations' should come as no surprise. Moreover, the French have been as active as anyone else in this important field. France deploys its own GCHQ-type organization that is no less sophisticated than that to be found in Britain – it is located at Domme in the Dordogne Valley. Ironically, some of its more modern equipment has been supplied by the United States. The future appears to be one in which there will be more communications and more complex alliances, which in turn will mean more rather than less work for the new GCHQ.

22

Bletchley Park in Post-War Perspective

CHRISTOPHER ANDREW

As several chapters in this volume have demonstrated, Ultra was an Allied rather than a purely British triumph. Bletchley Park was the centre of a great Imperial and Commonwealth Sigint network which spanned the globe. The British–American Sigint alliance forged during the war has remained ever since the most special and the most secret part of the 'special relationship'. Remarkably, Bletchley Park collaborated more closely with the US military and naval Sigint agencies than those agencies collaborated with each other. At the end of the war, Telford Taylor, the head of the Special Branch (US military Sigint) mission at Bletchley Park, expressed 'pride at the ease, goodwill and success' with which his mission had worked with the British, but reported that the problems of US inter-service Sigint rivalry 'have not been solved by this war'. They were to recur in an acute form at the beginning of the Korean War and were not adequately resolved until the foundation of the National Security Agency (NSA) in November 1952 established roughly the same level of co-ordination achieved by the (admittedly much smaller) British GC&CS a generation earlier and continued after the war by GCHQ.

The first step in the transformation of wartime Sigint collaboration into a peacetime alliance was a tour of imperial, Commonwealth and US Sigint stations in the spring of 1945 by Sir Edward Travis, head of Bletchley Park, his assistant Harry Hinsley (the main British negotiator of the wartime British–American Sigint agreements), Rear-Admiral Edmund Rushbrooke, the Director of Naval Intelligence, and Commander Clive Loehnis (a future Director of GCHQ) of the Admiralty Operational Intelligence Centre. Travis, Hinsley and Loehnis visited Washington towards the end of their tour to put proposals for a peacetime Sigint alliance to representatives of the War, Navy and State Departments. Though ignorant of intelligence and deeply suspicious of peacetime espionage, Harry S. Truman, who became President on Roosevelt's death, shortly before the British delegation reached Washington, was impressed by the insights given him by Sigint into the final months of the war against Japan. On 12 September 1945 he signed a top-secret one-sentence memorandum, providing for the peacetime continuation of the wartime Sigint alliance:

> The Secretary of War and the Secretary of the Navy are hereby authorized to direct the Chief of Staff, U.S. Army and the Commander in Chief, U.S. Fleet, and Chief of Naval Operations to continue collaboration in the field of communication intelligence between the United States Army and Navy and the British, and to extend, modify or discontinue this collaboration, as determined to be in the best interests of the United States.

The details of the postwar Sigint alliance were embodied in still-classified British–American agreements of March 1946 and June 1948 (the latter known as the UKUSA agreement), also involving Australia, Canada and New Zealand, which divided the world up into spheres of Sigint influence assigned to each of the five powers, and provided for extensive sharing of the intelligence obtained. British personnel continued for some years to play leading roles in the main Commonwealth Sigint agencies. The balance of power in the transatlantic Sigint alliance, however, which during the war had centred on Bletchley Park, passed decisively from Britain to the United States. A global Sigint network based on huge banks of advanced computers (which included both the first IBM mainframes and, later, the first Cray supercomputers), intercept stations around the world and Sigint personnel running eventually into six figures was simply too expensive for postwar Britain to afford, save as a junior partner.

Though Truman's interest in Sigint faded rapidly after the end of the war in the Pacific, Ultra had turned his successor, General Dwight D. Eisenhower, into a lifelong enthusiast. Soon after his arrival in Britain as commander of American military forces in June 1942, Ike had been briefed personally on Ultra by Churchill during a visit to Chequers. So committed was Eisenhower to the intelligence alliance with Britain that he insisted on having a British rather than American officer as his G-2 (intelligence chief), who oversaw his supply of Ultra. When he became Supreme Commander of Allied Forces in Europe at the end of 1943, the War Office attempted to remove his G-2, Brigadier (later General Sir) Kenneth Strong. Eisenhower appealed direct to Churchill and Strong was allowed to stay. 'The best time in a man's life', enthused Strong later, 'is when he gets to like Americans.' At the end of the war Eisenhower declared that Ultra had been 'of priceless value' to him and sent his 'heartfelt admiration and sincere thanks' to British cryptanalysts at Bletchley Park 'for their very decisive contribution to the Allied war effort'. Eisenhower's enthusiasm for Bletchley Park helps to explain his committed support as President for the NSA. Founded on the day of his election victory, the NSA received unprecedented resources during his two terms in the White House.

Although the total volume of Sigint available to the

superpowers during the Cold War was much greater than during the Second World War, Soviet high-grade cipher systems – based on the theoretically unbreakable one-time pad – were far less vulnerable than those of Nazi Germany and Imperial Japan. In the immediate aftermath of the Second World War, the failure to produce a Soviet Ultra led to what a later top-secret US official inquiry described as 'a sense of frustration and anti-climax'. Both American and British cryptanalysts, however, had some successes against Soviet traffic. Though most of these are still classified, one of them, the Venona operation, was declassified in the mid-1990s. Venona was the final codename given to approximately 3,000 Soviet intelligence and other classified telegrams intercepted during the period 1940 to 1948, which – as the result of errors in Soviet cipher production – used the same one-time pads more than once and thus became vulnerable to cryptanalytic attack. Most were decrypted, in whole or in part, by American code-breakers with some assistance from the British in the late 1940s and early 1950s.

Though the decrypts provided important information on Soviet espionage in regions of the world as far apart as Scandinavia and Australia, the most numerous and important revelations concerned intelligence operations in the United States. Venona revealed that over 200 Americans were working as Soviet agents during, and sometimes after, the Second World War, and that the leadership of the American Communist Party was hand-in-glove with the KGB. Every section of the wartime administration of Franklin D. Roosevelt, from the foreign intelligence agency, the Office of Strategic Services (OSS) to the atomic programme, had been penetrated by Soviet intelligence. Had the terminally ill Roosevelt died in 1944, the penetration would have been worse still. In 1944, Roosevelt would have been succeeded not by Truman but by his then vice-president, Henry Wallace. In preparation for this eventuality Wallace had already selected some of his future administration. The men he had chosen to be his Secretary of State and Secretary of the Treasury, Larry Duggan and Harry Dexter White, were both Soviet agents, codenamed respectively Frank and Jurist. Venona also identified agent Homer as the British diplomat Donald Maclean, one of the 'Magnificent Five' young Cambridge graduates recruited by Soviet intelligence in the mid-1930s. The unmasking of Maclean led eventually to the identification of the other four and to the belated discovery that the 'Fifth Man', John Cairncross, had worked as a Soviet agent inside Bletchley Park at the turning point of the war on the Eastern Front in 1942–3.

The legacy of Ultra influenced the handling of Venona in two ways. First, it was treated with at least the same level of extreme secrecy. Basking in the reflected glory of Ultra, Anglo-American cryptanalysts found it much easier than before the war to persuade those with access to their intelligence to keep secret both their past successes and current operations. Secondly, as with Ultra during the Second World War, collaboration on Venona during the early Cold War worked better within the transatlantic Special Relationship than within the US intelligence community. GCHQ liaison officers at the postwar US military Sigint service, the Army Security Agency (ASA), were informed of the initial Venona breakthrough even before the FBI. By 1948, according to a recent CIA/NSA study, 'there was complete and profitable US–UK cooperation' on the project. As well as collaborating closely with GCHQ, the chief American cryptanalyst working on the Venona project, Meredith Gardner, had regular meetings in the later 1940s with the representatives in Washington of MI6 and MI5, Peter Dwyer and Geoffrey Patterson, both of whom provided information on individuals referred to in the Soviet telegrams to assist the process of decryption. GCHQ also regularly briefed MI6 and MI5 on Venona.

But while ASA, and later the Armed Forces Security Agency (AFSA), kept the British intelligence agencies informed of progress on Venona, they concealed the entire project from the

Central Intelligence Agency (CIA), founded in 1947. Ironically, therefore, as MI6 liaison officer in Washington, Peter Dwyer had to be careful not to mention the decrypts in his meetings with CIA officers. The initial decision to keep the CIA in the dark seems to have been taken by the ASA at the urging of J. Edgar Hoover, the autocratic, long-serving director of the Federal Bureau of Investigation (FBI), which was responsible for internal security. Hoover regarded the CIA as a dangerous upstart, which prevented him achieving his ambition of extending Bureau operations into the field of foreign intelligence, and also wrongly suspected it of being, like its wartime predecessor the OSS, penetrated by Soviet intelligence. General Omar Nelson Bradley, who became Chairman of the Joint Chiefs of Staff in 1949, probably at Hoover's prompting, also opposed sharing Venona with the CIA. Bradley regarded the new Agency as insecure and as an unwelcome threat to the service intelligence agencies; he also resented the fact that, unlike the OSS, it was not placed under the authority of the Joint Chiefs. Most remarkably of all, Truman also appears not to have been informed of Venona – probably for fear that he would mention it to the Director of Central Intelligence (DCI, head of the CIA) at his weekly meetings with him. As a result the President remained confused about the nature and reality of Soviet intelligence penetration of the United States. Significantly, in over 1,200 pages of presidential memoirs, Truman never mentioned the Rosenbergs, Alger Hiss or anyone else publicly accused of being a Soviet agent during his presidency. The CIA was not briefed on Venona until Eisenhower (who had probably been briefed at the outset) was elected to succeed Truman in November 1952.

Even though the relevant British files have yet to be declassified, there is no reason to doubt that the British Prime Minister, Clement Attlee, and at least a few of his senior ministers were briefed on Venona. One remarkable consequence of the British–American Sigint alliance forged during the Second World

War was that until November 1952 the British Government and intelligence community were better informed on both the achievements of American cryptanalysts and Soviet espionage in the United States than the President and the DCI. So was Joseph Stalin. In 1950, the AFSA was shocked to discover that one of its employees, William Weisband, had been a Soviet agent ever since he joined the wartime army Sigint agency in 1942. Thus it was that the Venona secret was communicated to Moscow almost six years before it reached either the President or the CIA. Although Weisband was arrested in 1950, Philby, who succeeded Dwyer as MI6 liaison officer in Washington in 1949 and was fully briefed on Venona, continued to inform Moscow until his recall in 1951.

The attempt to keep the Ultra secret continued for over a quarter of a century after the Second World War. The British Chiefs of Staff agreed on 31 July 1945 that 'It is imperative that the fact that such intelligence was available should NEVER be disclosed.' This demand for perpetual secrecy was based chiefly on the conviction that revelation of the past Sigint successes would alert foreign powers to the possibility that their current ciphers were being broken by GCHQ and cause them to introduce cipher systems which would be difficult, if not impossible, to crack. GCHQ adduced one further, shorter-term reason for keeping the Ultra secret. If the Germans knew that their codes had been broken and that this had hastened their defeat, they might come to believe, as after the First World War, that they had not been 'well and fairly defeated' and succumb once again to a variety of the 'stab in the back' myth which had been exploited by Adolf Hitler.

GCHQ feared from the outset, however, that it might prove impossible to preserve the Ultra secret: '[T]he comparing of the German and British documents is bound to arouse suspicion in [historians'] minds that we succeeded in reading the enemy ciphers.' It now seems astonishing that for over a quarter of a century the great majority of historians suspected no such thing.

With the gift of hindsight, some of the clues now seem remarkably obvious. The fact that American cryptanalysts had broken the main Japanese diplomatic cipher in 1940 was extensively publicized during the Congressional inquiry into Pearl Harbor at the end of the war. It was also common knowledge that British cryptanalysts had broken German codes during the First World War; indeed, one well-publicized German decrypt – the Zimmermann telegram – had hastened American entry into the war. But, until the revelation of Ultra in 1973, almost no historian even discussed the possibility that German ciphers had been extensively broken during the Second World War as well as the First. The minority of academic historians who had served at Bletchley Park, or had been 'indoctrinated' into Ultra while writing official histories, were thus in the remarkable position of knowing that colleagues in their university departments who wrote about the Second World War had misunderstood an important aspect of the war, and of being forbidden by the Official Secrets Act to discuss this with them.

To a remarkable degree, the lack of interest in Sigint by historians and specialists in international relations has survived even the revelation of the Ultra secret. Although no historian of the Second World War nowadays fails to make some mention of Ultra, few stop to consider the influence of Sigint on the rest of the twentieth century. Even after the disclosure of Ultra's role in British and American wartime operations, it took another fifteen years before any historian raised the rather obvious question of whether there was a Russian Ultra on the Eastern Front as well. The great majority of histories of the Cold War do not refer to Sigint at all. Although most studies of US Cold War foreign policy mention the CIA, there is rarely any reference to the NSA – despite the public acknowledgement by George Bush (the first) that Sigint was a 'prime factor' in his foreign policy. The small circle of those in the know in Washington used to joke that NSA stood for 'No Such Agency'. The NSA, however, has a bigger budget than the CIA, employs far more people, and generates far more intelligence.

The abrupt disappearance of Sigint from the historical landscape immediately after VJ Day has produced a series of curious anomalies, even in some of the leading studies of policy-makers and postwar international relations. Thus, for example, Sir Martin Gilbert's magisterial multi-volume official biography of Churchill acknowledges his passion for Sigint as war leader but fails to discuss his continuing interest in it as peacetime Prime Minister from 1951 to 1955. Similarly, although Eisenhower's wartime enthusiasm for Ultra is well known, none of his biographers, so far as I am aware, mentions the enormous resources he devoted to Sigint as President of the United States from 1953 to 1961. There is even less about Sigint in biographies of Stalin. Indeed, it is difficult to think of any history of the Soviet Union which devotes as much as a sentence to the enormous volume of Sigint generated by the KGB and GRU. The US embassy in Moscow, however, appears to have been successfully bugged during the Second World War and for almost twenty years afterwards, and for a significant part of the Cold War, thanks to the achievements of Soviet cryptanalysts, France, Italy and some other NATO countries seem, without realizing it, to have been conducting open diplomacy in their dealings with the Soviet Union.

Although the neglect of Sigint by many leading historians is due partly to the overclassification of intelligence archives, it derives at root from what educational psychologists call 'cognitive dissonance' – the difficulty all of us have in grasping new concepts which disturb our existing view of the world. For many twentieth-century historians, political scientists and international relations specialists, secret intelligence was just such a concept. At the beginning of the twenty-first century, however, the traditional academic disregard for intelligence is in serious, if not yet terminal, decline. A new generation of scholars has begun to emerge, less disoriented than their predecessors by the role of intelligence and its use (or abuse) by policy-makers. A vast research agenda awaits them.

In the meantime, the story of Bletchley Park and what has begun to emerge about the history of cryptanalysis in the remainder of the twentieth century confronts all historians of the Cold War and international relations specialists with a major challenge, which most have avoided so far: either to seek to take account of the role of Sigint since the Second World War or to explain why they do not consider it necessary to do so.

Appendix I

<u>The very simple cipher which 'Snow', the first Double Cross agent, was given by his German controllers</u>

The code is based on the word CONGRATULATIONS, and the grid is set out as follows:

C	O	N	G	R	A	T	U	L	A	T	I	O	N	S
3	9	7	4	11	1	13	15	6	2	14	5	10	8	12
				░						░				
		░								░				
				░										░
										░				
							░							
					░									
									░					
							░							
				░										
░										░				
				░								░		
				░						░				

KEY ░ blank space

1st blank = 5
2nd blank = 5 + 6 = 11
3rd blank = 11 + 7 = 18
4th blank = 18 + 8 = 26
5th blank = 26 + 9 = 35
6th blank = 35 + 10 = 45
7th blank = 45 + 11 = 56
8th blank = 56 + 12 = 68
9th blank = 68 + 13 = 81

The grid is 15 squares long (to fit the 15 letters of CONGRATULATIONS) and 12 squares deep, this last figure being chosen for convenience.

The blank spaces are decided as follows:

The first blank space is placed, quite arbitrarily, at the 5th space, reading from left to right and starting at the left-hand top corner.

The next is 6 spaces after, i.e. at the 11th space, the next is 7 spaces after that, i.e. at the 18th space, and so on in arithmetical progression until the 9th blank, placed at the 81st space, is reached. It will be found that this is in the 6th row of the grid, i.e. halfway down.

The grid is now turned upside down and the same procedure followed as above, so that the blanks are symmetrical.

The message to be coded is now written in the grid, ignoring the blanks, that is to say, no letter must be written in a blank space. The blanks are then filled in with any letter which can be chosen quite arbitrarily.

At the top of the grid, the word CONGRATULATIONS is filled in, and underneath this each letter is numbered in order of the alphabet. Thus, A is 1, the second A is 2, C is 3, G is 4, and so on, until each column of the grid is numbered.

The procedure for sending out the message is as follows:

A line should be drawn at the end of the message when written out in the grid to separate it from the unused portion of the grid.

Each column (downwards) of letters is then written out, the order depending on the date on which the message is being sent. Thus if the date is the 8th of the month, the column headed 8 is written out, followed by the column headed 9, then 10 and so on until the string of letters is ended with the column headed 7. Should the date be more than 15, e.g. the 20th of the month, subtract 15 from the date and start on the difference, i.e. 5. This long string of letters is then counted off into blocks of 5 letters each, and in this form the message is transmitted.

Before the actual message is sent, the time, date and number of letters in the message is given. These are coded as follows:

The word CONGRATULATIONS is written out and those letters which recur, i.e. A, T, O and N are struck out, and the remaining letters numbered thus:

C	O	N	G	R	A	T	U	L	~~A~~	~~T~~	I	~~O~~	~~N~~	S
1	2	3	4	5	6	7	8	9			0			0

I and S are numbered 0 (nought) and can be used indiscriminately to represent this number.

The time of transmitting is then coded on this scale. E.g. if the time is 10.30 p.m., i.e. 2230 hours, this would be coded as OONI (or OONS); or 1245 hours would be coded as COGR.

The date on which the transmission is taking place is similarly coded, the day and month only being sent.

The total number of letters (i.e. including the 'bogus' letters used to fill in the blanks) is then sent using the same code.

N.B. If the message being transmitted is in answer to a message just received, and the time and date are therefore very much the same, it is possible that they may be omitted.

(Reproduced with thanks to the Public Record Office. PRO KV 2/453)

Appendix II

Wehrmacht Enigma Indicating Systems, except the *Kriegsmarine's Kenngruppenbuch* System

RALPH ERSKINE

Heer and *Luftwaffe* indicating system from 1 May 1940 onwards (except on Yellow): singly enciphered message keys.

To encipher a message, the operator first set up his machine according to the daily key (rotor order, *Stecker* and ring settings). He then –
a) chose a random group of three letters for the *Grundstellung* (the setting of the rotors when starting to encipher or decipher the message key) (e.g. WEP), wrote it down, and set his rotors to those positions;
b) chose three letters (e.g. RNL) as a message key, and typed them once only (RNL), producing perhaps HFI, which he again wrote down;
c) turned the rotors to RNL, and entered the plain-text of the message, writing down each letter as it lit up on the lampboard (generally a two-man operation, with one man writing as the other typed the text).

*

The transmitted message included –
d) the sender's and receiver's call signs;
e) a five-letter group consisting of two null letters (which were dropped later), followed by a three-letter discriminant, which showed which Enigma cipher was being employed. This allowed the recipient to look up and use the correct key-list (e.g. that for Red);
f) the unenciphered *Grundstellung*, followed by the three letters of the enciphered message key;
g) the enciphered text, in five-letter groups.

A typical *Heer* or *Luftwaffe* Enigma message is shown in Figure AII.1, with its various components marked.
To decipher the text, the receiving operator set up his machine according to the daily key (rotor order, *Stecker* and ring settings). He then –
h) set his rotors to the *Grundstellung* (WEP);
i) typed HFI – which lit up the lamps for RNL;
j) turned his rotors to RNL, and entered the cipher text, writing down the resulting letters as they lit up (again, often a two-man operation).

Heer and *Luftwaffe* indicating system from 15 September 1938 to 30 April 1940: doubly enciphered message keys.

The system was the same as that above, except that the operator typed the message key twice (say RNLRNL), producing perhaps HFIKLB. The group following the *Grundstellung* therefore consisted of six letters.

Figure AII.1 ***Heer* or *Luftwaffe* signal, as intercepted in September 1942**

The following is a typical *Heer* or *Luftwaffe* Enigma signal, as intercepted by a US Army station in September 1942:

9UL[1] DE[2] C[3] 6350 KCS[4] S 2/3[5] R 2/3[6] US 20[7] KA[8] 2005[9] BT[10] KR[11]

BT[10] 2TLE[12] BT[10] 1 TLE[13] 249[14] BT[10] YHX[15] LVI[16] WHX[17] BT[10] MBXSS . . . EYEMW[18] AR[19]

13SE[20] 2023Z[21] HH[22]

1. Station being called
2. From
3. Station calling (C = control)
4. Frequency
5. Signal strength (between 2 & 3)
6. Readability (between 2 & 3)
7. Intercept station no.
8. Beginning of preamble
9. German time of origin
10. Separator
11. Urgency signal (not always present)
12. Total number of parts in the signal
13. No. of this part (*Teile*) of the signal
14. No. of letters in this part
15. Cipher discriminant
16. *Grundstellung*
17. Enciphered message key
18. Cipher text
19. Message *Teil* complete
20. Date of intercept – 13 September 1942
21. Time of intercept
22. Operator's identification

Heer and Luftwaffe indicating system before 15 September 1938.

This system was the same as that in force from 15 September 1938 to 30 April 1940, except that the *Grundstellung* was set out in a key-list as part of the daily key, and not chosen by the operator.

'Throw-on' ('boxing') naval Enigma indicator system used before 1 May 1937, and for six wartime ciphers.

The naval indicating system employed before 1 May 1937 (called a 'throw-on' system by GC&CS) was the same as the *Heer* and *Luftwaffe* indicating system before 15 September 1938, with the *Grundstellung* being set out in a key-list, as part of the daily key. The message key may have been chosen from a list of 1,700 trigrams, and not left to the operator's discretion, but that is not clear. No *Kenngruppenbuch* or bigram tables were used. It is not known whether a cipher discriminant was incorporated then: only one cipher may have been in operation. The combination of doubly enciphered message keys and a single daily *Grundstellung* made it an appallingly weak system (see Chapter 10). The *Kriegsmarine* changed to the much more secure *Kenngruppenbuch* system (see Appendix III) on 1 May 1937.

However, in a series of catastrophic blunders, the *Kriegsmarine* employed the pre-1 May 1937 system for six naval wartime ciphers: Porpoise, Seahorse, Sunfish, Trumpeter, Bonito and Grampus, enabling Hut 8 and OP-20-G to penetrate them. Operators were permitted to choose their own message keys for these ciphers, subject to some very simple rules (e.g. words, and alphabetical sequences, such as HIJ, were banned): there was no list to choose from. This greatly assisted Hut 8 in breaking what was already a very weak system, which the *Heer* and *Luftwaffe* had discarded on the grounds of its insecurity in September 1938 (dropping of the daily *Grund*) and 1 May 1940 (abandonment of doubly enciphered message keys).

Appendix III

The Naval Enigma *Kenngruppenbuch* Indicator System – used with the main wartime ciphers

RALPH ERSKINE

At the start of each cipher day (often 1200 hrs), a naval Enigma operator had to set up his machine. If it was the first day of a pair in a key-list, an officer had first to insert the rotors in the order set out in the key-list, after setting the rotor rings to the letters indicated in the list. The operator then set the external connections (*Stecker*) on his machine in accordance with the key-list.

When enciphering a signal, an operator had to let the recipient know what the message key (the rotor positions when starting to encipher a specific signal) was, without revealing its clear text to the enemy. The principal naval Enigma ciphers, such as Dolphin and Shark, therefore disguised the message key by an indicating procedure known as the *Kenngruppenbuch* (recognition group book) system. Part A of the *Kenngruppenbuch* listed all 17,576 three-letter groups (trigrams – 'BSY' and so on) in random order. Each standard naval Enigma signal had its own message key. There was a separate system for short signals.

To encipher a message with the system, the operator –

a) looked up an allocation list to see which columns in Part A had been assigned to his cipher net (e.g. columns 251–320 or 561–620 for Shark (Triton) in July 1944), selected one of the three-letter groups in one of those columns at random for the *Schlüsselkenngruppe* (cipher indicator group, for example, for Triton), and wrote it in a special cipher form;
b) picked any column at random and chose another trigram (say VFN) as the *Verfahrenkenngruppe* (procedure indicator group, but actually the message key), and wrote it in the form under the first group;
c) inserted a letter as a null (say X), as the first letter in the *Schlüsselkenngruppe*, giving XHYU;
d) added another null letter (say K) as the last letter of the *Verfahrenkenngruppe*, making VFNK. He then had:

X H Y U
1 2 3 4
V F N K

e) encoded the vertical bigrams (XV, HF and so on) with bigram tables (which substituted pairs of letters), with XV and HF here giving BM and OG, for example. Written horizontally, these resulted in:
BMOG as the first indicator group
PYUD as the second indicator group.
He then went to his machine, and
f) turned the rotors to the *Grundstellung*, say GRD, set out in the key-list: each naval key-list contained a series of daily *Grundstellungen*, which were employed for all signals using the cipher in question;
g) obtained the message key by typing the unencoded version of the *Verfahrenkenngruppe* (VFN) once, giving e.g. SPL;
h) set the rotors to SPL as the message key;
i) keyed the plain-text of the signal, writing down each cipher text letter as its lamp lit up (often a two-man operation).

The cipher text was transmitted in four-letter groups, preceded by BMOG PYUD. A typical message is set out in Figure AIII.1. The indicator groups were repeated at the end to reduce deciphering mistakes, making naval Enigma signals instantly recognizable to friend and foe alike.

To decipher a message, the receiving operator went through the above steps in reverse (assuming that his machine was already set to the daily key for the cipher in question), first decoding the indicator groups, using the relevant bigram tables to obtain the enciphered message key, VFN. By typing it, he obtained SPL, to which he set his rotors. He then typed the cipher text, and wrote down the resulting letters as they lit up.

Using the *Kenngruppenbuch* system, Enigma slowed down a cipher system that was far from speedy in the first place. During a monitored discussion with a fellow prisoner, one captured U-boat radio operator was heard to comment: 'To be frank, it takes a considerable time to encipher a WT message – even if you are right up to the mark. When I enciphered a message of 40 groups [160 letters] with the *Funkmaat* [radio petty officer], it

Figure AIII.1 **Typical naval Enigma signal, as intercepted**

MMA'[1] 0141/4/370[2] 22[3]

HNMX[4] UOLP[4] FZNM HSNS CENH VHKQ TDEB XMTR GSRK DJYP XUWQ SWED NTET MWVI AUXP XXDK TYQF QBZO DDND ULDA HNMX[4] UOLP[4]

0812[5] 6790[6]

1. Call sign of shore transmitting station. A' was Ä
2. Time of origin, date and serial number
3. Group count
4. Indicator groups
5. Time of intercept
6. Frequency

used to take five minutes at least – and that was good going.'

The system was a strong one, except for the single daily *Grundstellung*, which made Banburismus possible, when combined with the fact that rotors I to V each had their turnover notches in different places.

Appendix IV

Cillies

RALPH ERSKINE

When cillies were discovered by Dilly Knox in late January 1940, they reduced enormously the work involved in using the Zygalski sheets, which was otherwise a very laborious process indeed, since up to sixty rotor orders might have to be checked. After 1 May, when the Zygalski sheets became useless, following the dropping of doubly enciphered message keys, cillies became a vital part of breaking Enigma by hand during most of 1940, even when the first usable bombe entered service in August. Although more bombes became available in 1941, cillies greatly eased the burden on them, thereby making bombes available for work against ciphers which could not otherwise have been attacked. Cillies were still valuable in 1943, and probably until a German procedural change in mid-1944.

Cillies resulted from a combination of two different mistakes in a multi-part message by some Enigma operators. The first was their practice of leaving the rotors untouched when they reached the end of the first part of a multi-part message, so that the letters then in the rotor windows, for example VEI, formed the basic setting, which was therefore transmitted in unenciphered form as usual, in the second part. Since the letter count of each message part was included in its preamble, the starting letters (the message key) of the preceding part could be calculated within fine limits, after allowing for rotor turnovers. The second error was the inclusion of non-random message keys in the same multi-part message: the use of keyboard sequences such as 'DFG', 'pronounceables', such as 'CIL' itself, and guessable ends of words such as 'LER' (for the unenciphered message key) following 'HIT' (for the *Grund*). The second type of error corroborated the first. It was vital: without it, the cryptanalysts would have been searching for will-o'-the-wisps.

The Hut 6 cryptanalysts used cillies, in conjunction with the different turnover points for rotors I to V, to find which rotors could, and which could not, be in any given slot in the machine, which often reduced the number of rotor orders to be tested to six or under – a very considerable saving. The information derived from cillies about message keys, for example the use of keyboard sequences such as QWE or PAW, also provided the cryptanalysts with up to five three-letter cribs for a five-part message.

Figure AIV.1 **Part of Imaginary Blist**

(The headings in the fourth and fifth columns would read 'Indicator' in a real blist)

Blist no.	Part	No. of letters	[Grund]	[Enciphered message key]	German time of origin	Time of intercept	Call sign
5/1	1	238	GXO	QPG	0300	0305	9QZ v APL
5/2	2	241	BDH	RZL	0300	0315	9QZ v APL
5/3	3	244	FPO	PRB	0300	0300	9QZ v APL
5/4	4	141	QKI	FML	0300	0345	9QZ v APL
5/5	5	95	PGH	MOT	0300	0400	9QZ v APL

Figure AIV.1 sets out part of an imaginary blist for a *Luftwaffe* cipher net. Let's test the first message part for a cilli by subtracting its length, 238 (9 × 26 + 4) from BDH, the basic setting of message part 5/2. The following starting points (message keys) for the message are therefore possible: BUD, BTD, ATD, *ASD*. Similarly, in message 2, counting back 241 (9 × 26 + 7) letters from FPO gives *FGH*, FFH, EFH or EEH, as potential message keys, after allowing for various rotor turnover positions. In message 3, subtracting 244 (9 × 26 + 10) letters from QKI gives QBY, *QAY*, PAY or PZY, while in message 4, we get PBW, *PAW*, OAW or OZW. Since we have four clear keyboard sequences here (italicized – see Figure AIV.2), it is almost certain that we do indeed have a cilli.

In message 5/2, counting back four letters from H (in the fast, right-hand slot) gives D. Counting back nine letters from D in the middle position gives U. However, the right-hand rotor may have passed through a turnover point between D and H – we don't know until we can limit the choice of rotors – which would result in the middle rotor moving ten times, so starting at T. The middle rotor may have advanced the slow rotor once, depending on the position of its turnover, so the slow rotor must have been set at B or A. If it started at A, the middle rotor has made an extra movement, making ten or eleven, and its starting position S or T. Since the *Luftwaffe* Enigma operators often use keyboard sequences, such as 'horizontals' like DFG or UZT (see Figure AIV.2), or 'diagonals' like WAP or RDX, the message key is almost certainly ASD.

Figure AIV.2 ***Wehrmacht* Enigma's keyboard**

QWERTZUIO

ASDFGHJK

PYXCVBNML

Figure AIV.3 **Rotor turnover positions**

Rotor	I	II	III	IV	V
Turnover position	Q/R	E/F	V/W	J/K	Z/A

With message key ASD, and finishing position BDH, the notch on the middle rotor must be between S and D. Only rotors III and V have turnover notches between those letters (see Figure AIV.3). We have found ten of the eleven movements by the middle rotor from S to D. The fast rotor's movements from D to H must have caused the middle rotor to advance, making its total eleven. The fast rotor's notch is therefore between D and H, and it can only be II. The possible rotor orders to test when finding the *Stecker* are (5–2), III/V, II: six permutations instead of sixty, a very considerable reduction indeed. We can also use the message keys in the remaining parts of the message to obtain short cribs. In message 5/2, we have FGH, a horizontal keyboard sequence, in message 5/3, QAY, a diagonal, and in 5/4, PAW, another diagonal. The cilli has therefore also provided us with four three-letter cribs: ASD, FGH, QAY and PAW plain-text, giving QPG, RZL, PRB and FML as cipher text. We are well on the way to a solution by hand so long as the *Ringstellungen* have been found by a Herivel tip. And if bombes are available, the reduction in the number of rotor orders will save a great deal of scarce bombe time, just as in Banburismus.

Cillies seem very obvious once they are pointed out, but the German authorities cannot have realized for many years that they were providing so much useful information, including cribs, in messages. However, in August 1944, the *Heer* introduced a procedure requiring operators to generate and use fully random lists of message keys. From 15 September 1944, the same order required operators sending long messages to advance the slow rotor by at least five places between the 70th and 130th letters, and to indicate the change by the letters 'CY'. The two procedures prevented Hut 6 from tracing cillies, but they had been introduced much too late in the day. Had the *Luftwaffe*, in particular, used them from 1940 onwards, the story of Hut 6 would have been very different indeed.

Notes and References

1 Bletchley Park in Pre-War Perspective

Page 2 Hinsley's 1979 lecture: information provided by the late Sir Harry Hinsley to Christopher Andrew.

Page 2 Turing on the Abdication: Turing to his mother, 11 December 1936 (King's College Archives, Cambridge, AMT K/1/50); Andrew Hodge, *Alan Turing: The Enigma* (Burnett Books, London, 1983), pp. 121–2.

Pages 3–4 British breaches of Sigint security in the 1920s: Christopher Andrew, *Secret Service: The Making of the British Intelligence Community*, 3rd edition (Sceptre, London, 1992), chaps 9, 10.

Page 5 Sinclair's instructions to Denniston: A. G. Denniston, 'The Government Code and Cypher School between the Wars', in Christopher Andrew (ed.), *Codebreaking and Signals Intelligence* (Frank Cass, London, 1986), p. 52.

Pages 5–6 Recruitment of 'professor types': Andrew, *Secret Service*, chap. 14.

Page 6 Turing to his mother: letter, 14 October [1936] (King's College Archives, Cambridge, AMT K/1/43).

Page 6 Turing and codebreaking: Hodge, *Alan Turing: The Enigma*.

Page 7 *Alice in ID25*: Frank Birch, *Alice in ID25*, privately printed, copy in A. G. Denniston papers (CCAC).

Page 7 Breaking down Knox's bathroom door: unpublished memoirs by Professor E. R. Vincent (Cambridge Professor of Italian and Bletchley Park veteran), p. 107 (Corpus Christi College Archives, Cambridge).

Page 7 'Hockey or Watching the Daisies Grow': drawing at the end of the third volume of Turing's correspondence with his mother (King's College Archives, Cambridge).

Page 7 Turing's silver ingots: Hodge, *Alan Turing*, pp. 344–5.

Page 8 Hinsley's recruitment: Christopher Andrew, 'F. H. Hinsley and the Cambridge Moles: Two Patterns of Intelligence Recruitment', in R. T. B. Langhorne (ed.), *Diplomacy and Intelligence in the Second World War: Essays in Honour of F. H. Hinsley* (CUP, Cambridge, 1985).

Page 8 later co-edited: F. H. Hinsley and Alan Stripp (eds), *Codebreakers* (OUP, Oxford, 1993).

Page 8 Ewing and recruitment to Room 40: Andrew, *Secret Service*, chap. 3.

Page 9 Twinn's recruitment: letter from Peter Twinn to Christopher Andrew, 29 May 1981.

Pages 9–10 Recruitment of mathematicians and chess players to Bletchley Park: Andrew, *Secret Service*, chap. 3; David Kahn, *Seizing the Enigma* (Souvenir Press, London, 1992), pp. 92 ff.

Page 10 Origins and early history of GC&CS: Denniston, 'The Code and Cypher School'.

Pages 10–11 US Sigint in the decade before Pearl Harbor: Christopher Andrew, *For the President's Eyes Only: Secret Intelligence and the American Presidency from Washington to Bush* (HarperCollins, London/New York, 1995), chap. 3.

Pages 12–13 Roosevelt and Magic: Andrew, *For the President's Eyes Only*, chap. 3; David Kahn, 'Roosevelt, MAGIC and ULTRA', *Cryptologia*, 16 (1992), 289.

Pages 12–13 Churchill and Sigint: Andrew, *Secret Service*, chaps 3, 9, 10, 14; Christopher Andrew, 'Churchill and Intelligence', in Michael Handel (ed.), *Leaders and Intelligence* (Frank Cass, London, 1988); David Stafford, *Churchill and Secret Service* (John Murray, London, 1997).

Page 13 Kennedy diary: John Ferris (ed.), 'From Broadway House to Bletchley Park: The Diary of Captain Malcolm D. Kennedy, 1934–1946', *Intelligence and National Security*, 4(3) (1989), 421.

Pages 13–14 JN-25B: Frederick D. Parker, 'The Unsolved Messages of Pearl Harbor', *Cryptologia*, 15 (1991), 295.

Page 14 'ACTION THIS DAY': Sir Stuart Milner-Barry, '"Action This Day": The Letter from Bletchley Park Cryptanalysts to the Prime Minister, 21 October 1941', *Intelligence and National Security*, 1(2) (1986), 272.

2 The Government Code and Cypher School and the First Cold War

Page 16 Army resentment, lack of co-operation and 1917 exchange of results: 'Record of Conference held at the Admiralty on 5 August 1919 on amalgamation of MI1b and NID25' (PRO HW 3/35); Christopher Andrew, *Secret Service: The Making of the British Intelligence Community* (Sceptre, London, 1986), p. 142; and 'Notes of Formation of GC&CS' (PRO HW 3/33), 1.

Page 16 Admiralty conference: 'Record of Conference held at the Admiralty on 5 August 1919 on amalgamation of MI1b and NID25' (PRO HW 3/35).

Page 16 Creation and roles of GC&CS: 'Notes of Formation of GC&CS', 1; A. G. Denniston, 'History of GC&CS' (PRO HW 3/32), 1.

Page 17 Main GC&CS targets and 'only real operational intelligence': ibid., C: Development 1919–1939, 3.

Page 17 'devotee of his art': translation of German newspaper article by former Russian codebreaker (PRO HW 3/12).

Page 18 Role in capture of the *Magdeburg* codebook: Andrew, *Secret Service*, pp. 143, 376.

Page 18 Details of Fetterlein's flight from Russia: P. William Filby, 'Bletchley Park and Berkeley Street', *Intelligence and National Security*, 3(2) (1988), 272.

Page 18 Fetterlein's wartime work: 'Work Done by Staff of ID25 During the War'. Summary. 15/5/1919 (PRO HW 3/35).

Page 18 Fetterlein's working practice: Filby, 'Bletchley Park and Berkeley Street'.

Page 18 British early success: Denniston, 'History of GC&CS', C: Development 1919–1939, 3.

Page 19 Contents of Russian BJs: John Johnson, *The Evolution of British Sigint 1653–1939* (HMSO, Cheltenham, 1997), p. 48; [John Curry], *The Security Service 1908–1945: The Official History* (PRO, London, 1999), p. 93.

Page 19 Wilson and Sinclair demand action: Andrew, *Secret Service*, pp. 383–6.

Page 19 Kamenev declared persona non grata: Johnson, *Evolution*, p. 48.

Page 20 Further press leaks and Krasin to Litvinov: ibid.

Page 20 Frunze complaint and change of ciphers: Christopher Andrew and Oleg Gordievsky, *KGB: The Inside Story* (Hodder & Stoughton, London, 1990), p. 55.

Page 20 Fetterlein success with new ciphers: Johnson, *Evolution*, pp. 48–9.

Page 20 Sources of telegrams: Denniston, 'History of GC&CS', pp. 10–15; 'History of Military Sigint', chap. 1 (PRO HW 3/90), 15–17; 'Historical Notes on Formation of GC&CS' (PRO HW 3/33), 1–3.

Page 21 Curzon embarrassment: W. F. Clarke, 'Naval Section of GC&CS' (PRO HW 3/1), 12.

Page 21 Sinclair appointment and move to Queen's Gate: 'Historical Notes on Formation of GC&CS', 1–3.

Page 21 Curzon ultimatum: Andrew, *Secret Service*, pp. 417–19.

Page 21 Russian messages deciphered in India: Johnson, *Evolution*, p. 53.

Page 21 Tiltman career: ibid.; 'History of Military Sigint', chap. 1, 9–21; Ralph Erskine, 'Brigadier John H. Tiltman: One of Britain's Finest' (unpublished paper).

Page 21 Tiltman recollections of work in India: Tiltman, 'Some Reminiscences' (NACP HCC Nr. 4632).

Page 22 Details of Sigint operations in India: 'History of Military Sigint', chap. 1 (PRO HW 3/90), 9–21, 12–24; Johnson, *Evolution*, p. 53; GC&CS (Naval Section) 1919–1941' (PRO HW 3/1), 5.

Page 23 Change of Soviet ciphers: John Ferris, 'Whitehall's Black Chamber: British Cryptology and the Government Code and Cypher School', *Intelligence and National Security*, 2(1) (1987), 73–5.

Page 23 Cooper recruitment: J. E. S. Cooper, 'Personal Notes on GC&CS 1925–39' (PRO HW 3/83), 1.

Page 24 New sources of Soviet traffic: ibid.

Page 24 Move to Broadway: Denniston, 'History of GC&CS', 1.

Page 24 Co-opting of Metropolitan Police unit: H. C. Kenworthy, 'A Brief History of Events Relating to the Growth of the "Y" Service' (PRO HW 3/81), 1; C. L. Sinclair Williams, 'H. C. Kenworthy' (unpublished). The latter document makes clear that the unit remained in the attic at Scotland Yard until the mid-thirties. Denniston appears to suggest that the police unit was co-opted almost immediately following the SIS takeover of GC&CS (Denniston, 'History of GC&CS', 16). But Kenworthy specifically dates the first contact to the 1926 General Strike.

Page 24 £2 million Soviet subsidies to miners: *The Security Service 1908–1945*, p. 93.

Page 25 *Daily Mail* transmitter: Kenworthy, 'A Brief History of Events Relating to the Growth of the "Y" Service', chap. 1, 1–2.

Page 25 ARCOS as base for espionage against Britain: *The Security Service 1908–1945*, pp. 96–8; Nigel West and Oleg Tsarev, *The Crown Jewels: The British Secrets at the Heart of the KGB Archives* (HarperCollins, London, 1998), pp. 29–32; Andrew, *Secret Service*, pp. 463–71.

Page 25 Chamberlain's acceptance of need to review relations: Chamberlain to Cunliffe-Lister, confidential letter, 19 January 1927, Chamberlain Papers (PRO FO 800/260).

Page 25 Doubts over cabinet acceptance: Chamberlain to Balfour, private and personal letter, ibid.

Page 26 Tehran and Peking cables and breaking of complete additive tables: Cooper, 'Personal notes on GC&CS 1925–1939', 1.

Page 26 Knox beats Maynard Keynes: Penelope Fitzgerald, *The Knox*

Brothers (London, Macmillan, 1977), pp. 187–9; work on Zimmermann Telegram: Johnson, *Evolution*, p. 38.

Page 26 Knox celebration: Fitzgerald, *The Knox Brothers*, pp. 187–9.

Page 26 ARCOS raid: Andrew, *Secret Service*, pp. 469–71. Warning of impending raid: West and Tsarev, *Crown Jewels*, p. 29.

Page 27 Sequence of events on Government's revelations of deciphered Soviet telegrams: *The Times* and the *Daily Telegraph*, 25–27 May 1927.

Page 27 Change to one-time pad system: Denniston, 'History of GC&CS', 6.

Page 27 Brief period during which the old ciphers continued to be used: Ferris, 'Whitehall's Black Chamber', 73–5.

Page 27 Denniston on 'HMG found it necessary': Denniston, 'History of GC&CS', 6.

Page 27 Tiltman reads Russian OTP: Cooper, 'Personal Notes on GC&CS 1925–1939', paras 28, 29.

Page 28 Comintern role: *The Security Service 1908–1945*, pp. 90–108. See also Jan Valtin, *Out of the Night* (Fortress Books, London, 1988).

Page 28 First appearance of Comintern transmissions: Kenworthy, 'A Brief History of Events Relating to the Growth of the "Y" Service', 5–6.

Page 28 Denniston on 'successful work on clandestine traffic': Denniston, 'History of GC&CS', 6.

Page 28 Tiltman running of Mask and experience in Soviet wireless and cipher practice: Erskine, 'Brigadier John H. Tiltman'.

Page 28 Denniston on the attack on the Comintern ciphers: Denniston, 'History of GC&CS', 6.

Page 28 Make-up of Section V: *The Security Service 1908–1945*, pp. 103–5.

Page 29 Curry on subjects dealt with in the messages: ibid.

Page 29 SIS use of deciphered messages to penetrate Comintern: ibid.

Page 29 Best source within the Comintern was Jonny X (Johann Heinrich de Graf): Michael Smith, *Foley: The Spy Who Saved 10,000 Jews* (Hodder & Stoughton, London, 1999), pp. 51–61; *The Security Service 1908–1945*, pp. 103–5.

Page 30 Curry on 'close and fruitful collaboration' and value of Jonny X: *The Security Service 1908–1945*, pp. 103–5.

Page 30 Move to Denmark Hill: Williams, 'H. C. Kenworthy'. GC&CS accounts of the Metropolitan Police unit normally refer to it as being at Denmark Hill. Sinclair Williams makes clear that it was not until some time in the early 1930s that it moved from Scotland Yard.

Page 30 Direction-finding operation: Kenworthy, 'A Brief History of Events Relating to the Growth of the "Y" Service', 5–6.

Page 31 MI5 surveillance operation and names of those involved: *The Security Service 1908–1945*, pp. 103–5. Curry gives later dates for this operation. He says, for instance, that the station did not begin operating until January 1934. But it is clearly the same operation and the evidence of the GC&CS files on the Mask operation, in particular the index of decrypts in PRO HW 17/80 (Index to Communist Party of Great Britain COMINTERN messages) makes clear that the Wimbledon transmitter was already being intercepted in March 1930.

Page 31 Operation to find Wheeton: Kenworthy, 'A Brief History of Events Relating to the Growth of the "Y" Service', 5–6.

Page 32 Co-operation with French: Tiltman memo to Goodall on Col. Bertrand, 29 May 1974 (PRO HW 25/16), 1.

Page 32 Mask operation continues until mid-1937: Moscow to Basle message serials: 29–30. April 1937 (PRO HW 17/35).

Pages 32–3 Mask operation of great importance to GC&CS: Cooper, 'Personal Notes on GC&CS 1925–1939', para. 18.

Page 33 For Tiltman work in India, see J. H. Tiltman, 'Some Reminiscences', 3; for Simla and Sarafand work on Russian military traffic see Robert Louis Benson and Cecil Phillips, *History of Venona* (NSA, Fort Meade, 1995), 1:9.

Page 33 Work on OGPU: Naval Section Report for 1930 dated 24.3.31. Annex A, 'Russian Black Sea Naval Ciphers', Paper 29 (PRO HW 3/1). The Russian Secret Service went through a number of name changes during the twentieth century, of which OGPU was just one. For ease of understanding, the abbreviation KGB will be used throughout.

Page 33 Clarke unhappy and setting up of naval section: W. F. Clarke, 'Naval Section of GC&CS' (PRO HW 3/1), 3–5.

Page 33 Use of Sarafand: ibid.

Page 33 1927 difficulties: Paper 22. Naval Section Report for 1927 dated 6.1.28 (PRO HW 3/1).

Page 34 Clarke tour: Naval Section Report for 1928 dated 25.2.29, Paper 27 (PRO HW 3/1).

Page 34 Improvement: Naval Section Report for 1929 dated 27.2.30, Paper 28 (PRO HW 3/1).

Page 34 Cooper survey, Titterton returns as Russian interpreter, and concerted effort: Naval Section Report for 1930 dated 24.3.31, Paper 29 (PRO HW 3/1).

Page 34 Cooper's report of his Sarafand survey on Russian traffic: attached as Annex A to ibid.

Page 34 Titterton departure and lack of success: Denniston memo to Rear-

Admiral G. C. Dickens DNI, 20 October 1932, Paper 31b (PRO HW 3/1); 'W. Bodsworth's Account of the Naval Section 1927–1939', Paper 91 (PRO HW 3/1), 6.

Page 34 Russian Navy dropped in 1935 because of insufficient staff: 'Naval Section GC&CS Reorganisation Proposals' dated 29.6.36. Paper 40 (PRO HW 3/1); 'Will cryptography be of use in the next war?' dated 1.9.38, Paper 47 (PRO HW 3/1).

Page 35 Tiltman Army Section: Johnson, *Evolution*, p. 53; Estonian material: Air Section GC and CS and the Approach to War 1935–1939. 'Reminiscences of J. E. S. Cooper June 1949' (PRO HW 3/83), 4–6.

Page 35 Recruitment of P. K. Fetterlein: ibid.

Page 35 Creation of Air Section under Cooper and lack of air messages in the Estonian material: ibid.

Page 35 Cooper quotes: ibid., 4–6.

Page 35 Titterton return: Naval Section Standing Orders, September 1937, Paper 43 (PRO HW 3/1).

Page 35 Home Fleet working on Russian naval traffic: papers placed between items 60 and 60a, detailing ciphers monitored by various RN stations and ships (ibid.).

Page 35 Recruitment of Vlasto and another specifically for their Russian skills: Air Section GC&CS and the Approach to War 1935–1939. 'Reminiscences of J. E. S. Cooper, June 1949', 11–12.

Page 35 Vlasto details: *The Times*, 12 September 2000.

Page 36 India break into super-enciphered code: Russian Section Report on Work for 1940 (PRO HW 14/11).

Page 36 Military Section takes over Russian material: Air Section GC&CS and the Approach to War 1935–1939. 'Reminiscences of J. E. S. Cooper, June 1949', 22–23.

Page 36 Origins of Station X: Michael Smith, *Station X: The Codebreakers of Bletchley Park* (Channel 4 Books, London, 1998), p. 20.

Page 36 Number of codebreakers: 'Personnel at BP' (PRO HW 3/82).

Page 36 Co-operation with French expanded: Expansion of Anglo-French Co-operation in Naval Work – German, Russian and Italian. Item 10 dated 6 April 1940 (PRO HW 14/4).

Page 36 Russian section at Wavendon: 'Russian Naval Section at Wavendon (Combined Section)', handwritten notes (PRO HW 3/151).

Page 36 Russian section at Sarafand: Denniston Minute, Item 35, dated 26 April 1940 (PRO HW 14/4).

Page 36 High-grade military cipher broken during Finnish-Russian War:

Russian Section Report on Work for 1940 (PRO HW 14/11); Denniston Minute, Item 35, dated 26 April 1940 (PRO HW 14/4). These breaks were to be the last into any high-grade Russian armed forces traffic for at least another decade. See Benson and Phillips, *History of Venona* 1:29.

Page 37 Tiltman foresight in arranging deal with Finns: Denniston to Menzies dated 29 April 1940, Item 47 (PRO HW 14/4).

Page 37 Tiltman's role in breaking Japanese super-enciphered codes and JN-25 in particular: see Michael Smith, *The Emperor's Codes* (Bantam Press, London, 2000), pp. 54–60.

Page 37 Details of exchange deal and subsequent difficulties: Tiltman résumé of information obtained during recent tour of Finland, 10 April 1940, Item CC/27 (PRO HW 14/4).

Page 37 Finns provided an increased flow of Russian military and KGB traffic and two Russian Army codebooks: 'Narrative of Liaison between British and Finnish General Staffs on the subject of cryptography and Wireless Interception', 16 April 1940, Item 27 (PRO HW 14/4); Denniston to Menzies, 29 April 1940, Item 47 (PRO HW 14/4); Denniston to Menzies 7 July 1940, Item 12 (PRO HW 14/6); Tiltman to CSS 30 May 1941, Item 82 (PRO HW 14/15).

Page 37 Finns' supply of codebooks: Godfrey to Tiltman, 2 September 1940. Report on the letterwriter's liaison visit to the Finns, Item 4 (PRO HW 14/7); Russian Section Report on Work for 1940 (PRO HW 14/11). Since Godfrey appears to indicate these were full codebooks, they must have been 'pinches', i.e. captured codebooks. Finns' supply of military and KGB (NKVD) traffic: Benson and Phillips, *History of Venona*, 1:29.

Page 38 Stockholm receivers: 'Russian Naval Pre-War, 1924–1939' (PRO HW 3/151), 2.

Page 38 Flowerdown and Scarborough: second page of handwritten notes on 'Russian Naval' (ibid.).

Page 38 Vlasto sent to Sarafand: two trained cryptographers for Middle East, 28 May 1940, Item 31 (PRO HW 14/5).

Page 38 India, Sarafand and RAF experiment on Caucasus traffic: Wavell Report on Item 2 of the Agenda for the India Middle East Intelligence Conference held at Cairo, 3–8 April 1940, dated 9 April 1940, Item 38/5/1 (PRO HW 14/4).

Page 38 RAF in Cairo, minute 18 April 1940, Item 8a (PRO HW 14/5).

Page 38 Dingli and Ismailia: extract from CinC Mediterranean Most Secret Letter, 27 April 1940, Item 39 (PRO HW 14/4).

Page 38 Alexandria: Naval Y Service Proposed Expansion, Item 65 (PRO HW 14/6).

Page 38 FECB watch on Vladivostok and Kiel: second page of handwritten notes on 'Russian Naval', entry marked 'GCCS papers', 10 March 1940.

Page 38 Australian and New Zealand codebreakers: Papers on Visit of Captain F. J. Wylie to Australia and New Zealand (National Australian Archives (Melbourne)) MP1185 2021/5/529, 82–4.

Page 38 French codebreakers: 'Russian Naval Pre-War, 1924–1939', 4.

Page 38 Polish operators and codebreakers: Denniston to Menzies. Ref. No. 2572, 5 October 1940, Item 12 (PRO HW 14/7). It is interesting to note, given the minor degree of controversy surrounding the decision that the Poles should concentrate on Russian material, that both these references appear to indicate that it was they who first suggested it.

Page 38 Interception of traffic in Ukraine: Capt. A. C. Stuart Smith to Tiltman, 7 January 1941, Item 17 (PRO HW 14/10).

Page 39 Denniston on importance of Finnish liaison: Denniston to Menzies, 14 January 1941, Item 46 (PRO HW 14/10).

Page 39 Concern over increasing collaboration between the Finnish General Staff and the Germans: letter to General Tadeusz Klimecki re W/T Operators for Soviet military and air interception. Dated 6 June 1941, Item 18 (PRO HW 14/16).

Page 39 Poles asked to reinforce their operation: ibid.

Page 39 Tiltman query: Tiltman to Helsinki MI6 Head of Station, 16 June 1941, item 58 (PRO HW 14/16).

Page 39 According to popular mythology: F. H. Hinsley et al., *British Intelligence in the Second World War* (HMSO, London, 1979), 1:199. The discretion of the official historian of British wartime intelligence was again in evidence when he stated inaccurately but perhaps at the request of GCHQ that 'All work on Russian codes and ciphers was stopped from 22 June 1941, the day on which Germany attacked Russia.'

Page 39 Debate over when to stop Russian work: War Diary No. 5 Intelligence School, entry for 28 June 1941 (PRO WO 169/2578); CinC Med to Admiralty, 10 September 1941, Item 42 (PRO HW 14/19); CinC India to War Office, 9 September 1941, Item 46 (PRO HW 14/19); Denniston memo, 30 September 1941, Item 153 (PRO HW 14/19); minute dated 2 October 1941 (PRO HW 14/20); CinC India to WO, 9 September 1941, Item 46 (PRO HW 14/19); War Diary No. 5 Intelligence School, entry for 28 August 1941 (PRO WO 169/2578).

Page 40 Poles asked to continue covering Russian material and watch kept by British sites on known frequencies: Denniston memo, 30 September 1941 (PRO HW 14/19).

Page 40 Resurgence of Soviet illicit traffic: Benson and Phillips, *History of Venona* 1:30; Jefferson, Petrie-Menzies meeting, and 'Bundles of Russian traffic': *The Security Service 1908–1945*, pp. 358–9.

Page 40 Russian coverage refined: Benson and Phillips, *History of Venona* 1:30–1.

Page 40 GC&CS secret Russian section: John Croft, 'Reminiscences of GCHQ and GCB, 1942–45', *Intelligence and National Security*, 13(4) (1998), 138–9.

4 Breaking Air Force and Army Enigma

Ralph Erskine would like to thank Philip Marks, Geoff Sullivan, Derek Taunt and Frode Weierud for their comments on Chapter 4.

Page 48 'was won, in a very large measure. . .': 'The History of WO "Y" Group', 109 (PRO HW 41/119).

Page 49 Navy adopted two simple versions: minute, 15 September 1926 (PRO HW 25/6).

Page 51 Figure 4.1: based on a figure in A. Ray Miller, *The Cryptographic Mathematics of Enigma* (NSA, Fort Meade).

Page 52 'Practical knowledge of [*Wehrmacht*] enigma nil': [D. Knox?], minute, 13 January 1939 (PRO HW 25/12).

Page 52 'a stony silence', etc.: A. G. Denniston [nd], 'How News was brought from Warsaw at the end of July 1939' (PRO HW 25/12).

Page 52 'Mrs B.B.' . . . 'had seriously contemplated': Knox to Denniston, letter [nd, but c. late July 1939, or early August, on Hotel Bristol, Warsaw, notepaper] (PRO HW 25/12).

Page 53 actual punching: A. D. Knox, and others, memorandum, 1 November 1939 (PRO HW 14/2).

Page 53 one third of the time predicted: ibid.

Page 53 contravene Denniston's orders: Knox, memorandum, 3 December 1939 (PRO HW 25/12).

Page 53 could not solve any Enigma: F. H. Hinsley, E. E. Thomas, et al., *British Intelligence in the Second World War: Its Influence on Strategy and Operations* (HMSO, London, 1979–88), 3(2):952.

Page 53 rotors IV and V had been incorrect: 'De Grey's History of Air Sigint', 95 (PRO HW 3/95).

Page 53 Denniston asked Menzies: Denniston, letter, 9 January 1940 (PRO HW 14/3).

Page 53 Menzies duly wrote: Menzies, letter, 10 January 1940 (ibid.).

Page 54 on 28 December 1939: Note from X to Y, 28 December 1939 (PRO HW 25/12).

Page 54 Jeffreys sheets: 'Mathematical theory of ENIGMA machine by A. M. Turing', 95 (PRO HW 25/3). Gordon Welchman, *The Hut Six Story: Breaking the Enigma Codes* (Allen Lane, London, 1982), pp. 71–2, errs in describing these sheets as being the same as the Zygalski perforated sheets. However, John Jeffreys was probably also working on a British version of the Zygalski sheets.

Page 54 around 7 January 1940: Knox, letter, 7 January 1940.

Page 54 threaten to resign: ibid.

Page 54 decision taken in early December: 'De Grey's History of Air Sigint', 91.

Page 54 first wartime key: Hinsley et al., *British Intelligence*, 3(2): 952 states that 6 and 17 January and 25 October 1939 were broken before 23 January. However, those dates of breaking do not quite coincide with a detailed list maintained by Colonel Gwido Langer, the head of the Polish Cipher Bureau: see Tables 1 and 2 in Gordon Welchman, 'From Polish Bomba to British Bombe: The Birth of Ultra', *Intelligence and National Security*, 1(1) (1986), 104.

Page 54 might have changed: 'De Grey's History of Air Sigint', 90.

Page 54 about fifty daily keys: Hinsley et al., *British Intelligence*, 1:108.

Page 55 until it went out of service: 'De Grey's History of Air Sigint', 102.

Page 55 'unversed in the ways of military intelligence': Ralph Bennett, *Behind the Battle: Intelligence in the War with Germany, 1939–45* (Sinclair-Stevenson, London, 1994), p. 72.

Page 55 were insufficiently organized: Hinsley et al., *British Intelligence*, 1: 137.

Page 55 made Enigma vulnerable: TICOM I-45 (OKW/Chi Cryptanalytic Research on Enigma, Hagelin and Cipher Teleprinter Machines – by Dr Erich Hüttenhain and Dr Fricke), 4.

Page 55 Red for 20 May: 'De Grey's History of Air Sigint', 105.

Page 55 discovered by Knox: minute of 25 January 1940, by Denniston to 'C' (PRO HW 14/3); [Denniston], telegram, 7 February 1940, apparently to Bertrand (PRO HW 25/12).

Page 55 1,000 messages on Red: minute, 26 August 1940, by Hut 6 cryptanalysts, 7 (PRO HW 14/6).

Page 55 Whitehall was ready: Hinsley et al., *British Intelligence*, 1: 144.

Page 56 completely vulnerable: Knox to Denniston, letter [nd; on Hotel Bristol, Warsaw, notepaper].

Page 56 before 1 November 1939: A. D. Knox, and others, memorandum, 1 November 1939 (PRO HW 14/2).

Page 56 14 March 1940: 'Squadron-Leader Jones' Section', 1 (PRO HW 3/164).

Page 56 much easier to devise: C. A. Deavours and Louis Kruh, 'The Turing Bombe: Was it Enough?', *Cryptologia*, 24 (1990), 331.

Page 56 99 per cent: Donald W. Davies, 'Effectiveness of the Diagonal Board', *Cryptologia*, 23 (1999), 131.

Page 57 thirty-five to fifty minutes: W. F. Friedman, 'Report on E Operations of the GC&CS at Bletchley Park', 59 (NACP HCC Box CBTE 28, Nr. 3620).

Page 57 preliminary check: 'Operations of the 6812th Signal Security Detachment', 14 (NACP HCC Box 970, Nr. 2943).

Page 57 peak of 9,064: 'Squadron-Leader Jones' Section', 9 (PRO HW 3/164).

Page 57 US Navy bombes: see Chapter 19.

Page 57 for about twenty-five days: DMI, minute, 19 March 1942, 'Brief for C.I.G.S. on 20.3.42' (PRO WO 208/5027).

Page 57 7 per cent of the total bombe time: memorandum, 3 May 1942, 'Proportion of Bombe Time Spent on Various Colours for April, 1942' (PRO HW 14/36).

Page 58 justified priority being given to the naval work: Hinsley et al., *British Intelligence*, 2: 216 fn.

Page 58 five 'bombe controllers': C. H. O'D. Alexander, 'Cryptographic History of Work on the German Naval Enigma', 37 (PRO HW 25/1).

Page 58 fifty-eight 'standard' three-rotor bombes: Friedman, 'Report on E Operations', 60.

Page 58 1,675 Wrens: 'Squadron-Leader Jones' Section', 14 (PRO HW 3/164).

Page 58 6812th Signal Security Detachment: memorandum, 15 June 1945, 'Operations of the 6812th Signal Security Detachment'.

Page 58 from October onwards: 'Times', 17 February 1945 (PRO HW 14/122).

Page 58 average of 71.5 runs: 'Figures Relating to the Use of Standard Type Bombes During April, 1945' (PRO HW 14/126).

Page 58 between twenty and thirty letters: S. Milner-Barry, memorandum of 25 July 1944, 'Operation D', 3 (PRO HW 14/108).

Page 59 'Sultan's Meldung': Friedman, 'Report on E Operations', 46–8; 'Cryptanalytic Report on the Yellow Machine', 84 (NACP HCC Box 1009, Nr. 3175).

Page 59 crib on Phoenix: ibid., 88.

Page 59 To Welchman's regret: Friedman, 'Report on E Operations', 7.

Page 59 reluctance to make the *Stecker*: ibid., 38; 'Cryptanalytic Report on the Yellow Machine', 42.

Page 60 basic mistakes: Friedman, 'Report on E Operations', 36; 'Cryptanalytic Report on the Yellow Machine', 71.

Page 61 indirect warnings: *X-Gerät* to be jammed: Hinsley et al., *British Intelligence*, 1: 326.

Page 61 'peculiarly incautious in their W/T chat': 'Report on the Work of 3G(N)', 11 (PRO HW 3/121).

Page 61 six or seven pairs: ibid., 81.

Page 61 *Heer* cipher discipline: Friedman, 'Report on E Operations', 38–9.

Page 61 Babbage . . . was worried: ibid., 40.

Page 61 1,400 intercepts: '"E" situation 20th June 1942', Tables I, IV (PRO WO 208/5028). This figure excludes the Green traffic. Since Green was essentially unbreakable, Hut 6 found that its inclusion in the intercept figures gave a misleading picture.

Page 61 between 3,300 and 6,000: Friedman, 'Report on E Operations', 4, 7 (NACP HCC, Box 1126, Nr. 3620), 4.

Page 62 five main sections: on the organization of Hut 6, see ibid., passim.

Page 62 two-thirds of the messages: ibid., 68.

Page 62 processed 'duds': ibid., 66.

Page 64 1,125 per day: Hut 6 Report, week ending 7 October 1944, in Fried Report # 103 (NACP HCC Box 880, Nr. 2612).

Page 64 'the best that we can do': ibid.

Page 64 'were ever likely to help': 'History of Military Sigint', 76 (PRO HW 3/92).

Page 64 'deeply suspicious': ibid.

Page 64 'Fusion Room': ibid., 34.

Page 65 'is not a pretty one': 'De Grey's History of Air Sigint', 116.

Page 65 Denniston informed Blandy and Butler: ibid.

Page 66 'an act of grace': ibid., 134.

Page 66 prevent Enigma coverage being transferred: minute, 26 August 1940, by Hut 6 cryptanalysts (PRO HW 14/6).

Page 66 'My only comment . . .': 'History of Air Sigint', 135.

Page 66 '. . . lamentable and inexcusable': 'Notes on a Most Secret Document', 9 September 1941 (PRO HW 14/19).

Page 66 'astonishingly and lamentably slow': 'History of Military Sigint', 198 (PRO HW 3/92); 'not then functioning well': 'History of Air Sigint', 118.

Page 66 190 sets were needed: minutes of 'E' Sub-Committee Meeting, 7 August 1941 (PRO WO 208/5125).

Page 66 Army, RAF and Foreign Office sets: 'Distribution of Sets Allocated to Interception of "E" Traffic', 2 November 1941 (PRO HW 14/22).

Page 67 with thirty-six sets: 'History of Military Sigint', 205.

Page 67 Chiefs of Staff authorized: ibid., 210–11.

Page 67 increased from 210: ibid., 214A.

Page 67 64 per cent: ibid.

Page 67 second Y expansion: ibid., 216. The memorandum to the Chiefs of Staff is set out in AZ 244 (PRO WO 208/5026).

Page 67 105 sets: Friedman, 'Report on E Operations', 17.

Page 67 'as short of sets as ever': J. Coleman, minute, 15 January 1945 (PRO HW 14/120).

Page 68 unable to break Yellow: minute, 26 August 1940, by Hut 6 cryptanalysts, 5 (PRO HW 14/6).

Page 68 sometimes even six: 'The History of WO "Y" Group', 48 (PRO HW 41/119).

Page 68 first-rate operators: 'Appreciation of the "E" Situation, June to December 1942', 7 (PRO HW 3/164).

Page 68 a burst of Morse: Barbara Littlejohn, 'Eavesdropping on the Enemy', in Hugh Skillen (ed.), *The Enigma Symposium 1994* (privately printed, Pinner, 1994).

Page 68 sixty-eight sets: 'Interception of Discriminant Groups in England', 20 July 1941 (PRO HW 14/17).

Page 68 35 per cent: 'Distribution of Sets Allocated to Interception of "E" Traffic' (PRO HW 14/22).

Page 68 380 *Teile*: 'Appreciation of the "E" Situation, June to December 1942', Table III (PRO HW 3/164).

Page 69 an invaluable source: Hinsley et al., *British Intelligence*, 2: 69, 374.

Page 69 *Luftwaffe* 'Light Blue' cipher: ibid., 1: 391.

Page 69 The only other *Luftwaffe* cipher: ibid., 2: 69.

Page 69 *Luftwaffe* key-lists except Brown: 'Appreciation of the "E" Situation, June to December 1942', 8.

Page 69 April Foxglove keys: ibid.

Page 69 were briefly revived: 'Cryptanalytic Report on the Yellow Machine', 81; cf. 'Report on E Operations', 46.

Page 70 140 and 290 decrypts: 'Appreciation of the "E" Situation, June to December 1942', 22, Table IV.

Page 70 prolific Red: Hinsley et al., *British Intelligence*, 2: 375.

Page 70 complete key repeats: 'Appreciation of the "E" Situation, June to December 1942', 22, Table IV (cf. 11); employed by *Luftwaffe* close support units: Hinsley et al., *British Intelligence*, 2: 375.

Page 70 used on the Russian front: ibid., 2: 294.

Page 70 broke no Vulture keys: 'Huts 6 and 8: Summary for August and September 1941', 4 October 1941 (PRO HW 14/20).

Page 70 Vulture and Chaffinch: 'Graphs Illustrating the Work of Hut 6 from September 1941 to November 1942' (PRO HW 3/164).

Page 70 broke Chaffinch: 'Huts 6 and 8: Summary for August and September 1941'.

Page 70 part of October: Hinsley et al., *British Intelligence*, 2: 294.

Page 71 2,800 *Heer* signals: '"E" situation 20th June 1942', Table IV.

Page 71 Even *Heer* Mediterranean ciphers: 'Appreciation of the "E" Situation, June to December 1942', 15.

Page 71 the Mediterranean *Heer* keys: ibid., 13.

Page 71 only *Heer* cipher to produce cillies: ibid., 5.

Page 71 success rate in 1942: the figures are from 'Graphs Illustrating the Work of Hut 6' and '"E" situation 20th June 1942', Table IV.

Page 71 eight or more ciphers: 'Graphs Illustrating the Work of Hut 6', note on Graph 6.

Page 72 increased from 32,000; Unidentified traffic: 'Graphs illustrating the work of Hut 6'.

Page 72 first five *Stecker* pairs; sent by land line: 'Cryptanalytic Report on the Yellow Machine', 82.

Page 72 solved the Railway traffic: letter, 17 August 1940, to Col. Hatton-Hall (PRO HW 14/6); 'GCCS Report for 1940. German section No 4. Intelligence School' (PRO HW 14/11); Hinsley et al., *British Intelligence*, 2: 668. For the decrypts, see GRD 1-59 (PRO HW 5/745).

Page 72 90 per cent success rate: 'Graphs illustrating the work of Hut 6'.

Page 72 stopped using discriminants: Ultra/Zip CCR 22, 27 February 1944, 'German Signals Security Improvements Since the Battle of El Alamein (October/November) 1942', 2 (NACP RG 38, Radio Intelligence Publications, Box 169, RIP 403).

Page 73 identified many of the *Heer*'s ciphers: Hinsley et al., *British Intelligence*, 3(2):779.

Page 73 UKD would be widely used: S. Milner-Barry, memorandum, 25 July 1944, 'Operation D' (PRO HW 14/101).

Page 73 about twenty-five *Luftwaffe* ciphers: Hinsley et al., *British Intelligence*, 3(2): 847.

Page 74 enciphered call signs: Ultra/Zip CCR 38, 22 December 1944, 'German Signals Security Improvements During 1944', 2, 6 (RIP 403).

Page 74 retained their fixed frequencies: 'The History of WO "Y" Group', 67.

Page 74 a system under which: 'History of German Air Section', Section V of Part I: 11 (PRO HW 3/106); cf. Hinsley et al., *British Intelligence*, 3(2):848 (referring only to 'improved security precautions' then, even though the nature of the precautions had been published in 1986).

Page 74 fell from 1,800 to 1,000 daily: ibid.

Page 74 a postwar history concluded: *ULTRA and the History of the United States Strategic Air Force in Europe vs. the German Air Force* (University Publications of America, Frederick, MD, 1986 – a reprint of SRH 13), p. 179.

Page 75 Figure 4.3, Enigma breaks (Hut 6) 1942 and 1944: '"E" situation 20th June 1942', Tables I, IV; 'Appreciation of the "E" Situation, June to December 1942'; IR 4082, Annex E, 'Figures for November' ('Capt. Walter J. Fried Reports', NACP HCC, Box 880, Nr. 2612).

Page 76 special 'traffic watch': 'History of German Air Section', Section V of Part I, 12.

Page 76 thirteen occasions: Hinsley et al., *British Intelligence*, 2: 662.

5 Hut 6 From the Inside

Page 77 'an exaggerated view of security . . .'; '. . . not at first satisfactory': 'De Grey's History of Air Sigint', 135 (PRO HW 3/95).

Page 78 main *Luftwaffe* cipher had just been broken: 'The History of WO "Y" Group', 48 (PRO HW 41/119).

Page 78 Milner-Barry on the 6813th Signal Security Detachment: Milner-Barry, letter 10 May 1945, to William Bundy, 'Technical History of the 6813th Signal Security Detachment', 13 (NACP HCC Nr. 4685).

Page 78 Welchman on the management of Hut 6: Gordon Welchman, *The Hut Six Story: Breaking the Enigma Codes* (Allen Lane, London, 1982), pp. 126–7.

Page 78 Milner-Barry on Welchman: 'In Memoriam W. Gordon Welchman', *Intelligence and National Security*, 2(1) (1986).

Page 82 'hankies': these were charts (sometimes called 'hanky-pankies') in which a 'discriminatrix' recorded cipher discriminants, plus the name of the ciphers and the radio frequencies used. The name was derived from John Hancock, who designed the chart.

6 Breaking Italian Naval Enigma

Page 96 rang through to Bletchley Park: letter from Edward Clarke, Nobby's son, who was on duty when the message came through.

Page 97 He suspected dactyls and a rhyme: Penelope Fitzgerald, *The Knox Brothers* (Macmillan, London, 1977), pp. 145–6.

Page 97 *Alice in ID25*: CCAC MSS DENN 3/3.

Page 99 The story of the Polish contribution: see Chapter 4.

Page 99 '. . . not mathematical but classical': Christopher Andrew, *Secret Service: The Making of the British Intelligence Community* (William Heinemann, London, 1985), p. 96.

Page 99 'very strange beasts indeed . . .': Michael Smith, *Station X: The Codebreakers of Bletchley Park* (Channel 4 Books, London, 1998), p. 16.

Page 99 'Knox grasped everything very quickly: Wladyslaw Kozaczuk, *Enigma* (University Publications of America, Frederick, MD; Arms and Armour Press, London, 1984), pp. 60, 236.

Page 99 He enclosed a set of rods: ibid., p. 60.

Page 100 Welchman, who had given much thought to the necessary organizational methods: see Gordon Welchman, *The Hut Six Story: Breaking the Enigma Codes* (New York, McGraw Hill; Allen Lane, London, 1982), pp. 74–6.

Page 100 Denniston recalled later: Denniston, letter to Knox, 11 November 1941 (PRO HW 14/22).

Page 104 'treatise on the Enigma': 'Mathematical theory of ENIGMA machine by A. M. Turing', also known as Turing's 'Treatise on the Enigma' (PRO HW 25/3). Turing's example of rodding is from the unsteckered Railway Enigma. Its wiring was solved by Hut 8 in 1940, using established methods (see p. 72).

Page 105 'the work did not really need mathematics': F. H. Hinsley and Alan Stripp (eds), *Codebreakers: The Inside Story of Bletchley Park* (OUP, Oxford, 1993), p. 113.

Page 105 Cunningham came down: John Winton, *Cunningham* (John Murray, London, 1998), p. 139.

Page 106 ready with a poem: personal possession.

Page 106 *Ultra Secret*: F. W. Winterbotham, *The Ultra Secret* (Weidenfeld & Nicolson, London, 1974), p. 66.

Page 107 accompanying book: Richard Deacon and Nigel West, *Spy!* (BBC, London, 1980), pp. 76–7.

Page 108 *The Times*, 18 February 1980.

7 A Biographical Fragment: 1942–5

Page 111 Many of the signals translated: decrypts of the Coral signals are in PRO ADM 223/264–83, as the SJA series, and at NACP as RG 457, SRNA series, Translations of Japanese Naval Attaché messages.

8 An Undervalued Effort: How the British Broke Japan's Codes

Page 128 Hobart-Hampden success: A. G. Denniston, 'GC&CS Between the Wars', *Intelligence and National Security*, 1(1) (1986), 55–6.

Page 129 Difficulties with Japanese interception: Jones to Lambert, 22 August 1924 (PRO HW 3/1), Folio 15; W. F. Clarke, 'Documents Relating to Naval Section' (PRO HW 3/1), Folio 1. 4–5; W. F. Clarke, 'History of Naval Section, The Years Between' (PRO HW 3/16), 5, 20, 21.

Page 129 Problems finding Naval Japanese experts: 'GCCS Requests Treasury Approval for Four new junior Assistant posts for new Sigint Bureau Proposed for Hong Kong' (PRO HW 3/55).

Page 129 Nave on recruitment by Royal Navy and Admiralty instructions: Eric Nave, 'An Australian's Unique Naval Career' (unpublished memoir, Australian War Memorial, MSS 1183), pp. 168–79. NB. This appears to be the first record of the use of 'Y' for interception.

Page 129 Nave progress and Flintham: Nave, 'An Australian's Unique Naval Career', pp. 168–200; Nave Notes on Procedure Y, 30 March 1926 (Australian National Archives Melbourne, MP 1049, 1997/5/196).

Page 130 Improvement in Japanese codes and ciphers: Michael Smith, *The Emperor's Codes: Bletchley Park and the Breaking of Japan's Secret Ciphers* (Bantam, London, 2000), p. 34.

Page 130 Tiltman on breaking Japanese military attaché system: J. H. Tiltman, 'Some Reminiscences' (NACP HCC Nr. 4632), 5.

Page 130 Foss and Strachey break the Japanese naval attachés' machine cipher: Nave, 'An Australian's Unique Naval Career', pp. 338–45. NB. This was the machine referred to by the US Navy codebreakers as Orange and broken by them in February 1936, apparently as a result of a 'pinch' of information, possibly even a machine, from the apartment of the Japanese naval attaché in Washington. See L. F. Stafford, 'History of Japanese Cipher Machines', 3 February 1944 (NACP HCC Nr. 2344), 1–2.

Page 131 Those working on the Japanese diplomatic material: John Ferris, 'From Broadway House to Bletchley Park: The Diary of Captain Malcolm D. Kennedy, 1934–46', *Intelligence and National Security*, 4(3) (1989), 430.

Page 131 Details of the Type A machine: Nave, 'An Australian's Unique Naval Career', pp. 338–45. Kenworthy: John Johnson, *The Evolution of British Sigint: 1653–1939* (HMSO, Cheltenham, 1997); H. C. Kenworthy, 'A Brief History of Events leading to the Growth of the "Y" Service' (PRO HW 3/81), 9. The Americans broke the Type A machine, which they called Red, in late 1936: see Stafford, 'History of Japanese Cipher Machines', 3 February 1944, 1–2; Frank B. Rowlett, *The Story of Magic: Memoirs of an American Cryptologic Pioneer* (Aegean Park Press, Laguna Hills, 1998), pp. 112–32.

Page 131 Setting up of FECB: see R. T. Barrett, 'HMS Anderson and Special Intelligence in the Far East' (PRO HW 4/24), 1–3; Paymaster-Captain H. L. Shaw, 'History of the Far East Combined Bureau' (PRO HW 4/25), 1–3.

Page 132 Tiltman breaking army codes: J. H. Tiltman, 'Some Reminiscences' (NACP HCC Nr. 4632), 8–9.

Page 133 Tiltman break into JN-25: Shaw, 'History of the Far East Combined Bureau', 14–15, 18; Ralph Erskine, 'Brigadier John H. Tiltman: One of Britain's Finest', unpublished paper.

Page 133 Moves of FECB and Bletchley Park: Barrett, 'HMS Anderson and Special Intelligence in the Far East', 4; Shaw, 'History of the Far East Combined Bureau', 15–17; Ferris, 'From Broadway House to Bletchley Park'; Michael Smith, *Station X: The Codebreakers of Bletchley Park* (Channel 4 Books, London, 1998), pp. 1–3.

Page 133 FECB JN-25 capabilities: 'Collaboration of British and US Radio Intelligence' (PRO ADM 223), 1; Lt.-Cmdr. Neil Barham, 'Japanese Cipher Notes' (PRO ADM 223/496), 3; Shaw, 'History of the Far East Combined Bureau', 23–4.

Page 133 Break into Purple: Rowlett, *The Story of Magic*, pp. 151–9.

Page 134 American gift of a Purple machine: 'History of the Signal Security Agency', Vol. Two, 'The General Cryptanalytical Problems' (NARA, RG 457 SRH 361), 13.

Page 134 Details of co-operation: 'Report of Technical Mission to England', A. Sinkov and Leo Rosen, 11 April 1941, 'Army and Navy Comint Regs & Papers' (NACP HCC Nr. 4632).

Page 134 Barham on introduction of JN-25B: Barham, 'Japanese Cipher Notes', 3.

Page 135 Early co-operation between FECB and Corregidor: 'Collaboration of British and US Radio Intelligence' (PRO ADM 223/496), 1; Shaw, 'History of the Far East Combined Bureau', 31–3; Nave, 'An Australian's Unique Naval Career', pp. 398–9.

Page 135 Exchanges with US Army and Dutch: 'History of the Far East Combined Bureau', 31–3.

Page 136 Nave return and exchange deal: Nave, 'An Australian's Unique Naval Career', pp. 405–11, 429–32; Nave to Shaw, 28 August 1941 (PRO ADM 223/496); Central Bureau Technical Records. Part A – Organisation (in author's possession), 1; Smith, *The Emperor's Codes*, p. 80.

Page 136 Oshima messages and GC&CS difficulty in making Whitehall believe that Germany was about to attack Russia: Carl Boyd, *Hitler's Japanese Confidant: General Oshima Hiroshi and Magic Intelligence* (University Press of Kansas, Kansas, 1993), pp. 18–21; F. H. Hinsley, *British Intelligence in the Second World War* (revised abridged edition) (HMSO, London, 1994), pp. 106–9; Smith, *Station X*, p. 73.

Page 136 Oshima messages revealing German attempts to draw Japan into war with Russia and Japanese intention to attack Indochina: diary of Captain Malcolm D. Kennedy (Kennedy Papers, University of Sheffield Library), 13–22 July 1941.

Page 137 FECB tracking of Japanese Fleet: 'Pearl Harbour and the Loss of Prince of Wales and Repulse' (PRO ADM 223/494), 2–8.

Page 137 'intelligence covering a wide field': Barham, 'Japanese Cipher Notes', 3.

Page 137 warnings to the Japanese embassy in London to await the Winds messages: PRO HW 1/240 and HW 1/303.

Page 138 Additive and call sign changes: Smith, *The Emperor's Codes*, pp. 98–9.

Page 138 Winds message received: Shaw, 'History of the Far East Combined Bureau', 28.

Page 139 British surprise: Nave, 'An Australian's Unique Naval Career', pp. 420–2; diary of Captain Malcolm D. Kennedy, 7 December 1941.

Page 139 FECB move to Colombo and capture of Hong Kong: Shaw, 'History of the Far East Combined Bureau', 30, 35–6; Peter Elphick, *Far Eastern File: The Intelligence War in the Far East 1930–1945* (Coronet, London, 1997), pp. 96–7.

Page 139 MacInnes on disruption caused by move from Singapore: John MacInnes, 'History of Anderson', chap. IX, Production (PRO HW 4/25), 119–21.

Page 140 Nave on Fabian security issues: Nave, 'An Australian's Unique Naval Career', pp. 409–11, 429–32, 449–51; Sharon A. Maneki, *The Quiet Heroes of the Southwest Pacific Theater* (NSA, Fort Meade), pp. 63–6, 88–91.

Page 140 MacInnes on advantages from Japanese failure to replace JN-25B book: MacInnes, 'History of Anderson', chap. IX, Production, 138–9.

Page 140 Codebreakers predict attack on Colombo: Hugh Denham, 'Bedford–Bletchley–Kilindini–Colombo', in F. H. Hinsley and Alan Stripp, *Codebreakers: The Inside Story of Bletchley Park* (OUP, Oxford, 1993), pp. 274–5; MacInnes, 'History of Anderson', chap. IX, Production, 131.

Page 140 MacInnes on further disruption caused by move to Kilindini: ibid., 119.

Page 141 Midway: For a fuller description of the role of Sigint in the Battle of Midway, see Smith, *The Emperor's Codes*, pp. 134–41.

Page 141 Problems caused by lack of co-operation from Fabian unit: Robert Louis Benson, *A History of US Communications Intelligence during World War II* (NSA, Fort Meade), pp. 87–8; Maneki, *The Quiet Heroes of the Southwest Pacific Theater*, pp. 88–91.

Page 141 Senior officer on US view of co-operation: Elphick, *Far Eastern File*, p. 399.

Page 142 Possibility of British breaking with US: Birch to Hastings, 2 July 1944 (PRO HW 14/142).

Page 142 Breaking of JN-40 and other codes/ciphers by Kilindini: MacInnes, 'History of Anderson', chap. IX, Production, 138–9.

Page 143 Tiltman on Japanese military attaché code: Tiltman, 'Some Reminiscences' (NACP HCC Nr. 4632), 10–11.

Page 144 Setting up of Japanese military section under direction of Tiltman: Nigel de Grey, 'History of Air Sigint', chap. IX, The Japanese War (PRO HW 3/102), 517–20; 'History of Military Intelligence Section at Bletchley Park' (PRO HW 3/156), 25–6.

Page 144 Tiltman sets up Japanese courses: Tiltman, 'Some Reminiscences', 9–10.

Page 144 Locations of various British outposts: Smith, *The Emperor's Codes* pp.231–2.

Page 146 Breaking of Water Transport Code: author's various correspondence with Joe Richard, January–February 2000; Alan Stripp, *Codebreaker in the Far East* (Frank Cass, London, 1989), p. 71; Hugh Skillen, *Spies of the Airwaves* (Hugh Skillen, London, 1987), p. 517; MacInnes, 'History of Anderson', chap. IX, Production, 139.

Page 146 Yamamoto shoot-down: John Prados, *Combined Fleet Decoded* (Random House, New York, 1995), pp. 459–63; Maneki, *The Quiet Heroes of the Southwest Pacific Theater*, p. 90.

Page 146 Bletchley success against Army Air code: Edward J. Drea, 'Were The Japanese Army Codes Secure?', *Cryptologia*, 19 (1995), 122; interview with Maurice Wiles, 22 December 1999; Minutes of Conference on Japanese

Military Ciphers held at Bletchley Park, 7 May 1943–17 May 1943 (PRO WO 208/5074).

Page 147 Conference on army codes: De Grey, 'History of Air Sigint', chap. IX, 'The Japanese War', 517–20; Minutes of Conference on Japanese Military Ciphers held at Bletchley Park, 7 May 1943–17 May 1943.

Page 147 Expansion of Japanese sections: Smith, *Emperor's Codes*, pp. 186–7.

Page 147 Move to Colombo and Redman softens attitude to co-operation: R. T. Barrett, 'HMS Anderson and Special Intelligence in the Far East' (PRO HW 4/24), 8; Benson, *US Communications Intelligence*, p. 119.

Page 148 Saunders on FRUMEL: Cdr. Malcolm Saunders, 'Report on Visit to US and Other Signals Intelligence Centres', 28 December 1943 (PRO HW 223/496), 3.

Page 148 Hinsley: Birch to Washington, 28/5/44 (PRO HW 14/142); Benson, *US Communications Intelligence*, pp. 120–1.

Page 148 Alexander role in breaking of Coral: Smith, *Emperor's Codes*, pp. 218–20.

Page 149 codebooks found at Sio: Central Bureau Technical Records. Part A – Organization, 6; 'History of Military Intelligence Section at Bletchley Park' (PRO HW 3/156), 42.

Page 149 Melinsky quotes: Hugh Melinsky, *A Code-breaker's Tale* (Lark's Press, Denham, 1998), pp. 19–67.

Page 150 BULBUL break: Leonard 'Joe' Hooper to Arlington Hall, 14 September 1944 (PRO HW 14/142).

Page 150 Kerry quote: interview with Sir Michael Kerry, 15 February 2000.

9 Most Helpful and Co-operative: GC&CS and the Development of American Diplomatic Cryptanalysis, 1941–2

David Alvarez would like to thank Ralph Erskine and Michael Smith for providing copies of certain documents from the Public Record Office.

Page 153 a staff of about sixty-five, etc.: GC&CS annual report for 1940, Diplomatic sections, 13 January 1941 (PRO HW 14/11).

Page 153 The Foreign Office received, etc.: D & R Berkeley Street, Diplomatic Section [nd] (PRO HW 3/162).

Page 153 recipient was Major Anthony Blunt: Chart, Sources of Material (as at 31 March 1944) (PRO HW 3/32).

Page 153 The Russians have recently claimed: David Kahn, 'Soviet Comint in the Cold War', *Cryptologia*, 22 (1998), 11.

Page 153 On 27 July 1942: Carl Boyd, *Hitler's Japanese Confidant: General Oshima Hiroshi and Magic Intelligence, 1941–1945* (University Press of Kansas, Lawrence, 1993) p. 63; Kahn, 'Soviet Comint in the Cold War', 13.

Page 155 brief existence in the 1920s: David Alvarez, *Secret Messages: Codebreaking and American Diplomacy, 1930–1945* (University Press of Kansas, Lawrence, 2000), p. 38.

Page 155 five Japanese diplomatic ciphers: 'History of the Signal Security Agency, vol. 2: The General Cryptanalytic Problem', pp. 31–2 (NARA, RG 457, SRH-361).

Page 156 at least one Mexican cipher: Alvarez, *Secret Messages*, p. 54.

Page 156 low-grade consular and administrative traffic: ibid.

Page 156 neither of these systems was readable: 'Italian Codes and Ciphers, 1939–1943' (NACP HCC Box 1388).

Page 157 still struggled with its target: Alvarez, *Secret Messages*, p. 61.

Page 157 was hardly better: ibid., p. 62.

Page 158 window into Japanese diplomacy had closed: ibid., p. 63.

Page 160 joint staff conference in London: Alan Harris Bath, *Tracking the Axis Enemy: The Triumph of Anglo-American Naval Intelligence* (University Press of Kansas, Lawrence, 1998), p. 25.

Page 160 exchange information on their cryptanalytic operations: Alvarez, *Secret Messages*, p. 76.

Page 160 'please expedite reply': quoted in Robert Louis Benson, *A History of US Communications Intelligence During World War II: Policy and Administration* (NSA, Fort Meade, 1997), p. 17.

Page 161 concerning specific foreign codes and ciphers: Alvarez, *Secret Messages*, pp. 78–9. The Akin–Friedman memorandum is undated but is generally thought to have been written on or about 1 September 1940.

Page 163 a few Red Army and Comintern systems: Robert Louis Benson and Cecil Phillips, *History of Venona*, (NSA, Fort Meade, 1995), 1:29. I am indebted to Lou Benson for arranging for the declassification of parts of this multi-volume history.

Page 164 it was the breakthrough: Stephen Budiansky, *Battle of Wits: The Complete Story of Codebreaking in World War II* (Free Press, New York, 2000), pp. 165–6.

Page 164 quashed their opposition: Alvarez, *Secret Messages*, p. 83.

Page 164 'have a look around': Prescott Currier oral history, NSA-OH-38-80 (National Cryptologic Museum Library, NSA, Fort Meade).

Page 165 'almost empty': Donald Gish, 'A Cryptologic Analysis', *International Journal of Intelligence and Counterintelligence*, 6(4) (1993), 387, fn 17. By January 1941, OP-20-G had recovered only 3 per cent of the values in JN-25B.

Page 166 had been working this system: Michael Smith, *The Emperor's Codes: Bletchley Park and the Breaking of Japan's Secret Ciphers* (Bantam, London, 2000), pp. 78–9.

Page 166 'a fairly large staff': [Abraham Sinkov], 'Report of Cryptographic Mission' (NACP HCC Box 1296).

Page 167 committed to the Italian problem: 'Cryptographic Codes and Ciphers: Italian' (NACP HCC Box 1388); 'Annual Report of the Chief Signal Officer and Miscellaneous Studies, FY 1942–1943' (NACP HCC Box 832).

Page 167 abandoned work on these formidable ciphers: 'Report on German Diplomatic Section', 8 January 1941 (PRO HW 14/4).

Page 168 ciphers used by Germany in the First World War: Alvarez, *Secret Messages*, p. 130.

Page 169 'all our technical documents': 'Report by Lieut. Colonel J. H. Tiltman on his visit to North America during March and April 1942' (PRO HW 14/46). The material passed by Tiltman to the Americans is enumerated in this report.

Page 169 'results from me': [Solomon Kullback], 'The British GC&CS', 1 August 1942, 6–7, Sinkov Papers (NACP HCC Box 1413).

Page 170 had been especially fruitful: 'Notes on Diplomatic Liaison with U.S.', 8 March 1942 (PRO HW 14/16); 'Report on present position of legibility of Foreign Government Cyphers', 25 July 1942 (PRO HW 14/38).

Page 171 'we wonder if they are actually deeply interested': Denniston to Stevens, 22 December 1942 (PRO HW 14/62).

Page 171 direct requests for assistance: for a survey of exchanges between Berkeley Street and Arlington Hall in the period 1943–5, see 'Governments on which there has been no substantial impediment to liaison', Clark Files (British Liaison, 1940–1945) (NACP HCC Box 1413).

Page 172 including American policies: Cadogan to 'C', 3 July 1944 (PRO HW 37/4).

Page 172 South American systems: for an overview of areas in which collaboration faltered, see 'Governments on which there is a present obstacle to liaison', Clark Files (British Liaison, 1940–1945) (NACP HCC Box 1413).

Page 172 Russian civil traffic: Benson and Phillips, *History of Venona*, p. 31.

Page 173 'very great indeed': (NACP, RG 457. SRH-349), 'Achievements of the Signal Security Agency in World War II', 9.

10 Breaking German Naval Enigma on Both Sides of the Atlantic

Ralph Erskine wishes to thank David Alvarez, Stephen Budiansky and Frode Weierud for supplying some of the documents used in Chapter 10.

Page 174 Even Knox found: Dillwyn Knox, undated notes on senior staff [nd c. end 1939] (PRO HW 14/1).

Page 175 'almost as conveniently as if . . .': C. H. O'D. Alexander, 'Cryptographic History of Work on the German Naval Enigma', 90 (PRO HW 25/1).

Page 176 were never broken: F. H. Hinsley, E. E. Thomas, et al., *British Intelligence in the Second World War: Its Influence on Strategy and Operations* (HMSO, London, 1979–1988), 2:664.

Page 176 Poles had given GC&CS a reconstructed Enigma: on the Polish contribution to GC&CS's Enigma work, see Appendix 30 to Hinsley et al., *British Intelligence*, 3(2).

Page 176 Birch and Turing on breaking Enigma: Alexander, 'Cryptographic History of Work on the German Naval Enigma', 19; 'all German codes were unbreakable': Birch, as quoted in A. P. Mahon, 'History of Hut Eight', 14 (PRO HW 25/2).

Page 176 Turing solved: 'Mathematical theory of ENIGMA machine by A. M. Turing', 136 (PRO HW 25/3). This version of 'Prof's Book' is much more legible than the poor photostat copy, 'Turing's Treatise on the Enigma' (NACP HCC Nr. 964), which lacks many figures; see also Alexander, 'Cryptographic History', 20.

Page 177 little headway: Alexander, 'Cryptographic History', 24.

Page 177 rotors, VI and VII were recovered: Hinsley et al., *British Intelligence*, 3(2): 957.

Page 177 *Schiff* 26 captures: Ralph Erskine, 'The First Naval Enigma Decrypts of World War II', *Cryptologia*, 21(1) (1997), 42; Hugh Sebag-Montefiore, *Enigma: The Battle for the Codes* (Weidenfeld & Nicolson, London, 2000), p. 74. *Schiff 26* is erroneously called VP 2623 in Hinsley et al., *British Intelligence*, 3(2): 959.

Page 177 Rotor VIII was captured: Hinsley et al., *British Intelligence*, 3(2): 957. For full details of the numerous captures of Enigma material, see Sebag-Montefiore, *Enigma*, but no one has discovered how rotor VIII was captured.

Page 177 'Foss's day' etc.: Alexander, 'Cryptographic History', 22.

Page 177 diagonal board: see p. 56.

Page 177 not getting 'fair does': Birch, 21 December 1940, as quoted in Mahon, 'History of Hut Eight', 29.

Page 178 Banburismus: see Alexander, 'Cryptographic History', chap. ix; Mahon, 'History of Hut Eight', 16. The most detailed account is in 'Home Waters Enigma' (NARA RG 38, Radio Intelligence Publications, Box 172, RIP 610).

Page 178 Enigma key-list for February: documents at NHB.

Page 179 'Germet 3': on this cipher, see 'German Naval Meteorological Cypher', Met 65 (NACP HCC Box 187 Nr. 874).

Page 179 broke the DAN meteorological cipher: G. C. McVittie, diary entry for 8 February 1941, with 'Autobiographical Sketch' prepared for Royal Society of Edinburgh (RLEW, CCAC).

Page 179 delay of fifty hours: Hinsley et al., *British Intelligence*, 2: 174.

Page 179 reconstructing . . . new bigram tables: Alexander, 'Cryptographic History', 31.

Page 179 a further two months: ibid.

Page 179 dummy signals . . . falsified: ibid., 30.

Page 180 unable to solve: ibid., 31.

Page 180 changed every two days: ibid., 5.

Page 180 only officers were permitted: *Der Schlüssel M. Allgemeine Bestimmungen* (M. Dv. Nr. 32/3), para. 130 (NHB).

Page 180 within thirty-six hours: Hinsley et al., *British Intelligence* (1979), 1: 338.

Page 180 *Werftschlüssel*, as well as Enigma: see e.g., identical *Werft* and Enigma signals in 'German Reports of British Mining on 29/7/41', ZG 45 of 31 July 1941 (PRO ADM 223/2). On the *Werftschlüssel* (M. Dv. Nr. 103) (NHB), see Michael van der Meulen, 'Werftschlüssel: A German Navy Hand Cipher', *Cryptologia*, 19(4) (1995), 349 and 20(1) (1996), 37.

Page 181 Shark . . . introduced . . . 5 October: MND signal 27 September 1941 (NACP microfilm T1022/2325). Alexander, 'Cryptographic History', 34, suggests that the change occurred on 3 October, but the German signal is very specific.

Page 181 bigram tables . . . changed: Alexander, 'Cryptographic History', 35.

Page 181 tables . . . captured from *Geier*: documents at NHB. The tables, but not the *Kenngruppenbuch*, had also reached Bletchley Park from *Donner* on 30 December, when they were immediately borrowed by Turing.

Page 181 M4: see Ralph Erskine and Frode Weierud, 'Naval Enigma: M4 and its Rotors', *Cryptologia*, 11 (1987), 235.

Page 181 M4 lid . . . from U-570: documents at NHB. The lid was from machine M 3172.

Page 181 already solved the wiring: 'Memorandum No. 3. "Schlüssel M (Form M 4)" ' (NACP RG 38, Radio Intelligence Publications, Box 169, RIP 403); cf. Alexander, 'Cryptographic History', 36.

Page 181 only three Shark keys: Alexander, 'Cryptographic History', 36.

Page 182 referred to the Y Board: DMI, minute, 19 March 1942, 'Brief for C.I.G.S. on 20.3.42' (PRO WO 208/5027).

Page 182 Soaring shipping losses: see table in Appendix O in S. W. Roskill, *The War at Sea*, Vol. 2 (HMSO, London, 1956).

Page 182 *Wetterkurzschlüssel* . . . seized: documents at NHB. For a description of the incident, see Sebag-Montefiore, *Enigma*, pp. 218–21.

Page 182 Hut 8 believed: McVittie, diary, 2 December 1942.

Page 183 Germet 3 additive tables . . . were repeated: 'WW and other crib processes into U-Boat traffic', nd, but between 12 December 1942 and 11 January 1943 (PRO HW 14/64).

Page 183 begin to be repeated on 8 December: memorandum of 15 December 1942 by RAF Section, 'Report of Research and Exploitation' (PRO HW 14/61).

Page 183 'hotted up': McVittie, diary, 2 December 1942.

Page 183 sent a teleprint: ZTPGU 1 (PRO DEFE 3/705).

Page 183 'Eighty-eight out of ninety-nine days': Mahon, 'History of Hut Eight', 77.

Page 183 pessimistically advised: as quoted in Rear-Admiral J. H. Edelsten, minute of 9 March 1943 (PRO ADM 205/29).

Page 183 could not build: Alexander, 'Cryptographic History', 50.

Page 184 90 out of the 112: ibid., 49.

Page 184 proved invaluable: ibid., 50.

Page 184 serious delays: see e.g. PRO ADM 223/OIC SI 641, 648 (weeks ending 19 and 26 July, when Shark had been partially read up to 19 June and 16 July, respectively); also OP-20-GM war diary (NACP RG 38, Crane Library, 5750/176), entries in July and August.

Page 184 British and US Navy . . . bombes: as to June, Hinsley et al., *British Intelligence*, 2: 751; as to August, ICY 51, 82 (NACP HCC Box 705, Nr. 1736). An early British four-rotor bombe had been available since April 1943, but for some reason (perhaps a lack of cribs) did not give any results against Shark until June: Alexander, 'Cryptographic History', 43.

Page 184 forty-five hours: OP-20-GY-A-1, memorandum, 3 November 1944 (NACP RG 38, Crane Library, 5750/205).

Page 185 Feynman adopted: Richard P. Feynman, *Surely You're Joking, Mr. Feynman* (Unwin Hyman, London, 1985, pbk), p. 128.

Page 185 score over 100 tetras: Alexander, 'Cryptographic History', 108.

Page 185 Decibans played a vital part: they were also used in breaking Tunny, the Lorenz SZ 40/42 teleprinter cipher attachment.

Page 186 'to succeed where it would otherwise have failed': Alexander, 'Cryptographic History', 108.

Page 186 Initially, Hut 8 consisted of: this section is based on ibid., 86–92.

Page 186 '. . . veil of considerable opacity': ibid., 38.

Page 187 visitor from Hut 6 pointed out: ibid., 39.

Page 187 *Süd*: *Kenngruppenverfahren Süd Januar 1944* (M. Dv. Nr. 608) (PRO ADM 223/331).

Page 187 Alan Turing had written: 'Mathematical theory of ENIGMA machine by A. M. Turing', 130.

Page 188 Sunfish . . . was broken: 'German Supply Ship ['Versorgungsschiff'] Traffic', ZG 240, 19 August 1943 (ADM 223/4).

Page 188 broke Seahorse: 'War diary of SCHIFF 28, Mar–June', ZG 244 of 15 September 1943 (PRO ADM 223/4).

Page 188 broken, '[a]fter a certain amount of trouble': Alexander, 'Cryptographic History', 71.

Page 189 *Kriegsmarine* . . . fully informed: see *Deckblätter* Nr. 1–8 '*Schlüsselanleitung zur Schlüsselmaschine Enigma vom 13.1.40*'; cf. *Der Schlüssel M Verfahren M Allgemein* (M. Dv. Nr. 32/1 – August 1940 edition), para. 140, referring to single encipherment for *Heer* Enigma.

Page 189 about 460 intercepts each day . . . : Mahon, 'History of Hut Eight', 7.

Page 190 by about one year: Alexander, 'Cryptographic History', 9 (although not mentioning HF-DF).

Page 190 twenty-three . . . stations: 'The Communication Intelligence Organizations of the British Empire', 73–6 (NACP RG 38, Radio Intelligence Publications, RIP 99).

Page 190 Tina: see 'Tina, 1946' (NACP HCC Box CBCB 43 Nr. 901), 'Tina, 1941' (ibid., Nr. 902), 'Tina, 1942–1943' (ibid., Nr. 903); 'Rep/Tina Historical Documentation' (ibid., Box CBKH 68 Nr. 1540); on RFP, see 'Report on R.F.P. Identifications', 15 November 1942 (PRO HW 14/58); 'Sample Oscilligrams – RFP Groups, 1944' (NACP HCC Box 585 Nr. 1451); 'RFP Manuals' (ibid., Box 806 Nr. 2330).

Page 190 seldom do more than distinguish: 'Report on R.F.P.', 19 November 1944 (PRO HW 18/89).

Page 190 Ultra: 'Ultra' was a short title for 'special intelligence': signal of 20 August 1944 (quoted in full in G. E. Colpoys, 'Admiralty Use of Special Intelligence in Naval Operations', 43 (PRO ADM 223/88)).

Page 190 all attempts . . . should be abandoned: minute of 19 November 1944, 'Summary of R.F.P. Classification of Naval Units during the German War' (PRO HW 18/89).

Page 190 US Navy RFP gave worse results: minute of 9 March 1944, 'R.F.P. and Tina Effort on German U-boats', 9 March 1944, para. 8 (PRO HW 18/89).

Page 191 Mrs Agnes Driscoll: 'Naval Security Group History to World War II', 400 (NARA RG 457, SRH 355); on her work against Enigma, see Colin Burke, 'Agnes Meyer Driscoll v the Enigma and the Bombe', *Cryptologia* (forthcoming).

Page 191 exasperated by GC&CS's failure: Cdr. J. N. Wenger, Cdr. H. T. Engstrom, Lt-Cdr. R. I. Meader, memorandum of 30 May 1944, 'History of the Bombe Project', para. 5 (NARA HCC, Box Zema 34, Nr. 4584).

Page 191 an extensive bombe programme: J. N. Wenger, memorandum of 3 September 1942, endorsed as approved by Admiral Horne, the Vice-Chief of Naval Operations (NACP RG 38, Crane Library, 5750/441).

Page 191 Desch . . . had completed: memo of present plans for an electro-mechanical bombe, 15 September 1942 (NACP RG 38, Crane Library, 5750/441). The report can be downloaded from http://frode.home.cern.ch/frode/crypto/USBombe/desch.pdf.

Page 191 Holden Agreement: PRO HW 3/193, f. 69; on the Agreement, see Ralph Erskine, 'The Holden Agreement on Naval Sigint: The First BRUSA?', *Intelligence and National Security*, 14(2) (1999), 187.

Page 191 British official history errs: see Hinsley et al., *British Intelligence*, 2: 57.

Page 192 Adam . . . delivered: serial 003 of 27 May 1943 (NACP RG 38, Crane Library, 5830/116).

Page 192 Neither machine was running well: see e.g., serials 852 of 3 July 1943 ('Adam out of operation'), 439 of 31 July 1943 ('Eve still out') (ibid.); cf. OP-20-GM war diary, 3 June 1943.

Page 192 production models began to be shipped: ibid., 31 August 1943.

Page 192 'semi-continuous operation': ICY 51, 82 (NACP HCC Box 705, Nr. 1736).

Page 192 530 and other USN bombes: 'Tentative Brief Description of Equipment for Enigma Problems' (NACP HCC Box 1419, Nr. 4640).

Page 192 ninety-five Navy 530 bombes (and other production figures): ibid.

Page 193 forty-eight and sixty three-rotor runs: as to forty-eight, C. H. O'D. Alexander, minute of 4 November 1943 (PRO HW 14/91); as to sixty, 'The Standard #530 Bombe' in 'Tentative Brief Description of Equipment for Enigma Problems'.

Page 193 down time was about 2.7 per cent, etc.: OP-20-GM-3 war diary, summary for 1–30 April 1944 (NACP RG 38, Crane Library, 5750/159).

Page 193 'still poor, . . .': Alexander to Church, 24 March 1944 (ibid., 5750/441).

Page 193 still attacking old wartime ciphers: OP-20-GE war diary, summary for 1–31 March 1946 (ibid., 5750/159).

Page 194 about seventy-five bombes in service: OP-20-GM-7 war diary, summary for 1–15 July 1943 (ibid.).

Page 194 four cryptanalysts: Alexander, 'Cryptographic History', 73.

Page 194 only five Shark keys: OP-20-GM war diary. Figures for April and May are not available.

Page 194 very apprehensive: see e.g. E. E. Stone, memorandum of 16 September 1943 for director naval communications (NACP RG 38, Crane Library, 5750/225).

Page 194 it agreed to run Hut 6: Alexander, minute of 4 November 1943 (PRO HW 14/91).

Page 194 Travis was pressed: Travis, letter of 31 March 1944 to Colonel Carter Clarke (NACP RG 38, Inactive Stations, Box 55, 3200/2).

Page 194 chided Travis and Redman: Clarke, letter of 4 April 1944 to Travis, memorandum of 4 April to Redman (ibid., 3200/3).

Page 194 about 45 per cent: memorandum of 2 February 1945, 'Summary of Attack on January Enigma Traffic', para. 84 (NACP RG 38, Crane Library, 5750/205); 115 bombes: 'History of OP-20-G-4E' (NACP HCC Box 1419, Nr. 4640).

Page 194 three-rotor bombes in service: 'Squadron-Leader Jones' Section', 9, 13 (PRO HW 3/164).

Page 195 fifty additional bombes, etc.: Travis, letter, 19 February 1944, as quoted in P. R. Kinney, memorandum of 18 November 1944 (NACP RG 38, Crane Library, 5750/205).

Page 195 OP-20-GM recovered: memorandum of 15 July 1944, 'Brief Resumé of OP-20-G and British Activities vis-à-vis German Machine Ciphers' (ibid., 5750/205).

Page 195 *Stichwort*: on this procedure, see p. 376.

Page 195 until mid-November: the first *Sonderschlüssel* intercept was on 17 November, OP-20-GY-A-1 war diary, 19 November 1944 (NACP RG 38, Crane Library, 5750/176).

Page 195 5,300 bombe hours: ibid., 5 April 1945.

Page 195 three *Sonderschlüssel* were broken: on 19 and 20 January, and 5 April, 1945 – ibid. for those dates.

Page 195 virtually all operational intelligence: Hinsley et al., *British Intelligence*, 3(2): 853.

Page 195 'one of the most formidable changes': Alexander, 'Cryptographic History', 83.

Page 196 broke about 1,120,000: NS 31 May 45 (PRO HW 14/142).

11 Hut 8 From the Inside

Page 198 Birch was able to write: A. P. Mahon, 'History of Hut Eight', 24 (PRO HW 25/2).

12 Bletchley Park and the Birth of the Very Special Relationship

Page 212 series of increasingly exasperated despatches: Geoffrey Stevens, letter, 31 July 1942 (PRO HW 14/47); Stevens, letter, 17 August 1942 (PRO HW 14/49); Stevens, letter, 28 September 1942 (PRO HW 14/53).

Page 214 swagger stick: author's interview with Cecil Phillips, November 1998.

Page 215 'we are entitled to recall': Alastair Denniston to the Director (personal), 15 November 1940 (PRO HW 14/8).

Page 215 'I find myself unable to devise': Stewart Menzies to Prime Minister, 24 June 1941 (PRO HW 1/6).

Page 216 Safford rejected any exchange: 'Chronology of Cooperation' (NACP HCC, Nr. 2738), 2–3.

Page 217 letter to President Roosevelt: Louis Kruh, 'British-American Cryptanalytic Cooperation and an Unprecedented Admission by Winston Churchill', *Cryptologia*, 13 (1989), 126.

Page 217 'lots of fun': Memorandum for Colonel Clarke, 15 June 1943, 'Army and Navy Comint Regs & Papers' (NACP HCC, Nr. 4632). The British also broke American naval codes in the interwar years, a fact that did not come out until many decades later; see DENN 1/4, A. G. Denniston Papers, CCAC.

Page 217 had begun in the 1930s: DENN 1/4, 12 (CCAC); F. H. Hinsley and Alan Stripp (eds), *Codebreakers: The Inside Story of Bletchley Park* (OUP, Oxford, 1993), p. 257.

Page 218 supply the needed translators: Report of Technical Mission to England, A. Sinkov and Leo Rosen, 11 April 1941, 'Army and Navy Comint Regs & Papers' (NACP HCC, Nr. 4632).

Page 218 Red machine . . . Purple machine: 'Chronology of Cooperation' (NACP HCC, Nr. 2738), 5; 'Naval Security Group History to World War II' (NACP RG457, SRH–355), 8; Report of Technical Mission to England, A. Sinkov and Leo Rosen, 11 April 1941, 'Army and Navy Comint Regs & Papers' (NACP HCC, Nr. 4632).

Page 218 British staff officials were astonished: Robert Louis Benson, *A History of US Communications Intelligence During World War II: Policy and Administration* (NSA, Fort Meade, 1997), p. 17.

Page 219 Army was essentially devoid of knowledge: Monitoring Activities, S. B. Akin to Signal Officer, Eighth Corps Area, 17 October 1939, 'Intercept/Crypto Correspondence 1927–1941' (NACP HCC, Nr. 2123).

Page 219 proposed giving to the British: J. O. Mauborgne, memorandum to Assistant Chief of Staff, G-2, 25 October 1940, 'Chronology of Cooperation' (NACP HCC, Nr. 2738).

Page 220 'Should this expert make a favourable impression': letter, C/5392, 22 November 1940 (PRO HW 14/45).

Page 220 'As proposed': Stewart Menzies to Prime Minister, C/5906, 26 February 1941 (PRO HW 1/2).

Page 221 handwritten agreement: R. H. Weeks to Commander Denniston, 3 March 1941 (PRO HW 14/45).

Page 221 sent each other recovered code groups: 'History of GYP-1' (NACP RG 38 Crane Library, CNSG 5750/202), 21; Benson, *US Communications Intelligence*, p. 20.

Page 221 At the time of Pearl Harbor: 'OP-20-GY' (NACP RG 38 Crane Library, CNSG 5750/198).

Page 222 not permitted to take notes: Briefs for Field Marshal by Colonel Tiltman, ref: General Marshall's letter to Field Marshal of 23 December 1942, 'Copies of Letters Between the Field Marshal and General Marshall, etc.' (PRO HW 14/60).

Page 222 'still being copied': Washington & E. Traffic, Notes on Correspondence, 'Bombe Correspondence' (NACP RG 38 Crane Library, CNSG 5750/441).

Page 222 memorandum to 'C': Denniston to the Director (personal), 5 August 1941 (PRO HW 14/45).

Page 223 'a little uneasy': Memorandum to Commander Denniston, 5 August 1941 (ibid.).

Page 223 cleared the matter up: Washington & E. Traffic, Notes on Correspondence, 'Bombe Correspondence'; Memorandum for Director of Naval Communications, Subj: History of the Bombe Project, 'Captain Wenger Memorandum' (NACP HCC, Nr. 4419), 1–2.

Page 223 'No results are being passed out': CSS to Washington, CXG 105–109, 1 December 1941 (PRO HW 14/45).

Page 224 Denniston . . . at once sent a message: personal from Denniston for Washington, CXG 139, 23 December 1941 (PRO HW 3/33).

Page 225 all sixteen bombes that were available: 'Squadron Leader Jones' Section' (PRO HW 3/164), 4.

Page 226 Tiltman cabled to London: Travis from Tiltman, [18 (?) April 1942], 'Bombe Correspondence' (NACP RG 38 Crane Library, CNSG 5750/441).

Page 226 Travis informed OP-20-G: for OP-20-G from GC&CS, 13 May 1942, 'Bombe Correspondence'.

Page 227 were concealing the fact: J. N. Wenger, Memorandum for OP-20-GM, Subject: Recent information on 'E', 6 August 1942, 'Bombe Correspondence'.

Page 227 to build 360 four-wheel bombes: Memorandum for OP-20, Subject: Cryptanalysis of the German (Enigma) Cipher Machine, 3 September 1942, 'Bombe Correspondence'; Wenger to GC&CS for Eachus, 4 September 1942, 'Bombe Correspondence'.

Page 227 tried to head off the American move: Memorandum for Director of Naval Communications, Subj: History of the Bombe Project, 'Captain Wenger Memorandum' (NACP HCC, Nr. 4419), 4.

Page 227 only had about thirty bombes: 'Squadron Leader Jones' Section' (PRO HW 3/164), 4.

Page 227 overloaded the available bombes: Hut 6 Report of July and August 1942 (PRO HW 14/51).

Page 227 'most alarming': Memorandum, 5 January 1943 (PRO HW 14/63).

Page 227 negotiated an agreement: Ralph Erskine, 'The Holden Agreement on Naval Sigint: The First BRUSA?,' *Intelligence and National Security*, 14(2) (1999), 187.

Page 228 GC&CS memorandum in late 1942: memorandum, 21 December 1942 (PRO HW 14/62).

Page 228 Army was proposing to build its own machine: William Friedman, memorandum for Colonel Bullock *THRU* Colonel Minckler, Subject: Project in the Cryptanalysis of German Military Traffic in their High-Grade Cipher Machine, 14 September 1942, 'Project 68003' (NACP HCC, Nr. 3815).

Page 228 $530,000 contract: 'Project X68003-Army Bombe' (NACP HCC, Nr. 2723).

Page 229 Turing went to Dayton: visit to National Cash Register Corporation of Dayton, Ohio, 'Bombe Correspondence' (NACP RG 38 Crane Library, CNSG 5750/441), 3.

Page 229 Arlington Hall received permission: Frank W. Bullock, Memorandum for File, 4 January 1943, 'Project 68003' (NACP HCC, Nr. 3815).

Page 229 'had better get together': author's interview with Dale Marston, September 1998.

Page 229 Turing was shown the actual prototype: Major G. G. Stevens, Report on Visit to Bell Laboratories, 'Project 68003' (NACP HCC, Nr. 3815).

Page 229 Tiltman tactfully responded: William F. Friedman, Memorandum for Colonel Corderman, 8 February 1943, 'GCHQ/US Cooperation' (NACP HCC, Nr. 2820), 2.

Page 230 OP-20-G was involved in solving Enigma keys by hand: 'OP-20GM-6/GM-1-C-3/GM-1/GE-1/GY-A-1 Daily War Diary' (NACP RG 38 Crane Library, CNSG 5750/176).

Page 231 internal GC&CS memorandum: 'Co-operation with US & Allocation of Tasks on "E" signals', 8 January 1943 (PRO HW 14/63).

Page 232 followed up with additional pressure: Taylor to Clarke, 5 April 1943, 'Army and Navy Comint Regs & Papers' (NACP HCC, Nr. 4632).

Page 232 more acerbic internal memoranda: 'Briefly stated the reasons why the British are averse to the Americans exploiting the intercepted German signals encyphered on their machine', 4 May 1943 (PRO HW 14/75).

Page 232 Taylor advised: Taylor to Clarke, 5 April 1943, 'Army and Navy Comint Regs & Papers' (NACP HCC, Nr. 4632), 6–7.

Page 233 'never on God's green earth': Scope of E Operation – other than Personnel, excerpt from Cable V4772, 13 May 1943, 'Col. McCormack Trip to London, May–June 1943' (NACP HCC, Nr. 3600).

Page 233 Gordon Welchman urged moderation: Welchman to Travis, 'The Americans and "E"' (PRO HW 14/68).

Page 233 BRUSA Agreement: memorandum for Assistant Chief of Staff, G–2, 'Special cryptanalytic Project in SIS ETOUSA, Project Beechnut' (NACP HCC, Nr. 3049); the full text of the BRUSA agreement has also been published in 'The BRUSA Agreement of May 17, 1943', *Cryptologia*, 21 (1997), 30.

Page 233 Telford Taylor to select decrypts: Benson, *US Communications Intelligence*, p. 111.

Page 233 summary of State Department cables: memorandum for Colonel Clarke, 15 June 1943, 'Army and Navy Comint Regs & Papers' (NACP HCC, Nr. 4632).

Page 234 British were equally suspicious: signal, To Corderman from Fried from Bicher, 1 November 1944, 'Clark Files' (NACP HCC, Nr. 4566); Report IB 32164, 'Clark Files' (NACP HCC, Nr. 4566), 15.

Page 234 behind a plywood partition: author's interview with Cecil Phillips, November 1998; Stephen Budiansky, 'A Tribute to Cecil Phillips – and Arlington Hall's "Meritocracy"', *Cryptologia* 23 (1999), 97.

Page 235 on 24 March 1944 GC&CS cabled: memorandum for Director of Naval Communications, 30 May 1944, 'History of the Bombe Project' (NACP HCC, Nr. 4584), 10.

Page 235 'dudbusting': C. H. O'D. Alexander, Dud-busting, 'Capt. Walter J. Fried Reports/SSA Liaison With GCCS' (NACP HCC, Nr. 2612).

Page 236 nearly automatic system for decryption: Stephen Budiansky, 'Codebreaking with IBM Machines in World War II', *Cryptologia*, 25 (2001) 241.

13 Mihailović or Tito? How the Codebreakers Helped Churchill Choose

All references, except where otherwise stated, are to documents held at the Public Record Office.

Page 239 'extreme elements': WO 208/2014, Enclosure 22A.

Page 240 pigeons: HW 19/53, ISOS 58952 and HW 19/137, ISK 60438.

Page 240 'decrypted about so little': HW 11/10, 10.

Page 241 start time: HW 5/11, CX/JQ/822.

Page 242 monitoring station: Noel Currer-Briggs describes the operation in 'Army Ultra's Poor Relations' in F. H. Hinsley and Alan Stripp (eds), *Codebreakers: The Inside Story of Bletchley Park* (OUP, Oxford, 1993), p. 209.

Page 242 somewhat smugly: HW 13/14.

Page 243 Brig. E. T. Williams: 'The Use of Ultra', WO 208/3575.

Page 243 identical to BP decrypts: e.g. an *Abwehr* decrypt of 17 August 1943, HW 19/60, ISOS 66091 is virtually the same as a decrypt of a Comintern message to Tito on 16 September, HW 17/51, ISCOT 1038.

Page 244 regular oral briefings: Davidson wrote notes for the Cabinet Office Historical Section in 1972. He referred to frequent telephone briefings to Churchill as well as visits to No. 10 and Chequers. Davidson papers, Liddell Hart Centre, King's College London, Document F.

Page 245 *Zwei Fischer*: HW 19/51, ISOS 56939.

Page 245 attacks on railway lines: HW 19/11, ISOS 8537.

Page 245 Italian aircraft: HW 5/24, CX/MSS/79.

Page 245 law and order: HW 16/6, ZIP/MSGP/27.

Page 245 bodies mutilated: HW 19/12, ISOS 9699.
Page 245 pacification of Bosnia: HW 19/12, ISOS 9841.
Page 245 'to crush the rebellion': HW 5/26, CX/MSS/265 and HW 1/82, C/7641.
Page 245 Italian divisions: HW 5/35, CX/MSS/364.
Page 245 German divisions: HW 5/37, CX/MSS/406.
Page 246 'clashes': HW 5/38, CX/MSS/437 and HW 1/218, C/8072.
Page 246 'Russia would win': HW 19/18, ISOS 148591.
Page 246 'caps over the fence': WO 208/4604, CAB 79/15–COS(41)354.
Page 246 revolt could be maintained: WO 208/4604, Minute 31.
Page 246 'in human power': quoted in F. W. D. Deakin, *The Embattled Mountain* (OUP, London, 1971), p. 144.
Page 247 situation reports: including HW 5/71, CX/MSS/784 and HW 1/402, C/8923.
Page 247 'only ones to be reckoned with': HW 19/89, ISK 3514.
Page 247 becoming steadily worse: HW 5/76, CX/MSS/823.
Page 247 time was right: WO 208/2014, Minute 11.
Page 247 all-out offensive: WO 208/2014, Enclosure D to Minute 11.
Page 247 movement of trains: HW 5/95, CX/MSS/1021.
Page 247 'smash the resistance': HW 5/90, CX/MSS/976.
Page 247 Churchill commented: WO 208/2014, Minute 22.
Page 248 Italians wished to withdraw: HW 5/126, CX/MSS/1333.
Page 248 had seized control: HW 5/130, CX/MSS/1390.
Page 248 'really ticklish situation': HW 5/132, CX/MSS/1394.
Page 248 'to do their part': WO 208/2014, Minute 30.
Page 248 vigorous action: HW 5/138, CX/MSS/1458.
Page 249 under German command: HW 5/138, CX/MSS/1455.
Page 249 'needlessly sacrificing': HW 5/139, CX/MSS/1468.
Page 249 clean up the Livno area: HW 5/148, CX/MSS/1559.
Page 249 antimony mine: HW 5/149, CX/MSS/1562.
Page 249 during the winter: HW 5/171, CX/MSS/1781.
Page 249 Operation *Weiss* and Operation *Schwarz*: HW 5/182, CX/MSS/1891 and HW 5/191, CX/MSS/1986.
Page 250 surround the Partisans: HW 5/194, CX/MSS/2015 and HW 1/1332; HW 5/194, CX/MSS/2011; HW 5/196, CX/MSS/2031.
Page 250 operation in mid-winter: WO 208/2019, Minute 7.
Page 250 prestige and influence: WO 208/2026, Minute 3.
Page 250 'active and vigorous Partisans': WO 208/3102. Minute 1.
Page 251 advancing on bauxite area: HW 5/208, CX/MSS/2156.

Page 251 left flank was exposed: HW 5/208, CX/MSS/2136.
Page 251 towns had fallen: HW 19/48, ISOS 53156.
Page 251 Löhr said he did not have: HW 5/207, CX/MSS/2141, 2144.
Page 251 to relieve: HW 5/210, CX/MSS/2174.
Page 251 thirteen and sixty: HW 19/49, ISOS 54524.
Page 252 Italian-officered Chetnik units: HW 5/216, CX/MSS/2236.
Page 252 German fire: HW 5/215, CX/MSS/2228.
Page 252 transporting them: HW 19/50, ISOS 55961.
Page 252 negotiation with the Partisans: HW 19/51, ISOS 56608, 56699.
Page 252 'current policy of supporting': WO 208/2019, Minute 3.
Page 252 Partisans should be contacted: CAB 80/68: COS(43) 142(0).
Page 253 yet to play a decisive part: HW 1/1474, C/2604.
Page 253 Chetnik reinforcements: HW 19/50, ISOS 55961.
Page 253 Mihailović barely escaped: HW 19/51, ISOS 56734.
Page 253 said to have joined the Partisans: HW 19/52, ISOS 57654.
Page 253 captured large quantities: HW 19/52, ISOS 55915, 58191, 58888.
Page 253 organizing in the towns and villages: HW 17/51, ISCOT 1040.
Page 253 headquarters near Foca: HW 19/53, ISOS 59368.
Page 254 Mihailović and his Chetniks: WO 208/2026, Minute 8.
Page 254 Hitler's instructions: HW 5/255, CX/MSS/2627.
Page 254 Djurisić had fallen out with Mihailović: HW 19/54, ISOS 59683, 59969.
Page 254 providing transport: HW 19/54, ISOS 60020.
Page 254 protect as many of the Chetniks: HW 5/250, CX/MSS/2574.
Page 255 near Jajce: HW 19/127, ISK 51991.
Page 255 Partisan and Chetnik losses: HW 5/271, CX/MSS/2782 and HW 1/1765, C/3654.
Page 255 Churchill argued in a note circulated: Winston S. Churchill, *The Second World War, Closing the Ring*, vol. V (Cassell, London, 1952), pp. 736–7.
Page 255 report from the intelligence services: PREM 3/510/7 124298.
Page 256 'satisfied from information': CAB 121/674.
Page 256 British efforts to unify the resistance: CAB 121/674.
Page 256 'of the highest importance': PREM 3/510/7 124298.
Page 256 could be sent to the Partisans: ibid.
Page 256 'hunting in the next field': CCAC, CHR/20/131.
Page 256 'the great disorder': HW 1/1820 Personal Minute Serial No. 122/3.
Page 256 the marvellous resistance: CCAC, CHR/20/131.
Page 257 conserve his forces: HW 17/51, ISCOT 1048.

Page 257 'main object of an Allied attack': HW 19/134, ISK 57401.
Page 257 'the first to be invaded': HW 36/1, GERDI 0460.
Page 257 their attention on the Balkans: HW 19/136, ISK 59589.
Page 258 'must strengthen her defences': HW 11/10, BJ 120793.
Page 258 Italians were withdrawing: HW 19/60, ISOS 65953.
Page 258 'a planned evacuation': HW 5/229, CX/MSS/3126.
Page 258 Italians were offering arms: HW 19/135, ISK 59221.
Page 258 to seize Italian naval installations: HW 5/340, CX/MSS/3180.
Page 258 5,000–6,000 Chetniks: HW 19/61, ISOS 67118.
Page 258 Mihailović would act only: HW 19/237, ISOSICLE 5863.
Page 259 German troops were marching: HW 11/10, BJ 122406.
Page 259 'firmly in our hands': HW 5/343, CX/MSS/3196.
Page 259 28,000 Italians: HW 19/62, ISOS 68601.
Page 259 'extremely bad effect': HW 19/88, ISOS 64286.
Page 259 'major operations': HW 5/363, CX/MSS/3299.
Page 259 actions of the Partisans: HW 19/141, ISK 66865.
Page 259 removed from Yugoslavia: HW 5/359, CX/MSS/3276.
Page 259 to seize Jews and others: HW 19/62, ISOS 69043.
Page 260 Partisan leader's complaints: HW 17/51, ISCOT 1063, 1192.
Page 260 a shopping list: HW 17/51, ISCOT 1092, 1303.
Page 260 sole recipient: WO 208/2026, Minute 22.
Page 260 sent to the resistance: HW 5/366, CX/MSS/3313/3328, HW 1/2078, C/4555, HW 1/2085, C/4574.
Page 260 could soon be sent: John Ehrman, *Grand Strategy* (HMSO, London, 1956), August 1943–September 1944, p. 58.
Page 260 provision of supplies: HW 1/2108, C/4643.
Page 260 threat to the major towns: ZIP/MSGP/50, GPD/1688-1905 and HW 5366/367.
Page 261 death of 3,200 Partisans: HW 5/381, CX/MSS/3431.
Page 261 'unsatisfactory': HW 5/411, CX/MSS (Series 2) R11.
Page 261 'the more active body': WO 208/4628, Appn/710/43/MI3b.
Page 261 Lukacević treaty: HW 19/146, ISK 73795 and HW 1/2259, C/5058.
Page 262 should be intensified: Ehrman, *Grand Strategy*, p. 111.
Page 262 'to overcome certain difficulties': HW 17/51, ISCOT 304/1459 (a signal of 28 September 1943, decrypted on 28 December 1945).
Page 262 alleged by a number of commentators: e.g. Michael Lees, *The Rape of Serbia* (Harcourt Brace Jovanovich, New York, 1990); David Martin, *Web of Disinformation: Churchill's Yugoslav Blunder* (Harcourt Brace Jovanovich, New York, 1990).

Page 262 'agent of influence': Christopher Andrew and Vasili Mitrokhin, *The Mitrokhin Archive: The KGB in Europe and the West* (Allen Lane, London, 1999), p. 167.

Page 263 Ralph Bennett . . . and others: Ralph Bennett et al., 'Mihailović or Tito', *Intelligence and National Security*, 10(3) (1995), 526.

Page 263 addressed the House of Commons: Parliamentary Debates (Hansard) Fifth Series, 397, House of Commons, 22 February 1944, 692–7.

14 Traffic Analysis: A Log-reader's Tale

The author was given access to 'The Sixta History'. This unpublished source is retained under the Public Records Act 1958.

Page 265 'My Y Service exists to produce intelligence . . .': Michael Smith, *Station X: The Codebreakers of Bletchley Park* (Channel 4 Books, London, 1998), p. 24.

Page 265 'a difficult and dangerous art' etc.: J. E. Cooper, memorandum, 24 June 1941, 'Relationship of Cryptography and W.T.I.' (PRO WO 208/5125).

Page 265 inference 'solely based upon radio studies . . .': W. F. Friedman, 'Report on E Operations of the GC&CS at Bletchley Park', 30 (NACP HCC, Box CBTE 28 Nr. 3620).

15 Bletchley Park, Double Cross and D-Day

Page 279 Jones said: Eric Jones, Memo to All Hut 3 Personnel, 6 June 1944 (PRO HW3/125); Brig. E. T. Williams, The Use of Ultra, 6 June 1944 (PRO WO 208/3575).

Page 280 Jellyfish information: Hinsley et al., *British Intelligence in the Second World War*, (HMSO, London, 1988), 3(2): 777–80; Michael Smith, *Station X* (Channel Four Books, London, 1998), pp. 157–8.

Page 280 Allied assessments of German defences fairly good: Hinsley et al., *British Intelligence*, 3(2): 771–6.

Page 281 Codebreaker's memories of Oshima message: Carl Boyd, *Hitler's Japanese Confidant: General Oshima Hiroshi and Magic Intelligence, 1941–1945* (University Press of Kansas, Kansas, 1993), p. 106.

Page 281 Japanese military attaché's message: Hinsley et al., *British Intelligence*, 3(2): 18.

Page 281 Japanese naval attaché report: see Hinsley et al., *British Intelligence*, 3(2): 787–92.

Page 282 Bennett on location of German divisions: Peter Bate interview with Ralph Bennett, for the Channel 4 television series *Station X* (Darlow Smithson Productions, 1999).

Page 282 White proposal: Tom Bower, *The Perfect Englishman* (Heinemann, London, 1995), pp. 37–8.

Page 283 Details of Snow: Summary of the Snow Case (PRO KV 2/452), 1–3; Transcript of shorthand notes taken at Scotland House, London SW1, on 24 September 1938 at the interrogation of [Arthur Owens] by Col. Hinchley Cooke (KV 2/452), 6, 21–2.

Page 283 Details of code sent to GC&CS: Robertson to Vivian, 19 September 1939 (PRO KV 2/453).

Page 283 Alert operator and GC&CS scepticism: [John Curry], *The Security Service 1908–1945: The Official History* (PRO, London, 1999), pp. 206–7.

Page 284 Broken by Gill and Trevor-Roper: ibid., pp. 178–9, 206–7.

Page 284 Setting up of GC&CS *Abwehr* section: ibid., pp. 178–9.

Page 284 Use of Pear codename: Report entitled 'ISOS', 25 September 1945 (PRO ADM 223/793), 1.

Page 285 Astor on MI5 and MI6 responsibilities: author's interview with Hugh Astor, 23 January 1998.

Page 285 Twenty Committee set up: J. C. Masterman, *The Double Cross System in the War of 1939 to 1945* (Pimlico, London, 1995), pp. 10–11.

Page 285 Astor on Robertson, Masterman and White: author's interview with Hugh Astor.

Page 285 Workings of the Double Cross system: Masterman, *The Double Cross System*, pp. 1–35; Michael Howard, *British Intelligence in the Second World War* (HMSO, London, 1990), 5: 8–9; Report entitled 'ISOS', 25 September 1945.

Page 286 Astor on consultations with the Twenty Committee: author's interview with Hugh Astor.

Page 286 Montagu quotes: Ewen Montagu, The XX System (PRO ADM 223/794).

Page 287 Knox solution of *Abwehr* Enigma: Denniston to Menzies, minute, 10 December 1941 (PRO HW14). Lever solution of GGG machine: private information.

Page 288 Robertson quotes: Howard, *British Intelligence in the Second World War*, 5: 20–1.

Page 288 Philby quotes: Nigel West and Oleg Tsarev, *The Crown Jewels* (HarperCollins, London, 1998), p. 309.

Page 288 Montagu quotes: Report entitled 'ISOS', 25 September 1945, 2–3.

Pages 289–90 Garbo and ISBA reports bring situation to a head: *The Security Service 1908–1945*, pp. 207–11; F. H. Hinsley and C. A. G. Simkins, *British Intelligence in the Second World War* (HMSO, London, 1990), 4: 125–7; Howard, *British Intelligence in the Second World War*, 5: 19.

Page 290 A few weeks later: *The Security Service 1908–1945*, pp. 206–9.

Page 290 Petrie takeover bid for Section V and Menzies compromise: Michael Smith, *Foley: The Spy Who Saved 10,000 Jews* (Hodder & Stoughton, London, 1999), pp. 242–3.

Page 291 Masterman quotes: Masterman, *The Double Cross System*, p. 65.

Page 291 Problems of accepting that German perception different from that of the British: PRO DEFE 28/49.

Page 291 Quotes on improvements in MI5–MI6 liaison following Foley appointment: Smith, *Foley*, pp. 243–4.

Page 292 Details of Mincemeat: PRO ADM 223/794; Currer-Briggs quotes: Smith, *Station X*, pp. 121–2.

Page 294 Astor on 'impression of tremendous rivalry': author's interview with Hugh Astor.

Page 294 Radio Security Intelligence Conference: Report entitled 'ISOS', 25 September 1945, 6.

Page 294 Astor on relations between MI5 and MI6 and use of Ultra: author's interview with Hugh Astor.

Page 295 Bodyguard: Roger Hesketh, *Fortitude: The D-Day Deception Campaign* (St Ermin's Press, London, 1999), pp. 17–19.

Page 295 Number of double agents: ibid., p. 46.

Page 295 Evolution of Fortitude: ibid., pp. 25–7.

Page 296 Main agents: ibid., pp. 46–56.

Page 297 Treasure comes close to giving away Fortitude: Summary of Treasure Case (PRO KV 2/464).

Page 297 Treasure 'saves Bletchley's bacon': Page to Masterman and Masterman memo, both 29 November 1944, Summary of Treasure Case (ibid.).

Page 297 Garbo networks: Howard, *British Intelligence in the Second World War*, 5: 231–3.

Page 298 mobile wireless vehicles: Operation Neptune Radio Deception (PRO WO 208/5050), 2; Notes on Army Wireless Deception for Operation Overlord (ibid.), 2.

Page 299 Garbo message and shown to Hitler: Howard, *British Intelligence in the Second World War*, 5:188.

Page 300 Garbo reports and German acceptance of them: ibid., pp. 188–9.

Page 300 Interrogation of relieved German: Hesketh, *Fortitude*, pp. 489–90.

16 How Dilly Knox and his Girls Broke the *Abwehr* Enigma

Page 303 His note, dated 28 October: PRO HW 14/21.

Page 304 the abomination of desolation: Daniel 12: 11; Matthew 24: 15.

Page 308 Denniston's reply: PRO HW 14/22.

17 Breaking Tunny and the Birth of Colossus

Page 319 Thrasher: Thrasher appears to have been the Siemens and Halske T43 teleprinter cipher machine, which employed a one-time tape.

Page 319 Sturgeon: The GC&CS attack against Sturgeon is fully described by Frode Weierud, 'Sturgeon, The FISH BP Never Really Caught', in David Joyner (ed.), *Coding Theory and Cryptology: From Enigma and Geheimschreiber to Quantum Theory* (Springer Verlag, New York, 1999), p. 18; Frode Weierud, 'BP's Sturgeon, The FISH that Laid No Eggs', in B. J. Copeland (ed.), *Colossus: The First Computer* (OUP, Oxford, forthcoming).

Page 332 Mrs Miles: 'General Report on Tunny, With Emphasis on Statistical Methods', 369 (PRO HW 25/4). Mrs Miles of Eynesbury had quadruplets in 1935 at St Neots (http://www.sntc.co.uk/history.htm).

18 Colossus and the Dawning of the Computer Age

The author is indebted to Diane Proudfoot for her detailed and valuable comments.

Page 343 'band of brothers': A.W. Coombs, 'The Making of Colossus', *Annals of the History of Computing*, 5 (1983), 259.

Page 344 'eyes dropped out': unless indicated otherwise all material directly relating to Flowers derives from (1) Flowers in interviews with Copeland, 1996–98; (2) Flowers in interview with Christopher Evans in 1976 ('The Pioneers of Computing: an Oral History of Computing', Science Museum, London).

Page 344 February 1944: 'General Report on Tunny, With Emphasis on Statistical Methods' (PRO HW 25/4, 25/5). Much of the detailed information in this chapter concerning Tunny and Bletchley's attack on Tunny comes from this report, which except in the case of direct quotation will not be referenced again. A digital facsimile of the typescript is available at <http://www.AlanTuring.net/tunny_report>.

Page 344 taken to Newman's newly created Computing Machine Laboratory:

K. Myers, 'Dollis Hill and Station X', in B. J. Copeland (ed.), *Colossus: The First Computer* (OUP, Oxford, forthcoming).

Page 344 1960: Donald Michie, personal communication, 2000. The author is indebted to Michie for a number of conversations about Colossus, Tunny and the Newmanry.

Page 345 photographs of Colossus (PRO FO 850/234).

Page 345 outlines of Colossus: I. J. Good, 'Some Future Social Repercussions of Computers', *International Journal of Environmental Studies*, 1 (1970), 67; I. J. Good, 'Early Work on Computers at Bletchley', *Annals of the History of Computing*, 1 (1979), 38; D. Michie, 'The Bletchley Machines', in B. Randell (ed.), *The Origins of Digital Computers: Selected Papers* (Springer-Verlag, Berlin, 1973); B. Randell, 'The Colossus', in N. Metropolis, J. Howlett and G. C. Rota (eds), *A History of Computing in the Twentieth Century* (Academic Press, New York, 1980).

Page 345 hardware of Colossus I: T. H. Flowers, 'The Design of Colossus', *Annals of the History of Computing*, 5 (1983), 239.

Page 346 'disciplined but unintelligent manner': A. M. Turing, 'Programmers' Handbook for Manchester Electronic Computer' (University of Manchester Computing Laboratory, 1950), 1. A digital facsimile is available at <http://www.AlanTuring.net/programmers_handbook>.

Page 347 Lovelace envisaged: A. A. Lovelace and L. F. Menabrea, 'Sketch of the Analytical Engine Invented by Charles Babbage, Esq.' (1843), in B. V. Bowden (ed.), *Faster than Thought* (Pitman, London, 1953).

Page 347 Difference Engine: C. Babbage, *Passages from the Life of a Philosopher*, M. Campbell-Kelly (ed.), *The Works of Charles Babbage*, vol. 11 (William Pickering, London, 1989); B. Randell (ed.), *The Origins of Digital Computers: Selected Papers* (Springer-Verlag, Berlin, 1982 – 3rd edn.), chap. 1.

Page 347 Analytical Engine: Babbage, op. cit.; Lovelace and Menabrea, op. cit.; Randell, op. cit., chap. 2; A. Bromley, 'Charles Babbage's Analytical Engine, 1838', *Annals of the History of Computing*, 4 (1982), 196.

Page 348 Vannevar Bush and Howard Aiken: V. Bush, 'Instrumental Analysis', *Bulletin of the American Mathematical Society*, 42 (1936), 649 (the text of the 1936 Josiah Willard Gibbs Lecture); H. Aiken, 'Proposed Automatic Calculating Machine', in Randell, op. cit.

Page 348 mealtime discussion at Bletchley: Flowers in interview with Copeland, 1996.

Page 348 ENIAC: A. W. Burks, 'From ENIAC to the Stored-Program Computer: Two Revolutions in Computers', in Metropolis, Howlett and Rota, op. cit.; H. H. Goldstine, *The Computer from Pascal to von Neumann*

(Princeton University Press, Princeton, 1972); H. H. Goldstine and A. Goldstine, 1946, 'The Electronic Numerical Integrator and Computer', in Randell, op. cit.

Page 349 given by Newman: Newman in interview with Christopher Evans in 1976 ('The Pioneers of Computing').

Page 349 'all numbers which could . . .': A. M. Turing, 'On Computable Numbers, with an Application to the Entscheidungsproblem', *Proceedings of the London Mathematical Society*, Series 2, 42 (1936–37), 230.

Page 349 emphasized that the Analytical Engine was universal: A. M. Turing, 'Computing Machinery and Intelligence', *Mind*, 59 (1950), 433.

Page 349 works on both using exactly the same operations: this is emphasized by Robin Gandy in his 'The Confluence of Ideas in 1936', in R. Herken (ed.), *The Universal Turing Machine: A Half-Century Survey* (OUP, Oxford, 1998).

Page 350 later to suggest: A. M. Turing, 'Lecture to the London Mathematical Society on 20 February 1947', in B. E. Carpenter and R. W. Doran (eds), *A. M. Turing's ACE Report of 1946 and Other Papers* (MIT Press, Cambridge, Mass., 1986).

Page 350 Right from the start: Newman in interview with Evans, op. cit.

Page 350 Differential Analyser: V. Bush, 'The Differential Analyser: A New Machine for Solving Differential Equations', *Journal of the Franklin Institute*, 212 (1931), 447; V. Bush, 'Instrumental Analysis', *Bulletin of the American Mathematical Society*, 42 (1936), 649; V. Bush, S. H. Caldwell, 'A New Type of Differential Analyser', *Journal of the Franklin Institute*, 240 (1945), 255.

Page 351 joined the Telephone Branch of the Post Office: 'Mr T. H. Flowers, MBE, BSc, MIEE', *Post Office Electrical Engineers Journal* (October 1950), 156.

Page 352 pay occasional visits to the London office: letter from Peter Twinn to Copeland, 2001.

Page 352 at the British Tabulating Machine Company: 'Enigma–Position' and 'Naval Enigma Situation', two notes, 1 November 1939, by Knox, Twinn, Welchman and Turing (PRO HW 14/2).

Page 352 Fellow since 1923: W. Newman, 'Max Newman: Mathematician, Codebreaker and Computer Pioneer', to appear in Copeland (ed.), *Colossus: The First Computer*.

Page 353 letters about mathematical logic: there are five letters from Turing to Newman during this period in the Modern Archive Centre, King's College Library, Cambridge.

Page 353 academic paper, published in March 1942: M. H. A. Newman, A. M. Turing, 'A Formal Theorem in Church's Theory of Types', *Journal of Symbolic Logic*, 7 (1942), 28.

Page 353 wrote to the Master of St John's: W. Newman, op. cit.

Page 354 William Tutte made the crucial break: W. T. Tutte, 'At Bletchley Park', to appear in Copeland (ed.), *Colossus: The First Computer*.

Page 354 rest of the Research Section joined in: ibid.

Page 354 designed by C. E. Wynn-Williams: C. E. Wynn-Williams, 'A Thyratron Scale of Two Automatic Counter', *Proceedings of the Royal Society of London*, series A, 136 (1932), 312.

Page 355 'other people's problems': Newman in interview with Evans, op. cit.

Page 355 Construction started in January 1943: the following paragraphs are indebted to accounts by three Dollis Hill engineers involved with Heath Robinson and Colossus, H. Fensom, 'How the Codebreaking Colossus was Conceived, Built and Operated: One of its Engineers Reveals its Secrets', K. Myers, 'Dollis Hill and Station X', and N. T. Thurlow, 'The Road to Colossus', all to appear in Copeland (ed.), *Colossus: The First Computer*.

Page 356 Dollis Hill made: letter from Harry Fensom to Copeland, 2001.

Page 357 'a knowledge of . . .': 'General Report on Tunny', 22.

Page 361 considered the offer derisory: Peter Hilton in interview with Copeland, 2001. The author is indebted to Hilton for numerous conversations about Bletchley Park; also to P. Hilton, 'Living With Fish: The Work of the Newmanry and the Testery', to appear in Copeland (ed.), *Colossus: The First Computer*.

Page 362 'didn't really understand . . .': Flowers in interview with Copeland, 1996.

Page 362 'got out'; 'in close touch with Turing': letter from Newman to von Neumann, 8 February 1946. A digital facsimile of the letter is available at <http://www.AlanTuring.net/newman_vonneumann_8feb46>.

Page 363 During the remainder of 1945: Michael Woodger in interview with Copeland, 1998. According to Woodger (Turing's assistant at the NPL from May 1946), an NPL file gave the date of Turing's technical report as 1945. Unfortunately, this file has since been destroyed. Woodger believes that Turing probably wrote the document between October and December 1945.

Page 363 'Proposed Electronic Calculator': reprinted in full under the title 'Proposal for Development in the Mathematics Division of an Automatic Computing Engine (ACE)', in Carpenter and Doran (eds), *A. M. Turing's ACE Report of 1946 and Other Papers*. A digital facsimile of the original typescript is available at <http://www.AlanTuring.net/proposed_electronic_calculator>. Much other material concerning the ACE, Pilot ACE and DEUCE is available at <http://www.AlanTuring.net>. See also B. J. Copeland (ed.), 'The Turing-Wilkinson Lecture Series on the Automatic Computing

Engine', in K. Furukawa, D. Michie and S. Muggleton (eds), *Machine Intelligence 15* (OUP, Oxford, 1999).

Page 363 'First Draft of a Report on the EDVAC': reprinted in full in N. Stern, *From ENIAC to UNIVAC: An Appraisal of the Eckert-Mauchly Computers* (Digital Press, Bedford, Mass., 1981).

Page 364 'one machine would suffice . . .': C. Darwin, 'Automatic Computing Engine (ACE)', 17 April 1946. NPL document. A digital facsimile is available at <http://www.AlanTuring.net>.

Page 364 Bendix G-15 computer: H. D. Huskey, 'From ACE to the G-15', *Annals of the History of Computing*, 6 (1984), 350.

Page 364 other derivatives: D. Yates, *Turing's Legacy: A History of Computing at the National Physical Laboratory 1945–1995* (Science Museum, London, 1997).

Page 364 a 'minimal ACE' would be ready: 'Status of the Delay Line Computing Machine at the P.O. Research Station', 7 March, 1946. NPL document. A digital facsimile is available at <http://www.AlanTuring.net>.

Page 364 'too busy . . .': Flowers in interview with Copeland, 1998.

Page 364 Turing suggested that the NPL: A. Turing, 'Report on visit to U.S.A., January 1st – 20th, 1947'. 3 February 1947. NPL document. A digital facsimile is available at <http://www.AlanTuring.net/visit_to_usa>.

Page 364 'probably as far advanced 18 months ago': NPL Executive Committee Minutes, 20 April 1948, 7. A digital facsimile is available at <http://www.AlanTuring.net>.

Page 364 pioneering work on Artificial Intelligence: A. M. Turing, 'Intelligent Machinery', National Physical Laboratory Report, [1948]. Reprinted in full in B. Meltzer and D. Michie (eds), *Machine Intelligence* 5 (Edinburgh University Press, Edinburgh, 1969). A digital facsimile of the report is available at <http://www.AlanTuring.net/intelligent_machinery>. See also B. J. Copeland and D. Proudfoot, 'Alan Turing's Forgotten Ideas in Computer Science', *Scientific American*, 280 (April 1999), 76.

Page 365 'very fed up': Robin Gandy's description of Turing in interview with Copeland, 1995.

Page 365 approved in July 1946: Council Minutes, Royal Society, 11 July 1946. Turing's salary was paid wholly from Newman's grant; letter from Newman to D. Brunt, 22 December 1948.

Page 365 It was one room in a Victorian building . . . : F. C. Williams, 'Early Computers at Manchester University', *The Radio and Electronic Engineer*, 45 (1975), 237.

Page 365 he designed: letter from Williams to Randell, printed in B. Randell,

'On Alan Turing and the Origins of Digital Computers', in Meltzer and Michie (eds), *Machine Intelligence*, 9.

Page 365 programming manual: 'Programmers' Handbook for Manchester Electronic Computer'.

Page 366 Artificial Life: A. M. Turing, 'The Chemical Basis of Morphogenesis', *Philosophical Transactions of the Royal Society of London*, series B, 237 (1952), 37.

Page 366 programming digital computers to think: A. M. Turing, 'Computing Machinery and Intelligence', *Mind*, 59 (1950), 433.

Page 366 perhaps given too little credit: Peter Hilton in interview with Copeland, 2001.

Page 366 '. . . Newman explained the whole business . . .': Williams in interview with Christopher Evans in 1976 ('The Pioneers of Computing'). See further B. J. Copeland (ed.), 'A Lecture and Two Radio Broadcasts on Machine Intelligence by Alan Turing', in K. Furukawa, D. Michie and S. Muggleton (eds), *Machine Intelligence 15* (OUP, Oxford, 1999).

Page 366 'number of different computing projects . . .': Turing, 'Report on visit to U.S.A., January 1st – 20th, 1947'.

Page 366 contract with the US Army Ordnance Department: Goldstine, op. cit., 150.

Page 367 consultant to the Eckert–Mauchly project: John Mauchly recalled that 7 September 1944 'was the first day that von Neumann had security clearance to see the ENIAC and talk with Eckert and me' (J. Mauchly, 'Amending the ENIAC Story', *Datamation*, 25(11) (1979), 217). Goldstine (op. cit., 185) suggests that the date of von Neumann's first visit may have been a month earlier: 'I probably took von Neumann for a first visit to the ENIAC on or about 7 August'.

Page 367 circulated bearing only: N. Stern, 'John von Neumann's Influence on Electronic Digital Computing, 1944–1946', *Annals of the History of Computing*, 2 (1980), 354.

Page 367 gave his engineers Turing's 'On Computable Numbers': private communication from Julian Bigelow to William Aspray, reported in W. Aspray, *John von Neumann and the Origins of Modern Computing* (MIT Press, Cambridge, Mass., 1990), 313.

Page 367 was working by the summer of 1951: J. Bigelow, 'Computer Development at the Institute for Advanced Study', in Metropolis, Howlett and Rota, op. cit.

Page 368 'the great positive contribution of Turing': letter from von Neumann to Wiener, 29 November 1946 (Library of Congress Manuscript Division,

Washington DC).

Page 368 'The importance of Turing's research is just this': the text of von Neumann's lecture 'Rigorous Theories of Control and Information' is printed in J. von Neumann, *Theory of Self-Reproducing Automata*, A.W. Burks (ed.) (University of Illinois Press, Urbana, 1966), 50.

Page 368 'I know that in or about 1943 or '44': letter from Frankel to Randell, 1972, printed in Randell, 'On Alan Turing and the Origins of Digital Computers', p. 10.

19 Enigma's Security: What the Germans Really Knew

Ralph Erskine would like to thank Philip Marks for his comments on aspects of Chapter 19.

Page 372 Army's Signal Security Agency exploited: 'Report on the Work Carried Out at S.S.A. on GEE' (NACP HCC Box 202, Nr. 970); Cecil Phillips, 'The American Solution of a German One-Time-Pad Cryptographic System', *Cryptologia*, 24 (2000), 324. Despite claims to the contrary by a former member of GC&CS, GEE was not solved by GC&CS.

Page 372 set out the *Grundstellungen*: *Der Schlüssel M Allgemeine Bestimmungen* (M. Dv. Nr. 32/3 – NHB), paras 23, 90.

Page 372 a second 'Greek' rotor (gamma): see p. 184.

Page 373 should replace Enigma by a codebook: 'German Naval Communications Intelligence' (NACP HCC Box 625, Nr. 1695), 256.

Page 373 carried out many inquiries: see R. A. Ratcliff, 'Searching for Security: The German Investigations into Enigma's Security', *Intelligence and National Security*, 14(1) (1999), 146.

Page 373 capture of *Schiff* 26: see p. 177.

Page 373 special *Stichwort*: 'Verlust Schiff 26 und 37 und Schlüsselsicherheit', 3 May 1940, OKM KTB 2/SKL (NHB, microfilm); on U-13, ibid., 11 June 1940.

Page 374 'Either our ciphers have been compromised': BdU, KTB, 28 September 1941 (NACP microfilm T1022, reel 4063) – translation from Ministry of Defence (Navy) [Günter Hessler], *The U-Boat War in the Atlantic* (HMSO, London, 1989), 1: 163.

Page 374 'The more important ciphers': Skl, Chef MND 2557/41, 24 October 1941, cited in ibid.

Page 374 BdU recorded that: BdU, KTB, 25 March 1943, as cited in Lt.-Cdr.

K. W. McMahan, 'The German Navy's Use of Special Intelligence and Reactions to Allied Use', 211.

Page 375 disturbing report: 'Entzifferung deutschen Marinecodes', OKM/A Ausl/Abw IM/T B.Nr. 1663/43, 18 August 1943; cf. 'Operative Geheimhaltung Allgemeines SKL Chef MND Ia 10-OKM' (NACP HCC Box 192, Nr. 908), 5; BdU, KTB, 13 August 1943 (copy held by author – this page was excised from the copy filmed for NACP T1022, reel 4063).

Page 375 '. . . out of the question': BdU, KTB, 13 August 1943.

Page 375 'At present no possible way . . .': 'Operative Geheimhaltung Allgemeines', 2.

Page 375 '. . . could *not* have taken place': ibid., 7.

Page 375 report on *Kriegsmarine* cipher security: 'Naval Cyphers and WT Procedures', 10 July 1944, 4/SKL, 2339/44 (PG 17626 – ADM 223/505).

Page 376 *Stichwort* procedure: this is set out in *Der Schlüssel M – Allgemeine Bestimmungen*, as amended, paras 100 ff., and described in Ralph Erskine, 'Ultra and Some U. S. Navy Carrier Operations', *Cryptologia*, 19 (1988), 93. The procedure was made much more complicated as the war progressed, but to no avail.

Page 376 protected captured key-lists: 'Operative Geheimhaltung Allgemeines', 2.

Page 377 'infallible confirmation': 'Naval Cyphers and WT Procedures', 5.

Page 377 'no trace or even hint . . .': ibid., 5–6.

Page 377 the contents of Allied signals: see e.g. ZTPGU 751 of 4 December 1942 (orders to RN submarine), ZTPGU 14736 of 27 May 1943 (destination of US Navy submarine).

Page 377 true HF-DF: signals 0142Z/10 April 1943 (true HF-DF) and 0959B/11 April 1943 (HF-DF as Ultra cover) (PRO ADM 199/575, 370).

Page 378 As Tranow observed: TICOM I-38 (Lt. Frowein), para. 33.

Page 379 made little real progress: 'German Naval Communications Intelligence', 259.

Page 379 also convinced: Wladyslaw Kozaczuk, *Geheim-Operation WICHER: Polnische Mathematiker Knackenden den deutschen Funkschlüssel 'Enigma'* (Bernard & Graefe, Koblenz, 1989), p. 340.

Page 379 MND's major report : 'Naval Cyphers and WT Procedures'.

Page 379 the dropping of double encipherment: see Appendix II.

Page 379 'change in the system': TICOM I-92 (Wachtmeister Otto Buggisch), cited in 'German Naval Communications Intelligence', 12.

Page 380 remained a dead letter: TICOM I-96 (Oberstlt Mettig), cited in 'German Naval Communications Intelligence', 255.

Page 380 'secure when used according to regulations': TICOM I-45 (OKW/Chi Cryptanalytic Research on Enigma, Hagelin and Cipher Teleprinter Machines – by Dr Erich Hüttenhain and Dr Fricke), 4.

Page 380 were well aware: Buggisch as quoted in 'European Axis Signal Intelligence in World War II as Revealed by "TICOM" Investigations', vol. 2 (EASI, 2), 12, 'Notes on German High Level Cryptography and Cryptanalysis'. My thanks to David Alvarez for supplying this document.

Page 380 'given extraordinary mechanical outlay . . .': 'Naval Cyphers and WT Procedures', 21; cf. TICOM I-45, 5; cf. EASI, 2: 10.

Page 380 catalogues of the enciphered letter 'e': TICOM I-45, 4.

Page 380 whether a practical solution: ibid., 5. A manuscript note on this file adds 'the army did according to [TICOM] DF 190'.

Page 380 rewired Enigma used by the Swiss: 'Analysis of the Cipher Machine "Enigma," Type K' (NACP HCC Box 1112, Nr. 3448), cited in David H. Hamer, Geoff Sullivan and Frode Weierud, 'Enigma Variations: An Extended Family of Machines', *Cryptologia*, 22 (1998), 222.

Page 380 re-enciphered at a different setting: TICOM I-92 (Wachtmeister Otto Buggisch), cited in EASI, 2: 9.

Page 380 to solve Railway Enigma traffic so successfully: see p. 72.

Page 380 cribs of only ten letters: TICOM I-77 (Dr Hüttenhain, Dr Fricke on *Zählwerk* (counter) Enigma).

Page 381 started to use a new reflector: Ultra/Zip CCR 38, 22 December 1944, 'German Signals Security Improvements During 1944', para. 1 (RIP 403, NACP RG 38, Radio Intelligence Publications, Box 169).

Page 381 beta rotor/thin reflector Bruno combination: see p. 181.

Page 381 *Umkehrwalze* D: for an outstanding study of UKD, see Philip Marks, 'Umkehrwalze D: Enigma's Rewirable Reflector, Part I', *Cryptologia*, 25 (2001), 101.

Page 381 3.2×10^{11} different possible wirings: ibid., 112. The letters J and Y could not be rewired.

Page 382 did not enter service until November: OP-20-GY-A-1 war diary, 4 and 13 November 1944 (NACP RG 38, Crane Library, 5750/159).

Page 382 'a pathetically meagre result': S. Milner-Barry, memorandum, 25 July 1944, 'Operation Dora', 2 (PRO HW 14/108).

Page 382 much less than anticipated: S. Milner-Barry, memorandum, 7 August 1944, 'Uncle D', in Fried Report #73 of 8 August 1944 (NACP HCC Box 880, Nr. 2612).

Page 383 The Autoscritcher: the Autoscritcher, Superscritcher and Duenna are fully described in Philip Marks, 'Umkehrwalze D: Enigma's Rewirable Reflector, Part II', *Cryptologia*, 25(2) (2001).

Page 383 four successful solutions: 'Signal Security Agency General Cryptanalytic Branch – Annual Report FY 1945', 20 (NACP HCC Box 1380, Nr. 4360).

Page 383 solved only eleven keys: 'Summary of Duenna Operations to June 1945', Exhibit 1, RIP 608, E6 – 147 (NACP RG 38, Radio Intelligence Publications, Box 171).

Page 383 without any warning: 'German Signals Security Improvements During 1944', 2, 6.

Page 383 *Uhr*: the *Uhr* is referred to, but not by name, in Gordon Welchman, *The Hut Six Story: Breaking the Enigma Codes* (McGraw Hill, New York, 1982; Allen Lane, London, 1982), pp. 136–7. It is fully described in Heinz Ulbricht, 'The Enigma Uhr', *Cryptologia*, 23 (1999), 193.

Page 384 embodying a rewirable reflector: TICOM I-53 (Construction of 'Schlüsselgerät 39'); EASI, 2: 16.

Page 384 Allies could not have broken: EASI, 2: 14.

Page 384 Plans were made in December: minutes of conferences held by OKW/Chi on 13 December 1943, as quoted in EASI, 2: 14.

Page 384 SG 41: for a description, see TICOM I-72 (Buggisch on SG 41).

Page 384 A post-war United States Army study concluded: EASI, 2: 13.

20 From Amateurs to Professionals: GC&CS and Institution-Building in Sigint

Page 388 displayed a greater flair: Alan Judd, *The Quest for C: Mansfield Cumming and the Founding of the Secret Service* (HarperCollins, London, 1999).

Page 389 intelligence . . . a departmental concern: Philip H. J. Davies, 'Organisational Politics and Britain's Intelligence Producer/Consumer Interface', *Intelligence and National Security*, 10(4) (1985), 114; Philip H. J. Davies, 'MI6's Requirements Directorate: Integrating Intelligence into the Machinery of British Central Government', *Public Administration* 78(1) (2000), 29.

Page 389 '50 per cent . . . drawn from overt published sources': Reginald Hibbert, 'Intelligence and Policy', *Intelligence and National Security* 5(1) (1990), 112.

Page 389 Hence, during the Napoleonic Wars: on military intelligence in the Peninsular Wars, see for example, Jock Hasswell, *The First Respectable Spy: The Life and Times of Colquhoun Grant, Wellington's Head of Intelligence* (Hamish Hamilton, London, 1969) and Julia Page's *Intelligence Officer in the Peninsula: the Letters and Diaries of Major the Hon. Edward Charles Coles 1786–1812* (Hippocrene, New York, 1986).

Page 389 Just as the Indian government . . . the Great Game: see, for example, Peter Hopkirk, *The Great Game* (John Murray, London, 1990).

Page 389 Secret Department of the Post Office: on the Post Office see, variously, P. Aubrey, *Mr. Secretary Thurloe* (Athlone, London, 1990), K. Ellis, *The Post Office in the Eighteenth Century* (OUP, Oxford, 1958).

Page 389 the Boer war: for the Boer War influence on pre-war thinking in MI6 and MI5's predecessor MO 5, see 'Secret Service in the Event of a European War', cover letter dated 17 October 1905 (PRO HD 3/124).

Page 389 Admiralty and War Office before the Haldane Committee: 'Report and Proceedings of the Sub-Committee of the Committee of Imperial Defence Appointed by the Prime Minister to Consider the Question of Foreign Espionage in the United Kingdom' (PRO CAB 61/8).

Page 389 MacDonough Scheme: Judd, *The Quest for C*, pp. 391–3.

Page 390 'independent sections . . . known as the SIS': Vivian to Menzies, appendix to Robert Cecil, 'C's War', *Intelligence and National Security*, 1(2) (1986), 186.

Page 391 led to a postwar scheme: H. A. R. 'Kim' Philby, *My Silent War* (Ballantine, New York, 1983), p. 124; Davies, 'MI6 Requirements Directorate'.

Page 391 interwar and early wartime years: F. H. Hinsley and C. A. G. Simkins, *British Intelligence in the Second World War, Volume Four: Security and Counter-Espionage* (HMSO, London, 1990).

Page 391 excessively rigid bureaucracy: see, for example, criticisms of the Security Service in the Security Commission Report on the Michael Bettaney Case, *Report of the Security Commission* (HMSO, London, 1985), Cmd. 9514.

Page 392 rivalry and hostility existed: Andrew, *Secret Service*, p. 141.

Page 392 Foreign Office and SIS control of GC&CS: ibid., p. 421.

Page 392 six senior assistants . . .: ibid., pp. 374–5.

Page 392 'technical success and organizational confusion': John Ferris, 'Whitehall's Black Chamber: British Cryptology and the Government Code and Cypher School 1919–1929', *Intelligence and National Security*, 2(1) (1987), 54.

Page 393 service branch complaints: Andrew, *Secret Service*, p. 421.

Page 393 naval, air and army sections formed: F. H. Hinsley et al., *British Intelligence in the Second World War: Its Impact on Strategy and Operations* (London, HMSO, 1979), 1: 22.

Page 393 commercial section was set up: ibid., p. 26; A. G. Denniston, 'The Government Code and Cypher School Between the Wars', *Intelligence and National Security*, 1(1) (1986), 63; 'ATB and (EPG) 13 and 14, Item 2(b) Organization of an Intelligence Service, Interim Report' with cover noted from Morton to Jones, 31 March 1938, FCI 968 (PRO BT 61/69/2).

Page 393 GPO-manned system of stations: Hinsley et al., *British Intelligence*, 1: 26; Denniston, 'The Government Code and Cypher School Between the Wars', 68.

Page 393 meteorological section: Hinsley et al., *British Intelligence*, 1: 339.

Page 393 MI6 circulating sections which tasked: Denniston, 'The Government Code and Cypher School Between the Wars', 57.

Page 394 acute lack of receivers: Hinsley et al., *British Intelligence*, 1: 51.

Page 394 moved mainly to landlines: ibid., p. 52.

Page 394 increasingly crowded circumstances: ibid., p. 270.

Page 394 demanded an investigation: ibid., pp. 270–1.

Page 394 the reconvened Y Board and its conclusions: ibid., p. 271.

Page 395 traffic analysis proved a very valuable auxiliary method: see, for example, Gordon Welchman, *The Hut Six Story* (Allen Lane, London, 1982).

Page 395 Y Board, the Y and cryptanalysis sub-committees: Hinsley et al., *British Intelligence*, 1: 271.

Page 395 cryptanalysis sub-committee petered out, ADI based at the OIC: ibid., p. 272.

Page 396 GC&CS quadrupled: ibid., p. 273.

Page 396 GC&CS staff numbers in 1941, 1942: F. H. Hinsley et al., *British Intelligence in the Second World War* (HMSO, London, 1981), 2: 25.

Page 396 exotic assortment of civilians, 'loose collection of groups', senior staff still performed: Hinsley et al., *British Intelligence*, 1: 273.

Page 397 'undisciplined' wartime staff: ibid., p. 274.

Page 397 appeal directly to Churchill: Hinsley et al., *British Intelligence*, 2: 25; the letter is set out at pp. ix–xii in the present book; for a personal account of the events, see also S. Milner-Barry, 'Action This Day: the Letter from Bletchley Park Cryptanalysts to the Prime Minister, 21 October 1941', *Intelligence and National Security*, 1(1) (1986), 272.

Page 397 Double Cross, volume of work and MI5's managerial crisis: see in particular Hinsley and Simkins, *British Intelligence in the Second World War*, vol. 4, John Masterman, *The Double-Cross System in the War of 1939 to 1945* (Yale University Press, London, 1972) and Nigel West, *MI5: British Security Service Operations 1909–1945* (Granada, London, 1983).

Page 399 'total operational control'; fell to quarrelling: Hinsley et al., *British Intelligence*, 2: 26.

Page 399 GC&CS subdivided and civil side moved: ibid.; for a personal account, see P. William Filby, 'Bletchley Park and Berkeley Street', *Intelligence and National Security*, 3(2) (1988), 272–4.

Page 400 subsequently received replacements, etc.: Hinsley et al., *British Intelligence*, 2: 26–7, Hinsley et al., *British Intelligence in the Second World War* (London, HMSO, 1984), 3(1): 460.

Page 400 redesignated himself Director General, etc.: ibid., p. 461.

Page 401 the Cold War GCHQ: for GCHQ's Cold War internal management structure, see Duncan Campbell, Friends and Others, *New Statesman and Society*, 26 November 1982, 6; Michael Smith, *New Cloak, Old Dagger* (Gollancz, London, 1996), pp. 185–7.

Page 401 JIC in the Cabinet Office: For the current version of the JIC's role in Britain's National Intelligence Machinery, see the Open Government webpage on Central Intelligence Machinery, downloadable at http://www.official-documents.co.uk/document/caboff/nim/nat-02.htm (10 July 2001).

21 Cold War Codebreaking and Beyond: The Legacy of Bletchley Park

Page 404 As early as 1943: R. Aldrich and M. Coleman, 'The Cold War, the JIC and British Signals Intelligence, 1948', *Intelligence and National Security*, 4(3) (1989), 538–40; F. H. Hinsley et al., *British Intelligence in the Second World War* (HMSO, London, 1980), 2: 618–19.

Page 405 The team returned: P. Whitaker and L. Kruh, 'From Bletchley Park to the Berchtesgaden', *Cryptologia*, 11 (1987), 129: M. Smith, *Station X: The Codebreakers of Bletchley Park* (Channel 4 Books, London, 1998), pp. 174–6.

Page 405 GCHQ relocated: R. Lewin, *Ultra goes to War* (Hutchinson, London, 1978), pp. 129–33; R. V. Jones, *Reflections on Intelligence* (Heinemann, London, 1989), p. 15.

Page 406 'From his remarks': Wilson to Crombie, with attached memo, 'Sigint Centre – Conditions of Service', 13 November 1945 (FO 366/1518 PRO); Travis to Crombie with attached memo, 'Sigint Centre', n.d. [30 November 1945?] (ibid.); Travis to Crombie, 19 December 1945 (ibid.).

Page 407 Moscow and its satellites: JIC (48) (0) (second revised draft), 'Sigint intelligence requirements' 1948, 11 May 1948 (L/WS/1196, IOLR).

Page 408 Several tunnels: C. Andrew and O. Gordievsky, *KGB: The Inside Story* (Hodder & Stoughton, London, 1990), pp. 308–9. I am also grateful to Matthew Aid and David Stafford for their views on this matter.

Page 408 During the Azerbaijan crisis: A. Stripp, *Codebreaker in the Far East* (Frank Cass, London, 1988), pp. 50–60; Jones, *Reflections*, pp. 14–16.

Page 408 Each of the three services: A. Thomas, 'British Signals Intelligence after the Second World War', *Intelligence and National Security*, 3(4) (1988), 103–4.

Page 408 GCHQ had overseas stations: Thomas, 'British Signals Intelligence', 106, J. Sawatsky, *For Services Rendered* (Penguin, London, 1983), pp. 23–4.

Page 409 But the main British Sigint centre: D. Ball, 'Over and Out: Signals Intelligence (sigint) in Hong Kong', *Intelligence and National Security*, 11(3) (1996), 32; Thomas, 'British Signals Intelligence', 107; Sawatsky, *For Services Rendered*, pp. 25–6.

Page 409 'very sensitive' areas: Eubank (COS) to Rowlands (MoS), 31 January 1952, DEFE 11/350 PRO; Eubank to DRPC, 31 January 1952, ibid.

Page 409 GCHQ was moving: COS (52) 152nd mtg. (1) Confidential Annex, 4 November 1952 (DEFE 11/350 PRO).

Page 409 In the autumn of 1945: C. Andrew, *For the President's Eyes Only: American Presidents and Intelligence From Washington to Bush* (HarperCollins, London, 1995), pp. 150–6.

Page 410 During the winter of 1946–7: C. Andrew, 'The Growth of the Australian Intelligence Community and the Anglo-American Connection', *Intelligence and National Security*, 4(2) (1989), 223–5; J. Bamford, *The Puzzle Palace: America's National Security Agency and Its Special Relationship with GCHQ* (Sidgwick & Jackson, London, 1983), pp. 314–17; J. Richelson and D. Ball, *The Ties that Bind: Intelligence Co-operation between the UKUSA Countries* (Allen & Unwin, Boston, 1985), pp. 141–5.

Page 410 'No Room for Canadians': W. Wark, 'Cryptographic Innocence: The Origins of Signals Intelligence in Canada in the Second World War', *Journal of Contemporary History*, 22 (1997), 639; Sawatsky, *For Services Rendered*, p. 29. I am much indebted to the guidance of Matthew Aid on these matters.

Page 411 In the late 1940s: M. Aid, 'US Humint and Comint in the Korean War: From the Approach of War to the Chinese Intervention', *Intelligence and National Security*, 14(4) (1999), 15.

Page 411 For example: O. Riste, *The Norwegian Intelligence Service, 1945–70* (Frank Cass, London, 1999), pp. 95–7; R. Tamnes, *The US and the Cold War in the High North* (Dartmouth, Aldershot, 1991), pp. 76–7.

Page 412 But Truman's mind: Samford (D of I USAF) to Twining, 6 August 1952 (224400, Box 66, USAF D of I records, RG 341, NACP).

Page 412 The efforts of the NSA: Brief on Fifth Report to the President by

PBCFIA (Recommendation concerning Fusion of Comint-Elint Activities), 11 March 1960, File: 1960 Meetings with the President Vol. 1 (5), Box 4, Presidential Subseries, Special Assistant Series, OSANA, WHO, Dwight D. Eisenhower Library, Abilene, Kansas.

Page 412 Elint was first: R. V. Jones, *Most Secret War* (Hamish Hamilton, London, 1978), p. 92.

Page 412 Towards the end: SEAC Noise Investigation Bureau report for May 1945 (WO 203/4089 PRO).

Page 412 Initially: McMurtie (JSM), to Moore (Pentagon), 20 November 1948 (File 2-8300 – 2-8399, USAF D of I records, RG 341, NACP).

Page 413 In 1948 they began: Partridge Memorandum, 'Northern European Ferret Flights', 20 August 1947 (File 2-800 – 2-899, USAF D of I records, RG 341, NACP).

Page 413 A British undercover team: I am indebted to Matthew Aid's forthcoming study of US Sigint for this point.

Page 413 Most of the airfields: AFOIN-T to D of I USAF, 16 April 1952 (223200, Box 64, USAF D of I records, RG 341, USAF).

Page 414 His headless body: R. R. James, *Anthony Eden* (Weidenfeld & Nicolson, London, 1986), pp. 436–7.

Page 414 Eden intended: Eden to Bridges, M.104.56, 9 May 1956 (AP20/32/78, Avon Papers, Birmingham University Library (BUL)).

Page 415 Eden gave this job: Prime Minister, Anthony Eden, to Minister of Defence, Antony Head, 22 December 1956 (AP20/21/228, Avon Papers, BUL).

Page 415 In April 1956: R. M. Bissell, Jr., *Reflections of a Cold Warrior: From Yalta to the Bay of Pigs* (Yale University Press, New Haven, 1996), pp. 115–16.

Page 415 'a bigger and better': Elkins (BJSM) to Mountbatten, 16 October 1956 (ADM 205/110 PRO).

Page 416 But the question: Inglis (DNI) to Flag Officer, Submarines, 19 October 1956, ibid.; Coote, USS Stickleback report, ibid.

Page 416 But he also warned: Elkins (BJSM) to Mountbatten, 31 December 1956, ibid.

Page 417 Serious airborne Sigint: M. Mikesh, *Canberra, B-57* (Ian Allan, Sheparton, 1980), pp. 124–9; G. Pedlow and D. Welzenbach, *The CIA and the U-2 Program, 1954–74* (CIA, Washington, 1998), pp. 49–51; Tamnes, *High North*, pp. 128–9; C. Pocock, *The U-2 Spyplane: Toward the Unknown* (Schiffer, Atglen, PA, 2000), pp. 16, 42, 50.

Page 417 The aircraft crew: S. Ambrose, *Eisenhower the President, Vol. 2, 1952–59* (Allen & Unwin, London, 1984), p. 584.

Page 417 The twin shoot-downs: The JIC paper was JIC (60) 43 (Final), 'Soviet Threats Against Reconnaissance Flight Bases Following the U-2 Incident', and is summarized in DEFE 13/342 PRO.

Page 418 The impact of these: Minutes, 'Surveillance Meeting', 26 April 1960, 16/W/160 (ADM 1/27680 PRO).

Page 418 By March 1961: minute by Head of Military Branch II, 10 March 1961, ibid.

Page 418 Macmillan now required: memorandum from PS to V.C.A.S. to PS to S. of S., 'Aircraft Approach Restrictions – Operation TIARA/GARNET', October 1960 (AIR 20/12222 PRO). The JIC paper prepared for Macmillan was JIC (60) 62 (Revised), 1 September 1960.

Page 419 Somewhat safer: on continuing British submarine intelligence operations in the 1960s see Riste, *Norwegian Intelligence Service*, p. 228.

Page 419 Both the NSA: http://users.ox.ac.uk/-daveh/Space/Military/milspace_sigint.html, accessed 21 June 2001.

Page 420 Nimrod maritime patrol aircraft: JCG/S/24, Operational Requirements Committee, 19 July 1967 (AIR 20/11747 PRO).

Page 421 'and a failure would threaten: DCDS (I) Maguire memo, 'Elint Collection in NATO', 27 November 1967 (ibid.); DASB Brief for mtg. with CDS, 22 November 1967 (ibid.).

Page 421 The cost of the Nimrod: Aiken (AC(I)) memo, 'Replacement Aircraft – No 51 Squadron', 1 August 1967 (AIR 20/12072 PRO).

Page 422 Current proposals: Sinclair to Strang, enclosing LSIB (53) 3 (Final), 'Policy for the Higher Direction of the Radio war', 6 October 1953 (CAB 125/193 PRO).

Page 422 Instead, the 1950s and 1960s: Evidence for the Department of Forward Plans, 21 August 1954 (CAB 125/175 PRO); Neale, for head of GCHQ Radio Division to Sec. Cabinet Communications Electronics and Space Committee, 31 December 1965 (CAB 21/5395 PRO).

Page 422 There were inevitable tussles: comments of Clive Loehnis at JIC (58) 8th mtg. (7), 23 January 1958 (CAB 159/29 PRO); also JIC (58) 55th mtg. (6) 14 August 1958 (CAB 159/30 PRO).

Page 423 By the late 1950s: Aldrich, *Espionage, Security and Intelligence*, pp. 147–9. See also Radford (JCS) memorandum, 'Clandestine Listening Devices', 6 April 1956, file: Presidential papers 1956 (8), Box 3, Presidential subseries, Special Assistant Series, OSANA, WHO, Dwight D. Eisenhower Memorial Library.

Page 423 This hermetic separation: private information.

Page 424 Around the main buildings: R. D. Cole, 'GCHQ: A Doughnut on the

Landscape', *Eye Spy*, 1 (2001), 89–91.

Page 424 Moscow maintained: D. Ball, *The Use of the Soviet Embassy in Canberra for Signals Intelligence (Sigint) Collection* (ANU Strategic and Defence Studies Centre Working Paper No. 134, Canberra, 1987), p. 1.

Page 424 This is a long: http://www.fas.org/irp.agency/navsecgru/digby/, accessed 26 June 2001.

Page 425 These developments: http://users.ox.ac.uk/-daveh/Space/Military/milspace_sigint.html, accessed 21 June 2001; Mark Urban, *UK Eyes Alpha* (Faber and Faber, London, 1996), pp. 56–69.

Page 425 The Iraqi attack: Loehnis comments at JIC (65) 3rd mtg. (9), 21 January 1965 (CAB 159/31 PRO). On the wider issues see R. Mobley, 'Deterring Iraq: the UK Experience', *Intelligence and National Security* 16(2) (2001).

Page 425 During the Gulf War: Andrew, *For the President's Eyes Only*, pp. 518–20; http://www.fas.org/spp/military/docops/operate/ds/signals.htm, accessed 23 June 2001.

Page 427 To present: private information.

Page 427 There is no doubt: R. Reeves, 'E-squad launched to crack criminal codes on the net', *Guardian*, 5 September 1999; N. Rufford, 'Blair's Spy Summit on Red Mafia', *Sunday Times*, 5 December 1999; P. Soomer, 'Protection or persuasion?', *Guardian*, 30 March 2000.

Page 428 It now appears: S. Singh, *The Code Book* (Fourth Estate, London, 1999), pp. 286–9; D. Campbell, 'Great Idea – Hide It', *Guardian*, 6 May 1999.

Page 428 The advent: J. Werran, 'CESG Securing the GSI', http://sourceuk.net/articles/a00445.html, accessed 20 June 2001.

Page 429 The future shape: R. D. Cole, 'GCHQ: A Doughnut on the Landscape', *Eye Spy*, 1 (2001), 91–2; R. Norton-Taylor, 'GCHQ to get new headquarters for £800m', *Guardian*, 7 March 2000: M. Evans, 'Spies pack their tea-chests for £300m move', *The Times*, 7 March 2000; M. Evans, 'Spy HQ bill overshoots by £227m', *The Times*, 26 November 1999.

Page 430 France deploys: Duncan Campbell, 'I Spy an Ally', *Guardian*, 15 March 2000.

22 Bletchley Park in Post-War Perspective

Page 431 Telford Taylor on Sigint co-operation with Bletchley Park: Telford Taylor, 'Anglo-American signals intelligence co-operation', in F. H. Hinsley and Alan Stripp (eds), *Codebreakers: The Inside Story of Bletchley Park* (OUP, Oxford, 1993).

Page 431 Taylor on US inter-service Sigint rivalry: 'Operations of the Military Intelligence Service War Department London' (MIS WD London), 11 June 1945, Tab A, 38 (RG 218, NACP). On the background to US inter-service rivalry, see my Chapter 1 above, 'Bletchley Park in Pre-War Perspective'.

Page 431 Korean War and origins of NSA: Christopher Andrew, *For the President's Eyes Only: Secret Intelligence and the American Presidency from Washington to Bush* (HarperCollins, London/New York, 1995), pp. 185–7, 196–7.

Page 432 'Round the World Tour by Sir Edward Travis and Rear-Admiral Rushbrooke and Staffs [Commander Loehnis, RN and F. H. Hinsley Esq], 14 March–27 April 1945', map showing the detailed route taken by each with dates: copy given by Sir Harry Hinsley to Christopher Andrew, published as endpaper in Hayden B. Peake and Samuel Halpern (eds), *In The Name of Intelligence: Essays in Honor of Walter Pforzheimer* (NIBC Press, Washington, DC, 1994). While Travis, Loehnis and Hinsley went to Washington near the end of their tour, Rushbrooke went to Canada. Despite the date on the title of the map, the detail on it shows that the British delegation did not leave North America until May.

Page 432 Truman and Sigint: Andrew, *For the President's Eyes Only*, pp. 150–6, 161–3. Truman Sigint memo: Truman, Memorandum for the Secretaries of State, War and the Navy, 12 September 1945 (Naval Aide Files, box 10, file 1, Harry S. Truman Library, Independence, Missouri). Bradley J. Smith, *The Ultra-Magic Deals* (Presidio, Novato, California, 1993), p. 212.

Page 432 Origins of UKUSA agreement: Christopher Andrew, 'The Making of the Anglo-American Sigint Alliance, 1940–1948', in James E. Dillard and Walter T. Hitchcock (eds), *The Intelligence Revolution and Modern Warfare* (Imprint Publications, Chicago, 1996).

Page 433 Eisenhower, Sigint and the Special Relationship: Andrew, *For the President's Eyes Only*, pp. 199–200, 216–17.

Page 434 The Venona decrypts, together with some explanatory material, are accessible on the NSA website: http://www.nsa.gov:8080/. Robert Louis Benson and Michael Warner (eds), *VENONA: Soviet Espionage and the American Response, 1939–1957* (National Security Agency/Central Intelligence Agency, Washington, DC, 1996) provide a valuable introduction to, and a selection of, the decrypts.

Page 434 Venona and Soviet espionage: Christopher Andrew and Vasili Mitrokhin, *The Mitrokhin Archive: The KGB in Europe and the West* (Penguin, London, 1999), chaps 7–9. Allen Weinstein and Alexander Vassiliev, *The Haunted Wood: Soviet Espionage in America – The Stalin Era* (Random House, New York, 1999).

Page 435 US–UK co-operation on Venona: Benson and Warner (eds), *VENONA*, p. xxii, n45. GCHQ has released no details of British participation in Venona. Internal evidence in the decrypts, such as British rather than American spelling and a distinct British numbering system, shows, however, that a minority of the Soviet telegrams were decrypted by GCHQ cryptanalysts.

Page 435 Gardner and British intelligence: information to Christopher Andrew from Meredith Gardner and interview with Gardner broadcast in BBC radio documentary, *VENONA*, written and presented by Christopher Andrew (producers: Mark Burman and Helen Weinstein), first broadcast on Radio 4 on 18 March 1998. Gardner later became NSA liaison officer with GCHQ in Cheltenham.

Page 435 Keeping the Venona secret from the CIA: Christopher Andrew, 'The VENONA Secret', in K. G. Robertson (ed.), *War, Resistance and Intelligence: Essays in Honour of M. R. D. Foot* (Macmillan, London, 1999).

Page 437 Weisband and Philby: Benson and Warner (eds), *VENONA*, pp. xxvii–xxviii, 167–70. Andrew, 'The VENONA Secret'. KGB files show that Weisband had been recruited as a Soviet agent in 1934; Weinstein and Vassiliev, *The Haunted Wood*, p. 291.

Page 437 Case for perpetual secrecy of Ultra and fears that historians might discover it: COS (45), confidential annexe, 31 July 1945 (PRO CAB 76/36); Special Order by Sir Edward Travis (Director GCHQ), 7 May 1945 (PRO FO 371/39171): both cited by Richard J. Aldrich, *The Hidden Hand: Britain, America and Cold War Secret Intelligence* (John Murray, London, 2001), pp. 1–3.

Page 438 no historian of the Second World War: The significance of Sigint was made clear by David Kahn's pioneering *Codebreakers*, published in 1967. Although a bestseller, however, its contents appeared to stun, rather than to inspire, most historians of international relations.

Page 438 whether there was a Russian Ultra: Geoff Jukes, 'The Soviets and "Ultra"', *Intelligence and National Security*, 3(2) (1988), 323. Though Jukes's conclusions are debatable, his article remains a path-breaking study. Cf. Andrew and Mitrokhin, *The Mitrokhin Archive*, pp. 125–7, 135–6.

Page 438 Bush and Sigint: Andrew, *For The President's Eyes Only*, p. 5 and chap. 13.

Page 439 Eisenhower and Sigint: Andrew, *For The President's Eyes Only*, chap. 6.

Page 439 Soviet Sigint successes: Andrew and Mitrokhin, *The Mitrokhin Archive*.

Page 440 vast research agenda: for examples of current research on Sigint history, see Matthew M. Aid and Cees Wiebes (eds), *Secrets of Signals Intelligence during the Cold War and Beyond* (Frank Cass, London, 2001); also published as special issue of *Intelligence and National Security*, Spring/Summer 2001. A number of research students at Cambridge University are currently writing dissertations which deal with various aspects of twentieth-century Sigint.

Appendix II: *Wehrmacht* Enigma Indicating Systems, except the *Kriegsmarine's Kenngruppenbuch* System

Page 444 *Heer* and *Luftwaffe* indicating system from 1 May 1940: *Schlüsselanleitung zür Chiffriermaschine Enigma* (H. Dv. g. 14) of 13 January 1940, as amended.

Page 444 typed them once only: ibid., para. 11; Gilbert Bloch and Ralph Erskine, 'Enigma: The Dropping of the Double Encipherment', *Cryptologia*, 10 (1986), 134.

Page 445 *Heer* and *Luftwaffe* indicating system from 15 September 1938: *Schlüsselanleitung zür Chiffriermaschine Enigma* (H. Dv. g. 14) of 8 June 1937, as amended.

Page 447 *Heer* and *Luftwaffe* indicating system before 15 September 1938: *Schlüsselanleitung zür Chiffriermaschine Enigma* (H. Dv. g. 14) of 8 June 1937.

Page 447 naval indicating system used before 1 May 1937: 'Mathematical theory of ENIGMA machine by A. M. Turing', 129 (PRO HW 25/3).

Page 447 may have been chosen from a list: ibid.

Page 447 the *Kriegsmarine* employed the pre-1 May 1937 system: on the throw-on indicating system for *Süd* and its sub-systems, see *Kenngruppenverfahren Süd Januar 1944* (M. Dv. Nr. 608) (PRO ADM 223/331).

Appendix III: The Naval Enigma *Kenngruppenbuch* Indicator System

Page 449 the *Kenngruppenbuch* (recognition group book) system: *Der Schlüssel M Verfahren M Allgemein* (M. Dv. Nr. 32/1 – August 1940 edition), paras 46–76; *Kenngruppenbuch* (M. Dv. Nr. 98).

Page 451 'it takes a considerable time': SR 323, 6 January 1943 (PRO WO 208/4201).

Appendix IV: Cillies

Page 453 Cillies: for a full discussion of cillies, see 'Cryptanalytic Report on the Yellow Machine', 71–4 (NACP HCC Box 1009, Nr. 3175). Some of the examples in this Appendix are based on that Report. Gordon Welchman later acknowledged that his account of the cillies (called 'Sillies' by him) in *The Hut Six Story: Breaking the Enigma Codes* (Allen Lane, London, 1982), pp. 99–101, was wrong: Gordon Welchman, 'From Polish Bomba to British Bombe: the Birth of Ultra', *Intelligence and National Security*, 1(1) (1986), 71.

Page 455 test the first message part for a cilli: readers who would like to test these examples may download excellent *Wehrmacht* Enigma simulators (which have been fully tested against real versions) from any of the following three sites in zipped (compressed) form:
http://frode.home.cern.ch/frode/crypto/
http://www.eclipse.net/~dhamer/download.htm
http://www.blueangel.demon.co.uk/crypto

Page 456 fully random lists: 'Changes in encyphering with machine keys', 27 August 1944 (PRO HW 25/13 Nr. 9879/44).

Glossary and Abbreviations

Abwehr the *Wehrmacht*'s intelligence service.
additive a series of random numbers (occasionally letters) added to a code to encipher it.
angoo-ki taipu a *see* Red (Japanese).
angoo-ki taipu b *see* Purple.
ATS (Women's) Auxiliary Territorial Service; also applied to members of that Service.
Banburismus a Bayesian probability process using specially prepared punched sheets to identify the right-hand and middle rotors in the Enigma M3 machine by relating distances in message keys.
basic setting *see Grundstellung.*
B-Dienst (*Beobachtungsdienst* – observation service). Cover name for the *Kriegsmarine*'s codebreaking section.
bigram tables (naval Enigma) sets of tables which substituted pairs of letters (e.g. AA=DF, AB=UA, and so on); used to encode the indicator groups in the *Kenngruppenbuch* indicating system for naval Enigma.
BJ (blue jacket) decrypt being circulated to a government department (derived from the distinctive blue file cover).
blist Bannister list – a register of Enigma messages, listing important components such as call signs, length of messages etc. (see example in Appendix IV). Designed to help the detection of cillies and the identification of messages with cribs.

bombe ultra-fast machine for recovering Enigma daily keys by testing a crib and its implications, at all possible rotor orders and initial settings.
BP Bletchley Park.
BRUSA British United States Agreement of May 1943, between the United States War Department and GC&CS on attacking the military codes and ciphers of the Axis powers.
'C' the head of the British Secret Intelligence Service.
CCAC Churchill College Archives, Cambridge.
cilli a German mistake, found by Dilly Knox, in using the rotor finishing positions in one part of a multi-part Enigma message as the *Grund* of the next part. Derived from CIL, the *Grund* of the message in which the mistake was first discovered.
cipher a cryptographic system in which letters or numbers represent plain-text units (generally single letters) in accordance with agreed rules.
cipher indicator group (naval) group indicating the cipher net for message (and therefore the key-lists to look up when enciphering or deciphering it).
cipher text text produced by a cipher.
closure the linking of the same letter in a chain in an Enigma menu (e.g., ACHIA) that returns to its starting point.
code a cryptographic system, generally set out in a codebook, in which groups of letters or numbers represent plain-text units of varying lengths.
counter Enigma (German *Zählwerk*) the *Abwehr* three-rotor Enigma machine using rotors with 11, 15 and 17 notches, but without a plugboard.
crib probable plain-text, which for Enigma was generally derived from a re-enciphered message (whether using Enigma or a manual cipher) or standard message (e.g., 'nothing to report').
CSS Chief, Secret Service ('C').
depth the correct alignment of ciphered text that has been enciphered by the same length of key.
DF direction finding – locating the position of a transmission by plotting two or more bearing lines.
diagonal board a circuit in the bombes that eliminated a considerable number of superfluous stops. By enabling the effective use of menus that did not consist entirely of closures, it greatly increased the power and flexibility of the bombes.
discriminant (German *Kenngruppe*) a group showing the cipher system being used.
doubly encipher to encipher something (e.g. text or a message key) twice (cf. *Offizier*).

dud a ciphered message which cannot be deciphered because of a faulty message setting or discriminant.
Duenna a US Navy machine which used long cribs to find the wiring of the rewirable Enigma reflector, UKD.
enciphered code code enciphered by a cipher system (generally a series of random figures known as an additive). The 'additive' figures are lined up under the encoded message, and added to the code digits using non-carrying arithmetic (5 plus 7 producing 2 rather than 12) to produce the enciphered message.
false stop a position at which a bombe stopped, but giving an impossible result for the *Stecker* (e.g., B steckered to X, but also to Y).
FECB Far East Combined Bureau. British intelligence organization, covering all fields of intelligence including special intelligence – interception, breaking and analysis of foreign encoded radio messages. Based in Hong Kong from 1934 and in Singapore from September 1939 until January 1942.
female (Enigma) a letter in the second group of a doubly enciphered Enigma message key, which repeats a letter in the corresponding position in the first group (e.g. AFO CFK).
Fish GC&CS cover name for traffic enciphered on the Sturgeon or Tunny teleprinter cipher machines.
FRUMEL Fleet Radio Unit (Melbourne). US Navy wartime intercept and codebreaking organization based in Melbourne, Australia.
FRUPAC Fleet Radio Unit (Pacific). US Navy intercept and codebreaking organization in Hawaii.
garble a distorted part of a message.
GC&CS the Government Code and Cypher School.
Green (later renamed Greenshank) an intractable Enigma cipher.
Grund short for *Grundstellung* (q.v.).
Grundstellung (Enigma) the basic initial position of the rotors at which the message key is enciphered or deciphered.
HCC RG 457, Historic Cryptographic Collection, Pre-World War I Through World War II (NACP).
Heer the German Army.
Herivel tip a method used to deduce the daily *Ringstellungen*, especially in *Luftwaffe* Enigma ciphers, from a series of *Grundstellungen* at the start of a cipher period. Named after John Herivel, who first realized that some operators would use the ring settings as *Grundstellungen* in this way.
Herivelismus the application of the Herivel tip.
Hut 3 the GC&CS section responsible for translating, analysing Enigma

decrypts received from Hut 6, together with related intelligence, and distributing the resulting intelligence.

Hut 4 the GC&CS section responsible for translating, analysing Enigma decrypts received from Hut 8, and for all naval cryptanalysis, except Enigma, and for sending the translated Enigma and other naval decrypts to the Admiralty.

Hut 6 the GC&CS section responsible for solving *Heer*, *Luftwaffe* and Railway Enigma ciphers.

Hut 8 the GC&CS section responsible for solving *Kriegsmarine* Enigma ciphers.

indicator a group of letters or symbols showing the cipher system being used.

indicator groups (naval Enigma) two groups setting out the cipher recognition group and procedure indicator group (from which the message key was derived).

IOLR India Office Library and Records.

ISK Illicit Services, Knox (also Intelligence Services, Knox).

ISOS Illicit Services, Oliver Strachey (also Intelligence Services, Oliver Strachey).

Jeffreys sheets a catalogue of the effect of any two rotors and the reflector in Enigma. Not to be confused with Zygalski sheets (q.v.).

JIC Joint Intelligence Committee.

JN Japanese naval. Used with a number to denote a Japanese naval code or cipher, such as JN-25 (the principal naval code).

JNA Japanese naval attaché.

JN-25 the principal Japanese Navy general operational code, a super-enciphered code introduced in June 1939 and used in numerous versions throughout the war. The JN-25 code and cipher additive books were allocated different letters and numbers by the Allies, as in JN-25B7, where 'B' denoted the 'Baker' codebook being used, and the final figure ('7' here), the relevant additive book.

kana Japanese syllable depicting a phonetic sound.

kanji the familiar Japanese ideographs on which the written language is based.

Kenngruppenbuch (naval Enigma) recognition group book; a book containing trigrams, used with the main naval Enigma indicating system (see Appendix III).

key a) as respects Enigma, an Enigma cipher, such as Red, Phoenix, etc.; b) as respects Enigma, the machine set-up for a day or period, consisting of the *Walzenlage*, *Ringstellungen* and *Stecker* (also the *Grundstellung* for *Kriegsmarine* Enigma ciphers); c) generally, a series of numbers or symbols used to encipher text.

key-list a list of keys, generally daily, for a cipher.

KGB *Komitet Gosudarstvennoi Bezopasnosti*, or Committee for State Security, the commonly understood title for the Russian state secret services.

These had a variety of different titles throughout the period covered. The title KGB was not introduced until March 1954 and was abolished in October 1991, but for ease of understanding it is used throughout.

Kriegsmarine the German Navy.

Luftwaffe the German Air Force.

MI1b the department of British military intelligence dealing with Sigint during the First World War.

MI5 the Security Service, title dates from the First World War and the immediate aftermath of the Armistice when it was part of Army intelligence and in theory its only role was to root out subversion within the armed forces.

MI6 common wartime name for the British Secret Intelligence Service, technically the Army intelligence branch that liaised with SIS. It was not introduced until 1940, but for ease of understanding it is used throughout.

MI8 the department of British military intelligence dealing with Sigint during the Second World War.

MND *Marinenachrichtendienst* (*Kriegsmarine* Communications Service).

M3 the *Kriegsmarine* three-rotor Enigma machine.

M4 the *Kriegsmarine* four-rotor Enigma machine.

menu a series of linked plain-text/cipher text letters used for giving instructions to bombe operators on setting up the bombes.

message key (Enigma) the rotor starting positions for a specific Enigma signal.

message setting the message key (q.v.).

NACP the National Archives, College Park, Maryland.

NHB Naval Historical Branch, Ministry of Defence, London.

NID25 Naval Intelligence Department 25. The Royal Navy's Sigint branch during the First World War, better known as Room 40 from the room in the Old Admiralty Buildings in Whitehall that it occupied.

NSA National Security Agency.

Offizier a system for doubly enciphering naval Enigma signals, which ensured that only officers could read their substantive text.

OKH *Oberkommando des Heeres* (High Command of the Army).

OKW *Oberkommando der Wehrmacht* (High Command of the *Wehrmacht*).

OKW/Chi OKW's *Amtsgruppe Wehrmachtnachrichtenverbindungswesen Chiffrierabteilung* – the section responsible for cipher security.

OTP one-time pad. A series of random additives intended for use once only. If used correctly, the system is unbreakable.

perforated sheets *see* Zygalski sheets.

PRO the Public Record Office, Kew, Surrey.

psilli psychological cilli. An Enigma message setting which is so closely related to the message *Grundstellung* that it can be guessed (e.g., *Grund* 'HIT' might give message setting 'LER'). Also a guessable keyboard sequence, such as 'QWE'.

Purple the Japanese diplomatic cipher machine, *angoo-ki taipu b* (Type B machine), codenamed Purple by the US Army.

RAF Royal Air Force.

Red the principal *Luftwaffe* Enigma cipher (codename assigned by Hut 6).

Red (Japanese) the Japanese diplomatic cipher machine, *angoo-ki taipu a* (Type A machine), codenamed Red by the Americans.

re-encipherment the encipherment of the same plain-text in two or more ciphers.

Ringstellung ring setting. The setting of the ring (or tyre) on an Enigma rotor.

romaji system of transliteration allowing *kana* to be spelt out in Roman letters.

rotor (Enigma) rotating disc (or wheel) with randomly wired electric contacts used for encipherment in Enigma.

rotor order (Enigma) the order in which rotors were inserted in Enigma (e.g., III, I, IV), looking at the machine from the front.

R/T radio telephone.

Schlüsselkenngruppe (naval Enigma) *see* cipher indicator group.

Schlüsselzusatz cipher attachment.

SD the *Sicherheitsdienst* (the intelligence service of the Nazi party).

Sigint signals intelligence. All intelligence derived from studying radio and other signals.

SIS (American) Signal Intelligence Service – the US Army's codebreaking unit (the name was changed on several occasions during the war).

SIS (British) the Secret Intelligence Service (MI6).

SKL *Seekriegsleitung* (the German naval war staff).

Spruchschlüssel *see* message key.

SS *Schutzstaffeln*. Protection squads formed in the 1920s, which became a powerful organization in the Nazi party, and Germany, with a military section, the *Waffen SS*.

SSA Signal Security Agency. The codebreaking unit of the US Army (which had a variety of names during the war; cf. SIS (American)).

SSD Signal Security Detachment. A codebreaking section in the US Army.

Stecker short for *Steckerverbindungen* (plug connections).

Steckerverbindungen the plug connections in Enigma's plugboard.

Stichwort (naval Enigma) cue word – a procedure modifying a daily key when a key-list had been compromised.

stop the position at which a bombe stopped, corresponding to a possible Enigma key.
Sturgeon GC&CS codename for the Siemens and Halske T52 series of teleprinter cipher machines.
success rate decrypts as a percentage of the signals intercepted.
superenciphered code *see* enciphered code.
SZ 40 or 42 the Lorenz *Schlüsselzusatz* (cipher attachment) for teleprinters.
TA *see* traffic analysis.
traffic radio signals, generally encrypted, between two or more stations, or using a common code or cipher.
traffic analysis the study of the external characteristics of signals (such as call signs and frequencies used) in order to derive intelligence.
trigram a group of three figures or letters.
Tunny GC&CS codename for the Lorenz SZ 40/42 teleprinter cipher attachment.
Typex the British cipher machine, based on Enigma (but without an entry plugboard). Never broken by the German codebreakers.
Uhr a device which made Enigma's plugboard largely non-reciprocal (*see* Chapter 19).
UKD *see Umkehrwalze* D.
Ultra 'special intelligence' – intelligence derived from high-grade codes and ciphers, such as Enigma and Fish.
Umkehrwalze (Enigma) reflector.
***Umkehrwalze* D** (Enigma) reflector Dora (UKD), which was rewirable in the field as part of an Enigma key (see Chapter 19). Used almost exclusively by the *Luftwaffe*.
Walzenlage (Enigma) rotor order (e.g., II, V, III).
WEC Wireless Experimental Centre. British signals intelligence site set up just outside Delhi in June 1942.
WED Wireless Experimental Depot. British intercept and decryption site based at Abbottabad on the North West Frontier, set up in the 1920s.
Wehrmacht all three branches of the German armed forces.
Werftschlüssel dockyard cipher – a manual cipher system used by the *Kriegsmarine*.
wheel *see* rotor.
Wren member of the WRNS (q.v.).
WRNS Women's Royal Naval Service.
Y service the intercept and DF service (before October 1943, the service also dealt with traffic analysis and broke some low-grade codes and ciphers).

***Zählwerk* Enigma** *see* counter Enigma.

Zygalski sheets lettered sheets with holes punched in them, showing which combinations of rotor starting positions and wheel orders produced females. By suitably aligning the relevant sheets on top of each other, the *Ringstellungen* and rotor order were revealed by the coincidence of holes in some sheets.

Notes on Contributors

Richard J. Aldrich holds a chair in politics at the University of Nottingham and is co-editor of *Intelligence and National Security*. His previous publications include *The Key to the South: Britain, the United States and Thailand During the Approach of the Pacific War, 1929–1942* and *Intelligence and the War Against Japan: Britain, America and the Politics of Secret Service*. He has recently completed *The Hidden Hand: Britain, America and Cold War Secret Intelligence*.

David Alvarez is the author of *Secret Messages: Codebreaking and American Diplomacy, 1930–1945* and the editor of *Allied and Axis Signals Intelligence in World War II*. He is a professor at St Mary's College of California and has served as scholar in residence at the US National Security Agency.

Christopher Andrew is Professor of Modern and Contemporary History at Cambridge University, Chair of the History Faculty, Fellow and President of Corpus Christi College, and former Visiting Professor at Harvard, Toronto and the Australian National University. He is also Chair of the British Intelligence Study Group, founding co-editor of *Intelligence and National Security* and a regular presenter on BBC Radio Four, which in 2001 broadcast his twelfth series of *What If?*. His latest book (with Vasili Mitrokhin) is *The Mitrokhin Archive: The KGB in Europe and the West*.

Keith Batey was recruited to Bletchley Park by Gordon Welchman after completing his Maths Tripos at Cambridge in June 1940, and worked in Hut 6 until transferring to ISK in November 1941. After the war he joined the Dominions Office, moving to the Ministry of Supply in 1951. He was appointed Secretary of the Oxford University Chest in July 1964, and became Treasurer of Christ Church, Oxford, in April 1972. He retired in 1986.

Mavis Batey (*née* Lever) joined Bletchley Park in May 1940, when she was nineteen, after breaking off German studies at University College, London. She worked with the famous codebreaker Dilly Knox, initially on Italian naval Enigma messages and later on German *Abwehr* Enigma traffic. An historian of landscape and literature, her books include *Arcadian Thames*, *The Historic Gardens of Oxford and Cambridge*, *Jane Austen and the English Landscape* and *Alexander Pope, the Poet and the Landscape.*

Stephen Budiansky is the author of *Battle of Wits: The Complete Story of Codebreaking in World War II.*

John Chadwick was educated at St Paul's School and Corpus Christi College, Cambridge, where he read classics. During the war, he served in the Royal Navy as a codebreaker in the Middle East and as a Japanese translator at Bletchley Park. His most famous book is *The Decipherment of Linear B*, an account of how he and Michael Ventris unravelled the ancient Minoan script. He was Perceval Maitland Laurence Reader in Classics, University of Cambridge, and an Honorary Fellow of Downing College, Cambridge. He died in December 1998.

Jack Copeland is Professor of Philosophy at the University of Canterbury, New Zealand, and Director of the Turing Archive for the History of Computing. He works in mathematical and philosophical logic, cognitive science, and the history and foundations of computing. He wrote the academic bestseller *Artificial Intelligence: A Philosophical Introduction* and is currently writing and editing several books on Alan Turing, including one on Turing's Automatic Computing Engine, and editing *Colossus: The First Computer* for Oxford University Press. He has also edited *Logic and Reality* and contributed numerous articles to philosophical and scientific journals.

John Cripps is a solicitor who studied Balkan history as a mature student at Southampton University. He is currently completing his Ph.D. dissertation at Southampton on 'The British, Signals Intelligence and the War and Civil War in Yugoslavia 1941–1944'.

Philip H. J. Davies is an Associate Professor in the Department of International and Strategic Studies at the University of Malaya in Malaysia. He specializes in development and institution-building in the intelligence services and has published extensively on intelligence issues in *Intelligence and National Security*, *Public Administration*, *Journal of Conflict Studies* and other journals. His survey of the literature on British intelligence was published in 1996. He is completing his Ph.D. dissertation 'Organisational Development of Britain's Secret Intelligence Service 1909–1979' for publication by Frank Cass, and is writing a comparative study of the British and American intelligence systems.

Ralph Erskine is a retired lawyer, and a member of the editorial board of the *Journal of Intelligence History*. His research interest is Sigint in the Second World War, on which he has published extensively in journals such as *Annals of the History of Computing*, *Cryptologia* and *Intelligence and National Security*.

Hugh Foss was born in Kobe, Japan, where his father was a missionary bishop. He was educated at Marlborough and Christ's College, Cambridge. He joined GC&CS in December 1924, and was head of the Japanese Naval Section (Hut 7) in 1942 and 1943. He retired from GCHQ in 1953, and died in December 1971.

Rolf Noskwith was born in Germany in 1919 and came to England with his parents in 1932. He was educated at Nottingham High School and Trinity College, Cambridge, where he read mathematics. He worked at Bletchley Park on the German naval Enigma traffic from 1941 to 1945 and subsequently on other ciphers. Since 1946 he has worked for Charnos, the well-known textile company founded by his father. He is now non-executive Chairman of Charnos plc.

Michael Smith is the Defence Correspondent of the *Daily Telegraph*. He is a former member of the Intelligence Corps, who worked for a number of years with GCHQ. His books include *New Cloak, Old Dagger: How Britain's Spies Came In From the Cold*, *Station X: The Codebreakers of Bletchley Park*, *Foley: The Spy Who Saved 10,000 Jews* and *The Emperor's Codes: Bletchley Park and the Breaking of Japan's Secret Ciphers*.

Derek Taunt was educated at Enfield Grammar School and the City of London School, entering Jesus College, Cambridge, to read Mathematics in 1936. After graduating in 1939, he spent the war years in various backrooms, notably Hut 6 at Bletchley Park from August 1941 until VE Day. After returning to

Cambridge as a research student in 1945, he won a Smith's Prize in 1947 and was a university lecturer from 1949 (with the honorific title of 'Cayley Lecturer' from 1965 until retirement in 1982). As a fellow of Jesus College he was at various times a director of studies, tutor, bursar and, from 1979 to 1982, President.

James W. Thirsk (known as Jimmy at Bletchley Park) was born in 1914. He was a librarian (FLA) before and after the Second World War, retiring in 1974. During the war he served in the King's Own Royal Regiment/Royal Artillery (Maritime Regiment) and, from 1942, as a company sergeant-major in the Intelligence Corps, working as a traffic analyst in Sixta (attached to Hut 6 at Bletchley). He is married to Dr Joan Thirsk (*née* Watkins) who was an ATS subaltern in the Fusion Room at Bletchley.

Shaun Wylie was at Bletchley Park from 1941 to 1945. He then took a Fellowship at Trinity Hall and became a lecturer in Mathematics at Cambridge University. In 1958 he went to become chief mathematician at GCHQ. After retiring in 1973 he taught for seven years at the Hills Road Sixth Form College in Cambridge.

Index

THE EMPEROR'S CODES
by Michael Smith

The wartime exploits of Britain's codebreakers continue to fascinate and amaze. In the bestselling Station X, Michael Smith wrote about the breaking of the Enigma cipher. Now, to continue this previously untold story, he turns to the Far Eastern theatre to reveal how Japan's secret codes were broken, and the consequences for the Second World War.

Drawing on recently declassified British files, Australian secret official histories and the memories of an unprecedented number of surviving codebreakers, *The Emperor's Codes* is the first full account of the vital role played by British and Australian codebreakers in the last war, and a classic contribution to our understanding of that tumultuous time.

Revised and updated for this paperback edition, with new material on how to break the Japanese superenciphered codes.

'Tells the full riveting story of the breaking of the Japanese codes . . . an enthralling tale, the stuff of John le Carré or Robert Harris, yet true'
Martin Booth, *Daily Telegraph*

'A former code-breaker . . . [Michael Smith] frankly accuses the US Navy of causing thousands of unnecessary casualties, most of them American, by its refusal to join in the common effort . . . Smith writes partly from other people's books, partly from his own knowledge of what the job is like, and partly from recently released archives; out of these last, he proves his point'
M. R. D. Foot, *Times Literary Supplement*

0 553 81320 X